Principles of MANAGEMENT

A Modern Approach

Third Edition

HENRY H. ALBERS
Chairman, Department of Management
University of Nebraska, Lincoln, Nebraska

John Wiley & Sons, Inc.
NEW YORK · LONDON · SYDNEY · TORONTO

Copyright ©1961, 1965, 1969 by John Wiley & Sons, Inc.

All rights reserved. No part of this book may be reproduced by any means, nor transmitted, nor translated into a machine language without the written permission of the publisher.

10 9 8 7 6 5 4

Library of Congress Catalog Card Number: 69-13675
SBN 471 01917 8
Printed in the United States of America

For Marjorie, Patricia, and Elliott

PREFACE

The core of this book is concerned with the basic elements of managerial action—planning, communication, and motivation—within an organized managerial structure. The knowledge and skills involved in managing are assumed to have universal properties that can be applied in different kinds of organization, in the various functional areas (production, finance, marketing, and personnel), and at any level of the hierarchy (president, department head, foreman). I have leaned toward an analytical approach, but I have not neglected to use descriptive material to build a necessary factual background and give content to analytical tools. However, I have assumed that many of the "facts" involved in managerial action are sufficiently similar to warrant the same classification.

This book is designed to serve the needs of a course in general management in colleges of business administration, engineering, and liberal arts. It can also be used to provide a foundation for executive development in business and other organizations. Technically educated persons (such as engineers and chemists) and the general reader may find the book helpful in gaining a familiarity with the management field.

The electronic computer and all that it implies are given a much more prominent place in this edition. There is a lengthy section on what Norbert Wiener called "the second industrial revolution" and a new chapter on computerized informational systems. A number of other chapters also give attention to the manner in which computers have affected management theory and practice. This edition gives more consideration to the systems concept and its relationship to the management process. The cybernetics model and such basic concepts as feedback and the black box are discussed in some detail. However, a systems approach has not necessitated any basic change in the conceptual framework of this book. The decisional and informational processes still occupy the center of the stage. The problems of managing American business and governmental organizations in foreign countries are given particular attention. A section on the impact of managerial strategy upon organizational structure has been added. The chapter concerned with decision making has been expanded to emphasize the particular importance of this managerial activity. Every effort has been made to bring the book up to date in the light of recent developments in theory and practice.

This book is "interdisciplinary" in the sense that it draws upon many fields of learning. Such subjects as operations research, information theory, group dynamics, economic theory, accounting, semantics, budgeting, quality control, and electronic data-processing form an integral part of the discussion. The functional areas of management, such as marketing, finance, and purchasing, are brought into play as aspects of the strategy developed through the planning process. Environmental forces, such as the economy, product and resource markets, government, and society, are analyzed in terms of their relationship to organizational dynamics. The manner in which such socio-psychological phenomena as status and primary groups influence behavior is given comprehensive consideration. The social foundations of authority, leadership succession in a democratic society, property and power, and the question of managerial responsibility are discussed at length.

There are four fundamental integrating themes: hierarchy, process, perspective, and economy. The hierarchical theme begins in Part II in which consideration is given the nature of the managerial structure. Part III gives emphasis to organization as a dynamic phenomenon and relates organization to the functions of planning, communication, and motivation. These functions are also viewed as a process which can be analytically traced through the following phases: (1) executives make planning decisions; (2) such decisions are activated by forward communication to subordinate managerial and nonmanagerial personnel; (3) the appropriateness of superior planning and subordinate performance is indicated by feedback or control communication; and (4) feedback forms the basis for revised planning decisions or for motivational decisions. Another important integrating theme is that the knowledge and techniques that relate to the managerial problem are discussed from the perspective of particular organizations. For example, economics is approached from an organizational rather than a social perspective; accounting is discussed from a managerial instead of a "professional accounting" viewpoint; and operations research is oriented toward the needs of the executive as opposed to those of the specialist. Finally, the problem of limited resources or economizing pervades much of the discussion. The practice of good "human relations" and the quest for a "social consciousness" have not repudiated the profit norm. Profits are assumed to be both necessary and moral. What is good for General Motors may not always be good for the country, but it is good for General Motors.

The introductory chapters include a brief description of Taylor's Bethlehem research and the Hawthorne study. I felt that the student of management should have more than a passing familiarity with these developments. The chapters in Part VII are extensively used to provide further insights into the nature of management skills and the manner in which they relate to educational curricula and company training programs. The conclusions made in the Gordon-Howell and Pierson reports on business education are scrutinized from the vantage point of executive development. The intent is to promote an understanding of the difficult problem of creating executive talent; it is not designed to be a "how to do it" guide for specific curriculum development or course scheduling.

Although the nature of mathematical techniques (such as operations research) and the manner in which they relate to managerial problems are discussed in depth, a background in mathematics is not required for any part of this book. The analysis of electronic data-processing systems assumes no prior knowledge of computer hardware and programming techniques. Every effort was made to provide sufficient background for a meaningful application of such knowledge areas as economics, semantics, information theory, and group dynamics to the management problem.

I hope that I have contributed in some small measure to the advancement of management knowledge. But there are many obligations to others, which are only partially indicated by footnote references. Complete acknowledgment of my intellectual debt to professors and practitioners in many fields is not possible in the space available here. I give particular thanks to Professor Francis J. Bridges, Georgia State College, for reading the entire manuscript and for his most helpful criticisms and comments. Many helpful suggestions also came from Professor Norman Bonnema, Buena Vista College; Professor Norman Brammer, Colorado State University; James O. Jensen, U.S. Army Management Engineering Training Agency; Professor Robert E. Lane, Northern Illinois University; Professor Fred Luthans, University of Nebraska; Dr. William E. Reif, Iowa-Illinois Gas and Electric Company; Professor James W. Walker, Indiana University; and Professor Donald C. Wright, Washburn University. The following executives gave me the advantage of their extensive managerial experience: Robert A. Bulen, Manager, Business Systems, Deere and Company; A. Lynn Bryant, Director, U.S. Army Management Engineering Training Agency; Dr. Roger J. Fritz, Director, Management Development and Personnel Research, Deere and Company; Ellis Maxcy, President, Southern New England Telephone Company; and John R. Mulhearn, Vice President, New York Telephone Company. I am also indebted to Lester A. Digman, D. C. Gibson, Roger Grinstead, Robert Kerber, Richard Lutz, Gordon A. Morse, William Scott, Richard Tussing, and William H. Vroman. My thanks to Marie Smith, who has proved that she is an outstanding organizer and administrator, and to Darlene Finnegan, Eileen Harms,

Phyllis Irwin, and Diane Thede for their secretarial support. A special word of thanks goes to Candace R. Luse for the facility and fervor with which she typed the manuscript, and to Gerry Jacobs for solving some last minute problems. Finally, appreciation is expressed to Patricia Albers for her help with the index.

Henry H. Albers

Lincoln, Nebraska
January 1969

CONTENTS

PART I   THE MANAGEMENT PROBLEM: PAST AND PRESENT   1

  1 Preliminary Perspectives   3
  2 Toward Scientific Management   31
  3 The Emerging Pattern   57
  4 Organizational Systems: The Decisional and Informational Processes   74

PART II   ORGANIZATION FOR MANAGEMENT   99

  5 The Organizational Structure   101
  6 Departmentation   120
  7 Line-Staff-Functional Relationships   155
  8 Centralization and Decentralization   185
  9 Committee Organization   212
  10 Boards of Directors and Other Committees   230

PART III   MANAGERIAL ORGANIZATION: BEHAVIORAL ASPECTS   253

  11 Authority, Status, and Power   255
  12 Organizational Dynamics   270
  13 From Organization to Process   300

PART IV   DECISION MAKING: PLANNING STRATEGIES   317

  14 Surveying the Environment   319
  15 The Development of Planning Strategies   345

16	Dynamic Planning I	373
17	Dynamic Planning II	399

PART V COMMUNICATION AND CONTROL — 419

18	Information and Communication	421
19	Communication Media: Message Construction and Reception	447
20	Specialized Informational Systems	473
21	Computerized Informational Systems	516

PART VI LEADERSHIP AND MOTIVATION — 551

22	The Problem of Motivation	553
23	Dynamic Leadership	585
24	The Responsibility of Management	605

PART VII EXECUTIVE DEVELOPMENT — 625

25	Executive Qualities and Executive Education	627
26	Company Executive Development Programs	660

NAME INDEX	683
SUBJECT INDEX	691

PRINCIPLES OF MANAGEMENT: A MODERN APPROACH

PART I

THE MANAGEMENT PROBLEM: PAST AND PRESENT

chapter 1

PRELIMINARY PERSPECTIVES

This book presents a systematic body of knowledge related to the practice of management in formal organizations. Although particular attention is given to business organizations, the basic principles can be applied in political, military, educational, religious, and other kinds of organized endeavor.

An Organizational Society

Organizations are playing an increasingly important part in modern living. Their objectives express the alpha and omega of human activity—to wage war and to preserve peace, to manufacture cribs, baseballs, and coffins, to sell books, coffee, and cigarettes, to worship God and to serve Bacchus. There is an exceedingly large number of organizations, many of which are impressive in size. Some of them encompass more resources than the entire nation at its birth.

Business Enterprises

The preponderance of business employment and industrial effort is found in enterprises that employ more than twenty persons. Some 20 million are employed in business enterprises with more than 100 employees; 14 million of these are in companies with more than 1000 employees.[1] Large corporations with 10,000 or more employees account for 22 per cent of all business employment.

[1] A. D. H. Kaplan, *Big Enterprise in a Competitive System* (Washington, D.C: The Brookings Institution, 1954), pp. 64, 65, 68.

The 500 largest United States industrial corporations produced over 359 billion dollars' worth of products and services in 1967 with a capital investment of more than 182 billion and about 13 million employees.[2] At the top of the list was the General Motors Corporation with sales of 20 billion, 9.2 billion in invested capital, and 728,198 employees. A total of almost one hundred companies in all categories had sales of over one billion dollars.

The number of companies in an industry ranges from as few as twenty to many thousands.[3] The extent to which output is concentrated in a small number of companies also varies a great deal.[4] Eight companies manufacture most of the nation's cigarettes with four companies producing 80 per cent of the total. The four largest manufacturers in the industry account for 79 per cent of the automobiles, 74 per cent of the metal cans, and 70 per cent of the tires and tubes produced in the United States. Three television networks provide most of the programs channeled into American homes. One company owns and operates six out of every seven telephones in the country. At the other extreme are industries in which there is little concentration of output. For example, the top four companies account for a relatively small percentage of the total output of such products as bakery products, dresses, animal feeds, metal stampings, and aircraft equipment.

Other Kinds of Organization

One out of every five Americans is employed by local, state, and federal governments. A single governmental "organization," the Department of Defense, has more than 4 million persons within its domain. About 17 million Americans hold membership in some 185 national and international labor unions. Two hundred and fifty religious organizations play a part in the catechizing process for Catholics, Lutherans, Methodists, Mormons, Baptists, and Jews. There are about 2000 cities with over 10,000 inhabitants, which require police, fire, and other services. Thou-

---

[2] *The Fortune Directory*. The 500 Largest U. S. Industrial Corporations, June 15, 1968, pp. 20–21. On p. 2 is this list of the 25 largest industrial corporations in the United States: General Motors, Standard Oil (N.J.), Ford Motor, General Electric, Chrysler, Mobil Oil, International Business Machines, Texaco, Gulf Oil, U.S. Steel, Western Electric, Standard Oil of California, Du Pont, Shell Oil, Radio Corporation of America, McDonnell Douglas, Standard Oil (Ind.), Westinghouse Electric, Boeing, Swift, International Tel & Tel, Goodyear Tire & Rubber, General Telephone and Electronics, Bethlehem Steel, Union Carbide.

[3] Kaplan, *op. cit.*, p. 93.

[4] *Ibid.*; U.S. Bureau of the Census, *Statistical Abstract of the United States:* 1967 (Eighty-eighth edition), Washington, D.C., 1967, pp. 751–752.

sands of educational organizations with specialized personnel prepare some 35 million young people for vocational and life tasks.

Future Prospects

The number and size of organizations will undoubtedly increase at a rapid rate in the years that follow. Many companies will be added to the "billion dollar club"; twenty new members were welcomed during a recent year. Government will probably become even larger unless radical revisions are made in defense and space programs. Primary and secondary schools will expand in size and become more specialized as the result of rural consolidation and population concentration. Universities and multiversities, to use Clark Kerr's term, will have to contend with an increasingly larger influx of students. Continued urbanization will give rise to more comprehensive and complex organized endeavor to meet the needs of mass living.

Cooperation and Technology

Organizations are the means through which man has sought to enhance his welfare by cooperating with his fellow man. They have endowed mankind with accomplishments that would not otherwise have been possible.

The Advantages of Cooperative Endeavor

Cooperation amplifies human capacities. What one man cannot do, two can; what one can do, two can do better. Two men may be able to move a stone that cannot be moved by one man. In Aesop's fable the blind man who could walk carried the man who could see but not walk. Such elemental examples of cooperation are the building blocks of the elaborate cooperative endeavor in the organizations of modern industrial civilization.

Cooperation assumes some kind of work division among the participating individuals.[5] When two men cooperate in moving a stone, the work is

---

[5] Work division has its corollary in specialization. Work is divided; persons specialize. Individual differences caused by heredity and environmental factors form a basis for both work division and specialization. Work division makes possible a more efficient utilization of the diverse capabilities available in a society. On the other hand, individuals tend to specialize in tasks for which they are best suited. Much of the specialization that exists in modern industrial civilization results from the work division that takes place in organization. Men learn skills and acquire knowledge that will fit them into one of the niches made in the work division process. Luther Gulick,

somehow divided between them. Work division solves problems of space, time, and limitations in human capabilities. One man within his life-span cannot acquire all the knowledge necessary in an advanced industrial society. People differ in natural qualities and can acquire greater proficiency by limiting the range of their activity.

Informal Cooperation

Much of the cooperation that occurs in society is spontaneous in origin and development. Man assembled into groups to take advantage of cooperation in coping with his environment. The earliest forms of cooperation were probably a matter of trial and error. Successful cooperative endeavor was repeated until particular patterns of behavior became routine and customary. These group experiences were then passed on to succeeding generations.

Informal cooperation is both a cause and a result of social living. It is often interwoven with other elements of social behavior. The quilting bee of early America illustrates a mixture of economic cooperative endeavor with an elaborate social by-product. As one writer on the subject put it: "Starting from the grimness of economic need, the quilt became a social factor. Soon no function was more important than the quilting-bee, in town or country." [6] Invitations were sent to the neighbors and elaborate preparations were made for the event. The quilters arrived early in the day and began work at once. At the same time the tongues wagged with glee about the latest neighborhood news and scandal. The men compared notes on farming and neighborhood affairs, while the children entertained themselves with games. Two big meals were served at noon and early evening. After the evening meal, "there was a grand frolic—singing, kissing-games, dancing and courting." [7] Then, in the words of an old ballad written by Stephen Foster:

> In the sky the bright stars glittered,
>   On the banks the pale moon shone,
> And 'twas from Aunt Dinah's quilting party
>   I was seeing Nellie home.

"Notes on the Theory of Organization," *Papers on the Science of Administration* (New York: Institute of Public Administration, Columbia University, 1937), pp. 3–6; Chester I. Barnard, *The Functions of the Executive* (Cambridge: Harvard University Press, 1951), pp. 127–132.

[6] Ruth E. Finley, *Old Patchwork Quilts* (Philadelphia: J. B. Lippincott Company, 1929), p. 33.

[7] *Ibid.*, p. 34.

It is evident that many of these activities were unrelated to the function of making quilts. The quilting bee provided an opportunity for social interaction and served other social functions, such as bringing young damsels into contact with eligible young men.

Cooperation in Formal Organizations

How would a modern business executive organize the production of quilts? He would most certainly take a dim view of many of the social activities that formed an integral part of the quilting bee. His initial consideration would be the technology of quilt making. He would organize the activities of people around the functions necessary to accomplish the primary objective. Such a change in emphasis denotes the essential difference between cooperation in formal organizations and informal modes of cooperation.

Formal organizations are consciously directed and designed to accomplish a predetermined objective. The cooperative endeavor necessary to achieve the objective is no longer a passive feature of social activity. This aspect of human behavior is abstracted from the totality of social behavior and given a separate dynamics.

Formal organizations have made possible the rich material rewards of modern industrial civilization. They have cut through a web of social custom and tradition that tends to impede change. But they have not eliminated the need for the social bonds that have always been an integral part of group living and cooperative activity. Unlike a machine or a production process, man is not designed for a specific functional purpose. Man does not leave behind the behavioral requirements of social living when he enters the factory gate or opens the office door.

The Will to Cooperate

The advantages of cooperation cannot be realized without the will to cooperate. The problem of motivation in cooperative endeavor has often been viewed in purely economic terms. Man was assumed to be an individualist who attempts to maximize his economic status. This highly abstract concept of man, although useful for certain kinds of economic analysis, is not an adequate basis for understanding organized human behavior. Chester I. Barnard, a leading business executive, asserts that he did not understand human behavior in organizations until he had "relegated economic theory and economic interests to a secondary—though indispensable—place. . . ." He found that "noneconomic motives, interests, and processes, as well as economic, are fundamental in behavior from the boards of directors to the last man." [8]

It has only recently been recognized that the social satisfactions of the quilting bee are important ingredients of successful cooperation in formal organizations. The significance of the social aspect of cooperation is indicated by the following comment about the quilting bee: "The social, gossipy interchange of neighborhood news did not interrupt the swiftly flying fingers of those expert quilters, but seemed rather to add to their agility." [9] The social satisfactions and the social sanctions that form a part of group living in organizations are important, if not primary, factors in achieving successful cooperation.

Technology and Cooperation

Technology has advanced the power and possibilities of cooperation. If four people are required to move a large stone, the use of a simple leverage device (technology) might make possible the achievement of the same task with half the personnel. The relationship between cooperation and technology in modern industrial society may be likened to the Marshallian question as to "whether it is the upper or the under blade of a pair of scissors that cuts a piece of paper." [10] A society, with a given state of technology, can enhance its accomplishments by better cooperation. Improvements in technology can likewise improve the outcome of a given quality of cooperation.

Some historians regard technological innovation as the prime moving force of economic history. "The technological sciences," writes Professor Usher, "furnish the account of the most important single factor in the active transformation of environment by human activity." [11] The accomplishments of technology during and since the industrial revolution are indeed impressive, but the important role played by cooperation should not be neglected. Modern technology would not have been possible without cooperation. Technology on any large scale demands a corresponding ability to integrate human resources and technology into effective organizations.

---

[8] Barnard, *op. cit.*, p. xi.

[9] Carrie A. Hall and Rose G. Kretsinger, *The Romance of the Patchwork Quilt in America* (Caldwell, Idaho: The Caxton Printers, Ltd., 1935), p. 21.

[10] Alfred Marshall, *Principles of Economics,* 8th ed. (London: Macmillan and Company, Ltd., 1938), p. 348.

[11] Abbot Payson Usher, *A History of Mechanical Inventions* (New York: McGraw-Hill Book Company, Inc., 1929), p. 1.

The Social Problems of an Industrial Civilization

Industrial society must balance the requirements of technology with the needs of the human side of industry.[12] The behavior of people in industry involves more than the totality of functions necessary to attain a given objective, such as making shoes or producing steel ingots. Organized behavior should be viewed in terms of a social system that transcends the functional demands of technology.

The future welfare of civilization rests on the ability to live and work in harmony. Social skills are as important as the development of technical skills. A science of human behavior is necessary to prevent destruction by the science of matter. The problems of industrial and international conflict cannot be solved without an understanding of the underlying reasons for such conflict.

Antecedents to Modern Management

Although the systematic study of management as a separate branch of human knowledge has a recent origin, the practice of management is as old as human society. The history of man is replete with the evidence of organizational activity that implies a knowledge of many of the ideas that later appeared in the writings of Frederick W. Taylor, Henri Fayol, Elton Mayo, and Chester I. Barnard. Archaeology has unearthed extensive accumulations of relics from past civilizations that reflect elaborate organizational achievements. The mammoth walls of ancient Babylon, the pyramids of the Pharaohs, and the temples of the Aztecs rival the accomplishments of modern industrial civilization, considering the then existing state of technology. Hannibal's crossing of the Alps in 218 B.C. with troops and equipment was a remarkable organizational feat.

---

[12] This problem is brought into focus by Elton Mayo in *The Social Problems of an Industrial Civilization* (Boston: Division of Research, Graduate School of Business Administration, Harvard University, 1945). Living and working in an industrial civilization were given careful scrutiny by leaders from management, labor, government, and education at the Corning Conference in 1951. The report of this conference is found in Eugene Staley (editor), *Creating an Industrial Civilization* (New York: Harper & Brothers Publishers, 1952). See also Douglas McGregor, *The Human Side of Enterprise* (New York: McGraw-Hill Book Company, Inc., 1960).

The Roman Empire

The glory that was Rome must be credited in great part to superior organizational abilities. The Roman legions conquered an empire that in the second century of the Christian era "comprehended the fairest part of the earth, and the most civilised portion of mankind." [13] This vast domain was linked together by an elaborate system of roads that reached from Rome into the outlying provinces. Relay stations with a supply of horses were established to facilitate rapid communication throughout the empire in the manner of the pony express of the American West. A short distance from the capital, the great port of Ostia sent ships to the provinces beyond the Mediterranean. Commerce extended overland to the shores of the Baltic and by sea to ports that supplied Rome with the riches of Asia. These accomplishments with a technology that must be considered primitive by modern standards give emphatic testimony to the genius of Roman organizers. Furthermore, Roman administrators were successful in making the organizational changes necessitated by the growth of a small city into a world empire.[14] The modern business corporation has had to contend with a similar situation. The Romans solved the matter in a way that would not be at all foreign to the executives of today. They had a clear understanding of the problems associated with decentralization, delegation, and coordination. Their success in solving these problems is adequately attested by the fact that the Roman Republic and later the Empire spanned centuries.

The Roman Catholic Church

The Roman Catholic Church successfully solved the organizational problems of large size long before today's industrial giants came into being. It developed organizational practices that made possible comprehensive control over the religious lives of more than half a billion people in every corner of the world. The central administrative organization of the Catholic Church, known as the Curia Romana, corresponds to the top levels of complex governmental and military organizations. Two American business executives from General Motors and Remington Rand came to the following conclusion in a historical study of organization: "It can be said in

---

[13] Edward Gibbon, *The Decline and Fall of the Roman Empire,* Vol. I (New York: The Modern Library, 1932), p. 1. Gibbon's classic study of Rome contains some excellent descriptions of Roman organization and accomplishments.

[14] James D. Mooney and Alan C. Reiley, *Onward Industry!* (New York: Harper & Brothers Publishers, 1931), pp. 109–144; Mooney, *The Principles of Organization* (New York: Harper & Brothers Publishers, 1947), pp. 62–72.

general of the Curia Romana that as an example of efficient departmentalization and executive coordination it is perhaps without a parallel in the entire realm of organization." [15] The Catholic Church followed a geographical pattern in its basic departmentation, but it also developed a highly effective functional approach to problems that can be better handled on this basis. The staff concept is utilized at all levels of the organization to permit specialized and subordinate participation in the decisional process without destroying unity of command.

The Arsenal of Venice

An outstanding example of the application of many of the ideas later advanced by the pioneers of scientific management is found in the famous Arsenal of Venice. The Arsenal anticipated the direct line production of the modern meat packing and automobile assembly plants. This fact is indicated by the Spanish traveler, Pero Tafur, who in 1436 described what he saw at the Arsenal in the following words.

And as one enters the gate there is a great street on either hand with the sea in the middle, and on one side are windows opening out of the houses of the arsenal, and the same on the other side, and out came a galley towed by a boat, and from the windows they handed out to them, from one the cordage, from another the bread, from another the arms, and from another the balistas and mortars, and so from all sides everything which was required, and when the galley had reached the end of the street all the men required were on board, together with the complement of oars, and she was equipped from end to end. In this manner there came out ten galleys, fully armed, between the hours of three and nine.[16]

The Arsenal was probably the largest industrial establishment of the fifteenth century, covering sixty acres of ground and water and employing between one and two thousand workers.[17] See Figure 1-1. It had a threefold task: the manufacture of galleys, arms, and equipment; the storage of these items; and assembly and refitting. The work of the Arsenal was divided into several functional departments with a foreman in charge of each department. Shipbuilding was divided into three stages of production and was carefully preplanned. The first step was the building of the frame by the ship carpenters. Then the planking was fastened and the cabins and superstructures were built. Both carpenters and caulkers participated in

[15] Mooney and Reiley, *op. cit.*, p. 241.
[16] Malcolm Letts (editor and translator), *Pero Tafur, Travels and Adventures, 1435–1439* (London: George Routledge & Sons, Ltd., 1926), p. 170.
[17] Frederic Chapin Lane, *Venetian Ships and Shipbuilders of the Renaissance* (Baltimore: The Johns Hopkins Press, 1934), pp. 129–175.

12   THE MANAGEMENT PROBLEM: PAST AND PRESENT

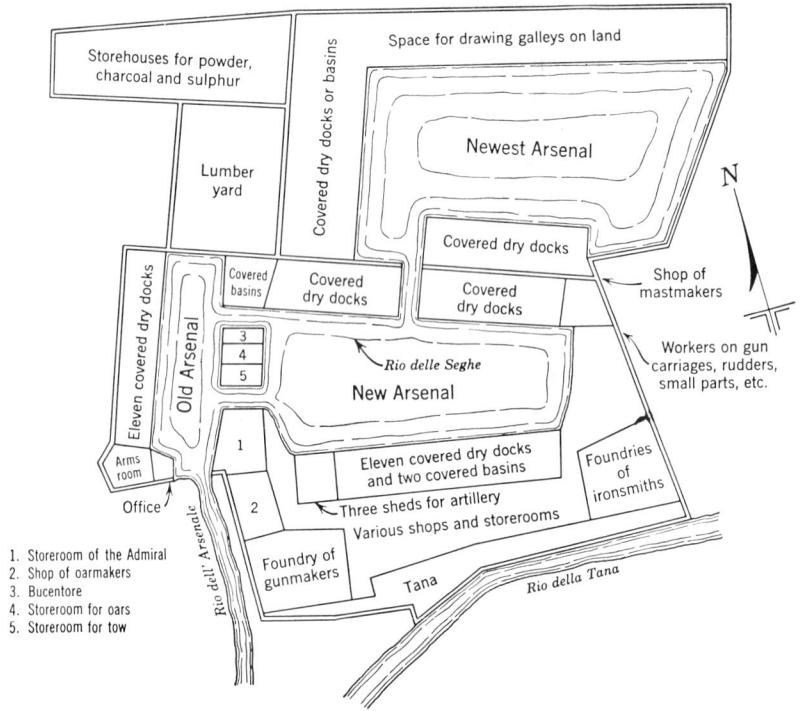

Figure 1-1. The Arsenal of Venice about 1560. Reproduced with permission from Frederic Chapin Lane, *Venetian Ships and Shipbuilders of the Renaissance*. Baltimore: The Johns Hopkins Press, 1934.

this work. The final stage of production was completed when the ship was called into service. All the departments of the Arsenal participated in this final assembly stage. The ship's seams were filled with tow and pitch, and the hull was covered with tar or grease. Then came the launching of the ship, after which the deck fixings were fastened in place. Finally the ship was provided with the rigging, moorings, and oars and arms for the crew. The efficiency attained in this stage of production is indicated by the assembly, launching, and arming of a vessel in less than one hour during a visit by Henry III, King of France, in 1574.

The Industrial Revolution

History books are filled with glowing accounts of the technological innovations of the industrial revolution in Great Britain and the United States.

Relatively little is known about the management methods and techniques that helped make this progress possible. As Urwick and Brech point out in their study of the development of scientific management, it seems highly unlikely that Great Britain could have made the industrial progress of the nineteenth century without a foundation of successful management.[18] A comprehensive study of the management practices of the Birmingham (England) plant of the Boulton and Watt Company is one bit of evidence to support this view.[19] The following observation is made in the introduction of this study.

Neither Taylor, Ford, nor other modern experts devised anything in the way of plan that cannot be discovered at Soho [the Birmingham factory of Boulton and Watt] before 1805; and the Soho system of costing is superior to that employed in very many successful concerns to-day. This earliest engineering factory, therefore, possessed an organisation on the management side which was not excelled even by the technical skill of the craftsmen it produced.[20]

As the name of the firm implies, one of the original participants in the organization was James Watt, whose developmental work on the steam engine supplied the power of the industrial revolution. The evidence presented in the Boulton and Watt study points to the development of managerial methods that equal the progress made in the purely technical areas. For example, an incentive system for cylinder borers was devised by determining the average time necessary for different size and type cylinders. A list of machines required in the production process with data on machine speeds was found in one of the company documents. A complete list of all subassemblies and components with full details of operation sequences was found. A detailed list of jobs assigned to individuals and groups of workers indicates a fixed standard job. Forecasting was used as a basis for production planning, and elaborate cost control records were maintained by the company.

The Background of Modern Management

The Factory System

The ascendancy of the factory as the primary mode of production and the tremendous rise in the volume of production after the industrial revolu-

[18] L. Urwick and E. F. L. Brech, *The Making of Scientific Management,* Vol. II (London: Management Publications Trust, 1946), p. 7.

[19] Erich Roll, *An Early Experiment in Industrial Organisation* (London: Longmans, Green and Co., 1930). A summary of this study is found in Urwick and Brech, *op. cit.,* pp. 24–39.

[20] Roll, *op. cit.,* p. xv.

tion created a need for large numbers of managers. Factory organization brought about a more complete differentiation between management and nonmanagement functions and between managers and workers. It also enlarged the scope of the management function.

The factory system may be distinguished from other modes of production by the following characteristics. (1) Workers, raw material, machinery, and equipment are concentrated in a building or a group of buildings used exclusively for production. Before the advent of the factory system a great deal of production was performed in the home by a single or a small group of craft workers. (2) The factory system brought centralized control of raw material, production, and output. The earlier merchant-employer or putting-out system lacked such unified control. The merchant furnished the raw materials and provided the markets; production was generally controlled by the craft workers. (3) The ultimate development of the factory system brought a clear distinction between the employer and the employed. Under earlier forms of craft organization, the master was more a fellow worker than an employer. An elaborate complex of customs and traditions governed the relationship between master and worker.

The industrial revolution was a major contributing factor in the rapid development of the factory system. It furnished both the power and the machines for large-scale production. The specialized machine performing one operation in a total sequence of hundreds of operations required the concentration of many workers to produce the final product. Large amounts of capital were required to finance the mechanized factories which shifted the control of production to the capitalist. The craft worker who lacked the resources to buy the machine or to compete with it assumed the role of an employee.

The factory required more planning and supervision than the smaller and simpler handicraft production units. The function of work division became more important and complex. The worker's part in the production process became ever more minute. His perspective became the specialized job. The task of integrating his job with other jobs passed to the manager. The relationship between the employer and the worker became more impersonal, and the problem of motivation became more difficult. The customs and traditions of craft production had played an important role in promoting cooperation. Pride of craftmanship and the social status that evolved from craft status were also important factors. The worker in the evolving factories no longer felt that he was an organic part of the enterprise. His interest in the enterprise rested in its ability to pay him a wage with which to nurture his body and soul. The difficulty of achieving cooperation in factory organization is indicated by the effort of the pioneers of scientific management to devise improved wage systems. The importance of the noneconomic motivations of the early craft organizations is emphasized by the attention now being given to the social system in organization and the attempts to reproduce smaller-scale production units through decentralization.

The examples of the previous section show that the practice of successful management preceded the factory system and the industrial revolution. Many of the problems that evolved from the rise of the factory as the dominant mode of production existed in preindustrial revolution factories, such as the Arsenal of Venice. The functions of management were important in these early organizations, and fragmentary historical accounts indicate that they were often well performed. But industrial production in factories was not quantitatively significant during earlier periods. Agriculture and craft production in small shops or homes were the dominant forms of economic activity. The industrial revolution greatly magnified industrial production in factories and at the same time created a managerial class. With the factory system came larger and more complex organizations in other areas of endeavor, which further expanded the need for management and managers.

The Rise of a Managerial Class

Corporations constitute the legal framework within which the organizations of modern industrial civilization have developed. The corporate form of organization overcame certain limitations imposed by a private control of property. It provided the means whereby the property of innumerable individuals could be combined and brought under unified control. In a world in which the life-span of the personal property holder is limited, the corporation provided a greater continuity in time.

With the development of capitalism, the control of the enterprise passed to the property owner or the capitalist. But the age of the capitalist was soon to become the age of the manager. Control has in great part shifted from the property owner to a nonpropertied managerial class. This shift in control has been expressed by such terms as "the managerial revolution" and "managerialism." It has resulted in a change in the manner of speaking. As Peter Drucker has noted, we now talk about the "responsibilities of management" rather than the "responsibilities of capital." [21] The term "management and labor" has generally replaced "capital and labor" in the vocabulary.

The rise of large corporations brought into being a large class of hired managers. The property owners could at best assume only a few top-

[21] Peter F. Drucker, *The Practice of Management* (New York: Harper & Brothers Publishers, 1954), p. 3.

management positions; the middle and lower ranks of management were filled with professional managers. Frequently the property owners were more interested in finance than in the active management of industrial organizations, which gave many top-management positions to the nonpropertied professional. Simultaneously the managerial class began to assume more complete control of the corporation. Management control was facilitated by a number of factors that evolved from the nature of corporate organization and its ultimate development. A wide dispersion of stock ownership occurred in many corporations—in some cases the largest stockholder held only a fraction of one per cent of the controlling stock. Stockholders began to view stock ownership primarily as a financial investment rather than an instrument of control. So long as a reasonable financial return was forthcoming, little difficulty was experienced by management in obtaining a sufficient number of proxies to control. In other instances the use of nonvoting stock made possible legal control with a relatively small investment. Even though unqualified legal control requires a majority of the voting stock, actual control can be obtained by minority stockholders if the remaining stock is well dispersed. Through these and other devices a clear differentiation between property and control began to appear in many corporations. The capitalistic system began to give way to the managerial system.

Similar developments occurred in other fields. In government, the professional public administrator has replaced the politician in many areas. University and college administrators have taken away many of the functions formerly performed by the professor and in some cases have taken active control of the curricula.

Trade Unionism

The development of industry on a large scale has been followed by a trade union movement in every democratic society. A number of explanations have been advanced for this phenomenon. The radicals have viewed trade unionism as one aspect of a class-conscious revolt of the proletarian worker against the capitalist, which they assumed to be the ultimate consequence of the new industrial system. The realization of this prophecy has been repudiated by the events of history. Industrial workers did not become the proletariat. The long-run consequence of the new industrial system was a higher standard of living than ever before experienced by the large masses of people. Anachronistically, the dictatorship of the proletariat was initially established in a nation that had not developed industry or capitalism on a significant scale.

The workers of the Western industrial nations have generally repudiated the ideas of the radicals. They have not been interested in destroying the basic institutions of capitalism. They sought higher wages and better conditions of work by extending control over the supply of labor through trade union organization. They rejected the views of the radicals and accepted the market mechanism of the private enterprise system.[22]

Beginning with small craft unions of carpenters, printers, and shoemakers in the early 1800's, the American trade union movement has resulted in the organization of 17 million workers in some 185 national and international unions. These unions range in size from 200 members for the smallest to well over a million for the largest. Some of these unions are craft unions including only workers in a particular craft, such as painters or bricklayers. The industrial unions, as the name implies, have organized workers in a particular industry. A number of the larger unions are actually multicraft-industrial unions because they have members in a number of crafts or industries or both.

American trade unions have generally accepted the philosophy that the best way to promote the welfare of the worker is through collective bargaining with the employer for wages, hours, and conditions of work. The nature of collective bargaining involves a union challenge to management control.[23] Collective bargaining is joint union-management action about certain matters. Contract negotiation results in important decisions about wages, hours, and conditions of employment, which are formally set forth in a trade agreement. Joint decision making is also involved in the procedure generally established in the trade agreement to resolve difficulties that arise in the administration of the agreement. What is the proper dividing line between the subject matter of collective bargaining and those areas that remain the exclusive domain of management? Management has generally conceded that unions have a right to participate in matters that directly affect the interest of the worker. But they have opposed attempts of unions to expand beyond this point. The management argument is that they are legally responsible to the stockholder and that they can assume this responsibility only if they are given a free hand in managing the enterprise. Union leaders argue that they represent the worker and should have a voice in any matter that directly concerns the interests of the worker.

---

[22] One account of the philosophy of American trade unionism is found in Selig Perlman, *A Theory of the Labor Movement* (New York: The Macmillan Company, 1928).

[23] Neil W. Chamberlain has made an outstanding contribution to a better understanding of this problem in *The Union Challenge to Management Control* (New York: Harper & Brothers Publishers, 1948).

Government Regulation of Business

The manner in which government intervention in the economic sphere has affected decision making by private business leaders is now considered.[24] Some government activity is designed to promote the exercise of private business leadership. The protection of property rights and the development of contract and corporation law are examples of this form of government intervention. This type of government control is usually taken for granted by business leaders. Of greater concern have been government activities that restrict the action of business leadership.

The Ideal of Competition

The American attitude toward the role of government in a private enterprise system has been greatly influenced by Adam Smith's *Wealth of Nations* and the Classical School of economists who promulgated his basic philosophical premises.[25] The fundamental thesis of the classical economists was that government intervention in the economic sphere should be minimized and that the pursuit of self-interest and competition would promote the greatest social welfare. Ironically, this doctrine of *laissez faire* and competition laid the initial basis for government intervention in the activity of businessmen. This intervention proceeded on the assumption that competition is good and that any attempts by business firms to become

---

[24] Many of the ideas in this section were originally presented by Robert A. Gordon in *Business Leadership in the Large Corporation* (Washington, D.C: The Brookings Institution, 1945), pp. 222–245.

[25] Adam Smith was particularly concerned with the government restrictions recommended by some of the mercantilists in the field of foreign trade. In the following oft-quoted passage he recommends *laissez faire* as a better policy: "As every individual, therefore, endeavours as much as he can both to employ his capital in the support of domestic industry, and so to direct that industry that its produce may be of the greatest value; every individual necessarily labours to render the annual revenue of the society as great as he can. He generally, indeed, neither intends to promote the public interest, nor knows how much he is promoting it. By preferring the support of domestic to that of foreign industry, he intends only his own security; and by directing that industry in such a manner as its produce may be of the greatest value, he intends only his own gain, and he is in this, as in many other cases, led by an invisible hand to promote an end which was no part of his intention. Nor is it always the worse for the society that it was no part of it. By pursuing his own interest he frequently promotes that of the society more effectually than when he really intends to promote it." Adam Smith, *The Wealth of Nations,* Cannan edition (New York: The Modern Library, 1937), p. 423. Originally published in 1776.

monopolistic had to be controlled. The businessman was given the freedom to control the destiny of his enterprise with one important exception: he could not engage in activities that threatened the survival of competition. Another important postulate of early government intervention was that competition should be fair and constructive. Originally enforced by the common law, this policy was soon enunciated by the statute law. The first legislation designed to promote competition was the Sherman Anti-Trust Act of 1890, which prohibited combinations in restraint of commerce. The Sherman Act was followed by the Clayton Act (1914), which prohibited local price discrimination, tying contracts, and interlocking directorates.[26] The Federal Trade Commission, an administrative agency, was created in 1914 to enforce statutory provisions against unfair competition. Additional amendments to the statutory law governing unfair competition were made in the Robinson-Patman Act of 1936. These and other Federal statutes, the administrative rulings of the Federal Trade Commission, the common law on the subject, and state legislation provide a voluminous body of rules within which the business leader must operate. The fact that enforcement has not always been stringent does not alter the basic idea that business decision making must take into account the fact or possibility of governmental action.

Other Forms of Government Intervention

The Federal labor laws have resulted in a comprehensive body of law governing the relationship between management and unions in industries engaged in interstate commerce. The Wagner Act (1935) with the amendments and additions made by the Taft-Hartley Act (1947) makes recognition of a union mandatory if the majority of employees in the bargaining unit vote for the union. The employer is also required to bargain in good faith with a union certified under the law. Although the law does not force the employer to come to an agreement with a union, the practical exigencies of the relationships created by the law have led to the establishment of joint union-management decision making about a number of important issues.

The Fair Labor Standards Act (1938) set a minimum wage and required the payment of time-and-one-half for work beyond forty hours per week. Legislation passed in the early 1930's forbade certain practices in

[26] An example of local price discrimination is price reduction by a local branch of a large firm to drive out independent merchants. Tying contracts were often used to force a buyer to purchase an entire line of goods produced by the manufacturer. An interlocking directorate exists when an individual is a director in two or more supposedly competing firms.

the securities markets and created the Securities Exchange Commission to administer the law. Railroads, telephone companies, electric light and power companies, and other public utilities were excluded from the regulatory efforts to enforce competition. Public policy in this field has been guided by the idea that the absence of competition necessitated more comprehensive government regulation. Administrative agencies, such as the Interstate Commerce Commission and the Federal Communications Commission, have placed severe restrictions on management decision making.

Although not expressly designed to regulate business, social security legislation (such as the Social Security Act) makes necessary accounting procedures and reports beyond the ordinary requirements of business. Corporation and personal income taxes have imposed similar responsibilities and also influence business decisions in a wide area. The requirements of national security have increased government participation in private decision making in numerous ways. Government contracts generally involve a great deal of such participation. The experiences of World War II and Korea indicate the extent to which government controls can be imposed in a private enterprise system when the national security demands it.

The role of government in a private enterprise system has been and will be the subject of a great deal of debate. A private enterprise system is founded on the idea of private rather than government decision making in the primary areas of economic activity. The principal form of government intervention has been regulation rather than government ownership. This regulation has placed limits on private decision making and also frequently involves the transfer of decision making to a government agency, such as the Interstate Commerce Commission and the National Labor Relations Board. The pursuit of self-interest is also a fundamantal premise of a private enterprise system. The question of when the pursuit of private self-interest begins to interfere with the public welfare frequently presents a difficult problem. Some of the policy problems in this area involve the rights of one economic group relative to another. The tariff question, for example, often leads to controversy between exporters and domestic producers over what is proper public policy.

The Second Industrial Revolution

In the first industrial revolution machines displaced man as a source of power, but it did not, as Norbert Wiener has pointed out, greatly affect other human functions.[27] The second industrial revolution represents an important forward step through the use of machines to perform mental operations. The primary instrument of this revolution is the electronic computer, which has made a profound impact upon many aspects of human living in a relatively short period of time.

The Development of Electronic Computers

Some of the theories upon which the modern electronic computer is founded can be traced back well over one hundred years. The difficulty in putting theory into practice stemmed from the lack of technological capacity. Charles Babbage, the British mathematician who developed the ideas for two kinds of automatic computers early in the nineteenth century, spent ten years visiting British and French workshops and factories in an unsuccessful attempt to overcome the limitations imposed by the then existing state of technology. A differential analyzer, something like the one envisioned by Babbage, was built in the early 1930's by Vannevar Bush of M.I.T. But the final gap between computer theory and practical application was not bridged until shortly after World War II. The key to the solution was found in the form of the already available vacuum tube, which made possible high-speed off-on switching. The basic core of a modern electronic computer is a large number of off-on switching devices, such as the vacuum tube or the more recently developed transistor. The requirements of the military gave impetus to the development of large-scale electronic computers designed to solve scientific and technical problems. The potential value of computers in the solution of informational problems in business, governmental, and other organizations became apparent almost immediately. Computers adapted to these requirements became commercially available in the early 1950's.

The Nature of Electronic Computers

Modern computing machines can generally be categorized as analogue and digital machines. An analogue machine is composed of devices that represent each variable of the problem by a corresponding physical quantity, such as gear ratios and relative voltage. The slide rule is a simplified version of an analogue-type computing instrument. Digital machines are counting machines like the ancient abacus or the desk calculators still found in most business offices. The discussion that follows is primarily

[27] Norbert Wiener, *The Human Use of Human Beings,* Second Edition Revised (Garden City, New York: Doubleday & Company, Inc., 1954), pp. 153–154.

restricted to electronic digital computers and their use in the solution of informational problems.

Digital computers can "read" perforations in paper cards or tapes, and magnetically charged tapes. They can perform arithmetic and logical operations with high accuracy and speed. They have the capacity to memorize or store information and to transmit information through printing devices. Two basic characteristics differentiate modern electronic computers from the computers of the past. One is the high speed implied by the word "electronic," which means that modern computers can perform operations in thousandths (milliseconds) and millionths (microseconds) of a second. Another is that modern computers can be programmed to solve simple and relatively complex informational problems automatically without further human intervention. This characteristic, together with its extremely high speed, gives it the capacity to perform elementary thinking operations.

In addition to routine and rapid information processing, computers have engaged in tasks that involve thinking when they are done by human beings. Computers have played checkers, chess, and other games with a facility that exceeds that of many human players. They have been successful in proving theorems in geometry and logic, and have solved problems in calculus. A large manufacturing company has used computers extensively to design electric motors. A computer was used to compose music that sounds about as good as some of the music that comes from humans. Computers have also written short cowboy movies which are fully as interesting as many of the late movies on television. But in spite of these and other successes, many people still assert with an air of finality that computers cannot think.

Thinking Machines

The question as to whether electronic computers can think has generated a great deal of controversy. On one side of the question are those who assert quite emphatically that computers cannot think. To quote a government report on the use of electronic data processing in the federal government:

However, for all their speed and efficiency, digital computers are totally unable to "think." The term "electronic brain" is a misnomer. Rather, they are super-efficient robots totally lacking in imagination—they do exactly what they are told to do, and no more.[28]

[28] *Use of Electronic Data Processing Equipment in the Federal Government,* House Report No. 858, 88th Congress, 1st Session, October 16, 1963, p. 96.

Another point of view is that computers can "think" in an elementary fashion, but that they are extremely stupid. A textbook on the subject presents this position.

The point is that electronic computers are not smart—they are stupid and far from being "brains." Consider the question in this light: Would you be willing to call the flush box of a toilet a brain—even a very small one? Actually, this utilitarian device does have one logical ability. It can determine when the water has risen to a certain predetermined level and then controls shutting off the incoming water. An electronic computer is a little smarter than a toilet, since it can recognize, not a single condition, but several possibilities and can then use that information to select appropriate succeeding operations.[29]

It is true that one toilet (a single off-on switch) would be rather stupid, but several thousand toilets flushing in elaborate combinations would have considerable "thinking" capacity. The off-on switching devices in a computer make possible complex patterns of logical thought. As the mathematician John von Neumann has written:

"And" and "or" are the basic operations of logic. Together with "no" (the logical operation of negation) they are a complete set of basic logical operations—all other logical operations, no matter how complex, can be obtained by suitable combinations of these.[30]

Present-day computers can "think" in the sense that they have the capacity to make such logical choices. The programmer provides the instructions as to when and how a choice is to be made; the computer then automatically makes these choices as information is processed. In solving complex problems, the outcome may not be apparent even to the man who did the programming.

A more comprehensive and demanding test of whether computers can think was devised by A. M. Turing, a British mathematician. Turing proposed that a machine could be said to be capable of thinking if it could communicate with a human being through a speaker system or a teletype in such a way that the person would not know whether he had been communicating with a machine or a man. A computer program designed to engage in a discussion about the weather was written with a reasonable amount of success. Most of the problems presently solved by computers are quantitative and primarily involve the computational routines of mathematics. However, symbolic logic and other techniques can be used to construct programs that permit the solution of nonquantitative problems. It

---

[29] William D. Bell, *A Management Guide to Electronic Computers* (New York: McGraw-Hill Book Company, Inc., 1957), p. 101.

[30] John von Neumann, *The Computer and the Brain* (New Haven: Yale University Press, 1958), p. 53.

seems reasonable to conclude that computers have the capacity for handling ideas and that, at some distant future date, they will be able to meet the essential requirements of Turing's test.

Some people are willing to concede that computers can think logically, but they immediately add that computers will never be able to think creatively. A contrary view is held by Herbert A. Simon and Allen Newell, who have developed a number of experimental computer programs concerned with this problem.[31]

"Creativity" is defined by Simon and Newell as the capacity to produce effective surprise. Since a computer is a determinant instrument, a simple program could not result in effective surprise because the end of the process is always readily apparent. The solution to the problem lies in a highly complex program, which, according to Simon and Newell, will need to have the following properties. Such a program must first of all contain a large number of instructions introduced by different programmers working independently over a long period of time. Furthermore, the computer must have access to a large amount of information about environmental phenomena that it can identify and from which it can make selections. In addition, the computer must have the capacity to change what it will do next in response to changing environmental conditions, and to modify its own program (through the use of higher level programs) to enable it to react more effectively at a future time. As the complexity of computer behavior increases, Simon and Newell suggest that "it may reach a level of richness that produces effective surprise."[32]

Such a computer program duplicates the process through which humans appear to derive creative potential. A possible difference is that humans may not be determinate beings, which might add (it could subtract) something to human capacities. But creativity by computers is not necessarily precluded by this possibility. Indeed, the creative potential of computers may be far greater than that of human beings.

Further Thoughts on Computer Thinking

Few people objected when machines became substitutes for human muscle power. But many people seem to feel that thinking is a unique capacity of man. To them the idea that a machine can think is tantamount to giving it human attributes. Computer designers and programmers

---

[31] Herbert A. Simon and Allen Newell, "What Have Computers to do with Management?" in George P. Shultz and Thomas L. Whisler (editors), *Management Organization and the Computer* (The Free Press of Glencoe, Illinois, 1960), pp. 43–45.

[32] *Ibid.,* p. 45.

thereby take on godlike qualities. No mere mortal should be so presumptuous. But none of these ideas precludes the development of nonhuman thinking machines. Such machines would be no more human than an automatic washer or a bulldozer. Even if a computer were someday to have more thinking capacity than a human being does not change this conclusion. An automatic washer washes, but it is not a woman. An airplane flies, but it is not a bird. A computer thinks, but it is not a man.

Some people concede that computers can think, but they contend that the human programmer, not the computer, does the thinking. A similar statement can be made about human thinking. Modern man has been programmed to think by those who have gone before him. In this sense, Euclid and Leibnitz think for the modern engineer; Einstein and Faraday for the modern physicist; Taylor and Fayol for the modern manager; Galen and Harvey for the modern physician; and Blackstone and Marshall for the modern jurist. The instructions and data fed into the memory of a computer are something like the information absorbed by the human brain in the learning process. Much of human knowledge is transmitted in the form of symbols that are translated into whatever kind of code is involved in the physiological phenomenon of memory. Computer programming duplicates at least some of the features of this process.

A large memory is an important ingredient in the human thinking apparatus. The computer is still outdistanced by the human system in terms of the number of memory elements. But there is little reason to doubt computer information storage may eventually reach, and probably surpass, the human memory capacity. Professor Richard P. Feynman, a physicist at the California Institute of Technology, has speculated that the entire twenty-four volume *Encyclopedia Britannica* could conceivably be "etched" on the head of a pin at some future date.[33] With proper coding, Feynman surmised that all of the world's books might be contained in a cube of material 1/200 of an inch wide—the size of a speck of dust. Although technology is not likely to achieve such goals for some time, the breakthroughs that have already been made in the development of tiny electronic devices called "semiconductors" indicate that computer memory capacity will be greatly increased during the next few years.

There would appear to be no absolute barrier to the development of computers that simulate the human thinking apparatus. Such an assertion is founded on the assumption that human physiology involves the same physical laws as the rest of this portion of the universe. Present neurophysiological research does not indicate a contrary conclusion. Indeed, there is some evidence that the human system utilizes off-on switching (a neuron

[33] Richard P. Feynman, "The Wonders that Await a Micro-Microscope," *Saturday Review,* April 2, 1960, pp. 45–47.

either responds or it does not), similar to that of a digital computer. There is still a great deal of mystery about the manner in which humans perform thinking operations. But there is good reason to believe that the essential process can eventually be duplicated in an electronic computer.

The Human System and Machine Systems

The author has asked students to indicate how much they would pay to have their brain kept alive after their deaths. Most students were not especially eager to take advantage of this form of eternal life. They recognized that what makes man man is as much his stomach and his sex organs as his thinking apparatus. Although man is made up of many parts, none of them in isolation even if alive can be called man. A man should be viewed as a total system. A computer represents only an aspect of the human process and, therefore, could not be called human even if it became as effective in thinking as the brain.

Should an attempt be made to build a mechanical man like the Frankenstein of movie fame? The answer is that little purpose would be served by such a being. It is much simpler and less costly to create a human being through normal physiological means. But a useful purpose can be served by constructing machine systems composed of parts that duplicate aspects of the human system. Electronic computers can be given sensory capacities through radar, temperature gauges, and Geiger counters. They can be provided with mobility through aircraft, automobiles, and rockets. They can be given instruments for modifying the environment such as machine tools and earthmoving equipment. In other words, computers can become something more than simply informational and thinking devices. They can be used as the "brains" for automated machine systems designed to perform particular functions. Computers can also be used in combination with both machines and man to form man-machine systems.

Computer Speed and Logic

Electronic computers are able to perform their basic operations much more rapidly than human beings. Electronic off-on switching can be measured in terms of thousandths (millisecond) and millionths (microsecond) of a second. The human neuron functions in much larger fractions (hundredths) of a second. But the human mental system makes up for its lack of speed through much more comprehensive and complex logical capacities.

Computers make up for some of their logical inadequacies through the tremendous speed with which they can solve problems. Even with a relatively simple logical system, a computer can frequently create surprising conclusions. For example, a computer can perform the computations for each period of a ten firm interacting business game in less than a minute. The ability of the computer to operate on incoming data at a rate which far exceeds that of human beings gives it the capacity to surprise even the man who programmed it. Norbert Wiener has warned that "by the very slowness of our human actions, our effective control of our machines may be nullified." [34]

Some of the problems solved by computers are difficult decisional problems when performed by human beings. For example, a computer has the capacity to dispatch fighter aircraft from airfields in different locations in response to radar reports on incoming enemy bombers. A general with the same information but without the computational speed of the computer would undoubtedly feel that he is faced with a major decisional problem. With sufficient time, the general might well have clerical personnel go through the same computational routines as the computer. But the fact that the time is not available means that the general must resort to a combination of objective and subjective techniques. The general's education and experience may well bring about some highly effective decisions. His advantage is much more sophisticated logical capacities than the computer. The computer compensates for the simplicity of its logical system through accuracy and high speed.

The Pace of the Computer Revolution

The pace of the computer revolution is partially indicated by the rapid growth in the number of computer installations in the United States. Beginning with almost no installations in 1951, the number of computers reached 1000 in a period of five years. Within the next five years this number had multiplied by ten and in another five years there were well over 30,000 computer systems. In late 1967, there were more than 50,000 such systems throughout the world.[35] General David Sarnoff, Chairman of the Board of the Radio Corporation of America, has estimated that the computer population may well reach 100,000 by the year 1976.[36]

The technical capacities and the economic efficiency of computers and related devices will continue to expand in the years ahead. Sarnoff estimates that in a recent ten year period "the typical electronic data processor has become ten times smaller, 100 times faster and 1,000 times less ex-

---

[34] Norbert Wiener, "Some Moral and Technical Consequences of Automation," *Science*, Vol. 131, May 6, 1960, p. 1355.
[35] *Computers and Automation,* June 1967, p. 77; December 1967, p. 71.
[36] *Saturday Review,* July 23, 1966, p. 22.

pensive to operate."[37] In terms of the total information processed, the computers that existed in 1956 were capable of some 12 billion computations an hour. By 1966 this total exceeded 20 trillion, and by 1976 computers will attain up to 400 trillion computations or about two billion per hour for every person in the United States.

The Impact of the Computer Revolution upon Management Science

The computer has already had a profound impact upon the philosophy and practice of management. It has made possible more efficient information processing and problem solving in business and other organizations, and has been highly instrumental in advancing management knowledge. The nature of some of the changes that have occurred in organizational practices as a result of computer technology is indicated in a number of chapters of this book. However, many of the innovations of the computer revolution are founded in the systematic approaches developed by earlier pioneers of scientific management. The chapter that follows is concerned with these important contributions.

[37] *Ibid.*

SELECTED REFERENCES

Adolf A. Berle, Jr., *The 20th Century Capitalist Revolution.* New York: Harcourt, Brace and Company, Inc., 1954.

Adolf A. Berle, Jr., and Gardiner C. Means, *The Modern Corporation and Private Property.* New York: The Macmillan Company, 1933.

Kenneth E. Boulding, *The Organizational Revolution.* New York: Harper & Brothers, 1953.

Howard R. Bowen, "Business Management: A Profession?" *The Annals of the American Academy of Political and Social Science,* Vol. 297, pp. 112–117 (January 1955).

Howard R. Bowen and Garth L. Mangum, *Automation and Economic Progress.* Englewood Cliffs, N.J.: Prentice-Hall, Inc., 1966.

Harvey C. Bunke, *The Liberal Dilemma.* Englewood Cliffs, N.J.: Prentice-Hall, Inc., 1964.

Gilbert Burck, *The Computer Age.* New York: Harper & Row, 1965.

Neil W. Chamberlain, *The Union Challenge to Management Control.* New York: Harper & Brothers, 1948.

Hershner Cross and others, *Computers and Management.* The 1967 Leatherlee Lectures. Boston: Graduate School of Business Administration, Harvard University, 1967.

William V. D'Antonio and Howard J. Ehrlich (editors), *Power and Democracy in America.* Notre Dame, Indiana: University of Notre Dame Press, 1961.

Richard Eells and Clarence Walton, *Conceptual Foundations of Business.* Homewood, Ill.: Richard D. Irwin, Inc., 1961.

Milton Friedman, *Capitalism and Freedom.* Chicago: The University of Chicago Press, 1962.

John Kenneth Galbraith, *The New Industrial State.* Boston: Houghton Mifflin Company, 1967.

Robert A. Gordon, *Business Leadership in the Large Corporation.* Washington, D.C.: The Brookings Institution, 1945.

Martin Greenberger (editor), *Computers and the World of the Future.* Cambridge: The M.I.T. Press, 1962.

Luther Gulick, "Notes on the Theory of Organization," *Papers on the Science of Administration,* pp. 3–45. New York: Institute of Public Administration, Columbia University, 1937.

Antony Jay, *Management and Machiavelli.* New York: Holt, Rinehart and Winston, 1967.

Elton Mayo, *The Social Problems of an Industrial Civilization,* Part I, Chaps. 1 and 2. Boston: Division of Research, Graduate School of Business Administration, Harvard University, 1945.

Joseph W. McGuire, *Business and Society.* New York: McGraw-Hill Book Company, Inc., 1963.

Wayne A. Meinhart, "Artificial Intelligence, Computer Simulation of Human Cognitive and Social Processes, and Management Thought," *Academy of Management Journal,* Vol. 9, No. 4, pp. 294–307 (December 1966).

C. Wright Mills, *The Power Elite.* New York: Oxford University Press, 1959.

James D. Mooney and Alan C. Reiley, *Onward Industry!* New York: Harper & Brothers, 1931. An abbreviated version of this book: James D. Mooney, *Principles of Organization.* New York: Harper & Brothers, 1947.

C. Northcote Parkinson, *Parkinson's Law.* Boston: Houghton Mifflin Company, 1957.

Selig Perlman, *A Theory of the Labor Movement.* New York: The Macmillan Company, 1928.

Karl Polanyi, *The Great Transformation.* New York: Rinehart & Company, Inc., 1944.

Robert Presthus, *The Organizational Society,* Chap. 3. New York: Alfred A. Knopf, Inc., 1962.

Jesse S. Raphael, *Governmental Regulation of Business.* New York: The Free Press, 1966.

F. J. Roethlisberger, *Management and Morale.* Cambridge: Harvard University Press, 1941.

Leonard R. Sayles (editor), *Individualism and Big Business.* New York: McGraw-Hill Book Company, Inc., 1963.

Scientific American, Vol. 215, No. 3, September 1966. The entire issue is devoted to information technology.

Herbert A. Simon, *The Shape of Automation.* New York: Harper & Row, 1965.

Eugene Staley (editor), *Creating an Industrial Civilization.* New York: Harper & Brothers, 1952.

Frank Tannenbaum, *A Philosophy of Labor.* New York: Alfred A. Knopf, Inc., 1951.

Norbert Wiener, *The Human Use of Human Beings,* 2nd ed. rev. Garden City, N.Y.: Doubleday & Company, Inc., 1954 (Doubleday Anchor Books).

chapter 2

TOWARD SCIENTIFIC MANAGEMENT

The development of management as an area of knowledge involved the contributions of many individuals from many kinds of endeavor. Some contributions came from practicing executives and engineers who translated the product of their experiences into published form. Others came from professors in business and engineering schools who sought to meet the educational requirements of the emerging profession. Still others were made by people in such fields as sociology, psychology, economics, mathematics, accounting, and statistics.[1]

Few publications on the subject of management were available before the beginning of this century. Fragmentary accounts of what might be called principles of management can be found in the writings of early historians, church officials, and military and political leaders. A few treatises in the fields of military and political organization are antecedent to the modern book on management.[2] An early contribution came from Charles Babbage

---

[1] For a study that brings together contributions that have been made to organization and management theory by sociologists, psychologists, economists, political scientists, and others: James G. March and Herbert A. Simon, *Organizations* (New York: John Wiley and Sons, Inc., 1958).

[2] One of the oldest military treatises is *The Art of War,* written about 500 B.C. by Sun Tzu Wu (Harrisburg: The Military Service Publishing Company, 1944). Other well-known classics in the field of military organization and strategy are Karl von Clausewitz's *On War* (Washington, D.C.: The Infantry Journal Press, 1950); Maurice de Saxe's *Reveries on the Art of War* (Harrisburg: The Military Service Publishing Company, 1944); and Frederick the Great's *Instructions for His Generals* (Harrisburg: The Military Service Publishing Company, 1944). Early examples from the field of political organization and policy are Plato's *Republic* and Machiavelli's *The Prince.*

as a result of his ideas for an automatic computer.[3] Babbage, as was noted in Chapter 1, visited many British and French factories and workshops in search of the technical capacities to construct an automatic computer. A by-product of this activity was a book in which he presented "some principles that seemed to pervade many establishments."[4] He dealt with such problems as work division and specialization, better methods for doing work, the utilization of machines and tools, and the maintenance of cost records.

Scientific Management: Frederick W. Taylor and his Lieutenants

The development of scientific management in the United States is generally considered to have begun with the experiments of Frederick W. Taylor at the Midvale Steel Company in the early 1880's. Taylor was born in Germantown, Pennsylvania, in 1856.[5] During his early youth he attended school in France and Germany and traveled extensively in Europe. In the fall of 1872 Taylor entered the Phillips Exeter Academy to prepare for Harvard College. The high scholastic standards at Exeter severely taxed Taylor's already poor eyesight. Although he passed the Harvard entrance examinations with "honors," he was not able to continue his academic pursuits. Late in the year 1874, at the age of eighteen, he decided to learn the pattern maker and machinist trades in the shop of a small Philadelphia pump manufacturing company owned by friends of his family.

The Midvale Experience

In 1878 Taylor went to work at the Midvale Steel Company as a laborer because employment was difficult to find in the machinist trade. A short time later he was given a machinist job with the lathe gang and within two months became the gang boss. His promotion at Midvale was rapid. In six years he rose from gang boss to foreman of the machine shop, to master mechanic in charge of all repairs and maintenance in the works, to chief

---

[3] Charles Babbage, *On the Economy of Machinery and Manufactures* (Philadelphia: Carey and Lea, 1832).

[4] *Ibid.*, p. vii.

[5] The "official" Taylor biography was written by Frank Barkley Copley, *Frederick W. Taylor, Father of Scientific Management*, Vols. I and II (New York: Harper & Brothers Publishers, 1923). The biographical material in this section is drawn from this source.

draftsman, and finally to chief engineer. To facilitate his advancement in industry Taylor took correspondence courses in mathematics and physics from Harvard professors and then through home study completed the requirements for the M.E. degree at Stevens Institute.

A factor in Taylor's promotion to gang boss was his good production record as a machinist. He knew that greater output was easily possible and that workers were engaged in what he termed "systematic soldiering." When he became gang boss and later foreman, he was determined to do something about the problem. The solution, he thought, was a careful study by management as to what constituted a proper day's work. The company granted him money to conduct experiments to find the time required for various kinds of work. Time study was begun in the machine shop in 1881, and after two years of preliminary experimentation, a full-time man was hired. Taylor considered the Midvale studies the beginning of the "profession" of time study.

The Bethlehem Experiments: Pig Iron Handling

In 1898 Taylor was hired by the Bethlehem Steel Company to increase the output of one of the larger machine shops, which had been a serious production bottleneck. Taylor's most noted achievements at Bethlehem were his studies of pig iron handling and shoveling and his metal-cutting experiments.[6] These studies are good illustrations of the practice of scientific management during the formative period.

The product of Bethlehem's five blast furnaces was handled by a gang of about seventy-five men. A railroad switch paralleled the piles of pig iron in the yards. Pig iron handling consisted of picking up a pig of iron (about 92 pounds in weight), carrying it up an inclined plank, and dropping it into a railroad car. Before Taylor began his study each man moved about 12½ long tons per day. A fourfold increase in output resulted from a scientific study of pig iron handling, a better selection of workmen, and training workers in the improved method.

To find the best method for handling pig iron, Taylor conducted a series of experiments. These experiments showed that a man should be able to handle 47½ long tons per day. In order to handle this much pig iron, research results indicated that the man would have to rest about 57 per cent of the time. This amount of rest was made necessary by the heavy load that the workman had to carry all day long. With a lighter load the amount of work time could be increased.

[6] Taylor's account of his work at Bethlehem can be found in his book, *The Principles of Scientific Management* (New York: Harper & Brothers Publishers, 1915), pp. 42–48, 58–77, 97–115.

The next step in the project was to select a man and train him to handle the amount of pig iron that the experiments indicated was possible. A man, to whom Taylor gave the pseudonym of Schmidt in his writings, was trained to work in accordance with the methods derived by experimentation. Schmidt was told when to work and when to rest, and by 5:30 of the first afternoon he had loaded 47½ tons. He rarely failed in meeting this standard during the time that Taylor spent at Bethlehem. After the success with Schmidt, other men were trained to work at the 47½ ton rate until all pig iron was handled at this rate. Wages under a new task system averaged $1.85 per day compared with $1.15 previously paid on a day basis.

The Shoveling Experiments

The Bethlehem yards employed a large crew of men to shovel iron ore and rice coal. The shoveling experiment began with a systematic study of shoveling. What is the best shovel load for a given type of material? When Taylor came to Bethlehem each worker brought his own shovel. A worker would shovel rice coal, which gave him a shovel load of 3½ pounds, and then use the same shovel for iron ore, which involved a load of 38 pounds. Taylor selected several first-class shovelers and paid them extra for following his directions. His experimentation indicated that an average load of 21 pounds gave the best results.

A large tool room was built to stock different-sized shovels designed to give a 21-pound shovel load for various types of material handled in the yards. The tool room also stocked other implements, such as picks and crowbars, designed and standardized for particular jobs. A detailed system of work assignment was developed. Two slips of paper were placed in a pigeonhole assigned to each worker, one indicating the implements he would have to use and where he was to work that day and the other reporting output and earnings of the previous day. When output was below par, a yellow slip served as a warning to improve, and a failure to meet the standard meant transfer to other types of work if available. The work was planned in advance, and workers were moved around the yard by clerks in the labor office. Elaborate maps and diagrams of the yard were used for this purpose, and telephone and messenger services were established to facilitate communication.

Studies were also conducted to determine the best way to shovel various types of material. For example, the best method for forcing the shovel into iron ore or bituminous coal was to hold the shovel so that the weight of the body could be used. This method takes less energy than when the arms are used alone. Workers were trained to use the new methods and were checked periodically to see whether they were using them.

The results of the shoveling experiments were phenomenal. The number of yard laborers was reduced from between 400 and 600 to 140. The average number of tons handled by each man per day increased from 16 to 59; handling cost per ton decreased from 7.2 to 3.3 cents. The cost included the office and tool-room expenses, the wages paid to foremen, clerks, and time study men, and an increase in wages from $1.15 per day to $1.88.

The Metal-Cutting Experiments

Taylor continued a study of cutting metals that he had begun at Midvale. This experimentation was carried on over a period of twenty-six years. Over 30,000 experiments were recorded, more than 800,000 pounds of iron and steel were cut into chips by experimental tools, and the total cost was estimated to exceed $150,000. One result was the discovery (by Taylor and Maunsel White) of high-speed steel which greatly increased the output of metal-cutting machinery. Another was information about the proper speed and feed for lathes, planers, drill presses, milling machines, and related equipment. The achievements of the metal-cutting experiments were in many respects more important than Taylor's other contributions. They represented a major breakthrough in American industrial development. High-speed and precision cutting tools are an essential ingredient of large-scale production.

The Taylor Differential Piecework Plan

Taylor developed an incentive piecework plan that made use of standards developed through time study. The plan called for high wage rates for performance above the standard and relatively low rates for work below standard. It did not guarantee a basic day wage as did later plans.

Publications on Scientific Management

After 1903, Taylor spent most of his time writing and lecturing on scientific management. In his paper "Shop Management," presented to the American Society of Mechanical Engineers in 1903, Taylor outlined the essential features of his system.[7] In 1907, he presented the results of his metal-cutting experiments.[8] In 1911, *The American Magazine* published a

[7] Frederick W. Taylor, "Shop Management," *Transactions of the American Society of Mechanical Engineers,* Vol. 24, June 1903, pp. 1337–1480.

[8] Frederick W. Taylor, "On the Art of Cutting Metals," *Transactions of the American Society of Mechanical Engineers,* Vol 28, 1907, pp. 31–350.

series of three articles by Taylor, which were later combined in book form as *The Principles of Scientific Management*.[9] *Shop Management*, originally published in the *Transactions of the American Society of Mechanical Engineers,* was also brought out in a more popular format.[10]

The Eastern Railroads Rate Hearings

Taylor had gained considerable fame from his metal-cutting and mechanical achievements at Bethlehem. But few people were familiar with his ideas on management. Wilfred Lewis, president of the Tabor Company, had asked Taylor to help his company out of a bad financial situation. Taylor announced that he would help only if his system of management was adopted. Lewis made the following comment about this stipulation: "We were only too glad to do this without having any conception of what it was." [11] A few years later editors of popular magazines were flocking to Taylor's home to learn about scientific management. The reason for this sudden popularity was a hearing before the Interstate Commerce Commission involving a request by eastern railroads for a rate increase. A number of engineering consultants and business executives testified that the lack of net income about which the railroads were complaining could be corrected by the techniques of scientific management. The press headlined this testimony and introduced the term "scientific management" into the homes of the average American.

Taylor's Lieutenants

The accomplishments of civilization are often symbolized by great men. Their names are inscribed into the marble and stone of libraries, museums, and science halls. Such innovators as Copernicus, Newton, Darwin, Pasteur, Freud, and Keynes became centers around which "schools of thought" assembled for identity and recognition. These men wear the laurels and at the same time bear the burden of claims made in their names. Similarly, Taylor became what his biographer, Frank B. Copley, terms "the soul of the whole Scientific Management movement." [12] He became the rally point around which the forces of scientific management gathered. He has undoubtedly received far more credit and criticism than he deserves. As his associate Carl G. Barth once remarked to Taylor: "You have received credit for a lot of things you didn't do; but, on the

[9] New York: Harper & Brothers Publishers, 1915.
[10] New York: Harper & Brothers Publishers, 1919.
[11] Copley, *op. cit.,* Vol. II, p. 176.
[12] Copley, *op. cit.,* Vol. II, p. 253.

other hand, you have been *blamed* for many things you didn't do, and I should say that the account was about even." [13]

The contributions of a number of other individuals were as important in the development of scientific management as those of Taylor. The names of Henry L. Gantt, Morris L. Cooke, and Frank and Lillian Gilbreth must be placed high on the list of original contributors. Gantt first came into contact with Taylor's work at Midvale and later played a part in the Bethlehem experiments.[14] He developed a wage incentive system that proved superior to Taylor's and devised a planning and control technique, the Gantt Chart, which is still extensively used in the United States and abroad. He applied scientific management techniques in more than fifty companies and achieved results as impressive as those of the shoveling and pig iron handling experiments. Morris L. Cooke adapted scientific management to the problems of university and municipal administration.[15] His tenure as the Director of the Department of Public Works in Philadelphia from 1912 to 1916 increased departmental efficiency and reduced costs by large margins.[16] Frank B. Gilbreth is best known for his work in motion study, but he also developed a comprehensive body of planning and control techniques for the construction industry.[17] Lillian M. Gilbreth collaborated in many of her husband's research and writing ventures and, after his death in 1924, independently developed and applied scientific management techniques. Many others can be categorized as pioneers of the scientific management movement. The scrolls of history have accorded them a better fate than they suffer here.

[13] *Ibid.,* (Italics in the original.)

[14] L. P. Alford, *Henry Laurence Gantt* (New York: The American Society of Mechanical Engineers, 1934); Alex W. Rathe (editor), *Gantt on Management* (New York: American Management Association and the American Society of Mechanical Engineers, 1960).

[15] Morris L. Cooke, *Academic and Industrial Efficiency* (New York: The Carnegie Foundation for the Advancement of Teaching, Bulletin No. 5, 1910).

[16] Cooke's experiences in this capacity are described in his book, *Our Cities Awake* (Garden City, N.Y.: Doubleday, Page & Co., 1918).

[17] Frank B. Gilbreth, *Field System* (New York: The Myron C. Clark Publishing Company, 1908). This book deserves more attention than it has received in the literature of management history. It represents the application of scientific management techniques to a complete organization. It sets forth standard practices and procedures for all phases of construction including the paperwork necessary for efficient field and home office operations. It was used as early as 1902 as a "confidential" company manual. The effectiveness of the system is indicated by a number of outstanding construction accomplishments of the Gilbreth Company and the fact that competitors frequently attempted to obtain a copy by dubious means.

The Planning Postulates of Scientific Management

The pioneers of scientific management gave emphasis to the importance of scientific methods in planning and helped promote their cause by the results obtained in practical applications. They also gave impetus to a shift in planning responsibilities from the performance level to management. In the words of Taylor:

All of the planning which under the old system was done by the workman, as a result of his personal experience, must of necessity under the new system be done by the management in accordance with the laws of science; because even if the workman was well suited to the development and use of scientific data, it would be physically impossible for him to work at his machine and at a desk at the same time. It is also clear that in most cases one type of man is needed to plan ahead and an entirely different type to execute the work.[18]

Henry K. Hathaway, vice-president of the Tabor Manufacturing Company, described the changes that occurred at his company after Taylor introduced scientific management.

At the Tabor Manufacturing Company we have succeeded through the application of the Taylor principles of Scientific Management in increasing our production to about three times what it formerly was, with the total cost approximately the same and approximately the same total of men; of course with a very much smaller proportion of the men in the shop, and *a very much increased proportion of men in the planning department, or on the management side.*[19]

The ultimate consequence of this development was a large increase in the size of the management hierarchy and its adjuncts. Many planning functions formerly performed by supervisors and workers were shifted to specialists in personnel, purchasing, production engineering, quality control, and other areas. At the same time, as Hathaway's experience indicated, personnel requirements at the performance level were reduced. Scientific planning increased the costs of managing, but it reduced the costs of operations. The net result has been a higher level of economic efficiency in business and other organizations.

[18] Taylor, *Principles, op. cit.,* p. 38.
[19] *First Conference on Scientific Management,* October 12, 13, 14, 1911 (Hanover, N.H.: The Amos Tuck School of Administration and Finance, Dartmouth College, 1912, p. 339). (Italics added.)

Scientific Management and Human Behavior

Although the scientific management pioneers emphasized the importance of scientific techniques in maximizing the productive capacities of machines and men, their assumptions about human behavior were founded in the "rabble hypothesis" and the concept of the economic man.[20] The idea that society is a rabble of individuals is implicit in much political and economic theory.[21] An empirical examination of the marketplace or society indicates that behavior is significantly influenced by social factors. The concept of "the individual" developed by political and economic theorists is a useful analytical technique. It has also played an important part in developing a democratic ideology. But the behavioral problems of management involve a lower level of abstraction and require a more pragmatic basis.

Taylor's ideas on cooperation were predicated on the assumption that the primary interest of management and the worker is economic gain in the form of lower labor costs and higher wages. The amount of work that the worker would have to do was to be measured by careful scientific investigation. Taylor believed that once the worker became aware of the great advantages of scientific management, he would acquire "a friendly mental attitude toward his employers and his whole working conditions, whereas before a considerable part of his time was spent in criticism, suspicious watchfulness, and sometimes in open warfare." [22]

In his experiments at Midvale and the Bethlehem Steel Company, Taylor was aware of the influence of the group upon individual behavior. He wrote that "there are few foremen indeed who are able to stand up against the combined pressure of all the men in the shop." [23] The possible consequences of a refusal to restrict output had he been a worker rather than a foreman were described by Taylor.

---

[20] John T. Diebold writes in reference to Taylor's emphasis upon the individual: "This unfortunately seems to be what scientific management has done. And I feel that here we hit upon the central weakness of Taylor's entire conceptual scheme." Diebold, "Scientific Management and Human Relations," *Advanced Management*, Vol. 17, No. 2, February 1952, p. 14. Some of the paragraphs in the latter portion of this section have been reproduced from: Henry H. Albers, "Frederick W. Taylor: An Evaluation," *Current Economic Comment*, Vol. 15, No. 2, May 1953, pp. 45–50.

[21] Elton Mayo, *The Social Problems of an Industrial Civilization* (Boston: Division of Research, Graduate School of Business Administration, Harvard University, 1945), pp. 34–56.

[22] Taylor, *Principles, op. cit.*, pp. 143–144.

[23] *Ibid.*, p. 50.

If the writer had been one of the workmen, and had lived where they lived, they would have brought such social pressure to bear upon him that it would have been impossible to have stood out against them. He would have been called "scab" and other foul names every time he appeared on the street, his wife would have been abused, and his children would have been stoned.[24]

At the Bethlehem Steel Company he attempted to solve this problem by breaking up the group. He concluded that a workman is much less efficient when herded into a gang "than when his personal ambition is stimulated."[25] Taylor related the action taken to effectuate this idea at Bethlehem.

For this reason a general order had been issued in the Bethlehem Steel Works that not more than four men were to be allowed to work in a labor gang without a special permit, signed by the General Superintendent of the works, this special permit to extend for one week only. It was arranged that as far as possible each laborer should be given a separate individual task. . . . Each of these men was given a separate car to unload each day, and his wages depended upon his own personal work.[26]

At the Simonds Rolling Machine Company, Taylor attempted to impede the socializing of behavior by seating girls inspecting bicycle ball bearings "so far apart that they could not conveniently talk while at work."[27] This process of "individualizing each workman" would, according to Taylor, give workers "what they most want, namely, *high wages*. . . ."[28]

These illustrations show that Taylor recognized the socializing of behavior by the work group. In part he attempted to solve the problem by breaking up the group. He assumed that group behavior was undesirable and that, if the individual worker were permitted to pursue his "natural" self-interest, the problem of output would be solved. He thought that the individual would dominate the scene with a little help from management. However, Taylor did not realize that social satisfaction may also play an important role in organization. By attempting to individualize the worker he was removing this kind of reward. Moving the workers so far apart they couldn't talk is a good case in point.

It should not be assumed that the other pioneers of scientific management completely agreed with Taylor's views on the human problem. Henry L. Gantt, for example, was much more willing to compromise with the

[24] *Ibid.*, p. 51.
[25] *Ibid.*, p. 72.
[26] *Ibid.*, p. 73.
[27] *Ibid.*, p. 92.
[28] *Ibid.*, p. 93.

human situation that did not always show itself ready to adapt to the dictates of the system.[29] Many of the early contributors to scientific management undoubtedly practiced "good human relations" in making their applications, but they did not use the scientific method to study the dynamics of human behavior in organization. The development of this aspect of management science had to await the experiments that began at the Hawthorne plant of the Western Electric Company in 1924.

Systematic Managerial Organization

Frederick W. Taylor and his lieutenants were primarily concerned with problems at the operating level. They did not give emphasis to the relationship between managerial organization and the performance of managerial functions. This section is concerned with those who systematized the work of the managers.[30]

The Contribution of Henri Fayol

A major contribution to the development of management science was made by Henri Fayol, a French executive and mining engineer. Fayol made several important advances in the field of metallurgy for which he received two awards. In 1888, he became general manager of Commentry-Fourchambault, a mining concern that was in critical financial condition; and his able management did much to put the company on a sound financial basis. Fayol credited the management methods he employed rather than personal qualities for this success. He first presented his views on these matters at the International Mining and Metallurgical Congress held in 1900 and continued to play an active part in the French management movement until his death in 1925. His ideas on management organization

---

[29] Differences in the attitudes of Taylor and Gantt in this respect are noted by the biographers of the two men. Copley, *op. cit.*, Vol. II, p. 23; Alford, *op. cit.*, pp. 129–130.

[30] A great deal of attention has been given in the management literature to Taylor's recommendation that the "military type" of organization should be replaced with functional organization and to his "functional foremanship" plan. However, Taylor's perspective was shop management, and his insight into the managerial process was not particularly sophisticated. He failed to appreciate the implications of functionalization at higher managerial levels and underestimated the importance of "unity of command" in the management hierarchy. Henri Fayol made some pointed comments on this aspect of Taylorism: (Constance Storrs, translator), *General and Industrial Management* (London: Sir Isaac Pitman & Sons, Ltd., 1949), pp. 69–70.

and functioning represented an important addition to management knowledge.[31]

Fayol divided the management process into five parts: (1) planning, (2) organization, (3) command, (4) coordination, and (5) control.[32] He thought that planning was the most important and difficult managerial responsibility and that a failure to plan properly leads to "hesitation, false steps, untimely changes in direction, which are so many causes of weakness, if not of disaster, in business."[33] Fayol viewed organizing as a problem of material and human organization; his discussion was confined to the human aspects of the organizing function. He compared the part played by man in an organization to that of the cell in the animal.

> Man in the body corporate plays a role like that of the cell in the animal, single cell in the case of the one-man business, thousandth or millionth part of the body corporate in the large-scale enterprise. As the development of the organism is effected by the grouping together of elemental units (men or cells) the organs appear, they are differentiated and perfected in proportion as the number of combined elements increases. In the social organism, as in the animal, a small number of essential functional elements account for an infinite variety of activities. Countless approximations may be made between the functions of the two kinds of organic units. The nervous system in particular bears close comparison with the managerial function. Being present and active in every organ, it normally has no specialized member and is not apparent to the superficial observer, but everywhere it receives impressions which it transmits first to the lower centres (reflexes) and thence, if need be, to the brain or organ of direction. From these centres or from the brain the order then goes out in inverse direction to the member or section concerned with carrying out the movement. The body corporate, like the animal, has its reflex responses or ganglia which take place without immediate intervention on the part of the higher authority and without nervous or managerial activity the organism becomes an inert mass and quickly decays.[34]

After the organization is formed, the function of command is necessary to make it work. Fayol listed a number of precepts that facilitate the performance of this function: (1) thorough knowledge of personnel, (2) elimination of the incompetent, (3) a good understanding of the agree-

---

[31] English translations of Fayol's writings can be found in the following sources: Henri Fayol (J. A. Coubrough, translator), *Industrial and General Administration* (Geneva: International Management Institute, 1929); Fayol (Constance Storrs, translator), *General and Industrial Management, op. cit.;* Fayol, "The Administrative Theory in the State," *Papers on the Science of Administration* (New York: Institute of Public Administration, 1937), pp. 99–114.

[32] Fayol, *General, op. cit.*, pp. 43–110.

[33] *Ibid.*, p. 44.

[34] Fayol, *General, op. cit.*, pp. 58–60.

ments between the organization and its employees, (4) setting a good example, (5) periodic audits of the organization structure, (6) utilization of the conference method of arriving at decisions, (7) refusal to become engrossed in details, and (8) development of unity, energy, initiative, and loyalty among personnel.[35]

Coordination and control are essential to the success of an enterprise. Fayol recommended weekly meetings of department heads and liaison officers to improve coordination. Control was defined as "verifying whether everything occurs in conformity with the plan adopted, the instructions issued and principles established."[36] The purpose of control is to find mistakes, correct them, and prevent them in the future. Effective control, Fayol warned, must operate within a reasonable time period and be followed up quickly with appropriate corrective action. Furthermore, control must not produce a duality of management between those who manage the departments and those who exercise the control functions.

Fayol's contribution to management has only recently been accorded appropriate recognition in the American management literature. There are a number of possible reasons for Fayol's late arrival in the United States. An obvious one is that Americans do not generally read French. But this fact hardly explains the failure to comprehend the content of the first English edition, which appeared in 1930. Although a small number of copies was printed, an adequate supply of this edition was available in American research libraries. A more fundamental factor was probably the tremendous popularity of Taylor's ideas. Taylorism did not produce a systematic theory of management, but it did provide the basis for great accomplishments on the production line. What could a European possibly add to a management system that made possible the production of 10,000 Model T Fords in a single day? Such an attitude was reinforced by the intellectual and political isolationism of the period. A vested interest in knowledge also helped keep Fayol's contributions in the background for so long. A reluctance to accept ideas that upset the existing "climate of opinion" is by no means confined to the management field. Every field of knowledge has at some time experienced long lags in introducing major innovations.

Max Weber's Theory of Bureaucracy

The contributions of Max Weber, the German sociologist, have also been long neglected in American management circles. Weber thought bureaucratic organization to be "the most rational known means of carry-

[35] *Ibid.*, pp. 97–98.
[36] *Ibid.*, p. 107.

ing out imperative control over human beings." [37] Although he recognized the importance of personal (charismatic) leadership, Weber concluded that bureaucratic leadership was indispensable for the mass administration required in a modern society.

Weber set forth his conception of the attributes of a model bureaucratic structure.[38] The organization of positions follows the principle of hierarchy, each lower office being subject to the control of a higher one. There is a systematic division of labor; each office has a clearly defined sphere of responsibilities. The occupants of the offices are selected on the basis of technical qualifications. The office should be the sole or primary occupation of the occupant and constitute a career with promotion based on seniority, achievement, or both. Official activity should be considered as something apart from the private sphere.

The bureaucratic model presented by Weber corresponds to what many management people call the formal organization. It incorporated the primary functional properties of a bureaucratic system, but it did not recognize the importance of informal organization. Weber was correct about the necessity for bureaucratic organization in modern society. His principles of bureaucratic structure were similar in many respects to those developed by early organization theorists from the business field.

Alfred P. Sloan, Jr., and the General Motors Revolution

Much of the credit for the development of a systematic approach to managerial organization must be given to practicing executives. The founders of large corporate enterprises in the United States possessed a combination of unique qualities and aspirations that were well suited to the requirements of the evolving industrial order. But many of them failed to give the enterprises to which they gave birth the properties that make for longevity in a dynamic environment. The executives who assumed the seat of power after the passing of the founders provided the lifeblood necessary for survival. As Ernest Dale has pointed out:

This second generation of managers, who used a systematic approach to maintain, expand, and perpetuate the corporations founded by the geniuses, were often those who made the enterprises successful over the long term. They were

[37] Max Weber (translated by A. M. Henderson and Talcott Parsons), *The Theory of Social and Economic Organizations* (New York: Oxford University Press, 1947), p. 337.

[38] *Ibid.*, pp. 329–341; *From Max Weber: Essay in Sociology,* translated and edited by H. H. Gerth and C. Wright Mills (New York: Oxford University Press, 1946), pp. 196–198.

the "great organizers" of American business, and the real value of their contributions has seldom been acknowledged. These contributions were of both practical and theoretical significance to the knowledge of administration.[39]

Although the laurels could be placed on other heads, the contributions of Alfred P. Sloan, Jr., make him an outstanding candidate for top honors. In May, 1920, Sloan prepared a comprehensive organizational plan for the General Motors Corporation.[40] The plan was initially presented to William C. Durant, the corporation's founder, who ignored it. However, when the Du Ponts assumed control, the Sloan report was accepted and became the basis for the reorganization that followed. A great deal of credit for the subsequent success of the GMC must be given to the organizational system created by Sloan and such collaborators as Donaldson Brown, John Lee Pratt, and James D. Mooney. A further basis for evaluating the importance of Sloan's contributions is the fact that a large number of corporations have adopted the essential features of the GMC organizational plan.

The General Motors reorganization symbolizes a major turning point in the management philosophy of the American corporate enterprise. It expressed the idea that management involved something more than financial manipulation and control and emphasized the need for operating integration rather than purely financial integration. During the past forty years, many companies have made organizational changes that denote such an emphasis. Corporate subsidiaries that were formerly tied to the parent company by loose financial strings became an integral part of a highly organized managerial and operating system. Many of them lost their corporate identity in the process and became operating divisions or departments. Presidents of subsidiary corporations became subordinate executives within a broader managerial framework. This kind of centralization has been fully as important as the much-lauded trend toward decentralization. These organizational changes have been accompanied by a rationalization of the mangement function. The scientific philosophy that Frederick W. Taylor first applied to factory operations has also systematized the activities of the managers. This development has increased the extent to which knowledge about management can be transferred to the neophyte. Education rather than experience has become the starting point in the manager's career.

[39] Ernest Dale, "Contributions to Administration by Alfred P. Sloan, Jr., and GM," *Administrative Science Quarterly,* Vol. 1, No. 1, June 1956, p. 31.
[40] *Ibid.*, pp. 39–43.

Principles of Organization and Management

An early contributor to organization theory was Russel Robb, who in 1910 gave a series of lectures on organization at Harvard University.[41] Robb felt that there is no "royal road" or easy formula for effective organization. He warned against particular approaches to organization, such as functional specialization, and pointed to the danger of too many records and statistics.

Much of the American literature on organization followed Robb's contribution by almost two decades. A book on the basic principles of organization and their historical origins by two executives, from General Motors and Remington Rand, was published in 1931.[42] A New England industrialist, Henry S. Dennison, came out in the same year with a book on structural and human problems in organizations.[43] An important contribution was made in 1938 by Chester I. Barnard, former president of the New Jersey Bell Telephone Company, with the publication of *The Functions of the Executive*.[44] Barnard emphasized the socio-psychological and ethical aspects of managerial organization and functions.

[41] Russel Robb, *Lectures on Organization* (privately printed, 1910); reprinted in: Catheryn Seckler-Hudson (editor), *Processes of Organization and Management* (Washington, D.C.: Public Affairs Press, 1948), pp. 99–124, 269–281; a portion of this work is found in: Harwood F. Merrill (editor), *Classics in Management* (New York: American Management Association, 1960), pp. 161–175.

[42] James D. Mooney and Alan C. Reiley, *Onward Industry!* (New York: Harper & Brothers Publishers, 1931). The title was changed to *Principles of Organization* in a 1939 edition, and a later abbreviated edition (1947) with this title was published without Reiley's name. There is a great deal of biographical information about James D. Mooney in standard sources, but little seems to be known about Alan C. Reiley. Some published material has given the impression that Reiley was a General Motors executive. To fill in the record and set it straight: Reiley was born in 1869 in the President's House of Rutgers University. His father was Professor DeWitt Ten Broeck Reiley of Rutgers and his maternal grandfather was the Rev. Dr. William H. Campbell, past president of Rutgers. He was employed as advertising manager of the Remington Company (now Remington Rand Division of Sperry Rand Corporation) from 1900 to 1928. He was an organizer (1910) of the Association of National Advertisers and organized a Fiftieth Anniversary of the Typewriter Celebration held at Ilion, New York, in 1923. In addition to the above cited book, Reiley wrote "The Story of the Typewriter" and the article on typewriters in the *Encyclopaedia Britannica*. Reiley died on February 3, 1947 at the age of 77. (Mr. W. C. Rockwell of the Remington Rand Division of Sperry Rand Corporation has been most helpful in locating this and other biographical information.)

[43] Henry Dennison, *Organization Engineering* (New York: McGraw-Hill Book Company, Inc., 1931).

[44] Chester I. Barnard, *The Functions of the Executive* (Cambridge: Harvard University Press, 1938).

Professors of industrial management began to approach their subject from an organizational perspective in the 1920's. Such early contributors as Richard H. Lansburgh (1923) and Ralph C. Davis (1928) gave attention to the importance of organizational structure and such basic management functions as planning and control.[45] Lansburgh gave explicit recognition to this development.

Stress has been placed on general organization problems, not only in the chapters on organization, but throughout the text, with the deep conviction that if a satisfactory structure be developed for any enterprise, all other phases of management are simplified.[46]

Oliver Sheldon, a British management consultant, made a contribution in *The Philosophy of Management* published in 1923.[47] Sheldon approached the problems of industrial management from the broader perspective of organization, administration (top policy making), and management (execution of policy). He also gave emphasis to the social responsibilities of management and the need to develop ethical as well as scientific principles.

Two basic lines of development can be noted in the early publications in management. The field of industrial management stressed the application of scientific methods to such operating problems as factory layout, operating standards, methods and procedures, material storage and movement, and illumination. But increasing attention was given to managerial organization and functions and such concepts as departmentation, line, staff, leadership, planning, and control. University courses in industrial management were frequently categorized as courses in management rather than courses in a functional area of management.

A second line of development followed the conceptual framework of Henri Fayol. Management was not viewed from the shop management perspective of Taylor, but as a universal set of principles applicable to any kind of functional and organizational setting. It is indeed unfortunate that Fayol's outstanding contribution remained undiscovered for so long. More rapid progress would have undoubtedly been made had this work been available at an earlier date. However, some of the contributions cited

---

[45] Richard H. Lansburgh, *Industrial Management* (New York: John Wiley & Sons, Inc., 1923); Ralph C. Davis, *The Principles of Factory Organization and Management* (New York: Harper & Brothers Publishers, 1928).
[46] Lansburgh, *op. cit.*, p. iii.
[47] Oliver Sheldon, *The Philosophy of Management* (London: Sir Isaac Pitman & Sons, Ltd., 1923). An American edition (Englewood Cliffs, N.J.: Prentice-Hall, Inc.) came out in the same year.

above and the work of such people as Mary Parker Follett and Lyndall Urwick soon gave this aspect of management science a firm foundation.[48]

A New Light from Hawthorne

The first intensive study of human behavior in an industrial situation was made at the Hawthorne Works of the Western Electric Company, which produces telephone and electrical equipment for the telephone industry.[49] The perspective of Taylor and his lieutenants had its roots in the logic of engineering. The Hawthorne Study applied socio-psychological techniques to managerial problems and gave impetus to the development of a theory of human behavior in organizations. It focused attention upon the importance of social forces and corrected some earlier misconceptions about cooperative behavior.[50]

The Illumination Experiments

The experiments at Hawthorne were begun in November, 1924, with a study of the "relation of quality and quantity of illumination to efficiency in industry." [51] The illumination studies were conducted with the usual controls of scientific experimentation. The original assumption was that there was a correlation between the intensity of illumination and worker output. Workers were divided into a test room in which illumination was

---

[48] The collected papers of Mary Parker Follett are found in: Henry C. Metcalf and L. Urwick, *Dynamic Administration* (New York: Harper & Brothers Publishers, 1942). An early contribution of Urwick: *Management of Tomorrow* (New York: Harper & Brothers Publishers, 1933).

[49] A comprehensive account of the Hawthorne experiments is found in: F. J. Roethlisberger and William J. Dickson, *Management and the Worker* (Cambridge: Harvard University Press, 1939). See also George C. Homans, "The Western Electric Researches," in S. D. Hoslett (editor), *Human Factors in Management* (New York: Harper and Brothers Publishers, 1951), pp. 210–241; Henry A. Landsberger, *Hawthorne Revisited* (Ithaca: Cornell University Press, 1958).

[50] A distinction should be made between personnel management and the development of a "human relations" approach in management. Personnel management, like production management, financial management, traffic management, and advertising, is a functional area of management. The subject matter of "human relations" should be viewed as an organic part of management and organization theory. Some of the most important decisions of every executive involve human problems. The large majority of such decisions cannot be delegated to a personnel department. The responsibility must be shared by every executive in the organization.

[51] The original illumination experiments are reported in Roethlisberger and Dickson, *op. cit.*, pp. 14–18.

varied and a control room with constant conditions. Output increased in the test room, but it also increased in the control room. Illumination was then cut, in one case to an amount of light equivalent to moonlight, with no appreciable decline in output. The results were all negative.

The researchers also experimented with rest periods, shorter working days, and wage incentives; and they tested the influence of fatigue and monotony on output. They began to realize that they "had not been studying an ordinary shop situation but a socially contrived situation of their own making." [52] In the words of Roethlisberger and Dickson:

> The experiment they had planned to conduct was quite different from the experiment they had actually performed. They had not studied the relation between output and fatigue, monotony, etc., so much as they had performed a most interesting psychological and sociological experiment. In the process of setting the conditions for the test, they had altered completely the social situation of the operators and their customary attitudes and interpersonal relations.[53]

After this point the investigators discontinued testing the effects of single variables and turned to a study of the socio-psychological factors that seemed to exert a greater influence than changes in rest periods, wages, hours of work, and the like.

The Interview Program

Thousands of interviews were conducted to determine employee attitudes on a variety of matters. The first interviews sought to determine the worker's attitude toward the company, supervision, insurance plans, promotion, and wages. It soon became clear that this method resulted in comments on the subject considered important by the interviewer rather than what was important to the employee. The interviewing method was changed to a nondirective approach with the interviewer assuming a passive role. The worker was no longer guided along predetermined lines but was permitted to talk about anything that came into his mind. The problems that bothered him were not as logical or as easily identified as was originally assumed. Many of the responses were founded in nonlogical sentiments.

A Sociological Perspective

Although the interview program gave valuable insight into the nature of human behavior in organization, it was not completely satisfactory. The

[52] *Ibid.*, p. 183.
[53] *Ibid.*

social situation that had played an important role in the responses that employees gave in the interviews seemed to require further attention. A detailed study of a shop situation was begun to develop new research methods and to find out something about the behavior of people in small groups.

The Bank Wiring Observation Room. The Bank Wiring Observation Room Group was composed of fourteen workers engaged in wiring, soldering, and inspecting equipment used in telephone exchanges.[54] The physical layout, the tools and equipment, and the operating methods were planned by the use of scientific techniques. The workers were under a group piecework wage plan that conformed to the basic precepts developed by Taylor, Gantt, Emerson, and others. The research results showed that the actual behavior of the group departed in a marked degree from the behavior planned by the company.

Systematic Soldiering. Systematic soldiering or output restriction caused Taylor difficulty when he became gang boss at the Midvale Steel Company. The research people at Hawthorne also found that workers gave a great deal of attention to output. Out of the thirty-two men interviewed before the group study began, twenty-two discussed output rates. The observations of the group observer led to the conclusion that "there existed a group norm in terms of which the behavior of different individuals was in some sense being regulated." [55] In view of the comments made by Taylor on the importance of the group in restricting output,[56] this conclusion was not particularly original. What was significant was that output restriction occurs even when the techniques recommended by Taylor are utilized. The Hawthorne researchers did not assume that the problem could be solved by time study and wage incentives. They sought a solution through a better understanding of group dynamics.

A Group Output Norm. Each individual in the group was restricting his output a significant amount below the company standard of 7312 terminals per day. The group seemed to agree that two equipments constituted a "proper" day's work. An output of two equipments required 6600 terminal connections for connector equipments and 6000 for selector equipments. Operators would frequently stop working before the official stopping time when they had met the group standard. Each individual seemed to know how much he had accomplished at a given time and, also, how much his neighbors were producing. One wireman was able to tell the time within two minutes by computing the amount he had wired that morning. Workers

---

[54] For more detailed information about this aspect of the Hawthorne research: *Ibid.*, pp. 379–548. The material that follows is indebted to this source.
[55] *Ibid.*, p. 423.
[56] Frederick W. Taylor, *Principles, op. cit.*, pp. 50–52.

who attempted to exceed the group output norm were generally looked upon with disfavor, and group pressure was directed against them.

Why Restrict Output? Why did the group restrict output? Some of the following reasons were given by individuals in the group. One thought that working at the rate set by the company would result in unemployment for one out of four people and another that higher output "would mean that somebody would be out of a job." [57] Still another thought that the "bogey would be raised, and then we would just be turning out more work for the same money." [58] Others thought that the supervisor "might 'bawl out' the slower men," [59] and most of the workers seemed to agree that something would happen.

Who Set the Norm? How did two equipments come to be the output norm of the group? The investigators were not able to find a satisfactory explanation. Fatigue did not seem to be a limiting factor, and there was no evidence that the foreman or his assistants originated the norm, even though the foreman agreed that, if a man did more than 6600 connections a day, "he would wear his fingers out." [60] The supervisors generally felt that the norm represented a satisfactory day's work. Another possible explanation for the norm is that the workers could finish two equipments, but not three, and therefore might prefer to stop with two rather than leave a partially completed equipment for the next day. This explanation is discounted by the fact that they frequently stopped work during the wiring of an equipment. Another factor that probably influenced the group's thinking about the norm was indicated by one worker. "I turn out 6,600 regularly. . . . Of course you could make out less and get by, *but it's safer to turn out about 6,600.*" [61] In other words, the norm seemed to satisfy supervision and higher management. A lower norm might, in the opinion of the group, cause "something to happen"; a higher norm might also bring bad consequences. It caused no difficulties—why risk the possible consequences of change.

Although the logic of either output restriction or the norm of two equipments cannot be completely explained, the fact that individuals seemed more concerned about the group norm than the company standard indicates that the social consequences of not conforming played an important role in their output behavior. How important was scientific management in the output situation at the Hawthorne plant? The methods work of the

---

[57] Roethlisberger and Dickson, *op. cit.*, p. 419.

[58] *Ibid.*, p. 418. The bogey was a psychological incentive and was not related to the amount of pay the worker received.

[59] *Ibid.*, p. 417.

[60] *Ibid.*, p. 455.

[61] *Ibid.*, p. 413. (Italics added.)

company industrial engineers and the scientifically derived output standards were undoubtedly important variables. Actual output and the output norm developed by the group would probably have been lower in the absence of scientific management. As it was, the norm of two equipments and also the output of the group seemed satisfactory to the company. Output had increased over a period of years, and the group was turning out considerably more than workers in other companies.

Regulated Output Patterns. The fact that the group norm set forth two equipments as a "proper" day's work did not mean that all individuals produced this number of equipments.[62] There were significant differences in the actual output of different individuals in the group. However, the weekly average output of individuals showed little change from week to week. They felt that, if their output was not reasonably constant, "something might happen." Too high an output would indicate that they could do better; low output might cause supervisors to "bawl them out." They resorted to subterfuge to prevent undue fluctuation in individual output records. One technique was to underreport or overreport actual output; another was to control the output rates by reporting a greater amount of daywork, which increased the output *rate* because output was divided by a smaller amount of time. Daywork allowances were permitted only for a number of specific reasons, such as material shortages and defective wire, but they were frequently used to control the recorded output rate.

Psychological Testing. A seemingly logical explanation for the differences in the output of individuals was that it reflected differences in ability. To test this hypothesis, each person in the group was given dexterity and intelligence tests. The three slowest wiremen scored higher on the dexterity test than did the three fastest men, and the lowest producer ranked first in intelligence and third in the dexterity tests. This relationship between the test results and actual output suggests the importance of the group to these workers. An individual could by increasing his output receive a larger share of the total group "wage fund" and also reduce the possibilities of unemployment. But these material rewards had a penalty in the form of group censorship.

Job Trading and Helping. The company rule against job trading expressed the logic of greater efficiency through specialization. The assumption was that a worker could become a more proficient wireman, solderer, or inspector by concentrating his attention on one type of work. Workers were not supposed to trade jobs, but they frequently did. They were per-

[62] Orvis Collins, Melville Dalton, and Donald Roy, "Restriction of Output and Social Cleavage in Industry," *Applied Anthropology* (now *Human Organization*), Vol. 5, No. 3, Summer 1946, pp. 1–14; Donald Roy, "Quota Restriction and Goldbricking in a Machine Shop," *American Journal of Sociology*, Vol. 57, No. 5, March 1952, pp. 427–442.

mitted to help a fellow worker only when conditions prevented them from working on their own equipment. A shortage of parts, for example, would be a valid reason for helping someone until parts could be obtained. Most of the helping that occurred during the study could not be justified on this basis. Everyone in the group, except inspectors, participated in this practice, but the helping hand was not extended equally to all. Friendship increased willingness to help one another, and those who received help were expected to return the favor. An informal leader, who was popular with the group, received the most help even though he did not actually need it. One of the faster wiremen, who showed a great desire for leadership, helped the most, but his help was rarely returned.

Other Social Activities. Almost everyone in the group participated in games, such as matching coins, shooting craps, card games, pools on horse races, baseball and quality records, and "binging,"[63] which were played during lulls in the work and lunch periods. Financial gain was not the primary consideration in the games of chance—the winnings ranged from one to ten cents. A great deal of controversy occurred about whether windows should be open or closed. The subject of group conversations ranged from arguments about religion to a discussion of a shapely woman. They talked about the possibility of war and the role that they would play. One worker liked to imitate "Popeye the Sailor" and tell long yarns about his virility. There were many off-color stories and much good-humored kidding. One of the solderers was the "clown" of the group and frequently entertained the group with his comments. An inspector with three years of college liked to impress the group with his superior knowledge; he once walked over to a worker and told him he was going to test his vocabulary.

Group Norms. The Bank Wiring Observation Room Group responded to norms that they themselves made about their behavior. Some norms had reference to output; others involved personal conduct.[64] The following norms seemed to influence behavior.

1. You should not turn out too much work. If you do, you are a "rate-buster."

2. You should not turn out too little work. If you do, you are a "chiseler."

---

[63] "Binging" was a game that involved hitting someone as hard as possible. The person who was hit had the privilege of returning one "bing" or hit. An object of the game was to see who could hit the hardest, but it was also used to restrain high-output individuals. Roethlisberger and Dickson, *op. cit.,* p. 421.

[64] The first four norms listed here were originated by Roethlisberger and Dickson, *ibid.,* p. 522; the fifth norm was added by George C. Homans, *The Human Group* (New York: Harcourt, Brace & Co., Inc., 1950), p. 79. Norms are what people think behavior ought to be.

3. You should not tell a supervisor anything that will react to the detriment of an associate. If you do, you are a "squealer."

4. You should not attempt to maintain social distance or act officious. If you are an inspector, for example, you should not act like one.

5. You should not be noisy, self-assertive, and anxious for leadership.

These norms were enforced by such social sanctions as binging, ridicule, and ostracism from social activities. A relationship was found between conformity to these norms and standing in the group. The best-liked worker in the group conformed closely to the group norms. Although his actual production was generally higher than the group norm, he underreported his output and also claimed less daywork, which would have increased his hourly output rate. Another worker respected the output norm of the group, but he was not as well liked because he violated the norms that related to personal conduct. One of the most disliked persons in the group had an acceptable output record, but he "squealed" to the foreman, an extremely serious offense in the eyes of the group.

SELECTED REFERENCES

L. P. Alford, *Henry Laurence Gantt*. New York: The American Society of Mechanical Engineers, 1934.

Frank Barkley Copley, *Frederick W. Taylor, Father of Scientific Management*, Vols. I and II. New York: Harper & Brothers, 1923.

Horace B. Drury, "Scientific Management, A History and Criticism," *Studies in History, Economics, and Public Law*, Vol. 65, No. 2, pp. 275–489. New York: Columbia University, 1915.

Henri Fayol, *General and Industrial Management*. London: Sir Isaac Pitman & Sons, Ltd., 1949.

Claude S. George, Jr., *The History of Management Thought*. Englewood Cliffs, N.J.: Prentice-Hall, Inc., 1968.

Frank B. Gilbreth, Jr., and Ernestine Gilbreth Carey, *Cheaper By The Dozen*. New York: Thomas Y. Crowell Company, 1948. An account of the Gilbreth family life written in a humorous vein.

Haruki Iino, "Management Theory of C. Barnard and His Followers," *The Shogaku Ronshu*, The Business Review of Kansai University, Osaka, Japan, Vol. 8, No. 2, pp. 133–158 (June 1963).

John F. Mee, *Management Thought in a Dynamic Economy*. New York: New York University Press, 1963.

Harwood F. Merrill (editor), *Classics in Management*. New York: American Management Association, 1959.

Henry C. Metcalf and L. Urwick (editors), *Dynamic Administration*. New York: Harper & Brothers, 1942.

Alex W. Rathe (editor), *Gantt on Management*. New York: American Management Association and the American Society of Mechanical Engineers, 1960.

F. J. Roethlisberger, *Management and Morale*. Cambridge: Harvard University Press, 1947.

F. J. Roethlisberger and William J. Dickson, *Management and the Worker*. Cambridge: Harvard University Press, 1939.

Oliver Sheldon, *The Philosophy of Management*. London: Sir Isaac Pitman & Sons, Ltd., 1923. American edition: Englewood Cliffs, N.J.: Prentice-Hall, Inc., 1923.

Alfred P. Sloan, Jr., *My Years With General Motors*. Garden City, N.Y.: Doubleday & Company, Inc., 1964.

Harold F. Smiddy and Lionel Naum, "Evolution of a 'Science of Managing' in America," *Management Science,* Vol. 1, No. 1 (October 1954), pp. 1–31.

William R. Spriegel and Clark E. Myers, *The Writings of the Gilbreths.* Homewood, Ill.: Richard D. Irwin, Inc., 1953.

Frederick W. Taylor, *Scientific Management.* New York: Harper & Brothers, 1947. This book contains *Shop Management, The Principles of Scientific Management,* and (Taylor's) *Testimony Before the Special House Committee.*

L. Urwick, *The Meaning of Rationalisation.* London: Nisbet & Co., Ltd., 1929.

chapter 3

THE EMERGING PATTERN

This chapter builds a bridge between the contributions of the pioneers and more recent developments. Brief attention is first given to the relationship that management has to other fields of knowledge. The significance of the management process concept in systematizing management knowledge is given consideration. The discussion then turns to the basic elements that make up the process and the way in which they have evolved from the early beginnings. The future prospects for a more comprehensive science of management are analyzed in the next part. The final section is devoted to problems concerned with the development of a profession of management.

Knowledge for a Profession of Management

A large army of workers from economics, sociology, psychology, statistics, mathematics, and electrical engineering has invaded the field of management with new theories and techniques. The management literature is now replete with references to mathematical programming, decision theory, communication networks, cybernetics, semantics, interaction theory, status systems, and motivational theory. This development has brought about a vast accumulation of useful knowledge for potential and practicing executives.[1] But the newly sprouted branches of management

[1] Some management experts have expressed concern about the present state of management knowledge. Professor Harold Koontz has lamented what he has termed a jungle of approaches and approachers to management theory, "The Management Theory Jungle," *Journal of the Academy of Management,* Vol. 4, No. 3, December 1961, pp. 174–188. The diversity of terminology and theoretical concepts, differences in defining management as a body of knowledge, and a failure of latecomers to give adequate recognition to the contributions of the past are some of the things about

knowledge have not all found the tree. An important reason is that the academic fields from which many of the recent theories have evolved do not necessarily classify knowledge to satisfy the needs of management. A distinction should be made between the discipline of management and the disciplines that may contribute to management knowledge. Many of the contributions made by economists, sociologists, psychologists, and related professionals form a part of a conceptual framework appropriate to their fields rather than that of management. Much of this knowledge must be modified in some manner if it is to become a part of the science of managing.

The relationship between the social sciences and management is similar to that between the basic sciences and medicine. Medical practitioners are exposed to pharmacology, but they do not study it in depth. A pharmacologist knows more about the properties of drugs than most physicians or surgeons. Similarly, economists, sociologists, and psychologists know more about their respective fields than most practitioners and professors of management.[2] Management, like medicine, is an applied field which involves a part of many disciplines. An executive makes use of economics, sociology, psychology, and other sciences in performing his functions, but he does not need to be a full-fledged professional in any of these fields.

Frederick W. Taylor and his lieutenants did not develop a systematic body of knowledge, in spite of the significant contributions they made to management. A major reason is that they lacked an adequate conceptual framework. The solution came in the form of the management process concept which incorporated the basic functions performed by the practitioner. Such a classification of knowledge would appear to be highly appropriate for any field that seeks professional status. The knowledge that forms the basis for professional development should be related to the skills required for application.

The management process provides an excellent framework for the diverse knowledge required for effective executive action. Some of this

which Professor Koontz expressed concern. Similar problems have existed in other fields that have experienced a dynamic period of growth. Many economists, for example, were at a loss as to what to do about the Keynesian innovation. Some of them refused to accept a theoretical formulation that could not be neatly fitted into the traditional model. For other views on recent developments in management knowledge: Waino W. Suojanen, "Management Theory: Functional and Evolutionary," *Academy of Management Journal,* Vol. 6, No. 1, March 1963, pp. 7–17; William C. Frederick, "The Next Development in Management Science," *Academy of Management Journal,* Vol. 6, No. 3, September 1963, pp. 212–219; Lyndall F. Urwick, "Management in Perspective: The Tactics of Jungle Warfare," *Academy of Management Journal,* Vol. 6, No. 4, December 1963, pp. 316–329.

[2] However, an individual can have professional status in more than one field, particularly if the content is closely related.

knowledge represents the contributions of persons who were directly concerned with management problems. Such contributions correspond to those made by medical practitioners and professors. Some knowledge comes from disciplines that have purposes and practices that differ in some or many respects from those of the profession of management. Such contributions are like those made in medicine by such sciences as chemistry, biology, pharmacology, and physiology.

The Management Process Concept

Henri Fayol was the father of the management process concept even though, as Professor Harold Koontz has written, "many of his offspring did not know their parent."[3] The management process represents an attempt to develop a conceptual framework for management knowledge. It assumes that the totality of what managers do can be divided into different functions. Fayol included planning (*prévoyance*), organization, command, coordination, and control in his list of administrative or managerial functions.[4] Another early list is expressed by the word POSDCORB which represented the following functions: planning, organizing, staffing, directing, coordinating, reporting, and budgeting.[5] Such functions as forecasting, leadership, delegating, and investigating have also been used by pioneers of the process approach.[6] Some of the differences in these lists are not as great as they appear to be. Fayol does not include staffing because it is considered under organization. The reporting function in the POSDCORB list could be called control; budgeting could have been categorized as an aspect of planning.

The logic of the process concept is that management functions are performed in a sequence through time. Planning comes first, then organizing, which is followed by staffing, directing, and controlling. One function is assumed to lead logically to the next. Thus, planning provides the basis for organizing, which in turn sets the stage for staffing, and so on. There may be significant departures from the sequence idea in actual practice. There are generally many plans which give the appearance that executives are performing their functions out of order. But aside from such a fusion of functions, the sequence may begin with different functions and come to an

---

[3] Koontz, *op. cit.*, p. 176.

[4] Henri Fayol, *General and Industrial Management* (London: Sir Isaac Pitman & Sons, Ltd., 1949), p. 3.

[5] Luther Gulick, "Notes on the Theory of Organization," in L. Gulick and L. Urwick, *Papers on the Science of Administration* (New York: Institute of Public Administration, Columbia University, 1937), p. 13.

[6] A comprehensive list of management functions is found in: L. Urwick, *The Elements of Administration* (New York: Harper & Brothers Publishers, 1943).

end without completing the whole cycle. Changes in the organizational structure are often made without regard to particular plans. Staffing problems may lead to planning rather than the other way around. Companies with an excess of executive personnel resulting from reduced demand may plan new programs rather than lay off personnel. Directing may simultaneously involve several or all plans (including future plans) rather than a specific plan. Staffing may be constantly carried on to strengthen the organization in a general sense.

The process concept is basically static in nature. Everything is held constant except for the elements involved in the process. A truly dynamic model would incorporate environmental and other changes during the various stages. A similar state of affairs exists in most of the models used in economics and other social sciences.

The functions that make up the management process have become the basis for specialized research and teaching. Such specialization is a sound development. It indicates that management has taken a long step forward and that there is now adequate knowledge for a good beginning. The following discussion gives brief consideration to the evolution of specialized areas of management knowledge.

Organization Theory

The early contributions to organization theory had a functional orientation. Harlow S. Person, a leading proponent of Taylorism, had the following to say on the subject: "The older procedure in organization, for instance, of the administrative and executive section of an enterprise, was to secure the men first and then consider their positions and authorities; the newer procedure is to determine the functional requirements of the enterprise and then secure the proper human capacities for assignment to the several responsibilities." [7] A great deal of attention was given to the problem of efficient functional design. Taylor proposed his famous functional foremanship plan. Fayol, Mooney and Reiley, Graicunas, Gulick, and Urwick were concerned with principles of specialization, span of control, the scalar process, unity of command, and functionalization.

The importance of socio-psychological factors in organization was noted by Chester I. Barnard in his classic contribution, *The Functions of the Executive*.[8] Barnard gave emphasis to the idea that managerial organization cannot be explained purely in terms of a set of principles about formal

[7] "The Taylor Society" (H. S. Person, editor), *Scientific Management in American Industry* (New York: Harper & Brothers Publishers, 1929), p. 29.

[8] Chester I. Barnard, *The Functions of the Executive* (Cambridge: Harvard University Press, 1951).

organization structure. The actual behavior of organizational participants departs in many ways from the behavior that is planned. Organized executive action involves nonlogical factors not unlike those that influenced the behavior of the Hawthorne Bank Wiring Observation Room workers.

Some recent research in organization theory builds on the foundations of the functional theorists by drawing on the experiences of the practitioner. A two-year study of organization structures by the American Management Association provides a good example.[9] This study dealt with such subjects as departmentation, delegation, span of control, staff specialists, committee action, and decentralization.

Organization research has also attempted to gain greater knowledge about actual organizational behavior. An investigation of human relations in a large telephone company and union gave significant insights about such behavior.[10] A study of restaurants in a large metropolitan area also represented a major milestone for this kind of research.[11] Similar research was performed by people who used Weber's bureaucratic theory as a point of departure. A good example is Alvin W. Gouldner's study of the bureaucratic process in a gypsum plant.[12] Other research related to organization theory is considered in the paragraphs that follow. Research involving small group behavior and communication networks could be categorized under organization theory.

The research of the last two decades has given rise to a large variety of theories about organization. There is as yet no unified or universal organization theory. Such a theory is probably impossible in a society in which freedom prevails. Present knowledge provides a useful point of departure for those who must live and work in an organization. The least that can come of it is a recognition that there are no simple solutions to organizational problems. Consideration is now given to the development of knowledge about planning and other functions performed by executives in organized systems.

[9] Ernest Dale, *Planning and Developing the Company Organization Structure* (New York: American Management Association, 1952).

[10] E. Wight Bakke, *Bonds of Organization* (New York: Harper & Brothers Publishers, 1950).

[11] William Foote Whyte, *Human Relations in the Restaurant Industry* (New York: McGraw-Hill Book Company, Inc., 1948). Also significant in this respect are: Melville Dalton, *Men Who Manage* (New York: John Wiley & Sons, Inc., 1959); Rensis Likert, *New Patterns of Management* (New York: McGraw-Hill Book Company, Inc., 1961); Rensis Likert, *The Human Organization: Its Management and Value* (New York: McGraw-Hill Book Company, 1967).

[12] Alvin W. Gouldner, *Patterns of Industrial Bureaucracy* (Glencoe, Ill.: The Free Press, 1954). See also: Philip Selznick, *TVA and the Grass Roots* (Berkeley and Los Angeles: University of California Press, 1949); Peter M. Blau, *The Dynamics of Bureaucracy* (Chicago: University of Chicago Press, 1955).

Planning Methodology

Planning is presently viewed from a broader perspective than the "technological efficiency" approach of the early pioneers of scientific management. A scientific approach to the study of markets and other environmental forces and the development of techniques to control them has become an important part of planning methodology. The static and dynamic models of the economist have provided a point of departure. The theory of the firm as presented in principles of economics courses defines the basic problems with which the executive must contend. This broader framework has imposed limitations upon the applicability of the scientific method. An important limitation is that science cannot completely solve the problem of uncertainty in a dynamic economy. Market forecasts are much less reliable than the estimates involved in the technologically oriented studies of Taylor at Midvale and Bethlehem.

A recent development in planning methodology is the use of mathematical techniques. These techniques translate planning problems into mathematical or symbolic models which are then manipulated to obtain a solution. They have been used for such purposes as planning production programs, determining inventory levels, and scheduling sequences of activities. This approach to planning has been given the status of a separate branch of knowledge generally referred to as "operations research." [13] Particular attention should be given to the impact of "game theory" upon decisional methodology. The basic elements of this theory were presented by Oskar Morgenstern and John von Neumann in the *Theory of Games and Economic Behavior* in 1944.[14] Game theory gives emphasis to the idea that planning should take into account the strategies developed by others. For example, the appropriateness of a price increase or reduction may be significantly influenced by the pricing strategies of other companies.

The attention that has been given to scientific methods should not blind students of management to the importance of subjective methods. A subjective approach to planning is necessary because some problems *cannot* be solved by the methods of science. Another consideration is that executives frequently cannot delay action long enough for a comprehensive scientific study. The question of ultimate values cannot be given a scientific answer, and the creation of new ideas involves subjective consideration. Relatively little attention has been given to subjective decision-making techniques. An

---

[13] A comprehensive survey of operations research methodology and techniques is found in: C. West Churchman, Russell L. Ackoff, and E. Leonard Arnoff, *Introduction to Operations Research* (New York: John Wiley & Sons, Inc. 1957).

[14] Princeton: Princeton University Press, 1944.

important barrier to the development of subjective theories is limited knowledge about the capacities of the human brain. However, research in the fields of neurology and psychology indicates that some progress may be made in the years to come.

Communication and Control

The early management literature, except for some rather perfunctory statements about command and control, gave little attention to communication problems and processes. Barnard was one of the first to stress the importance of communication in the managerial process. "The need of a definite system of communication," wrote Barnard, "creates the first task of the organizer and is the immediate origin of executive organization."[15] The *system* of communication evolves from the structuring of executive positions into a hierarchy; the executives as persons are the *means* through which communication takes place.

Many insights into the nature of the communication process were derived from the behavioral studies noted in the section on organization theory. All of these studies showed that informal communication played an important part in the communication process. Particular attention has been given in recent research to communication networks. Professor Keith Davis' study of managerial communication in a leather goods company provides a good example of this type of research.[16] Experimental research has also been conducted to obtain knowledge about communication networks.[17] This kind of research makes use of experimental groups in laboratory situations to design and test different types of communication patterns.

Another important development has been the application of ideas from the subject of semantics to communication problems in organization. The contributions of such pioneers as C. K. Ogden, I. A. Richards, and Alfred Korzybski on the relationship between language and human behavior have helped overcome many barriers to effective communication.[18] A more

[15] Barnard, *op. cit.*, p. 217.

[16] Keith Davis, "A Method of Studying Communication Patterns in Organization," *Personnel Psychology,* Vol. 6, No. 3, Autumn 1953, pp. 301–312; Davis, "Management Communication and the Grapevine," *Harvard Business Review,* Vol. 31, No. 5, September–October 1953, pp. 43–49.

[17] Alex Bavelas, "Communication Patterns in Task-Oriented Groups," in Daniel Lerner and Harold D. Lasswell (editors), *The Policy Sciences* (Stanford: Stanford University Press, 1951), pp. 193–202.

[18] C. K. Ogden and I. A. Richards, *The Meaning of Meaning,* 8th ed. (New York: Harcourt, Brace & Company, Inc., 1956; 1st ed., 1923); Alfred Korzybski, *Science and Sanity,* 4th ed. (Lakeville, Conn.: The Institute of General Semantics, 1958; 1st ed., 1933).

recent innovation came in the form of two mathematical theories which presented a conceptual framework for the study of communication and control in organizations, society, animals, and machines.[19] These theories, categorized as "information theory" and "cybernetics," have provided useful insights about the behavior of complex systems, the problem of control, the idea of feedback, and the nature of information. Information theory will probably have the greatest impact through the electronic computer. The computer may well bring about a revolution in thinking about organization and management. Many changes in the communication process and the structuring of managerial positions have already been anticipated.[20]

Motivation and Leadership

The Hawthorne Study initiated a period of intensive research to provide information about human behavior in organization.[21] This research indicated that something more is required than the efficiency precepts of scientific management. The problem of motivation is not solved simply by installing an incentive wage system. Group norms, social satisfactions, informal leadership, status, and other socio-psychological factors are also important. Motivation is a highly complex problem involving the interdependence of many factors. A change in any part of the system affects every other part in some fashion.

A great deal of attention has been given during recent years to the study of small groups. However, little that is really new has been added to the

---

[19] Norbert Wiener, *Cybernetics, Control and Communication in the Animal and the Machine* (New York: John Wiley & Sons, Inc., 1948); Claude E. Shannon and Warren Weaver, *The Mathematical Theory of Communication* (Urbana: The University of Illinois Press, 1949). Shannon's theory was originally published in the *Bell System Technical Journal* in 1948.

[20] George P. Shultz and Thomas L. Whisler (editors), *Management Organization and the Computer* (Chicago: Graduate School of Business, The University of Chicago; The Free Press of Glencoe, Illinois, 1960); William E. Reif, *Computer Technology and Management Organization* (Iowa City: Bureau of Business and Economic Research, 1968).

[21] The nature of and the results obtained in this kind of research are found in the following references: William F. Whyte, *Money and Motivation* (New York: Harper & Brothers Publishers, 1955); George C. Homans, *The Human Group* (New York: Harcourt, Brace & Company, Inc., 1950); Michael S. Olmsted, *The Small Group* (New York: Random House, Inc., 1959); Eleanor E. Maccoby, Theodore M. Newcomb, and Eugene L. Hartley (Editorial Committee), *Readings in Social Psychology*, Third Edition (New York: Holt, Rinehart and Winston, Inc., 1958); Timothy W. Costello and Sheldon S. Zalkind, *Psychology in Administration* (Englewood Cliffs, N.J.: Prentice-Hall, Inc., 1963).

results that were obtained by the Hawthorne researchers. Small group theory presents important insights, but it cannot provide knowledge about some aspects of human behavior. Much more knowledge about individual behavior is needed if management is to effectively control.

What is the present state of knowledge in the field of psychology? A prominent psychologist had the following to say on this subject: "While it is probably safe to say that some areas of psychology have attained a respectable level of scientific development, it would nevertheless have to be admitted that much of the field does not qualify." [22] This psychologist emphasized that psychological phenomena are extremely complex and that human behavior exhibits such a multiplicity of forms as to defy easy analysis.[23]

Behavioral theory has also been concerned with people in large organizations. Individual and small group behavior generally occurs within more comprehensive organized systems. Some useful insights about the integration of individuals and small groups into business and other kinds of organizations has been gained by several recent contributions.[24] Large organizations impose special conditions that can significantly influence human behavior. The problems created by large organizations are complex problems which can only be partially solved with the knowledge presently on hand.

Scientific Management: Future Prospects

The scientific method has played an important part in building management knowledge and improving managerial skills. The field of management has taken a long step forward during the past twenty years. There is now adequate knowledge for a solid foundation. But it should not be assumed that the scientific method will soon provide all of the answers. Executives will continue to be plagued with problems that cannot be resolved by objective means. They will have to contend with uncertainties that cannot be removed by scientific endeavor. The nature of the limitations imposed by the forces involved in the work of managing are indicated in the pages that follow.

[22] Kenneth W. Spence, *Behavior Theory and Conditioning* (New Haven: Yale University Press, 1956), p. 2.
[23] *Ibid.,* p. 21.
[24] For example: Harold J. Leavitt, *Managerial Psychology,* 2nd ed. (Chicago: University of Chicago Press, 1964); Douglas McGregor, *The Human Side of Enterprise* (New York: McGraw-Hill Book Company, Inc., 1960).

The Nature of Science

The philosophical root of science is that some degree of order exists in the universe. Without uniformity and recurrence in the behavior of things and people, the development of scientific knowledge would not be possible. Science may be viewed as an attitude, a method, and an accumulation of knowledge. The scientist must be willing to accept the conclusions he derives from the scientific method even when they repudiate his most cherished beliefs. Scientific investigation begins with a problem that arises when something is unsatisfactory, when traditional beliefs are in question or inadequate, when the facts necessary to resolve the situation are not apparent, and when possible hypotheses have not yet been formulated.[25] The method of science involves the development of hypotheses and gathering facts about the nature of things.[26] A hypothesis is a tentative theory about the nature of the phenomena that are to be studied. It forms the basis for investigation into the facts of the subject matter under consideration. As the investigation proceeds, the initial hypothesis may be frequently revised as the facts dictate a different conclusion. There is no such thing as pure empiricism in science.[27] Facts do not classify or measure themselves. Hypotheses are necessary to make sense out of the facts and to provide the basis for further observation and experimentation. Hypotheses are never considered to be final truths; every law of science is a hypothesis for further investigation.

The end product of the scientific method is an accumulation of knowledge. This knowledge results in a better understanding of man and his environment. It forms a basis for predicting the future and arriving at desired ends consciously. The degree to which the latter condition can be attained depends in great part on the stability of the data. For this reason, the fields of knowledge concerned with material things have experienced the greatest scientific development. The behavior of the atom is more predictable than the behavior of man.

A Science of Management?

The development of a science of management is related to the properties of the subject matter of management decision making. Oliver Sheldon, a

---

[25] F. S. C. Northrop, *The Logic of the Sciences and the Humanities* (New York: The Macmillan Company, 1947), p. 17.

[26] Morris R. Cohen and Ernest Nagel, *An Introduction to Logic and Scientific Method* (New York: Harcourt, Brace & Company, Inc., 1934), pp. 197–222, 391–403.

[27] Werner Heisenberg, *Physics and Philosophy* (New York: Harper & Brothers Publishers, 1958).

British industrial consultant and author of an outstanding book on management, has observed that "in so far as management deals with things, its methods can be reduced to terms of scientific principle; but in so far as it deals with men and women, it can only use scientific principles to the extent that the men and women are willing to subject themselves to them." He concluded that "there can be no science of co-operation." [28] Frederick W. Taylor, the American scientific management pioneer, was much more optimistic about the possibilities of developing a comprehensive science of management.[29] Taylor thought he had found the principles that would lead to an era of cooperation in industry. Although Sheldon's views reflect an appreciation of the difficulty in developing a science of human behavior, they were unduly pessimistic in the light of modern developments. Taylor's optimism about his system of management was founded in oversimplified assumptions he made about human behavior.

The Problem of Uncertainty

Werner Heisenberg, the physicist, challenged Einstein's dictum that "God does not play dice" with experiments which indicate that the universe is characterized by probability.[30] The fact that God does seem to play dice places an ultimate limitation on the knowledge that can be obtained about the universe. The difficulty cannot be overcome by improved experimental design and better theories. Theories must remain probabilistic because the behavior of the forces being theorized about is probabilistic.

The manager is faced with an even more difficult problem than the physicist. Many of the forces with which he must deal are enveloped by uncertainty. There is a dearth of probability values to guide him. The results sometimes seem to come from a dice game being played in the dark with constantly changing rules.

Partial Theories

Frederick W. Taylor's experiments were restricted to a shop situation in which the behavior of things played a primary part. His experiments were as much engineering as they were management. Scientific techniques have always seemed more successful when the behavior of things and human behavior are interrelated in a system. The reason is probably that things help structure a relatively unstructured human situation. The Hawthorne

---

[28] Oliver Sheldon, *The Philosophy of Management* (London: Sir Isaac Pitman & Sons, Ltd., 1923), p. 35.
[29] Taylor has summarized his views in *The Principles of Scientific Management* (New York: Harper & Brothers Publishers, 1915).
[30] Heisenberg, *op. cit.*

study was similar to Taylor's experimentation in that it was concerned with a shop situation. It differed in that it used human behavior as a point of departure. However, the results were rigidly structured by a social interaction model which served the function of things in the Taylor experiments.

An imporant reason for the success of the Taylor and the Hawthorne experimentation is that both ignored important internal and external factors.[31] All knowledge is made up of partial systems which exclude a larger environment. A theory that incorporates the totality of forces that can affect even a simple organizational situation is impossible at the present time. Those who accumulate knowledge about management should continue to build partial theories in the manner of Taylor and Hawthorne. But they should recognize that the solutions obtained from such theories may be significantly modified by a more comprehensive and complex environment.

The Black Box

Many theories give good solutions for the wrong reasons. The content of the "black box" frequently remains hidden even when theories predict well. For example, the increases in output achieved by Taylor at Bethlehem can at least partly be credited to changes in the attitude of workers as a result of the experiment. The Hawthorne researchers would undoubtedly have considered worker attitude as an important variable in the Taylor experiments. Many business concerns accepted Taylor's ideas about improved methods and incentive wages with good results. The fact that other important, but then unknown, variables were involved in the results did not make the Taylor ideas less useful.

Theories and Realities

The realities with which executives must contend are not as structured as the theories that seek to explain. Theories help create a degree of certainty in a world characterized by uncertainty. Man perceives much of his environment in terms of learned symbols and thus substitutes a symbolic world for the real one. Much of the symbolic world created by man does not have a counterpart in reality. But it plays an important part in molding human behavior. Similarly, many of the theories that relate to management influence the behavior they attempt to predict.

[31] For some interesting insights on this matter: Sherman Krupp, *Pattern in Organization Analysis: A Critical Examination* (Philadelphia: Chilton Company, 1961).

Management Knowledge and Executive Development

An important argument for the accumulation of scientific knowledge about management is the need to develop large numbers of executives. Even though such knowledge is limited, the student can be given some significant insights into the nature of the management problem. A university cannot train "finished" executives. It can only provide a useful point of departure for further executive development through experience. The same is true for professional pursuits such as medicine, law, engineering, and the military.

A Profession of Management

Can management be categorized as a profession? The answer to this question is partly dependent on the definition of a profession.

The Nature of a Profession

The terms "profession" and "professional" have been given a variety of meanings.[32] They may be broadly used to refer to any occupation by which a person earns a livelihood. They may also be used in a restricted sense to include only "the three learned professions" of theology, law, and medicine. The majority of definitions fall somewhere between these two extremes. The conditions that seem to be most often used to differentiate a profession from an ordinary vocation are: (1) the learning of a systematic body of knowledge together with the skills necessary for application, and (2) conformity to an established body of standards governing professional and personal behavior. Other factors (some of which are related to the above) that have assumed varying degrees of importance in this respect are

---

[32] The entire issue of *The Annals of the American Academy of Political and Social Science,* Vol. 297, January 1955, is devoted to problems relating to professional status, standards, and conduct in such vocations as accounting, engineering, medicine, business, and architecture. Of particular interest for present purposes are the articles by Morris L. Cogan, "The Problem of Defining a Profession," pp. 105–111, and Howard R. Bowen, "Business Management: A Profession?" pp. 112–117. The problems of professionalization in the area of business are, also considered in: Robert A. Gordon and James E. Howell, *Higher Education for Business* (New York: Columbia University Press, 1959), pp. 69–73; and Frank C. Pierson and others, *The Education of American Businessmen* (New York: McGraw-Hill Book Company, Inc., 1959), pp. 16–33.

the existence of an association, such as the American Medical Association or the American Institute of Accountants; a relationship of responsibility toward patients or clients; legal or other restrictions to entry into the profession, or both; an oath, such as the Hippocratic Oath of the physician; and a high degreee of altruistic motivation. The nature of educational requirements and social status also seem to have importance. Some unionized crafts meet many of the conditions cited above, but they are not usually categorized as a profession.

The Executive as a Professional

The executive role seems to satisfy at least some of the conditions that make a vocation a profession. Executives require knowledge and skills which can be acquired through formal education or experience or both. The problem of executive development is much like that of medicine, law, and other fields, where some knowledge and skills can be acquired through formal education and some through practical experience. The physician or lawyer is not a "finished product" on graduation from medical or law school. A similar statement can be made about the executives produced by university executive development programs. Much of the knowledge and skill that make for professional competence is gained after a long period of practical experience.

Executives have given some attention to the development of professional standards, but such standards have by no means been systematized or universally accepted or applied.[33] There is no Hippocratic Oath or Engineer's Vow of Service to which an executive must testify before he practices his "vocation." A number of management associations, chambers of commerce, and better business bureaus do set forth various norms of behavior, but they do not enforce them in the manner of the American Medical Association. However, such associations may represent the basis for more complete professionalization in the future.

The traditional professions of law and medicine have generally involved a personal relationship between practitioners and clients or patients.[34] The Principles of Medical Ethics of the American Medical Association, for example, stress the personal role of the family physician. The relationship between executives and customers, stockholders, suppliers, creditors, and labor is generally impersonal. This difference, however, would not seem to preclude professional status since large specialized medical clinics and hos-

[33] The attitudes of executives toward ethical standards and the nature of such standards are indicated in: Stewart Thompson, *Management Creeds and Philosophies, Research Study No. 32* (New York: American Management Association, Inc., 1958).

[34] Bowen, *op. cit.,* p. 114.

pitals have significantly reduced the importance of the family physician without a marked "deprofessionalization" of medicine in the public mind. A high degree of altruistic motivation has been given a great deal of emphasis in the traditional professions. It is generally assumed that executives qualify least with respect to this quality. Yet, physicians are not completely immune to the quest for money, and executives have been known to make great personal sacrifice in the interests of organization. There are many "organization men" who are dedicated to their responsibilities within the meaning of the Oath of Hippocrates. The executive "profession" does not control entry in the manner of many of the traditional professions, but the educational requirements of the future may well provide a similar consequence.

Professional status for executives and their work should not be viewed as a matter of definition or nomenclature. Some of the techniques employed by the traditional professions to enhance the quality of practitioners would seem to apply to executives. The basic elements of professionalization are important irrespective of whether they lead to formal professional status. The development of skill in executive work through education or experience is a primary consideration in executive development. Appropriate motives for effectiveness in the executive role should also have a high place in the scheme of things. Some of the other conditions that make for professionalization may also be important in that they provide means to control standards relating to skills and motives.

Knowledge and Skills for Professional Development

A systematic body of management knowledge that can be used for professional development has evolved during the past sixty years. The progress that has been made in this respect was reviewed in Chapter 2 and the earlier portions of this chapter. An important step toward management professionalization is provided by the management process concept. The management process gives emphasis to the idea that management involves skills as well as knowledge. The nature of these skills and the manner in which they relate to management are elaborated in Chapter 4.

SELECTED REFERENCES

Gustav Bergmann, *Philosophy of Science*. Madison: University of Wisconsin Press, 1957.

Paul M. Dauten, Jr. (editor), *Current Issues and Emerging Concepts in Management*. New York: Houghton Mifflin Company, 1962.

Paul J. Gordon, "Transcend the Current Debate on Administrative Theory," *Academy of Management Journal*, Vol. 6, No. 4, pp. 290–302 (December 1963).

Robert A. Gordon and James E. Howell, *Higher Education for Business*, Chap. 4. New York: Columbia University Press, 1945.

Luther Gulick, "Notes on the Theory of Organization," *Papers on the Science of Administration*, pp. 3–45. New York: Institute of Public Administration, Columbia University, 1937.

Harold Koontz (editor), *Toward a Unified Theory of Management*. New York: McGraw-Hill Book Company, Inc., 1964.

Sherman Krupp, *Pattern in Organization Analysis: A Critical Examination*. Philadelphia and New York: Chilton Company, 1961.

Huxley Madeheim, Edward Mark Mazze, and Charles S. Stein, *Readings in Organization and Management*, Part VI. New York: Holt, Rinehart and Winston, 1963.

John F. Mee, *Management Thought in a Dynamic Economy*. New York: New York University Press, 1963.

Hildegard Nordsieck-Schroer, *Organisationslehren*. Stuttgart: C. E. Poeschel Verlag, 1961.

F. S. C. Northrop, *The Logic of the Sciences and the Humanities*. New York: The Macmillan Company, 1947.

Thomas A. Petit, "A Behavioral Theory of Management," *Academy of Management Journal*, Vol. 10, No. 4, pp. 341–350 (December 1967).

Frank C. Pierson and others, *The Education of American Businessmen*, Chap. 2. New York: McGraw-Hill Book Company, Inc., 1959.

Alex W. Rathe, "Projection 1976: New Demands on Management," *Michigan Business Review*, Vol. 20, No. 3, pp. 20–24 (May 1968).

Bernard Sarachek, "A Comment on the Interdisciplinary Approach to Administrative Thought," *Academy of Management Journal*, Vol. 10, No. 4, pp. 365–370 (December 1967).

Bernard Sarachek, "Elton Mayo's Social Psychology and Human Relations," *Academy of Management Journal,* Vol. 11, No. 2, pp. 189–197 (June 1968).

Leonard R. Sayles, *Managerial Behavior,* Chap. 1. New York: McGraw-Hill Book Company, Inc., 1964.

William G. Scott, *Human Relations in Management,* Part I. Homewood, Ill.: Richard D. Irwin, Inc., 1962.

Fremont Shull, Jr., "The Nature and Contribution of Administrative Models and Organizational Research," *Journal of the Academy of Management,* Vol. 5, No. 2, pp. 124–138 (August 1962).

Fremont A. Shull, Jr. (assisted by Andre L. Delbecq), *Selected Readings in Management, Second Series,* Part III. Homewood, Ill.: Richard D. Irwin, Inc., 1962.

Waino W. Suojanen, *The Dynamics of Management.* New York: Holt, Rinehart and Winston, 1966.

A. N. Whitehead, *Science and the Modern World.* New York: The Macmillan Company, 1925.

Richard J. Whiting, "Historical Search in Human Relations," *Academy of Management Journal,* Vol. 7, No. 1, pp. 45–53 (March 1964).

Joan Woodward, *Industrial Organization: Theory and Practice,* Chap. 12. London: Oxford University Press, 1965.

chapter 4

ORGANIZATIONAL SYSTEMS: THE DECISIONAL AND INFORMATIONAL PROCESSES

The first part of this chapter is concerned with the nature of the systems concept and its relationship to the process and problems of management. Attention is then directed to the decisional and informational processes and the manner in which they interrelate in an organized managerial endeavor. The last part of the chapter presents a conceptual framework for this book that closely follows the cybernetics model.

A Systems Approach to Management

A great deal of attention has been given in recent years to a systems approach to management. Such terms as "management systems," "systems management," and "systems theory" are frequently found in the management literature.

System Defined

A system is commonly defined as consisting of parts that are connected or combined to form a whole.[1] Such a definition is so universal as to

---

[1] For example: Richard A. Johnson, Fremont E. Kast, and James E. Rosenzweig, *The Theory and Management of Systems* (New York: McGraw-Hill Book Company, Inc., 1963), p. 4; Stafford Beer, *Cybernetics and Management* (New York: John

include almost any variety of phenomena. Indeed, it would be difficult to find something that cannot be so categorized. The universe, the solar system, a society, an economy, an industry, an automobile, a house, a football game, a coffee pot, a book, a human being, a wolf, a worm, and a dictionary are examples of systems. Some of these systems are aspects of other systems and are themselves composed of subsystems. Scientists are still not sure they have found the basic building block of the universe or whether there is a more comprehensive system than the universe.

Model Building and the Systems Concept

A distinction should be made between a model of a system and the system itself. Most models involve the use of some kind of general or specialized language system to represent various aspects of the real thing. Some examples are the following: maps are models of a territory; demand and supply curves may be used to denote a market; an organization chart can represent a management hierarchy; a process chart is often used to portray manufacturing operations; and algebraic equations can be constructed to show an inventory situation. An important advantage of models is that they can be used to gain better insights about the system being represented. Models can provide the basis for prediction if they adequately express the nature of the real system.

Another advantage of models is that they can often be used to represent more than one kind of system. This idea was expressed on a grand scale by Professor Norbert Wiener's concept of cybernetics. The basic elements of the cybernetics model correspond to the attributes of many kinds of systems, in particular systems that are exceedingly complex. Cybernetics is concerned with the communication and control problems necessary to achieve some purpose. Control is partly a problem of *feedback* which provides self-regulation through a comparison of the system's output with a predetermined standard. The input into the system may be modified if there is too much variation from the output norm.

Control in the cybernetic model may also be expressed in terms of the theory of information. A system can be conceived as a mechanism for handling information. The variety (or uncertainty) of an exceedingly complex system is related to the information contained in it. The efficiency of such a system can be increased by some highly sophisticated statistical techniques that increase the amount of information, thereby reducing the uncertainty. Another cybernetic mode of control is found in the concept of

Wiley & Sons, Inc., 1959), p. 9. Some representative readings on the systems concept are found in: Peter P. Schoderbek (editor), *Management Systems: A Book of Readings* (New York: John Wiley & Sons, Inc., 1967).

the *black box*. Since the contents of the black box are assumed to be unknown, the only approach to its control is through an analysis of the relationship between its inputs and outputs. Such an analytical device offers a useful approach to the control of exceedingly complex systems.

The basic cybernetics model is pertinent in many fields of endeavor—electrical engineering, neurophysiology, economics, physics, and sociology. The universality of such a model provides a new perspective for thinking about problems and increases the possibility of applying ideas from one field to others. The interdisciplinary and interdepartmental walls that serve to restrict the flow of information are at least partly breached for the benefit of all concerned.

Some management problems can be approached through the concepts of the cybernetics model. The concept of feedback, for example, corresponds to the control problems that arise in business and other organizations. The theory of information and the black box have parallels in management practices to overcome the problem of uncertainty. However, it should not be assumed that cybernetics presents a large array of practical applications for management purposes. Cybernetics is a highly abstract mathematical model, which can provide insights that lead to practical innovations. Einstein's abstract mathematical formulations lead to the use of atomic power for many purposes, but only after a large number of more mundane but nonetheless difficult engineering problems had been solved.

The Electronic Computer and the Systems Concept

The informational capacities provided by electronic computers have given impetus to the use of models to help solve managerial problems. Much more comprehensive and complex economic models have been constructed for the purpose of predicting changes in the economic system or in an industry. Elaborate models that simulate environmental and organizational realities can be used to test alternative planning strategies. The large variety of planning problems can be solved through resource allocation, inventory, queuing, and other kinds of mathematical models. Analogue models, such as PERT, have played an important part in planning and controlling highly complex projects. Business game models have been used extensively for purposes of executive development with a significant amount of success.

The computer has made possible more complete information about environmental and organizational conditions and more rapid communication of such information to management. Much of the routine paperwork in many organizations is done by computers. A large part of the informational functions performed in production, purchasing, finance, marketing, and accounting departments is now performed by computers. Computers have also been used on an "on line" and "real time" basis to collect and process data about events as they occur and to directly control all elements of a system.

The primary ingredient of systems control is information. The efficiency with which electronic computers can handle information has expanded the size of the system that can be controlled from a single control center. For example, the Polaris submarine and the Main Battle Tank weapons projects were controlled by a computerized analogue model (PERT) containing thousands of events in an interrelated network. The informational functions formerly performed on a decentralized basis in individual functional (such as production and purchasing) departments are now often processed by a centralized information department.

Application of the Systems Concept to Organization and Management Theory

Some systems are sufficiently similar to justify the same classification. A highly abstract model can be made to represent selected aspects of many realities. The same mathematical symbol can denote a man, a neuron, or a planet. Mathematical logic can be used to describe the relationships involved in many systems. But the fact that something is similar in certain respects does not mean that it is not different in certain other respects. The differences may not be significant for some purposes, but they may be highly significant for others. A man is not a neuron or a planet; the relationships among men are not the same as those found in neurological or solar systems. Highly abstract models with universal attributes can point to important truths about the nature of systems. But, at the same time, other significant insights can only be derived from an assumption that one system is not like any other.

The field of management involves the systems concept, but it does not deal directly with all categories of systems. Management is far more concerned with social systems than with physical and biological systems. But by no means all social systems fall within the scope of management science. A distinction must also be drawn between management science and the economic and political sciences. Executives (as executives) are not economists, political scientists, or sociologists. The systems that fall most directly within the domain of the traditional field of management are business and industrial organizations. In recent years, military, health, religious, and educational organizations have often been added to the list. The boundaries of such systems are probably best defined by the fact that they are bureaucratic. There appear to be sufficient similarities among different bureaucracies to warrant a similar classification for many purposes. Much has been done in recent years to bring about a single field of administration applicable to military, health, religious, and educational as well as business organizations. The foregoing should not be construed to mean that executives can ignore economic and other social systems. The point is that executives and economists are concerned with different systems and, for that reason, cannot be given the same professional preparation.

To repeat: the informational capacity of the electronic computer has expanded the size of the system that can be controlled from a single decision-making center. In other words, business and other organizations can be increased to a larger size without a loss of managerial efficiency. It might even be possible to control entire industries or even the economy through a single organizational system. But such a state of affairs should not arise simply because there are now informational techniques that make it possible. The philosophy of "systems management" with the stress that is given to the construction and use of comprehensive models for system control does not mean that we should reorganize the social system simply in order to take advantage of informational innovations. Let us not assume that we should impose centralized control over social systems that are not now so controlled.

Business and other organizational systems are controlled through decisions and information. The management process corresponds to the control process portrayed in the cybernetics model. Attention is given in the next section to decision making and is followed by a section that shows how decisional and informational activities combine to form the management process.

Management Decision Making

Few people would be inclined to resist the idea that decision making is a highly important managerial responsibility. Professor Herbert A. Simon has suggested that it might be well to treat "decision-making as synonymous with managing." [2]

Decision Making Defined

Decision making may be narrowly defined as the making of a choice from among alternative courses of action. More broadly construed, deci-

[2] Herbert A. Simon, *The Shape of Automation* (New York: Harper & Row, 1965), p. 53.

sion making also involves all of the actions that must take place before a final choice can be made. Probably the most important of these is to determine whether something needs to be done. This aspect of decision making is similar to the initial step in a scientific investigation. Neither decisional nor scientific endeavor can begin unless there is a problem that requires solution. To paraphrase Professor F. S. C. Northrop, the scientist must begin not with the facts nor with deductive reasoning nor with a hypothesis but with the problem and the problematic situation.[3] The problem may arise from changing or previously unnoticed environmental conditions being observed by the scientist. It may also result from an essentially subjective insight that evolved from prior experience with particular phenomena. In a similar sense, executives spend a great deal of time surveying the economic, political, social, and technical environment in search for situations that require decisional action.[4]

After a decisional problem has been identified, alternative strategies for the solution of the problem may be developed. This aspect of decision making generally involves both the question of ends and means. Are the ends presently sought by the organization appropriate in terms of changing environmental conditions? Are the means now being utilized adequate for existing or changed ends? The final step in decision making is to make a choice from among two or more alternatives. Strictly speaking, at least some of the alternatives must appear to be equally appropriate. If such were not the case, there would be no real problem of choice. The best alternative would be obvious and automatically eliminate the other alternatives.

Rationality in Decision Making

To what extent is decision making a rational process?[5] Decisions can be subjected to a test of truth or falsity to the extent that they accurately describe a future factual situation. However, as Professor Simon points out, they have an additional quality in that a selection is made from among

---

[3] F. S. C. Northrop, *The Logic of the Sciences and the Humanities* (New York: The Macmillan Company, 1947), p. 17.

[4] Simon, *op. cit.*, p. 54.

[5] A comprehensive discussion of this problem is found in: Herbert A. Simon, *Administrative Behavior,* 2nd ed. (New York: The Macmillan Company, 1958), pp. 45–109. This question is also given scrutiny by Robert Tannenbaum, "Managerial Decision-Making," *The Journal of Business* (University of Chicago), Vol. 23, No. 1, January 1950, pp. 22–39. Conclusions on this matter from the point of view of economics are found in: Lionel Robbins, *An Essay on the Nature and Significance of Economic Science* (London: Macmillan and Co., Ltd., 1935).

several behavioral possibilities.[6] In other words, decisions have ethical properties in that they assert that one course of action is better than another or none.

A Differentiation of Means and Ends

An approach to the problem of rationality is to differentiate between means and ends. The choice of alternative means can be subjected to a test of rationality. Such a choice is rational if the means result in the achievement of a given end. Thus, a man who decides to drink water (means) to quench his thirst (end) has made a rational decision. A decision to eat an ounce of salt would not be rational without a prior decision to change the end sought. Rationality may also be defined as the selection of the best of several possible alternative means. Thus, a man who desires to quench his thirst may have the choice of water or whisky to solve his problem. His choice is rational if he chooses the better thirst quencher. To end further speculation, it will be arbitrarily assumed that water is most effective. But there is a more subtle implication in this problem. If the man decides to drink whisky to quench his thirst, the consequence might well be a state of inebriation or an unanticipated end. Therefore, if his sole objective is to quench his thirst, he would clearly choose water. If his objective is a combination of thirst quenching and inebriation, he might be considered rational if he chose whisky.

A Means-Ends Chain or Hierarchy

The aspects of decision concerned with means cannot easily be differentiated from those relating to ends. The translation of ends into means is a continuous process in all individual and group behavior. Decisions generally involve a consideration of both means and ends. The ends become embodied in the means employed to achieve them. Furthermore, a particular end frequently is the means to more final ends. The whole process should be viewed as a means-ends chain or hierarchy. One thing always seems to lead to something else either by plan or chance. For example, Jones obtains a part-time job to earn money for a date with a beautiful blonde. In this case money is an intermediate end toward a more final one. If Jones were perfectly rational, he would take into consideration all the other consequences his decision to date the blonde might have. It could lead to marriage and children. It might also lead to drunkenness and remorse. In making his decision to work in a part-time job, Jones should

---

[6] Simon, *Administrative Behavior, op. cit.,* p. 46.

have considered all possible future consequences. If he knew them all, he might have refused the job and the blonde. The problem is made even more difficult by the fact that perfectly rational decision making would require knowledge of all of the consequences of *not* taking the part-time job. It is immediately evident that life is never so well planned. The decisions we make today have unplanned future consequences, some good and some bad. Many decisions evolve from the force of circumstances rather than the plan of man. It is possible to know only a few of the totality of major and minor consequences that may follow a decision.

Ethical Elements in Executive Decision Making

The ethical problems in executive decision making are somewhat mitigated by the fact that organizations generally occupy the middle of the means-ends chain. To some extent the problem is that of adapting to externally imposed value systems. A business organization, for example, responds to consumer demand and market prices. But it would be incorrect to say that executives are not significantly involved in the making of value decisions. Business and other ogranizations frequently limit the range of choice available to the consumer and play a positive part in the creation of values through advertising and other techniques. The fact that the consumer does respond in a positive fashion does not necessarily prove the correctness of the action. Other possible alternatives might have been better from the point of view of both consumer and organizational welfare.

Risk and Uncertainty

The purpose of managerial decision making is the conscious direction of human behavior toward some future end. Rationality presupposes an ability to make some kind of judgment about the future. To what extent can the consequences of decisional action be accurately predicted?

The problem of predicting the outcome of a decision can be categorized as follows. (1) *Certainty* is present if an action is known to lead invariably to a specific outcome. (2) *Risk* exists when an action leads to one of a set of possible outcomes, each outcome occurring with a known probability. (3) *Uncertainty* prevails if the probabilities of possible outcomes are completely unknown or are not even meaningful.[7]

The regularity in the behavior of some phenomena through time permits prediction with a high degree of certainty. It is reasonably certain that the sun will "rise" in the morning and that an ice cube will melt in a pot of

[7] R. Duncan Luce and Howard Raiffa, *Games and Decisions* (New York: John Wiley and Sons, Inc., 1957), p. 13.

boiling water. The question of probability values can be safely ignored in solving some problems. But such a situation prevails only for a limited number of the decisional problems that face executives. The impossibility of highly accurate prediction in the actual conduct of organizational affairs should not create frustration or despair. It should in fact lead to a sigh of relief for those who aspire to become executives. With complete certainty there would be no real decisional problems and, according to Professor Frank Knight, executives "would be laborers merely, performing a purely routine function, without responsibility of any sort, on a level with men engaged in mechanical operations." [8]

Statistical Probability

The probability theory developed by mathematicians and statisticians has been useful in solving some decisional problems. It is based on the assumption that a large number of past events can be used to predict similar future events. A good example of the application of this principle is in the field of insurance. The number of fires or deaths that will occur during a given period can be calculated with a low margin of error if the sample is large enough and randomly distributed. But probability theory cannot determine which house will be destroyed by fire or who will pass through the pearly gates.

Several difficulties are implicit in the use of statistical probability theory in decision making. One difficulty is that many of the events a business executive must predict are significantly different from events that occurred in the past. There is also the lack of a sufficient number of past events for statistical probability computation. Furthermore, there must be a large enough number of future events if prediction is to be reasonably accurate. Thus, a gambler who has thrown a pair of dice 10,000 times can forecast the consequences of another 10,000 throws with a fair degree of certainty. But he faces the future with a great deal more uncertainty if his fate is to be decided on the basis of 1 rather than 10,000 throws.

Subjective Probability

Statistical techniques provide a basis for predicting such events as the number of machine breakdowns, quality rejects, employee turnover, and customer returns. There remains the problem of making predictions under conditions that do not permit the use of statistical probability techniques. The executive is then forced to form an essentially subjective conception of

[8] Frank H. Knight, *Risk, Uncertainty and Profit* (Boston: Houghton Mifflin Company, 1921), p. 268.

what he thinks the future might hold. Previous experience cannot provide more than a few fragments of what can be called objective measurement, which means that the executive must fill the void with his own imagination and creative thought. Subjective probability judgments are less reliable than statistically derived probability values. Socio-psychological factors may cause variances in the probability judgments made about the same future event. The only way to eliminate this difficulty is to accumulate empirical knowledge that would permit executives to view the problem apart from their subjective selves. Since such knowledge is lacking, the only alternative would seem to be an approach that makes possible the utilization of whatever subjective insights the executive may possess.

Types of Decisions

Professor George Katona has made a distinction between routine and genuine decisions.[9] Routine decisions involve the application of familiar principles to a situation. The decisions made by experienced automobile drivers, for example, can generally be placed in this category. Although the driver always faces a somewhat different environmental situation in passing another automobile, the principles necessary to solve the problem are well understood. On the other hand, genuine decisions require the formulation of new principles through conscious thought processes.

Professor Herbert A. Simon has utilized computer terminology in formulating a similar dichotomy. As shown in Figure 4-1, Simon has categorized decisions as programmed or nonprogrammed. The programmed decisions are the routine and repetitive decisions for which the organization has developed specific processes. The nonprogrammed decisions are the one-shot, ill-structured, novel policy decisions that are handled by general problem-solving processes.

Although the above dichotomies are useful for analytical purposes, it should not be assumed that all decisions can be neatly categorized. Many of them fall somewhere between the two extremes. Another consideration is that the experience of the executive is important. A recent college graduate in his first executive position might well testify that few of his decisions are routine or habitual.

Decision-Making Techniques

The types of decisions categorized in Figure 4-1 are related to corresponding sets of traditional and modern decision-making techniques. Ha-

[9] George Katona, "Psychological Analysis of Business Decisions and Expectations," *American Economic Review,* Vol. 36, No. 1, March 1946, pp. 48–49.

Types of Decisions	Decision-Making Techniques	
	Traditional	Modern

Programmed
 	
Routine, repetitive decisions
Organization develops specific processes for handling them
	1. Habit
	2. Clerical routine
	  Standard operating procedures
	3. Organization structure
	  Common expectations
	  A system of subgoals
	  Well-defined informational channels
		1. Operations Research
		  Mathematical analysis
		  Models
		  Computer simulation
		2. Electronic data processing

Nonprogrammed One-shot, ill-structured novel, policy decisions Handled by general problem-solving processes	1. Judgment, intuition, and creativity 2. Rules of thumb 3. Selection and training of executives	Heuristic problem-solving technique applied to (a) training human decision makers (b) constructing heuristic computer programs

Figure 4-1. Traditional and modern techniques of decision making.

Source: Figure I, p. 62 in *The Shape of Automation* by Herbert A. Simon (Harper & Row, 1965). Reprinted by permission of the publisher.

bitual responses are developed for handling many of the programmed decisional problems. Such responses may become recorded as standard operating procedures, which are particularly useful in training new members to contend with routine problems. The organizational structure provides another approach to programmed decision through a system of well-defined managerial responsibilities and relationships.

A more modern approach to programmed decisional problems has resulted from the second industrial revolution. Electronic computers have made possible the practical application of complex mathematical and comprehensive analogue models to help solve decisional problems. Somewhat less dramatic is the use of computers to make many of the routine "decisions" involved in the informational processing that occurs within accounting, finance, marketing, production, and purchasing departments.

The traditional techniques for solving nonprogrammed decisions are expressed by such words as judgment, intuition, and creativity. The subjective processes involved in these techniques are still not well understood. There may gradually develop rough but not really satisfactory rules of thumb for handling some such decisional problems. The education and experience of executives appear to be helpful in overcoming some of the difficulty. People seem to acquire the capacity to become more successful in solving nonprogrammed problems through the learning process. A few small steps forward have been taken to develop improved techniques for these problems. One approach is to study the manner in which humans solve such problems with the idea of developing systematic techniques. Computer programs that simulate some aspects of human thought processes have been developed.

The Decisional Problem in a Business Organization

The basic decisional problem in business organization is to develop strategies that give rise to a favorable balance between revenues and costs. Business organizations generally cannot survive if costs are consistently greater than revenues. Whether such organizations attempt to maximize profits in the short or the long run need not be answered for present purposes.

The Static Theory of the Firm

The static theory of the firm developed by economists is a good first approximation of the problems faced by the executive. It is assumed that the prices of products and factors (wages, rent, and interest) and the physical facts of production are known.[10] The decision maker begins with data about the amounts of output that will occur with various inputs of land, labor, capital, and management. These data show him that some factor combinations are more efficient from a purely technical standpoint than others. The initial problem is to correlate the advantages of more efficient physical productivity with those that can be derived from a substi-

[10] In monopoly and monopsony theory a schedule of product and factor prices and quantities is known.

tution of less expensive factors for more expensive ones. In other words, whenever possible more labor and less capital will be used if labor costs less than capital. However, costs have little meaning until they are related to revenues or the amount a firm will receive for the product. Since the price or a price schedule for different outputs is known, the problem is to determine the point of greatest profit or least loss. If the firm is capable of producing more than one product, further adjustments need to be made to determine the best relationship between costs and revenues for all the products of the firm.

The decisional problem in the static theory of the firm is essentially mathematical. Personal motives and production capabilities are translated into quantitative data and assumed to be known. The solution to every problem is given by what economists call the marginal analysis. The decision maker solves the problem of maximizing profits by making a series of adjustments or incremental changes in the production plan. Each adjustment is appraised in relationship to its contribution to the total revenue and the amount by which it adds to the total cost.[11] The extent to which total revenues are greater or less than total costs measures the degree of failure or success. In the long run, revenues must be greater than costs if the firm is to survive.

Decision Making in a Dynamic Environment

In the static theory of the firm the executive makes marginal adjustments in the production and marketing program until the maximum profit point is reached. The problem can be solved by an appropriate set of simultaneous equations. Once solved it stays solved because the data that make up the problem are static. The actual problems of the executive are greatly complicated by the fact that the forces with which he must contend are constantly changing. The executive cannot assume that consumer demand, technology, productivity, costs, and factor prices will remain fixed. A change in any one of these values may require significant adjustments in organizational activity. The problem is further complicated by the fact that

[11] In the language of the economist, the firm is said to be in equilibrium when the following results are achieved. Within the limits set by technical considerations, one type of productive resource (such as labor or capital) is substituted for another until the last dollar spent for each resource makes an equal contribution to the firm's revenues. In a similar manner one product is substituted for another until the contribution made to revenues by the last dollar spent for productive resources is the same for every product. Additional resources are employed until the marginal revenue product of each resource equals its market price. Under such conditions the firm cannot improve its economic status.

it takes time to make some of these adjustments. An increase in demand, for example, may require additional machines, equipment, tooling, and personnel. For this reason the executive must attempt to anticipate the changes that will occur in the future. The difficulty of predicting the future with a high degree of accuracy means that some decisions will complicate rather than facilitate matters. A decision to hire and train additional personnel will create obvious difficulties if an expected increase in demand does not occur. The executive is then forced to make further decisions to correct the consequences of his failure to accurately predict the future. But even if the future were well known the difficulty of measuring the values involved in decision presents another problem. Statistical and accounting techniques are not sufficiently developed to give the executive more than a rough approximation of the situation. Many successful executives feel that the development of an elaborate cost accounting system is money down the drain. At any rate, a precise measurement of marginal costs or revenues is impossible in actual practice. Thus, the difficulties of measurement together with the problem of predicting the future limit the applicability of the quantitative techniques used in the static theory of the firm. Yet, in spite of such limitations, this theory is a useful framework for an analysis of some of the dynamic problems that face the executive.

Adaptation and Modification

Although the preciseness of the marginal analysis of economic theory is lacking, the approach of the practical executive is similar in many respects. Executive decision is concerned with incremental rather than complete changes in the organizational program. The past always imposes a high degree of inflexibility upon future executive action. Some things cannot be changed within any pertinent period of time even when change might be highly desirable. Furthermore, there is generally some degree of stability in behavior over time. For example, consumer demand for a product is rarely reduced to zero except over a relatively long period. The process of executive decision involves a constant sequence of incremental changes in the scope and nature of organizational activities. Some decisions evolve from the need to adapt to such environmental forces as product and resource markets, governmental policies, innovations, and cultural factors. Others express an attempt to modify the environment through product line changes, price policies, advertising, and research and development. Still others are concerned with more economical procurement of labor, materials, supplies, and other resources and with the achievement of greater managerial and operating efficiency.

The Management Process

This section shows how decisional and informational activities combine to form the management process. This process closely corresponds to the cybernetics model and forms the conceptual framework for the chapters that follow.

Planning and Motivational Decisions

Decision making is partly a matter of planning organizational objectives and the methods that will be used to achieve them. Planning imposes organizational responsibilities on subordinate managerial and nonmanagerial personnel. Decision making is also concerned with the problem of motivating subordinates. A decision to adopt an incentive wage system or to offer stock options is an illustration. The distinction between planning and motivating is similar to the relationship between production and distribution theory in economics.

Management and Nonmanagement Decisions

Management decisions are concerned with organizational objectives, and executives are those who accept the responsibility for making such decisions. The leader of an informal group within the organization, though he may make decisions that govern the behavior of others, is not an executive. The same conclusion can be made about a labor leader who participates in the negotiation of a collective bargaining agreement. The decisions made by informal group leaders and labor leaders involve the personal goals of organizational participants.[12]

Policy Making as a Management Function

Policy making is sometimes included as an important function of management. However, there seems to be little basis for differentiating between policy making and decision making. Policies may be defined as standards or norms that govern behavior in an organization. They are the product of past decisions by management. Some policies have been in effect for a longer period of time than others. Some of them apply to the entire organi-

---

[12] However, a labor leader is an executive in his own organization.

zation rather than to a part of it. Similar statements can be made of any of the norms that evolve from management decisions. Policy making does not appear to be a separable management function.

The Organizing Function

The organizing function is often categorized as an important management function. In this book "organizing" is assumed to be a part of the management process as an aspect of the planning function. Organization and organizing are given comprehensive consideration in chapters specifically concerned with these subjects.

The Importance of Communication

Decision making is a cooperative activity performed by executives who occupy positions in an organizational structure. The positions and persons in such a structure are interrelated by a communication system. Communication may be defined as the transfer of information from one person to another through signs, signals, or symbols from a mutually understood language system. The part that is played in this respect by the English language, accounting, statistics, and mathematics is almost too obvious to mention. The social sign language expressed by frowns, smiles, gestures, and silence is also an important communication instrument.

The Management Process

The management functions can be fitted into the traditional management process framework. The process begins with planning (decision making) which sets forth norms (standards, rules and regulations, procedures, plans, policies) to guide subordinate behavior. These norms are then communicated to subordinate managerial and nonmanagerial personnel. The process would end at this point if it were not for possible failures in communication and motivation. Subordinates cannot assume responsibilities they do not understand; they will not accept them if they are not motivated. Communication is at best imperfect, and authority (acceptance by subordinates) is not always present. A control mechanism to compare actual with planned behavior is necessary if organizations are to achieve their objectives. Control is partly a problem of obtaining information about subordinate performance. It may also involve motivational decisions by superiors if performance is not in accord with planned behavior. The nature of this process is shown in Figure 4-2.

```
                    Superior
                 decision making
                   (planning or
                motivational decisions)
         ↗                              ↘
  Forward                                  Feedback
communication                            communication
                                       (information about
                                           performance)
         ↘                              ↗
                    Subordinate
                    performance
```

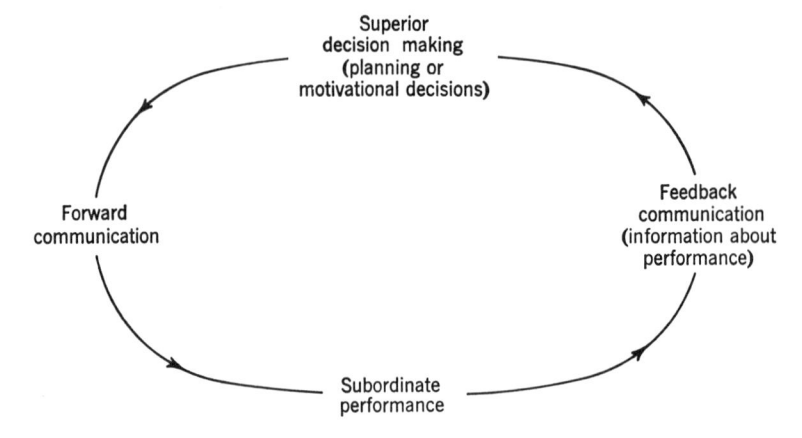

Figure 4-2. The management process. The process begins with planning decisions setting forth previously nonexistent behavioral norms, which are communicated to subordinate managerial or nonmanagerial personnel. Performance information is relayed back to the superior, who may make motivational decisions if behavior is not in accord with the norms of planning decisions.

The management functions may not be performed in the order indicated in the management process. Decisions involving motivation are often made without regard to particular plans. Some plans are not activated by the communication function because they may not now be pertinent. Planning for an event that does not occur is common and a price often paid for uncertainty.

Planning and Control: Information and Decision

The planning process translates the profit norm into a variety of interrelated subsidiary standards or norms. Budgets, standard cost data, mechanical drawings, purchase specifications, procedures and methods, quality standards, and wage incentive standards represent some of the ways in which standards are set forth. Such standards are communicated to subordinate managerial and operating personnel who are expected to carry them out by delegation (to lower levels) or by performance. The intended result is a change in the behavior of subordinates through authority or acceptance by subordinates. Nothing further would be required if communication were perfect and authority complete, but such an ideal is not and cannot be achieved in human organization. For this reason, information about the performance of subordinate managerial and operating personnel is a vital ingredient of effective executive action. This information forms the basis for control decisions to create greater conformity to planning decisions.

The Problem of Measurement

Control involves a comparison of planning and performance information to evaluate the proficiency of subordinates. However, a favorable or unfavorable relationship between plan and performance should not always be accepted at face value. A lack of conformity to plan can result from inappropriate plans rather than inadequate performance. Planning decisions frequently have to be revised because of errors in judgment and forecasts. Whether the plan or the nonconforming subordinate is the villain is sometimes difficult to determine. Subordinates are sometimes penalized for the superior's planning failures rather than their own performance failures.

The logic used to formulate planning and performance information should be the same. For example, the premises used in preparing budgets should be the same as those used to compile accounting and other performance data. The mechanical drawings used for inspection purposes should contain the same specifications as those used to plan operations. A similar statement can be made about oral and written messages prepared in the English language. A major difficulty in this respect is the deliberate and nondeliberate (semantic) distortion of information. The intent of superiors may not be properly communicated because subordinates impute a different meaning.

Executives should recognize that a comparison of planning norms and performance information may not adequately measure efficiency. The words or data in messages do not necessarily express the actual state of affairs. A great deal of knowledge about environmental, technological, and socio-psychological factors is necessary to understand the significance of messages about plans and performance.

Feedback and Oscillation

The purpose of a control system is to determine whether the performance of an organization or a department is in accord with planning goals and norms. The possibility of planning errors also requires a constant inflow of information about such environmental forces as product markets, resource markets, and innovation. Control or feedback information indicates planning inadequacies and variations from plans. It provides a basis for adjustments in organizational behavior and proper adaptation to environmental changes.

A thermostat used to regulate the temperature of a house is a good example of a control or feedback system. The desired temperature is communicated to the system by setting an indicator. The furnace responds by turning on or off as the actual temperature varies by some amount from the desired level. Thus, it begins to heat at 69°F and shuts off at 71°F. A good thermostat will keep a house at fairly even temperature, but a badly designed thermostat will send the temperature into violent oscillations.[13] A similar situation can arise from feedback failures in business and other organizations.

A lag in the flow of information about an environmental change and a failure to take prompt action can cause a sequence of adjustments in wrong directions. A company faced with severe fluctuations in the demand for its products may find itself increasing production when it ought to cut production, and conversely. Production schedules may never be in accord with the actual market situations because information about an increase or reduction in demand is received or acted upon *after* demand has again moved in an opposite direction. Although the transformation period, lead time requirements, and planning considerations limit adaptability, an organization can often increase its survival power if information about an environmental change is received in sufficient time. Similar problems can arise with respect to factors that are internal to the organization. For example, a relatively minor morale problem can become a serious labor relations problem because a lack of information precluded prompt corrective action. Top management may not become aware of the problem until a horde of union officials storm "the executive suite" with loud voices. Such a development might have been avoided by timely information about the problem. Costly consequences can also result from inadequate information about such matters as the quality of production, customer complaints, industrial accidents, a shortage of personnel, and research and development difficulties.

The Cost of Control

Some degree of control information is necessary for effective managerial action. However, there is a level beyond which additional information is too costly from an economic standpoint. The revenues or savings that result from a correction of planning and performance errors must be at

[13] The problem of feedback and oscillation in physiological, mechanical, and other feedback systems is considered by Norbert Wiener, *Cybernetics* (New York: John Wiley and Sons, 1948), pp. 113–136.

least equal to the cost of obtaining the required information. Some companies undoubtedly spend far too much money for budgeting, accounting, and other types of control information. Others are too niggardly in this respect and would reap rewards from additional information facilities. The difficulties of measurement and differences in the control problems of particular companies preclude an exact solution or a universal formula. But executives should not ignore the problem because they may be wrong by a few cents or a few hundred dollars. They should give constant attention to the problem and carefully scrutinize present and proposed control devices.

Supervision as an Instrument of Control

The importance of supervision or direct observation of a subordinate should not be neglected. Every executive below the apex of the hierarchy, whether he be a vice-president or a foreman, is subject to supervision from a higher level. Observing a subordinate's behavior under various conditions is sometimes the best way to evaluate his performance or potential. Much of the process is informal and indirect and becomes an aspect of the sociopsychological dynamics of the superior-subordinate relationship. However, a superior cannot constantly keep watch over his flock if he is not to be overwhelmed with work. There are also good motivational reasons for not carrying supervision to an extreme. Accounting and other indirect control devices make possible a greater degree of decentralization and tend to give more personal freedom to subordinates. The control process generally involves some combination of supervision and indirect techniques.

Planning and Control Decisions

Control decisions enforce conformity to the behavioral pattern planned by management. Planning makes the rule; control enforces it. The control function is similar to the judicial function in political organizations. It cannot be legitimately exercised without prior planning decisions that stipulate the kind of behavior expected from subordinates. Control decisions bestow rewards or impose penalties for conformity or nonconformity to norms that define appropriate behavior. The problem of control is fundamentally the problem of motivation. Organizations cannot long survive if they must constantly use firing squads or layoffs to achieve cooperation. In this book "control" communication is treated as an aspect of the total communication problem. Control or judicial decisions are viewed as a kind of motivational decision.

The Universality of the Management Process

The management process is a necessary feature of all organized activity. Although the purposes of organizations differ, the management process remains constant.[14] It is present in factories, banks, retail establishments, military organizations, churches, universities, and hospitals. It is a common denominator which pervades the functional areas of specialization, such as production management, marketing management, and financial management. It is also an attribute of the various levels of management from the foreman to the chairman of the board.

A Fusion of Functions

A distinction should be made between managerial and other functions performed by the people who occupy managerial positions. Most managers are part-time managers and part-time something else. The head of an accounting department, for example, is often engaged in accounting activities in addition to managing subordinates. The president of a steel company employs both a knowledge of management principles and the technology of steel producing and marketing in performing his duties. The director of an art museum combines a knowledge of art with his management tasks. A university dean makes use of his teaching and research experiences in performing managerial functions.

A High Degree of Substitution

The common properties of the managerial process make possible a high degree of substitution among managers in different kinds of endeavor. Army officers have become successful university administrators and business executives. Governmental posts have been filled by business executives with a large measure of success. Executives in one kind of business, such as retailing, have successfully moved to industries with radically

---

[14] Oliver Sheldon has this to say on this subject: "It is because management is the one inherent necessity in the conduct of any enterprise that it is possible to conceive of it as a profession. Whether capital be supplied by individuals or by the State, whether labour be by hand or by machine, whether the workers assume a wide control over industry or are subjected to the most autocratic power, the function of management remains constant." *The Philosophy of Management* (London: Sir Isaac Pitman & Sons, Ltd., 1923), p. 48.

different technologies, such as manufacturing or publishing. Equally important in this respect are transfers from one area of functional specialization to another. A vice-president of finance or advertising often becomes the chief executive of a manufacturing concern.

Management as Process and People

A distinction should be noted between management as a process and the use of that word to denote the people who perform the function. When the word "management" is used to mean people, it is often restricted to those who manage business and industrial organizations. The management process has a broader scope than this usage implies. It includes the activities of anyone who manages the affairs of any kind of formally organized endeavor.

The Management Process and Management Organization

Executive action is organized. Decision making is a cooperative activity performed by executives who occupy positions in a managerial structure. The positions and persons are interrelated by a communication system. The management process can only be properly understood if it is viewed in an organizational context. It involves complex sets of social interaction within an already established structure of relationships. The structure is self-generating in the sense that it constantly reconstructs itself in response to changing conditions.

From Organization to Process

The problem of developing a managerial structure is considered in Part II. Part III is concerned with the impact of formal and informal sociopsychological forces on the organized management process. The functions that make up the management process are portrayed as organized phenomena in Chapter 13 to provide a point of departure for Parts IV–VII. Part IV deals with decision making with particular emphasis on planning the organizational program. Part V deals with communication problems and processes, and Part VI directs attention to motivation decisions. The last two chapters (Part VII) relate the material in the preceding parts to the problem of executive development.

SELECTED REFERENCES

Marcus Alexis and Charles Z. Wilson, *Organizational Decision Making*, Section 2. Englewood Cliffs, N.J.: Prentice-Hall, Inc., 1967.

Stafford Beer, *Decision and Control*. New York: John Wiley & Sons, Inc., 1966.

Stafford Beer, *Management Science*. Garden City, N.Y.: Doubleday & Company, Inc., 1968.

Sune Carlson, *Executive Behavior*. Stockholm: C. A. Stromberg Aktiebolag, Publisher, 1951.

Andre L. Delbecq, "The Management of Decision-Making Within the Firm: Three Strategies for Three Types of Decision-Making," *Academy of Management Journal*, Vol. 10, No. 4, pp. 329–339 (December 1967).

Editors of Fortune, *The Executive Life*. Garden City, N.Y.: Doubleday & Company, Inc., 1956.

Comstock Glaser, *Administrative Procedure*. Washington, D.C.: American Council on Public Affairs, 1941.

William I. Gore, *Administrative Decision-Making: A Heuristic Model*. New York: John Wiley & Sons, Inc., 1964.

Crawford H. Greenewalt, *The Uncommon Man*, pp. 59–76. New York: McGraw-Hill Book Company, Inc., 1959.

Richard A. Johnson, Fremont E. Kast and James E. Rosenzweig, *The Theory and Management of Systems*, 2nd ed. New York: McGraw-Hill Book Company, 1967.

Craig C. Lundberg, "Administrative Decisions: A Scheme for Analysis," *Journal of the Academy of Management*, Vol. 5, No. 2, pp. 165–178 (August 1962).

Max D. Richards and Paul S. Greenlaw, *Management Decision Making*, Homewood, Ill.: Richard D. Irwin, Inc., 1966.

Leonard R. Sayles, *Managerial Behavior*, Chap. 3. New York: McGraw-Hill Book Company, Inc., 1964.

Herbert A. Simon, *The Shape of Automation*, Part III. New York: Harper & Row, 1965. The same material can be found in: Simon, *The New Science of Management Decision*. New York: Harper & Row, 1960.

Robert Tannenbaum, "The Manager Concept: A Rational Synthesis," *Journal of Business of the University of Chicago*, Vol. 22, No. 4, pp. 229–240 (October 1949).

Seymour Tilles, "The Manager's Job: A Systems Approach," *Harvard Business Review,* Vol. 41, No. 1, pp. 73–81 (January–February 1963).

Stanley Young, *Management: A Systems Analysis.* Glenview, Ill.: Scott, Foresman and Company, 1966.

Van Court Hare, Jr., *Systems Analysis: A Diagnostic Approach.* New York: Harcourt, Brace & World, Inc., 1967.

Norbert Wiener, *Cybernetics, Control and Communication in the Animal and the Machine.* New York: John Wiley & Sons, Inc., 1948.

PART II

ORGANIZATION FOR MANAGEMENT

chapter 5

THE ORGANIZATIONAL STRUCTURE

The organizational structure is the framework within which managerial and operating tasks are performed. The development of a sound structure generally has a high priority in the thinking of executives. Many executives view decisional and operating problems as organizing problems. This statement, taken from an *Annual Report* of the Ford Motor Company, indicates the importance of organizing in the total scheme of things: "One of the most important ways in which the Company has improved its competitive position in the past decade has been the rebuilding and strengthening of its management and organization."[1] A top General Electric executive lauded organizational changes made by his company in these words: "This sound new organization has been designed to enable the Company to realize the full market potential in each of its diversified product lines."[2] Deere and Company stressed the significance of its new managerial structure in giving it the "ability to deal effectively with the opportunities and challenges that lie ahead."[3]

The Management Hierarchy

The "individualistic" entrepreneurial concept of economic theory does not have many counterparts in practice. Most organized endeavor is managed by a group ranging in size from a few persons to several thou-

[1] *Annual Report,* Ford Motor Company, 1955, p. 13.
[2] *Annual Report,* The General Electric Company, 1955, p. 1.
[3] *Annual Report,* Deere and Company, 1966, 15.

101

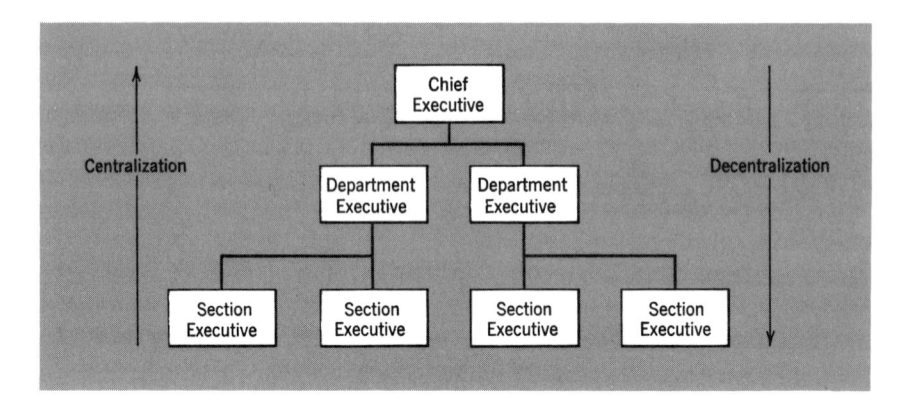

Figure 5-1. A simplified management hierarchy.

sands. Such groups are generally structured in the form of a hierarchy as the result of formal planning or informal processes.

The Nature of Hierarchical Organization

The management hierarchy ranks and relates positions and persons in the manner indicated in Figure 5-1. It represents simultaneously a decentralization and centralization of decision making. Decisional responsibilities are decentralized in the sense that they are dispersed among whatever number of executives is necessary to do the job. The work division involved in organized endeavor generally is applied to managerial work. But organization requires a coordination of effort if a common purpose is to be achieved. Two people who cooperate in pushing a stalled automobile will accomplish little if they push in opposite directions. Coordination is a necessary consequence of organization; an absence of coordination is disorganization.[4] The ranking of executives in a hierarchy provides a means for coordinating management action. Conflicting and contradictory decisions can be resolved by executives at higher levels.

Every executive below the chief executive is subject to planning and control decisions from higher levels. Proceeding from the bottom to the top of the hierarchy, decision-making responsibilities are centralized in fewer

[4] James D. Mooney and Alan C. Reiley call coordination the first principle of organization. To them, coordination "expresses the principles of organization in toto; nothing less." *Onward Industry!* (New York: Harper & Brothers Publishers, 1931), p. 19.

and fewer numbers of executives until the apex is reached. All persons in the organization, managerial and nonmanagerial, are required to respond to decisions from that point.

Cooperative Executive Action

The hierarchy sets the stage for cooperative executive action. Each executive is assigned some part of the total decisional burden. Executives at lower levels function within an area of discretion determined by executives at higher levels. They make decisions on their own initiative, but they are also required to respond to decisions from superiors. The decisional responsibilities at the various levels are differentiated by a process called "departmentation." The executives who occupy the basic positions in the hierarchy are generally assisted by staff and service personnel. Committees may also be used to perform decisional responsibilities and serve other purposes.

Hierarchical Spans and Levels

The limited capacity of the executive makes hierarchical organization essential. An executive can reduce his work-load by the delegation of work to the next lower level, but delegation simultaneously increases the work-load by the amount of supervision that must be given to subordinate executives. The reduction in work-load by delegation is usually greater than the resulting increase in supervisory responsibilities. Another level in the hierarchy may become necessary when the amount of supervision begins to exceed the executive's capacity. The number of subordinates under an executive, which is often referred to as "the span of management," is related to the number of levels in a hierarchy. A larger span generally means fewer levels, and conversely.

The Span of Management

The term "span of management" is used here rather than "span of control," which is frequently used in the management literature, because, as Koontz and O'Donnell point out, "the span is one of management and not merely of control. . . ."[5] How many subordinates can be effectively managed by an executive? Is there an ideal number or a minimax solution

[5] Harold Koontz and Cyril O'Donnell, *Principles of Management*, 4th ed. (McGraw-Hill Book Company, Inc., 1968), p. 241n.

to the problem? An early reference to this matter is found in the Biblical account of the Exodus.

The Thing That Thou Doest Is Not Good

After leading the Israelites safely out of Egypt, Moses experienced many difficulties in the journey that led ultimately to the promised land of Canaan. One such difficulty is recorded in the Book of Exodus. His father-in-law, Jethro, observed that Moses was kept busy from morning until evening giving counsel to the people, who had to stand for long periods of time. Jethro said to Moses:

The thing that thou doest is not good. Thou wilt surely wear away, both thou, and this people that is with thee; for this thing is too heavy for thee; thou art not able to perform it thyself alone. Hearken now unto my voice, I will give thee counsel . . . thou shalt provide out of all the people able men, such as fear God, men of truth, hating covetousness; and place such over them, to be rulers of thousands, and rulers of hundreds, rulers of fifties, and rulers of tens. And let them judge the people at all seasons; and it shall be, that every great matter they shall bring unto thee, but every small matter they shall judge; so shall it be easier for thyself, and they shall bear the burden with thee.[6]

A Conclusion from Military History

Sir Ian Hamilton, a British general, concluded from the history of military organization that spans should range from three to six. He wrote that three would keep an officer fairly busy while six would probably require a ten-hour day. Hamilton thought that "the nearer we approach the supreme head of the whole organisation, the more we ought to work towards groups of three; the closer we get to the foot of the whole organisation (the Infantry of the Line) the more we work towards groups of six."[7]

Fayol's Hypothetical Hierarchy

Henri Fayol, the French industrialist, uses these data in constructing a hypothetical hierarchy.

Each fresh group of ten, twenty, thirty workers brings in a fresh foreman; two, three or four foremen make necessary a superintendent, two or three superin-

[6] Exodus 18:17–22.
[7] Sir Ian Hamilton, *The Soul and Body of an Army* (New York: George H. Doran Company, 1921), p. 230.

tendents give rise to a departmental manager, and the number of links of the scalar chain continues to increase in this way up to the ultimate superior, each new superior having usually no more than four or five immediate subordinates.[8]

A Hoover Commission Recommendation

The Hoover Commission on the Organization of the Executive Branch of the Government noted that a total of sixty-five departments, administrations, agencies, boards, and commissions is directly responsible to the President.[9] This number does not include quasi-judicial and quasi-legislative regulatory agencies. Some of the departments under the President are larger than the entire Federal government of twenty-five years ago. If the President spent one hour a week supervising the primary units, he would be working a 65-hour week. When other time-consuming obligations of the President are considered, such as news conferences, meetings with foreign dignitaries, and speeches, the situation becomes even more intolerable. To reduce this burden, the Hoover Commission recommended the consolidation of the organizational units under the President into about one-third the present number.

Industrial Spans

The American Management Association surveyed 141 companies to obtain information about actual industrial spans.[10] The sample was composed of companies "with good organizational practices," and the study was limited to the span of the president. Data were obtained from 100 large concerns (over 5000 employees) and 41 medium-sized firms (500 to 5000 employees).

As indicated in Table 5-1, the number of subordinates reporting to the president ranged from 1 to 24. In 9 out of 141 companies only one executive, usually an executive vice-president, reported to the president. The presidents of 55 companies had a span of 10 or more. The median for the 100 large organizations surveyed was between 8 and 9; for the 41 medium-sized concerns, between 6 and 7.

---

[8] Henri Fayol (Constance Storrs, translator), *General and Industrial Management* (London: Sir Isaac Pitman & Sons, Ltd., 1949), p. 55.

[9] *The Hoover Commission Report on Organization of the Executive Branch of the Government* (New York: McGraw-Hill Book Company, Inc., 1949), p. 25.

[10] The results of this survey are reported in Ernest Dale, *Planning and Developing the Company Organization Structure,* Research Report No. 20 (New York: American Management Association, 1952), pp. 56–60.

Table 5-1. Number of Executives Reporting to President in 100 Large and 41 Medium-Sized Companies

Number of Executives Reporting to President	Number of Large Companies	Number of Medium-Sized Companies
1	6	3
2	—	—
3	1	2
4	3	2
5	7	4
6	9	8
7	11	7
8	8	5
9	8	2
10	6	4
11	7	1
12	10	—
13	8	1
14	4	1
15	1	—
16	5	—
17	—	1
18	1	—
19	—	—
20	1	—
21	1	—
22	—	—
23	2	—
24	1	—
Totals	100	41

Adapted from data presented in Ernest Dale, *Planning and Developing the Company Organization Structure,* Research Report No. 20 (New York: American Management Association, 1952), pp. 57, 59.

The data on actual spans warn against any dogmatic conclusions as to numbers.[11] There is no general rule that can be used to determine the proper span for particular situations. Spans should probably be smaller at higher levels than at the first-line supervisory level. There would also seem to be an upper limit to the number of subordinates a superior can effec-

---

[11] The span of management concept has generated a great deal of controversy in recent years. One rather unrestrained exchange on the subject began with an article by Waino W. Suojanen which concluded that the span of management (control) is

tively supervise; 100 subordinates are too many under almost any circumstances, but whether the number should be 5 or 25 cannot be given a definite answer. An executive with 10 subordinates may have a lighter work-load than one with only 3 or 4. The reason is that the amount of work involved in different superior-subordinate relationships may vary a great deal. Some subordinates require frequent and extensive supervision; others can work out their problems with little attention from above.

Factors Indigenous to the Executive

A variety of factors influence the span of management. Some of them have general applicability and others help explain the wide divergence of spans in different organizations.

The Problem of Fatigue

Managerial activities, like other kinds of activities, result in fatigue. Fatigue may be defined as a lower ability to do work because of previous work. The energy of the human being is restricted by body mechanics and chemistry, and it cannot be expended through time without intervening periods of sleep. In extreme cases, fatigue can result in a temporary inability to engage in further physical activity. Roger Bannister, the first man to run the four-minute mile, suffered a physical collapse on completing some of his record runs.

Psychological fatigue is generally a more serious problem among executives than the fatigue that results directly from physical activity. Research conducted during World War II by the military services suggests that normal persons may show the usual symptoms of the psychoneurotic if they

not a valid concept to the extent that coordination can be achieved through formal and informal group activity. "The Span of Control—Fact or Fable?" *Advanced Management*, Vol. 20, No. 11, November 1955, pp. 5–13. Suojanen's article brought about a lengthy response from Lt. Col. Lyndall F. Urwick, the British management expert, who contended among other things that Suojanen was wrong and that the span of management (control) concept is still a most important precept in the array of management principles. "The Span of Control—Some Facts about the Fables," *Advanced Management*, Vol. 21, No. 11, November 1956, pp. 5–15. See also: Herbert A. Simon, "The Span of Control: A Reply," *Advanced Management*, Vol. 22, No. 4, April 1957, pp. 14, 29; Waino W. Suojanen, "Leadership, Authority, and the Span of Control," *Advanced Management*, Vol. 22, No. 9, September 1957, pp. 17–22; Lyndall F. Urwick, "The Manager's Span of Control," *Harvard Business Review*, Vol. 34, No. 3, May–June 1956, pp. 39–47.

are subjected for long periods of time to frustration and emotional conflict. This phenomenon has been expressed by such terms as "anxiety reaction," "combat fatigue," and psychoneurosis. Typical symptoms include rapid heart rate, insomnia, sweating, loss of appetite, loss of weight, irritability, inability to concentrate, tension, depression, and low motivation.[12] Many executives have experienced psychological fatigue, but the problem is frequently bypassed with remarks about Jim's change in attitude or Frank's irritability. The following comments by Dr. Frederick W. Dershimer, Director of Psychiatry at the Du Pont Corporation, indicate that the problem should be given more attention.

Sometimes a supervisor or a manager comes in with a problem to discuss. This may or may not mean that the subject of his discussion comes in later because in many cases—and here is where the question of diagnosis becomes important—conversation with the superior about the supposed patient reveals that the real patient is not the man who is being discussed at all, but the man who is doing the discussing. In other words, it is not the worker but the boss. It has been surprising and very gratifying to find how ready our management is to examine the possibility that they may be promoting the very condition they are worried about, and how ready to accept suggestions for correcting the real fault. This is doubly important because from long observation I am convinced that mental disease, like smallpox, is infectious. Where you have leaders who are in a state of excellent mental health, mental health spreads down the line. But the contrary is also true—where you have leaders who are in a poor state of mental health, their organization becomes increasingly unhealthy, as if it were exposed to an actual infection by germs. Members of the group become more and more insecure. More and more they demand this and that in the effort to cure their feelings of insecurity, when actually the real focus of the infection is a weak leader.[13]

A temporary reduction in responsibilities or a vacation is all that is needed to "cure" the majority of cases. The executive should not be made to feel that he is no longer wanted. The resulting insecurity can give rise to more anxiety than the pressure of work. Nervous tension and stomach ulcers seem to be a by-product of the pace and problems of an industrial

---

[12] Many of these symptoms appeared among combat air force personnel during World War II. John C. Flanagan (editor), *The Aviation Psychology Program in the Army Air Forces,* Report No. 1 (Washington, D.C.: U.S. Printing Office, 1948), p. 220. The other military services and industry had similar experiences with this problem. Physicians who handled industrial cases during World War II reported many cases of psychological fatigue, though the patient generally thought his difficulty to be physical.

[13] Frederick W. Dershimer, "The Practical Application of Psychiatry to Business Problems," *Industrial Applications of Medicine and Psychiatry,* Personnel Series, No. 130 (New York: American Management Association, 1949), p. 13.

society. Such a society should probably make more use of the knowledge of the psychologist and the psychiatrist than is presently the case. Many "normal" people can be helped in making adjustments to difficult work and life situations.

Knowledge and Personality

The range of knowledge necessary to conduct the affairs of organization may affect the span of management. For example, engineering and accounting are often given separate status even though the number of people involved could otherwise be organized into a single department. Specialized knowledge plays an important part in structuring managerial responsibilities.

The diversity of spans found in industry can also be explained by differences in executive personality. An "empire builder" may significantly enlarge his span over a period time. A submissive individual's span may become smaller as others gradually take over his domain.

Exogenous Factors

The manner in which factors external to the executive relate to the span of management is considered in this section.

The Theory of V. A. Graicunas

The number of human relationships in a span is greater than the number of subordinates. The nature of these relationships is indicated in a study by V. A. Graicunas, a French management consultant.[14] Graicunas categorized the various relationships as direct single, direct group, and cross relationships. If S has two subordinates, X and Y, he may confer with each of them individually, which constitutes two direct single relationships. Two direct group relationships result when S talks to X when Y is present and to Y with X present. The assumption is that the behavior of each subordinate is influenced by the presence of the other. Two cross relationships result from interaction between the two subordinates when the supervisor is not present. In some cases X's work may require consultation with Y,

[14] V. A. Graicunas, "Relationship in Organization," *Papers on the Science of Administration* (New York: Institute of Public Administration, Columbia University, 1937), pp. 183–187; an analysis of managerial relationships is also found in: Fayol, *op. cit.*, p. 55.

110 ORGANIZATION FOR MANAGEMENT

and conversely. Graicunas' analysis results in a total of six possible relationships.

Direct Single Relationships	
S to X; S to Y	2
Direct Group Relationships	
S to X with Y; S to Y with X	2
Cross Relationships	
X with Y; Y with X	2
Total Relationships	6

With other assumptions, the relationships that might result from a combination of two subordinates and one superior are greater than six.[15] Furthermore, it cannot be assumed that relationships remain constant over a period of time. The possibility of promotion, difficulties at home, personal financial problems, or a hangover make Jones a different person today than he was last week or yesterday.

Graicunas computed the number of relationships that might arise with different numbers of subordinates. The result shows a highly progressive rate of increase in relationships as the number of subordinates is increased.[16] Increasing the number of subordinates from 11 to 12 results in 13,334 additional relationships. Table 5-2 shows the relationships with various numbers of subordinates. Fortunately, it is not likely that they will be present or pertinent at the same time.

Table 5-2. Number of Relationships with Various Numbers of Subordinates

Number of Subordinates	Number of Relationships
4	44
8	1,080
12	24,708
16	524,528
20	10,486,140
24	201,327,144

[15] Among other relationships not recognized by Graicunas are: (1) either one subordinate or both may initiate action from the superior; (2) the superior may assume the role of an equal in group relationships with one or both subordinates.

[16] Where n is the number of subordinates, the relationships r can be obtained by solving: $r = n(2^{n-1} + n - 1)$.

The significance of Graicunas' theory is that it recognizes that the problem of managing others is both an individual and a social problem. Management must deal not only with a variety of individual personalities but also with different combinations of individuals or group "personalities." Social interaction, group norms and sentiments, and informal leadership are important in understanding subordinate behavior. A hostile clique or conflict among subordinates presents problems that do not exist with a spirit of teamwork.

An Expanded System of Relationships

Additional relationships result from interaction with executives at the same and higher levels. Also important are contacts with customers, union officials, suppliers, the public, and government. Organizational reasonsibilities frequently extend beyond the regular schedule of work. An invitation from a customer or a supplier to engage in a round of golf cannot usually be ignored. A company-sponsored picnic for employees and their families has a similar implication. Membership in service and social clubs may also impose a burden on an executive. These and other relationships form an integral part of the work and life of many executives.

The Type of Activity

The nature of organizational activities makes for variations in hierarchical spans and structure. Executive work in a manufacturing plant, an investment house, an educational institution, and a military unit differ in some or many respects. Similar differences exist between departments within an organization. The pace and pattern of work in the production department is not the same as that of the financial department. A change in activities over time can also affect the problem of organizing the hierarchy. Organizations may have to develop and maintain a hierarchy that is not equally efficient for various kinds of activities. For example, the military retains combat-ready structures during the routines of peacetime garrison life. Companies in seasonal industries often maintain a larger than necessary management force during the slack periods to meet the demands of the busy season.

Spatial Dispersion

To what extent and how does a geographical dispersion of organizational activities affect managerial organization? Technological innovations in transportation and communication have given new dimensions to the concept of distance. Many organizations have branch factories and offices in every corner of the globe. A distance of three thousand miles meant several months of travel under difficult conditions during early American history. Today a journey from New York to Paris or Rome can be accomplished in hours. Distance has also been conquered by communication devices that transmit messages for any number of miles in a fraction of a second. But in spite of the advantages afforded by modern technology, spatial dispersion presents a number of management problems. Modern transportation and communication facilities are efficient, but they are also expensive. Traveling to a distant branch factory or office still involves more time than an elevator ride to the seventh floor. The preparation of reports for home and branch offices takes time and effort. The need for important spot decisions may require the presence of major executives in regional offices. These and other factors make for variations in the nature and size of management hierarchies with different degrees of spatial dispersion.

Flat versus Tall Structures

Some organizations have constructed a "flat" or "horizontal" structure by increasing the span of management and reducing the number of levels. Others have developed a "tall" or "vertical" structure through shorter spans and more levels. Some of the advantages and disadvantages of the two types of organization are considered in this section.

The Argument for Flat Structures

James C Worthy, a management consultant and a former Sears Roebuck vice-president, contends that "the emphasis is constantly on *shortening* the span, without giving much more than lip service to the fact that circumstances often differ and that under certain conditions there may be positive advantages in *lengthening* the span." [17] One argument for longer spans is that it makes close supervision impossible and forces subordinates to rely on their own resources. A subordinate cannot expect much help from his superior, and the resulting responsibilities in turn make for less supervision of those under him. Such a situation tends to bring about a better selection of subordinates, because more delegation with less supervision is risky with incompetent personnel. Executive development is en-

[17] James C. Worthy, *Big Business and Free Men* (New York: Harper & Brothers Publishers, 1959), pp. 100–102.

hanced by earlier decisional experience for people who show promise. As Worthy has noted, "if they have to wait until middle age before having a chance to carry bona fide responsibility, they are not likely to develop into strong, self-reliant leaders and executives." [18] An opportunity to move rapidly to important responsibilities can have favorable motivational consequences for personnel at lower levels. However, it should not be assumed that all people can function well in this kind of environment. The system is not conducive to persons who lack self-confidence and competence.

The argument for longer spans is supported by empirical studies which indicate that productivity may be higher when close supervision is impossible.[19] The data accumulated in these studies show that the heads of low-producing departments supervised their subordinates more closely than those who headed high-producing departments. Supervisors of high-producing subordinates clarified the objectives and then gave few instructions on how to achieve them. Subordinates were permitted to pace themselves and to use their own ideas and techniques in carrying out their responsibilities. Effective supervisors tended either to ignore mistakes or to use them as a learning device. The heads of lower-producing groups were inclined to give frequent and specific instructions and to be critical and punitive when mistakes were made.

A flat structure has fewer hierarchical levels, thereby tending to reduce the "administrative distance" between top and bottom levels. The concept of administrative distance has reference to the understanding and intimacy which characterize the relationship between persons at different levels of the organizational structure. Too much administrative distance can create communication difficulties. As Worthy has pointed out:

> In the vertical structure the administrator is forced to rely less on knowledge growing out of direct contact and more on formal reporting systems in information which is filtered up to him through successive levels of supervision and perhaps considerably distorted in the process. A great deal is lost if the facts about problems have to work their way up through too many hands—and too many "censors"—before they reach the man who has to act on them.[20]

Many hierarchical levels or "layering" increases impersonality and reduces understanding between higher and lower levels. The personal touch is lost and informal ties becomes tenuous. Top executives tend to be excluded from the socializing that occurs at lower levels, an exclusion which can seriously disrupt the cooperative process.

[18] *Ibid.*, p. 112.
[19] The results of some of this research have been summarized in: Rensis Likert, *New Patterns of Management* (New York: McGraw-Hill Book Company, Inc., 1961), pp. 9–12; 20–25.
[20] Worthy, *op. cit.*, pp. 102–103.

Flat versus Tall Structures: A Comparative Analysis

A flat structure can complicate the communication process by the burdens it imposes upon cross communication. Fewer levels may facilitate communication between superiors and subordinates, but larger spans can produce communication problems among subordinates. Communication among equals does not necessarily have an advantage over communication among unequals. Conflicts among individuals and groups of subordinates can become barriers to effective communication.

Authority can be a highly useful communication instrument. An authoritative message from superior to subordinate is often given far more attention than messages from one subordinate to another. The impetus given by authority can bring about a rapid flow of information among the larger numbers of levels in a tall structure in spite of the greater administrative distance. The adverse consequences that the reduced administrative distance in flat structures can have on the authority relationship should also be noted. Authority is reinforced by inequalities in status; it can be reduced by too much socializing among superiors and subordinates.

The emphasis on equality in the flat structure can cause coordination problems. In a world pervaded by uncertainty, differences of opinion cannot always be resolved by the logic of the scientific method. The democratic process cannot be completely depended upon to provide an appropriate outcome. Authority is frequently necessary if an organization is not to be disrupted or even destroyed by a lack of coordination. The fact that flat structures tend to develop capable and self-confident subordinates can complicate the problem. Such subordinates are inclined to push their prerogatives and build strong subsidiary departments. Departmental interests may become far too important in the total scheme of things. Subordinates must frequently be "forced" to conform to the requirements of superior levels.

The flat structure fits the cultural norms of the United States better than does the tall structure. Most people appear to have a preference for leaders who use a democratic approach and who do not overtly use their authority. The reaction against close supervision reflects such sentiments. A related factor is that a flat structure with less social stratification is more in accord with an egalitarian political and social philosophy. However, preachments on this subject do not always correspond to actual practices. Indeed, a tall structure is sometimes more satisfactory from a motivational standpoint because it offers a greater number of status gradations.

People in a democratic society are not normally opposed to an authoritarian approach when it is necessary to achieve an important purpose.

They rarely refuse to accord authority during an emergency. The relatively tall structure of the military with its authoritarianism is widely accepted during time of war. Such structures are probably more effective in situations requiring rapid adaptations and precise coordination.

Related to Decentralization

The problems considered above are closely related to the subject of decentralization, which is discussed in Chapter 8. Decentralization or a lack of it can bring about different behavioral patterns in structures that have a similar shape.

An Hourglass Structure

The information processing made possible by the electronic computer may have a profound impact upon the shape of the organizational structure. The structures of the future may look something like an hourglass, or, to use the words of two early contributors on the subject, "a football balanced upon the point of a church bell." [21]

Management in the 1980's

Professors Harold J. Leavitt and Thomas L. Whisler in their now famous article, "Management in the 1980's," predicted that the decisional and information capacities of electronic computers will make major changes in organizational structures.[22] They felt that computers and related mathematical and statistical techniques, which they called "information technology," would have the greatest effect upon middle and top management. The reason for this is that information technology would move the boundary between planning and performance to higher levels. The scientific management school of Frederick W. Taylor shifted the responsibility for planning from the worker to first line supervision and then to specialized line and staff personnel at the middle management level. Many managerial responsibilities at the middle-management level, according to Leavitt and Whisler, will become more highly structured and susceptible to computer programming and processing.

Not all of the jobs at the middle levels will be affected in the same way.

[21] Harold J. Leavitt and Thomas L. Whisler, "Management in the 1980's," *Harvard Business Review*, Vol. 36, No. 6, November–December 1958, p. 47.
[22] *Ibid.*, pp. 41–48.

The more routine responsibilities will move downward in status and pay because they will require relatively less skill, but others will become more challenging and move upward in the structure. Included in this category are the positions concerned with the implementation of the new information technology (such as computer programmers) and those relating to research and development. Creativity and innovation will become increasingly important at the top management level.

Leavitt and Whisler point to a recentralization of management decisional responsibilities and a relative increase in the number of people at the top of the structure. The increased flow of information from all parts of the organization to the top level will put a great deal of pressure upon the top decision makers. Additional staff personnel will be required to provide necessary knowledge for effective decision, and the diversity of decisional subject matter will bring about a greater reliance upon group management.

An Opposing Opinion

Not all people agree with the above predictions. The increased information that can be provided by electronic computers may well bring about an even greater trend toward decentralization. An executive in a large electrical company has said that there is "a very reasonable basis for concluding that decentralization and the middle manager are much more likely to *grow* and *flourish* than to wither and die in the decades ahead." [23] Whether an organization is centralized or decentralized is at least partly if not primarily related to management philosophy. Information technology can be used to move the organization in either direction. It can improve the centralized control that makes greater decentralization possible. An important reason for centralization at the present time is a lack of sufficient information for effective centralized control over decentralized operations. But, at the same time, a greater amount of information simultaneously makes possible more centralization.

Empirical Research and Organizational Experiences

Empirical research and experience support some of the conclusions made in the original Leavitt and Whisler article. The findings of one study on the subject are "that (1) fewer decisions are being made at lower levels in the management hierarchy, (2) less important decisions are being made by decentralized managers, and (3) there is greater control of local operations by high level executives." [24] But this study also indicates that there is

[23] John F. Burlingame, "Information Technology and Decentralization," *Harvard Business Review,* Vol. 39, No. 6, November–December 1961, p. 121.
[24] William E. Reif, *Computer Technology and Management Organization* (Iowa City: Bureau of Business and Economic Research, 1968), p. 110.

a discretionary element. "The ability of the computer to process and disseminate information required for company-wide planning and control decisions to virtually anyone in the organization has enabled the firm to become highly discriminate in designating whom it wants to make the decisions." [25]

Another study on computer induced organizational changes concludes that in all of the eleven firms studied "some of middle management's decisions had been abrogated by the computer." [26] Furthermore, "instances of recentralized movement of decisions were found in virtually every firm in the sample." [27] A few of the middle managers had been shifted to lower levels in the organization, but none of them had been eliminated or financially downgraded.

Other research indicates that changes have occurred in the pattern of information processing within organizations, but that the point at which decisions are made has not been changed. Information processing has been centralized, but decision making has not. As Ernest Dale has concluded in a study of the decision-making process in organizations with electronic computers: "Predictions foreshadowing pronounced trends toward either centralization or decentralization have so far not materialized." [28]

Some Preliminary Conclusions

Which of the conclusions made above best expresses the actual state of affairs? The answer is that they are all correct in certain respects. All agree that electronic computers have already greatly affected information processing in many organizational structures. The disagreements that exist are more apparent than real. The decisional responsibilities of middle managers have not been markedly centralized or for that matter decentralized as a result of information technology. There appear to be some changes, but the extent to which such changes are discretionary is difficult to say at this time. An organizational structure like that envisioned by Leavitt and Whisler is undoubtedly possible and may well set the pattern for the future. But there is also a possibility that there will evolve equally efficient decentralized structures with a strong middle management.

[25] *Ibid.*
[26] Roger C. Vergin, "Computer Induced Organization Changes," *MSU Business Topics,* Vol. 15, No. 3, Summer 1967, p. 64.
[27] *Ibid.,* p. 65.
[28] Ernest Dale, *The Decision-Making Process in the Commercial Use of High-Speed Computers* (Ithaca, New York: Cornell Studies in Policy and Administration, Graduate School of Business and Public Administration, Cornell University, 1964), p. 42.

SELECTED REFERENCES

Michael Beer, "Organizational Size and Job Satisfaction," *Academy of Management Journal*, Vol. 7, No. 1, pp. 34–44 (March 1964).

Ernest Dale, *Planning and Developing the Company Organization Structure*, Research Report No. 20, pp. 49–60. New York: American Management Association, 1952.

Gerald G. Fisch, "Stretching the Span of Management," *Harvard Business Review*, Vol. 41, No. 5, pp. 74–85 (September–October 1963).

V. A. Graicunas, "Relationship in Organization," *Papers on the Science of Administration*, pp. 183–187. New York: Institute of Public Administration, 1937.

John G. Hutchinson, *Organizations: Theory and Classical Concepts*. New York: Holt, Rinehart and Winston, 1967.

Elliott Jaques, "Too Many Management Levels," *California Management Review*, Vol. 8, No. 1, pp. 13–20 (Fall 1965).

Harold Koontz, "Making Theory Operational: The Span of Management," *The Journal of Management Studies*, Vol. 3, No. 3, pp. 229–243 (October 1966).

Harold J. Leavitt and Thomas L. Whisler, "Management in the 1980's," *Harvard Business Review*, Vol. 36, No. 6, pp. 41–48 (November–December 1958).

Edward A. Nelson, "Economic Size of Organizations," *California Management Review*, Vol. 10, No. 3, pp. 61–72 (Spring 1968).

William E. Reif, *Computer Technology and Management Organization*. Iowa City, Ia.: Bureau of Business and Economic Research, 1968.

F. L. W. Richardson, Jr., and Charles R. Walker, *Human Relations in an Expanding Company*. New Haven: Labor and Management Center, 1948.

Waino W. Suojanen, "The Span of Control—Fact or Fable?" *Advanced Management*, Vol. 20, No. 11, pp. 5–13 (November 1955).

Henry Tosi and Henry Patt, "Administrative Ratios and Organizational Size," *Academy of Management Journal*, Vol. 10, No. 2, pp. 161–168 (June 1967).

Jon G. Udall, "An Empirical Test of Hypotheses Relating to Span of Control," *Administrative Science Quarterly*, Vol. 12, No. 3, pp. 420–439 (December 1967).

Lyndall F. Urwick, "The Manager's Span of Control," *Harvard Business Review*, Vol. 34, No. 3, pp. 39–47 (May–June 1956).

Albert K. Wickesberg, *Management Organization*. New York: Appleton-Century-Crofts, 1966.

J. C. Worthy, "Organizational Structure and Employee Morale," *American Sociological Review*, Vol. 15, No. 2, pp. 169–179 (April 1950).

James C. Worthy, *Big Business and Free Men*, Chap. 7. New York: Harper & Brothers, 1959.

chapter 6

DEPARTMENTATION

Hierarchical organization represents a two-dimensional definition of executive responsibility. The first of these evolves from the delegation of responsibilities to different levels of the hierarchy. This aspect of the organizing problem is discussed in Chapter 8. The second dimension concerns the division of responsibilities among executives situated at the same level. This kind of differentiation results from the process of departmentation.

Departmentation Defined

Departmentation divides the work of the organization into semi-autonomous units or departments. The consequence of departmentation is a delineation of executive responsibilities *and* a grouping of operating activities. Every level in the hierarchy below the apex is departmentalized, and each succeeding lower level involves further departmental differentiation.

Types of Departmentation

The activities necessary to achieve the organizational objective are a basic consideration in organizing. The nature of such activities may differ significantly with such diverse objectives as making steel, waging war, selling insurance, and educating students. However, the types of departmentation have general applicability and can be applied in many different situations. The types most commonly used are the following: (1) functional, (2) product, (3) service, (4) territorial, (5) time, (6) equipment, and (7) alpha-numerical.

Table 6-1. Typical Patterns of First-Order Functional Departmentation in Various Fields

Bank (large)
  Comptroller
  Economics and business research
  Legal
  Maintenance
  Operations (generally divided by type of service, such as pension, personal and corporate trust, banking)
  Personnel
  Public relations
Department Store
  Controller
  Merchandising
  Personnel
  Sales promotion (publicity, advertising)
  Store superintendent (a group of service functions, such as maintenance, traffic, delivery)
Insurance
  Accounting
  Actuarial
  Advertising
  Agency
  Claim adjustment
  Investment
  Medical
  Personnel
  Underwriting
Manufacturing
  Engineering
  Finance (comptroller)
  Industrial relations (labor relations, personnel)
  Marketing (sales)
  Production (manufacturing)
  Purchasing
  Research and Development
Public Utility (Electric)
  Accounting
  Construction
  Controller
  Engineering
  Operations
  Personnel (industrial relations, employee relations)
  Purchasing
  Sales

Terminological Variations

The terms used to denote the "departments" that result from departmentation vary a great deal. Business organizations use such terms as division, department, and section; the military uses regiment, battalion, group, and company; governmental units are called branch, department, bureau, and section. Terminology may vary in different fields of endeavor (Table 6-1) and from company to company. The principal operating units may be called departments in one company and divisions in another. Similar variations appear in the descriptions of functional departments. Production departments are sometimes called manufacturing and operations departments, and the terms employee relations, industrial relations, and personnel may be used synonymously. The types of departmentation are also subject to problems of nomenclature. Territorial departmentation is often called geographical or location departmentation, and commodity departmentation is substituted for the term product departmentation.

Functional Departmentation

Departmentation based on such primary functions as production, sales, finance, engineering, and personnel is common. Some kind of functional departmentation is present in nearly every organization. Functional departmentation may begin at different levels of the management hierarchy. Some organizations make almost exclusive use of this kind of departmentation; others interlace functional, product, customer, and territorial departmentation. See Figures 6-1 and 6-2.

Nature of Functional Differentiation

The terms "function," "functional," and "functionalism" have reference to distinctions between kinds of duties.[1] Some of the duties in different functional departments differ significantly, but others are similar in nature. An interviewer in the personnel department and a design engineer in the engineering department are engaged in dissimilar activities. A typist in the purchasing department seems to be doing something similar to that of a typist in the personnel department. However, there is generally a difference even when the activity seems exactly alike. The typist in the purchasing

---

[1] James D. Mooney and Alan C. Reiley, *Onward Industry!* (New York: Harper & Brothers Publishers, 1931), pp. 45, 491.

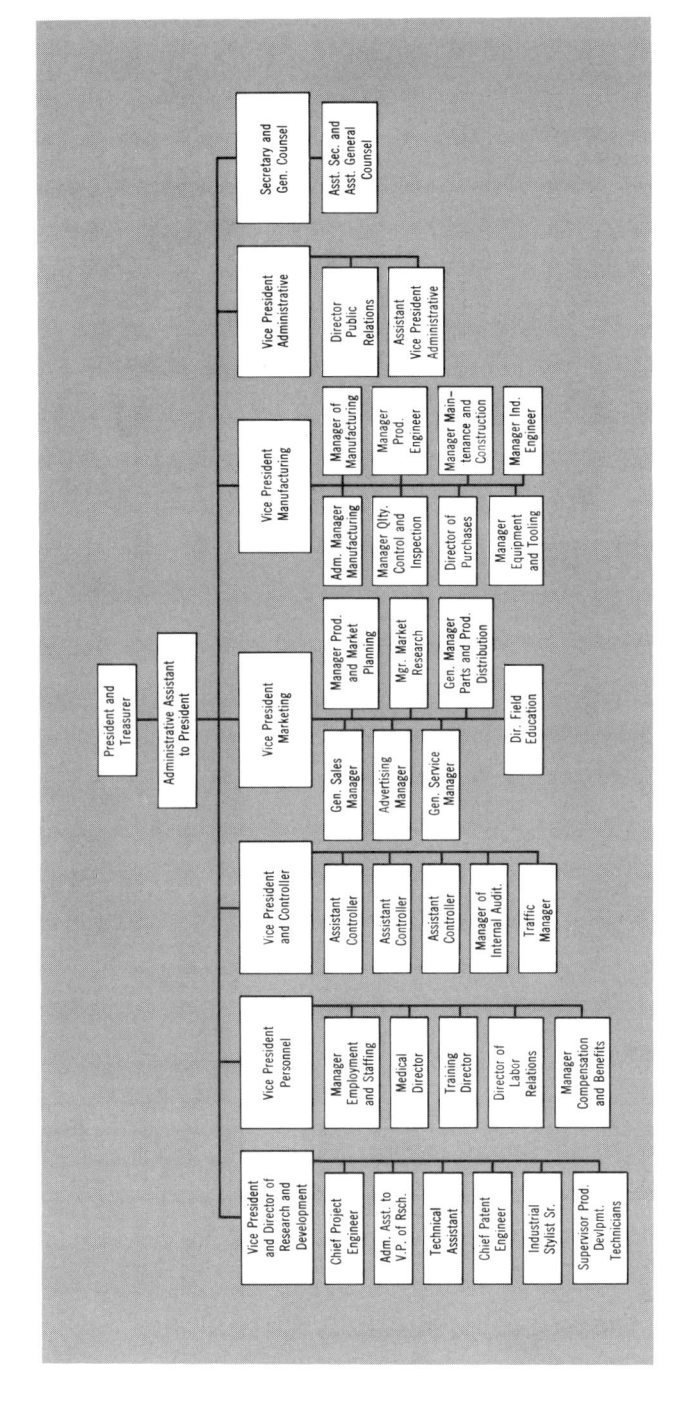

Figure 6-1. Functional departmentation: The Maytag Company organization. Courtesy of The Maytag Company, Newton, Iowa.

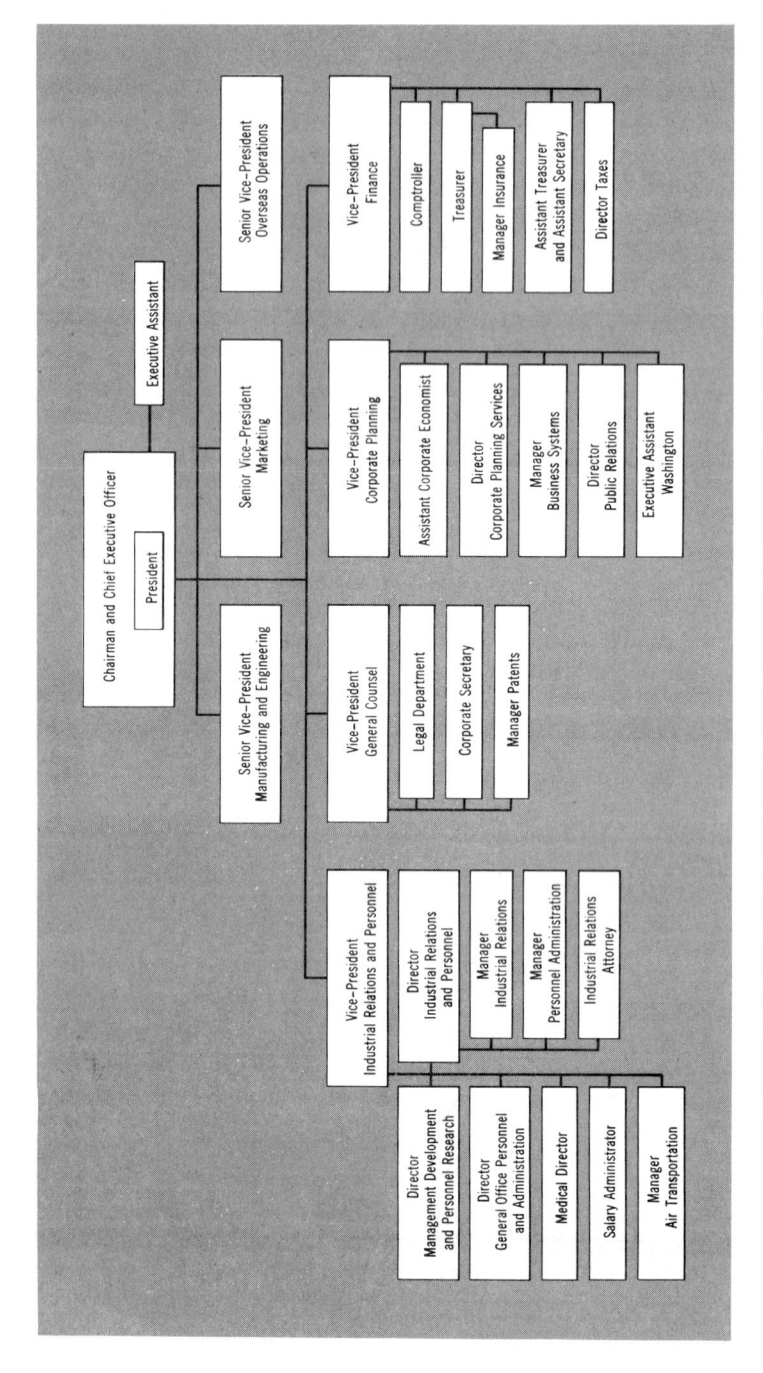

Figure 6-2. Functional departmentation: Deere and Company. Courtesy of Deere and Company, Moline, Illinois.

department types purchase orders; the one in personnel types employee classification forms. Functional differentiation may also involve the different ways in which similar and dissimilar duties are interrelated and combined.

Parallel Functionalization

A differentiation between kinds and combinations of duties has little meaning without an objective. Functional departments, such as sales, production, engineering, and industrial relations, are responsible for a functionally defined objective. But such subsidiary objectives cannot be planned without a consideration of the activities that will be necessary to achieve them. Professor Herbert A. Simon points out that functional departmentation "assumes the possibility of a parallel functionalization of objectives and of activities." [2] The activities of each functional department should contribute toward the achievement of a necessary functional objective. If activities cannot be grouped in this manner, departmentation should not take place. It may be possible to redefine the objective to facilitate a logical grouping of activities. However, a combination of activities that does not result in the achievement of an essential objective does not serve a useful purpose.

Primary Functions

Some functions that seem to be basic in the operation of business and industrial organizations are almost universally given important departmental status. These functions have been called "organic functions" because their performance is vital and essential to the survival of the organization and the values they create are indispensable.[3] Although there are some differences of opinion on the subject, the functions that are generally so classified are production, sales, and finance.[4]

The importance of a functional department is indicated by the level a

---

[2] Herbert A. Simon, *Administrative Behavior,* 2nd ed. (New York: The Macmillan Company, 1958), p. 191.

[3] Ralph C. Davis, *The Fundamentals of Top Management* (New York: Harper & Brothers Publishers, 1951), pp. 205–213.

[4] Davis, *ibid.,* p. 207; Henri Fayol divides all the operations of a business organization into six basic functions: (1) the technical functions (production), (2) commercial functions (sales, purchasing), (3) financial functions, (4) security functions (protection of property and persons), (5) accounting functions, (6) management functions. Only the first five are horizontal functional differentiations. *General and Industrial Management* (London: Sir Isaac Pitman & Sons, Ltd., 1949), p. 3.

ORGANIZATION FOR MANAGEMENT

Table 6-2. Types of Executives Reporting to the President in 100 Large Companies

Function [a]	Number of Companies
Production, Operations, Manufacturing	94
Marketing, Sales	88
Industrial relations, Personnel administration	64
Legal counsel, General counsel	55
Controller, Comptroller	46
Treasurer	45
Finance	42
Purchasing	38
Research, Development, New products	38
Plant managers	37
Assistant to president	37
Engineering	37
Secretary	37
Public relations	34
Executive vice-president	29
Advertising	15
Overseas operations	13
Traffic	13
Organization	9
Economic research	7
Quality control	4
Patents	4
Special assignments	3
Government relations	3
Maintenance	2
Office management	1
Safety	1
Claims	1
Production control	1
Coordination	1

Source. Ernest Dale, *Planning and Developing the Company Organization Structure,* Research Report No. 20 (New York: American Management Association, 1950), p. 58.
[a] The functions listed in Tables 6-2 and 6-3 are as described in the companies' organization charts. Their importance and content are obviously not the same in all cases. When two functions were combined, each was counted as one-half. In the case of plant managers and heads of subsidiaries, the function itself was counted once in the case of every company, even though there were several of them.

functional executive occupies in the hierarchy. Production, sales, and financial executives frequently report directly to the president or the executive vice-president. A study conducted by the American Management Association on this matter provides some interesting data. The results are presented in Tables 6-2 and 6-3.

Table 6-3. Types of Executives Reporting to the President in 41 Medium-Sized Companies

Function	Number of Companies
Production, Operations, Manufacturing	38
Marketing	32
Treasurer	21
Industrial relations	20
Engineering	17
Executive vice-president	14
Purchasing	14
Controller	13
Plant managers	13
Finance	12
Research	12
Secretary	12
Assistant to president	10
Legal counsel	6
Overseas operations	6
Organization	3
Public relations	3
Advertising	2
Economic research	2
Transportation	2
Production control	1

Source. Ernest Dale, *Planning and Developing the Company Organization Structure,* Research Report No. 20 (New York: American Management Association, 1950), p. 60.

The high status occupied by production and marketing executives in the management hierarchy indicates the importance of these functions to the survival of the organization. The rank of industrial relations and personnel executives reflects the extensive practice of company-wide collective bargaining, the importance of the decisions made in collective bargaining, and the emphasis given in recent years to "human relations." The legal and financial complexities of modern corporate existence help explain the high standing of the executives responsible for the solution of such problems.

Although some functions occupy an important hierarchical position in almost every organization, a wide diversity can be found in the status accorded particular functions. In some companies the quality control executive reports directly to the executive vice-president or president, and in others this department is a subdivision of the production department. Public relations is sometimes a top echelon function, but it may also be a subdepartment in the sales department. Engineering and purchasing may be found in the production department, or they may appear at the same level as production.

The answer given to the problem of functional departmentation by a particular organization depends on a variety of intraorganizational and environmental factors. A company engaged in the production of defense material for the government may establish a contract administration or a government relations department. A desire to improve public and community relations may prompt the creation of a public relations department. One company set up a consumer service department, independent of sales and production, because the sales department complained that production caused consumer dissatisfaction by not meeting production schedules. The avalanche of taxes with which industry has been endowed during the last two decades has brought about specialized tax departments in many organizations. A company faced with serious customer credit problems may attempt to correct the situation with a credit department. A highly competitive market may bring about a sales promotion or an advertising department, and greater emphasis may be given to the research and development function.

Secondary Functions

The process of functional differentiation may continue through several successive levels in the hierarchy. The organization or a subdivision thereof (such as a territorial or product division) may first be divided into sales, production, finance, personnel, and purchasing departments. If further differentiation is necessary, functional subdepartments may be created and such units may in turn be departmentalized. Table 6-4 shows this process through three successive levels. However, functionalization can continue only so long as there exists a sound basis for further differentiation. Another type of departmentation may be employed when functional departmentation has been utilized to the fullest extent. For example, large accounts receivable departments are often subdivided on an alphanumerical basis, purchasing departments frequently use product as a basis for further departmentation, and sales departments may turn to territorial units.

Table 6-4. Levels of Functional Departmentation in a Manufacturing Company

FIRST LEVEL FUNCTIONAL DEPARTMENTATION

    Finance
    Industrial relations
    Marketing
    Production
    Research and development

SECOND LEVEL FUNCTIONAL DEPARMENTATION

Production
    Engineering
    Manufacturing
    Production control
    Purchasing
    Quality control

THIRD LEVEL FUNCTIONAL DEPARTMENTATION

Purchasing
    Buying (usually divided by product or type of supplier)
    Expediting
    Receiving and storage

The Lower Levels

Departmentation at higher levels follows a similar pattern in many organizations, but there may be a marked dissimilarity in the departmentation that occurs at lower levels. The lowest level in an automobile body manufacturing plant includes the following departmental units: wet sand, wheel polish, trim line, hang doors and lids, and spot weld quarters. Similar departments in basic steel are melting, combustion, and dolomite; in an automatic washer plant such departments as porcelain finishing, sheet metal, and paint finishing are common.

Functional Centralization and Decentralization

Should the purchasing function be centralized in a purchasing department, or should it be decentralized in production, sales, and other departments? Should each department provide its own stenographic service, or would a central stenographic department be more efficient? What are the advantages of a centralized plant maintenance department? Should there be a personnel department, or should each department do its own personnel work? Under what circumstances should an organization department be established? Some of the factors that relate to these questions are considered in this section.

Size and Specialization. Size is an important determinant of the extent to which functional centralization is feasible. Departmental status cannot be given to an otherwise separable function if the volume of work does not justify it. For this reason such departments as purchasing, quality control, public relations, and personnel are not generally found in small organizations. These functions are performed by the existing departments. Such a situation may be illustrated by a manufacturing establishment with a sales, production, and finance department. The various executives handle their own personnel problems, purchase whatever is required, and carry out public relations functions, such as sending material to a college professor or giving a speech at the Lions Club. The quality control function is handled as an integral part of production work. Foremen inspect the quality of the work in addition to their other duties. When a serious quality problem arises, the head of production may give it his personal attention and confer with his foremen, workers, the sales manager, and the chief executive.

Company growth often leads to some higher degree of functional specialization. A particular function may be assigned to one or several persons on a full-time or part-time basis. The purchasing function, for example, may gradually become the primary responsibility of someone in the production department, possibly a foreman who shows interest and capacity in this work. A full-fledged purchasing department may eventually emerge as the company grows and prospers. A similar evolutionary process applies to personnel, quality control, research and development, and other functional areas.

An argument for functional centralization is the greater efficiency that may result from a reduction in the diversity of functions in a department. The time and talent of a production specialist, for example, may be better utilized by limiting his responsibility to purely production matters. Furthermore, executives in such primary functions as sales and production may not give adequate attention to peripheral functions. They may neglect what to them is a less important functional responsibility. Centralizing such functions as purchasing, personnel, research and development, and public relations tends to give them higher status in the total picture. It also makes possible the employment of specialized personnel and the use of specialized machines and equipment.

Control and Coordination. Functional centralization is sometimes used to promote control and coordination. A need for greater uniformity in wage and salary schedules can often be facilitated by a centralization of the personnel function. An organization department can be helpful in coordinating organizational planning and development. The channeling of outgoing information through a public relations department may become necessary to prevent a release of contradictory statements and information detrimental to the interests of the organization. Control over the flow of paperwork can often be improved by a centralized procedures department. This kind of departmentation frequently results in better coordination and control with respect to the functions being centralized, but the resulting increase in the number of functional departments can have consequences in an opposite direction.

Revenues and Costs. An important factor in determining the relative merits of functional centralization or decentralization is monetary return in the form of lower costs or additional revenue. Centralization may reduce costs through greater managerial and operating efficiency, but such gains must compensate for any additional expenditure for personnel and physical facilities. The determination of costs before and after centralization presents many difficulties. However, functional centralization sometimes promotes improved cost control by bringing hidden cost into the open.

Functional centralization should pay its way on the revenue side of the ledger. A statistics department may develop quality control techniques that result in increased customer satisfaction and sales. A public relations department may increase revenues through inproved customer relations. However, such consequences are often indirect and, as in the case of cost evaluation, difficult to measure in objective terms.

Functional Empires. Although a reason for centralization is to give greater emphasis to a necessary function, the result is sometimes an expansion beyond the needs of the organization. Functional executives are not immune to "empire building," which can overemphasize the importance of a function in the total scheme of things. They may engage in projects that cannot be economically justified. For example, an executive in one organization asked the research department to provide information about the influence of temperature upon product behavior.[5] He wanted an approximate answer, which he thought would cost about $100. He was amazed a few months later to receive a research report that had cost the company $10,000. Some functional departments find themselves pushed into overexpansion by other departments. This problem seems to be most prevalent in cases that involve an intraorganizational service, such as engineering,

[5] P. E. Holden, L. S. Fish, and H. L. Smith, *Top-Management Organization and Control* (New York: McGraw-Hill Book Company, Inc., 1951), p. 175.

research, statistics, and personnel. As Holden, Fish, and Smith point out, these departments are expected to give speedy and adequate service and as a consequence frequently feel compelled to maintain larger than necessary facilities to prevent criticism from other departments.[6] This situation in turn invites more work from other departments and requires even more resources. The result is too much use of service personnel for work they should not be doing. For example, research engineers may be engaged in functions that can be more economically performed by production engineers.

The Problem of Jurisdictional Delineation

The responsibilities of functional departments cannot always be clearly differentiated, which is illustrated by the centralization of human relations functions in personnel departments. As an executive has written:

By centralizing the personnel function in a personnel department, too many people have assumed that you can centralize human relations. That was perhaps the error in the thinking of the production people and general managers who felt that it would be very helpful if we could just put all our personnel headaches into one hat and let somebody else worry about them for all of us. And it did bring some measure of relief to many production people. But I am not sure that the process helped human relations. The personnel function is by no means a one-man function or a one-department function.[7]

The centralization of the purchasing function presents similar difficulties. The purchasing department is usually in a better position to evaluate the alternative ways for meeting a requirement than are the departments that use the materials. But, as one purchasing executive has said, it "should not necessarily have the authority to over-rule the experience and judgment of those who use materials." [8] Where should the line be drawn? Under what circumstances should the purchasing department be permitted to modify or change specifications designated by the using departments? Who should have the final word on the determination of the quality of the items requested on a requisition? The final verdict on specifications and quality generally comes from production and other user departments, with purchasing having the right to question specifications, but the nature of this relationship differs from company to company. Similar peripheral problems

---

[6] *Ibid.*

[7] Glenn Gardiner, "The Operating Executive and the Personnel Department," *Personnel Functions and the Line Organization,* Personnel Series No. 121 (New York: American Management Association, 1948), pp. 3–4.

[8] R. C. Moffitt, *Purchasing,* Technical Paper No. 138 (New York: United States Steel Corporation), p. 8.

are present in many other areas. Credit departments sometimes experience jurisdictional difficulties with sales departments; manufacturing and production control departments have disagreements over their respective responsibilities for production scheduling; and public relations, advertising, and sales promotion departments experience similar difficulties.

Interdepartmental Coordination

The problem of achieving coordination among functional departments have been a recurring subject of discussion in management circles.[9] Much of the work of the organization flows across functionally differentiated departmental lines with each department contributing some portion of the total activity necessary to achieve the organizational objective. Implicit in these ideas are two potentially conflicting forces. On the one hand, the responsibility of a departmental executive is the successful accomplishment of a functional objective. By pursuing his departmental interests, the executive serves the interests of the organization, but the two interests are not always compatible. Under such circumstances, a subordination of departmental interests to organizational interests becomes necessary. However, the balance should not be tipped too far in this direction as Urwick has so aptly noted.

Many people argue that the departmental manager should subordinate his departmental point of view to the good of the whole. That is nonsense. Either his department has no excuse for existence or its point of view is *needed in the whole*. It must be reconciled with all the other points of view involved, but it must not be abandoned. Men should never be encouraged to de-departmentalise themselves. They should be taught to inter-departmentalise themselves.[10]

Interest Conflicts. Conflicts of interests among functional departments are not uncommon. Sales executives are inclined to promise delivery dates that cannot be met by production or to approve customer-initiated design changes that cause production difficulties. Production executives sometimes fail to appreciate that customer demands cannot be ignored if the company is to survive. Sales personnel may make sales even when they in-

---

[9] For example: Henry H. Farquhar, "The Anomaly of Functional Authority at the Top," *Advanced Management*, Vol. 7, No. 2, April–June 1942, pp. 51–54, 83; *Personnel Functions and the Line Organization*, Personnel Series No. 121, *op. cit.*, pp. 3–12; *Coordination between Engineering, Production and Sales*, Production Series No. 193 (New York: American Management Association, 1950), pp. 10–20; L. Urwick, *The Load on Top Management—Can It Be Reduced?* (London: Urwick, Orr & Partners Ltd., 1954), pp. 26–32.

[10] L. Urwick, *The Elements of Administration* (New York: Harper & Brothers Publishers, 1943), p. 115. (Italics in the original.)

volve considerable credit risk. The credit executive, on the other hand, is generally more interested in keeping down bad debt losses than in an additional customer. The safety engineering department's effort to reduce hazards is often considered to be unreasonable by production executives.

Interest conflicts are frequently founded in differences about how best to achieve the organizational objective. Urwick has emphasized that different functions always involve different points of view.[11] Nothing much would be accomplished if there were no difference of opinion. An absence of internal conflict is not necessarily a good sign, but the line between constructive disagreement and destructive dissension is sometimes difficult to draw.

Personal Conflicts. When executives are primarily motivated by self-interest, interdepartmental differences can become a serious obstacle to effective action. A sales executive who seeks only to make a good impression upon the chief executive, irrespective of the difficulties he creates for other departments, is generally a detriment. His desire to break sales records may cause him to accept orders that cannot be fitted into the production schedule and then blame the production executive for failures to meet delivery schedules. Although some such propensities are the property of humans generally, they cannot dominate the scene without doing serious damage. Functional departmentation is probably more susceptible to this kind of problem than other types of departmentation. The difficulty of defining jurisdiction and pinpointing responsibility makes a fertile field for personal conflict. A further aggravating factor is the narrow perspective of some functional specialists.

Functionalization versus Unity of Command

Frederick W. Taylor introduced functional foremanship at the Midvale Steel Company in the early 1880's. This experience convinced him that functional foremanship should be considered an important principle in management. His views on the matter were presented in *Shop Management,* which was originally published in 1903.

Throughout the whole field of management the military type of organization should be abandoned, and what may be called the "functional type" substituted in its place. . . . If practicable the work of each man in the management should be confined to the performance of a single leading function.[12]

Under the Taylor plan, workers were subject to the dictates of as many as five foremen on different functional matters. Such a differentiation of managerial responsibility may not cause serious difficulties if coordination

---

[11] L. Urwick, *Top Management, op. cit.,* pp. 26–30.
[12] Frederick W. Taylor, *Shop Management* (New York: Harper & Brothers, 1911), p. 99.

occurs at a level not too far removed from the foreman level. Taylor assumed that this would take place, but he envisioned a more complete functionalization of management. Only a few years after Taylor announced his plan, Henri Fayol wrote that it is "dangerous to allow the idea to gain ground that unity of command is unimportant and can be violated with impunity." [13] More recent critics have lamented the extent of functionalization, particularly at the upper levels of the hierarchy.[14] Urwick has this to say on the subject.

When the principle is applied at higher levels where the sense of unity is less, where personal contact is not so close and real differences of outlook and emphasis inevitable and desirable, the chief executive is apt to be overwhelmed with problems of co-ordination.[15]

A number of solutions have been given to the unity of command problem. An oft-used arrangement is a line-staff system that retains many of the advantages of functional specialization without violating unity of command. Under such a system, functional departments and executives perform activities in a staff relationship to the operating departments. Some companies have product or territorial operating departments and facilitating functional staff and service departments. Formal committees are also used to improve coordination and develop interfunctional communication. Chapters 7, 8, and 9 give comprehensive consideration to these organizational techniques.

Functionalization and Motivation

Too much functional specialization can cause teamwork and motivation problems. Both management and workers may feel that the work they are doing is unimportant and that they are an insignificant part of the total picture. Some organizations have attempted to overcome this problem by enlarging functional responsibilities. For example, personnel functions may be shifted from a centralized department to first-line supervision.[16] The argument is not that functional specialization is suddenly all wrong but that it can have adverse consequences if carried to an extreme.

[13] Fayol, *op. cit.*, pp. 69–70.
[14] For example: Farquhar, *op. cit.*; Urwick, *Top Management, op. cit.*, pp. 26–32.
[15] Urwick, *ibid.*, p. 28.
[16] This was done at the IBM Endicott Plant, as reported by F. L. W. Richardson, Jr., and Charles R. Walker, *Human Relations in an Expanding Company* (New Haven: Labor and Management Center, Yale University, 1948), pp. 23–26. The problem is also discussed in James C. Worthy, "Organizational Structure and Employee Morale," *American Sociological Review*, Vol. 15, No. 2, April 1950, pp. 169–179. Also pertinent is: Fritz J. Roethlisberger, "The Foreman: Master and Victim of Double Talk," *Harvard Business Review*, Vol. 23, No. 3, Spring 1945, pp. 283–298.

The Impact of Information Technology

In many organizations, informational functions formerly performed within production, purchasing, marketing, finance, and personnel departments are now performed by centralized and computerized informational systems. The extent to which information processing cuts across functional lines is expected to increase rapidly in the near future.[17] The effect of such informational integration upon functional departmentation is difficult to forecast, but many people believe that major changes in organization will undoubtedly occur.

An executive in a large shoe manufacturing concern has said that "it is not at all difficult to conclude that the basic functions of sales, procurement of materials, personnel management, production, marketing, financing, and accounting will be strongly cemented together by an automated data processing system which is unlike anything in existence today."[18] In describing the changes in his company, this executive said: "Through our system of estimates and information processing we have achieved a state in which production, merchandising, and procurement no longer function as semi-independent entities."[19] A departmental consequence of these changes was that "today we have a vice-president of *merchandising and production*, whereas up until recently these had been separate functions."[20] An executive from a large oil company emphasized the need to develop "an integrated functional system crossing departmental lines."[21] Another executive reports that his company had centralized the staff work formerly done in the various functional departments in a central planning department.[22]

It would not be appropriate to assume that computerized planning and informational systems will make all the decisions involved in the traditional functional departments. Such systems can be given the capacity to make many programmed-type decisions, and they can provide highly useful information to functional executives. The number of line and staff specialists in particular functional fields will probably be reduced as comprehensive computerized planning and informational systems are developed.

[17] Neal J. Dean, "The Computer Comes of Age," *Harvard Business Review*, Vol. 46, No. 1, January–February 1968, pp. 89–90.
[18] Leonard F. Vogt, "The International Shoe Company," in George P. Schultz and Thomas L. Whisler (editors), *Management Organization and the Computer* (Illinois: The Free Press of Glencoe, 1960), pp. 133–134.
[19] *Ibid.*, p. 151.
[20] *Ibid.*, p. 160.
[21] *Ibid.*, p. 181.
[22] *Ibid.*, pp. 237–238.

Important decisions will still be made by executives who have specialized knowledge in such fields as production, marketing, purchasing, personnel, and finance.

The continued existence of functional executives does not necessarily mean that functional departments will remain. Some fusion of closely related functional departments has already occurred in some organizations. All functional executives could be placed within a single department at some future time. But there is also reason to believe that the traditional type of functional departmentation will not be completely abandoned. Computerized planning and informational systems will make significant changes in the specific line and staff responsibilities involved in a functional field. But the way in which functional responsibilities are departmentalized will still be subject to considerable discretion. There does not appear to be a one-best pattern of departmentation at the present time, and there is not apt to be one in the future.

A major problem in bringing about necessary reorganization to take full advantage of the capacity of computerized systems is resistance to change on the part of executives. As one data processing executive remarked: "EDP and systems actually are cutting across department lines. Because management still clings to old-fashioned, historic ideas about organization, there is a lot of chaos. With these conditions, it's very difficult to know how to organize for computers." [23]

Product Departmentation

Products can be used for departmentation purposes in many companies. Some product departments are multifunctional in the sense that they encompass the major functions, such as production, marketing, sales, personnel, and purchasing. In other cases, a company may have a product structure with the exception of one or more functional areas, such as finance or sales. Product may also be used to further departmentalize sales, purchasing, production, and other functional departments.

Organizational Fission

Product departmentation is widely used to make little "organizations" out of big ones. The General Motors Corporation is divided into operating divisions consisting of a plant or group of plants manufacturing one or a number of related products. See Figure 6-3. Other large organizations, such

[23] M. Valliant Higginson, *Managing with EDP*, AMA Research Study, No. 71 (New York: American Management Association, Inc., 1965), p. 12.

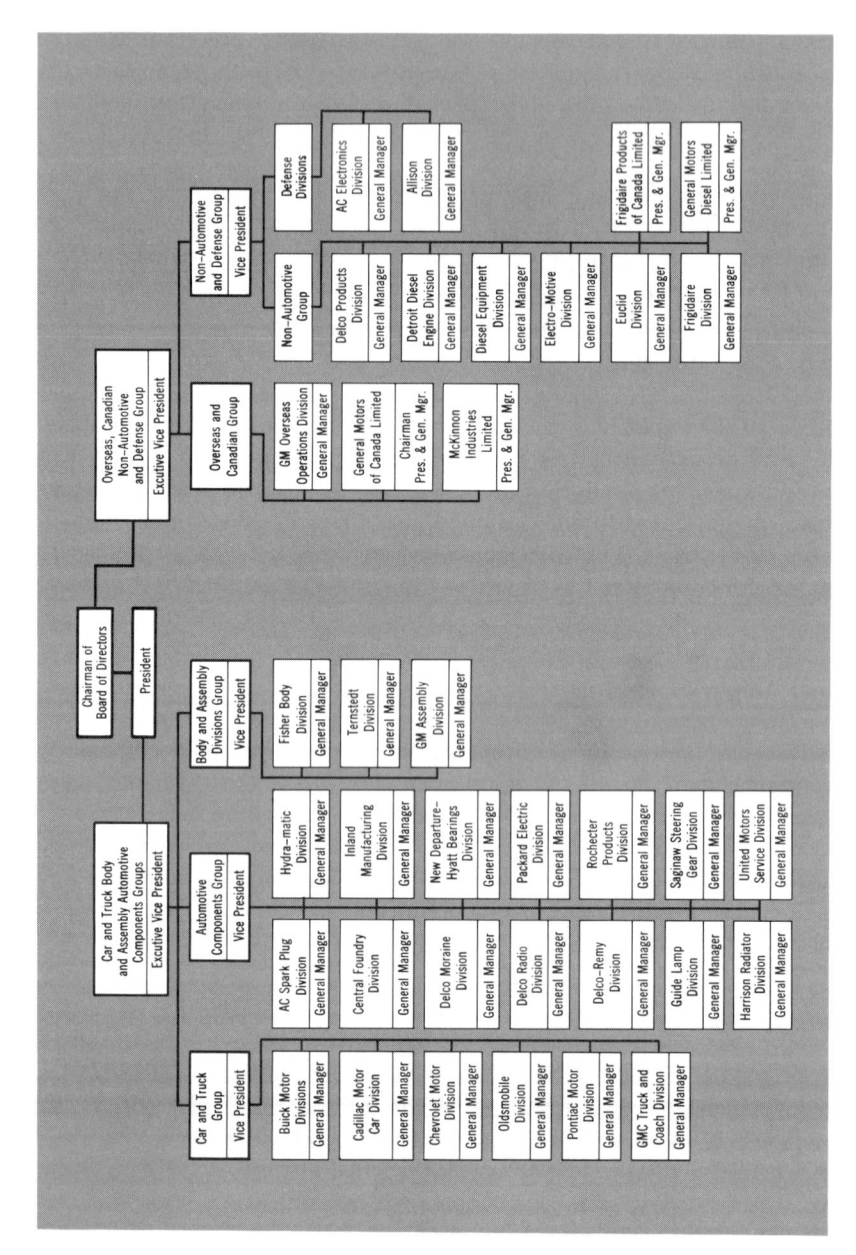

Figure 6-3. Product departmentation: General Motors Corporation. Courtesy of GMC.

as General Electric, Ford, International Harvester, Du Pont, and RCA, have followed a similar pattern. Product departments, such as GMC's Delco Remy Division or GE's Clock Department, can be managed much like an independent company. This kind of structure helps retain the flexibility and initiative of small enterprise and, at the same time, provides advantages of large size through centralized staff and service facilities.

Product-Functional Combinations

Some departments involve a fusion of product and functional departmentation. The basic operating units of a department store, for example, result from a product differentiation of the merchandising function. Each of these departments handles a particular line of merchandise, such as home furnishings, shoes, apparel, and linens. Department managers, usually called buyers, are responsible for both the buying and selling functions. Production departments frequently manufacture different products, subassemblies, and parts in separate plants. The purchase of such items as steel, glass, and specialized equipment is often departmentalized in large purchasing departments. Industrial, consumer, and other product categories are used in the departmentation of the sales function. Research and development activities are often conducted on a product-project basis.

Product Specialization

Educational programs in business and related fields generally give a great deal of emphasis to functional specialization. They sometimes fail to give sufficient attention to specialization on the basis of product or industry. Knowledge about the economics and technology of such industries as steel, coal, oil, and automobile would seem to be important for future executives. An industrial organization course with a strong economic theory emphasis would probably be most useful for this purpose. The present areas of functional specialization, such as production and marketing management, should generally not be presented from the perspective of particular industries. Product specialization is also an important aspect of the knowledge and skills accumulated through experience. The executive who heads a battery manufacturing department generally knows more about production than other functional executives, but he also knows more about batteries than other production executives.

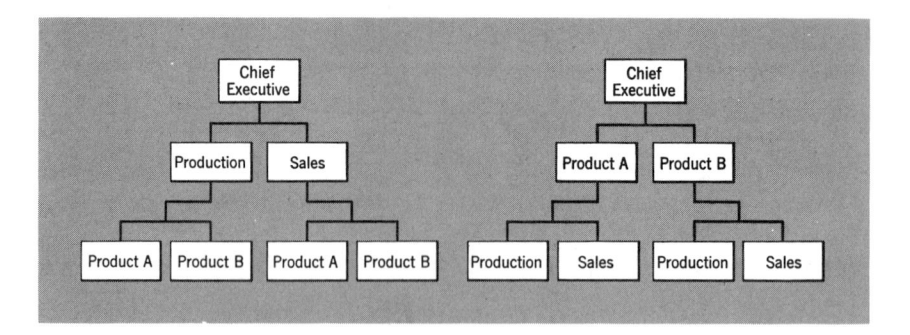

Figure 6-4. Alternative structures for company with two products.

Coordination Advantages

Some people contend that product departmentation at higher levels can reduce the coordination problems of functional departmentation. A functional perspective is assumed to be more disruptive to a unity of purpose than a product perspective.[24] Also important is that product departmentation provides interfunctional coordination centers at lower levels of the hierarchy. This idea is illustrated in Figure 6-4, which shows alternative structures for a firm producing two products. In the functional structure the chief executive is faced with the problem of coordinating sales and production for both products *A* and *B*. In the product structure these functions are coordinated by the executives who head the product departments. However, these alternatives are not available to every company. Some companies are not large enough for functional specialization in more than one structure. The lack of a diversified product line or a product that can be divided into distinct subassemblies and parts is another limiting factor. But as Urwick has emphasized, a company does not have to be as large as General Motors to organize on a product basis.[25]

Control Advantages

Product departmentation may facilitate the measurement and evaluation of managerial and operating performance. Revenues and costs can generally be more readily differentiated and assigned in a product than a functional structure. Market and profit criteria can be directly applied in

[24] Urwick, *Top Management, op. cit.*, p. 32.
[25] *Ibid.*, p. 31.

product departments that incorporate the major functions of an independent company. The GMC divisions, for example, are subject to controls of this kind. Another advantage of product departmentation is that an unprofitable department can be dropped with less disruption to the rest of the organization. Product differentiation within functional departments may also help pinpoint responsibility for particular difficulties.

Executive Development

A product department provides an excellent training and proving ground for executive personnel. The problems of many multifunctional product departments are much like those of a complete company. The top executives of such departments gain a diversity of functional experience, which seems to be generally more important than a diversity of product experience. Functional executives are sometimes too inclined toward the perspective of their specialization after they become chief executives. However, such an orientation may be appropriate under certain circumstances. A cigarette company, for example, may prefer a president who thinks like an advertising executive.

Service Departmentation

Some organizations are exclusively in the business of producing services, and in others, services represent an aspect of product producing and selling activities. Different kinds of services become the basis for departmentation in the manner of product departmentation. A distinction is sometimes made between customer and service departmentation. Some basis for this kind of differentiation is provided by the idea that the nature of the customer may dictate different departmentation even though the services rendered are essentially the same. For example, universities generally maintain separate physical education departments for male and female students for reasons other than differences in the activities involved. The logic of product, service, and customer departmentation is similar, but such differentiations may serve a practical purpose.

Service and Customer Differentiations

The qualities of customers, such as sex, age, and income, are sometimes used as a point of departure for departmentation. Such distinctions generally, but not always, involve different kinds of services, which provide another approach to the problem. The manner in which various factors are applied in actual situations is illustrated by the following examples. Churches usually maintain separate departments for the religious instruction of children and adults. Steamship lines and railroads generally divide passenger accommodations into various classes that involve differences in services and customer demands. Sales departments frequently differentiate on the basis of industrial users, wholesale buyers, and ultimate consumers. Department stores organize bargain basement departments that duplicate items found in other departments to attract certain kinds of customers.

The Customer Is Not Always Right

Customer satisfaction is an important ingredient in business success, but it is by no means the only consideration. An organization should not be fragmentized into economically inefficient service departments merely to cater to the whims and fancies of customers. Customers can become a costly resource, and a loss of some of them is better than negative profits.

Territorial Departmentation

Territorial departmentation is frequently used when the activities of an organization are dispersed over a wide area.[26] However, the fact that an organization is dispersed territorially does not mean that departmentation is territorial. All types of departments occupy different physical locations, which does not make all departmentation territorial. Departmentation is territorial only when location is the primary consideration in defining and differentiating executive responsibility. However, something more is involved in territorial departmentation than an arbitrary subdivision of geographical area. This idea is illustrated by a problem in government.

The Area Problem in Local Government

Governmental organizations have experienced difficulties because geographical area measured in square miles was used to delineate administrative responsibility. The spatial symmetry of land surveys and the dictum of legislative bodies were highly influential forces in the organization of local government. The famous Land Ordinance of 1785, for example, desig-

[26] The factors that cause organizations to locate in particular areas are considered in Chapter 15.

nated that the territories west of the original colonies should be surveyed in the following manner.

> The Surveyors, as they are respectively qualified, shall proceed to divide the said territory into townships of six miles square, by lines running due north and south, and others crossing these at right angles, as near as may be, unless where the boundaries of the late Indian purchases may render the same impracticable, ...[27]

The townships thus created by legislative act were generally accepted in the Middle West as the territorial boundary of the civil township.[28] In other words, government surveyors laid out the areas within which local government developed in early rural America. State legislatures also imposed area limitations governing the creation of counties.[29] As a result, important administrative units of state government were to a great extent carved out on an area basis.

Whether the area delineations of local political organization were ever efficient from an administrative point of view will not be dealt with here. It must be said that the land ordinances of early United States history provided for the orderly development of civil government on the frontier.[30] The political boundaries that evolved from these ordinances and subsequent legislation by the states were made without any knowledge about such matters as the nature of economic development or future population growth and structure. Furthermore, no one could have prophesied the extent to which the spatial concepts of the horse and buggy era were to be changed by modern transportation and communication facilities. Although hindsight affords a tremendous advantage to the critic of past folly, the fact remains that the area delineations that presently dominate the administrative structure of many states are obsolete and inefficient.

The consensus among students of government is that there are too many counties. As one writer on the subject put it: "Given a clean slate, no legislature to-day would tessellate a state into hundreds of counties." [31] The Brookings Institution, which has studied the administrative organization of a number of state governments, has concluded that area should not be treated as the only or even an important determinant of the proper size

---

[27] Henry S. Commager (editor), *Documents of American History*, 6th ed. (New York: Appleton-Century-Crofts, Inc., 1958), p. 123.

[28] Arthur W. Bromage, *American County Government* (New York: Sears Publishing Company, Inc., 1933), p. 26.

[29] John A. Fairlie and Charles M. Kneier, *County Government and Administration* (New York: The Century Co., 1930), p. 59.

[30] The Northwest Ordinance of 1787, for example, preplanned the development of political organization in the territories west of the original colonies.

[31] Bromage, *op. cit.*, p. 196.

144   ORGANIZATION FOR MANAGEMENT

of a county.[32] The Brookings studies indicate that county consolidation would generally improve administrative efficiency and significantly reduce the cost of state government. But consolidation is not easily accomplished. Tradition, politics, local pride, and vested interests are important obstacles in the road to better administrative organization.

A business enterprise could not long continue to use such area delineations as a basis for departmentation. Area has little meaning for purposes of departmentation without an analysis of the nature of the activities that occur within a spatial context. As these activities change, so should the area used to frame the boundaries of managerial action be changed.

The Nature of Territorial Departments

As in product departmentation, territorial departmentation can be used to divide larger organizations into relatively self-sufficient units. Grocery, drug, and department chain stores, local telephone exchanges, and branch banks exemplify such departmentation. Territorial differentiations may also be used to further subdivide functional and product departments. Different spatial spheres of managerial responsibility are often appropriate for different functions. A manufacturing company may organize territorial departments that include the functions of manufacturing, engineering, personnel, and accounting but develop a sales organization with different boundaries. In other instances, a number of functions, such as purchasing, sales, and production, may use different territorial delineations. A similar situation frequently prevails within a particular functional field. The sales manager in a metropolitan location may have a small territory compared to the manager in the wide open spaces of the western plains.

Territorial Specialization

Little emphasis has been given in the management literature to territorial specialization. As Chester I. Barnard points out, "the 'same kind' of work is always different when the location is different." [33] Knowledge of the local environment is an important element in effective managerial action.

Operations can be greatly affected by climatic conditions in different geographical regions. The problems faced on a construction project in

[32] Institute for Government Research of the Brookings Institution, *Report on a Survey of the Organization and Administration of the State and County Government in Mississippi* (Jackson, Miss.: The Research Commission of the State of Mississippi, 1932), p. 647.

[33] Chester I. Barnard, *The Functions of the Executive* (Cambridge: Harvard University Press, 1951), p. 129.

Minnesota during the winter differ from those of a similar project in Alabama. Operating a bus line in an area with heavy snowfall presents problems not encountered in a warm climate. The impact of climate upon military operations is illustrated by the Russian campaigns of Napoleon and Hitler; the planning and command problems in the deserts of North Africa or the jungles of Viet Nam are significantly different. The problems of operating a railroad or a trucking line in a mountainous area are not the same as those in a plains area.

Variations in the culture of different areas make for differences in managerial problems. Chain department stores are faced with dissimilarities in consumer preferences in various areas. Bikini bathing suits may sell like hotcakes in a "sophisticated" metropolitan community but not in the domain of the "bible belt." Specialty foods, such as rattlesnake meat, generally have a good market in areas infested with gourmets, but few sales are made in a "meat and potato" region. Business practices are also affected by similar factors. Businessmen have reported, for example, that sending out monthly statements is not well received by customers in some areas.

International Business Operations

The impact of cultural and social differences is even more apparent beyond the national boundaries. The international realm has become increasingly important during the past decade. In addition to a million and a half military personnel and dependents, something like 100,000 Americans now live abroad on a semi-permanent basis. Included in this number are almost 35,000 who own or are employed by private business enterprises.[34] Several hundred thousand individual business trips abroad are made by Americans during a typical year.[35] Approximately 4,100 American corporations control 14,000 foreign business enterprises, and the direct American foreign investment (involving some degree of managerial control) is roughly fifty billion dollars.[36] Companies with extensive foreign production and marketing facilities include General Motors, Ford, International Business Machines, Procter & Gamble, Deere and Company (see Figure 6-5), Eastman Kodak, Standard Oil (New Jersey), Sears Roebuck, Abbott Laboratories, and Kaiser Industries.

---

[34] Mira Wilkins, "The Businessman Abroad," *The Annals of the American Academy of Political and Social Science,* Vol. 368, November 1966, p. 84.

[35] Richard G. Lurie, *Passports and Profits* (New York: Pan American Airways, 1965), p. 9.

[36] Wilkins, *op. cit.,* pp. 84–85.

Figure 6-5. Deere and Company overseas operations.

Argentina:
- John Deere Argentina S.A.I.C.
  Rosario
  Tractors and planting and tillage equipment
- Cindlemet, Corporacion Industrial del Metal, S.A.
  Rosario
  Grey iron castings for John Deere Argentina S.A.I.C. and others
  (Associated Company)
- John Deere Argentina S.A.I.C.
  Buenos Aires
  Sales Branch

Australia:
- John Deere Limited
  Sydney
  Sales Branch

Mexico:
- John Deere S.A.
  Monterrey
  Tractors and farm implements
- John Deere S.A.
  Mexico City
  Sales Branch

John Deere Limited
Langar, England
Sales Branch

John Deere Svenska A.B.
Eslov, Sweden
Sales Branch

England and Sweden

John Deere Intercontinental Limited
Brussels, Belgium
Sales Branch

John Deere Werke
Zweibrucken, Germany
Combines, mowers and other harvesting equipment

John Deere Vertrieb Deutschland
Mannheim, Germany
Sales Branch

John Deere Export
Mannheim, Germany
Export Branch

John Deere Werke
Mannheim, Germany
Farm and industrial tractors

John Deere Italiana S.P.A.
Milan, Italy
Sales Branch

Deere and Company—European Office
Heidelberg, Germany
Administrative Offices

Belgium, Germany and Italy

Figure 6.5 (continued)

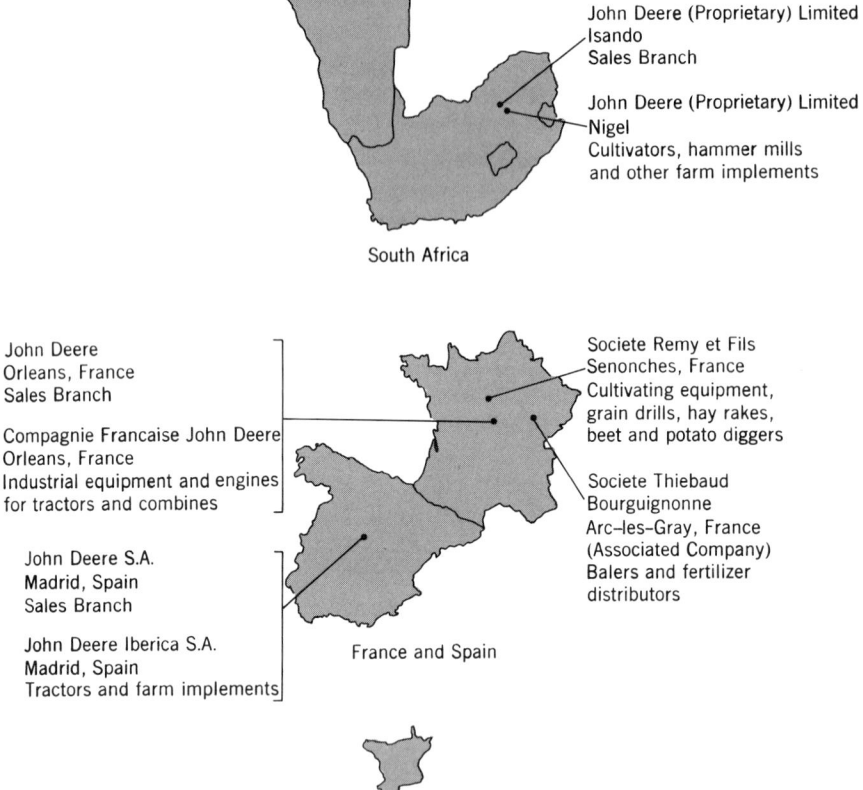

John Deere (Proprietary) Limited
Isando
Sales Branch

John Deere (Proprietary) Limited
Nigel
Cultivators, hammer mills
and other farm implements

South Africa

John Deere
Orleans, France
Sales Branch

Compagnie Francaise John Deere
Orleans, France
Industrial equipment and engines
for tractors and combines

John Deere S.A.
Madrid, Spain
Sales Branch

John Deere Iberica S.A.
Madrid, Spain
Tractors and farm implements

Societe Remy et Fils
Senonches, France
Cultivating equipment,
grain drills, hay rakes,
beet and potato diggers

Societe Thiebaud
Bourguignonne
Arc–les–Gray, France
(Associated Company)
Balers and fertilizer
distributors

France and Spain

Hitachi, Limited (Licensee)
Hitachi
under John Deere Intercontinental, Ltd.
Moline, Illinois (Export Branch)
manufactures and markets
products in Southeast Asia

Japan

Figure 6.5 (continued)

148

Many American executives have found themselves inadequately prepared for the problems of working and living in foreign lands. Most of them would probably agree that a background in foreign languages, geography, world history, international economics, and cultural anthropology can be as helpful as knowledge about marketing, production, and accounting. Part of the problem is that many colleges of business administration have failed to meet some of these needs. Foreign languages have not generally been given recognition as a business tool; in fact, language requirements were abandoned at some business schools at the very time that U.S. foreign commitments were increasing. Courses in world history and geography are not often required or even recommended for prospective executives. Fortunately, a little reading can make up for some of this sort of deficiency. A visit abroad should be preceded by a visit to a library for a selection of books on the country concerned.

Differences in language, currency, practices, politics, and social customs are a few of the factors that may affect business activities in foreign nations. Language barriers are difficult to overcome in a short period of time. Only a native or a long-term resident can fully comprehend the meaning of a foreign language. A language is far more than words; it is a way of life that must be lived to be truly understood. But, in spite of this fact, language training can be extremely helpful. A high school or college language course represents a good beginning and can become a valuable asset for those who venture abroad. Most people in foreign countries, with the possible exception of the French, appreciate the efforts of someone who attempts to speak their language. The French seem to feel that only the French should be permitted to speak French badly.

A visitor to a foreign country should become familiar with elementary facts about that country. A good beginning is to look at a map in order to learn the name of the provinces, major cities, and places of interest. It is amazing that so few U.S. college graduates can name the provinces of Canada. A much smaller number know the islands that make up Japan, the Länder of Germany, the provinces of France, the capital of Venezuela, or the country to which Kuala Lumpur belongs. Other seemingly minor facts to an American at home can be a source of difficulty in the countries concerned. For example, the Republic of South Africa is not the Union of South Africa nor is it any longer a part of the British Commonwealth. The Japanese have a high status in Okinawa, but they have experienced problems in dealing with the Republic of Korea.

There are as many differences within foreign countries as within the United States. Bavarians have customs that differ from those found in Schleswig-Holstein in north Germany; life in Normandy departs significantly from that of Paris; and social practices in Milan are not the same as those found in Naples. Another important consideration is that foreign societies have "class" distinctions not unlike those that exist in the United States. There is a tendency for Americans (as well as foreigners in the U.S.) to neglect this fact and treat everyone as though they were alike. Many of our problems with the people of Viet Nam and Korea can be credited to this kind of failure.

Sometimes the apparently little things, such as the ritual of eating and drinking, make a big difference. The American should recognize that his mode of living may not be acceptable abroad. For example, Europeans do not generally eat sandwiches with their fingers—they use a knife and fork. And they hold their forks with the left hand when they eat; forks are not transferred to the right hand in the American fashion. An invitation to a Japanese or Korean meal may mean eating with chopsticks with no western silverware in sight.

Probably the best advice to those who wish to work and live abroad is that they should attempt to understand the society in which they visit. Understanding does not mean they need to agree or approve. A visitor to some countries should not be surprised if a customer has four wives. He need not marry the first four women he finds, but it might not be a good idea to suggest to the customer that one wife is enough. A traveler in a foreign land, particularly if his mission is to gain cooperation from foreigners, should not generally play the part of a critic. He should remember that the United States has problems that are often no less difficult than those found in foreign countries. The South African policy of apartheid, for example, has a parallel in practices found in the United States. There have been people with the propensities of the Nazis in every country, not excluding the United States. Everyone should remember that it is easier to be a critic than to provide a practical solution to a problem.

Executives who need help in promoting their business interests in foreign countries will find many helpful sources of information. There are a large number of public and private agencies concerned with this kind of thing. For example, the commercial attaché attached to American embassies and consulates throughout the world has the responsibility of providing a wide variety of economic and business information to American concerns. There are American Chambers of Commerce in every major nation to help further the commercial interests of companies from the United States. American banks with foreign branches, advertising agencies, steamship lines, and management consultants can be most helpful in this respect.

The Importance of Innovation

The electronic computer and the jet airplane have already affected the pattern of territorial departmentation and promise more changes in the not too distant future. The rapid processing of information by electronic computers together with rapid data transmission devices make possible a much wider territorial dispersion of organizational units. To cite conclusions made by one report on data communications:

> As a result of advances in the science of electrical communications, business executives can be located completely in accordance with the needs of the organization. It is now practicable to send information anywhere in the nation, in almost any form, with accuracy and speed. In a matter of a few minutes, a sales report, financial statement, or production report can be transmitted wherever needed so that a decision may be based on timely information. Through the use of advanced communication techniques, a company can determine its geographic distribution solely on the bases of the demands of the business. Plant proximity is no longer a prerequisite for reliable communications.[37]

The more complete and timely information made possible by modern processing and transmission equipment can greatly facilitate planning and control in companies with distant offices, plants, and projects. Air mail may be used to provide information that cannot be sent through such electronic facilities. Also important is that executives from headquarters can be flown to the most distant organizational outpost in a matter of hours.

Time and Other Types of Departmentation

Departmentation may result from the fact that work is performed during different periods of time. When a company operates on a three-shift basis, a "department" is not one but three departments, although they all may be alike in terms of objectives and activities.

Equipment Departmentation

A heat-treat furnace or an electronic computer can give rise to a separate department, particularly when the equipment is required by a number of departments and cannot be duplicated for economic reasons. Such departmentation may also result because the equipment cannot be placed in the physical area occupied by the user department. Heavy equipment cannot always be installed on the second or third floor of a factory or office building. The difficulties of supervising personnel from a distance may justify an additional departmental unit. The specialized skill required to operate some equipment is another contributing factor.

[37] Edgar C. Gentle, Jr., *Data Communications in Business* (New York: American Telephone and Telegraph Company, 1965), pp. 19–20. Copyright © by American Telephone and Telegraph Company.

Alpha-Numerical Departmentation

This method is frequently used at lower levels of the hierarchy. Telephone companies divide work by a series of telephone numbers, personnel records departments use alphabetical differentiations, and accounts receivable sections allocate responsibilities by number or alphabet. Alpha-numerical departmentation is not as simple as it sounds and can present difficult problems under certain circumstances. An alphabetical system, for example, does not always result in even workloads when the number of persons so classified increase or decrease, because sampling techniques do not always provide the right distributions. Although numbers offer greater flexibility than the alphabet, changes that may occur in the problems of people so categorized can lead to unequal workloads. For example, the amount of work represented by the early numbers in a series used to identify customers may change because long-time customers often have different problems and attitudes than newcomers.

Functional, Product, Territorial, and Other Combinations

The responsibilities of executives may involve several types of departmentation. An executive may be responsible for the *production* of a particular *product* within a given *territory*. Actual departments cannot generally be neatly divided into the categories found in this chapter. The nature of the contents placed into a filing case does not always correspond to the system that has been planned. There does not seem to be one best pattern of departmentation even in similar situations; companies have solved the problem in a variety of ways with what are probably equally good results.

SELECTED REFERENCES

The Annals of the American Academy of Political and Social Science, Vol. 368, (November 1966). The entire volume is devoted to Americans abroad.

Eugene J. Benge, "Managers Abroad—They're Different," *Advanced Management Journal,* Vol. 33, No. 2, pp. 31–36 (April 1968).

Alvin Brown, *Organization of Industry,* Chaps. 10 and 11. Englewood Cliffs, N.J.: Prentice-Hall Inc., 1947.

Ernest Dale, *Planning and Developing the Company Organization Structure,* Research Report No. 20, pp. 21–38. New York: American Management Association, 1952.

Ralph C. Davis, *The Fundamentals of Top Management,* Chap. 7. New York: Harper & Brothers, 1951.

Major General Welborn G. Dolvin and the U. S. Army Management Engineering Training Agency, *Lessons Learned: Joint International Program Management for the US/FRG Main Battle Tank.* Rock Island, Illinois: USAMETA, 1966.

Edgar C. Gentle, Jr., *Data Communications in Business.* New York: American Telephone and Telegraph Company, 1965.

Mason Haire, Edwin E. Chiselli and Lyman W. Porter, *Managerial Thinking.* New York: John Wiley & Sons, Inc., 1966.

Frederick Harbison and Charles A. Myers, *Management in the Industrial World.* New York: McGraw-Hill Book Company, Inc., 1959.

Paul E. Holden, Lounsbury S. Fish, and Hubert L. Smith, *Top-Management Organization and Control,* Part B, Sec. 1 and 2. New York: McGraw-Hill Book Company, Inc., 1951.

James O. Jensen, *The Weapon System Acquisition Process.* Rock Island, Ill.: U. S. Army Management Engineering Training Agency, 1965.

Charles R. Klasson and Kenneth W. Olm, "Managerial Implications of Integrated Business Operations," *California Management Review,* Vol. 8, No. 1, pp. 21–32 (Fall 1965).

Walter Krause and F. John Mathis, *International Economics and Business: Selected Readings.* Boston: Houghton Mifflin Company, 1968.

Dalton E. McFarland, *Company Officers Assess the Personnel Function,* AMA Research Study, No. 79. New York: American Management Association, 1967.

Donald J. Porter, *Joint International Program Management.* Rock Island, Ill.: U. S. Army Management Engineering Training Agency, 1966.

Richard D. Robinson, *International Management.* New York: Holt, Rinehart and Winston, 1967.

George P. Schultz and Thomas L. Whisler (editors), *Management Organization and the Computer.* Glencoe, Ill.: The Free Press, 1960.

Maneck S. Wadia, *The Nature and Scope of Management,* Section IX. Chicago: Scott, Foresman and Company, 1966.

Charles R. Williams, "Regional Management Overseas," *Harvard Business Review,* Vol. 45, No. 1, pp. 87–91 (January–February 1967).

chapter 7

LINE-STAFF-FUNCTIONAL RELATIONSHIPS

Staff assistants are often employed to help executives with their work; staff departments perform facilitating functions for operating departments. The difference between line and staff relationships is that line executives have command prerogatives and staff personnel does not. However, as will be shown later in this chapter, staff may do everything except command and may exert a large amount of influence. The staff concept makes possible the utilization of functional specialists without violating unity of command. To quote one writer on the subject: "Specialists are necessary, but 'they should be on tap—not on top.'"[1] The military has always recognized the importance of maintaining unity of command in combat units. Staff personnel is attached to each position to assist the commander in the exercise of his responsibilities.

Military Staff Organization

At 6:30 on the morning of June 6, 1944, the first wave of Allied troops assaulted the beaches of Normandy to begin one of the most difficult and comprehensive military operations in the history of warfare. The invasion armada was composed of some 4,200 troop transports, 800 warships, and numerous other crafts. Bombers and naval guns pounded enemy fortifications, and over 11,000 aircraft formed a protective umbrella over the invasion fleet and forces. Within six days the beachhead was secure, and

[1] Henry H. Farquhar, "The Anomaly of Functional Authority at the Top," *Advanced Management,* Vol. 7, No. 2, April–June 1942, p. 51.

some 325,000 troops, 54,000 vehicles, and 100,000 tons of supply had been brought ashore.

Less than fifty years earlier a much smaller American force invaded the shores of Cuba in what was possibly the most unorganized operation in military history. Thousands of troops were forced to wear winter uniforms in the heat of the Cuban summer because no khaki cloth was available in the United States.[2] The meat furnished by the Commissary Department was so bad that soldiers complained that they had to eat "embalmed beef." Camp sanitation was so primitive that death from disease exceeded death on the battlefield thirteenfold. The conditions at one port of embarkation (Tampa, Florida) were described by General Nelson A. Miles in the following words.

Several of the volunteer regiments came here without arms, and some without blankets, tents, or camp equipage. The 32nd Michigan, which is among the best, came without arms. General Guy V. Henry reports that five regiments under his command are not fit to go into the field. There are over 300 cars loaded with war material along the roads about Tampa. . . . To illustrate the confusion, fifteen cars loaded with uniforms were side-tracked twenty-five miles from Tampa, and remained there for weeks while the troops were suffering for clothing. Five thousand rifles, which were discovered yesterday, were needed by several regiments. Also, the different parts of the siege train and ammunition for the same, which will be required immediately on landing, are scattered through hundreds of cars on the side-tracks of the railroads.[3]

The difference between the haphazard performance in Cuba and the highly efficient performance in Normandy was a well-organized military staff system. The Normandy invasion was preceded by careful and comprehensive staff plannning and preparation which began many months before the operating phase of the campaign.[4] Every possible strategy and countermove by the enemy were taken into consideration. Specialized landing craft and equipment were designed, tested, and constructed. Two harbors were prefabricated for assembly on the French shore during the initial phases of the campaign. Plans were made to lay pipelines under the English Channel to supply the necessary gasoline. Numerous invasion maneuvers were conducted against almost exact replicas of the Normandy beaches. Plans were made for the evacuation of battle casualties and captured enemy prisoners. Provisions were made for civil and military government in liberated and enemy territory. Complicated diversionary tactics

---

[2] Samuel Eliot Morison and Henry Steel Commager, *The Growth of the American Republic* (New York: Oxford University Press, 1950), p. 332.

[3] Quoted in, *ibid.*, p. 333.

[4] The planning and preparation that preceded the Normandy invasion are well described in: Albert Norman, *Operation Overlord* (Harrisburg, Pa.: The Military Service Publishing Company, 1952).

were planned to deceive the enemy concerning the time and location of the attack. After the invasion began, field command and higher echelon staffs continued to provide the planning, coordination, and supervision that made the ultimate victory possible.

Military Staff Development

Although history records the existence of staff organization in the armies of ancient Egypt, Assyria, Macedonia, and Rome, modern military staff development had its genesis with the contributions of Gustavus Adolphus of Sweden in the early seventeenth century.[5] The Swedish system contained the basic elements found in modern military staffs. It made an important imprint upon the staff organizations that were subsequently developed in France, Prussia, England, and Russia.

The Prussians have often been credited with perfecting military staff organization. After the disastrous defeat by Napoleon in 1807, General G. J. D. Scharnhorst initiated a series of reforms to improve the staff system. Scharnhorst greatly expanded the educational facilities for the officer corps and developed a system of rotation whereby staff officers became familiar with the problems of the line units. Staff coordination was improved by a better system of channeling staff work through the chief of staff. Line commanders were instructed to take cognizance of the recommendations of the chief of staff, which gave recognition to the idea that the best staff is useless if the commander refuses to use it. The ultimate development of this requirement gave the chief of staff almost equal status with the line commander, and, in some instances of military failure, the chief of staff rather than the commander was removed. On the other hand, a refusal to listen to the recommendations of the chief of staff was sometimes equally fatal for the commander. Through such measures the line commanders were forced to use the organized military brain made available by the staff system. Many military experts credit the subsequent victories over the Austrians and the French in 1866 and 1871 to the efficiency of the Prussian staff.

The emphasis given to Prussian staff development in management and military literature sometimes gives the impression that the modern military staff was entirely a Prussian innovation. Historical evidence indicates that they borrowed much of their material.[6] Some Prussian staff terminology is obviously of French origin. French instructors were used in the military academy established by Frederick the Great in 1765. Scharnhorst was a diligent student of the Napoleonic military method and theory and un-

[5] J. D. Hittle (Lt. Col.), *The Military Staff* (Harrisburg, Pa.: The Military Service Publishing Company [now The Stackpole Company], 1949), pp. 1–43.

[6] *Ibid.*, pp. 69–70.

doubtedly applied some of the knowledge thus acquired in his military reforms. The contribution of the Prussians, and later the Germans, was that they recognized the importance of an efficient staff and were willing to give it a high status in their military system.

Staff development in the United States Army began with the Revolutionary Army under the command of General George Washington, whose efforts were greatly hampered by the lack of competent staff personnel. The situation was partially remedied by the appointment of a former staff officer in the Prussian Army, Baron Frederick von Steuben, as inspector general. Unfortunately, the staff techniques introduced by von Steuben did not form the beginning of systematic staff development. It was not until the turn of the present century that steps were taken to give the United States an adequate staff system. The gross inefficiency of many aspects of the military effort during the Spanish-American War of 1898 emphasized the need for better staff organization. Elihu Root, who became Secretary of War in 1899, was largely responsible for the legislation of 1903 which created an American general staff that followed the basic European pattern.

The United States Military Staff System

The top military staff in the United States is the Joint Chiefs of Staff which together with the Joint Staff is composed of the chiefs of staff and officers from the army, navy, and air force. This group is responsible for strategic planning and the coordination of land, sea, and air power. The three military services maintain separate and comprehensive staff organizations to plan, coordinate, and supervise the activities of their respective departments. The Joint Chiefs of Staff and the departmental staffs, such as the Department of the Army General Staff in Washington, are top-level policy and planning groups. A distinction is usually made between these staffs and the field command staffs. Each field commander, from the highest to the lowest echelon, has some kind of staff assistance available to him.

Functions of the Military Staff

The staff officers of a military unit assist the commander in the performance of his command responsibilities. Paraphrasing Urwick, ostensibly the staff officer provides only information, yet he makes all the arrangements that enable the fighting forces to perform their duties with the maximum of unity and the minimum of friction.[7] The staff officer com-

[7] L. Urwick, "Organization as a Technical Problem," *Papers on the Science of Administration* (New York: Institute of Public Administration, 1937), p. 63.

LINE-STAFF-FUNCTIONAL RELATIONSHIPS

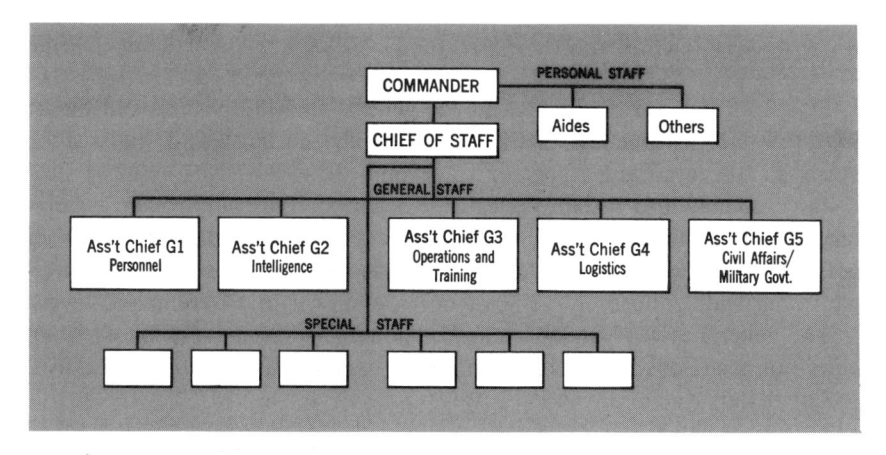

Figure 7-1. A simplified five-sectional general staff organization.

mands no one, yet he assists the commander to command everyone. More specifically, military staffs

... perform the basic functions of procuring information for the commander, preparing details of his plans, translating his decisions and plans into orders and then causing the orders to be transmitted to the troops. It is also ... the duty of the staff to bring to the commander's attention any matters which require his action, or about which he should be informed, and make a continuous study of the existing situation and prepare tentative plans for possible future action. Another important function of the staff officer is to supervise the execution of plans and orders and to carry out the commander's intentions.[8]

The commander and his staff should be viewed as a single entity relative to other commands in the military hierarchy. Each command acts as a coordinated unit in the name of the commander and the command headquarters.

Army Field Command Staff Organization: Division and Higher Headquarters

Three kinds of staff can be distinguished in higher army field commands: (1) personal staff, (2) general staff, and (3) special staff. The function of the personal staff, consisting of aides, messengers, secretaries, chauffeurs, and others the commander may designate, is to assist the commander directly and personally. The general staff is the primary planning and coordinating group within the command. The special staff is composed of technical specialists and administrative officers. A simplified five-sectional general staff organization is shown in Figure 7-1.

[8] Hittle, *op. cit.,* pp. 2–3.

The General Staff

Staff coordination is provided by the general staff in divisions and higher headquarters. The general staff consists of the chief of staff, the section chiefs or the assistant chiefs of staff, and their assistants. Higher field commands may also include a deputy chief of staff, a comptroller, a secretary of the general staff, and other kinds of personnel.[9] The staffs of commands below the division level are also organized somewhat differently, but staff philosophy and practice are similar at all command levels.

The general staff is divided into functional sections headed by assistant chiefs of staff. The basic responsibilities of each staff section in a five-sectional staff system are as follows.

1. *Personnel.* This section deals with matters pertaining to the personnel of the command, military and civilian. Its activities include such matters as the procurement of personnel, assignment, discipline, personnel services, control of prisoners of war and civilian internees, burials and grave registration, and other related subjects. The chief of this section is referred to as G-1.

2. *Intelligence.* This section is concerned with all matters relating to the collection, evaluation, interpretation, and distribution of information about enemy activities and capabilities. It also provides information about the weather and terrain to the commander and other interested parties. The intelligence chief is called G-2.

3. *Operations and Training.* Organization and training, operational planning and evaluation, the translation of operational decisions into orders, and the tactical employment of atomic weapons are some of the responsibilities of this section. This section chief, sometimes referred to as the operations officer, is known as G-3.

4. *Logistics.* This section deals with matters concerning the logistical support of an operational plan. Supply requirements, procurement, establishing priority systems, evacuation and hospitalization, transportation, and services are some of the specific functions that come under the jurisdiction of this section chief, referred to as G-4.

5. *Civil Affairs/Military Government.* This section deals with governmental, economic, and social problems of the areas in which the armed forces are engaged. The control of civil affairs and the establishment of military government are important responsibilities of this section chief, known as G-5.

---

[9] The basic levels in the military hierarchy are company, battle group, division, corps, and army. Such command echelons are army group, theater army, and theater may be organized above the army level.

The general staff functions encompass all the activities necessary to command a military unit. These functions are analogous to the organic functions in business organizations.[10] Functional differentiation in the military presents difficulties similar to those experienced in business enterprise. The chief of staff is charged with the task of resolving jurisdictional difficulties.

The functional subdivisions of general staff organization have evolved over a long history of military staff development. Except for differences in terminology and the allocation of some specific functions, the staff systems of the major military powers are similar in most respects. The United States Army has generally maintained a four-sectional staff, including personnel, intelligence, operations, and logistics, with a fifth section being added from time to time. During World War I, for example, a G-5 section was added to higher command staffs of the American Expeditionary Force to cope with the special problems of training large numbers of troops. The lower general staffs operated with three sections—personnel and supply, intelligence, and operations and training. During and subsequent to World War II, a fifth section has been organized in higher command echelons to deal with the problems of military government and general staff level (division level), a basic four-sectional staff is used. The functional organization of the general staff depends upon the nature and volume of particular kinds of military activity. Additional special functions are added to the staff sections whenever necessary. For example, the tactical use of atomic weapons and the growing importance of psychological warfare have created additional responsibilities for each of the general staff sections. Another important feature of the United States Army general staff system is equal status for the functional sections. This arrangement differs from the pre-World War II German staff system wherein the operations officer (G-3 in the United States Army) of the general staff was the senior general staff officer. Under such a system, the other functions were frequently subordinated to the operations function, with the possibility of a lack of balance in staff operations. However, formal equality can lead to similar consequences through informal modifications resulting from personality and other considerations.

The military staff function is a unified and coordinated function. The commander is not surrounded by autonomous staff advisors whose activities and counsel he must constantly evaluate and supervise. Such a staff might well be a hindrance rather than a help. All staff activities, including those of the special staff, are channeled through the five section chiefs who

[10] Production, sales, and finance are sometimes called organic functions in an industrial organization. A staff organization comprising these functions might be called a general staff in the same sense that the term is used in the military.

coordinate the staff work within their respective functional areas. The chief of staff coordinates, directs, and supervises the activities of the entire staff and assigns the staff responsibilities necessary to implement the orders of the commander.

The Special Staff

Special staff officers are technical specialists and administrative officers who assist the commander on matters pertaining to their particular specialty. Each general staff officer is charged with the responsibility for coordinating the special staff activities that fall within his jurisdiction. Some officers of the special staff have both command and staff responsibilities. Although vested in the same individual, these responsibilities are separate and distinct.[11]

Completed Staff Action

The function of the staff is to provide the commander with answers, not to plague him with questions. Staff activities are organized in the manner of an assembly line; the product is *completed staff action*, which is presented to the commander for approval or disapproval.

Staff Duties and Procedures

Military staff duties are performed within a general procedural framework designed to promote coordination among the various elements of staff action. Every general staff and special staff officer provides some part of the total plan. Each part of the plan is carefully evaluated in the light of every other part as the planning proceeds. A lack of replacements, a shortage of gasoline or mortar shells, or enemy troops movements may significantly influence the type of operational plan that can be instituted. In active warfare the entire planning process is in a constant state of flux.

In addition to the broader aspects of operational planning, a great many details must be taken into consideration. Maps of enemy territory have to be provided to combat units, and traffic to and from the front must be

---

[11] Some of the difficulties that may be experienced by an officer cast in such a dual role are presented by Major McGlachlin Hatch of the Corps of Engineers: *Method of Operation of the Division Engineer* (Fort Belvoir, Virginia: The Engineer School, 1949). This study and others like it emphasize the need for comprehensive operational studies of staff duties. The basic theory concerning what ought to be is well developed. But, specifically, how does it operate in an actual situation? What are some of the informal elaborations of the formal system?

controlled. Provisions have to be made for captured enemy troops and for the civilian population in the combat area. Issues of cigarettes, candy, soap, toothpaste, and shaving equipment must be made to troops. Hospital and evacuation facilities must be available, and the cemeteries for the dead cannot be forgotten. The outward confusion of battle is usually more apparent than real. The reason is that every detail has been given careful scrutiny by the military staff.

Staff Supervision

A frequent misconception about the staff function is that it is restricted to informational, planning, and advisory activities. As was pointed out above, the military staff provides the commander with completed staff action. Every detail required to implement a given course of action is worked out by the staff. But the process does not end with the completion of operational orders. The staff also supervises the execution of the orders issued in the name of the commander. The staff sees to it that the intent of the commander is carried out by subordinate and related commands and makes recommendations for modifications and elaborations when needed to cope with unforeseen and unusual circumstances. Supervision should be placed high on the list of basic staff responsibilities. A badly executed plan is tantamount to having no plan at all. The plans of mice and men go most often astray because the doing that is planned is not done.

Line and Staff Relationships

Many half-truths about the line and staff relationship have been perpetuated by nonoperational definitions. The idea that the line officer commands and the staff officer does not command affords little enlightenment about the relationship. Although a line commander is formally required to respond only to commands from a superior line commander, he obviously cannot ignore the superior's staff officers. Suggestions from higher echelon staff officers are rarely taken lightly. Every line commander knows that he is subject to the commands of the staff officer's headquarters and that a staff officer's suggestion can be followed by a formal order in the name of the superior commander. Even a staff officer of low rank may have considerable actual "authority" if he comes from a high headquarters. A classic example is provided by the mission of Lieutenant Colonel Hentsch of the German General Staff who ordered the withdrawal of an entire army in the first battle of the Marne in World War I.[12]

[12] Hittle, *op. cit.*, p. 74.

The line commander subjects himself to possible reversal when he refuses to deal reasonably with the superior's staff officers.[13] But the staff officer faces a similar consequence if he fails to conduct himself properly. The staff officer does not have to respond to the orders of a subordinate line commander, but he may be reversed by his commander. The relationship tends to promote cooperation because a lack of cooperation can have undesirable consequences for both the line and staff officer. In actual practice the superior line commander is rarely forced to resolve differences between his staff and a subordinate commander. When such difficulties do arise, they are generally settled informally.

Staff Functionalism

Staff organization found at different command levels is dissimilar in many respects, but the basic staff functions are found in some form at all command levels. The functional pattern found in lower command staffs follows that of higher staffs. Such staff functions as supply (logistics), intelligence, and operations are found at all levels in the hierarchy. At lower levels staff functions are frequently performed on a part-time basis by regular line officers, who may have a number of different staff responsibilities.

Although the formal rules governing line and staff relationships are generally observed, a great deal of interaction along functional lines occurs between staff specialists at different levels in the command hierarchy. Formal and informal contacts are made through staff visits, inspections, and conferences. Much of the written communication between different headquarters is channeled along functional lines. Reports from a subordinate to a higher headquarters are usually sent directly to the appropriate staff officer by the message control center.

Line, Staff, and Functional Relationships in Business Organizations

Military staff organization provides interfunctional coordination at every decision-making center in the hierarchy. It preserves unity of command without sacrificing the advantages of functional specialization. Many business organizations, faced with jurisdictional and coordination problems among functional executives, have turned to prototypes of the military staff system.

---

[13] An excellent synthesis of this relationship is made by L. Urwick, *op. cit.*, p. 64.

Staff Assistants

Part of the burden of an executive position can be reduced by clerical, technical, and administrative assistants. An important facilitating position is that of the private secretary, who generally assumes responsibility for planning and supervising the routine clerical work of an executive office. Many executives report that their secretaries keep track of business engagements and appointments, answer routine letters in their names, and decide who is going to talk to them over the telephone.[14] Some secretaries buy the boss' shirts, theater and football tickets, and write checks for his personal bills. A similar type of assistance is given by clerical and stenographic personnel. An efficient filing clerk assures the availability of important letters and reports when needed by the executive. A receptionist helps maintain control over the executive's personal contacts. An efficient office force familiar with the routine work of the executive position may frequently mark the difference between efficient and inefficient executive performance.

Many other types of staff assistance can be noted. A ghost writer may be extremely helpful to an executive who has to give many speeches; an attorney may be retained to advise on legal matters; a budget expert may be hired to assume responsibility for budgetary planning and control; an economist may be added to help appraise immediate and long-term economic prospects. Sometimes an executive delegates a variety of duties to general administrative assistants. The addition of staff assistants does not increase the number of decision-making positions in the management hierarchy. However, it does increase the number of individuals who perform the major and minor tasks that make up executive work.

The Pure Line-Staff Relationship

The line-staff relationship in business organizations is not always maintained with the formality of the military system. Business staff assistants are frequently permitted to give instructions and recommendations in their own names to subordinate line executives. Their responsibilities and relationships are usually not as rigidly defined as those of the military staff. Such departures from the formal doctrine do not alter the situation as long as line and staff executives understand the line-staff relationship and act accordingly.

[14] *Fortune,* Vol. 34, No. 4, October 1946, p. 14.

A Modified Line-Staff Organization

Some confusion exists in making distinctions between line and staff in business organizations. Personnel managers, purchasing agents, budget directors, and comptrollers are sometimes called staff personnel when they are in fact line executives.[15] The functional nature of their decision-making responsibilities does not necessarily make them staff. Functional executives may be staff, line, or a combination of the two. They are staff when they act as a representative of a superior in dealing with subordinate executives. They may have a line status with respect to the affairs of their own departments and, at the same time, serve in a staff capacity in relation to other departments. They may also have some functional decision-making prerogatives that cut across departmental lines.

Functional Line-Staff Relationships

A functional structure gives each executive decision-making responsibilities over a functional area, such as sales, production, personnel, purchasing, and finance. Under such an arrangement subordinate personnel is frequently subject to the decisions of several executives. The first step toward a line-staff organization is taken when functional executives are given exclusive decision-making prerogatives over activities and personnel in their departments. Such a change restricts the decision-making jurisdiction of functional executives and creates a dual line and staff role. Each executive has line prerogatives within his own department; he functions in a staff capacity in dealing with personnel in other departments.

The major operating departments, such as production and sales, are often formally designated as line departments, and executives in charge of these departments as line executives. A staff designation is frequently given to personnel, accounting, organization, and budgetary control departments and executives. Such formal descriptions do not change the basic functional line-staff relationships defined in the previous paragraph. Staff departments are frequently so designated because most of their activities involve personnel in the operating or line departments toward whom they function in a staff capacity. For example, personnel executives spend most of their time with people in other departments; production and sales executives are chiefly involved with people in their own departments, a line relationship. It should be noted that executives from line departments function in a staff capacity when they deal with subordinates in a staff department.

[15] Luther Gulick, "Notes on the Theory of Organization," *Papers on the Science of Administration* (New York: Institute of Public Administration, Columbia University, 1937), p. 31.

Operating executives generally assert the need for full decision-making prerogatives over the activities and personnel of their departments. There is a danger, however, in placing these executives in too dominant a position. If the counsel of staff executives is constantly ignored, the advantages of functional specialization may be lost. The staff executive must have an effective communication channel to the superior line executive and an opportunity to gain line support for his program. The proper execution of such a relationship inhibits line myopia to staff suggestions without eliminating unity of command.

Functional Decision Making by Staff Executives

Functional executives, who occupy an essentially staff status, may retain some decision-making prerogatives over the affairs of operating departments. For example, college-trained technical personnel is frequently hired on a company-wide basis by a centralized personnel department. Such a delegation of decision-making prerogatives to staff executives may present some of the coordination and control difficulties discussed in Chapter 6. The problem is to maintain a proper balance between the advantages of functional decision making and the need to preserve unity of command in operating departments.

Business executives have not always appreciated the possibilities inherent in a military-type line-staff organization.[16] The staff relationship, when properly executed, does not preclude the delegation of almost all the responsibilities of an executive position. The superior executive need only give a formal stamp of approval to the arrangements worked out by the staff. The personal intervention of the superior is needed only when staff and line executives cannot resolve their differences.

How does the delegation of functional decision-making prerogatives change the basic staff relationship? The pure staff system gives line executives direct access to the superior executive on all problems that arise between them and the superior's staff. Subordinate line executives do not have such access on those matters over which the staff executives are given decision-making prerogatives. Any direct communication with the superior is equivalent to skipping a level in the hierarchy. In other words, staff executives become duly constituted superiors over some functional activities. Although the line executive may theoretically appeal to a higher level, such action is not as feasible from a practical point of view. Ignoring a superior and "skipping levels" is not usually considered the best way to please the superior executive who did the delegating in the first instance. The delegation of functional decision-making prerogatives may provide

---

[16] Urwick, *op. cit.*, p. 63.

greater release from certain responsibilities. The superior may feel that an exclusively staff basis obligates him to give some personal attention to the arrangements made by staff executives. But if carried to an extreme, functional decision making can destroy the unity of command present in the pure line-staff system.

Product, Territorial, and Functional Line-Staff Relationships

The managerial structures of many large business organizations incorporate the advantages of two or more types of departmentation. The basic operating departments or divisions are generally organized on a product or a territorial basis with operating executives reporting directly to an executive vice-president or the chief executive. A second group of major executives is composed of functional specialists in production, engineering, personnel, public relations, research, and other functions. These executives frequently called general staff executives, report to the chief executive or to an executive who serves as the chief of staff. Such a managerial structure offers the coordination and control advantages of product or territorial departmentation in the operating part of the organization. At the same time, the knowledge of the functional specialist is made available to top management and the operating executives. This kind of organization has been used with a great deal of success by such well-known corporations as the General Electric Company, the General Motors Corporation, the Radio Corporation of America, and the Du Pont Company.

Line-Staff-Functional Relationships: Illustrations

The Standard Oil Company of California: The Management Guide

An excellent description of a well-organized line-staff managerial structure is found in *The Management Guide* of the Standard Oil Company of California.[17] Although this publication purports to describe a hypothetical organization, its contents enunciate the basic organizational theory and practice of the Standard Oil Company of California. The organizational structure presented in *The Management Guide* is called "a modified or hybrid form" of the pure line-staff structure (see Figure 7-2). It is described in the following words.

[17] George L. Hall and Franklin E. Drew (editors), *The Management Guide,* 2nd ed. (San Francisco: Department on Organization, Standard Oil Company of California, 1956).

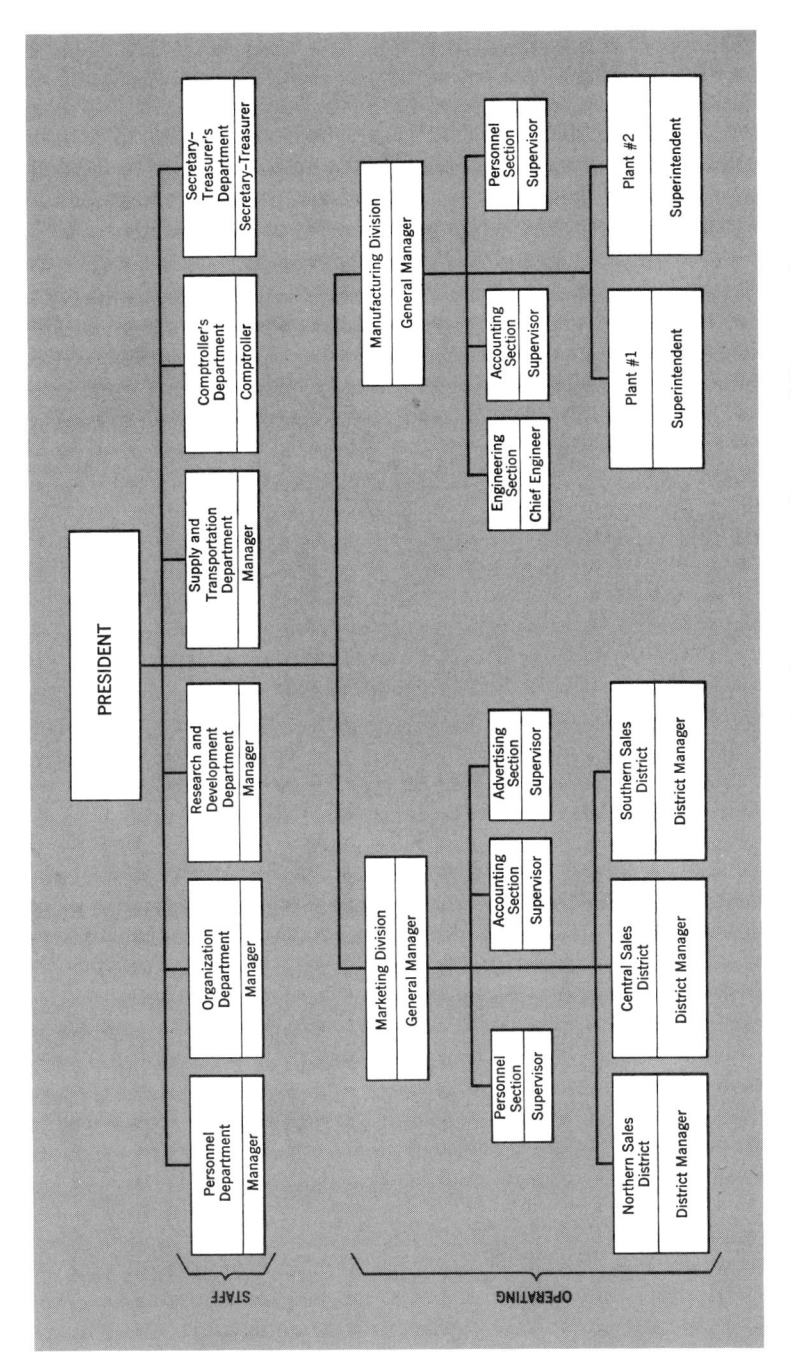

Figure 7-2. Line-staff departments in a functional structure. Courtesy of Department on Organization, Standard Oil Company of California, San Francisco, California.

In its pure form, line-and-staff organization has one top position from which the direct line of control runs to the operating component or components. However, since the head of a large enterprise cannot be expected to act as his own advisor in all specialized and technical matters, this top position is supplied with a staff, experts in the various phases of the operations and activities of the enterprise, who supply this necessary advice. Having been advised by his staff, the head of the enterprise then issues all orders and instructions downward through the direct line of control, and supervises their execution by the leaders of operating groups.

Today a modified or hybrid form of this pure line-and-staff organization is the type found in most general use. In this altered form the top position, the staff, and the operating groups have the same relative places in the structure as do those in the pure form. However, because of the large size and complexity of modern enterprises in the United States, it is impractical for the head of the enterprise to issue all instructions and personally to oversee compliance with them.

As a result, the staff exercises functional guidance over the operating components. This does not mean that staff members issue orders, supervise activities, or control any portion of the operating groups. Each staff man recommends policies to the head of the enterprise for his approval. Once these policies are approved, procedures in line with the policies are established, in some cases by the staff member concerned, and in other cases by the top position upon recommendation of the staff member.

After establishment of a procedure, the staff man within whose province the particular procedure falls, furnishes the appropriate operating component chief with technical or specialized advice and assistance in the application of the procedure. The staff member is responsible for furnishing this functional guidance, and is accountable to his principal for the fulfillment of this responsibility. The chief of the operating component is responsible for the application of the functional guidance which he receives, and is accountable to *his* principal for the fulfillment of *his* responsibility. In no case is the chief of the operating component subject to the orders, supervision, or control of the staff man, nor can he ever be held accountable to the staff member for fulfillment of his responsibilities.

Briefly, this hybrid type line-and-staff organization permits help and guidance to be given to the operators by the specialists, and at the same time ensures that an individual has only one person to whom he reports.[18]

The practical consequences of such an organizational structure and military line-staff organization are similar. Unity of command is retained in the operating divisions, and staff executives do not "issue orders, supervise activities, or control any portion of the operating groups." After the head of the enterprise has approved policy recommendations of staff executives,

---

[18] George L. Hall and Franklin E. Drew (editors), *op. cit.,* pp. 34, 36.

the staff deals directly with subordinate operating executives on these matters. This arrangement is similar to the military staff regulation that authorizes the staff officer to issue orders or directives in the commander's name to subordinate units when within a framework of established policies. Operating executives are required to apply functional guidance from the staff only after the superior line executive has given his approval. Strictly speaking, such a relationship does not give the staff executive functional decision-making prerogatives. The operating executive accepts the functional guidance of staff executives because the superior has decided to extend line support to staff suggestions. However, when such support becomes permanent with respect to certain functional subjects, the arrangement may, in a practical sense, amount to a delegation of functional decision-making prerogatives to staff executives.

Line-Staff Organization in the General Motors Corporation

The basic operating units of the General Motors Corporation are product divisions, such as the Buick Motor Division, the Chevrolet Motor Car Division, GMC Truck & Coach Division, Delco-Remy Division, and the Diesel Equipment Division. Within limits set by top corporate policy, the operating executives have full decision-making responsibility over the personnel and activities of their divisions. Division managers report to executives in charge of groups of divisions manufacturing related products, and these executives report to an executive vice-president or directly to the president. The group executive is the link between the operating divisions and the central organization; he works closely with the divisional managers and with the top-management line executives.

The GMC top-management organization includes four types of staff executives: the financial staff, the legal staff, the operations staff, and the public relations staff. Figure 7-3 shows these staff groups and their relationship to the line structure. The financial and legal staffs provide financial and legal information and advice to top management. Their activities are only indirectly concerned with manufacturing and sales activities. The structural differentiation of this staff group from the operations staff relates to the distinction made by GMC between top-level operating and financial policy formulation. A similar differentiation is made between the operating divisions concerned primarily with manufacturing and sales and the group of operating subsidiaries dealing with finance and insurance.

The operations staff is divided into the following functional sections: marketing, engineering, personnel, manufacturing, research, styling, and patents. These sections function in an advisory and service capacity to both divisional and central managements. Staff executives also participate in

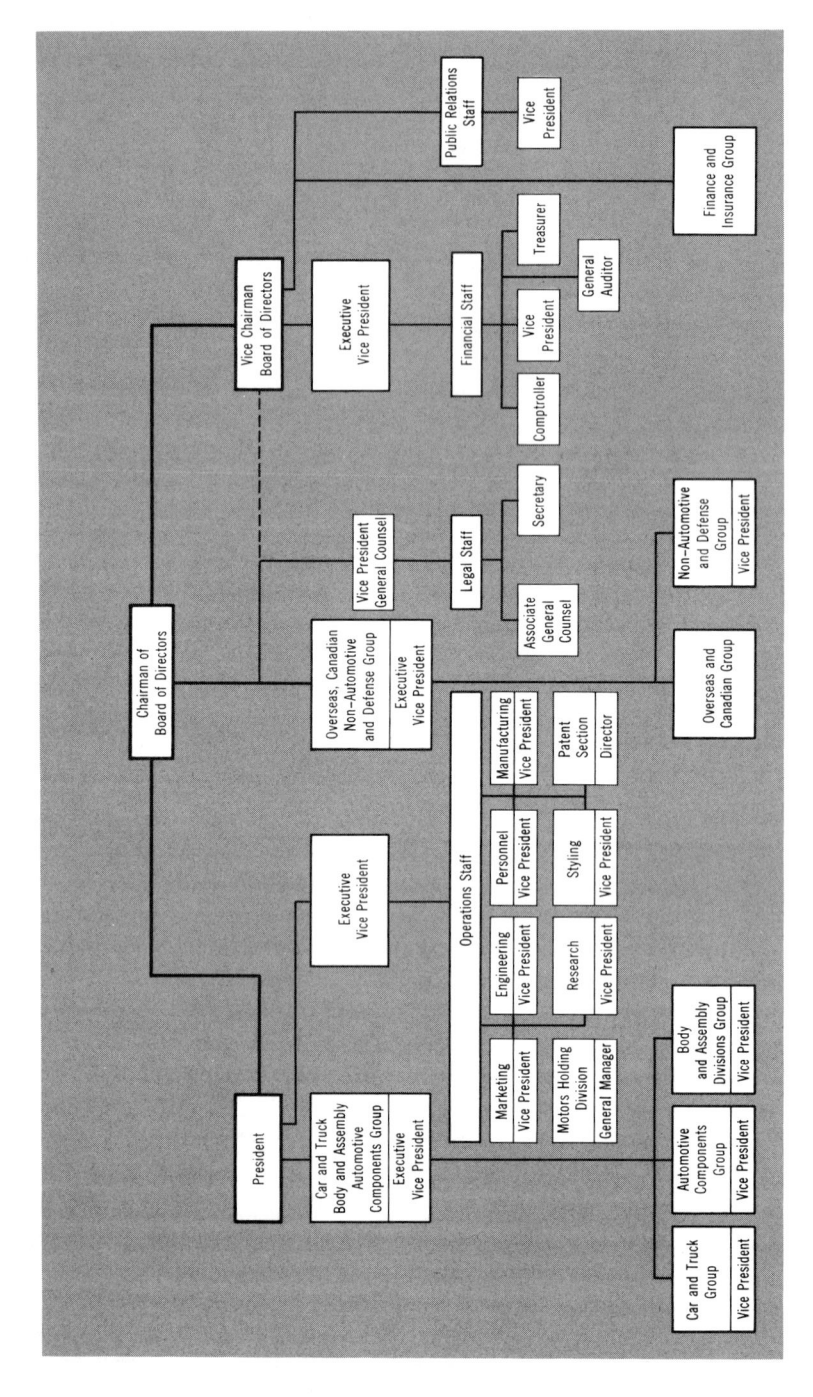

Figure 7-3. Line and staff relationships: General Motors Corporation. Courtesy of GMC.

corporate policy formulations through their membership in top-level policy groups. Within the limits designated by the top management, the functional staff executives deal directly with the operating executives. Although the mandate of the superior line executive is sometimes implied in such staff relationships, operating executives have a direct channel to the superior line executive if they disagree with staff recommendations or instructions. This relationship is similar to the line-staff relationships discussed in previous sections of this chapter. GMC staff executives have some functional decision-making prerogatives involving the affairs of the operating divisions. The personnel staff section of the operations staff, for example, has the responsibility for negotiating and administering agreements with numerous national labor unions.

The RCA Concept of Line and Staff Teamwork

The Radio Corporation of America has given a great deal of attention to the development of effective line and staff teamwork. The basic line structure of RCA comprises three levels: (1) top management (the chairman of the board and the president); (2) group executives and the heads of RCA Communications, RCA Laboratories, National Broadcasting Company, and RCA International; (3) executives in charge of product and service operating units, who report to the group executives.[19] It should be noted that RCA, like many other large organizations, has integrated subsidiary corporations into the over-all operating structure. Thus, the National Broadcasting Company is subject to direct operating control from the RCA top management, and its activities are coordinated with other subsidiaries and operating units.

Two major staff groups report to the chairman of the board and the president. The corporate staff is similar in most respects to the operations staff of the General Motors Corporation. The top management also has a special staff composed of executives who serve as special advisors and consultants. Like the special staff officers of the military, most of these staff executives also manage specialized operating units. In addition to the top executive officers, the group executives and heads of major corporate subsidiaries, such as the National Broadcasting Company and RCA Communications, also use the services of the top staff. The nature of these staff services is defined in the following words.

[19] The source for much of the material in this section is *The RCA Organizational Realignment* (New York: Radio Corporation of America, 1954). The author also received a great deal of helpful information from John L. Mastran, Manager, Organization Planning and Management Development, RCA.

The kind of service rendered is that which is needed and called for—it can range from purely advisory to that which activates a divisional or subsidiary function, or may be operational. For convenience, economy and over-all consistency, certain activities which cut across several divisions and subsidiaries are carried on by the Corporate Staff.[20]

This statement indicates that the staff relationship at RCA involves a significant amount of functional decision making.

Most of the functions represented on the corporate staff are duplicated in the basic operating divisions and subsidiaries. Whenever possible, functional activities are performed close to the point of use and decision. Although the heads of the operating units are the principal line executives, subordinate functional executives are given considerable functional decision-making prerogatives. For example, the division personnel manager is "functionally responsible for the development and maintenance of effective and sound personnel programs in all operating units of the division."[21] Plant personnel managers work in a close functional relationship with the division personnel manager. A great deal of decision making within operating units is therefore functionally differentiated. However, interfunctional coordination is provided at both division and plant level by the principal line executives who head these units. Functional executives at the division or plant level cannot ignore the division or plant managers. The plant manager can appeal directly to the division manager if he does not approve the decisions made by division functional executives. Thus, functional executives take into consideration the views of the principal operating executives in conducting their affairs. In actual practice, these relationships are not authoritarian; formal appeals to the superior line executive are rare. Differences of opinion are generally handled informally on a give-and-take basis until agreement is reached.

Managerial Relationships in Perspective

An important organizational problem is to strike a proper balance between the unity of command principle and the equally important need for managerial specialization. The military has generally given a priority to the unity of command principle. The need for specialized advice and services has been met through a highly efficient staff system. Business organizations have been more inclined to give decision-making prerogatives to functional specialists. However, the problems of overlapping spheres of

[20] *Ibid.,* p. 16.
[21] Information received from John L. Mastran, RCA.

responsibility, jurisdictional controversy, and coordination difficulties have caused many business organizations to adopt some kind of a line and staff management structure. The result has generally been a modified line and staff structure that retains some of the features of a functionally differentiated managerial structure, but at the same time assures a significant degree of unity of command in the operating units.

Staff Must Be Used

A line and staff organization cannot effectively serve the need for specialized knowledge if operating executives ignore the counsel of staff executives. An important reason for the success of the Prussian staff system was the requirement that the commander give full consideration to the recommendations of the staff. The following quotation from an RCA publication on managerial relationships also gives explicit attention to the problem: "It is the duty of every line executive to use staff services to best advantage in planning, directing, controlling and improving his operations." [22] The staff cannot become an effective instrument of management action without the cooperation and support of the line.

Functional Decision Making and Unity of Command

A modification of the pure line and staff relationship by giving functional decision-making prerogatives to staff executives gives recognition to certain functional activities. It assumes that the functional specialist should play a primary role with respect to these matters, even though the unity of command principle is violated in some degree. How much functional decision making is too much? The theory of organization does not offer a precise answer to this question. Organizational practice indicates that a significant amount of functional decision making can occur without seriously disrupting unity of command. The use of coordination centers at each level of the management hierarchy seems to provide an important safeguard against the difficulties that sometimes accompany functionally differentiated decision making. See Figure 7-4. A clear definition of functions and relationships also serves a useful purpose in this respect.

The Problem of Attitude

Operating executives are prone to regard the activities of staff executives with aversion. They sometimes feel that staff executives are barriers between them and their superior. Such an attitude may be reinforced if the

[22] *The RCA Organizational Realignment, op. cit.,* p. 10.

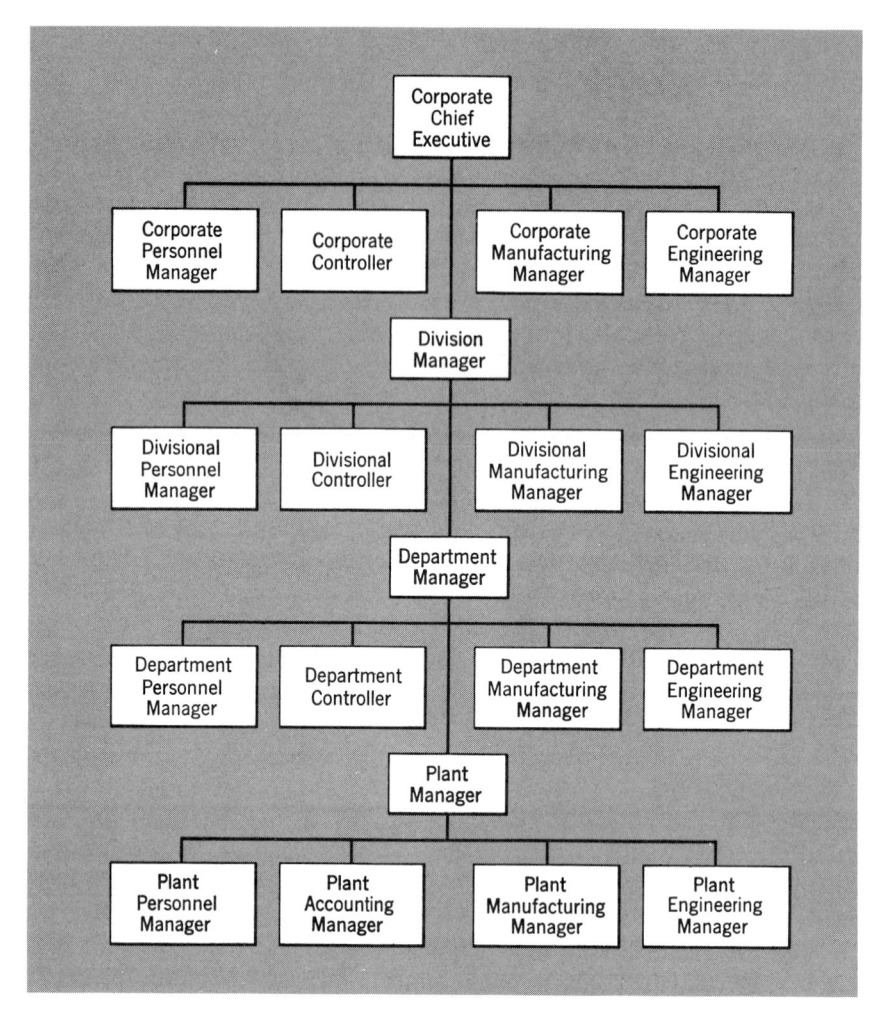

Figure 7-4. A simplified functional structure with coordination at each hierarchical level.

superior appears overzealous in his support of staff recommendations. Another frequently expressed view is that staff executives are "ivory tower" planners who do not understand the problems of operating departments. The fact that such attitudes are often a product of the imagination does not make the problem less difficult.

The staff should not constantly seek the support of the superior line executive to overcome resistance from operating executives. The function of the staff is to make the arrangements and solicit the cooperation of subordinate executives. Constant appeal to the superior increases his workload and repudiates the role that the staff should play. Many barriers to line and staff cooperation can be overcome by good human relations on the part of the staff. The staff executive cannot approach the operating executive like a bull in the china shop and expect to get anywhere. He should not assume that opposition to his ideas always results from a closed mind. Skepticism is not a synonym of stupidity. The staff executive must be willing to sell his ideas and show the operating executives how he can solve their problems; he must also sell himself as a person. He must convince operating executives that he is interested in *their* welfare. He must frequently subordinate his normal desire for recognition by giving credit for success to the operating executives.

The superior also has a responsibility for the development of good line and staff relationships. He should not hesitate to support or restrain his staff or operating executives whenever constructive differences of opinion begin to deteriorate into internecine warfare. He should not be content to sit back and let them fight it out. A policy of "let them read my mind" may be good sport, but it hardly helps mold constructive organizational behavior. Frequent intervention is generally not necessary, but when it does occur it should be positive and clearly understood by all parties concerned.

A Blurring of Line-Staff Distinctions

A number of organization and management theorists contend that the distinctions between line and staff are becoming blurred.[23] Some have pointed to the "coming death of bureaucracy" with a greater reliance upon organizational structures in which task-force teams play an increasingly important role. They assert that the traditional authoritarian relationships will become subordinated to the requirements of the task to a far greater extent than in the past. Some of the reasons given for such a change in managerial relationships are: (1) a tremendous rate of technological innovation that has increased the complexity of industrial products and processes; (2) the need to adapt to rapid and frequent changes, which

---

[23] Douglas McGregor, "The Role of Staff in Modern Industry," in George P. Shultz and Thomas L. Whisler (editors), *Management Organization and the Computer* (Illinois: The Free Press of Glencoe, 1960), pp. 105–118. Similar ideas are expressed in: Warren G. Bennis, "The Coming Death of Bureaucracy," *Think,* Vol. 32, No. 6, November–December 1966, pp. 30–35; William H. Read, "The Decline of the Hierarchy in Industrial Organizations," *Business Horizons,* Vol. 8, No. 3, Fall 1965, pp. 71–75.

tends to be impeded by the traditional structure of relationships; (3) a growth in the professionalization of specialized personnel, which makes them less inclined to accept the traditional authoritarian relationships.

There is undoubtedly some validity in these ideas. Line and staff relationships may have become more blurred, but it should be noted that they have never been as distinct as their definitions sometimes make them. Managerial relationships have always been informal, contradicting formally defined relationships. Informally induced teamwork has frequently become a substitute for authoritarian relationships. Some useful purpose may be served by giving some of this teamwork a formal status because of recent technological developments. But it would be highly inappropriate to assert that authoritarianism can be entirely abandoned. People appear to be less cooperative and willing to serve a common purpose than is often assumed.

Service and Auxiliary Functions

The establishment of staff relationships generally results in a grouping of activities. Staff executives are not isolated individuals who assist in the performance of the management function; they frequently manage personnel who provide a service to the basic operating departments. For example, the intelligence officer of the army general staff conducts intelligence operations, and the styling section of the General Motors Corporation is actively engaged in styling activities for the operating divisions.

A distinction is generally made between the departments engaged in primary operating activities and auxiliary or service departments. This kind of classification reflects the different values assigned to the various activities performed in the organization. Such functions as production and marketing are generally accorded higher status than personnel, research and development, purchasing, and budgeting. Although the success of the organization is closely related to the efficiency of the primary operating departments, the auxiliary departments also play a vital role. The activities of the personnel department often mark the difference between good and bad labor relations. A long strike can cost millions of dollars in sales and significantly affect the ability of the organization to survive in a competitive market. The failure to keep up with styling trends or to advance in the field of research and engineering may have equally fatal consequences. The appearance of functional decision making within the framework of a line and staff organization is partly explained by the importance of some activities to the organization. The result is both a centralization of decision making and a grouping of particular functional activities.

Information Technology and Line-Staff Relationships

The impact of information technology upon line-staff relationships can be pursued in a number of directions. One is that electronic computers have changed the relative number of line and staff personnel. Many organizations may eventually experience a marked reduction in the total number of staff people within the managerial structure.[24] Several research studies indicate that the installation of electronic data processing equipment tends to reduce the size of the clerical staff. However, a number of studies show a growth of management personnel relative to clerical employees.[25] In some organizations the number of staff people within the total management structure will not be reduced and may actually increase in order to take advantage of the informational capacities of the computer. The electronic computer can provide information not available with the technology of the past. There will be a demand for information that can improve planning and control.

The Computer and Job Changes

The introduction of electronic data processing has eliminated jobs, revised jobs, and created entirely new jobs. A good example is afforded by the changes that occurred in the customer accounting department of a large public utility.[26] Table 7-1 indicates the number and kind of changes in this instance. Only 8 of an original 28 job categories were not changed. Eleven job categories were entirely eliminated; 9 were revised to accommodate EDP; and 15 new job classifications were created.

Electronic computers have caused similar changes in jobs above the clerical level. Highly responsible jobs once performed by functional specialists, many of whom had college degrees, have been entirely eliminated by EDP. Many of the duties involved in production planning and scheduling, materials procurement, personnel assignments, inventory control, and the accounting process are now performed by computerized systems. Some job

---

[24] It should be noted that it is almost impossible to predict the ultimate impact of computerized informational systems upon employment in particular organizations or the total economy. The conclusions made in this section seem reasonable in terms of existing experience.

[25] Walter A. Hill, "The Impact of EDP Systems on Office Employees: Some Empirical Conclusions," *Academy of Management Journal*, Vol. 9, No. 1, March 1966, p. 18.

[26] Hill, *op. cit.*, pp. 13–15.

Table 7-1. Jobs Affected by the Introduction of the Electronic Data Processing System

UNCHANGED JOBS		REVISED JOBS	
Job Title	Pay Group	Job Title	Pay Group
Bill Information Clerk	10	Cash Proof Clerk	11
General Clerk, Bill Information	17	File Clerk—Customer Accounting	7
Head Clerk, Power Billing	19	Office Boy	3
Meter Order and Audit Clerk	11	Revenue and Statistics Clerk	16
Miscellaneous Accounts Receivable Clerk	13	Key Punch Operator—Trainee	3
		Key Punch Operator A	7
Power Billing and Accounts Clerk	19	Key Punch Operator B	10
Typist Clerk	8	Customer Accounting Machine Operator	9
Typist	8	Balance and Control Clerk	15

JOBS TO BE REMOVED FROM MANUAL— NO LONGER NEEDED		NEW JOBS	
Job Title	Pay Group	Job Title	Pay Group
Control Clerk	12	Senior Key Punch Operator	14
Balance Clerk	15	EDP Equipment Operator A-T	11
Customer Accounting Machine Operator—Special	13	EDP Equipment Operator B	14
		EDP Console Operator A-T	15
Calculating Punch Operator	12	EDP Console Operator B	18
Calculating Punch Operator—Special	13	EDP Programmer A-T	15
		EDP Programmer B	18
Review Sorter Operator	14	EDP Programmer C	20
Review Clerk	16	Tape Record Clerk	13
File Maintenance Lead Clerk	17	Burster Operator	9
Customer Tabulating Lead Clerk	17	Conversion Checking Clerk	10
		Conversion Reconciliation Clerk	13
Head Clerk—Customer Tabulating	21	Bill Checking Clerk	10
Key Punch Operator B—Special	10	Correction Clerk	10
		Meter Order Record Clerk	11

Source. Company Records. Walter A. Hill, "The Impact of EDP Systems on Office Employees: Some Empirical Conclusions," *Academy of Management Journal,* Vol. 9, No. 1, March 1966, p. 14.

descriptions have been changed to conform to the demands of information technology. For example, responsible accounting positions generally require the performance of duties involving computerized informational systems. Other jobs have evolved from information technology, for example, systems design engineers, computer programmers, and systems administrators or managers.

The Organizational Location of Staff Personnel

Information technology has already caused major shifts in the organizational location of staff personnel. Many line executives will have fewer staff people assigned to them in the future as centralized data processing departments become more firmly established. Production managers in some companies have already lost staff personnel concerned with production planning and scheduling. Staff executives may also find themselves on the losing end of the personnel game. For example, the information processing once performed within accounting and purchasing departments is now a centralized responsibility in some organizations. In other instances, such departments as accounting and finance will experience large gains in personnel if they are given the responsibility for all information processing.

Another development is the higher status sometimes accorded staff departments concerned with the new information technology. The managers of such departments frequently report to an executive at the top management level. Both line and staff departmental executives, who once had their own informational staffs reporting to them, now find that they have to deal with staffs who have strong support from higher executives. This sort of thing has occurred before. Executives in charge of such areas as industrial relations, safety engineering, and credit have frequently been given a higher organizational status to enable them to deal more effectively with line executives who are reluctant to cooperate.

The Proper Role of Information Technology

An important problem is to find the proper role of information technology in the organizational structure. Some organizations have used computers almost exclusively to process routine data. They have relegated computer specialists to a relatively low organizational status and have not taken full advantage of the decisional and informational potential of the computer. Other organizations have undoubtedly moved too far in the opposite direction. There will be much seesawing during the next few years as the new information technology finds its proper niche in the management process.

Information technology staffs will undoubtedly have much influence in the immediate future. They will serve a highly useful purpose through their systematic approach to management problems. But executives should recognize that some problems cannot be solved through these techniques. Indeed, a great deal of harm can result from an overextension of information technology. Professors Whisler and Shultz have pointed out that information technology, because of its imposingly objective nature, may cause qualitative judgments to be treated lightly and create too much rigidity in the decision process.[27]

Computers are by no means a panacea for the solution of all of the difficult problems. There will still be room for executives who make the nonprogrammed decisions. An authoritarian approach will be necessary to resolve some of the disagreements and differences involved in this kind of decision making.

Information Technology: Line or Staff?

The question of whether information technology is line or staff has been the subject of considerable controversy.[28] Some contend that the people who design and administer computerized systems are definitely line because their activity directly affects such strategic operating functions as marketing and production. Systems people are engaged in setting standards and procedures that have the effect of predetermining decisions in the primary operating departments. Others argue that there is a fundamental difference between the contribution of the information technologists and that of the line executives. For one thing, information technologists are primarily concerned with problems that can be systematized in objective terms. They provide partial solutions for the really important decisions made by line executives. Still other people assert that information technologists play both line and staff roles.

The distinctions between line and staff have always presented definitional difficulties. There is some truth in all of the above arguments. Information technologists, like other staff personnel, have taken away some of the prerogatives of line executives. But such a situation has always accompanied the introduction of a new kind of staff. For example, the establishment of personnel and industrial relations departments had a similar impact upon the prerogatives of line departments. There were complaints in many organizations that the new personnel technologists were unduly interfering with the operating departments.

Information technology is not primarily a line function in spite of the significant part it will play in the affairs of the operating departments. It is

[27] George P. Shultz and Thomas L. Whisler (editors), *Management Organization and the Computer* (Illinois: The Free Press of Glencoe, 1960), p. 10.

[28] Some of the basic arguments are presented in Schultz and Whisler, *ibid.* Other literature on the subject is indicated in William E. Reif, *Computer Technology and Management Organization* (Iowa City: Bureau of Business and Economic Research, 1968), pp. 24–34.

not likely that information technologists will make the really important marketing and production decisions although they will make some programmed decisions and influence other decision making. Such fields as marketing, production, finance, purchasing, and personnel involve more than the knowledge and techniques encompassed by information technology. There is a sufficient basis for separate specialization in the subject matter that makes up information technology. Mathematical model building, computer programming, and systems analysis and development all involve a great deal of education and experience. The people who become specialists in these fields are not thereby qualified to make the important marketing or production decisions. They can help improve performance in the operating departments by making some programmed decisions and providing analytical and informational support for nonprogrammed decisions. As such, they should be categorized as staff with some responsibilities that can be called line. Their status in this respect does not differ from other kinds of staff.

SELECTED REFERENCES

John R. Beishline, *Military Management for National Defense,* Chaps. 2, 10–13. Englewood Cliffs, N.J.: Prentice-Hall, Inc., 1950.

Warren G. Bennis, "The Coming Death of Bureaucracy," *Think,* Vol. 32, No. 6, pp. 30–35 (November–December 1966).

Francis A. Cartier, et al., *The Air Force Staff Officer.* Maxwell Air Force Base, Alabama: Air Force ROTC, Air University, 1961.

Ernest Dale, *Planning and Developing the Company Organization Structure,* Research Report No. 20, pp. 61–83. New York: American Management Association, 1952.

Ernest Dale and Lyndall F. Urwick, *Staff in Organization.* New York: McGraw-Hill Book Company, Inc., 1960.

J. D. Hittle (Lt. Col.), *The Military Staff.* Harrisburg, Pa.: The Military Service Publishing Company (now the Stackpole Company), 1949.

Douglas McGregor, "The Role of Staff in Modern Industry," in George P. Schultz and Thomas L. Whisler (editors), *Management Organization and the Computer,* pp. 105–118. Illinois: The Free Press of Glencoe, 1960.

James D. Mooney, *The Principles of Organization,* Chaps. 5, 14, 17, 18. New York: Harper & Brothers, 1947.

William H. Read, "The Decline of the Hierarchy in Industrial Organizations," *Business Horizons,* Vol. 8, No. 3, pp. 71–75 (Fall 1965).

Robert C. Sampson, *The Staff Role in Management.* New York: Harper & Brothers, 1955.

L. Urwick, "Organization as a Technical Problem," *Papers on the Science of Administration,* pp. 49–88. New York: Institute of Public Administration, 1937.

chapter 8

CENTRALIZATION AND DECENTRALIZATION

Several kinds of centralization and decentralization are found in organizations. One is the geographical concentration or dispersion of operations. In this sense an organization is centralized if all operating activities are performed in one geographical area; it is decentralized if plants and offices are located in different areas. Second, these concepts may have reference to the centralization and decentralization of particular functions. Thus, the function of purchasing is centralized in one department or performed on a decentralized basis by a number of departments. Finally, as used in this chapter, centralization and decentralization describe the manner in which decision-making responsibilities are divided among executives at *different* hierarchical levels.

As was noted in Chapter 5, the management hierarchy represents both a centralization and decentralization of decision making. Decision making is decentralized through delegation from higher to lower levels of the hierarchy. It is centralized to the extent that decision-making prerogatives are retained (or not delegated) by higher management levels. Centralization and decentralization should be viewed in relative rather than absolute terms. Complete centralization is the concentration of *all* decision making at the apex of the management hierarchy. If this were possible, there would be no need for a management hierarchy. Complete decentralization, or the delegation of *all* decision-making functions to the lowest level of the hierarchy, is equally absurd. The logical consequence would be the elimination of all managerial positions above the lowest level. Some centralized decision making is necessary to coordinate management effort and achieve a unity of purpose. The question is not whether centralization or decentralization should take place; it is a matter of finding the proper balance between these mutually dependent forces.

Centralization and Decentralization: Problems and Practices

Decentralization: Fact or Fiction

The words centralization and decentralization have been endowed with many subjective qualities. In recent years, decentralization has become the golden calf of management philosophy. It has been lauded by such terms as "more democratic," "a step toward world peace," "greater freedom of spirit," and "less authoritarian." The implicit assumption is that centralization reflects the opposite of these worthy qualities.

In spite of the verbal emphasis given to the virtues of decentralization, there appears to be some discrepancy between resolution and practice. As one executive put it:

I find myself just a little annoyed at the tendency of all of us to adopt certain clichés such as "decentralization" and then glibly announce that we are for it. I have been somewhat amused at some of my colleagues who are most vocal in expounding the virtues of decentralization and yet quite unconsciously are apt to be very busily engaged in developing their own personal control over activities for which they are responsible.[1]

A limited survey conducted by the American Management Association indicates that decentralization is not as widespread as commonly supposed.[2] As Ernest Dale has concluded, "an examination of the actual activities of chief executives discloses that they continue to make most or all major decisions, either directly or through a formal framework of strict rules, checks and balances, informal instructions, and through mental compulsion on the part of subordinates to act as the boss would act."[3] Decisions on relatively unimportant matters are made at the top of the hierarchy in many companies. Some of the following examples, listed by Dale, are not at all unrepresentative.

In several large companies the chief executive insists on approving all purchases over $2,500.

---

[1] Quoted in Helen Baker and Robert R. France, *Centralization and Decentralization in Industrial Relations* (Princeton, N.J.: Industrial Relations Section, Department of Economics and Sociology, Princeton University, 1954), p. 37.

[2] Ernest Dale, *Planning and Developing the Company Organization Structure*, Research Report No. 20 (New York: American Management Association, 1952), p. 118. The questionnaire used in this survey is found in: *ibid.*, pp. 108–109.

[3] *Ibid.*, p. 118.

CENTRALIZATION AND DECENTRALIZATION 187

At many companies all salary changes for those earning above $4,000 or $5,000 must be approved by the president. Sometimes this is done to prevent any unjustified applications for salary increases.

In a number of small companies the chief executive insists on opening all the mail himself and signing all the replies.

In many large companies the president must pass on every public appearance, however small the audience, of every member of management and approve whatever he may say.

Frequently any grievance that is at all unusual must be presented to the top echelon; any grievance settlement costing money may have to be approved by a vice president.

General managers of sizable divisions must go to headquarters for capital expenditures above a few hundred dollars, even if these are budgeted. This may, of course, be done to prevent piling up of many small expenditures.

Company presidents must approve the transfer of all production workers in a number of fairly large companies.

Every suggestion award, no matter what size, must be approved by the company president in a number of companies.[4]

There is some indication that decentralization is more widespread than it was fifteen years ago. But this does not mean that the wildly enthusiastic preachments of today will become tomorrow's reality. Donald K. David, former Dean of the Harvard University Graduate School of Business Administration, has pointed out that "delegation without control is irresponsible."[5] Too much decentralization is planned chaos and the antithesis of the very meaning of organized endeavor.

The Problem of Definition and Measurement

The broad statements often made about centralization and decentralization provide little enlightenment about the actual state of affairs. What specific changes occur in the structure of decision making when an organization embarks on a program of decentralization? How does the process of decision making differ in a highly centralized organization as compared with one that is decentralized? To what extent are the various functional areas of management decision making affected by higher or lower degrees of centralization? These questions indicate the importance of developing objective standards that permit quantitative and qualitative measurement.

[4] *Ibid.*
[5] Edward C. Bursk (editor), *The Management Team* (Cambridge: Harvard University Press, 1954), p. 4.

The kind of criteria that can be used to determine the nature and extent of centralization and decentralization is indicated by Ernest Dale.

1. The greater the number of decisions made lower down the management hierarchy.
2. The more important the decisions made lower down the management hierarchy. For example, the greater the sum of capital expenditure that can be approved by the plant manager without consulting anyone else, the greater the degree of decentralization in this field.
3. The more functions affected by decisions made at lower levels. Thus companies which permit only operational decisions to be made at separate branch plants are less decentralized than those which also permit financial and personnel decisions at branch plants.
4. The less checking required on the decision. Decentralization is greatest when no check at all must be made; less when superiors have to be informed of the decision after it has been made; still less if superiors have to be consulted *before* the decision is made. The fewer people to be consulted, and the lower they are on the management hierarchy, the greater the degree of decentralization.[6]

Such criteria make possible a more objective analysis of this aspect of organizational dynamics. However, the difficulties involved in developing a better understanding of managerial behavior should not be underestimated. Things are not always what they seem to be. Actual practice may differ significantly from the practices stipulated in organization manuals or proclaimed by executives. Thus, an organization which appears to be highly centralized may actually practice a high degree of decentralization on an informal basis. Many of the personal relationships between executives have subtle and subjective qualities that cannot be readily translated into objective terms.

What is the proper degree of centralization or decentralization? The answer to this question will vary under different conditions. Some organizations achieve more effective management by a higher degree of centralization. Others attain the same goal by greater decentralization. Some of the factors that influence the extent to which decision making is delegated are considered here.

The Process of Delegation: Problems and Limitations

Delegation becomes necessary when the workload of an executive position exceeds the physical and psychological capacity of the executive. The delegation process reduces the executive workload, but it also adds to the workload by increasing the number of subordinates or span of manage-

[6] Dale, *op. cit.,* p. 107.

ment. This process can continue until the workload that evolves from an increasing span of management exceeds the executive's capacity to carry the burden. Additional levels of management become necessary when this limit is reached.

The superior's responsibility is not absolved by the act of delegation. Delegation involves taking a risk on the capability of subordinates.[7] This risk cannot be entirely avoided, but it can be mitigated by exercising some degree of supervision over the activities of the subordinate. Decentralization is greater or less to the extent that executives are willing to delegate important decision-making responsibilities and exercise a minimum of supervision and control.

An important argument for greater decentralization is the need to develop initiative and self-reliance among subordinates. Many executives believe that the subordinate should be constantly challenged by greater responsibility. Sears, Roebuck and Company has deliberately followed a policy of creating long spans of management, which forces greater delegation and restricts the amount of supervision. Such a policy gives the executive more freedom of action and throws him on his own resources. It tends to weed out those who do not have the necessary potential and promotes the development of experienced and dynamic executives.

The extent to which a policy of decentralization can be carried out may be limited by the personality of the executive. The psychological make-up of some executives inhibits their willingness to delegate decision-making prerogatives. Henry Ford, Sr., for example, felt that he had to fit every piece into the puzzle. Having built a "billion dollar" corporation from a very humble beginning, he disliked giving anyone else a part of what he considered to be a "one-man show." He delegated decision-making responsibilities in the most haphazard fashion and frequently reversed subordinates without consulting them.

A refusal to delegate may also be prompted by the degree of risk involved. As Ernest Dale has written, "hard times and increased competition may foster centralization."[8] The organization's ability to absorb a mistake by a subordinate may be greatly reduced under such circumstances. As a consequence, the top executives may exercise more decision-making prerogatives than would otherwise be necessary and increase the extent to which subordinates are supervised.

The lack of competent executives frequently explains a reluctance to delegate. Although decentralization often enhances the development of executive talent, it is not always possible to make a silk purse out of a

---

[7] A discussion of some of the fine points of delegation is found in: Bursk, *op. cit.*
[8] Ernest Dale, "Centralization Versus Decentralization," *Advanced Management,* Vol. 20, No. 6, June 1955, p. 13.

sow's ear. A policy of decentralization, even under the most favorable circumstances, cannot be implemented overnight. Some executives do not have the ability to assume additional responsibility and have to be gradually removed through the retirement system or induced resignation. Younger executives generally require extensive supervision by experienced superiors before they can be given more responsibility.

Uniformity and Diversity of Conditions and Policy

A higher degree of centralization is generally more workable with uniform operating and environmental conditions. The experience of the Fisher Body Division of the General Motors Corporation is a good case in point.[9] This division manufactures bodies for the automotive divisions, such as Buick, Oldsmobile, and Chevrolet. Although the various body makes and styles differ in design and specification, the basic method of manufacturing is essentially the same. Before World War II, Fisher Body operated on a highly centralized basis, and relatively minor operating matters in the widely dispersed plants had to be referred to division headquarters for approval. This mode of management was significantly changed during World War II when the division divided into five product subdivisions, each of which produced one of the five major wartime products. The managers of the subdivisions were given greater freedom from the dictates of division management. As Peter Drucker has observed, they were "in pretty much the same position as the manager of a General Motors Division."[10] The change from the peacetime production of a single final product to the production of several distinct wartime products was undoubtedly a major consideration in Fisher Body's decision to decentralize. The resulting diversity in the nature of operations made highly centralized decision making more difficult.

Geographical decentralization sometimes creates an impetus toward greater managerial decentralization. Significant differences in local conditions tend to reduce the applicability of centralized decisions, which may impose a greater uniformity of policy than is warranted by differences in customer preferences, state and local laws, weather conditions, and business customs. The difficulty that can result from a failure to recognize such differences is illustrated by a situation described by Edwin R. Embree.

In a little school just outside Baton Rouge, Louisiana, the teacher had been hearing a class read a lesson on birds in one of the standard textbooks. To drive home a point from the lesson, she asked a boy, "When do the robins come?"

[9] Peter F. Drucker, *Concept of the Corporation* (New York: The John Day Company, 1946), pp. 120–122.
[10] *Ibid.*, p. 120.

The pupil promptly answered, "In the fall."

"Now, Jimmie," urged the teacher, "read the lesson carefully again."

After he had droned out the text a second time, she said cheerily, "Now, Jimmie, when do the robins come?"

More hesitantly and sullenly he answered again, "The robins come in the fall." "James, James," shouted the teacher, "read that lesson again. Now tell me when do the robins come?"

Almost in tears the boy finally answered, "The robins come in the spring."

And so they do—in Boston where the text was written. But in Louisiana, just in order to avoid the northern winter, they come in the fall, as the boy well knew.[11]

Managerial decisions made in Boston may similarly fail to take into account unique conditions facing a plant manager in Baton Rouge, Louisiana.

The advantages of standardization and specialization may dictate a greater uniformity of policy through centralization. The problem is to balance these advantages with those that may be gained by adapting to a dissimilarity of conditions. Lower levels of management often prefer more freedom of action in dealing with local problems. However, good policy at this level may be bad policy from an organizational point of view. The symmetry of the forest is not always apparent to one who views the individual trees.

A higher degree of centralization is sometimes imposed by external considerations. Employer and industry-wide collective bargaining has reduced the discretion that can be given to lower levels of management in the area of industrial relations. Modern communication facilities, such as television, tend to promote greater centralization in the areas of advertising and sales promotion. The size of business organizations with which a firm deals may also be important in this respect. The fact that raw materials are obtained from a large supplier may induce greater centralization over the purchasing function. Centralization of financial and accounting matters has been made necessary by Federal taxes and regulations.

The Problem of Size

The relationship between the size of an enterprise and its economic efficiency has been the subject of much speculation by economists and management experts. Economic theory indicates three phases of develop-

[11] Edwin R. Embree, "Can College Graduates Read?" *The Saturday Review of Literature*, Vol. 18, No. 12, July 16, 1938, p. 4.

ment as a firm increases in size. During the first phase of growth, greater specialization of capital and personnel and a better utilization of indivisible resources result in increasing economic returns.[12] After the firm is sufficiently large to take full advantage of these economies, it may enter a phase during which further growth results in constant rather than increasing returns. An increase in the scale of operations of 20 per cent will bring about an equal percentage of additional output. Eventually, however, further increases in size may bring about decreasing economic returns. After this point is reached, the percentage increase in output will be lower than the corresponding rate of growth.

The reason generally given for decreasing returns is that an increase in enterprise size beyond a certain point reduces managerial efficiency.[13] Increases in the scale of operations necessitate a corresponding expansion of the management hierarchy. A relatively larger number of executives is required, and the vertical and horizontal relationships become more complex. For a time the advantages of managerial specialization tend to increase efficiency, but the hierarchy cannot be infinitely expanded without creating conditions that lead to serious problems. Communication becomes more difficult as more levels of management are added. Top executives are farther removed from operating conditions and are generally forced to make decisions on the basis of information relayed by other executives. The number of communication centers is increased, which tends to create a greater distortion of information and delay the transmission of decisions. Effective control and coordination become more difficult, and morale may suffer as executives become smaller fish in a bigger pool. These and other factors, the argument goes, eventually cause a decline in economic efficiency, which serves as an automatic check on bigness in a competitive environment.

Empirical studies have not been particularly successful in substantiating the inevitability of decreasing returns to scale. Many American industrial corporations have challenged the concept by growing bigger. Some have doubled and tripled in size during the past ten years. Sixty of them have

[12] An indivisible resource may be roughly defined as one which cannot be divided into smaller units without complete or partial loss of efficiency from either a cost or technical standpoint. For example, the radar installation on a large ship is much the same as that on a smaller ship. A railroad must construct trackage of sufficient gauge to handle its rolling stock even if only one train a week is scheduled. A grocery store must have at least one clerk even though he may be busy only half the time.

[13] A distinction should be made between the concept of decreasing returns to scale and the law of diminishing returns. Diminishing returns results from combining additional variable factors with one fixed factor. The eventual lack of proportionality in factor combination causes a decline in output.

assets exceeding 1 billion dollars, and more than 80 have sales in excess of that amount. However, bigness is not a product of business activity alone. The size of military, religious, trade union, and governmental organizations has in many instances exceeded that of the business corporation.

An argument that the big business corporation is operating under conditions of suboptimal efficiency is not supported by existing data. However, such organizations have had to overcome a number of difficult managerial problems in coping with the problem of size. Many of them have drastically changed their management organization to solve coordination, communication, and control problems. Product and territorial departmentation were used to divide big organizations into relatively autonomous operating units. Staff organization helped reduce the coordination problems that often accompany functional specialization. The delegation of a major share of the responsibility for making operating decisions to lower managerial levels was another approach. Such organizational and managerial innovations have been highly instrumental in reducing the applicability of the theory of decreasing returns to scale.[14]

Although decentralization has been particularly advantageous in large organizations, it may also promote more effective management in medium-sized and small organizations. Size is an important consideration in determining the appropriate degree of decentralization, but it should not be viewed as the only consideration.

The Problem of Communication

The management hierarchy may be viewed as a structure of communication centers through which decisional and control information is transmitted to and from the performance level. The volume of information that flows through this system is closely related to the extent to which decision making is centralized. Decisions made at the apex of the hierarchy involve more communication centers than those originating at lower levels. Too much centralization can easily overload the system and create bottlenecks in the flow of information. This problem is amplified with increases in the size of the management hierarchy, and it may significantly reduce the speed of decision making and the ability to adapt to dynamic operating conditions. A further difficulty is that information is frequently distorted as it passes through a long maze of hierarchical positions.

---

[14] Large corporations take full cognizance of the relationship between operating efficiency and plant size and recognize that specialization in certain areas has limits. At the same time, the size of the entire enterprise has made possible more intensive specialization in some areas, such as research and development.

Coordination and Control

As was pointed out earlier in this chapter, decentralization always involves some degree of centralized planning and control. Every level of management below the chief executive is subject to decisions made at a higher level. Such an arrangement is necessary to coordinate activities and achieve an organizational unity of purpose. The freedom of action given to executives through decentralization is always restricted. The executive is on his own, but never completely. His situation is similar to that of the driver of an automobile on a public highway, who may drive as he pleases within the limits set by traffic regulations. Decentralization diminishes the amount of direct supervision exercised by a superior over the activities of a subordinate, but this reduction in personal supervision is replaced by other forms of control, such as budgetary, profit, and cost controls. Such controls are an essential feature of decentralization; without them there would be far less inclination to delegate important decision-making prerogatives.

Executive Development

Industrial and business leaders have often lamented the dearth of executive material, yet a part of the responsibility for this situation must be placed upon their doorsteps. Too many executives have failed to see that a puppet can never become a puppeteer. The experience of recent wars indicates the existence of a large reservoir of potential leadership material. A large part of military leadership below the division level came from men who were barely out of their teens. Many of these youthful company, battalion, and regimental commanders were eminently successful in the discharge of great responsibility. To be sure, considerable risk was involved in such an extensive delegation of decision-making prerogatives to an inexperienced officer corps, and some officers did not have the capacity for the responsibility imposed upon them. Failures as well as successes must be placed upon the scoreboard, but the over-all results probably exceeded expectations.

The experience of industrial establishments with a history of decentralization has been similar to that of the military. Although formal training is an important factor in executive development, experience molds the final product and gives a subordinate a chance to prove that he can make the grade. A willingness to risk delegation to lower levels reduces the hazards of promotion and helps provide a reservoir of qualified executives. It also helps indicate which executives do not have the capacity to assume greater responsibility.

Managerial Specialization

Centralization is sometimes favored because it permits a higher degree of managerial specialization. This argument undoubtedly has validity in the case of small enterprise. The advantages of specialization are generally greater than the disadvantages that may evolve from a higher degree of centralization. However, the net advantages that may be derived from specialization diminish rather rapidly as the size of the firm is increased. The coordination, control, and communication difficulties that tend to accompany centralized decision making by functional specialists are important elements in reversing the process. Large organizations have generally turned to product and territorial departmentation and decentralization to solve the problems of overspecialization. Many medium-sized and some small firms, as Urwick has suggested, can benefit from greater decentralization along similar lines.[15] An integral part of such a decentralization program has been the development of functional staff and service departments to advise and assist those who make the decisions. However, it should not be assumed that all centralized decision making by functional specialists has been eliminated. The most avid practitioners of decentralization on a product or territorial basis have retained important functional decision-making prerogatives at the top management level. A reason is that some forms of specialization become possible only in large organizations. Also, the point of decreasing returns from specialization is not reached at the same time in all areas of managerial decision making.

Centralization and Decentralization of Functional Areas

Decentralization has generally been accompanied by high degrees of centralization in some functional areas of decision making. In some instances, organizations have recentralized functions that were previously decentralized. To what extent has decision making been decentralized in various functional areas? What are the factors that influence policy on this subject? The answers to these and related questions form the content of this section. The discussion will be limited to the more important functions.[16]

[15] L. Urwick, *The Load on Top Management—Can It Be Reduced?* (London: Urwick, Orr & Partners, Ltd., 1954), pp. 30–31.

[16] Much of the material in this section is based on Ernest Dale's analysis of the findings of an American Management Association survey on decentralization in functional areas. *Planning and Developing the Company Organization Structure, op. cit.,* pp. 188–195.

Production Management

A number of factors promote greater decentralization in the production area. The size of a manufacturing plant cannot be expanded infinitely without a reduction in efficiency. The existence of more than one plant, particularly when accompanied by territorial dispersion, gives impetus toward decentralization. Centralized decision making is also made more difficult when radically different production processes are involved. The production of different products in the same or different plants frequently leads to extensive decentralization on a departmental or plant basis. Another consideration is that immediate action is often necessary to prevent a breakdown in manufacturing operations. A delay in decision may cause a chain reaction of difficulties in an integrated production situation, and an intimate knowledge of operating conditions is necessary for effective action. These and related factors have resulted in extensive delegation over strictly production activities. However, production executives are usually held accountable for results through centralized accounting and statistical controls. Centralized staff and service departments in such areas as research and development, engineering, and product design also impose direct and indirect limitations on decision making by operating executives.

Sales Management

One writer has concluded that decentralization is more extensive in sales management than in any other area of management.[17] The selling activity is frequently dispersed throughout a large territory, far removed from headquarters. The impact of regional differences upon sales promotion plans and practices and a diversity in products and product lines tend to induce decentralization. Differences in the types of customers, such as industrial users, retailers, and ultimate consumers, are also contributing factors, and the personal relationships involved in the sales activity reduce the applicability of centrally determined standards and procedures. Such problems account for the widespread use of branch sales offices differentiated on the basis of territory, product, or customer. Decentralization in sales management is generally accompanied by centralized control over results.

Although many factors promote decentralization in sales management, centralization does not always come out second best. A high degree of centralization is frequently found in enterprises in which the customer

[17] John A. Murphy, "Why Decentralization Takes Root in Sales Management," *Sales Management,* Vol. 57, No. 10, November 10, 1946, p. 80.

comes to the salesman, such as department stores and other retail establishments. Extensive use is also made of standardized sales promotion plans and presentations prepared by headquarters, and sales managers are limited in the discretion they can exercise over such matters as prices and discounts, credit policy, and the compensation of salesmen.

Financial Management

Decision making about financial matters tends to be highly centralized, even when a great deal of decentralization exists in other areas. There seems to be more reluctance to delegate responsibility in this field than in any other. An explanation is that the relationship between property rights and managerial power is legally expressed in financial arrangements. Any financial decisions that directly or indirectly concern this relationship are generally made by top management. The importance of this aspect of the finance function probably inhibits delegation over other financial matters— at least this would seem to be an important psychological factor. Financial information is the common denominator through which objectives and plans are expressed, and it provides a means for measuring the performance of executives and operating departments. Internal financial policy and control tend to become more important in larger and more decentralized organizations. The reduction in direct decision making and supervision by top management must be replaced by a mechanism through which overall planning and control can be instituted. Decentralization over operating matters and centralization in the financial area would seem to be mutually compatible forces.

The Industrial Relations Function

A majority of chief executives who contributed to a study by Baker and France were of the opinion that industrial relations generally requires more centralization than operating functions.[18] The study also indicated that centralization in the industrial relations area has increased during the past decade. Industrial relations policy is generally made at the top-management level, with centralized staff specialists assuming the responsibility for the standards and procedures necessary to effectuate policy. Not infrequently, relatively minor personnel matters in the operating areas are referred to higher levels by formal and informal means. Several considerations seem to dominate top management's preference for greater centrali-

[18] Baker and France, *op. cit.* The material in this section is derived from this comprehensive and excellent study. Industrial relations is broadly defined to include both personnel administration and labor relations.

zation in the area of industrial relations. One is the magnitude of the financial resources involved in wage and related decisions; another is management's trusteeship responsibility to the stockholder; and still another is the possible adverse effects of a lack of uniform policy upon motivation and morale. The existence of large national unions and the size of the bargaining unit in collective bargaining have reinforced the need for uniformity. Furthermore, many of the problems in the industrial relations area are matters of public policy.

Purchasing

There seems to be an absence of extreme tendencies either toward centralization or decentralization in the area of purchasing. A wide geographical dispersion of plants, a diversity of product lines, and the need to purchase locally are some of the factors that induce greater decentralization. However, an organization with decentralized purchasing frequently continues to purchase some materials centrally. The Ford Motor Company, which has delegated important purchasing powers to operating divisions, buys steel, glass, and tires on a centralized basis. Decentralized purchasing is usually accompanied by centrally determined standards and procedures. A common control technique is the audit of vendors' invoices and the records of decentralized purchasing points.

Advertising

Many factors contribute toward a centralization of decision making in advertising. Particularly important are the large amounts of money spent for advertising and the close relationship between advertising and success or failure. National advertising employing television networks and publications with nationwide circulation tends to promote centralization. Top management may also be inclined to carefully scrutinize the advertising program because it influences the status and prestige of the organization. Considerable mutuality exists between advertising and public relations.

Traffic Management

Traffic management is usually decentralized when shipments are made directly from branch plants to customers and when suppliers ship directly to the plants. Such decentralization often operates within centrally determined policies with respect to rates, routing, types of carriers, and related matters. Centralization tends to be greater in highly integrated production and distribution systems that require a coordinated flow of parts, subassemblies, and products.

The General Motors Corporation: Decentralization in Practice

The General Motors Corporation is the largest manufacturing company in the world.[19] Almost 40 divisions and subsidiaries employing over 700,000 people in some 150 plants produced 20 billion dollars' worth of goods and services in 1967. Its production and distribution facilities extend beyond the borders of the United States into more than a score of foreign nations. In addition to five domestic makes of automobiles, its consumer and industrial products include trucks and buses, Diesel locomotives and engines, earth-moving equipment, household appliances, aircraft engines, and tanks.

General Motors was organized in 1908 by William C. Durant, a man whose optimism and boldness accurately portrayed the future of the horseless carriage in American social and economic life. But Durant failed to give his bold ventures financial and operating stability. Twice during his regime the corporation suffered serious financial difficulties, the last of which resulted in a change in managerial control. The man who was largely responsible for the management philosophy that was to give Durant's dream an even greater reality was Alfred P. Sloan, Jr., who assumed the presidency in 1923. Some of the salient features of this philosophy are highlighted below.

The Formal Structure

The organizational structure of the General Motors Corporation is shown in Figures 8-1, 8-2, and 8-3. Viewed in sequence these organization charts present the management hierarchy from the top through the plant level. They also show the basic types of departmentation used to group activities and differentiate managerial responsibility. The major operating divisions (Figure 8-1) are divided on the basis of product; a functional plan of organization (Figure 8-2) is generally employed at the division

[19] Much of this section is based on information and material received from the General Motors Corporation. Another important source was Peter Drucker's *Concept of the Corporation, op. cit.,* a study of the managerial policies and organization of the General Motors Corporation.

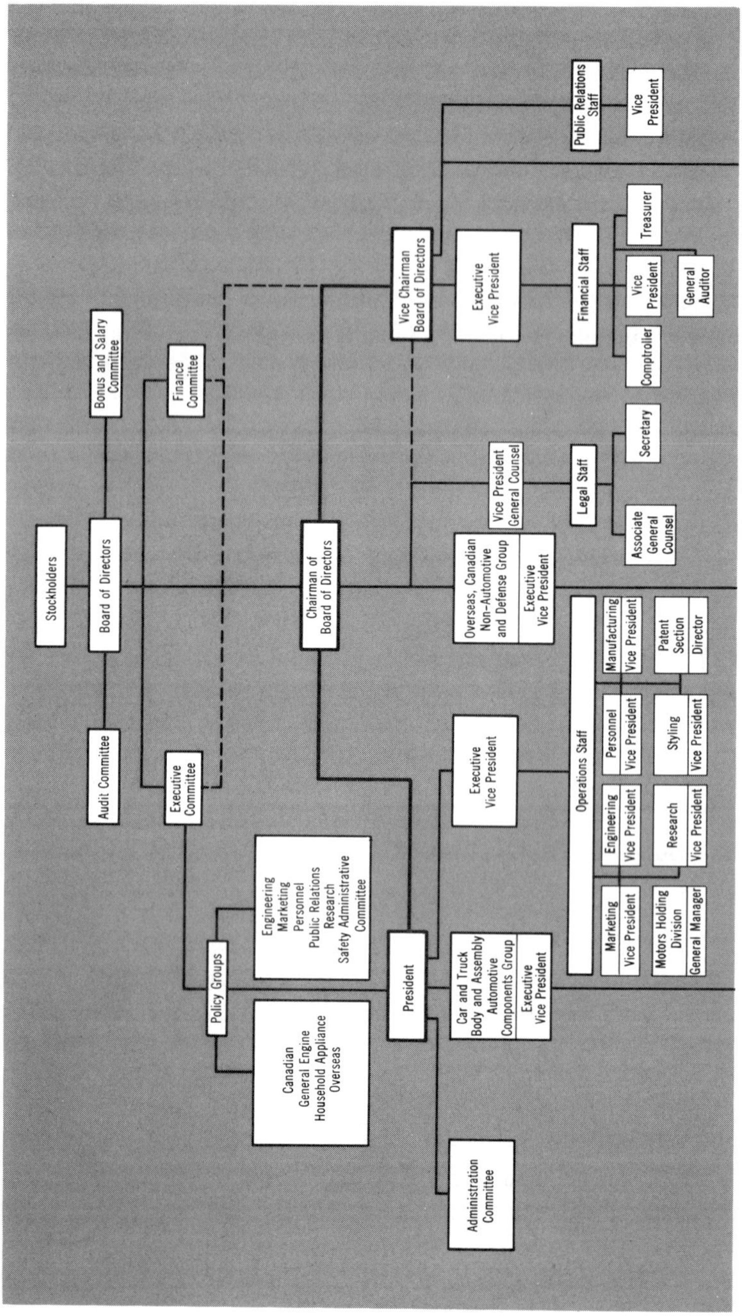
Stockholders
Board of Directors
Audit Committee
Bonus and Salary Committee
Finance Committee
Executive Committee
Chairman of Board of Directors
Vice Chairman Board of Directors
Policy Groups
Engineering
Marketing
Personnel
Public Relations
Research
Safety Administrative
Committee
Canadian
General Engine
Household Appliance
Overseas
President
Administration Committee
Executive Vice President
Car and Truck
Body and Assembly
Automotive
Components Group
Executive Vice President
Overseas, Canadian
Non-Automotive
and Defense Group
Executive Vice President
Vice President General Counsel
Legal Staff
Associate General Counsel
Secretary
Executive Vice President
Financial Staff
Comptroller
Vice President
Treasurer
General Auditor
Public Relations Staff
Vice President
Operations Staff
Marketing
Vice President
Engineering
Vice President
Personnel
Vice President
Manufacturing
Vice President
Motors Holding Division
General Manager
Research
Vice President
Styling
Vice President
Patent Section
Director

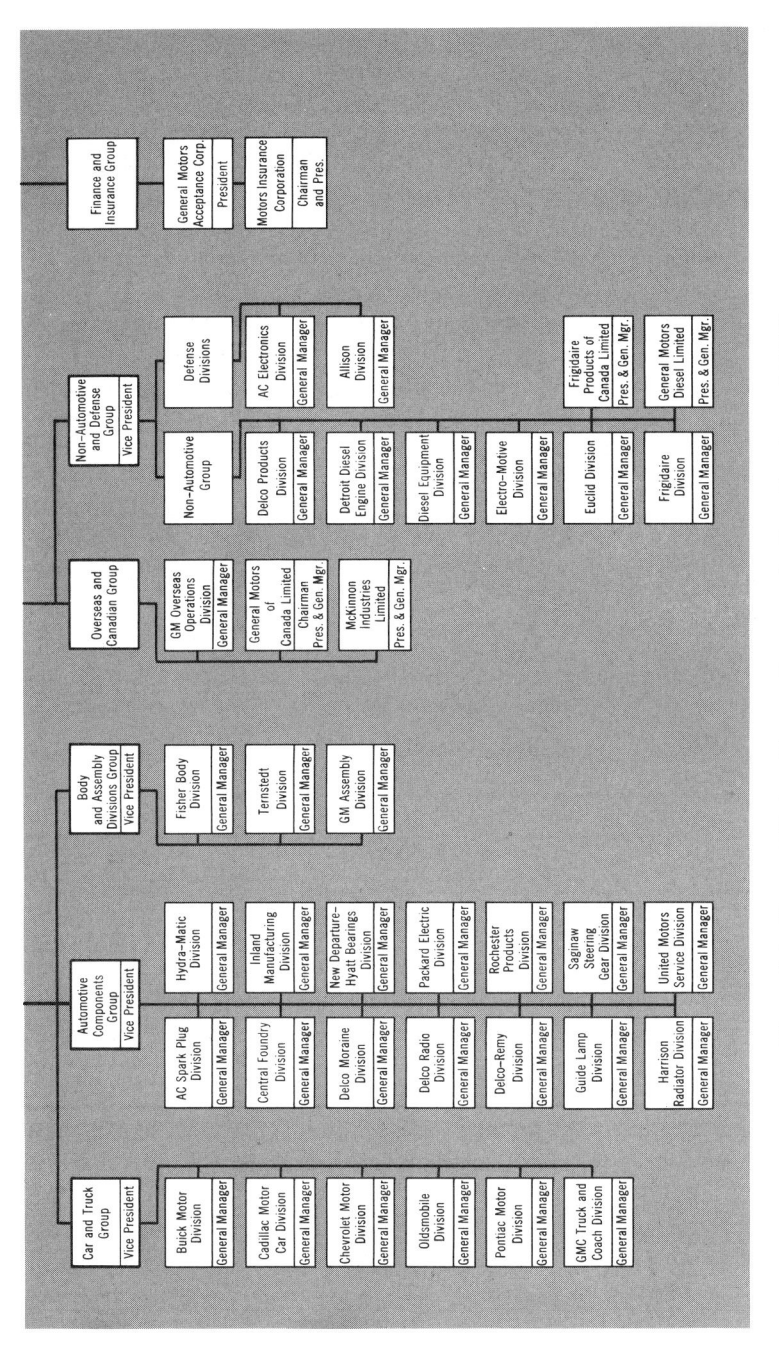

Figure 8-1. General Motors Corporation organization. Courtesy of GMC.

level; and divisions allocate production to plants on a product, territorial, and process basis. Figure 8-3 shows a standard organization chart for a plant of the Fisher Body Division. In divisions with only one plant, some of the positions found in the charts in Figures 8-2 and 8-3 would not appear. Three basic elements of the managerial structure will now be briefly described: (1) the line organization; (2) staff and service facilities, (3) the committee system.

The operating divisions are headed by general managers, who have wide discretion in planning division programs. The group executives are representatives of central management and serve in a liaison and advisory capacity to the division managers in their groups. In exercising these functions, they work closely with the executive vice-presidents, who report to the president and the chairman of the board. The president, who is designated as the chief operating officer, has responsibility for major operating phases of the business. The chairman of the board, the chief executive officer, has responsibilities for operations through the president and an executive vice-president, and has particular responsibility, with the assistance of a vice-chairman, for legal, financial, and public relations policies and practices.

As noted in Chapter 7, General Motors has four staffs: operations, financial, legal, and public relations. The activities of the staff groups are coordinated by an executive vice-president or a vice-president. The staffs provide advisory, informational, and other services to the operating divisions and central management. Staff executives have functional decision-making prerogatives over certain matters and participate in policy formulation through policy groups that make recommendations to the executive committee.

Top corporation policy is developed through the executive and the finance committees. Operating and staff executives participate in policy formulation through membership on four product and six functional product groups or subcommittees. Suggestions and recommendations from these groups are presented to the executive committee. The administration committee makes recommendations on manufacturing, marketing, and other activities to the president and considers problems that may be referred to it by the president or the executive committee. The finance committee, the other top policy-making body, is charged with the financial policies and affairs of the corporation. This committee and the executive committee are responsible to the board of directors. Overlapping memberships together with formal and informal contacts promote coordination in the activities of the two committees.

The Extent of Decentralization

Several GMC executives have estimated that 95 per cent of all decisions are made by the division managers.[20] Although such a measurement offers a number of definitional difficulties,[21] it does reflect a high degree of autonomy at the division level. Subject to broad policy control and centralization in certain areas, the division manager is much like the head of an independent business enterprise. The primary responsibility for planning the division's program and progress rests with him. His decision-making prerogatives encompass the major functional areas, such as manufacturing, distribution, design and development, purchasing, advertising, employment, and public relations. A further index of autonomy is that the division manager can refuse to purchase from another GMC division if an outside supplier can supply the same item at a lower cost.

Does the practice of extensive decentralization extend below the division level? Peter Drucker's study indicates that in general not all divisions have carried decentralization as far as has the corporation.[22] Some divisions have practiced a high degree of centralization, and a few senior executives believe that decentralization is more efficient only under special circumstances. One reason for such differences in practice and philosophy is that the management problems in one division may differ significantly from those of another. Differences in product, location, history, and size are important in this respect. A higher degree of centralization within a division would not seem to be incompatible with the top-management policy of decentralization. Although the corporation would probably experience serious difficulties with extensive centralization, an argument that the same proposition applies to every division would be difficult to support. Some of the more centralized divisions have shown themselves to be sufficient producers. There is no available evidence to show that such divisions have created any serious disrupting influences in the over-all managerial structure or process. One might even say that the diversity of division practices shows that top management means business when it speaks of decentralization. In other words, a division manager is not ordered to pursue a policy of decentralization if he gets better results from an opposite policy.

[20] Drucker, *op. cit.*, p. 56.

[21] One definitional problem is that all decisions are not equally important. Also, the locus of decision making is not always clear. If a decision evolves from a meeting of a central management executive and a division manager, who actually made the decision?

[22] Drucker, *op. cit.*, pp. 119–122.

Centralized Policy Formulation

Central management formulates top-corporate operating and financial policy. It establishes a broad framework within which the divisions are expected to operate. It plans the total manufacturing program and determines the amount of capital that is allocated to each division. It coordinates the activities of the divisions and provides a unity of purpose throughout the corporation. Perhaps the most important function of central management, as Peter Drucker has pointed out, is the responsibility of planning the long-term growth and development of the enterprise.[23]

In addition to the function of over-all corporate planning, central management has retained decision-making prerogatives for certain aspects of division operations. For example, it assigns minimum production quotas and sets a price range for major product lines. Contract negotiation with unions is essentially a top-management affair, and the appointment of top division executives is subject to central-management veto. Centrally determined standards and procedures are used in a number of areas, such as accounting and position classification for salaried employees.

The Integration Process

Decentralization has not precluded the development of management teamwork and cooperation throughout the entire enterprise. Several features of the system promote this kind of integration. The group executives perform an important liaison function between the operating divisions and the central management. They represent the central management and act as advisors to the divisions under their jurisdiction. The operations and financial staffs promote unity through the advice and services rendered to the operating divisions. The influence of the staff executives in operating matters is enhanced by participation in top-policy formulation. The group executives and many of the division general managers actively participate in central-management policy determination through membership on top level committees. Division managers are given an opportunity to express their opinions before a policy becomes effective.[24] Suggestions and objections from operating executives are never taken lightly, but central management does not make policy by polling the division executives. It may completely disregard their views and adopt an opposite policy, but, if it does, central management explains the reasons for doing so. Participation, persuasion, and understanding, rather than line commands, define the

[23] *Ibid.*, p. 51.
[24] *Ibid.*, p. 62.

normal relationship between divisional and central management. This formally established system of communication and authority is facilitated by numerous informal interactions among General Motors executives. For example, a major executive in one of the divisions receives frequent phone calls from former subordinates, who now hold responsible positions in two other divisions. He talks to them about their problems and gives them his point of view, but he emphasizes that the relationship is personal and that his advice and suggestions have no official status.

Centralized Controls

The group executives, the staff sections, and the committee system provide the central management with information about the activities of operating divisions. However, too much control through direct supervision presents the risk of reducing the actual degree of decentralization. Division managers may become less prone to make their own decisions and rely upon the formal and informal advice and suggestions of central-management executives. The result of too much supervision might well be "creeping centralization" and control through subjective personality-oriented standards. Such potential disruptive influences are reduced by the development of a number of objective yardsticks to measure the performance of divisional executives.

The relative performance of the operating divisions is measured in several ways. One yardstick is a costing system that eliminates extraneous factors, such as cyclical fluctuation, as much as possible. Second, the rate of return on capital invested in each division is compared. Finally, an analysis is made of the competitive standing of the products of each division in the market. The performance of divisions that sell principally to other GMC divisions is measured by their ability to supply these divisions at a lower cost than outside suppliers. Every attempt is made in the application of these standards to eliminate the impact of forces that cannot be controlled by the division managers. Thus, a significant reduction in sales resulting from a general decline in the demand for automobiles is not assumed to be a sign of managerial inefficiency. The division manager is held accountable only if the share of the total market going to a division begins to decline.

In addition to reducing the risks of delegation, control through objective performance standards is an important reason for the success of the General Motors system. It tends to reduce infringement by top management upon the decision-making prerogatives delegated to the division level. Division managers could hardly be held responsible for the results if too many important decisions were actually made by central management.

Such controls also reduce the need for division executives to cater to the whims and fancies of top executives. Clever political manipulations and subjective evaluations are less likely to play a dominant role in the relationships between superiors and subordinates. Success or failure is a matter of objective record that cannot be readily changed by personal likes or dislikes.

The Importance of Centralization

The emphasis given in recent years to the philosophy of decentralization should not cause the student of management to neglect the importance of centralization. The failure to develop a sufficient degree of centralization may have serious consequences. In spite of all the talk about decentralization, the General Motors Corporation faced this problem during its early history. Its former president, Harlow H. Curtice, has described the situation.

Prior to 1921 there existed no real concept of sound management in General Motors. Operations were neither integrated nor coordinated. There was no consistent policy with respect to product programs. Frequently poor judgment was exercised in making capital expenditures and establishing production schedules. The Corporation did not have a properly developed research and engineering staff nor any sound concept of budgetary control. The central administration did not exercise adequate control over the operations of individual divisions. There were wide variations in the competence of divisional managements. In short, the corporation was unorganized and the individual units largely out of control.[25]

Top management cannot simply sit back and watch the scores recorded by the financial and statistical control systems. It must play a positive and active role in the formulation and implementation of policies that concern the welfare of the organization as a whole. It cannot assume that a policy of *laissez faire* will somehow promote the best interests of the organization. Decentralization does give a subordinate greater freedom, but it is never freedom without restrictions from above. Decentralization without centralization is an invitation to internecine warfare. Organizations cannot survive without coordination and a unity of purpose.

[25] Portion of a statement by Harlow H. Curtice before the Subcommittee on Antitrust and Monopoly of the U.S. Senate Committee on the Judiciary, December 2, 1955. This point is also made by Alfred P. Sloan, Jr., in *My Years with General Motors* (Garden City, N.Y.: Doubleday & Company, Inc., 1964), p. 46.

Decentralization in Other Organizations

Other large and medium-sized organizations which have developed a system of management similar to that of General Motors are the Ford Motor Company; Sears Roebuck; Du Pont; International Harvester; Standard Oil Company (New Jersey); Unilever; J. C. Penney; General Electric; Sylvania; and the Sperry Corporation. However, it should not be assumed that these and other companies have simply copied the General Motors prototype. Every organization has developed its own particular version of decentralized management. For example, the vast Unilever combine, which operates in some forty countries, uses roving directors to keep in touch with its widely dispersed operating units. Some companies make greater use of committees than others, and differences can also be noted in the extent to which certain functions have been centralized or decentralized. Historical development, industry differences, and executive personality are some of the factors that cause variations in the manner in which a philosophy of decentralization is put into practice.

An Historical Perspective and Prospects for the Future

Strategy and Structure

Some interesting and useful insights on the development of American industrial enterprises are presented in an historical analysis by Professor Alfred D. Chandler, Jr.[26] Chandler's basic thesis is that organizational structure follows managerial strategy. Strategy involves the determination of long-term organizational objectives together with the adoption of plans and the resource allocation necessary to achieve them. Changes in structure do not immediately come about after a change in strategy. The vested interests of executives in an existing structure, a failure to see beyond operating problems, and a lack of sufficient knowledge to make necessary structural changes are some of the reasons for this state of affairs. But appropriate changes in structure cannot be delayed for a long period if an enterprise is not to become highly inefficient in the utilization of resources.

Chandler was primarily concerned with structural changes in four companies—Du Pont, General Motors, Standard Oil (New Jersey), and

---

[26] Alfred D. Chandler, Jr., *Strategy and Structure* (Garden City, N.Y.: Doubleday & Company, Inc., 1966—originally published by MIT Press in 1962).

Sears Roebuck. He was able to trace two periods of organizational growth and structural change. An initial period of rapid growth brought on by expanding product markets or a consolidation of smaller enterprises into larger ones. This growth was followed by the development of more efficient organizational structures. Then came a second period of growth as the enterprise reached the limits set by existing markets. Executives sought to overcome these limits through product diversification and territorial dispersion. This strategy gave rise to still another major structural change resulting in the kind of decentralization described earlier in this chapter.

The four companies studied by Chandler developed similar decentralized structures, but they did not all have the same problems or reach the solution in the same way. Du Pont moved from a centralized to a decentralized structure to contend with a strategy of aggressive product diversification after World War I. On the other hand, the problem of General Motors was too little centralized control over a diversity of functions and products. The solution was the Sloan organizational plan which called for centralized control with decentralized operations. Sears Roebuck moved from an unsuccessful decentralized structure to centralization and then to its present highly successful decentralized structure. Standard Oil (New Jersey) made successive structural adjustments on an *ad hoc* basis without a plan like that of Sloan at GMC.

A major determinant in the move to decentralization on the part of these and other companies was the extent to which they developed strategies that gave rise to product diversification and territorial dispersion. But it should not be assumed that the kind of structure that would best relate to this strategy was readily apparent. There was much floundering about and many uncertainties as to what to do. A problem in this respect was that higher executives were sometimes so immersed in immediate operating problems that they failed to see the implications of long-term strategic changes. The new decentralized structures clearly differentiated operating responsibilities from strategic planning.

Information Technology and Organizational Structure

An important lesson of the past is that management should not neglect the possible structural significance of such major innovations as information technology. The changes that may eventually evolve are by no means certain at this stage of development. Much of the impact of information technology to date has had tactical rather than strategic implications. But the future may bring about structural changes as profound as those that followed the strategy of product diversification.

Whether information technology will cause business and other organizations with decentralized structures to move to centralization has been the subject of a wide diversity of opinion. The matter has not been resolved by empirical research or industrial experience. It is impossible at this point to detect a decisive move in either direction.[27]

The basic argument of those who anticipate a trend toward centralization is that computerized informational systems will provide top management with sufficient information for centralized planning and control. A contrary view is that something more than information is involved in the problem of structure. Centralized informational systems do not necessarily mean centralized decision making. As John Dearden has said on the subject:

It is not lack of *information* that has required delegation; it is two other deficiencies: 1. Management lacks the *time* to make all but the important decisions. As the president of a multibillion-dollar corporation told me: "My scarcest resource is my time. I have to allocate my time to those activities where my contribution is greatest. In fact, as a rule of thumb, I try to make no decisions that involve less than a million dollars." 2. Managers are unable to maintain *expertise* in all of the different businesses in which their company is engaged. They cannot, therefore, make as good decisions as the expert *even with the same information*. It is not, therefore, lack of the right kind of information that has made it necessary to delegate authority; it is lack of the knowledge necessary to use the information most effectively.[28]

The fact that computerized informational systems frequently cross company boundaries may bring about consolidations among small and medium-sized enterprises. The large organizations of today may grow even larger as informational innovations make it possible. In other words, the ultimate product of information technology may well be a large increase in the size of business enterprise. Such a development could require a con-

---

[27] Some pertinent literature on the subject: Harold J. Leavitt and Thomas Whisler, "Management in the 1980's," *Harvard Business Review*, Vol. 36, No. 6, November–December 1958, pp. 41–48; George P. Shultz and Thomas L. Whisler (editors), *Management Organization and the Computer* (Glencoe, Ill.: The Free Press, 1960); John F. Burlingame, "Information Technology and Decentralization," *Harvard Business Review*, Vol. 39, No. 6, November–December 1961, pp. 121–126; Rodney H. Brady, "Computers in Top-Level Decision Making," *Harvard Business Review*, Vol. 45, No. 4, July–August 1967, pp. 67–76; John Dearden, "Computers: No Impact on Divisional Control," *Harvard Business Review*, Vol. 45, No. 1, January–February 1967, pp. 99–104; George Kozmetsky and Paul Kircher, *Electronic Computers and Management Control* (New York: McGraw-Hill Book Company, Inc., 1956); Ernest Dale, *The Decision-Making Process in the Commercial Use of High-Speed Computers* (Ithaca: Cornell Studies in Policy and Administration, Cornell University, 1964); William E. Reif, *Computer Technology and Management Organization* (Iowa City: Bureau of Business and Economic Research, 1968).

[28] John Dearden, *op. cit.*, pp. 100–101.

tinuation of decentralization rather than a move toward centralization. It would also necessitate a reexamination of economic and political philosophy; antitrust policy might have to be modified to meet the challenge.

Strategic and Tactical Planning

Perhaps the most important implication of past experiences with organizational planning is that a distinction should be made between strategic and tactical considerations. The organizational changes required for current planning purposes are generally given adequate attention because it is difficult to avoid them. The possible impact of longer-term strategic changes upon organizational structure are many times neglected because they can often be delayed without an immediate decline in profits and frequently because they involve vested interests of executives. Top management should constantly consider the manner in which strategy may affect the organization structure. The strategic as well as the tactical significance of such innovations as information technology should be periodically scrutinized.

SELECTED REFERENCES

Helen Baker and Robert R. France, *Centralization and Decentralization in Industrial Relations.* Princeton, N.J.: Industrial Relations Section, Department of Economics and Sociology, Princeton University, 1954.

Rodney H. Brady, "Computers in Top-Level Decision-Making," *Harvard Business Review,* Vol. 45, No. 4, pp. 67–76 (July–August 1967).

John F. Burlingame, "Information Technology and Decentralization," *Harvard Business Review,* Vol. 39, No. 6, pp. 21–126 (November–December 1961).

Edward C. Bursk (editor), *The Management Team.* Cambridge: Harvard University Press, 1954.

Alfred D. Chandler, Jr., *Strategy and Structure.* Boston: MIT Press, 1962.

Ernest Dale, "Centralization Versus Decentralization," *Advanced Management,* Vol. 20, No. 6, pp. 11–16 (June 1955).

Ernest Dale, *Planning and Developing the Company Organization Structure,* Research Report No. 20, pp. 98–119, 188–195. New York: American Management Association, 1952.

John Dearden, "Computers: No Impact on Divisional Control," *Harvard Business Review,* Vol. 45, No. 1, pp. 99–104 (January–February 1967).

Peter F. Drucker, *Concept of the Corporation,* Chap. 2. New York: The John Day Company, 1946.

H. J. Kruisinga, *The Balance Between Centralization and Decentralization in Managerial Control.* Leiden: H. E. Stenfert Kroese N. V., 1954.

Harold J. Leavitt and Thomas L. Whisler, "Management in the 1980's," *Harvard Business Review,* Vol. 36, No. 6, pp. 41–48 (November–December 1958).

John A. Murphy, "Why Decentralization Takes Root in Sales Management," *Sales Management,* Vol. 57, No. 10, pp. 80 ff. (November 10, 1946).

William H. Newman and James P. Logan, *Management of Expanding Enterprises.* New York: Columbia University Press, 1955.

Problems and Policies of Decentralized Management, General Management Series, No. 154. New York: American Management Association, 1952.

Alfred P. Sloan, Jr., *My Years with General Motors.* Garden City, New York: Doubleday & Company, Inc., 1964.

Perrin Stryker, "The Subtleties of Delegation," *Fortune,* Vol. 51, No. 3, pp. 94 ff. (March 1955).

L. Urwick, *The Load on Top Management—Can It Be Reduced?* London: Urwick, Orr & Partners, Ltd., 1954.

L. G. Wagner, "Computers, Decentralization, and Corporate Control," *California Management Review,* Vol. 9, No. 2, pp. 25–32 (Winter 1966).

Chapter 9

COMMITTEE ORGANIZATION

A committee may be defined as a group of people engaged in the performance of some aspect of the executive function. Committees may be used for informational and advisory purposes, to promote coordination, and to facilitate communication and cooperation. Some committees, which are often referred to as plural executives, exercise decision-making responsibilities.

A survey of executive attitudes on the subject of committee organization might well lead to the frustrating conclusion that committees must be the worst and the best means to achieve a goal. One side of the argument is illustrated by such comments as: the best committee is a three-man committee with two men absent; minutes are taken, but hours are wasted. In spite of such criticism, committees are found in many organizations and, when properly used, are important instruments of managerial action.

The Nature of Committees

Organizational practices indicate a variety of committee types and purposes. Some committees are a formally constituted part of the managerial structure with duly designated functions, procedures, and membership. Other committees are little more than informal gatherings of executives to discuss whatever subjects seem appropriate at the time. Committees cannot always be readily distinguished from the informal interactions that occur among executives; many organizations have the equivalent of a committee system through informal meetings.

Informal "Committee" Action

An informal gathering of executives rarely occurs without some reference to company business. Many organizational problems are solved during coffee breaks, luncheon engagements, golf games, or a round of cocktails. The organizational consequences of such informal meetings and committee meetings may be similar. The difference between the two types of group activities is that the formally designated purpose of a committee is to consider an organizational problem whereas informal meetings evolve from nonorganizational purposes. This distinction frequently involves some fine hairsplitting. A luncheon engagement is a committee meeting if its primary purpose is to discuss company business; it is an informal meeting if its primary purpose is to eat lunch. However, personal and organizational purposes are generally merged and cannot be readily differentiated. Although this chapter is primarily concerned with formally constituted committees, it recognizes that informal meetings frequently serve an equivalent function.

Permanent and Temporary Committees

Some committees are permanent; others have a relatively short life-span. Committees may be created for a special purpose and dissolved when their mission has been accomplished. Permanent or standing committees generally perform a continuing and vital managerial function. The life-span of committees is also influenced by the inclinations of their creators. Executives may delay the dissolution of temporary committees by giving them additional assignments. On the other hand, permanent committees can be dissolved and replaced by another organizational device. Committees sometimes have a propensity to perpetuate their own existence, particularly when membership has high status value to the participants.

Committees and Hierarchical Levels

Committees are used at all levels of the management hierarchy. At the apex of the hierarchy is the board of directors, which is the legally constituted governing body of a corporation. Some boards perform their managerial functions during regular board meetings; others delegate specific prerogatives to special and permanent committees of the board. Committees at the top-management level may also be established by the president and other top-level executives to assist them in the performance of their managerial functions. The extent to which committees are used in the major operating divisions or departments may vary a great deal. Some executives appoint committees at the drop of a hat; others take a negative attitude toward committees. When company policy dictates that committees be used, executives frequently place the imprint of their own personality upon this policy. A few may simply go through the motions and let the committees wither on the vine. At the plant level, joint employee-management and union-management committees are common.

Meeting Places and Committee Procedures

Committee meetings are held in a variety of physical settings, such as conference rooms, offices, the exective dining room, and the employee cafeteria. Organizations sometimes hold top-level conferences at resort hotels in distant places. A similar diversity can be found in committee procedures and methods of operation. Although most committees have a chairman, the role of the chairman differs a great deal. Some chairmen have only one vote; others have the right to veto committee action; and still others make the final decision after hearing the deliberations of the committee. Committee procedure ranges from strict "Robert's rules of order" methods to a highly informal "talk when you can or have an idea" approach. Some committees require members to submit formal reports on the subject matter under consideration, and others merely require a presence of person and mind. Committees may have a definite membership roll, or they may vary participation with changes in the nature of the problems being considered.

Advantages of Committees

Committees can be advantageously used to achieve a number of organizational goals. The benefits that may be derived from committees are discussed in this section.

Integrated Group Judgment

An important reason for committees is that a problem may require the coordinated application of a number of knowledge areas, such as engineering, production, and sales. A familiarity with conditions in different geographical areas and the perspective of executives situated at different managerial levels can also be brought to bear upon a situation.

Group judgment sometimes shields the organization against errors in judgment that evolve from unique personal qualities of individual executives. The views of the pessimist tend to be neutralized by those of the optimist; the arguments of the expansive executive are countered by more restrained points of view. Group action may provide a more balanced and reliable judgment by "averaging" extremes in the personalities of executives.

The advice and recommendations of executives could be obtained through memoranda and individual consultation. A committee meeting often gives better results because it involves more than a combination of individual points of view. It promotes a chain reaction of ideas as each member appraises the views expressed by others. Ideas are combined, reshaped, and created. Group dynamics is itself a creative force that frequently leads to a better solution.

Coordination

Much ot the work of the organization flows across departmental lines. The decisions made by one departmental executive often affect the activities of other departments. Delivery dates promised by the sales department can cause difficult scheduling problems in the production department. The work of the design and styling department is directly related to that of the production engineering department. Changes initiated by one department frequently create a series of problems in every other major department. For example, a successful advertising campaign may require a higher rate of production, the purchase of additional supplies and raw material, the recruitment of personnel, and an increase in training activities.

Committees offer an approach to the problem of coordinating interdepartmental activities. Executives are given insights into the problems faced by other departments. As a result, they may better understand the need for coordination and the means by which it can be achieved. The knowledge acquired about the plans and activities of other departments can help them better integrate their own area of endeavor. A narrow specialized perspective is frequently replaced by a more comprehensive point of view.

The differentiation of managerial decision-making responsibilities through the departmentation process sometimes results in what has been called "splintered authority." No one department has complete decision-making prerogatives over a given problem area. Although such difficulties can be referred to a higher level in the management hierarchy, committees can be used to bring together the departments that jointly have the decision-making prerogatives.[1] This approach makes possible the solution of the

---

[1] Harold Koontz and Cyril O'Donnell, *Principles of Management*, 4th ed. (New York: McGraw-Hill Book Company, Inc., 1968), p. 382.

problem at a lower level of the management hierarchy, helps ease the burden of top-level executives, and promotes cooperation among the departments concerned.

Committees and Executive Teamwork

Committee organization is a formal recognition of the cooperative nature of managerial action and the importance of personal association in the development of teamwork. Teamwork is achieved by integrating individuals into what sociologists have called primary groups with common purposes and sentiments. Primary groups evolve from face-to-face interaction with others over a period of time. The social satisfaction derived from such associations has a motivational significance, and the sanctions of the group can help obtain conformity to a common purpose. Group accomplishment, rather than individual competition, is encouraged. As one executive put it, the committee system "encourages co-operative thinking and quells the natural tendency to seek recognition and promotion through individual efforts. It is another tool in the emancipation of man from 'the tyranny of his own ego.'" [2]

Many of the personal associations among executives are initiated and established informally. However, informal interaction does not always provide the associations that may be necessary for organizational purposes. Formally constituted committees can frequently be used to enlarge the scope of executive contacts and develop face-to-face interactions among particular groups of executives. For example, geographically dispersed executives can be assembled for periodic committee meetings, and personal interactions between lower and higher levels of management can be increased.

Participation by Subordinates

Committees make possible participation by subordinate managers and employees in the decision-making process. Participation can become an important motivating factor and help develop a higher degree of co-operation.[3] The emphasis that is often given to subordinate participation can be partly explained by the democratic traditions of the political system.

[2] Charles P. McCormick, *The Power of People* (New York: Harper & Brothers Publishers, 1949), p. 28.

[3] An interesting discussion of participation as a managerial device is found in: Robert Tannenbaum and Fred Massarik, "Participation by Subordinates in the Managerial Decision-Making Process," *The Canadian Journal of Economics and Political Science,* Vol. 16, No. 3, August 1950, pp. 408–418.

A former executive vice-president of the United States Junior Chamber of Commerce relates the impact of this idea from his experiences.

I recall conversations with literally thousands of young men—the type of young men who were destined to be tomorrow's leaders—in which they conveyed an impression that business too often retained control so firmly at the top that they were not given opportunity to prove what they could do or train themselves to do well at the top when their time came. The old one-man boss plan simply failed to take them into account. Young men could not understand why the very business leaders who most hated dictatorship in government not only tolerated but fostered a virtual dictatorship in business.[4]

The author of this quotation adds that "it is good to see now that the times have brought a certain change to correct this situation." [5] He feels that democracy has proved its superiority in business as it has in the political system.

The willingness of subordinates to accept decisions is an important determinant of the actual authority of superiors. People frequently feel more inclined to accept decisions that they have helped make. They like to exercise some control over matters that affect their personal and organizational interests. However, too much participation can weaken rather than strengthen the authority of the superior. Leadership and decision-making responsibilities cannot be completely delegated to subordinates without subjecting the organization to the destructive forces of compromise and indecision. Economic democracy, like political democracy, cannot survive without leadership. Participation is not the antithesis of leadership; it should be viewed as a corollary of leadership.

Committees and the Communication System

Committees can become important instruments for disseminating and acquiring information. Face-to-face oral communication seems to be a more effective form of communication than written reports and memoranda. Opportunity is provided for questions about anything that is not properly understood, and participants can learn something about the attitudes and opinions of others toward particular problems.

Interest Group Representation

Committees are sometimes used to give representation to important interest groups, such as creditors, customers, suppliers, labor unions, and

[4] Thomas R. Reid, "Multiple Management Re-examined," *Advanced Management,* Vol. 7, No. 2, April–June 1943, p. 61.
[5] *Ibid.*

stockholders.[6] Financial institutions and large minority stockholders are frequently given a place on the board of directors to protect their financial interests. Labor unions play a representative role in contract negotiation and on grievance committees.

The composition of the board of directors of the Federal Reserve Banks provides a good example of diversified interest group representation. Of a total of nine directors, three are elected by and represent the ownership interests of small, medium-sized, and large member banks; three must be actively engaged in business, agriculture, or some other commercial pursuit; and three are designated by the Board of Governors, which supervises the operations of the Federal Reserve System and conducts the nation's monetary policy. Governmental boards and committees also make extensive use of interest group representation. The National War Labor Board was composed of three groups representing the interests of management, labor unions, and the general public. The Joint Chiefs of Staff includes in its membership the chiefs of staff of the three military services.

Cooperation is sometimes refused if participation rights are not granted. A bank may refuse to supply funds unless it is given a place on the board of directors, and labor unions may give emphatic notice of their unwillingness to cooperate through the strike. On the other hand, an organization may invite representation to obtain a higher degree of cooperation from an interest group, such as a large customer or supplier. Interest group representation may also be used to obtain better decision making through the information and experience brought into the organization.

Executive Development

Committees can make a contribution to executive development. Subordinates are given insights into the problems facing other executives and the organization generally and become concerned with matters beyond the scope of their present responsibilities. Younger executives are able to observe more seasoned executives in action and have an opportunity to develop more reliable judgments. Senior executives can teach them "the tricks of the trade" and familiarize them with the duties of higher executive positions. At the same time, the capabilities of a junior executive can be observed and evaluated for future vacancies.

---

[6] An analysis of the participation of interest groups in managerial decision making is found in: Robert A. Gordon, *Business Leadership in the Large Corporation* (Washington, D.C.: The Brookings Institution, 1945), pp. 147–267.

Disadvantages of Committees

The use of committees may also present a number of important disadvantages, which should be evaluated in the light of the advantages considered above.

The Cost of Committees

The monetary cost of committees is indicated by a summation of the salaries of the participants. With an average salary of $7000, a six-man committee costs roughly $21 per hour, and salaries of $25,000 would make the hourly cost about $75. Committee work can be extremely time-consuming. A six-man committee has one speaker and five listeners unless there is a babble of many tongues. It cannot be assumed that every individual will always cast "pearls of wisdom" or that every other person will necessarily listen when a pearl is cast. Committee members may have to obtain information and data or prepare comprehensive reports. The time consumed by the physical movement of people to and from the place of meeting should not be ignored; some individuals may have to travel a considerable distance, involving transportation, lodging, and other expenses.

The application of rigorous economic calculation to evaluate committee efficiency is difficult. Although some quantitative inferences can be made from comparative productivity data, the contribution of committees is often highly intangible. For example, the motivational consequences of committee organization cannot be easily translated into quantitative terms. What part of an increase in productivity should be credited to committees as compared with other possible reasons for such a phenomenon? The contribution that would have been made by executives had they not been busy with committee work is also difficult to estimate.

The lack of precise measuring devices does not preclude the formulation of some practical guideposts. Generally the use of committees should not significantly increase the amount of executive work. When committee work begins to interfere excessively with the performance of other vital functions and requires long hours, the situation demands scrutiny. Another gauge for determining committee effectiveness is the attitude of participating executives. Too many complaints about committee responsibilities may indicate that something is wrong.

Compromise and Indecision

Group accomplishment rather than individual aggrandizement should dominate the committee scene. When viewed solely as a means for achieving personal and departmental ends, committees tend to become negative rather than positive instruments of cooperation. The result is decision making by compromise and logrolling rather than by group action. Up to a point, compromise is an important feature of group activity. But, like castor oil, too much of it can be a destructive force.

The progress of committees can be seriously stifled by an excessive amount of bickering, bantering, and bargaining. One or a few individuals can sometimes delay the process for a considerable time. The least competent sometimes impede the efforts of the most competent. Some committees never seem to reach a meaningful decision; the conclusion may be so diluted by compromise that nothing much remains. The achievement of a group consensus demands considerable social skill and a positive will to cooperate. An absence of these qualities can easily make committees parasites which destroy the host that gives them sustenance.

A majority rule can be employed to reach a decision when compromise is not possible. It provides a means for breaking a stalemate, but majority rule does not always result in a good decision. None of the alternatives presented for voting purposes may offer a really satisfactory solution to a problem. A significant diversity in opinion is generally present in a committee that requires a majority rule to reach a decision. The end product of the process is a minority that felt strongly enough about the matter to register formal opposition. The minority group sometimes sabotages the goals of the majority.

A committee charged with decision making is under compulsion to continue the proceedings until some kind of group decision evolves. Informational and advisory committees, on the other hand, can present a number of alternatives to the problem under consideration. The burden of selecting *the* alternative is shifted from the committee to an executive. Individuals are often more inclined to accept an alternative with which they disagree if the decision comes from a superior executive. However, nominal acceptance without genuine cooperation can also result.

One-Man or Minority Domination

Committee decisions should reflect the best judgment of the group. The possibility of domination by a formally constituted or an informally derived leader is an ever-present danger. A strong chairman, for example, can browbeat the committee into accepting a decision. Committees composed of members from different levels in the management hierarchy may experience domination by higher ranking executives. Informal leaders and cliques may display similar propensities.

All groups eventually develop some kind of leadership hierarchy. The problem is not the existence of leadership, but the manner in which the formal or informal leader exercises his power. The leader serves a useful function if he uses his capabilities to help achieve a *group* consensus. He repudiates the basic premise of group action if he attempts to make the committee an instrument of his personal volition. Every committee participant should have the right and feel free to present his personal convictions about a problem. To paraphrase Charles P. McCormick, mutual respect is a necessary committee attribute; every man has the right to be heard.[7]

When the purpose of the committee is advisory and informational, restrictions upon the subject matter of committee deliberations may be in order. For example, the executive seeking information or advice may wish to limit the discussion to certain aspects of a problem. He may not want to restrict his freedom of action over some matters by strong expressions of opinion by committee members. However, too many restrictions can develop psychological barriers that hinder effective communication between himself and the committee. The committee may feel that the executive simply wants to reinforce his own point of view, even when such a conclusion is not warranted.

The Problem of Responsibility

The final product of committee action is the joint responsibility of every member of the committee. The individual participant has an obligation to play an active and cooperative role in the process that leads to a group consensus. But he cannot be held personally accountable for the recommendations or decisions made by the group. This conclusion is not altered by the possibility that his suggestions formed the primary basis for the group decision. Group acceptance translates a recommendation of an individual member into a group recommendation. Furthermore, the fact that an individual consented to a group decision does not necessarily mean that he is in complete accord with it.

An approach to the problem of responsibility is to make the entire group accountable for its actions. Such a policy may cause the committee to take its responsibilities more seriously and police its own activities by employing sanctions against recalcitrant members. Another possibility is to make the chairman responsible for committee performance. The chairman can fre-

[7] McCormick, *op. cit.*, p. 21.

quently facilitate the group decision-making *process* by careful guidance. He can be held accountable for failure to properly discharge his chairmanship responsibilities, but not for the group decision. He may in fact disagree with some or many aspects of the results achieved.

A committee that makes too many bad decisions or seems to be generally incompetent should be dissolved. However, the dissolution of a committee for such reasons can have undesirable consequences upon morale. Executives who occupy responsible positions outside the committee may view such action as a personal affront. Individuals who attempted to make the committee a success may have a similar reaction. An effort should be made to protect the personal and professional integrity of committee members, assuming they are otherwise competent. A failure to do so may reduce their effectiveness in discharging future organizational responsibilities.

Committee versus Individual Action

Particular organizational conditions are important determinants in evaluating the effectiveness of committee versus individual action. A suitable solution for one company may not be appropriate in another. This fact should be kept in mind in appraising the material that follows.

A Functional Analysis

The American Management Association interviewed executives and examined records in twenty organizations to determine the relative efficiency of committee and individual approaches to various problems.[8] The survey resulted in a breakdown of twelve types of functions into four categories of effectiveness (Table 9-1). The size of the sample and classification and enumeration difficulties limit the inferences that can be made from the data. However, the degree of preference expressed in some of the data gives support to several conclusions. Committees seem to be superior in handling jurisdictional questions or problems that involve the interests and affairs of a number of different departments. On the other hand, the functions of leadership, execution, decision making, and organizing fall rather definitely into the opposite category. The data show a preference for individual action with respect to most functions, but the importance of committees as facilitating instruments is indicated.

[8] Ernest Dale, *Planning and Developing the Company Organization Structure*, Research Report No. 20 (New York: American Management Association, 1952), pp. 92–93.

Table 9-1. Evaluation of the Effectiveness of Committee and Individual Action in the Performance of Specific Management Activities

Management Function	Can Be Exercised by Committee Effectively	Committees Effective but Can Be Exercised More Effectively by Individual	Individual Initiative Essential; May Be Supplemented by Committee Action	Individual Action Essential; Committee Ineffective
Planning	20	20	25	35
Control	25	20	25	30
Formulating objectives	35	35	10	20
Organization	5	25	20	50
Jurisdictional questions	90	10	—	—
Leadership	—	—	10	90
Administration	20	25	25	30
Execution	10	15	10	65
Innovation	30	20	20	30
Communication	20	15	35	30
Advice	15	25	35	25
Decision-making	10	30	10	50

Source. Ernest Dale, *Planning and Developing the Company Organization Structure,* Research Report No. 20 (New York: American Management Association, 1952), p. 92.

Plural Executives

A committee becomes a plural executive when it performs the decision-making function. Many organizations seem to have a great deal of success with this kind of management. However, formal structures and statements should not always be taken at their face value. An operational analysis of some situations would reveal that the actual executive is an individual rather than the group.

The Importance and Immediacy of the Problem

The time and cost of committee deliberations prohibit their use for trivial and routine matters. The use of a committee to determine whether the company should purchase round or square wastebaskets would seem to be an unwarranted waste of resources. One should not attempt to hunt moles with an elephant gun. The time consumed by committees inhibits their use for situations requiring immediate action. A delay in decision is frequently more costly than any gains that might be achieved through group action.

By-Products of Committee Organization

Management should recognize that committees may have secondary and unplanned consequences. Such consequences may be more significant than the achievement of the objective for which a committee was established. Thus, a committee organized primarily for advisory and informational purposes may make a greater contribution in the form of improved cooperation and motivation.

Fundamentals of Effective Committee Operation

The preceding sections have shown that committees may serve a useful purpose in certain respects. However, this conclusion must be modified if committees are not properly used. The means by which more effective committee action can be achieved are considered in this section.

Planning for Committee Action

The part that a committee will play in the managerial process should be planned. Committee responsibilities and relationships should be understood by everyone who is directly or indirectly involved. A detailed job description, illustrated in Table 9-2, is frequently useful for this purpose. The effectiveness of committees may also be enhanced by the following procedures.[9]

1. A membership list should be maintained together with other pertinent data, such as the dates and conditions of appointment. Each member should be formally notified and informed about his responsibilities.

2. Whenever possible, a schedule of meetings should be planned with the dates, length, time, and place of meeting. The schedule should take into

[9] A checklist of procedures developed by one large organization is found in Dale, *op. cit.*, p. 186.

Table 9-2. Job Description for a Manufacturing Committee

Manufacturing Committee

Basic Functions

Review, analysis, and coordination of basic manufacturing policies, procedures and methods of all operating groups and operating divisions to promote the greatest possible interchange of information and cooperation.

Scope

The duties and responsibilities of this Committee cover the production policies and operations of all operating groups and divisions.

Responsibilities

1. To develop basic policies, procedures and administrative techniques in regard to manufacturing, purchasing, packaging, and shipping.
2. To integrate manufacturing policy with that of other departments of the Company, especially sales.
3. To develop policies aimed at the maximum utilization of capital equipment and its intra-company availability, of managerial talent and of labor (incentives, safety, etc.) and the continuous consideration of labor-saving through the introduction of mechanical equipment.
4. To set up procedures and constantly review new and outstanding manufacturing developments and product cost reduction for materials control, handling and utilization.

Committee Members

Vice Presidents in Charge of Manufacturing, Engineering, Marketing. The six most competent executives from the operating divisions.

Authority

This Committee shall serve as a counseling and advisory group to the president. Recommendations resulting from Committee action shall be presented to the president for his consent where matters of general policy or extra budgeting expense are concerned.

Source. Ernest Dale, *Planning and Developing the Company Organization Structure,* Research Report No. 20 (New York: American Management Association, 1952), p. 180.

consideration other responsibilities of the participants and the amount of preparation required for a meeting.

3. A carefully prepared agenda can be an exceedingly helpful device. If possible, the agenda and other material, such as reports, recommendations, and proposals, should be made available to committee members well in advance of the meeting. This procedure makes possible a study and appraisal of the matters to be considered. Some members may wish to obtain the opinion and counsel of others before the meeting.

4. The duties of the chairman and committee staff personnel, such as secretaries, should be carefully defined.

5. Provision should be made for maintaining and distributing a record of committee proceedings, recommendations, and decisions.

6. A formal control mechanism should be devised to evaluate the effectiveness of committees. A periodic summary report from the committee chairman on the number of meetings, attendance, man-hours expended, committee progress and accomplishments and other such matters may be useful in this respect.

Type of Committee Membership

The question of who should be included in the committee membership is closely related to the nature of the committee purpose. A committee that is primarily concerned with informational, advisory, or problem-solving functions should include individuals who have the required knowledge and skills. Thus, if engineering or accounting talent is needed, one or several engineers or accountants should be included. Functional proficiency may not be the primary consideration in selecting membership for a committee designed to promote better coordination or cooperation. A coordinating committee, for example, should include executives from the departments concerned. When the purpose is to promote cooperation, the sociological structure of the organization is an important consideration. An attempt should be made to include informal leaders and provide representation for formal and informal interest groups. The ability of individuals to effectively participate in group activities also warrants attention in making up a committee roster.

The Size of Committees

Is there an optimum committee size? How many members are too many or too few? These questions have received a variety of answers, but, as Robert F. Bales of the Harvard Laboratory of Social Relations has pointed out, "so far they seem to come mostly from numerology rather than from scientific research."[10] The question of size is related to such factors as the purpose of the committee and the personalities and participational skills of the members. The optimum size differs under different conditions.

Individuals are never identical; the structure of group interaction may be significantly changed by one individual. Adding individual X may make the group seem large and unwieldy, which might not result if Y and Z, rather than X, were included. In spite of such difficulties, the concept of size should be given consideration. A large committee is not suited for certain types of group action, such as the achievement of a genuine group consensus. But a committee of fifty may not be too large if the primary purpose is to give information to the participants. At the other extreme, a committee can be too small for effective action. For example, a three-man committee is often unsuitable because "the tendency of two to form a combination against the third seems fairly strong."[11] The result is frequently a lack of a "healthy" amount of disagreement.

Effective Committee Procedures

Why are some committees effective and others not? One approach to this problem is to observe successful committees in action. The experiments conducted by the Laboratory of Social Relations at Harvard University indicate that most successful groups go through three stages in the solution of a problem.[12] First, they attempt to acquire the largest pool of common information about the facts of the situation. During the second stage they make inferences and evaluations and try to form common opinions in a general way. Finally, after an extensive groundwork has been laid, they get around to more specific suggestions and solutions to the problem.

It should not be assumed that an agreement on facts is always easy to achieve. Facts evolve from sensory perceptions, which make them vulnerable to the vagaries of individual interpretation, and they are often clouded by emotional reactions and hearsay. Yet, the accumulation of scientific knowledge assures us that proper methods and attitudes make possible agreement on many matters.

After agreement has been achieved on the essential facts of the situation, every participant should be given adequate opportunity to express his views. Individuals will frequently depart from the facts and express nonlogical sentiments and attitudes. They will express antagonism and harmony, agreement and disagreement, altruism and egotism. Such

---

[10] Robert F. Bales, "In Conference," *Harvard Business Review*, Vol. 32, No. 2, March–April 1954, p. 48.
[11] *Ibid.*, pp. 48–49.
[12] *Ibid.*, p. 47.

reactions should be viewed as an integral part of the committee process. They tend to become a deleterious force only if either extreme is permitted to completely dominate the scene. Too much agreement may be as bad as too little agreement, and conversely.[13]

A critical stage in the process occurs when the committee begins to consider specific solutions to the problem. However, the danger of stalemate or stagnation is mitigated if the facts are permitted to cast some light throughout the deliberations. In the words of Robert F. Bales:

> In an environment barren of consensus, only a fact can survive; and, where there is hostility, even facts find a slim foothold. But a rich background of common facts lays the groundwork for the development of common inferences and sentiments, and out of these common decisions can grow. No decision rests on "facts" alone, but there is no better starting point. To start the decision-making process at any other point is to multiply the risk of a vicious circle of disagreement—and at no saving of time in the long run.[14]

The Role of the Chairman

The chairman may play an important facilitating role in the committee process. He can help initiate the proceedings by a carefully worded statement of objectives and promote participation by directing questions to specific committee members. He can frequently lead the group away from digressions that take a great deal of time and go nowhere. A periodic summary by the chairman can help the group crystallize its thinking.

As was pointed out earlier, the chairman should not dominate the group. It is his duty to be impartial and assist the group in achieving a consensus, even though the final outcome differs with his own views. He should respect the opinions of every man on the committee and give each an opportunity to freely express his opinion. He should not put the committee into a "strait jacket" by too many formal procedural requirements. On the other hand, he cannot permit the proceedings to flounder in circumlocution. Effective chairmanship demands a high degree of social manipulative skills. The chairman must lead and yet not seem to be leading. He must be resolute, but never intolerant. He must solicit views with which he may disagree violently. He is frequently forced to intercede when antagonism begins to dominate the scene, but he must be careful not to antagonize the antagonists.

[13] *Ibid.*, p. 46.
[14] *Ibid.*, p. 47.

SELECTED REFERENCES

Robert F. Bales, "In Conference," *Harvard Business Review,* Vol. 32, No. 2, pp. 44–50 (March–April, 1954).

Ernest Dale, *Planning and Developing the Company Organization Structure,* Research Report No. 20, pp. 83–97. New York: American Management Association, 1952.

Ralph C. Davis, *The Fundamentals of Top Management,* pp. 468–487. New York: Harper & Brothers, 1951.

M. Joseph Dooher and Vivienne Marquis (editors), *Effective Communication on the Job,* Part VIII. New York: American Management Association, 1956.

P. E. Holden, L. S. Fish, and H. L. Smith, *Top-Management Organization and Control,* Part B, Sec. 4. New York: McGraw-Hill Book Company, Inc., 1951.

Charles P. McCormick, *The Power of People.* New York: Harper & Brothers, 1949.

Herrymon Maurer, "Management by Committee," *Fortune,* Vol. 47, No. 4, pp. 145 ff (April, 1953).

Robert Tannenbaum and Fred Massarik, "Participation by Subordinates in the Managerial Decision-Making Process," *The Canadian Journal of Economics and Political Science,* Vol. 16, No. 3, pp. 408–418 (August, 1950).

chapter 10

BOARDS OF DIRECTORS AND OTHER COMMITTEES

This chapter gives a comprehensive account of corporate boards of directors, which are legally constituted plural executives. Committees of the board and other kinds of management committees are also considered here.[1]

The Board of Directors

A corporation is a legal instrument through which large numbers of people engage in cooperative endeavor. It is a creature of the law with many of the legal rights and privileges of persons, but of course it has no intrinsic human qualities. It is a legal entity apart from the property and persons necessary to bring it into existence. The board of directors provides an important link between the corporation as an inert legal concept and the reality of the corporation as a dynamic phenomenon of human cooperation.

The laws of most states provide that the corporate powers shall be exercised by a board of directors. The board personifies the corporation; its powers are equivalent to those of the corporation. These powers are conferred upon the directors as a group, which means that top managerial control is legally vested in a committee or a plural executive. However, the legal status of the board does not necessarily describe its actual role in

[1] Some of the material in this chapter originally appeared in: Henry H. Albers, "The Managerial Functions of Boards of Directors," *Iowa Business Digest,* Vol. 30, No. 2, Winter Quarterly 1959, pp. 5–8.

corporate affairs. Some boards take an active part in management and in practice occupy the status prescribed by the law. Others operate as mere legal formalities through which some other group, such as the operating executives, exercises managerial control.

What is the legal relationship between the board of directors and the stockholders? The latter own the corporation, but the property of the enterprise belongs to the corporation. This legal distinction provides an important basis for differentiating between the managerial status of the board of directors and that of the stockholders. The managerial prerogatives of stockholders are essentially limited to the right to elect the directors and to appeal to the courts when the actions of management seem prejudicial to stockholder interests. The wide dispersion of stock ownership, the passive attitude of many stockholders, the use of the proxy and restricted issues of voting stock, and the expense and difficulty of court litigation tend to further limit the intervention of the stockholder in the affairs of the corporation. The limited legal rights of stockholders in management have corresponding limitation with respect to their liabilities. The stockholder is not liable for the acts of the corporation unless he is a director. The board of directors is solely responsible for action taken in the name of the corporation.

The managerial powers conferred by the law upon the board of directors are limited by the provisions of the corporate charter and state and federal laws that apply to corporations specifically and business enterprises generally. Within these limits, the legal authority of the board to manage the corporation is relatively unrestricted. However, a limitation imposed by the proprietary interests of the stockholder deserves particular attention. The board is generally viewed as a trustee with respect to these interests. Narrowly defined, trusteeship means that the interests of the stockholders should always be the primary consideration in managerial decision making. A broader interpretation is that the board is required to maintain an equitable balance among the claims of stockholders, employees, customers, and the general public. Thus, although the stockholders' interests are given particular legal recognition, the assumption of a broader responsibility is not specifically prohibited by the law. Such a conception of trusteeship seems necessary if the corporation is to maximize its potential as a cooperative system.

The Board of Directors and the Managerial Function

In spite of the important powers and duties conferred by the law, the boards of directors of some corporations are plural executives in name only. They exist because the law requires it. Actual control is in the hands of the board chairman, a few directors, large minority stockholders, or the operating management. Under such circumstances, the board is little more than a rubber stamp for the controlling interests and has little real voice in the affairs of the enterprise.

The extent to which boards of directors are powerless puppets in managerial affairs cannot be determined with any degree of accuracy. However, the past few years have brought a significant amount of speculation and introspection about the functions of boards of directors. There is evidence that boards are less inclined to be "backseat drivers," particularly in the larger corporation. As John C. Baker concluded in his study of directors and their functions:

Directors are awakening today to their responsibilities. There is a widespread concern among them to know their functions and a desire to perform them properly. Corporation directors are making exceedingly important contributions to business development, irrespective of the criticisms leveled against them and misunderstandings which have existed.[2]

The question of the role that directors should assume is subject to a diversity of opinion. Some executives and directors feel that the board should do little more than formally fulfill the requirements of the law; at the other extreme are those who believe the directors should actively participate in operating matters. Executives, particularly in larger corporations, seem more inclined to accept the board as an integral part of top management. Increasing recognition is being given to the idea that the individual and group judgments of well-qualified directors can make a significant contribution to the welfare of the corporate enterprise.

The managerial functions performed by a large number of boards of directors studied by the Harvard Graduate School of Business Administration differed from company to company.[3] But, as one of the Harvard studies concluded, "taken as a whole, they covered practically the entire range of top management functions."[4] The basic functions performed by boards of directors can be divided into three major categories.[5]

SELECTION OF EXECUTIVES. This function is often considered to be the most important of board responsibilities. Although boards sometimes select

---

[2] John C. Baker, *Directors and Their Functions* (Boston: Division of Research, Graduate School of Business Administration, Harvard University, 1945), p. 133.

[3] Melvin T. Copeland and Andrew R. Towl, *The Board of Directors and Business Management* (1947); Myles L. Mace, *The Board of Directors in Small Corporations* (1948); and Baker, *op. cit.* Published by the Division of Research, Graduate School of Business Administration, Harvard University.

[4] Baker, *op. cit.*, p. 12.

[5] Copeland and Towl, *op. cit.*

all top corporate officers, they frequently give the president the privilege of nominating his own immediate subordinates. In a few instances, boards reserve the right to approve the appointment of relatively low echelon managerial personnel. The directors sometimes temporarily fill an important gap in the executive ranks caused by death or resignation, and thus help assure a continuity of management.

POLICY FORMULATION. Boards of directors sometimes play an active role in the formulation of important corporation policies. Some of the problems considered by boards are illustrated by the following questions: Should the company embark on a major expansion program? How should an increased need for financial resources be met? Where should a new plant be located? Should the company expand or diversify its product line? Should electric power be produced or purchased? How much should be paid out in dividends to stockholders? Should the executive compensation plan be changed?

APPRAISING COMPANY AND EXECUTIVE PERFORMANCE. The appointment of the top corporate executives is accompanied by a delegation of important decision-making functions. Although a board should give the management significant freedom of action over operating matters, it should not ignore instances of executive incompetence. Removal and replacement may sometimes be necessary to assure effective management. Furthermore, the board should determine whether its decisions have been carried out by corporate executives. For this reason, the board should carefully scrutinize and evaluate financial and operating data and keep itself informed about company activities through contacts with executives and through personal observation.

Methods of Board Action

The procedures used by boards of directors indicate that there are at least four major variations in the way they carry out their functions.[6] One method is to *decide* what will be done about matters over which the board assumes jurisdiction. Second, boards *confirm* decisions made by the corporation executives on matters that are subject to board approval. The directors sometimes ask discerning questions to ascertain the soundness of executive judgment, but only in rare cases do they refuse confirmation. Another form of board action is to *counsel,* advise, and guide executives on major policy matters. Recommendations and suggestions from directors are especially helpful during the initial phases of policy determination. Finally, directors *review* management plans and financial and operating reports.

[6] Baker, *op. cit.,* pp. 16–20.

Table 10-1. Methods Used by Directors in Different Companies to Deal with Illustrative Problems

	Methods Used by Directors		
Problems	In Most Companies	In Many Companies	In Few Companies
Selection of president—his remuneration (and removal)	Decide		
Nomination of directors	Decide		
Changes in capital structure	Decide		
Capital budget or expenditures	Decide	Confirm	
Selection of outside auditors	Decide	Confirm	
Determination of dividends	Decide	Confirm	
Selection and remuneration of other executives	Confirm	Decide	
Formation of postwar plans	Counsel	Confirm	Decide
Formation of major policies in production, marketing, finance, personnel	Counsel	Confirm	Decide
Addition of new products	Review	Counsel	Confirm
Preparation of operating budget	Review	Counsel	Confirm
Union negotiations and settlement	Review	Counsel	Confirm
Reports on competitive position and operating results		Review	Counsel
Decisions on detailed advertising program			Review

Source. John C. Baker, *Directors and Their Functions* (Boston: Division of Research, Graduate School of Business Administration, Harvard University, 1945), p. 18.

Table 10-1 shows the manner in which these techniques are applied to various problem areas.

Informal Activities

Boards of directors perform many functions on an informal basis. Baker concluded from his study that "one popular misconception about directors was that they performed their most important function by attending formal board meetings." [7] Attendance at board meetings or an examination of minutes did not give an adequate basis for evaluating the contributions of many directors. A description of a week in the life of Sidney Weinberg,

[7] Baker, *op. cit.,* p. 132.

director of twelve corporations, by *Fortune* magazine provides a good illustration of a director in action.

Somewhat exceptional in the scope of his activities, Mr. Weinberg is not atypical in the way he pursues them. On a certain Saturday he went to Chicago so that he could spend Sunday talking with Sears' General Robert E. Wood. Monday there was a Sears Board meeting that lasted till lunch, after which there were talks with General Wood and with officers of the company. On Tuesday at 9:45 A.M. there was an executive-committee meeting of McKesson & Robbins in New York, which went over leases, salary increases, leaves of absence, business figures for the preceding six months, and estimates for the coming six months. There followed a luncheon meeting of the development committee of the Manufacturers Trust Co. (not a board—investment bankers are not allowed to serve on the boards of banks), and from 4:00 P.M. to 5:30 P.M. there was a Madison Square Garden Board meeting, which considered, among other matters, the new Garden. After that was over, Mr. Weinberg talked business with the President over a cocktail. On Wednesday his activity began at 7:30 A.M. with a call from the president of one of the companies he directs. The Board of Continental Can met from 9:30 A.M. to 11:45 A.M.; afterward Mr. Weinberg discussed Point Four with one of the company's executives. There were three phone calls during the day from Continental Can officers. There were also phone calls from President Barry Leithead of Cluett, Peabody on an employee-stock-purchase plan, from John Collyer, President, and George Vaught, Vice President, of Goodrich. After a third Goodrich call, there were two more to another company of which Mr. Weinberg is a director about a sinking fund for bonds. Thursday there was a Cluett, Peabody Board meeting, in the course of which the stock-purchase plan was passed. At four in the afternoon there was a meeting of G. E.'s finance committee, and President C. E. Wilson asked Mr. Weinberg to arrive at three-thirty for a private discussion. Friday, came the regular G. E. Board meeting, which lasted till noon. "As much or more," says Mr. Weinberg, "is done in a well-run company informally as is done formally." [8]

Formal meetings and minutes do have a place in the scheme of things. They emphasize the importance of major decisions, encourage critical review of performance and objectives, and help prevent future misinterpretations and misunderstandings. But a failure to recognize the informal aspects of board activities leaves out an important part of the picture.

The Question of Size

There are many opinions on the question of board size, and business practices indicate a diversity of answers. Table 10-2, which is based on

[8] Herrymon Maurer, "Boards of Directors," *Fortune,* Vol. 41, No. 5, May 1950, pp. 108, 122.

Table 10-2. Size of Corporate Boards, 1966

456 Manufacturing Companies	
Number of Board Members	Number of Companies
3	1
4	1
5	9
6	10
7	39
8	20
9	63
10	46
11	57
12	46
13	29
14	35
15	42
16	17
17	20
18	7
19	9
20 or over	5

Source. Jeremy Bacon, *Corporate Directorship Practices,* Business Policy Study No. 125 (New York: National Industrial Conference Board, Inc., 1967), p. 2.

National Industrial Conference Board data, shows the board size in 456 manufacturing companies surveyed in 1966. Comparison of these statistics with similar studies made in 1961 and 1958 indicates a slight increase in the size of boards. The data indicate a trend toward boards of 7 to 15 members with a median size of 11 members.[9] A study by Holden, Fish, and Smith of 31 large corporations, with a reputation for progressive and enlightened management practices, showed a range of 7 to 36 board members with an average size of 13.[10] A statistical tabulation made by Robert A. Gordon on the size of boards in 155 large corporations indicates a similar average.[11] Historical data assembled by Mabel Newcomer on the

[9] Jeremy Bacon, *Corporate Directorship Practices,* Business Policy Study No. 125 (New York: National Industrial Conference Board, Inc., 1967), p. 2.
[10] P. E. Holden, L. S. Fish, and H. L. Smith, *Top-Management Organization and Control* (New York: McGraw-Hill Book Company, Inc., 1951), p. 221.
[11] Robert A. Gordon, *Business Leadership in the Large Corporation* (Washington, D.C.: The Brookings Institution, 1945), p. 117.

boards of large corporations led to the conclusion that "there appears to be no trend toward either larger or smaller boards." [12]

Boards that exist only to meet legal requirements tend to be no larger than the minimum prescribed by the law. Such a situation is particularly prevalent in the small owner-managed corporation. On the other hand, the large corporation is frequently faced with pressures to increase the number of directors. Superannuated top executives are often given a place on the board as a reward for distinguished service and to take advantage of their mature judgments. In other cases, executives are "promoted" to a board position to get them out of the way. Growth through consolidation also tends to increase the number of directors through the representation often given the managements of acquired companies. Large corporations are sometimes inclined to accord greater interest representation or to increase the size of the board for public relations purposes.

What is the proper size of the board of directors? Some writers on the subject have suggested a minimum of from 5 to 6 and a maximum of 12.[13] Executive opinion on this matter ranges from rather definite limits to the idea that, like a burlesque queen's fan, a board should not be so large as to be unwieldy, but large enough to cover the subject—efficient management. If boards of directors are merely facades through which others manage the corporation, the question of size is not particularly important. But, if the board is viewed as an integral part of the process of managing, the ideas advanced in Chapter 9 on the size of committees have significance. Many directorates are too large for effective group management. However, a large board may be necessary for other reasons. As one executive commented:

We have found it necessary to have a large board in order to provide adequate representation for the principal foreign countries in which we and our subsidiaries are active and where large numbers of our shareholders are located.[14]

The question of size cannot be viewed entirely in terms of managerial efficiency.

The Composition of Boards of Directors

What proportion of the board should be composed of salaried corporate executives and to what extent should outside groups, such as stockholders,

[12] Mabel Newcomer, *The Big Business Executive* (New York: Columbia University Press, 1955), p. 25.

[13] Gordon, *op. cit.,* p. 118; George E. Bates, "The Board of Directors," *Harvard Business Review,* Vol. 19, No. 1, 1940, p. 86.

[14] Solomon Ethe and Roger M. Pegram, *Corporate Directorship Practices,* Studies in Business Policy No. 90 (New York: National Industrial Conference Board, Inc., 1959), p. 13.

financial, and other interests, be represented? Statistical data indicate that corporations have given a variety of answers to this question.

Gordon's data on the boards of directors of 155 large corporations show that 35.9 per cent of the directors were salaried executives.[15] In 31 corporations, executives held the majority of the directorships. The boards of industrial corporations had the largest executive representation; the railroads had the lowest. None of the railroad boards had a majority of directors from the executive group.

Studies conducted by the National Industrial Conference Board indicate a trend toward greater representation of outside interests during the past 30 years.[16] The manufacturing companies surveyed in 1938 split evenly between those with a majority of executives on the board and those with a majority of outside directors. Outside directors constitute a majority in 63 per cent of manufacturing boards in 1966 as compared with a majority of 61 per cent in 1961, 57 per cent in 1958, and 54 per cent in 1953.

Another important group on boards of directors are substantial stockholders or their representatives. Such directors were in a minority in most of 420 companies studied by the National Industrial Conference Board.[17] About 12 per cent of the companies reported that substantial stockholders other than officers held a majority of board positions. Approximately one-fourth of the companies indicated that none of their nonofficer directors were owners or representatives of large amounts of stock. Something like one out of five directors on the average board represents or has substantial proprietary interests. However, except for small and medium-sized corporations, the total percentage of corporate stock held by boards of directors is relatively small.

The roster of corporate directors also includes a significant number of executives from other companies, bankers, and lawyers. The principal occupations of outside directors in 436 manufacturing companies are shown in Table 10-3.

Many corporations seek to achieve "a balanced board." [18] There is general agreement that a balanced board should be composed of the following groups: (1) corporation executives, (2) outside interests, (3) representatives of large ownership interests, and (4) experts in general management.[19]

[15] Gordon, *op. cit.*, p. 119.
[16] Bacon, *op. cit.*, p. 6.
[17] Ethe and Pegram, *op. cit.*, p. 17.
[18] Ethe and Pegram, *op. cit.*, p. 16.
[19] Such a definition of a balanced board was advanced a number of years ago by George E. Bates of the Harvard Graduate School of Business Administration. Bates, *op. cit.*, pp. 83–84; also see Bacon, *op. cit.*, p. 6.

Table 10-3. Principal Occupations of Outside Directors.

Occupation	Number of Directors [a]	Number of Companies
436 Manufacturing Companies		
Bankers (commercial, investment, private)	420	260
Retired or former company officers	342	200
Corporate presidents [b]	337	167
Attorneys	308	249
Prominent businessmen, not otherwise classified	245	92
Corporate chairmen, vice-chairmen and committee chairmen	216	114
Retired businessmen [c]	193	127
Industrialists and manufacturers	139	65
Brokers (investment, real estate, commodity)	109	78
Investment and financial counsellors, financiers	106	82
Educators	101	86
Corporate vice-presidents	84	64
Consultants	82	64
Board directors	43	28
Professions other than law and education	39	35
Insurance executives	25	23
Trustees or officers of foundations, institutions	16	15
Business proprietors	15	13
Farmers and ranchers	10	10
Housewives	8	6
Government and military	6	6
Managers and other operating personnel	5	3
Religious or charitable	5	5
Founder of company or related	5	3
Total	2,859	

Source. Jeremy Bacon, *Corporate Directorship Practices,* Business Policy Study No. 125 (New York: National Industrial Conference Board, Inc., 1967), p. 15.
[a] No director is tabulated more than once, e.g., a banker may be president of his bank and also an investment counsellor, but he is counted only as a banker.
[b] Including two directors identified as chief executives of their companies.
[c] Including all directors identified as retired (other than retired former employees), regardless of previous occupation.

Several countervailing forces are implicit in the concept of a balanced board. The idea that the board's managerial responsibilities require directors who have managerial abilities and intimate knowledge about operating conditions is an important consideration. Interest group representation is often necessary to assure the continued cooperation of customers, suppliers, stockholders, and the community. It is also viewed as a means for making the corporation more responsive to the various interests.

If the board is to manage, directors with managerial talent are obviously needed. An equally good argument can be made for directorships which facilitate cooperation, even though such directors may add little in the form of managerial resources. However, the argument that representation is necessary to enforce responsibility has less validity in practice. Representation per se does not give substantive content to the rights of the interest groups. Baker has pointed out that, "the perfect board will not be found in form but rather in substance, that is, in the adaptation of the personnel and organization of a board to the specific problems of its social, political, and business environment." [20] Boards composed entirely of corporation executives may exhibit a greater degree of responsibility than a board that has a majority of directors from outside the corporate ranks. The fact that a board roster gives the appearance of balance does not necessarily mean that it is an ideal board.

Directors' Compensation

Some corporation directors could easily succumb to malnutrition if they tried to live on their compensation. A National Industrial Conference Board survey showed that 36 per cent of the responding companies paid a fee of $100 per meeting with 24 per cent reporting a fee of $200.[21] The fees paid by companies that do not pay annual retainers ranged from $25 up to $1,000. Only about 3 per cent of the companies do not compensate outside directors in any way. Larger corporations generally pay higher fees than medium-sized and smaller corporations There appears to be a trend toward paying directors on an annual retainer basis with or without an additional per-meeting fee. The median retainer paid to outside directors by the manufacturing companies surveyed is $3,000; the highest reported amount was $20,000. Extra compensation is sometimes received for serving on committees of the board. Most companies reported the payment of traveling and other expenses incurred in attending board meetings.

Financial compensation is not the only or necessarily the primary factor in inducing individuals from outside the corporation to serve as directors.[22] Other motivating factors noted by Copeland and Towl are the challenge of meeting new and complex problems, the experience that may be gained, the opportunity to associate with financial and business leaders,

[20] Baker, *op. cit.,* p. 136.
[21] Bacon, *op. cit.,* p. 30.
[22] Copeland and Towl, *op. cit.,* pp. 161–162.

and a sense of obligation to the business community. In spite of such evidently important nonfinancial incentives, there is still some question about the adequacy of the present level of financial compensation. Competent outside directors, who actively participate in the affairs of the corporation, would seem to be worth as much on a pro rata basis as top corporation executives.

Frequency of Board Meetings

The previously cited National Industrial Conference Board study indicated that almost half of the boards of the companies surveyed meet from 10 to 14 times a year, or approximately once a month.[23] Quarterly meetings are about as common as monthly ones in companies in the insurance and merchandising industries, and in companies performing miscellaneous services. A few boards meet only three times a year and some even less often. The boards of smaller corporations generally meet less frequently than those of larger corporations.

The Boards of Small Corporations

The management literature has given relatively little attention to the boards of directors in small corporations. A noted exception is a study by Professor M. L. Mace of the Harvard Graduate School of Business Administration.[24] The chief executive of a small corporation usually cannot confine his activities to the overall direction of the enterprise. He must frequently devote a great deal of time and effort to such specialized functions as production, sales, finance, advertising, and personnel. Too often, he is a jack-of-all-trades and a master of none.

It also became apparent to Mace in his study that the typical board of the small corporation exists simply to meet the formal requirements of the law. He found that directors are often appointed by the owner-manager and that they take no active part in management. In order to determine the possible contributions that could be made by boards of directors, a number of situations in which boards assumed a more active role were given scrutiny.[25] Mace concluded that a board composed of active and able directors makes for a more balanced judgment on many matters. They can broaden the manager's perspective and help him make better decisions by suggest-

[23] Bacon, *op. cit.,* p. 126.
[24] Mace, *op. cit.*
[25] The cases studied were those in which the management owned 51 per cent or more of the voting stock; no consideration was given in this respect to the less typical situation in which the managers did not have full legal control.

ing alternative solutions to particular problems. They can act as a sounding board for new ideas and give him counsel, encouragement, and moral support.

In some respects a board of directors is more useful in a small corporation than in a large one. The management of a small enterprise is not surrounded by an array of technical, professional, and executive talent. The possibility of obtaining the services of such personnel on a consulting basis is often precluded by limited financial means. The board of directors provides a possible source of much-needed advice and counsel. Considerations other than monetary provided the necessary incentives in many cases studied by Mace. Although a director should not be elected simply to obtain "free advice," many university professors, attorneys, bankers, accountants, and executives seem willing to give a great deal of time and effort to the affairs of a small enterprise. As Mace pointed out: "Many business and professional men served as board members for the business education they gained thereby; others served as contributions to the welfare of their communities." [26]

Owner-managers are sometimes so concerned with operating problems and their own stake in the business that they fail to recognize a broader framework of responsibility to minority stockholders, the community, employees, customers, and other interest and participating groups. A competent and active board can frequently help create an awareness of such responsibilities and their significance to the long-term welfare of the organization.

It should not be assumed that a more effective use of boards of directors is a panacea for all the ills of small corporate enterprises. The best physicians in the world cannot cure a patient who has been hacked to death by a quack. However, a competent group of directors and a willingness on the part of managers to heed their counsel provide a frequently neglected and important ingredient for better management in many small corporations.

Toward More Effective Boards

The fact that boards are often ignored as positive instruments of management does not eliminate any essential managerial functions. If the board does nothing, the burden must be carried elsewhere.

A strictly legal approach to the problems of corporation management tends to create a dichotomy between the board and the executives. The board is essentially a management committee with many of the characteristics of other such committees. One difference is that boards of directors

---

[26] Mace, *op. cit.,* p. 89.

continue to exist in form even when they are used only to satisfy legal requirements. The question of whether the board should take an active part in managing is closely related to the committee versus individual management argument. In spite of the legal requirement that the corporation be "managed" by a board of directors, a plural executive at the peak of the management hierarchy does not always provide the best solution to all problems. A board of competent directors can perform certain functions well; an individual executive, such as the board chairman or the company president, is better suited for some purposes.

How can the board of directors become a more effective instrument of corporate management? The asking of discerning questions has been called one of the most important contributions by directors to the management process.[27] A discerning question is one that opens up a situation and results in executive action or a review of policy. Such questions force the corporate executives to consider matters that may have been neglected or give further consideration to possible alternative solutions to a problem. It is not likely that every member of the board will have the ability to effectively ask discerning questions. But as Copeland and Towl point out, "a board which does not have any keen questioner in its membership is not likely to be a strong board."[28]

Corporations are sometimes faced with circumstances that force them to accept directors who may not be well qualified. Interest group considerations may result in the nomination of some directors who do not have the qualities that would be desirable from a strictly managerial point of view. A suggestion by a substantial stockholder cannot always be ignored. Yet, many corporations could improve their boards by more carefully scrutinizing the qualities of prospective candidates.

Good organizational practices should not be neglected. Some corporations specify board functions in the organization manual; others do not even include the board in the structure of management positions displayed in the organization chart. Although the powers and duties of the board are broadly defined in the bylaws of the corporation, a clear and concise differentiation of functions assigned to the board and corporate executives would seem to be desirable.[29]

Like committees generally, the effectiveness of a board can be increased by capable leadership. The functions of the board chairman vary a great deal from company to company and tend to reflect the personality of the incumbent. Baker's research on the subject led him to conclude that "the title suggested anything from a promoted but ineffective president to a

[27] Copeland and Towl, *op. cit.*, p. 95.
[28] *Ibid.*, p. 113.
[29] Holden, Fish, and Smith, *op. cit.*, p. 218.

strong chief executive."[30] The board chairman, whether he be the chief executive or a separate officer, can greatly enhance the effectiveness of a board.[31] The chairman can direct the attention of the board to important policy questions and matters that involve the concept of trusteeship. He can help maintain a good relationship between the board and the corporate executives. Planning the agenda, presiding at meetings, and developing effective procedures are other ways in which a board chairman can improve board operations.

The Directors as Philosophers of the Corporation

The last few years have witnessed a reappraisal of the role of the corporation in modern industrial society. The first phase of corporate development was often dominated by narrow financial interests and considerations. Operational efficiency became the primary goal during the second and most recent phase. It has been suggested that the continued existence of the corporation is no longer a question of operational policy, but of an ability to develop a social philosophy.[32] The development of such a philosophy demands introspection and speculation about the purpose and responsibility of the corporation. To some extent at least, the attention that has been given in recent years to boards of directors and their functions reflects this new perspective of corporate dynamics. Some students of management believe that the directors should assume the role of statesmen and philosophers of the corporation. The failure of the financial group to give sufficient attention to operating problems brought about the ascendancy of the operating executive in corporate affairs. If the operating executive fails to give proper attention to the broader horizons of corporate living, his role may be reshaped to meet the needs of the future. A competent board of directors may help provide a balance between a strictly operational approach to corporate management and a more comprehensive conception of purpose and responsibility.

Committees of the Board

Boards of directors, particularly in large corporations, often delegate responsibilities to special and permanent committees.[33] The types of committees most frequently organized are the following.

[30] Baker, *op. cit.*, p. 120.
[31] *Ibid.*, p. 137.
[32] Maurer, *op. cit.*, p. 132.
[33] The data used in this section are from Bacon, *op. cit.*, pp. 135–162.

EXECUTIVE COMMITTEE. The most frequently encountered committee in corporations surveyed by the National Industrial Conference Board is an executive committee. Membership on this committee varied from two to as many as 14 directors with an average of around 5. The importance of such committees in the management picture can be inferred by the frequency of meetings. Some corporations reported no meetings for a long period; weekly, biweekly, and monthly meetings were the rule in other companies.

FINANCE COMMITTEE. Although only about 1 out of 6 of 517 companies surveyed by the Conference Board reported a finance committee, this committee frequently occupies an important and powerful position. Budgetary policy, capital expenditures, and other financial matters fall within its province.

AUDITING COMMITTEE. This committee is generally concerned with the employment of auditors, auditing and accounting procedure, and the appraisal and transmission of accounting data.

SALARY, BONUS, AND PENSION COMMITTEES. One or several committees are sometimes established to scrutinize and make recommendations on executive compensation.

SPECIAL COMMITTEES. Such committees are sometimes organized to handle problems of a nonrecurring nature. Plant location, company reorganization, purchase or sale of important properties, and the recruitment of a new chief executive are some of the problems that may justify a special committee.

Of these committees, the executive and finance committees are generally the most important. In some larger corporations, they have equal status and in a *de facto* sense occupy the highest positions in the managerial hierarchy. The functional dualism expressed by these committees also reflects the tendency of the larger corporation to differentiate top-level operating and financial policy formulation. However, it should be emphasized that some such committees exist only in form and have no real voice in the affairs of the corporation.

Top-Management Committees

Many of the larger corporations have made extensive use of committees at the top-management level. Some of these committees have the official designation of committees of the board. Others include operating and staff executives in their membership. They may serve in an advisory capacity to the chief executive, make policy recommendations for his approval, or play the role of a plural executive with important decision-making responsibilities.

The following examples illustrate the use of committees at the top-management level. The corporations selected for this purpose have had a successful history of committee management. However, many other good examples can be cited.[34]

The Executive Committee of the Du Pont Company

The Du Pont executive committee, composed of the company president and eight vice-presidents, is the top policy-making group in the operating end of the business. Other than being the committee chairman, the president has no special prerogatives. The vice-presidents are not directly in charge of any of the operating components of the company. The committee operates on the basis of majority rule with each member having one vote.[35] It meets all day once a week and at such additional times as may be necessary.

The executive committee has two types of functions: (1) those performed as a committee; (2) those performed by individual members. As a committee, it is responsible for top policy making and control of company operations. It passes on policies and projects proposed by the operating departments and coordinates the diversity of activities in which the company is engaged. In addition to these important committee responsibilities, each member serves as the executive advisor for various phases of company activities. For example, one member acts as advisor on engineering and foreign relations, another on advertising, sales, and trade analysis, and so on. But it should be emphasized that these assignments are advisory only. The philosophy of this arrangement is that executive committee members should be free to give primary attention to the overall affairs of the corporation, without being burdened with the day-to-day tasks involved in the ordinary executive position. Their realm is major corporate strategy; the heads of the operating departments are the tacticians who put the plans into action.

Officially, the executive committee is a committee of the board of directors, and it submits a summary of all important activities for discussion and approval by the board. The board is composed of full-time executives of the company or retired company officials who function as elder states-

[34] Other companies with important committees at the top-management level are the Ford Motor Company, Bank of America, Westinghouse Electric Company, Continental Oil Company, American Can Company, Phillips Petroleum Company, Caterpillar Tractor Company, Carrier Corporation, Crown Zellerbach Corporation, Penn Fruit Company, and the Chesapeake and Ohio Railway Company. The General Motors Committee system was considered in Chapter 8.

[35] With the limitation that it takes a minimum affirmative vote of four to pass any resolution.

men. It meets once a month and takes an active interest in all important operating and financial matters. The board and its subcommittees, such as the executive committee and the finance committee, are a part of an effective system of checks and balances within the company. Thus, although the executive committee plays the primary role at the top-management level, its activities are subject to the scrutiny and review of the other groups.

Committee Management at New Jersey Standard

The top policy-making groups in the Standard Oil Company (New Jersey) are the board of directors and the executive committee.[36] The board, composed of fourteen inside directors, takes an active part in the management of the company. As *Fortune* has pointed out, "in the usual sense of the word, the Jersey Board members are not directors at all but a board of managers."[37] Since most of the directors have spent their entire business careers with the company or its affiliates, they come to the weekly board meetings with a personal understanding of operating conditions. Between meetings the full prerogatives of the board are assumed by the executive committee, which meets daily and is composed of five directors and any other directors who want to attend.

The board and the executive committee keep posted on the affairs of operating units through "contact" directors, who are assigned an area or a function with which they are expected to maintain contact. This system makes for reliable information and results in a chain of personal relationships involving the entire organization. Another important link between the operating companies and central management is provided by the coordinating committee. This committee serves both the board and the managements of affiliates by providing marketing information, reviewing capital expenditures, evaluating operating costs, and assisting in many other matters. It has the help of six departments specializing in production, pipelines, marine transport, refining, marketing, and economics. The coordinating committee is composed of coordinators who head these departments, representatives from affiliated companies, and two directors from the Jersey board who act as chairman and vice-chairman.

In addition to other board subcommittees, the Jersey board has established an advisory committee on human relations. This committee's primary function is to advise the board and the managements of operating

---

[36] A discussion of the top-management organization of New Jersey Standard is found in *Fortune*, Vol. 44, No. 4, October 1951, pp. 99–103, 174–184. Much of the material in this section is derived from this source.

[37] *Ibid.*, p. 103.

companies on matters involving the stockholders, the government, employees, and the public.

Committees at the Operating Level

Overall organizational policy, the desires of particular executives, and the size of the organization are some of the things that influence the use of committees in operating departments. Interdepartmental coordination committees are used extensively, and departmental executives sometimes make use of advisory committees composed of key departmental personnel. Special committees are also established to consider such specific problems as scrap reduction, employee morale, and industrial housekeeping. Committees at the operating level frequently include employees in their membership in order to promote cooperation through participation and to give employees a better understanding of the problems that face management.

Union-management committees have become more numerous in recent years. Some of these committees are a product of collective bargaining and are designed to administer the trade agreement. An example is the joint union-management grievance committee. Other committees are designed to promote union-management cooperation in areas not encompassed by collective bargaining relationships. Accident prevention, waste reduction, community chest drives, reduction of absenteeism, and recreational activities are some of the areas in which unions and management have assumed joint responsibilities. The manner in which committees have been used at lower managerial and operating levels is illustrated by the following examples.

A Junior Board of Directors

McCormick and Company, a Baltimore concern engaged in the spice and extract business, has had two boards of directors since the early 1930's. The company was hard hit by the depression and needed the proverbial "shot in the arm" to weather the storm. Among other things, the newly appointed president, Charles P. McCormick, decided to appoint a junior board of directors. McCormick has described the basis for this action.

. . . I was looking for a way to stimulate the thinking of McCormick's executives. Somewhere I had read that the average businessman utilizes only about half of his mental capacity. I wanted to find methods of lifting our men out of the routine ruts that suppress imagination and inventiveness. The solution came to me at the next meeting of the Board of Directors. Glancing around, I realized that while I was thirty-six years old, nearly all the members were over forty-five and several had passed sixty. . . . I had taken stock of myself and had arrived at the conviction that I possessed neither the ability nor the inclination to be a one-man manager of a multimillion-dollar business. I told the directors that I appreciated the value of their individual experience, mature judgment, and collective wisdom, but thought we should exhaust every source of ideas and information. To accomplish this, I suggested the formation of a Junior Board of Directors, to be chosen from among assistant department managers and others who had shown special zeal in their work. The purpose of the Junior Board then, as it is now, would be not to bypass the judgment of the more mature men, but to supplement that judgment with new ideas.[38]

In addition to the junior and senior boards, the McCormick Company organized a factory board, a sales board, and an institutional sales board. Suggestions from the subordinate boards are sent to the senior board for final approval, after which they are passed to the line organization for action. Members are given extra compensation for the time spent on board business. Since the establishment of the system in 1932, new members of the senior board of directors have, with one exception, previously served on one of the subordinate boards.

The Scanlon Plan

This plan represents a new approach to industrial productivity through formal and informal participative techniques.[39] Joseph Scanlon, formerly with the United Steel Workers of America, played a major part in its development. The Scanlon plan works through a formal system of committees that include both management and union members in their membership. Departmental committees are composed of union production committeemen, who are appointed or elected, and the foremen. Other interested parties, such as the grievance committeeman and employees directly concerned with a problem, may be invited to participate in committee deliberations. An administration or screening committee, with three management and three union members, handles matters referred to it by departmental committees and problems that involve the affairs of more than one department.

The Scanlon plan is concerned with the solution of two mutually related problems: (1) the initiation and implementation of suggestions for the improvement of productivity; (2) the development and administration of a

[38] Charles P. McCormick, *The Power of People* (New York: Harper & Brothers Publishers, 1949), p. 12.

[39] William Foote Whyte, *Money and Motivation* (New York: Harper & Brothers Publishers, 1955), pp. 166–188. The articles on which this material is based are indicated on: *ibid.,* p. 166.

formula through which the rewards of higher productivity are to be shared by management and workers. The sharing formula is based on a ratio of labor costs to the sales value of production and is adapted to the conditions that exist in a company. The ratio can be renegotiated at the initiation of management and the union when warranted by changes in external and internal conditions. The bonus is paid on a percentage of the regular wage basis, and both management (except top management) and workers participate.

Suggestions for productivity improvements are channeled through the committees described above. The rewards result from reductions in labor costs, which are translated into bonuses by the sharing formula. The individual who makes a suggestion does not receive direct payment as in other suggestion systems. He shares in the bonus that results from his suggestion and the ideas contributed by fellow workers and supervisors. Social satisfactions may also result through recognition from the group for outstanding individual contributions.[40]

The Scanlon plan takes into consideration the behavioral theories that evolved from the Hawthorne Study and related research. The assumption is that the individual is thwarted by group pressures in an individualistic approach to productivity and wage problems. The formal committee structure gives emphasis to this idea and provides a setting within which informal interactions can expedite matters. The individual is not pitted against the group but is directed to behave formally as he generally must behave informally. The plan attempts to take advantage of, rather than work at cross-purposes with, the behavioral patterns actually found in industrial situations.

Although good results have been achieved in a number of instances, the Scanlon plan should not be viewed as a panacea for all the ills of industrial relations. It is founded on a will to cooperate on the part of both management and unions and would undoubtedly fail in many companies. The wage incentive plans of scientific management were also successful under certain conditions. However, the Scanlon plan seems to be better adapted to the realities of industrial behavior than earlier plans.

Committee Management in the Future

In their pioneering article on management in the 1980's, Leavitt and Whisler predicted that information technology would bring about a marked move toward centralization in the not-too-distant future.[41] They envi-

---

[40] Whyte, *op. cit.,* p. 175.

[41] Harold J. Leavitt and Thomas Whisler, "Management in the 1980's," *Harvard Business Review,* Vol. 36, No. 6, November–December 1958, pp. 41–48.

sioned a highly interdependent top-management oligarchy in which "groupthink" would become commonplace. Included in this oligarchy would be operations researchers, mathematical programmers, computer experts, and other information technologists. An executive would still be responsible for making the final choice, but the decisional process leading up to this step would become a group affair.

Committees at the top management level preceded the birth of information technology. An important reason was that one man could no longer contend with the increasingly complex social and technological environment. It does not appear likely that information technology will radically reconstruct the group processes that already exist in such companies as General Motors, Du Pont, and Standard Oil (New Jersey). Information technology will provide additional information that will directly and indirectly affect top management decision making. Computerized models of the economic system or an industry may pave the way to more accurate forecasting. Some testing of alternative planning strategies will become possible through models that simulate environmental and organizational realities. But the extent to which information technology can be helpful in this respect is definitely limited. The problems of uncertainty and values will plague top management so long as a free society continues to exist.

Information technology will probably be a far more important instrument for solving middle-management problems than those of top management for quite some time. After top management has more or less arbitrarily determined the organizational objectives, electronic computers can be highly effective in translating these objectives into production plans and schedules, purchase programs, personnel requirements, and other subsidiary plans. The solution of programmed rather than nonprogrammed decisions will be the principal contribution of the computer even beyond the 1980's.

As was pointed out in Chapter 9, many companies have "committees" through informal group processes. Information technologists will often make a contribution to the decisional process through informal interaction and influence. Significant changes in the manner in which decisions are made may occur through informal means. Some part of the predictions made by Leavitt and Whisler may come about through informal "reorganization" rather than formal structural changes.[42]

[42] William E. Reif, *Computer Technology and Management Organization* (Iowa City: Bureau of Business and Economic Research, 1968), p. 113.

SELECTED REFERENCES

Jeremy Bacon, *Corporate Directorship Practices,* Business Policy Study No. 125. New York: National Industrial Conference Board, Inc., 1967.

John C. Baker, *Directors and Their Functions.* Boston: Division of Research, Graduate School of Business Administration, Harvard University, 1945.

George E. Bates, "The Board of Directors," *Harvard Business Review,* Vol. 19, No. 1, pp. 72–87 (Autumn Number 1940).

Gilbert Burck, "The Jersey Company," *Fortune,* Vol. 44, No. 4, pp. 98 ff (October 1951).

M. T. Copeland and A. R. Towl, *The Board of Directors and Business Management.* Boston: Division of Research, Graduate School of Business Administration, Harvard University, 1947.

Robert A. Gordon, *Business Leadership in the Large Corporation,* Chap. 6. Washington, D.C.: The Brookings Institution, 1945.

Carter F. Henderson and Albert C. Lasker, *20 Million Careless Capitalists.* Garden City, N.Y.: Doubleday & Company, Inc., 1967.

P. E. Holden, L. S. Fish, and H. L. Smith, *Top-Management Organization and Control,* Part D, pp. 213–238. New York: McGraw-Hill Book Company, Inc., 1951.

J. M. Juran and J. Keith Louden, *The Corporate Director.* New York: American Management Association, 1966.

Harold Koontz, *The Board of Directors and Effective Management.* New York: McGraw-Hill Book Company, Inc., 1967.

Frederick G. Lesieur (editor), *The Scanlon Plan.* New York: The Technology Press of M.I.T. and John Wiley and Sons, Inc., 1958.

L. P. Lessing, "The World of Du Pont—The Top Level," *Fortune,* Vol. 42, No. 4, pp. 88 ff (October 1950).

Myles L. Mace, *The Board of Directors in Small Corporations.* Boston: Division of Research, Graduate School of Business Administration, Harvard University, 1948.

Herrymon Maurer, "Boards of Directors," *Fortune,* Vol. 41, No. 5, pp. 107 ff (May 1950).

Mabel Newcomer, *The Big Business Executive,* Chap. 3. New York: Columbia University Press, 1955.

William Foote Whyte, *Money and Motivation,* Chap. 14. New York: Harper & Brothers, 1955.

PART III

MANAGERIAL ORGANIZATION: BEHAVIORAL ASPECTS

chapter 11

AUTHORITY, STATUS, AND POWER

Organized executive action is impossible without authority. The nature and foundations of authority are considered in the first part of this chapter. Attention is then given to the significance of status in maintaining the authority relationship. The importance of power in organizational behavior is analyzed in the final section.

The Nature of Authority

Power and authority are closely related concepts. Power may be defined as the capacity to change individual or group behavior. Brown has power if he can cause Smith to go to a poker party with the boys rather than to a dancing party with the wife. Power is present when an individual or a group is able to affect the activity of another individual or group. It gives rise to behavior that differs from the behavior that would have occurred otherwise. The power that evolves from a managerial position is usually categorized as authority. People with authority have power, but power does not always denote authority. A subordinate may have no authority, but he can have a great deal of power.

Authority of Position

The "authority of position" is the power (or authority) that a person has by virtue of his superior position.[1] Subordinates normally accord

[1] Chester I. Barnard, *The Functions of the Executive* (Cambridge: Harvard University Press, 1938), p. 173.

255

authority to those who occupy higher hierarchical positions. This authority is to a great extent unrelated to the particular person who occupies the position. Authority would arise even though the occupant does not have the personal capacity to create power.

Personal Power

The power of executives may far exceed the amount of power (or authority) that evolves from the authority of position. The reason is that some executives have personal and professional qualities that make subordinates more willing to accept organizational responsibilities. There are also executives who actually reduce the authority accorded them by their positions. The personal qualities they possess adversely affect the extent to which subordinates accept responsibilities.

The Power of Subordinates

Subordinates sometimes have considerable personal power even though they may not have authority.[2] This power can be used to challenge the authority of those in superior positions and to change the balance of power implied by the authority of position. The power of subordinates may significantly modify the planned structure of power (or authority). A superior may actually become a subordinate even though all of the attributes of his position indicate a higher status.

The Social Foundations of Authority

Society supports and sustains authority in business and other organizations. The factors that affect authority in a society are now analyzed.

Social Conditioning

People learn to play the role of a subordinate shortly after birth. The behavior of the child is initially conditioned by the intervention of his parents. The child may resent the intrusion of parents into his adventures with his environment and his attempts to express himself, but gradually he begins to accept his parents' decisions about certain matters and to develop

[2] David Mechanic, "Sources of Power of Lower Participants in Complex Organizations," *Administrative Science Quarterly*, Vol. 7, No. 3, December 1962, pp. 349–364.

an area of acceptance within which he will obey without too much question. This process of conditioning is reinforced as the child enters school, the church, the Boy or Girl Scouts, and other formal and informal associations.

People accept organizational responsibilities, including the duty to respond to superior decisions, in return for salaries and wages, status, social satisfactions, and other considerations. But the social conditioning referred to above reinforces the authority relationship in an organization. Obeying a superior has become an habitual mode of behavior for many people. Particular organizational authority systems are also given support by social sanctions imposed upon nonconformists. In other words, insubordination may have consequences beyond the penalties that may be imposed within the organization. To paraphrase Professor Simon, it can be as embarrassing as a failure to wear a necktie in church.[3]

The problem of insubordination in business and other organizations is related to the social conditioning that occurs before people assume a formal organizational role. The conditioning process in a democratic society is subject to many forces with respect to both goals and techniques. Parents, teachers, child psychologists, physicians, clergymen, school boards, textbook writers, television scriptwriters, veterans' associations, and others have a hand in producing the man who walks into a personnel office. There are differences of opinion about the extent to which children should be conditioned to accept superior decisions and the techniques that should be used to condition them. Professors John Dollard and Neal E. Miller have this to say about the problem.

Some of the elements of current child-training procedures are undoubtedly thousands of years old. They represent a long history of conflict and confusion, of survivals from older times and unassimilated increments of the present. For example, modern society attempts to make children meek and obedient in the family but strong and competitive outside. Sometimes training in docility is so strong that the child is never able to hold its own later in the world outside the family. In other cases, rebellious traits are strongly developed and barely restrained within family life but are later freely generalized to the adult milieu. The problem of getting meekness exactly where it is wanted and strength displayed where it is appropriate is not an easy one, and it is not surprising that children frequently fail to make the correct discriminations.[4]

A consideration in social conditioning is the development of the desired end product. The fact that large numbers of people are required to play the

[3] Herbert A. Simon, *Administrative Behavior,* 2nd ed. (New York: The Macmillan Company, 1957), p. 131.

[4] John Dollard and Neal E. Miller, *Personality and Psychotherapy* (New York: McGraw-Hill Book Company, Inc., 1950), pp. 127–128.

role of subordinate in organizations might become significant in this respect. Thus, if the manner in which society now rears its children causes psychological conflicts in later authority situations, some change in the attitudes of parents, teachers, child psychologists, and others may be appropriate. However, the training process in a democratic society is not under unified control, and changes in attitude are difficult to bring about. Furthermore, the psychology of human learning is not far enough advanced to provide more than rough approximations about the relationship between training techniques and personality development. The important point for purpose of this discussion is that the problem of insubordination may partly evolve because parents no longer spank their children or because mother has become the dominant personage in the family situation. Although the significance of such factors, if they are significant, cannot be readily measured, psychologists and educators might well give them attention in developing theories and giving counsel.

Sanctions and Authority: A Social Perspective

Sanctions may be defined as penalties that can be exacted for failure to accept a superior's decision. They may also be viewed in the positive sense that a willingness to respond to a decision may result in rewards. The possibility that present or potential rewards may be withheld is frequently as important to a subordinate as a more direct penalty. Some of the sanctions that can be imposed upon subordinates evolve from powers of the organization and have an existence apart from the person of the superior. They are ultimately based on authority in another part of the organization or outside the organization. Organizational sanctions are instrumental in creating authority, but they also result from authority. The nature of this relationship is illustrated in the mutiny in 1905 on the Russian battleship *Potemkin*.

The *Potemkin* incident began with complaints by the crew about maggoty meat that was being used to prepare *borsch*.[5] The matter caused so much commotion that the captain saw fit to call the senior surgeon to inspect the meat. The surgeon reported that the meat was excellent and that the white maggots were nothing but eggs laid by flies. A little washing with vinegar and water was the prescribed remedy. The crew refused to accept the solution suggested by the surgeon. The situation became increasingly serious as agitators continued to incite an attitude of rebellion. The controversy came to a rapid conclusion when the men refused to eat *borsch*

---

[5] Richard Hough, *The Potemkin Mutiny* (New York: Pantheon Books, 1961), pp. 13–41.

which contained the maggoty meat. The captain warned the crew that they could be strung up on the yardarm for their behavior. He asked those who were willing to eat the meat to step forward. Only a number of petty officers and bosuns and a few of the older men broke ranks. The rest of the crew stood in silence. The captain, sensing the seriousness of the situation, decided to seal some of the meat in a bottle for analysis and report the incident to the commander-in-chief for his action. He dismissed the crew and departed for his cabin. However, the second in command refused to let the matter stand. He reformed the ranks, and ordered the bosun to call out the guard and to bring a tarpaulin. An old naval practice was to throw a tarpaulin over mutineers before shooting them. All those who were prepared to eat the *borsch* were asked to step forward. Only a few of the men moved. The bosun was ordered to bring the ringleaders and throw the tarpaulin over them. The firing squad was ready. Suddenly one of the leading agitators called, "Don't shoot your own comrades—you can't kill your own shipmates! Don't fire, comrades!" Others called for rifles and ammunition to take over the ship. Most of the officers, including the captain, were shot or forced overboard.

This mutiny shows that even the threat of death may not be adequate to maintain authority. Most of the crew seemed willing to submit to a firing squad rather than obey orders to eat the *borsch*. Authority might have been reestablished if the firing squad had not hesitated in performing its duties. The insubordination of the firing squad removed the possibility of imposing sanctions, which gave impetus to the mutiny.

Complete breakdowns of authority illustrated by the *Potemkin* mutiny are unique rather than usual events in history. An organization, whether a state, a ship, or a business enterprise, cannot survive without authority. Society has a vital interest in the maintenance of authority in the organizations through which it pursues its purposes. A breakdown of authority in such organizations is a serious threat to the welfare of society and cannot generally be tolerated. Authority is supported by a formal system of laws and informal social norms backed by the powers of society. However, the established patterns of authority must have general acceptance if they are to survive. Too much use of force is disruptive and indicates a breakdown of existing patterns. Firing squads, electric chairs, discharge from employment, or excommunication may be necessary as examples for the few, but authority rests on a highly insecure foundation if the few become the many. A particular authority system can be supported by sanctions imposed by other organizations of the society. However, as the *Potemkin* incident illustrates, such sanctions may not reestablish authority and are themselves based on authority.

The Sanctions of Property

Authority in a business organization is supported by the sanctions that evolve from the law of property. A subordinate who does not obey an order can be physically removed from company property by the courts and the police if he does not do so voluntarily. This action is implied whenever anyone is discharged from employment. The power to discharge has a corollary in the power to hire and grant economic and other benefits. Executives as owners or as representatives of owners can determine the use that will be made of the property rights conferred by law. They possess the power to impose sanctions in the sense that actual and expected benefits from an employment relationship can be removed in whole or in part. This power is highly instrumental in creating authority or acceptance from subordinates. It differentiates executives from others in the organization and gives a basis for the idea that authority is delegated from the top. The sanctions of property, like the firing squad on the *Potemkin,* are based on authority in other parts of the society. They can be enforced by the courts, the police, and, if necessary, the military. However, the law of property has general social acceptance and is usually obeyed without the use of such instrumentalities of power. This situation did not prevail with respect to the Eighteenth Amendment prohibiting the sale of alcoholic beverages and the enforcement provisions set forth in the Volstead Act. The result of Prohibition was a large volume of illicit production offered for sale by thousands of bootleggers. There was a great deal of laxity in the enforcement of the law, and, in many instances, law enforcement personnel behaved like the firing squad on the *Potemkin* and refused to fire upon or arrest violators of the law. Thus, the failures in authority with respect to the law were given support by insubordination among those responsible for imposing sanctions.

The Impact of the Market

The potency of sanctions that may be imposed by management as a result of property rights is affected by economic and market conditions. An excess of jobs over job-seekers sometimes makes a subordinate more inclined to "tell the boss to go to hell." A large amount of unemployment or the lack of particular employment opportunities tends to enhance the compulsion of the power of discharge. Present and potential benefits of an employment situation can be made more or less attractive by alternative opportunities. The possibility of being promoted to a vice-presidency or of an increase in salary is not quite as alluring if a similar or a better opportunity is offered by another organization.

Unionism and Collective Bargaining

The power implied by property rights has found a countervailing force in the rise of powerful labor unions. Labor legislation and the strike weapon have given unions formidable power in bargaining with management. Collective bargaining is partly concerned with the manner in which the workers represented by the union will share in the distribution of income to stockholders, customers, and other interest groups. This aspect of union action is not unlike that of other organized groups with which management must contend. A "monopolistic" supplier or bank may exert as much pressure upon management as a labor union. However, there is a fundamental difference between the impact of unions upon the affairs of management and that of other groups. The interests of the workers are more closely related to matters internal to the organization because they are themselves subordinates and directly subject to managerial decisions. The power of the union is used to restrict the discretion of management in dealing with subordinates represented by the union. The trade agreement that evolves from the collective bargaining process sets forth norms that limit the actions of both parties for a given period of time. Differences involving such norms are generally resolved through a formal grievance procedure agreed to by both parties.

Many aspects of collective bargaining are applications of the political norms of a democratic society into the industrial area. This development has been lauded by such terms as "a system of industrial jurisprudence" and "industrial democracy." The difficulty is that there is frequently a difference between idealistic preachments and industrial practices. Unions and their constituents generally regard the trade agreement as a safeguard against "arbitrary" actions on the part of management. The history of labor-management relations is not without examples of management practices that would bring a ringing rebuke in the "climate of opinion" of today. But the pendulum can swing too far in the opposite direction. The restrictions imposed by unions can interfere with management's responsibility to the organization as an integrated system. Military commanders cannot be expected to assume the responsibility of fighting the nation's wars if they cannot order soldiers into battle. Soldiers might prefer not to face death on the battlefield, but they must if the nation is to survive. Industrial workers might also prefer not to face many of the hazards of the industrial order. They can and should be protected against some of them, but they cannot escape them all. Too much restriction on the power of management to make decisions can cause industrial organizations to bog down with inefficiencies. A production line might be paced at a rate that adversely affects the health of workers, but it need not be slowed to prevent a little perspiration. The welfare of the worker should be considered in making technological innovations, but it should obviously not be the only consideration. Workers should not be required to subject themselves to a hell on earth, but they and the unions that represent them should not assume that the "pie in the sky" can be obtained by merely asking.

Unionism and collective bargaining have also placed limitations upon management's power to impose sanctions. Workers have recourse in the grievance procedure if they believe their rights under the trade agreement have been violated by management actions. Thus, although management has the right to discharge and impose other sanctions for "cause," workers have procedural rights much like those extended by courts of law. The union is generally given a part in the proceedings through shop stewards and joint union-management committees. Many trade agreements make provision for arbitration by outside parties if the union and management cannot themselves resolve the dispute. The rights that are accorded by this procedure place a restraint upon arbitrary uses of power by management. However, unions and workers sometimes use the grievance procedure for other purposes. They may accumulate an unreasonable number of grievances to put pressure upon management and give the union bargaining power relative to other matters. The grievance procedure can also be used to avoid sanctions through "legalistic" strategies. It can be used to protect scoundrels as well as saints. Furthermore, management may not attempt to discipline workers for some improper acts because it involves a long sequence of power clashes with the union. The grievance procedure provides a useful instrument for those who deliberately seek to practice insubordination.

Management is sometimes forced to approach labor relations in terms of conflict with the union. A genuine desire to treat workers fairly may be thwarted by strategical and tactical considerations. Management may not make concessions it might otherwise make because they are spoils in the game of bargaining with the union. Unions sometimes view management's efforts toward better labor relations as a threat to their survival and deliberately create conflict situations to justify their existence to the worker.

Professional Associations

Associations of professors, physicians and surgeons, engineers, teachers, nurses, and other professional groups may also limit the power of management in the organizations in which they are employed. Although such associations do not usually bargain with management in the manner of labor unions, they are often highly effective in promoting the interests of their members through political, economic, and social pressures. The techniques used range from mild forms of "moral suasion" to a vigorous pursuit of legislative favor. The manner in which an association protects the interests of a professional group is illustrated by the way in which the American Association of University Professors (AAUP) endeavors to enforce standards relating to academic freedom and tenure. The universities in which professors are employed cannot be legally forced to conform to such standards. However, the AAUP censures or "blacklists" university administrations that violate its academic freedom and tenure standards and publishes a full account of the matter in its official journal. The American Medical Association and related associations have played an important part in promoting professional standards and protecting the status of their members in hospitals and other organizational situations. The decisional discretion that may be exercised by hospital administrators over the activities of resident physicians and surgeons is generally more limited than that which may be exercised over other employees even when matters relating to medical care are eliminated.

The Status System and the Authority Relationship

Status may be defined as the totality of attributes that rank and relate individuals in an organization. It is a product of group behavior; an isolated individual has no status. For example, A has a higher status than does B, C has a lower status than B and A, and D and E have equal status, and so on. The status accorded an individual is a product of the values prevalent in a society. In some societies an individual's status is enhanced by a large number of wives. In others polygamy predicates a lower status for the practitioner. An ability to drink a large volume of beer may have status value in a student club, but it would hardly confer high status among members of the WCTU.

Status and Authority

Status plays an important part in maintaining authority in organizations. A person generally does not like to take orders from someone he considers to be his equal. The status system makes compliance easier because a degree of inequality is rationalized. The instrumentalities of status impute qualities that reinforce the authority relationship.

Formal Status Factors

Some of the attributes that make for higher or lower status form an integral part of the position a person occupies in an organization. For example, the position of president generally carries with it such objects of status as a walnut-paneled private office, carpeting, and elegant furnishings. The discussion that follows is concerned with formal or planned aspects of the status system.[6]

Scalar and Functional Status

The levels in a hierarchy correspond closely to the amount of status accorded a position. Persons who occupy higher positions generally, but not always, have a higher status than those in lower positions. Functional specialization may also significantly affect status. The status value of a particular function varies from organization to organization. In a production-oriented organization the production manager may have higher status than the sales manager; the reverse may be true in an organization in which marketing is strategic.

Formal Ceremonies of Appointment and Achievement

Formal ceremonies are more common in military, political, educational, and fraternal organizations than in business organizations. One purpose of such ceremonies is to communicate to people in the organization and society that a particular person should be accorded the status associated with a given position or accomplishment. Ceremonies also remind those in and outside the organization that such positions as general of the army, secretary of agriculture, governor, and the president of a corporation or university are important. A university commencement announces that a certain number of students are entitled to the status accorded an academic degree and that the degree and the institution conferring it have a status value. In spite of esoteric and entertaining or at least energetic commencement speakers, the educational attainment of the graduating senior is not enhanced in any significant degree by the ceremony. In fact, some of the participants, including faculty members and university presidents, may be slightly bored with the proceedings. Nevertheless, the status implications of

[6] Chester I. Barnard first gave emphasis to the importance of the status system in "Functions and Pathology of Status Systems in Formal Organizations," in William Foote Whyte, *Industry and Society* (New York: McGraw-Hill Book Company, 1946), pp. 46–83. Many of the ideas in this section were derived from this source.

such ceremonies should not be taken too lightly in a world in which the power of empire is symbolized by the coronation of a queen with full pomp and circumstance. The contention is not that all ceremony is useful but that ceremony can be a useful status device.

Insignia and Other Status Identifications

Military organizations are probably most pronounced in their use of status identifications. Anyone familiar with the meaning of military symbols of rank can readily ascertain the approximate status of all noncivilian personnel in a military garrison. Such symbols become a common denominator of status throughout the organization. They make possible a degree of stability in the status system and give it universality throughout the organization. The importance of this fact can be seen in an armed force of ten million persons with considerable shifting of personnel and constantly changing personal associations. A high status individual does not have to take personal action to enforce his status. The general or colonel does not have to say: "I have high scalar rank and should be accorded high status." The insignia will assure a general or a colonel proper response from lower status personnel. It provides a cue to all participants in the organization as to how they should behave toward others in the organization.

Religious and educational organizations make frequent use of formal symbols of status. The vestment worn by officiants and assistants during a religious service in the Catholic Church and many protestant churches indicates the rite and the hierarchical rank of the wearer. Academic gowns used by educational organizations during ceremonial occasions identify the degree (Ph.D., M.A., B.A.), the institution that conferred the degree, and the area in which major work was done. In the legal profession a judge is identified by a black robe, and in England wigs are worn by attorneys and judges. Distinctive attire is often worn by medical doctors, nurses, and other hospital personnel. Police and fire services use uniforms and insignia that identify rank and specialization. Uniforms and insignia are also used by the Red Cross, Salvation Army, and many fraternal organizations.

Although generally not as formalized or widely used, various kinds of status identifications can be found in business organizations. Uniforms and insignia are generally worn by plant protection personnel. Identification badges used by some companies for security reasons usually become an integral part of the status system. Such badges generally identify scalar and functional position by shape and color. One company uses round badges with two colors for top executives, one-color round badges for other executives, rectangular badges for supervisors and workers. Supervisory rank is indicated by the number of black bars on the badge. All badges have a photograph of the wearer, except those worn by top executives. The status value of these badges is indicated by the fact that many people wear them after working hours. In the restaurant industry, standard uniforms are often worn by waitresses. The chef's hat is an important status symbol in the kitchen. In the better restaurants one can readily identify the functional position and the scalar rank of all personnel from the bus boy to the chef. Hotels also use uniforms and symbols of rank extensively; bellboys are almost always uniformed. Uniforms are also frequently used by trucking concerns, public transport companies, and theatres.

The Use of Titles

Scalar rank is indicated by such titles as vice-president, foreman, group chief, general, captain, bishop, mayor, governor, and maître d'hôtel. Functional designations are also vital ingredients of the organizational status system. The status distinctions inferred from the following titles are well understood by participants in organization: engineer, accountant, bookkeeper, filing clerk, private secretary, stenographer, machinist, janitor, chemist, physicist, typist, and laborer. Professional designations such as attorney, physician, C.P.A, psychiatrist, osteopath, and chiropractor have similar status implications. Academic achievement is indicated by such titles as Doctor of Philosophy (Ph.D.), Doctor of Medicine (M.D.), Master of Arts (M.A.), and Bachelor of Arts (B.A., A.B.).

The Status Implications of Privileges and Special Facilities

Status is also symbolized by the privileges and special facilities made available to organizational personnel. A distinction should be made between privileges and facilities as instruments of status and other organizational purposes that privileges and facilities may serve. A private office may improve the functional efficiency of an executive, and it may also be a material reward. In the following discussion, the emphasis is upon the status implications of privileges and special facilities. Someone taking a tour through the offices of any large organization will find significant differences in the physical facilities provided various kinds of personnel. The desks of top executives are usually more ornate and larger than the desks of lower-level personnel. The lowest-ranking office personnel use functional desk pens, while higher-ranking executive personnel have more elaborate marble-base desk pens. Sometimes the size of the base and the number of pens increase as one goes from lower executive ranks to the top ranks. In one concern, the top executives have real fireplaces; the next level of executives has artificial fireplaces; lower levels have no fireplaces. The carpeting in the offices of top executives is often more luxurious than the rugs, if any, at lower levels. The offices of some top executives are furnished by the best interior decorators and resemble penthouse apartments. The kind of automobile provided by the organization to various ranks may vary from Cadillac limousines (with chauffeurs) for top executives to a less opulent Ford, Chevrolet, or Plymouth for lower-ranking personnel. Less restricted working hours and longer lunch periods are privileges of rank. Access to company-owned hunting lodges and other facilities has an important status meaning. Also important is the type of traveling and entertainment facilities made available for business purposes. A similar distribution of privileges and facilities is found in universities, hospitals, churches, government, and military organizations.

Rationalization of Personality

The status of high-ranking executives is often enhanced by a public relations program. A good press agent can emphasize the "personal qualities" of an executive and "create" attributes that confer higher status within an organization and in the society. The techniques that were used to make an "Elvis Presley" are also used to promote the "personalities" of top leaders in business, governmental, religious, and military organizations.

Authority and Power

The institutions of the society and the formal instruments of status give support to a hierarchical structure of authority. Such a power structure is essential in complex cooperative endeavor. An important reason is that compulsion is sometimes required to achieve cooperation. But even with complete cooperation authority would still be required to resolve the problem of "uncertainty." Uncertainty means that there is no way to determine which of several alternatives provides the best solution to a problem. People with high intelligence and the best of intentions may disagree violently about the appropriateness of a decision. Authority is necessary to resolve such conflicts if cooperative endeavor is to survive.

A distinction should be made between the positions that make up the structure of authority and the persons who occupy them. Authority exists apart from particular persons who hold positions. However, persons may significantly affect the authority structure by the personal power they possess. Executive X may have far more power than executive Y with the same amount of initial authority. Superior authority is also affected by the power of subordinate personnel. The power of subordinates acts as a countervailing force which may increase or decrease the power of superiors. The nature of some of these relationships and the part they play in the managerial process are considered in Chapter 12.

SELECTED REFERENCES

Chester I. Barnard, *The Functions of the Executive,* Chap. 12, Cambridge: Harvard University Press, 1938.

Chester I. Barnard, "Functions and Pathology of Status Systems in Formal Organizations," in William Foote Whyte, *Industry and Society,* Chap. 4. New York: McGraw-Hill Book Company, Inc., 1946.

Reinhard Bendix and Seymour Martin Lipset (editors), *Class, Status and Power: A Reader in Social Stratification.* Glencoe, Ill.: The Free Press, 1953.

John Kenneth Galbraith, *American Capitalism: The Concept of Countervailing Power.* Boston: Houghton Mifflin Company, 1956.

Everett C. Hughes, "Dilemmas and Contradictions of Status," *American Journal of Sociology,* Vol. 50, No. 5, pp. 353–359 (March 1945).

Harold J. Leavitt, *Managerial Psychology,* 2nd ed., Chap. 11. Chicago: The University of Chicago Press, 1964.

Herbert A. Simon, *Administrative Behavior,* 2nd ed., Chap. 7. New York: The Macmillan Company, 1957.

William Foote Whyte, *Human Relations in the Restaurant Industry,* Chaps. 2 and 4. New York: McGraw-Hill Book Company, Inc., 1948.

chapter 12

ORGANIZATIONAL DYNAMICS

The organizational structure is constantly being "organized" and "reorganized" by informal and formal means. Actual behavior may depart significantly from the planned structure of responsibilities and authorities. The nature and importance of informal modifications are given comprehensive consideration in this chapter. Attention is also given to formal or planned changes in the organizational structure.

Functional Structure and Organizational Behavior

An organizational structure tends to develop even when no prior planning has taken place. A good example is provided by a street corner gang studied by sociologist William Foote Whyte.[1] Doc was the top man in the Norton gang. Danny, who was Doc's best friend, and Mike occupied the second rung in the Norton organization. Friendship with the three top leaders gave Long John a somewhat superior standing in the gang. Nine other members occupied subordinate positions and responded to directions from above. See Figure 12-1. Large and complex organizational structures do not simply evolve as a by-product of the social process. They are systematically planned for the achievement of predetermined organizational purposes.

Functional Design Theory

The theory of functional design is impersonal in its approach and is an attempt to construct an "ideal" organizational structure. The approach is

[1] William Foote Whyte, *Street Corner Society,* 2nd ed. (Chicago: The University of Chicago Press, 1955), pp. 3–51.

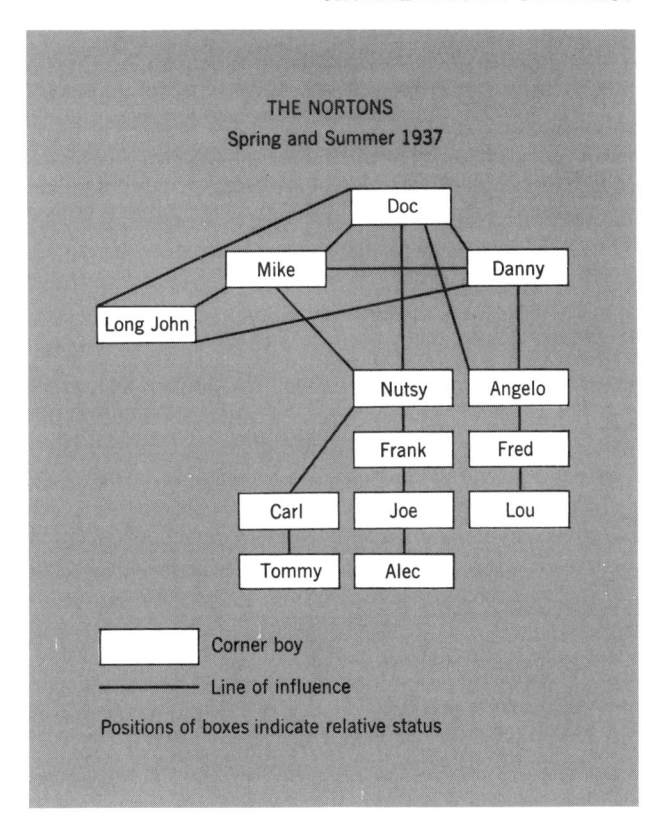

Figure 12-1. Informal hierarchial structure. Reproduced with permission from William Foote Whyte, *Street Corner Society,* 2nd ed. Chicago: The University of Chicago Press, 1955, p. 13.

human only to the extent that the planned responsibilities cannot exceed the capabilities of personnel available to the organization. It is evident that an organizer cannot plan positions that can be filled only by people with the intelligence of an Einstein or the physical stamina of a Tarzan. The motif of a functional design is how best to achieve the organizational objective. The organizer disregards the impact of personality and social behavior; his goal is the best possible functional plan.

The argument of the functional purist is that, although a good functional design will not necessarily assure efficient cooperation, a bad one will make it even more difficult. As the industrialist Henry S. Dennison has pointed out:

The importance of right structure of organization is sometimes undervalued, because with the right men almost any kind of organization can run well. This is true, but is by no means the whole truth. With the finest of personnel, an illogical organization structure makes waste through internal friction and lost motion; it fails to retain and develop good men and to invite into its membership new men of high quality.[2]

Some people have suggested that a purely functional design is inadequate. They contend that personality should be given consideration in planning the organizational structure.

Functional Design: The Personality Problem

The functional theorist does not ignore the impact of personality after the plan is put into effect. His argument is that personality should play a minimum part, if any, in planning the organization. A contrary view is held by Charles R. Hook, Jr., an experienced executive, who contends that:

An organization is people—not a collection of functions. Too much of the thinking devoted to organization planning has been done as though we were embarking upon the structuring and staffing of a brand-new but as yet nonexistent organization. If this were the case, our problems would be simple indeed! Under such a situation, it is not only possible but almost imperative that our planning should be carried on without regard to any particular human being. Aren't most of us, however, concerned with the improvement of an *already existing* organization, a *living,* breathing organism? . . . *Oftentimes the most important outcome of an organization plan is to give a really good man a chance to go to work.*[3]

Lyndall Urwick, on the other hand, laments the lack of attention given a functional approach to organizational structure.

Emphasis has been laid on this question of thinking consciously and technically about organisation, of laying out structure first and not thinking about individuals till structure has been determined, because it is still rare to find any general acceptance of this principle. The number of human institutions which do put correct structure first and politics second is very limited. The majority of social groups being left to grow like Topsy find, sooner rather than later, that Topsy has married Turvy.[4]

[2] Henry S. Dennison, *Organization Engineering* (New York: McGraw-Hill Book Company, Inc., 1931), pp. 5–6.

[3] Charles R. Hook, Jr., "Organization Planning—Its Challenges and Limitations," *Organization Planning and Management Development,* Personnel Series, No. 141 (New York: American Management Association, 1951), p. 21. (Italics in the original.)

[4] L. Urwick, *The Elements of Administration* (New York: Harper & Brothers Publishers, 1943), p. 39.

Although there appears to be some difference of opinion between Hook and Urwick, the area of disagreement is more apparent than real. Urwick is pointing to the danger of letting organizational politics play a dominant part in shaping and reshaping the organizational structure. Hook gives emphasis to the idea that professional and personal differences cannot be ignored or eliminated in organization planning. The relative weight that should be given to function and personality cannot be answered with any degree of certainty. It would obviously be a mistake to let either dominate the scene completely. The organizational structure should not become a strait jacket that restrains personal adaptation and initiative.[5] Executives rarely achieve results in exactly the same way. One executive may organize a particular department differently than another with no loss in productivity. There does not seem to be one best way to achieve an objective.

Executive personality may significantly affect the apportionment of managerial responsibilities. An aggressive "empire builder" will absorb available responsibilities; a submissive individual may give up important functions. An authoritarian leader will delegate responsibilities differently than a democratic leader. An executive who is heavily endowed with social skills will not have the same approach to managerial problems as one who lacks this quality.

Organizers are constantly forced to compromise between the needs of the system and the self-interests of the people who serve it. The organization should not be permitted to become an agency for personal goals that conflict with organizational goals. However, the dividing line between the two cannot always be readily determined. Something that appears contrary to organizational interests may have an opposite effect. For example, a vice-president of marketing may have more assistants than he really needs to perform his responsibilities. The reason (which is generally rationalized) is that he likes congenial people (possibly "yes-men") around the office and at company sales meetings. A neophyte might approach such a situation with a "suggestion" or an order that an assistant or two be transferred to another department. The result might well be the loss of an extremely valuable marketing executive to a company willing to indulge his whims. An executive's salary may involve payment in forms other than financial remuneration. A president who fires too many vice-presidents, a division manager who buys better than necessary office furnishings, a sales manager who hires a private secretary he doesn't really need, or an executive vice-president who travels more than he should may all be retained because their contributions to the organization far exceed their total cost.

[5] Ernest Dale, *Planning and Developing the Company Organization Structure*, Research Report No. 20 (New York: American Management Association, 1952), p. 40.

However, it should not be assumed that such personal goals can always be justified.

Functional Design: Informal Organization

An organizer cannot possibly plan the totality of activities and interactions that make up organizational behavior. The people in organization amplify and modify the formal or planned organization and create more comprehensive and complex behavioral patterns. The difference between the formal organization and the behavior that actually prevails can be categorized as the informal organization. The formal organization is the behavior that is planned by superiors. The informal organization is the behavior that subordinates themselves have "planned" to contend with organizational and personal problems. It can become a disruptive force that impedes progress toward an organizational objective. But it can also play a constructive part in achieving goals and provide a means for more effective organization.

Informal organization can compensate for inadequacies in the planned structure. If the organization plan fails to provide adequate communication channels, the informal system frequently corrects the difficulty. Much of the communication across departmental lines is informal; the formal communication chain is often short-circuited to facilitate information flow. Many organizations have an effective "committee system" even though none has been planned. Coordination in one large industrial company is achieved almost exclusively through informal means. A considerable amount of leadership comes from people who have not been charged with such responsibilities. Subordinates sometimes make up for failures on the part of superiors. They may even assume personal risks involving their careers to serve the organization. Such informal instrumentalities are often important ingredients of organizational efficiency. Organizers should take care not to disrupt them without providing equally effective alternatives. Zealous organizers who seek a functional ideal not infrequently destroy more than they create.

Authority and Power Structures

The actual structure of power in an organization may differ in a marked degree from the planned structure of authority. A good example of the

ORGANIZATIONAL DYNAMICS 275

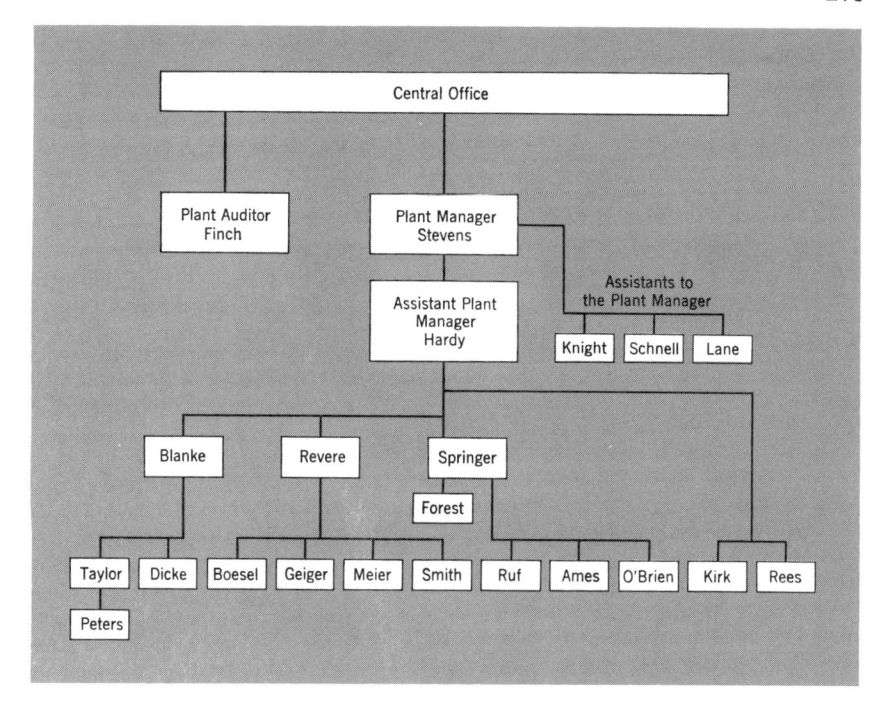

Figure 12-2. Milo formal structure simplified. Reproduced with permission from Melville Dalton, *Men Who Manage*. New York: John Wiley and Sons, Inc., 1959, p. 21.

extent to which the authority (or power) accorded by managerial positions may be modified is indicated in a study made by Melville Dalton.[6]

Authority versus Power: The Milo Plant

The formal organization chart of the Milo plant portraying the planned structure of authority is shown in Figure 12-2. The actual power of the people who occupied the positions is indicated in Figure 12-3. The power rankings were made by Milo personnel who were or had been close associates of the managers being ranked. The author of the study, Melville Dalton, who was himself a staff member, participated in the rating process by challenging rankings he thought to be out of line in terms of his own experiences. It should be noted that there were far more agreements than disagreements on what the rankings should be.

[6] Melville Dalton, *Men Who Manage* (New York: John Wiley & Sons, Inc., 1959), pp. 20–31.

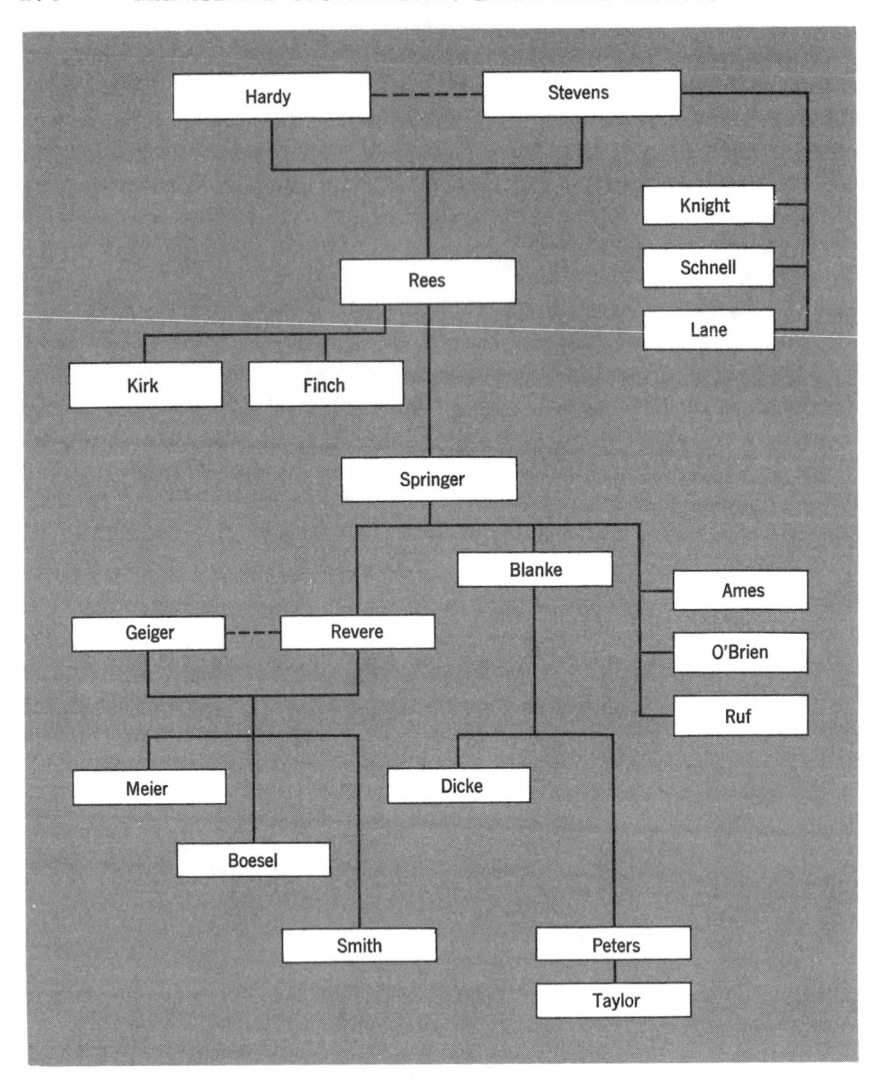

276 MANAGERIAL ORGANIZATION: BEHAVIORAL ASPECTS

Figure 12-3. Milo structure of unofficial power. Reproduced with permission from Melville Dalton, *Men Who Manage*. New York: John Wiley and Sons, Inc., 1959, p. 22.

The Plant Manager, Stevens, and the Assistant Plant Manager, Hardy, are given equal rank in the power structure. Some of the reasons for this departure from the formal authority structure were the following. Stevens was clearly less forceful than Hardy and generally gave way to Hardy in executive meetings. Most of the questions at the meetings were directed to

Hardy, who usually gave answers without consulting Stevens. Hardy's approval was considered to be strategic in the more important promotions. When production delays occurred, persons in charge were more concerned with Hardy's possible reaction than they were about the Plant Manager's. Stevens was considered to be "unsocial and distant" in contrast to the highly personable Hardy. These and other factors were sufficient to counterbalance the authority accorded Stevens by his superior position.

The third man in the power structure was Rees, who headed the Industrial Relations section. Rees, a bright young man with a degree in aeronautical engineering, had recently taken over the section from someone who was no longer capable of managing it. One of the first things Rees did was to challenge Hardy emphatically in a meeting on incentives, asserting that the "top management" had put the system here and "by God we're going to make it work, not just tolerate it!" [7] This and other incidents, together with the fact that Rees had spent three years at headquarters, led people to view Rees as an unofficial spokesman for top management. Hardy was assumed to be more powerful because he dominated more areas of Milo life, but he did not interfere with Rees' "functional" jurisdiction. As Melville Dalton points out: "Hardy almost certainly exceeded his assigned authority over all plant processes except those which Rees interpreted as lying in his sphere. Here Hardy exercised less than his formal authority." [8]

Springer, the superintendent of one of the three divisions, was placed slightly below Rees in the power ranking. He had developed a close personal bond with Hardy during the past. The other superintendents, Revere and Blanke, recognized this relationship and often consulted with Springer when they wanted something from Hardy. Revere had the lowest rank among the superintendents partly because he "no longer aspired to dominate plant events." [9] He was not particularly interested in higher income and he was reluctant to accept more responsibilities. Hardy had given him the job because there were no other good candidates.

The rank held by Ames in Springer's division resulted from his ability to get along with the men and the union. Both Hardy and Springer appreciated the support that Ames gave them in the shop. Geiger ranked at a par with his chief, Revere, partly because he headed a major production unit. He also had strong support from Blanke, one of the other division superintendents, as the result of favors in the past. The power situation was affected by the close cooperation among Blanke, Geiger, Dicke, Meier, and Boesel because of their German descent. Knight ranked above the other

[7] Dalton, *op. cit.*, p. 25.
[8] *Ibid.*
[9] *Ibid.*, p. 27.

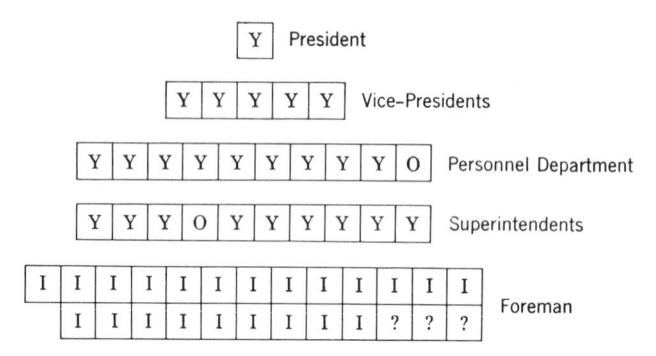

278   MANAGERIAL ORGANIZATION: BEHAVIORAL ASPECTS

				Y		President

| Y | Y | Y | Y | Y | Vice-Presidents

| Y | Y | Y | Y | Y | Y | Y | Y | Y | O | Personnel Department

| Y | Y | Y | O | Y | Y | Y | Y | Y | Y | Superintendents

| I | I | I | I | I | I | I | I | I | I | I | I |
| I | I | I | I | I | I | I | I | I | ? | ? | ? | Foreman

Figure 12-4. Legend: Y—Yankee; I—Irish; O—Others. Job-ethnic hierarchy in a New England factory. The non-Yankee at the superintendent level is a testing engineer. The non-Yankee member of the personnel group is a young Italian who does safety cartoons and acts as general errand boy. (Adapted from: Orvis Collins, "Ethnic Behavior in Industry: Sponsorship and Rejection in a New England Factory," *American Journal of Sociology,* January 1946, p. 294.)

two assistants to the Plant Manager because of his knowledge of internal affairs and his close personal relationship with Stevens.

Informal Status and Power Instruments

Status is a planned attribute of organizational positions which, in addition to other things, gives support to authority. It may also stem from the qualities of the person who occupies a position and can serve as an important instrument of power. The nature of some of these qualities is now considered.

Ethnic and Related Factors. Attitudes that relate to nationality, race, and religion can significantly affect the way in which people react to someone. Such identities as Catholic, Jew, Negro, Indian, Japanese, Italian, and Irish are important in status evaluation. Some people are antagonistic toward persons from particular ethnic groups and will not accord them "equality." One executive may have much less power than another executive with the same authority but the "right" ethnic background.

Ethnic groups, including those who are a minority, may form alliances to preserve their power and to prevent entry by "outsiders." The cooperation among "the Germans" in the Milo plant illustrates this kind of behavior. A study of a New England factory by Orvis Collins is another case in point.[10] Figure 12-4 shows the ethnic backgrounds of the people in the

[10] Orvis Collins, "Ethnic Behavior in Industry: Sponsorship and Rejection in a New England Factory," *American Journal of Sociology,* January 1946, pp. 293–298.

management hierarchy. The upper and middle positions are dominated by Yankees and the supervisory positions by Irish. The ethnic loyalties that were involved in this situation "enforced" a policy of hiring Irishmen for supervisory positions and Yankees for the higher positions. A departure from this policy was permitted only with the complete approval of the two in-groups. The promotion of a Yankee named Peters to replace Sullivan, an "old country" Irishman, caused an immediate uproar. The social pressure became so pronounced that Peters soon failed to show up for work for reasons of illness. Peters did not again report for work and was replaced by a man named Murphy.

The problem of cooperation may cause management to consider ethnic factors in recruiting and promoting personnel. An outsider may not be able to work effectively with a particular ethnic group. An example is provided by the problems experienced during World War II with a group of Indians recruited on a reservation for work in a shipyard.[11] The supervisor to whom they were assigned reported them a sullen, unmanageable crowd, soldiering on the job. He threatened to quit if he could not be given another assignment. His boss complained that he did not know what to do with these "maladjusted employees." An employee counselor finally took command of the situation. She talked to the chief and found that he had successfully supervised a work project on the reservation. On the suggestion of the counselor, the chief was given some training and put in charge of the group. The result was reported in the following words.

The Indians went to work with a will. The supervisor wisely ignored complaints that the Indians were loafers because they took their accustomed siestas, dozing in the shade. The work was done in unexpected ways, but the results were, by the highest production standards, excellent.[12]

Although an emancipation of the distaff side of the human species has occurred during recent decades, women are still accorded an inferior rank in many respects. Most males have many reasons for not wanting female supervisors, and even the women have doubts on this subject. Age also plays a part in status evaluation, even though it does not command its former respect. Older supervisors are often more effective than younger ones, other things being equal.

Education and Experience. Education is an important status factor partly because the knowledge it presumably produces is necessary in an advanced industrial society. It is in many instances the first step in the

[11] E. B. Strong, "Individual Adjustment in Industrial Society: The Experience of the Navy Employee Counseling Service," *American Sociological Review*, Vol. 14, No. 3, June 1949, p. 341.
[12] *Ibid.*

managerial and professional ladder. Many organizations will not look twice at an applicant who has not completed four years of college. Higher education has also become a bearer of social prestige.

Academic degrees have status value as titles irrespective of how they were earned. H. L. Mencken noted that Americans are particularly fond of such titles and observed that "the tendency to multiply degrees has been marked in the United States since the turn of the century." [13] There are now so many different kinds of bachelor, master, and doctorate degrees that they are generally followed by a designation denoting the field of study. In addition to the so-called earned degrees, honorary degrees are widely distributed in the United States. Such degrees are, to use Mencken's words, "conferred wholesale upon the presidents and other high officers of rich corporations, newspaper editors and columnists, eminent radio crooners, college presidents who may be trusted to reciprocate, and a miscellaneous rabble of contributors or potential contributors to college funds." [14]

The college or university from which a degree is received may also make a difference in status evaluation. The question, "Where did you get your degree?" frequently has status implications. Although "the school tie" is not as important in the United States as some European countries, the fact that someone has attended a "proper" preparatory school or college is usually noted in news items announcing engagements, marriages, promotions, and deaths.

The knowledge that comes from experience may significantly affect a person's status in an organization. Education is important, but it is not enough. Experience is generally assumed to be an essential quality of the successful man. Some kinds of experience have a higher value than others. A corporation executive with governmental experience may have less prestige than one who has the equivalent in business experience. The reverse may be true for administrators in the federal government. Experience in a well-known corporation is often worth more than experience in an ordinary company even when there is no real difference.

Administrative Skills and Related Factors. An executive who has had a great deal of experience in business or other bureaucracies is often much more effective than one without such experience. Familiarity with the ins and outs of the administrative process is highly important in this respect. Knowledge of people may also significantly influence the power structure. An executive who is personally acquainted with persons in key positions has an advantage over an executive who is not well known. A wide circle of friends, membership in a powerful clique, and support from higher

[13] H. L. Mencken, *The American Language, Supplement One* (New York: Alfred A. Knopf, 1945), p. 527.
[14] *Ibid.*, pp. 528–529.

executives are often strategic elements in the power structure. The adage "it is not what you know, but who you know" has much validity in the management field. The reason is that executives have to work through other people to get things done. An executive who knows many people has an important ingredient for the achievement of both organizational and personal goals.

Socio-Psychological Factors. A person with a large amount of drive often has more power than someone with less drive. Decisiveness or the ability to come to a decision may also be important in this respect. Another applicable quality is the extent to which an executive is motivated toward particular objectives. A strong desire for power and status can cause a person to expend much energy and take many risks to achieve this goal. On the other hand, there are people like Superintendent Revere in the Milo plant who have less power because they do not want to control events.

An ability to "manipulate" people is an important instrument of power in an organization. Social skills, communication capacities, and a talent for leadership can greatly enhance the power of an executive. However, it should not be assumed that effective executives are necessarily well liked. A "struggle" for power is not the same as a popularity poll. Indeed, a powerful executive is not infrequently "feared" as much as he is "liked."

Family, Clubs, Politics, and Other Factors. Family background may make a difference in the manner in which people behave toward a person. The situation that often prevails in family-controlled corporations is almost too obvious to mention. The influence of prominent families can also serve their siblings in many ways. The children of business and governmental leaders frequently have an advantage. They probably gain more from the fact that they are familiar with the intricacies of organizational behavior than they do from contacts made for them. They have learned something about "the rules of the game" and the techniques that make for success.

Fraternal and other forms of association can play a major part in the power formula. Melville Dalton cited constant references to the importance of the Masons in the Milo plant.[15] Of the 21 top managers of the plant only 2 were not Masons. Membership in the community Yacht Club was also related to progress in the managerial structure. It should be noted that membership in some clubs is possible only *after* high status is achieved. Power is both a prerequisite and a consequence with one reinforcing the other.

All of the higher managers in the Milo plant were or pretended that they were Republicans.[16] One of the executives expressed considerable anxiety

[15] Dalton, *op. cit.*, pp. 178–181.
[16] *Ibid.*, p. 91.

when a Democratic sticker was stuck to the rear of his automobile. He hoped that his superiors had not seen it. Although there are important exceptions, business executives tend to take a conservative position in their political thinking.

Participation in community affairs, such as heading the Community Chest, often provides a basis for higher status within an organization. The contacts that are made with influential people and the publicity that results from such activities are important in this respect. The wives of executives may also help determine their husband's place in the power structure. An executive can be helped by his wife's family background, her skills at company social affairs, and the psychological support she gives him. Social relationships among organization personnel in neighborhood groups, on the golf course, in poker clubs, and at dinner parties are often used for "politicking." Executives who do not participate in such affairs sometimes find themselves with a disadvantage. Informal alliances and "inside" information are important pawns in the power game.

A Combination of Factors. A person's power or lack of it is influenced by a combination of many factors. The part played by a particular factor is most difficult to determine. Some factors add to and others subtract from the total. Being a Catholic may be helpful, but not having a college degree may be a hindrance. A particular quality may be an advantage in one organization, but a disadvantage in another. A Republican, a Protestant, or a Mason may find himself with an asset or a liability in different situations. Some factors are not at all important in one company or locality, but highly strategic in another. Furthermore, status involves more than simply adding together a set of plus or minus attributes. A given factor may have a different value in different kinds of combinations.

The Power of Subordinates

Subordinates may have considerable power even though they do not have authority. The power of subordinates as individuals and as a group acts as a countervailing force upon the power of superiors. Indeed, as was shown for Stevens and Hardy in the Milo Plant, a formally constituted subordinate may actively assume the role of a superior. The factors that make for superior power also apply to subordinates. Ethnic qualities, personality, educational background, length and kind of experience, and administrative and social skills are highly important in this respect.

An important source of subordinate power, as Professor David Mechanic has noted, "is to obtain, maintain, and control access to persons, information, and instrumentalities." [17] A superior who is cut off from the

---

[17] David Mechanic, "Sources of Power of Lower Participants in Complex Organizations," *Administrative Science Quarterly,* vol. 7, no. 3, p. 356 (December, 1962).

informal stream of information will generally experience difficulty in performing his functions. Subordinates may also use formal rules and regulations as a weapon against a superior. They may use rules to justify inaction on their own part and to keep a superior from by-passing "red tape" to get an important job done.[18] Subordinates may form combinations to combat or to defend themselves against particular superiors. Such coalitions sometimes involve subordinates in a number of departments and, not infrequently, include superiors who dislike one of their own kind.

The form that subordinate power can take is illustrated by the actions of Joe Cook, an office manager in a gypsum plant. Cook disliked Peele, the new plant manager, and proceeded to make him "look bad" in the eyes of the main office executives. As described by sociologist Alvin W. Gouldner:

> When the main office would telephone the plant, Cook frequently would take the call in Peele's absence. When asked to put Peele on the phone Cook would make some effort to find him, but would finally report that he couldn't contact Peele. Instead of *"covering up"* for Peele—as he had for Doug [the former manager]—by pretending that Peele was in some inaccessible part of the mine, Cook would intimate that Peele had not let him know where he could be found. The main office was allowed to draw the inference that Peele was acting irresponsibly.[19]

The ultimate power of a subordinate is that he can quit his job. A subordinate who has strategic knowledge and skills and who cannot be readily replaced generally has a great deal of power. A lack of adequate rewards for the responsibilities that must be imposed to achieve organizational objectives can also put superiors in a highly vulnerable position. The ability to fire subordinates may have little meaning under such circumstances simply because it is difficult, if not impossible, to find replacements. Such a situation shows that authority in an organization is by no means absolute and that it may not be adequate for particular purposes.

The Power Structure: A Dynamic Process

The power structure in an organization is in a constant state of flux. Gradual and not so gradual changes occur in individuals. Smith may decide that he doesn't want a vice-presidency. Another addition to the family can cause Jones to really go after a promotion. The recruitment and retirement of personnel always alters the power structure in some fashion. Changes in informal groups or cliques also affect the relative power of individuals and groups.

[18] *Ibid.,* pp. 362–363.
[19] Alvin W. Gouldner, *Patterns of Industrial Bureaucracy* (Glencoe, Ill.: The Free Press, 1954), p. 75.

Formal Structural Modifications

Informal adaptations in the organizational structure are generally accompanied by planned or formal changes in managerial authorities and responsibilities. Executives should generally be given considerable discretion to reshape the structure to meet professional and personal needs. Too much autonomy and too little planning, however, can lead to problems over a period of time. There must be organizational planning if the parts are to properly relate to the whole.

A Continuous Sequence of Planned Changes

Organizing is a continuous process in a going concern. New departments are formed to take advantage of specialization and to contend with such matters as public and labor relations difficulties. Additional activities are assigned to existing departments and transferred from one department to another. Coordination problems lead to the establishment of committees, and too many committees result in their elimination or a committee to investigate committees. Staff assistants are added to reduce the burden of executives and to contend with special matters. The scope of organizing activities may range from changes in one or a few positions to comprehensive changes in the whole hierarchy. The term "reorganization" is often used to describe major structural and personnel adjustments.

The Development of an Organization Plan

An important step in organization planning is to survey and review the present structure. A good starting point is to assemble existing organization charts and manuals, job descriptions, salary schedules, written procedures, and executive orders. Questionnaire and interview techniques can be used to obtain information from executives. The questionnaire approach is less expensive and time consuming than interviews, but it generally provides little information about informal aspects of executive action. The more costly interview technique can be used to supplement results obtained from questionnaires. The benefits that can be derived from additional information must be balanced with the cost of that information. Another limiting factor is that many executives have an aversion to giving information about their activities. Subordinates tend to be cautious about anything that may directly or indirectly affect their status, and superiors are not inclined to want subordinates to know too much about activities in the "executive suite."

The information obtained from an organization survey should be carefully scrutinized and evaluated, and used to prepare organizational and departmental charts, written descriptions of responsibilities and relationships, procedures, and other pertinent instruments. The existing structure may be accepted as the point of departure for future planning with or without minor modifications. On the other hand, information about the present state of affairs can be used to develop a more adequate plan. The organizer should search for evidence of unsound structure and inefficient performance. Overlapping and duplicating functions, jurisdictional conflict, communication and control inadequacies, executive work-load difficulties, friction between line and staff, and delays in decision and execution represent some of the more common problem areas. Attention should also be given to the manner in which such environmental factors as secular economic development, changes in product demand, cyclical fluctuations, and technological innovation may influence the situation.

Implementing the Organization Plan

Phase charts and plans are sometimes used to indicate the time sequence of reorganization. Organizational changes can be put into effect immediately or over a period of time. An American Management Association study indicates the manner in which companies have solved this problem.[20]

The "Earthquake Approach." This method involves radical changes planned by a few executives that are announced and put into effect at once. A new management team sometimes takes this approach to reconstruct an inefficient organization or to reshape the organization in its own image. The "earthquake approach" should be used with a great deal of discretion because, as Ernest Dale has pointed out, "such a reorganization may result in loss of security for many able executives, loss of men who can move elsewhere, restraint of free expression, damage to prestige, and a widespread break in morale."[21] Although extreme measures are sometimes necessary to pump new blood into a dying organization, executives should recognize the difference between transfusion and bleeding.

The Short-Run Approach. Reorganization is spread over a six-month to three-year period with this method. A study is usually made of the existing

[20] Ernest Dale, *Planning and Developing the Company Organization Structure*, Research Report No. 20 (New York: American Management Association, 1952), pp. 131–133.
[21] *Ibid.*, p. 132.

structure, and executives are consulted for opinions and suggestions. The final plan is carefully explained in meetings in which executives are given an opportunity to make amendments. A short-run plan is sometimes a phase of a long-run reorganization program.

The Long-Run Approach. With this approach gradual changes are made over a longer period of time. The idea is to create as little disruption as possible and to assure continued cooperation. Some changes may be delayed until executives reach retirement or the hierarchies of the heavenly order. This approach leads to a continuous process of organization planning and change.

The Administration of the Plan

Organizing can be regarded as a part of the totality of planning that occurs in a company. The organized hierarchical process by which planned changes are made in the production or marketing program is also used to make changes in the organization The extent to which executives at various levels can institute changes without approval from higher levels differs from company to company. Some companies have centralized organization planning and maintain an elaborate system of control to enforce conformity to an overall plan. Organizing in other companies is more decentralized with less emphasis upon uniformity in the pattern of organization.

Organization Departments. Many companies have established organization departments to assist top executives in planning and controlling the organization.[22] Such departments may employ from one to a dozen persons and are usually headed by a manager who reports to the president. The following are some of the functions performed by organization departments.[23]

1. Developing short- and long-run organization plans.

2. Defining and clarifying the approved plan of organization by means of organization charts, job descriptions, training programs, and other devices.

3. Initiating changes in the organization plan and reviewing changes proposed by others.

4. Periodically reviewing organization plans and practices to determine their soundness and adequacy.

[22] P. E. Holden, L. S. Fish, and H. L. Smith, *Top-Management Organization and Control* (New York: McGraw-Hill Book Company, Inc., 1951), pp. 49–51.
[23] *Ibid.*, pp. 49–50; George L. Hall and Franklin E. Drew (editors), *The Management Guide*, 2nd ed. (San Francisco: Department of Organization, Standard Oil Company of California, 1956), pp. 42–43.

5. Conducting surveys to obtain information to facilitate planning and control.
6. Developing and administering plans to control manpower and payroll.

Organization departments are also given responsibilities over such matters as capital and operating expenditures, wage and salary structures, key appointments and promotions, and product line changes. As Holden, Fish, and Smith have pointed out, these activities "are an inseparable part of organization planning, involving the allocation of functions, assignment of responsibilities, and delegation of authority." [24] Companies without a full-fledged organization department often assign organizing activities to the personnel or industrial engineering department. But it should not be assumed that executives can wash their hands of organizing responsibilities by centralizing them in a departmental unit. The organizing function, like the human relations function, is not a one-man or a one-department function.

Organization Charts. An organization chart portrays managerial positions and relationships in a company or a departmental unit. Most companies use a pyramid-type chart with rectangular boxes [25] containing such information as position title, name and rank (as vice-president) of the person holding the position, and, sometimes, a brief description of responsibilities and duties. The boxes are generally linked together with solid lines to show line relationships and broken lines for functional and staff relationships. Lines of different colors may also be used to relate positions and indicate relationships. Some companies use horizontal-line charts that list positions in columns with indentations for different hierarchical levels.[26] A series of diverging circles may also be used to indicate reporting and communication lines.[27] However, the important consideration is not form per se, but the clarity and correctness with which a chart presents information. Organization charts are useful for the dissemination of information, but their limitations should also be noted. They picture only a small part of the totality of executive activities and interactions. Another limitation is that a chart is a static picture of a dynamic organism and needs constant revision

---

[24] Holden, Fish, and Smith, *op. cit.,* p. 50.
[25] Circular rather than rectangular "boxes" may be used.
[26] The National Industrial Conference Board has compiled organization charts of sixty-two companies, most of which are pyramid–rectangular box charts. Horizontal-line charts were used by two participating companies. Harold Stieglitz, *Corporate Organization Structures,* Studies in Personnel Policy, No. 183 (New York: National Industrial Conference Board, 1961). This report also contains information about good organizing practices and charting techniques.
[27] Dale, *op. cit.,* p. 32.

Table 12-1. General Manager, Manufacturing Division

I. FUNCTION

Conducts the manufacturing, packaging, plant facilities and equipment operation, engineering, maintenance, plant and process design, technical service, and plant and warehouse construction activities of the company, and warehousing.

II. RESPONSIBILITIES AND AUTHORITY

The responsibilities and authority stated below are subject to established policies.
  A. Operations and Activities
     1. Formulates, or receives and recommends for approval, proposals for policies on manufacturing, packaging, plant facilities and equipment operation, engineering, maintenance, plant and process design, technical service, and plant and warehouse construction activities; administers such policies when approved; and conducts such activities for the company.
     2. Establishes and administers procedures pertaining to manufacturing, packaging, plant facilities and equipment operation, engineering, maintenance, plant and process design, technical service, and plant and warehouse construction.
     3. Recommends new or altered products and the discontinuance of products.
     4. Operates such warehouses as are necessary to the accomplishment of his function.
     5. Conducts necessary buying activities, calling upon the services of the Supply and Transportation Department as necessary.
  B. Organization of His Division
     1. Recommends changes in the basic structure and complement of his Division.
     2. Recommends placement of positions not subject to the provisions of the Fair Labor Standards Act in the salary structure.
     3. Arranges for preparation of new and revised Management Guides and position and job descriptions.
  C. Personnel of His Division
     1. Having ascertained the availability of qualified talent from within the company, hires personnel for, or appoints employees to, positions other than in management within the limits of his approved basic organization.
     2. Approves salary changes for personnel not subject to the provisions of the Fair Labor Standards Act who receive not over $......... per month, and recommends salary changes for such personnel receiving in excess of that amount.

3. Approves wage changes for personnel subject to the provisions of the Fair Labor Standards Act.
4. Recommends promotion, demotion, and release of personnel not subject to the provisions of the Fair Labor Standards Act.
5. Approves promotion, demotion, and release of personnel subject to the provisions of the Fair Labor Standards Act.
6. Approves vacations and personal leaves, except his own.
7. Prepares necessary job and position descriptions.

D. Finances of His Division
1. Prepares the annual budget.
2. Administers funds allotted under the approved annual budget, or any approved extraordinary or capital expenditure program, or any appropriation.
3. Approves payment from allotted funds of operating expenses and capital expenditures not in excess of $......., which are not covered by the approved budget, any approved expenditure program, or an appropriation.
4. Recommends extraordinary or capital expenditures.
5. Administers fiscal procedures.
6. Receives for review and recommendation the items of the annual budgets of the staff departments and the field divisions coming within his province.

III. RELATIONSHIPS

A. President
Reports to the President.
B. General Manager, Marketing Division
Coordinates his activities and cooperates with the General Manager of the Marketing Division on matters of mutual concern.
C. Department Managers
Coordinates his efforts and cooperates with the Department Managers and seeks and accepts functional guidance from them on matters within their respective provinces.
D. Government, Labor and Vendors
Conducts such relationships with representatives of government and labor and with vendors as are necessary to the accomplishment of his function.
E. Others
Establishes and maintains those contacts necessary to the fulfillment of his function.

Source. Franklin E. Drew and George L. Hall (editors), *The Management Guide,* 2nd ed. (San Francisco: Standard Oil Company of California, 1956), p. 55.

if it is not to give wrong information about the actual situation. A chart can be manipulated apart from the thing it is supposed to represent and, if improperly constructed, can give a highly distorted representation of reality. People may also infer something that was not intended. For example, the fact that positions are shown on the same level does not necessarily mean that they have the same status.

Organization Manuals. Manuals can help promote an understanding of responsibilities and relationships, facilitate the training of managerial personnel, and provide a basis for the study of organization problems.[28] They may contain comprehensive information about the entire organization, or their contents may be limited to particular divisions, departments, plants, and functions. Although organization manuals differ in format, the following kinds of material are commonly included.

JOB DESCRIPTIONS. Many manuals present detailed descriptions of the responsibilities and relationships of executive positions. The number of descriptions may be limited by various criteria, such as scalar rank, nature of the function, salary level, and official corporate status. The material that may be included in a job description is indicated by Table 12-1.

ORGANIZATION OBJECTIVES. Objectives can be expressed in such subjective terms as "being a good citizen of the community" and "preservation of the American way." They are also defined operationally, that is, the objective is the same as the function necessary to achieve it. For example, the term "function" as used in the *Management Guide* of the Standard Oil Company of California "means the broadest course of action or task pertaining to a position. This includes the objective or purpose." [29] Overall objectives are broken down into such subsidiary objectives as production, sales, finance, purchasing, and personnel.

ORGANIZATION AND MANAGEMENT PRINCIPLES. Some manuals highlight good management practices: how to develop and train a suitable successor; line executives should take full advantage of staff and service facilities; it is the duty of the subordinate to keep his superior informed about certain kinds of contacts (the conditions are usually stipulated); and subordinates should not be praised or blamed before their equals or subordinates. Principles related to organizing might include such statements as every function necessary to achieve an objective should be assigned to an existing or a newly created department; hierarchical levels should be kept to a minimum; and responsibilities should be delegated to the lowest possible level.

TERMINOLOGY. Organization manuals sometimes devote space to a clarification of such terminology as "function," "responsibilities," and "ac-

---

[28] A more detailed discussion of manuals and their contents is found in Dale, *op. cit.*, pp. 149–158; Holden, Fish, and Smith, *op. cit.*, pp. 98–100.

[29] Hall and Drew, *op. cit.*, p. 18.

countability." They may also contain an organization creed, which expresses the philosophy of management on a variety of subjects, such as social responsibility, human relations, and economic values. A statement of the qualifications necessary to fill various positions is sometimes included, and a few manuals consider particular company organization problems.

Manuals and Charts Are Facilitating Instruments. Effective organizing involves more than drawing organization charts and writing manuals. Some executives, who feel that such devices create more difficulties than they cure, cite the danger of misinterpretation and rigidity, and the failure to adequately record complex and changing relationships. Although these problems cannot be completely overcome, they can be mitigated by good construction and composition, frequent revisions, and training in the use of the manual. The preparation and maintenance of manuals is costly and time consuming; annual sales of five million dollars have been mentioned as the minimum size at which a manual can be justified.[30] However, most companies can afford and many can advantageously use some kind of written presentation on organizational matters. Some hard thinking and a little elbow grease plus a typist and a mimeograph machine can accomplish much along these lines.

Organizational Problems and Policies

Formal organizations are formed to achieve predetermined objectives as efficiently as possible. In a business organization the basic problem is to make a profit. Efficiency is partly a matter of good functional design. People are brought into the organization for particular purposes. They cannot obviously behave in any manner that pleases them. But at the same time the nature of man and the power accorded him in a private enterprise system precludes any kind of perfect adaptation to the needs of an organization. The discussion that follows pinpoints some common organizational problems and indicates policies that can help overcome them.

Formal Organizing and Informal "Reorganizing"

A sound functional structure is a good point of departure for most organizational purposes. Particular personal qualities and social situations should be considered during the planning phase of organizational development only when there are substantial reasons. But a modification of a planned structure cannot be avoided, except in Aldous Huxley's *Brave*

[30] Dale, *op. cit.,* p. 150.

New World or George Orwell's *1984*. Human beings cannot be forced into a rigid functional structure without being reduced to the level of social insects.

Bureaucracy in a Gypsum Plant. The extent to which human behavior can be molded into a particular pattern varies with conditions. A good example is provided in Alvin W. Gouldner's study of bureaucratization of a gypsum plant.[31] The plant employed about 225 people in two basic operating divisions, a subsurface mine and a surface factory. There was much socializing among all levels in both the plant and the community. The management was informal in approach and lenient in attitude. Then the old manager died; a new manager, given the pseudonym of Vincent Peele, was brought in to put things in order. The highly informal approach of the past was drastically disturbed. New rules and regulations were formulated and old ones were enforced. A discharge and a demotion indicated to all concerned that Peele meant business. Many of the past informal arrangements and alliances were broken and gradually replaced by new attitudes and groupings. However, Peele's attempt to reduce the amount of informal action and replace it with more formal approaches was not universally accepted. The workers in the surface factory were far more willing to respond favorably than the subsurface miners. The miners refused to submit to close bureaucratic control. An important barrier to bureaucracy was the miners' belief system. For example, the miners believed and strongly supported the idea that "down here we are our own bosses." The hazards of working in the mine helped reinforce the miners' resistance to control. The miner felt that he had the right to oppose orders that might endanger his life. A refusal to abide by work rules and authoritarian demands was often justified on the basis of dangerous working conditions. The miner was thought to be entitled to an occasional release, such as getting drunk and not showing up for work the next morning. The danger also helped keep down the number of people willing to work in the mine, thereby reducing the power of management to replace an uncooperative miner. Informal solidarity among the miners increased the effectiveness of their resistance to management's attempts to impose rules and regulations.

The Importance of Informal Organizing. The organizational structure should generally be defined broadly enough to permit a significant amount of informal organizing. Some discretion is essential if people are not to be put into a strait jacket which stifles initiative and self-reliance. An attempt to place too many restraints on human behavior will create control problems and costs that repudiate any reasonable concept of efficiency. It would make necessary an elaborate policing system which could be far more costly than any revenues that might be derived from improved behavioral

[31] Gouldner, *op. cit.*

responses. Another important consideration is that people do not like to be treated as though they were normally incompetent and irresponsible. As Professor Douglas McGregor has noted: "Man will exercise self-direction and self-control in the service of objectives to which he is committed." [32] The notion that most human beings attempt to avoid responsibilities and have to be subjected to many rules and close supervision is not always a valid assumption. Organizations should be viewed as *means* rather than ends. There are generally a number of equally good ways to achieve an objective. Informal techniques that get the job done are better than formal techniques that fail.

Formal Reorganization

Formal reorganization, as used in this section, is assumed to involve major planned changes in an organizational structure. Such changes can produce higher profits, but they can also produce difficult problems. This discussion deals with strategic factors that relate to reorganization.

Should There Be Reorganization? The existing organizational structure is not always as bad as it may seem. Management should consider the possibility that the problem is not the structure, but the personnel. A relatively small number of ineffective people can seriously disrupt an otherwise sound structure. On the other hand, people can make a bad structure perform well. Another consideration is that behavior may only appear to be efficient or inefficient. A smart "military look" does not always mean that an individual or unit will perform well in combat. A business-like atmosphere does not always denote productivity. Efficiency also has stereotypes. Results rather than appearance should be scrutinized in evaluating an organization.

Reorganizations are often launched for the purpose of improving the profit situation. Such a goal is eminently proper. The difficulty is that a failure to make adequate profits can have many causes. Increased competition, high labor costs, ineffective advertising, changing consumer tastes, inadequate equipment and many other factors can paint a bad profit picture. Some organizations have undoubtedly gone through the throes of reorganization only to find that the diagnosis was wrong. A situation that seems to require a major reorganization can sometimes be corrected by minor adjustments. A problem in one part of the organization can cause a chain reaction of problems in many other parts. In one organization the removal of a vice-president through early retirement solved a whole series

[32] Douglas McGregor, *The Human Side of Enterprise* (New York: McGraw-Hill Book Company, Inc., 1960), p. 47. Professor McGregor compares the traditional concepts with the theories that have evolved from behavioral research.

of problems. In another the overhauling of a small department was all that was needed to correct a number of major production difficulties.

The Results of Reorganization. Reorganization frequently occurs only after productivity has begun to decline in a marked degree. Organizations often do not take action until they are pushed by a possibility of complete disaster. Too many people are like the grasshopper of Aesop's fables who starved to death because he failed to store sufficient food for the winter. However, the real culprit is sometimes a lack of knowledge rather than a lack of foresight. The efficiency of an organizational structure is difficult to measure. The factors that contribute to productivity or a lack of it cannot be readily isolated.

A long period of success under a diversity of economic conditions may indicate that a particular kind of structure is more efficient than another. The General Motors Corporation, for example, has experienced a high degree of success since its reorganization in the early 1920's. It survived the depression of the '30's (although it had difficulty surviving earlier relatively minor recessions before the reorganization). Ernest Dale has concluded that organizational shortcomings were predominant in the early GMC failures and that the new organization significantly increased survival power.[33] The frequency with which other companies have imitated the GMC organizational structure supports this conclusion.

The reorganization of the Westinghouse Electric Corporation during the late '30's provides important information on the consequences of major structural modifications.[34] Before the reorganization decision making at Westinghouse was concentrated in the hands of a headquarters group composed of the chairman of the board, the president, and four vice-presidents in charge of manufacturing, sales, engineering, and finance. Each of the vice-presidents had authority over his function from the top to the bottom levels, which meant that every plant was under the direction of four managers. Three basic changes were made in the reorganization: (1) plant operations were grouped on a product basis and the product division managers were given much more decisional responsibility; (2) functional staffs were established at headquarters to advise top management and assist the divisions; and (3) centralized budgetary and cost controls were instituted to assure a proper use of delegated decision-making powers.

Ernest Dale, who analyzed the Westinghouse data, divided the impact of the reorganization into three stages. During "the immediate impact" stage, which lasted about a year, the gains from reorganization outweighed the additional costs. Improved decisions, faster communication, better coordi-

[33] Ernest Dale, *The Great Organizers* (New York: McGraw-Hill Book Company, Inc., 1960), p. 83.
[34] *Ibid.*, pp. 143–174.

nation, and higher executive morale helped bring about this result. The second stage, which Dale called "the short-run impact," occurred during the second and third years of reorganization when the extra expenses increased and more than balanced the gains. Some of the factors that contributed to the increased costs were errors from lack of experience, status and motivational problems, a buildup of improved staff personnel, and larger administrative expenses. The final and third stage, which began after three or four years, gave rise to many benefits that were only beginning to bear fruit during earlier periods. Top management was able to give much more attention to the development of new profit-making ideas. Divisional managements were able to use their familiarity with the operating environment to good advantage. Staff specialists at headquarters gained the confidence of operating executives and made more contributions that improved productivity. Finally, the decentralized structure helped develop a larger supply of managerial talent.

Did the Westinghouse reorganization favorably affect productivity and profits? Before and after reorganization data were carefully evaluated. Financial and other kinds of performance information for Westinghouse were compared with similar data for its major competitor (General Electric), the industry as a whole, and the total economy. Factors of change other than organizational structure were eliminated by statistical and other techniques to the greatest possible extent. A comprehensive statistical analysis indicated "that Westinghouse's performance improved as a result of the reorganization and that the actual data probably understate the true extent of the improvement." [35]

Reorganization should be viewed as a long-run phenomenon. The money and human costs cannot normally be recouped in less than something like three to five years. The fact that reorganization frequently occurs when performance is down may further complicate matters. An improved structure may not become effective in time to prevent disaster. A reorganization should not normally be launched in the midst of other major problems. For example, a company engaged in a comprehensive plant modernization program might experience difficulty if it also made unrelated radical organizational changes.

The Process of Organizational Change

This section is concerned with socio-psychological problems that relate to changes in the organizational structure. Functional requirements can create havoc with human relationships, and conversely.

[35] Dale, *op. cit.*, p. 174. For a description of the data and the statistical methods that were used in the analysis: *ibid.*, pp. 217–238.

The Social System. Organizing and reorganizing involves far more than formally defined authorities and responsibilities. Indeed, formal organizing actually disorganizes in that it disrupts and in some instances destroys an informally organized social system. Such a system plays an important part in the process through which people cooperate in pursuing common purposes. The organizer should recognize this fact and retain as much social continuity as possible.

Informal groups can cause serious cooperative problems by supporting personal goals that are contrary to organizational needs. In such situations an organizer may deliberately attempt to break up the informal social pattern. Some structural changes may be made specifically for this purpose. Another approach is to change the leadership and membership of informal groups by personnel transfers and forced resignations. This technique represents an attempt to create favorable changes in attitude through different combinations of personalities. The organizer should give consideration to the *ultimate* consequences of changes in the formal structure. What will an enthusiastic "empire builder" do with it? Will it benefit those who are more concerned with personal aggrandizement than with organizational welfare? How can a particular change be used for purposes other than those intended? Will people be forced to unduly circumvent the formally constituted organization to get the work done? These and similar questions should be carefully scrutinized in making structural modifications. It should be remembered that there are many devious and ingenious ways to serve selfish interests. However, such ways are sometimes necessary to promote organizational purposes.

Developing Cooperation. The effectiveness of organizational planning is highly dependent on the cooperation of managerial and other personnel. People are usually reluctant to accept changes that might adversely affect their status. They may appear to approve the new organization and then use every available means to make sure it will not be successful. The social mechanisms that were used to help achieve the organizational objective and, not infrequently, to make an unsound structure function are now used to impede the cooperative process. This kind of redirection of effort explains why the "bad" structure of the past performed better than the "good" structure that followed.

A systematic training program can be helpful in overcoming resistance to change. Such a program should give recognition to the fact that reorganization creates socio-psychological problems that frequently require as much attention as functional matters. Some companies invite the active participation of subordinates through periodic conferences and meetings which provide information about organizational changes and help dispel conditions that create status anxiety. The burden of adverse changes in position can sometimes be eased by the manipulation of status instruments. A person who feels that his position is being lowered may be given a more impressive title, a higher salary, a larger office, and other compensating inducements. Such status instruments may also become important for face-saving purposes. Although organizational changes should be made as palatable as possible, management should not attempt to hide the obvious. Early retirement, demotions in position, and outright dismissal are necessary under some circumstances. An organization can be compromised to death by a lack of executive courage and resoluteness.

Pruning Deadwood. Reorganization may accomplish the transfer of incompetent executives from important positions and from the organization. Productive personnel during earlier years may no longer be effective. Some deadwood is a normal product of the difficulty of forecasting human capacities. Technological innovation can complicate a situation by causing radical changes in personnel requirements. Changes in the organizational structure, some of which may be superficial, can provide a good means for bringing about necessary personnel adjustments. However, an organization should not cut off its nose to spite its face. A little deadwood, even in high places, is better than a dead tree.

SELECTED REFERENCES

Chris Argyris, *Personality and Organization*. New York: Harper & Brothers, 1957.
Chris Argyris, *Understanding Organizational Behavior*. Homewood, Ill.: The Dorsey Press, Inc., 1960.
Gerald D. Bell (editor), *Organizations and Human Behavior*. Englewood Cliffs, N.J.: Prentice-Hall, Inc., 1967.
Reinhard Bendix, *Work and Authority in Industry*. New York: John Wiley and Sons, Inc., 1956.
Warren G. Bennis, *Changing Organizations*. New York: McGraw-Hill Book Company, 1966.
Warren G. Bennis, "Organizational Revitalization," *California Management Review*, Vol. 9, No. 1, pp. 51-60 (Fall 1966).
Peter M. Blau and W. Richard Scott, *Formal Organizations*. San Francisco: Chandler Publishing Company, 1962.
Michael Crozier, *The Bureaucratic Phenomenon*. Chicago: University of Chicago Press, 1964.
Ernest Dale, *Planning and Developing the Company Organization Structure*, Research Report No. 20. New York: American Management Association, 1952.
Ernest Dale, *The Great Organizers*. New York: McGraw-Hill Book Company, Inc., 1960.
Melville Dalton, *Men Who Manage*. New York: John Wiley and Sons, Inc., 1959.
Marshall E. Dimock, *Administrative Vitality*. New York: Harper & Brothers, 1959.
Amitai Etzioni, *A Comparative Analysis of Complex Organizations*. Glencoe, Ill.: The Free Press, 1961.
William F. Glueck, "Applied Organization Analysis," *Academy of Management Journal*, Vol. 10, No. 3, pp. 223-234 (September 1967).
Alvin W. Gouldner, *Patterns of Industrial Bureaucracy*. Glencoe, Ill.: The Free Press, 1954.
Mason Haire (editor), *Modern Organization Theory*. New York: John Wiley and Sons, Inc., 1959.
Mason Haire (editor), *Organization Theory in Industrial Practice*. New York: John Wiley and Sons, Inc., 1962.
Rensis Likert, *The Human Organization*. New York: McGraw-Hill Book Company, 1967.
Joseph A. Litterer, *Organizations: Structure and Behavior*. New York: John Wiley and Sons, Inc., 1963.

James G. March (editor), *Handbook of Organizations*. Chicago: Rand McNally & Company, 1965.
John M. Pfiffner and Frank P. Sherwood, *Administrative Organizations*. Englewood Cliffs, N.J.: Prentice-Hall, Inc., 1960.
Robert Presthus, *The Organizational Society*. New York: Alfred A. Knopf, Inc., 1962.
James L. Price, *Organizational Effectiveness: An Inventory of Propositions*. Homewood, Ill.: Richard D. Irwin, Inc., 1968.
William G. Scott, *Organization Theory: A Behavioral Analysis for Management*. Homewood, Ill.: Richard D. Irwin, Inc., 1967.
Victor A. Thompson, *Modern Organization*. New York: Alfred A. Knopf, Inc., 1961.
James C. Worthy, *Big Business and Free Men*, Chaps. 6 and 7. New York: Harper & Brothers, 1959.

chapter 13

FROM ORGANIZATION TO PROCESS

The functions that make up the management process are presented as organized phenomena in this chapter. The first part is concerned with the manner in which formal and informal "organizing" relates to communication. The second part describes and analyzes the organized decision-making process. This chapter is followed by a more comprehensive consideration of decision making and communication in Parts IV, V, and VI.

Organizational Communication Channels

Although the word "channel" is generally used in a more restricted sense, the line of persons through which written or oral messages pass may be viewed as a communication channel. Some persons in a channel play a passive role with respect to the content of the message. They transmit the message to another person who may be the ultimate recipient or yet another link in the channel. Other persons add to, subtract from, modify the content, or change the form of the message before transmitting it to another person. The communication problem is an important consideration in developing the organization structure. As Chester I. Barnard has pointed out: "The need of a definite system of communication creates the first task of the organizer and is the immediate origin of executive organization." [1] The executives who occupy positions in the management hierarchy are important links in the chain of information flow.

[1] Chester I. Barnard, *The Functions of the Executive* (Cambridge: Harvard University Press, 1951), p. 217.

Hierarchical Communication Channels

The hierarchical system gives direction to and imposes restrictions upon the flow of information. Decisional information flows from higher to lower levels and information about performance from lower to higher levels. Executives are required to respond to decisional information transmitted by superiors and provide information about the activities under their direction. If the "unity of command" principle is followed, a subordinate has only one superior from whom he receives orders and to whom he reports. A subordinate need not respond to the decisions of any other superior. Thus, personnel in the sales department is not subject to decisions made by the head of the production department. A functionally differentiated decision-making system modifies the "unity of command" principle by making subordinates subject to a number of functional executives. In such a system, people in the production department are required to respond to the personnel manager on matters that fall within his jurisdiction.

Information flow is also restricted by prohibitions against bypassing levels or "short-circuiting" the line of command. A superior should not directly give orders to anyone who is more than one level below him in the hierarchy. However, emergency conditions may cause a superior to take a personal hand in the affairs of subordinate executives. Restrictions are also imposed upon the subordinate's freedom to communicate with those at higher levels in the hierarchy. Bypassing one's immediate superior is generally considered to be a mortal sin in organizational life, but a distinction is usually made between hierarchical decisional relationships and other kinds of contact. The following instructions from an organization publication of the Radio Corporation of America are typical in this respect.

The organization structure and the organization chart define lines of responsibility and authority; but do not indicate channels of contact. The RCA organization permits and requires the exercise of common sense and good judgment, at all organizational levels, in determining the best channels of contact necessary for the expeditious handling of the work. Contact between units of the organization should be carried out in the most direct way. In making such contacts, however, *it is the duty of each member of the organization to keep his senior informed on:* (1) Any matters on which his senior may be held accountable by those senior to him. (2) Any matters in disagreement or likely to cause controversy within or between any units of the corporation. (3) Matters requiring advice by the senior or his coordination with other units. (4) Any matters involving recommendations for change in, or variance from, established policies. RCA could not operate without freedom of decision at many key action points down the line; yet those who carry senior responsibility must be kept in a position to exercise the direction and control for which they are held accountable. It is the job of everyone to make good use of channels of contact and communication in making this concept work throughout RCA.[2]

As was indicated in Part II, committee and staff organization influence the pattern of communication among executives. Committees create supplementary links in the communication chain and provide additional means for the dissemination of information. They may facilitate communication through the development of executive contact patterns that might not otherwise arise. For example, executives with different scalar ranks often feel more inclined to communicate with one another because a degree of equality is implied by membership on the same committee. Executives from different functional areas, such as production and sales, are given an opportunity to exchange ideas and discuss mutual problems. Staff and functional relationships represent additional elements in the hierarchical communication system. Although staff executives cannot directly transmit orders or commands, the possibility of support by superior line executives means that staff recommendations and advice cannot generally be ignored by subordinate executives. Functional decisional prerogatives give staff executives the same status as line executives with respect to certain functional matters. Thus, a staff executive may have the final word in negotiating a contract with the union or the hiring of certain kinds of personnel.

Planned Paperwork Procedures

It takes a mountain of paper to conduct the affairs of organization. The flow of forms, records, and reports connects the various elements of an organization. The personnel department is constantly engaged in the task of assembling information about prospective and present employees. The accounting department is concerned with information about cash disbursements, accounts receivable, accounts payable, operating expenses, and other financial matters. Production planning and control translates sales and forecast information into production schedules. Purchasing processes requisitions and orders, receiving reports, invoices, and inventory information. Some paperwork is directly related to the production of products or services. As one writer put it: ". . . the whole complex web of production is kept alive and moving by a network of pieces of paper held together by threads of interdependent and interrelated information which stem from the planning goal and lead to the finished product."[3] A large volume of

[2] *The Four Basic Organizational Concepts of the Radio Corporation of America* (New York: Radio Corporation of America, April 1954), pp. 4–5. (Italics inserted.)

[3] R. L. Forster, "Coordinating Office with Company-wide Cost Reduction," *Office Management Series Number 125* (New York: American Management Association, 1949), p. 27.

paperwork is also required to handle information requirements that are not directly related to production activities, such as social security and tax reports, employee medical records, and public relations material. Paperwork operations are linked together by planned procedures which guide the flow of such information within the organization.

Informal Communication Channels

Managerially planned communication channels represent only a portion of the actual communication channels found in an organization. Much of the communication system is informal in the sense that it is not planned by superior executives. Subordinates modify planned channels and create channels that have not been planned. As Professor E. Wight Bakke has concluded from a comprehensive study of a large telephone company:

Our respondents were reacting . . . not to the planned system of Communication even in those areas where it *was* planned; they were reacting to planned procedures, which they had remade; but what is equally important, they were reacting to unplanned procedures which they themselves had made.[4]

A diversity of opinion can be found on the subject of informal communication. Some executives look upon such communication as a noxious weed that should be eliminated. Others regard it as an important facilitating force in organization communication. Still others can be found somewhere between these two extremes. The problem of evaluating informal communication is partly semantic. The word "grapevine," which is often used to refer to such communication, seems to be used as a synonym for "rumor" and "gossip" by some executives. There is also a tendency to use the word to mean the dissemination of information detrimental to the interests of management. Furthermore, some executives seem to have the idea that the "grapevine" is found only among workers. Such conceptions are given credence by the fact that informal communication may spread false and harmful information, but they fail to take into account the positive role that informal communication can and does play in organizational life. Indeed, there is some question as to whether organizations can survive without such communication.

Management cannot possibly plan every communication channel that will be necessary to perform the work of the organization. The formal or planned system is the framework within which other communication channels are developed by managerial and nonmanagerial personnel. The distinction that is often made between "lines of responsibility and author-

[4] E. Wight Bakke, *Bonds of Organization* (New York: Harper & Brothers Publishers, 1950), p. 84.

ity" and "channels of contact" gives emphasis to the importance of supplementary informal channels. Some organizations explicitly sanction the development of informal channels for operational purposes. Other organizations give implicit recognition to the need for such channels by permitting them to develop with little or no intervention. But not all informal communication channels are concerned with the work of the organization. Some channels evolve from the efforts of people to satisfy purely personal motives. A promoter of a football pool may develop communication channels with individuals who normally buy chances. Other individuals may periodically contact one another for an exchange of jokes or gossip. The channels normally used for organizational purposes may also be used to conduct personal affairs. A "convention-returned" sales manager may describe the attractions of a burlesque show to the production manager during a meeting on changes in product design. The president may give a dissertation on his recent achievements in golf during the weekly meeting of vice-presidents. The foreman may tell the latest "traveling salesman" joke before he informs the machinist that tolerances have been revised. Social relationships that occur outside the province of the organization also have an informational significance. A country club party or an evening of bridge involving organizational personnel is rarely terminated without some reference to the affairs of organization.

Types of Informal Chains

Some important insights into the nature of informal communication channels were gained from an empirical study of management communication in a leather goods manufacturing company by Professor Keith Davis.[5] The informal communication channels were classified by Davis into four basic types: single strand, gossip, probability, and cluster. The *single-strand chain* involves the passing of information through a long line of persons to the ultimate recipient. *A* tells *B*, who tells *C*, who tells *D*, and so on. In the *gossip chain,* as the name implies, *A* actively seeks and tells everyone else. The *probability chain* is a random process wherein *A* transmits the information to others (*F* and *D* in Figure 13-1) in accordance with the laws of probability, and then *F* and *D* tell others in a similar manner. In the *cluster chain, A* tells selected persons who may in turn relay the information to other selected individuals. Most of the informal

[5] The research techniques used in this study are described in: Keith Davis, "A Method of Studying Communication Patterns in Organizations," *Personnel Psychology,* Vol. 6, No. 3, Autumn 1953, pp. 301–312; a report of the results of the study can be found in: Keith Davis, "Management Communication and the Grapevine," *Harvard Business Review,* Vol. 31, No. 5, September–October 1953, pp. 43–49.

FROM ORGANIZATION TO PROCESS 305

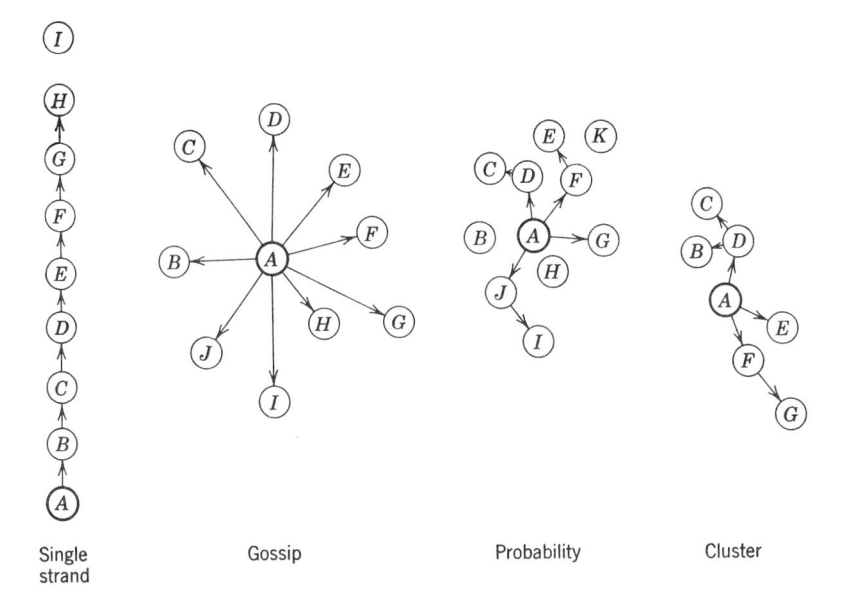

Figure 13-1. Types of communication chains in a management hierarchy.

communication among management personnel followed the pattern of this chain. In other words, the so-called grapevine can be highly discriminating in disseminating information. This point is emphasized by the following example.

The local representative of the company which carried the employee group insurance contract planned a picnic for company executives. The Jason Company [a pseudonym] president decided to invite 36 executives, mostly from higher executive levels. The grapevine immediately went to work spreading this information, but it was carried to *only two of the 31 executives not invited*. The grapevine communicators thought the news was confidential, so they had told only those who they thought would be invited (they had to guess, since they did not have access to the invitation list).[6]

Although additional empirical studies are required before any firm conclusions can be drawn, the cluster chain is probably the predominant type in most of the informal communication among executives. The psychological restraints of an authoritarian system would seem to give impetus to the development of this kind of chain. Too much talking can readily jeopardize the present and future status of an executive. As Professor E. Wight Bakke has written, the behavioral quality, "keeps mouth

[6] Davis, *op. cit.*, p. 44.

shut when should, avoids gossip," is generally an important element in the penalty and reward system in organizations.[7] This mandate is not restricted to information about organizational matters but also tends to apply to the personal domain of executives. There are strong taboos against the dissemination of information that might "embarrass" a fellow executive, particularly if he is a superior. Group loyalty also plays an important role in this respect. A propensity to gossip is often restrained when those who are not a part of the "social group" are present. For example, foremen are frequently left out of management communication chains.

What kind of informal communication chains are found among nonmanagerial personnel? There is every reason to believe that they are similar in form to those found among executives. Workers are highly selective in communicating certain kinds of information. Thus, the Bank Wiring Observation Room Group of the Hawthorne Study had a strong taboo against telling "a superior anything that will react to the detriment of an associate."[8] This kind of restraint is partly motivated by the efforts of "the group" to protect itself against the power of management. In situations involving a union, it may be used to play the interests of the union against those of management. In a similar sense, workers might be inclined to gossip about matters that are detrimental to the interests of the organization and the management group. Thus, although the form of informal patterns may be similar to those of management, the manner in which they are used is influenced by motives that may differ from those of managerial personnel.

Communication Channels and Information Flow

The communication channels in an organization can be determined by plotting the flow of information over a period of time. Such a diagram would show that some communication follows a regular and continuous pattern. Much of the information that flows through hierarchical positions and planned paperwork systems can be placed in this category. On the other hand, some communication patterns function on a highly intermittent basis; they may appear only once without any indication that they will ever be repeated. Should highly intermittent and nonrecurring patterns be categorized as communication channels? They could be excluded by defining a channel as a pattern of communication with some degree of recurrence. But the fact that a pattern appears intermittently or only once does

[7] Bakke, *op. cit.,* p. 110.
[8] F. J. Roethlisberger and W. J. Dickson, *Management and the Worker* (Cambridge: Harvard University Press, 1939), p. 522.

not exclude its potential usefulness. Such patterns may become important under emergency conditions or during particular difficulties. Some of them can be viewed as reserve communication facilities that can be activated under the pressure of necessity. A similar statement can be made about the channels that evolve from an exchange of purely personal information.

A major reorganization may significantly change formal hierarchical chains and informal contact patterns. Such forces as technological innovation and organizational growth can cause radical changes in the processing of paperwork. Also important are shifts in the pattern of informal communication caused by changes in work layout, transfer of personnel, status changes, retirement, hiring, and many other factors.

The Organized Decision-Making Process

Decision making in organizations beyond a certain size cannot be fully understood without the recognition that it is a cooperative process. The nature of a cooperative decisional process and its significance in solving decisional problems are considered in this section.

The Management Hierarchy in Action

The organized decision-making process translates broad objectives into more specific objectives as one proceeds from the top to the bottom of the hierarchy. Simultaneously there occurs a transformation of objectives into plans which indicate the activities that will be necessary to achieve them. As Barnard has expressed it, the organized decisional process "is one of successive approximations—constant refinement of purpose, closer and closer discriminations of fact—in which the march of time is essential." [9] At the upper levels primary attention is given to objectives with little attention to the means for achieving them. At the intermediate levels broad objectives are redefined into more specific objectives, and a great deal of attention is given to the solution of particular production, marketing, personnel, engineering, and financial problems. The type of departmentation used at various levels determines the manner in which subsidiary objectives are defined. Thus, the organization objective may be differentiated on a product basis at one level and on a functional basis at another. Decisions at the lower levels are essentially concerned with the specific activity through which objectives are achieved.

[9] Barnard, *op. cit.*, p. 206.

Other Types of Interaction

The hierarchical process is generally accompanied and frequently preceded by other types of executive interaction. The president of the company, for example, may call in lower echelon executives and specialists before he transmits a decision through the hierarchy. He may use a formal committee system or approach the problem informally. A major decisional problem frequently involves weeks or months of consultation with large numbers of people. Executives at lower levels also make use of this technique in working out their problems. In many instances everyone concerned will know something about the part he will play before the hierarchical process begins. Such a situation was described by the president of a department store: "This afternoon's meeting of department heads resulted in general agreement about the action we are going to take on a variety of matters. I will now draft a formal communication and transmit it through 'official' channels."

The Composite Organization Mind

The cooperative action that takes place within the hierarchical structure involves highly complex and subtle executive interrelationships. A decision is frequently little more than a formal expression of the results of cooperative activity. The question as to who originated an idea frequently cannot be determined, except in the sense that some executive in the hierarchy is formally responsible for the decision into which it is incorporated. This idea is well illustrated by the experiences of General Lucius Clay as Deputy Military Governor of Germany under General Dwight D. Eisenhower. Eisenhower gave Clay full responsibility for the establishment of military government. However, each week he traveled from Frankfurt to Clay's headquarters in Berlin to discuss occupation problems and policies. As Clay has expressed it, "so informal and broad were these discussions that it never occurred to me then, nor could I state now, from which of us came the major decisions which determined our course of action in Germany." [10] Alfred P. Sloan, Jr., of the General Motors Corporation has expressed a similar idea about the nature of the cooperative decision-making process:

Little can be said authoritatively regarding the exercise of individual business judgment in the modern corporation. It is an important but a limited and narrow subject. The big factors are engineering, knowledge of markets, and so forth, and organization. When the subject of decision is broadened to include

[10] Lucius D. Clay, "The Art of Delegation," in: Edward C. Bursk (editor), *The Management Team* (Cambridge: Harvard University Press, 1954), pp. 11–12.

the data, it is an enormous problem. In a big outfit, this is the work of many persons, or the group, you might say, with individual leadership of course playing a significant creative part.[11]

It is difficult to isolate and identify the manner in which the initiative and creativeness of individual executives affect the final outcome. To a great extent executives act as representatives or spokesmen for what might be called "the composite organization mind."

Decision-Making Centers

The decision-making problem may also be approached from the vantage point of each position in the hierarchy. Every executive, from the president to the foreman, is assigned a certain portion of the total decisional responsibility. The jurisdiction of each executive is defined by a two-dimensional process of delineation which was considered in the chapters on departmentation and on centralization and decentralization. For example, the executive who heads the production department has decisional responsibility over production problems which have not been delegated to his subordinates or retained by his superior. Within the area thus defined, decisions about production objectives and methods originate with him. The apportionment of the decision-making function reduces the magnitude of the decisional problem. The executive cannot and need not comprehend the vast array of technical and human problems that make up the total executive work-load. This function is to provide a solution to a relatively small part of the problem. Each executive should give primary attention to the decisional matters that have been assigned to him, but of course he need not ignore the problems of other executives in making his plans. Using Adam Smith's mode of expression, by pursuing their own particular interests, executives are led by an invisible hand to promote the welfare of the whole organization. Every executive adds a few pieces to a puzzle that cannot be solved by any one of them.

Executive Responsibilities in a Decentralized Decision-Making System

A prime ingredient of cooperative planning and control is effective executive action at each position in the hierarchy. The failure of an executive to properly discharge the decisional responsibilities assigned to him may seriously disrupt the process. But executives should also refrain from

---

[11] Quoted in *Fortune,* Vol. 52, No. 2, August 1955, p. 130.

making decisions that should be made by others.[12] Thus, the superior should not make decisions that ought to be made by subordinates. On the other hand, subordinates should not constantly shift their responsibilities to the superior. As Barnard has pointed out, an important problem of the executive is to determine whether he should or should not make a decision.[13] Although there are no absolute rules, decisional obligations generally evolve from three sources.

1. Decisions transmitted to an executive from higher levels in the hierarchy generally require further decisional action. As noted earlier in this section, broad objectives are redefined into more particular objectives, and objectives are translated into plans. Some superior decisions cannot be executed because they fail to take into consideration the nature of the problems at the subordinate level. Executives sometimes have to practice insubordination if they are to effectively promote what they consider to be the best interests of the organization. They often find themselves between the proverbial frying pan and the fire. A failure to respond to a decision from above is obviously a serious matter, but attempts to impose the decision may have equally serious consequences. It takes courage and social skill to successfully resolve such a dilemma. Some executives have the capacity to make insubordination appear as though it expressed absolute loyalty.

2. Decisional obligations may also evolve from appellate cases referred by subordinates. Such cases can arise from the unwillingness or the inability of the subordinate to make a decision. As Barnard has indicated, the capacity of most men to make decisions is limited and they often try to avoid decisions that involve more than a routine response to conditions.[14] Jurisdictional conflicts among subordinates, lack of information, and insubordination at lower hierarchical levels may also cause subordinate executives to solicit intervention. The executive cannot respond to every subordinate appeal for help without negating the very reason for delegation in the first instance. He should seek to develop self-reliance and initiative among his subordinates by forcing them to make decisions. Subordinates should not feel free to call for a superior decision whenever difficulties darken the horizon. Superiors should generally confine their intervention to important decisional problems, matters that require a precedent, serious jurisdictional questions, and informational deficiencies.

3. Every executive has some decisional responsibilities that are not

---

[12] An excellent discussion of the nature of a decentralized decisional system is found in Barnard, *op. cit.*, pp. 189–194.
[13] *Ibid.*, p. 190.
[14] *Ibid.*, pp. 189–190.

imposed by superior decisions or referred by subordinates. The nature of such responsibilities is generally defined by the formal plan of organization. The executive must determine whether changes should be made or corrective action should be taken within the subject matter area thus defined. Although he is held accountable for results, such decisions are made entirely on his own initiative. Barnard calls such decisions the most important test of executive capacity.[15] Decisional problems imposed by a superior or posed by a subordinate generally cannot be avoided. But executives can and often do avoid decision over matters that fall within their exclusive province. One reason for a failure to take action is the personal responsibility imposed by the act of decision. The fear of wrong decision is frequently more compelling than the possible adverse consequences of no decision.

The Dynamics of Delegation

The management literature is replete with double talk about delegation.[16] Greater delegation or decentralization has been lauded by many executives, but practice does not always reflect preachments. Executives are often more reluctant to delegate than they themselves will admit. Perhaps the most common problem in this respect is the failure to delegate responsibility over relatively minor matters. Far too many executives clutter their desks and minds with details that could be handled by a literate office boy. Some of them are so concerned with the position of the sheet music on the stand that they fail to conduct the orchestra. They frequently disrupt the work of subordinates by neglecting to develop a systematic approach to delegation. William C. Durant, founder of the General Motors Corporation, had the habit of assuming decisional responsibilities of subordinates without notice. Walter Chrysler, who headed the Buick organization and later served as GMC general manager, relates that Durant at one time sold the Detroit Buick Branch without consulting him.[17] At another time Durant hired one of Chrysler's principal superintendents without informing him about it.

The qualities of the superior play an important part in determining the kind of functional and social equilibrium that will be achieved in superior-subordinate relationships. The following situation, experienced and described by Sir Ian Hamilton, illustrates the importance of individual

[15] *Ibid.,* p. 191.
[16] A discussion of some of these problems is found in an article by Perrin Stryker, "The Subtleties of Delegation," *Fortune,* Vol. 51, No. 3, March 1955, pp. 94 ff.
[17] Ernest Dale, "Contributions to Administration by Alfred P. Sloan, Jr., and GM," *Administrative Science Quarterly,* Vol. 1, No. 1, June 1956, p. 36.

differences.[18] While serving as Deputy-Quartermaster-General with the British Army at Simla, Hamilton was constantly faced with an almost endless amount of night work. He described his boss, the Quartermaster-General, as "a clever, delightful work-glutton. . . ." When his chief was ordered back to Europe, Hamilton was asked to assume both the duties of the Quartermaster-General and the job he had been doing. He thought the task an impossible one, but decided to give it a try. To his surprise he found that when his chief departed so did the work. His twelve-hour workday was reduced as though by magic to a six-hour day. The reason was that his former chief liked to record his reasons for every decision, while Hamilton simply said "Yes" or "No." Many subordinates have experienced similar problems in working for and with superiors. They may consider the boss to be somewhat less than efficient or even a little touched in the head, but they rarely suggest that he change his work habits. If the boss likes to work early in the morning or late into the night, many subordinates are inclined to adjust their schedules. If he takes home a briefcase full of work every evening, the office will begin to sprout executives carrying briefcases. If he likes elaborate written reports, subordinates will load his desk with their literary efforts. The work habits of high-ranking executives often influence the behavior of large numbers of subordinate executives at lower levels.

The allocation of decisional responsibilities is also related to the qualities of subordinates. Some subordinates have the capacity to assume more responsibility than others. One may constantly seek to enlarge his domain and another may have opposite propensities. As Lucius D. Clay, who became chairman of the board of Continental Can, has said, "individuals with above average capacities will continually absorb the work and responsibilities of their weaker associates."[19] As a result the actual responsibilities of executives may differ significantly from those specified in the formal plan. Some executives believe that subordinates should be encouraged to add to their responsibilities and make decisions that others fail to make.[20] This idea can obviously be carried too far in a cooperative decision-making system. Anarchy would soon reign supreme if executives failed to abide by the basic pattern of responsibilities set forth in the plan of organization. However, there is generally a shadow area within which decisional responsibilities may shift between superior and subordinate. Delegation should be viewed as a dynamic rather than a static concept. Superiors frequently

---

[18] Sir Ian Hamilton, *The Soul and Body of an Army* (New York: George H. Doran Company, 1921), pp. 235–236.

[19] Clay, *op. cit.*, p. 6.

[20] *Ibid.*, p. 7. This view was also expressed by a number of executives interviewed by the author.

increase responsibilities as subordinates become more experienced. On the other hand, the responsibilities of "weak" subordinates are often reduced by redelegation to another subordinate or to the superior himself. An executive may permit a subordinate to make a decision about a certain matter at one time but not at another. A serious mistake by a subordinate may cause a superior to reassume responsibilities formerly delegated. Personal antagonism between superior and subordinate may also lead to shifts in responsibilities.

A Mutually Dependent System

The management hierarchy and its adjuncts produce a constant sequence of decisions made by different executives at the same time and at different times. An executive position is both an active and a passive force relative to other positions. The decisions made at each position have an impact on other parts of the organization, but at the same time decisions are made in response to changes that result from the decisions of executives in other positions. For example a decision by the president to reduce the budget of a department presents a decisional problem to the departmental executive. Decisions made by the sales executive may create problems for the production executive, and conversely. Each position in the hierarchy is simultaneously a decision-making, a communication, and a leadership (authority) center. Decisions are interrelated into a unified system by the hierarchical distribution of functional responsibility. Coordination is achieved by subjecting lower levels of the hierarchy to decisions made by higher levels. The decisional process is made dynamic through the communication or flow of information from one executive position to another. It becomes effective through the authority relationship or the willingness of managerial and operating personnel to make behavioral changes. However, the decisional process should not be viewed as a mechanistic system with precise differentiations and interrelationships. Unplanned or informal social interactions among executives and others are an integral part of the system. Such interactions may facilitate or impede the decisional process, but they cannot be eliminated in organizations composed of the human beings who presently inhabit this planet.

The Decision-Making Function: Planning and Motivational Decisions

Chapter 14 is concerned with environmental factors that relate to the problem of making planning decisions. The strategies that may be used to make a profit are elaborated in Chapter 15. The discussion is continued in Chapters 16 and 17 with an analysis of the planning process within an organization. After Part V on communication and control, the decision-making function is given further attention in Part VI on leadership and motivation. This sequencing of subject matter is in accord with the management process concept considered in Chapter 4.

SELECTED REFERENCES

Gerald Albaum, "Horizontal Information Flow: An Exploratory Study," *Academy of Management Journal,* Vol. 7, No. 1, pp. 21–33 (March 1964).

Helen Baker, John W. Ballantine, and John M. True, *Transmitting Information Through Management and Union Channels: Two Case Studies.* Princeton, N.J.: Industrial Relations Section, Department of Economics and Social Institutions, Princeton University, 1949.

E. Wight Bakke, *Bonds of Organization,* Chap. 4. New York: Harper & Brothers, 1950.

Chester I. Barnard, *The Functions of the Executive,* Chap. 13. Cambridge: Harvard University Press, 1951.

Keith Davis, "Management Communication and the Grapevine," *Harvard Business Review,* Vol. 31, No. 5, pp. 43–49 (September–October 1953).

Harold J. Leavitt, *Managerial Psychology,* 2nd ed., Chap. 15. Chicago: The University of Chicago Press, 1964.

Harold J. Leavitt, "Some Effects of Certain Communication Patterns on Group Performance," *The Journal of Abnormal and Social Psychology,* Vol. 46, No.1, pp. 38–50 (January 1951).

William W. Mussmann, *Communication Within the Management Group,* Studies in Personnel Policy, No. 80. New York: National Industrial Conference Board, Inc., 1954.

Herbert A. Simon, *Administrative Behavior,* 2nd ed., Chap. 8. New York: The Macmillan Company, 1958.

PART IV

DECISION MAKING: PLANNING STRATEGIES

chapter 14

SURVEYING THE ENVIRONMENT

The economic, political, social, and technical environment plays an important part in planning the program of business and other organizations. Organizational objectives evolve from responses to environmental forces and from attempts by organizations to change and control these forces. Executives spend a great deal of time surveying the environment in search of opportunities for their organizations. They also look for obstacles that may impede the achievement of organizational objectives. A complete evaluation of all of the factors that are pertinent in a particular situation is obviously impossible; the problems of every organization are unique in some or many respects. The purpose here and in subsequent chapters is not to provide specialized knowledge in such fields as economics, political science, labor economics, market research, procurement, and finance but to promote a better understanding of the manner in which such subject matter relates to the planning problem.

Market Forecasting and Analysis

The importance of market forecasting in planning for the future can hardly be overestimated. Such forecasts make possible planned adjustments to economic change. The adverse effects of a recession can often be mitigated by such prior changes as reductions in inventories, changes in the product line, and more aggressive merchandising. The opportunities made possible by favorable market trends can also be better exploited if time is available for adequate planning. Long-range market projections provide the basis for a systematic rather than haphazard approach to secular growth and development. Such projections are particularly important in coordinating short-run and long-run planning.

Some market forecasts, if indeed they can be called forecasts, are little more than hunches or guesses by executives, whereas others involve simple projections of the experience of the recent past into the future. There is also a tendency to go along with whatever the prevailing consensus on the economic future may happen to be. However, there seems to be a trend toward a more objective approach to the problem of forecasting. One reason is that greater objectivity has been made possible by more reliable business and economic statistics and improved forecasting techniques. Another is the realization that survival in a dynamic economic environment can be enhanced by the use of such information.

Demand Determinants

An "ideal" forecasting model would have to take into account a large number of independent and dependent variables and the changes that might occur in their interrelationship over time. It would have to be comprehensive enough to encompass such economic phenomena as cyclical turning points and inflation. A detailed knowledge of the manner in which a diversity of economic, technical, political, cultural, and psychological factors might influence a particular market situation would be required. The use of such a model for forecasting would involve a huge volume of empirical data and highly complex electronic computing facilities. There is little likelihood that the economist or statistician will ever achieve this kind of perfection. Yet, progress in the science of forecasting may be hastened by the construction of comprehensive models of the economy.[1] Such models together with more extensive use of available data and modern computing devices may afford valuable analytical insights and empirical knowledge.

The practical forecaster generally restricts his analysis to a few important demand determinants, such as personal income, population growth, inventory levels, steel output, and the cost of living. Although accurate forecasts sometimes result, the executive should recognize that such forecasts involve some rather broad assumptions about the general state of the economy. Thus, highly accurate forecasts of the demand for a product may result from a correlation with personal income during a relatively stable economic period, but a failure on the part of the forecaster to anticipate a forthcoming economic recession will upset the whole scheme. The accuracy of demand forecasts is closely related to an ability to forecast such dynamic phenomena as cyclical fluctuations, inflation, structural changes, and secular growth and development.

[1] Karl A. Fox, "Econometric Models of the United States," *The Journal of Political Economy*, Vol. 64, No. 2, April 1956, pp. 128–142.

Economic and Sales Forecasting

The forecasting problem is generally viewed as a process that begins with forecasts of general economic conditions and ends with a forecast of the sales prospects for a given company. However, a relatively small number of business organizations are actively engaged in economic forecasting. Even those who profess to make such forecasts are greatly dependent upon outside economic prognostication. The cost of a full-fledged economic forecast is prohibitive for all except some of the larger companies. The attitude of executives seems to be, why spend a lot of money trying to forecast general business conditions when good forecasts are available at practically no cost. Many companies use the market and economic information found in industry, trade, business, and government publications. These forecasts are generally prepared by people who make a business of forecasting, and there is little reason to believe that they are any less reliable than those prepared by company staffs. However, they may not be completely applicable to the needs of a particular company. For this reason some companies employ consultants to interpret and modify the data.

The importance of economic forecasts in formulating sales objectives varies from company to company. Some companies feel that such forecasts are highly significant.[2] Others express an opposite point of view. This diversity of opinion can be partly attributed to the degree of correlation that exists between general economic and industry data and the sales of a particular company. A lack of correlation would tend to reduce the value of external data. Furthermore, sales objectives are not entirely determined by external market factors. For example, a company may fail to maximize its sales potential because it lacks plant capacity or fears government antitrust intervention.

Many companies use the economic forecasts only as a general guide for officers and executives. Thus, the influence that an economic forecast may have upon planning cannot be entirely expressed in objective terms. Much of it enters the decisional process through the subjective judgments of executives. Economic factors tend to be blended with a wide variety of other considerations. As Barnard has pointed out, many of the elements that enter into a decision can only be understood by those intimately familiar with the complex and subtle socio-psychological forces that make up organizational behavior.[3] Some planning premises cannot be easily

[2] John A. Howard, "A Note on Corporate Forecasting Practices," *The Journal of Business of the University of Chicago,* Vol. 27, No. 1, January 1954, p. 105.

[3] Chester I. Barnard, *The Functions of the Executive* (Cambridge: Harvard University Press, 1951), p. 239.

translated into concrete terms even by executives who understand them.

The demand for a given product or service is defined in terms of both quantity and price. How many units will be purchased at a given price, or how much will be purchased at different prices? Some forecasting is concerned only with the sales potential of a particular company. A more general approach is to forecast the total industry demand which is then used to project the revenue potential for the firm.

Market Forecasting Techniques

Companies generally use a combination of different methods in making a market forecast. The most widely used forecasting techniques include the projection of past sales behavior (trend-cycle analysis), correlation analysis, and a variety of survey, interview, and judgment techniques.

Trend-Cycle Analysis. This technique assumes that there is a high degree of continuity between past and future demand or sales behavior. Historical sales data are studied to determine seasonal, cyclical, and secular patterns of behavior. A projection of these data forms the basis for forecasting future sales. Such projections may be highly reliable in forecasting seasonal and secular sales patterns, but the technique is not very dependable in forecasting cyclical variations because of the lack of regularity in such movements.

Correlation Analysis. This method is frequently used if a relationship can be found between sales and other economic and noneconomic phenomena, such as the national income, defense expenditures, population growth, and the weather.[4] Thus, if the national income and sales have moved together in the past, a forecast can be derived from national income data. Such forecasts are generally concerned with the sales volume for the entire industry. The forecaster arrives at a company forecast by estimating the company's share of total industry demand. The basic logic of correlation analysis is that the variables used (such as national income or building construction expenditures) can be forecasted more accurately than sales. However, if the forecaster is fortunate enough to find a sufficient lag between movements in a variable and sales, he can forecast directly from historical data. A six-month lag between a decline in national income and reduced sales illustrates such a situation. One difficulty with correlation analysis is that a past relationship may not continue into the future. Correlation techniques are most reliable when a causal relationship can be

[4] The term "simple correlation" is used to denote correlation with one variable; "multiple correlation" means the use of more than one variable.

established between the variables and sales. However, there is always the possibility that factors other than those used in forecasting may significantly change the outcome.

Correlation techniques have been used to develop *demand functions* for a number of products, such as furniture, refrigerators, and automobiles. Thus, the demand for furniture is a function of disposable personal income per household, the value of private residential construction per household, and the ratio of the furniture price index to the Consumer Price Index.[5] Some demand functions show a close correlation between actual and calculated demand over a relatively long period of time. But, like more simple types of correlation analysis, forecasting the variables used in the equation is a major problem. To paraphrase a market research specialist, it might be guessed that the errors in forecasting several variables would add up to a greater total than those of a straight "judgment" estimate of demand.[6]

Survey and Interview Techniques. Such techniques are used to obtain information about sales prospects from purchasers, the sales force, company executives, and others. A survey of purchaser intentions would seem to provide a useful source of data about future sales potential. The difficulties are that purchaser planning is based upon a variety of economic and noneconomic expectations and that many individuals, institutions, and business firms are not engaged in systematic forward planning.

Survey techniques can also provide historical and current sales data that may be useful for forecasting purposes. For example, information about consumer and dealer inventories may be helpful in many instances. Data on current purchasing provide a basis for predicting future purchases of wholesalers and retailers. Companies frequently turn to sales personnel for assistance in forecasting because they have information about local conditions. However, salesmen sometimes fail to see the forest for the trees and flavor their reports with too much optimism or pessimism. Also, the possibility that sales quotas may be derived from the sales forecast may tinge the estimates somewhat. Some sales forecasters find that interviews and conferences with company executives can frequently supply pertinent information about industry and intraorganizational matters. The forecaster may also obtain useful information from interviews with jobbers, wholesalers, retailers, and others in the industry.

---

[5] Walter Jacobs and Clement Winston, "The Postwar Furniture Market and the Factors Determining Demand," *Survey of Current Business,* May 1950, pp. 8–11.

[6] C. M. Crawford, Market Research Department, Mead Johnson and Company, *Sales Forecasting Methods of Selected Firms* (Urbana: Bureau of Economic and Business Research, College of Commerce and Business Administration, University of Illinois, 1955), p. 49.

New and Changed Products

Forecasting the demand for new products and services is complicated by the lack of historical data. The television and aircraft industries faced this problem during the initial phase of development. Changes in an established product present a similar difficulty, for, although an historical record is available, the data do not provide information about the possible influence of styling, technological, and other innovations upon future sales. Next year's automobiles, washers, refrigerators, television sets, and fountain pens may differ significantly from those sold last year or five years ago.

A number of techniques have been developed to contend with these problems.[7] One is to use past sales of an existing product as a basis for forecasting new product sales. For example, the sales potential for automatic washers may be derived from the sales history of wringer washing machines. An entirely new product may be viewed as a substitute for an established product or service. Overseas air and passenger ship travel illustrates such a relationship. An estimate of the rate of growth and ultimate demand potential for a new product can sometimes be inferred from an analysis of the growth curves of established products. The marketing history of a variety of household appliances may thus provide an empirical growth curve that can be used to forecast the potential market for a new appliance.

Another approach is to experiment in a restricted market, such as a metropolitan area or a chain of stores, in order to gauge the national or regional sales potential of the product. Consumer acceptance can also be tested by survey and interview techniques. A difficulty with this approach is that the consumer has limited knowledge of the product. However, this problem can sometimes be overcome by trial demonstrations in the home, office, and plant.

The Hazards of Forecasting

The hazards of forecasting are almost too obvious to mention. Forecasting seems most successful when there is nothing much to forecast. A successful forecast is something of a miracle and often occurs for the wrong reasons. The forecasting problem indicates the difficulties of developing a science of management. However, it should not lead to the assumption that nothing has been accomplished. There are good "rule of thumb" forecasts.

[7] Joel Dean, *Managerial Economics* (Englewood Cliffs, N.J.: Prentice-Hall, Inc., 1951), pp. 172–175.

A part of the problem is that too much is expected from forecasting. People want more precise answers than are possible in an environment characterized by uncertainty.

A major responsibility of top management is the determination of organizational objectives. The planning process appears more scientific after this step has been taken. Many of the techniques developed during recent years become highly useful at this point. But they have not significantly reduced the uncertainty that pervades the broader environment. The basic contribution of such techniques as linear programming is that they provide a systematic approach to the changes made necessary by uncertainty. Similarly, the solutions gained from partial theories are often more pertinent after certain environmental forces are excluded by top-management decision.

A number of factors help mitigate the consequences of inadequate forecasting. One is that all of the firms in an industry frequently respond to similar economic data in determining their objectives. The errors that are made will affect them in the same direction with essentially equal burdens or benefits. Another factor is that competition is by no means perfect, and this discrepancy supplies some margin for forecasting errors. Still another is that forecasters often bury their mistakes. For example, an automobile manufacturer decides to produce body design X rather than Y for his new model. The resulting profit of 6 per cent would seem to denote a good decision. But the profit might well have been 9 per cent with body design Y.

Short-Run and Long-Run Forecasts

A forecast is generally classified as a long-run forecast if it extends beyond one year. Although such forecasting is less prevalent than short-run forecasting, many companies have recognized the importance of a longer-range perspective, so that three-, five-, and ten-year forecasts are not at all uncommon. Long-range forecasts may afford vital information for decisions about capital outlay, plant location, executive development, and research programs. The forecasting problem changes as the time period of the forecast is lengthened. The vagaries of cyclical fluctuations become relatively less important, but basic structural and cultural changes in the economy become more significant. Demographic factors, such as population growth, age and sex distribution, and geographic distribution become more important in long-range forecasting. Fundamental changes may also occur in the size and distribution of real income, the state of technology, and socio-psychological patterns of behavior.

The Markets for Productive Resources

The markets for productive resources are subject to forces which are for the most part beyond the control of the individual enterprise. The prices of raw materials, equipment, plants and buildings, money, and personnel are important cost determinants. The supply of resources available to a particular enterprise is another planning factor. Although the problem of scarcity is generally solved by the price mechanism, an absolute scarcity may be present with respect to some resources.

Financial Markets

The revenues from consumers are used to compensate those who contribute productive resources to the firm. A company cannot long meet its financial obligations without sales receipts. However, current receipts are not always sufficient to match current expenditures even when the enterprise is operating under profit conditions. Some cash is needed to compensate for variations in the relative magnitude of expenditure and income flows. Companies must either possess the necessary cash or acquire funds in the money market. A money demand may also arise from investment in such current assets as inventories, work in process, supplies, and consumer receivables. The replacement and expansion of plant facilities, equipment, and other fixed assets require large amounts of money.

Where do companies obtain the money required for such purposes? A distinction is generally made between internal and external financing. The primary internal sources are depreciation allowances and retained earnings. External sources include the organized securities markets, insurance companies, banks, suppliers, and private individuals. The data presented in Table 14-1 indicate the manner in which corporations financed their capital requirements over a period of three years.[8]

Externally acquired funds have generally played a smaller quantitative role than funds accumulated internally. During the last few decades external sources have probably accounted for about 35 per cent of the total required for all kinds of capital expenditures. However, such factors as the age and size of the company, type of business, and economic conditions make for considerable variation from norm. A survey of small- and medium-sized businesses indicated that smaller companies were on the whole less interested in obtaining capital from outside sources than were

[8] *Survey of Current Business,* Vol. 47, No. 5, May 1967, p. 16.

Table 14-1. Sources and Uses of Funds, Nonfarm Nonfinancial Corporate Business, 1964–1966
[Billions of dollars]

	1964	1965	1966
Sources, total	70.5	88.1	96.1
Internal sources	50.8	55.3	58.7
Undistributed profits	18.5	21.7	23.3
Corporate inventory valuation adjustment	−.4	−1.5	−2.1
Capital consumption allowances	32.8	35.1	37.5
External sources	19.7	32.7	37.4
Stocks	1.4	.0	1.2
Bonds	4.0	5.4	10.2
Mortgages	3.3	3.2	2.1
Bank loans, n.e.c.	3.6	9.3	7.6
Other loans	1.3	1.3	2.1
Trade debt	3.4	7.3	7.7
Profits tax liability	.9	2.0	−.4
Other liabilities	1.8	4.2	6.8
Uses, total	67.2	87.4	93.5
Purchases of physical assets	52.2	61.9	73.2
Nonresidential fixed investment	44.1	51.3	59.4
Residential structures	3.7	3.9	2.9
Change in business inventories	4.4	6.8	10.9
Increase in financial assets	14.9	25.4	20.3
Liquid assets	.7	.6	1.1
Demand deposits and currency	−2.5	−1.9	.7
Time deposits	3.2	3.9	−.7
U.S. Government securities	−1.4	−2.1	−1.2
Finance company paper	1.5	.7	2.3
Consumer credit	1.0	1.2	1.1
Trade credit	9.1	13.7	10.9
Other financial assets	4.0	9.3	6.5
Discrepancy (uses less sources)	−3.3	−.7	−2.6

Source. Board of Governors of the Federal Reserve System.

the larger companies in the sample.[9] Significant industry differences can also be noted. For example, the communications and electric power industries have relied much more heavily in the postwar years on external sources than companies in the automobile and petroleum industries.[10] The kind of temporal variations that may occur in the pattern of financing is illustrated by the experience of the automobile companies. In the postwar years that preceded the Korean War, depreciation allowances and retained earnings exceeded capital outlays by a wide margin with a resulting increase in liquidity. However, this liquidity was greatly reduced during the years 1951 and 1952 when outlays were almost 75 per cent larger than the funds accumulated from operations. Liquidity was somewhat increased in 1953, but the extensive model changes in 1954 had an opposite effect and also led to a substantial amount of external financing.

Internal financing mitigates the impact of changes in the money markets upon business planning, but it does not by any means eliminate interest rates and money scarcity as strategic planning factors. A considerable diversity of opinion can be found on the importance of interest rates in business planning.[11] Interest rates should not be viewed apart from the many other factors that may influence planning, such as consumer demand, wage rates, raw material prices, and construction costs. A 1 per cent increase in the interest rate may have a negligible effect when profit expectations are high.[12] A 1 per cent decline may likewise have little effect if profit expectations fall to zero or below. But this polarity fails to take into account the many circumstances under which a change in interest rates might be important. Companies have modified their financial plans when interest rates advance. Although such actions generally evolve from a combination of economic factors, it seems reasonable to assert that the interest rate is sometimes the straw that breaks the camel's back.

Interest rates reflect in some degree at least the supply and demand conditions in particular money markets. However, it cannot be assumed that higher interest rates will always bring forth an adequate supply of money. The lending agent assumes a more strategic role during periods of short supply. The available funds tend to go to those who have relatively better financial standings and profit expectations, while otherwise good

[9] Loughlin F. McHugh and Jack N. Ciaccio, "External Financing of Small- and Medium-sized Business," *Survey of Current Business,* October 1955, p. 18.

[10] *Federal Reserve Bulletin,* June 1956, pp. 583–585.

[11] An excellent summary of the interest rate-investment argument is found in: Jan Tinbergen and J. J. Polak, *The Dynamics of Business Cycles* (Chicago: The University of Chicago Press, 1950), pp. 167–171. This study is based on statistical and econometric research by Professor Tinbergen over a period of fifteen years.

[12] Since such expectations are frequently based on high profits in the past, the impact of the external money market is further mitigated by greater internal financing.

credit risks may experience financial difficulties because the more affluent companies are at the front of the line. Larger concerns are usually more successful than small businesses in obtaining outside money.[13] Newly established companies are particularly vulnerable in this respect. However, even the largest and most successful corporations can be plagued by troubles in the money market. In 1957, for example, such companies were finding that Federal tax payments, higher operating costs, and large outlays for new plant and equipment were playing havoc with their cash position.[14] The consequence can be reduced expenditure for new plant and equipment if sufficient funds cannot be obtained at reasonable rates of interest. The money market may become a highly strategic planning factor under certain economic conditions. The plans of enterprising executives go oft astray because a banker frowned and uttered nay.

The Labor Markets

A glance at the want ad section of a newspaper or trade publication gives testimony to the importance of the labor market in planning. Every company experiences a continuous inflow and outflow of executive, professional, technical, and operating personnel over a period of time. Retirement, death, and discharge create a constant demand for replacement. The addition of a new plant, a large cutback in output, and changes in the nature of operations are also important in this respect.

The availability of labor is sometimes a critical factor in planning the company program. The supply of certain kinds of labor is inelastic in the short run. A great deal of time is required to develop such skilled and educated personnel as engineers, chemists, mathematicians, and tool and die makers. Regional variations in supply may also create planning difficulties. Labor is sometimes highly immobile and cannot always be attracted by higher wages. Companies requiring particular kinds of labor may find that some areas are better than others. Furthermore, such factors as local labor laws and union conditions can affect the situation.

The importance of the labor market in solving the cost-revenue problem is indicated by the following data. An average of about 60 per cent of the private national income from 1929 to 1950 was paid out as compensation of employees.[15] The percentages for different industries differ consid-

---

[13] The problem of external financing by smaller business firms has been explored by McHugh and Ciaccio, *op cit.*

[14] *Business Week,* August 3, 1957, pp. 75–76.

[15] W. S. Woytinsky and Associates, *Employment and Wages in the United States* (New York: The Twentieth Century Fund, 1953), p. 42. Private national income is defined as national income excluding compensation of government employees.

erably, varying from 18 per cent of income originating in agriculture to 75 per cent in transportation.[16] Data covered by the Census of Manufacturers show that wages have constituted roughly 40 per cent of the value added by manufacture over a long period of time.[17] A comparison of wage and salary payments and total costs shows somewhat lower percentage results—a random sample of various types of companies indicates that 30 to 40 per cent is a good approximation. Labor cost is generally the second highest item in the operating statement, which means that a relatively small change in wage and salary rates may significantly affect profit margins.

A lack of knowledge of economic opportunity and the prevalence of noneconomic motives make actual labor markets less than fully competitive. Companies can sometimes take advantage of market imperfections [18] and maintain their labor force with lower wages than are being paid by others in a particular market area. Regional wage differentials make possible movement from one market area to another to reduce labor costs. However, labor unions and collective bargaining have removed some of the opportunities afforded by such conditions. Many of the differentials within given market delineations have been wiped out by union efforts to achieve equalization in the level of wages. This kind of equalization may create difficulties for companies operating under higher cost conditions than others in the same line of business. The ability of companies in different types of endeavor to pay the same level of wages is partly related to the elasticities of product demand. Companies with inelastic demand curves for their products have a greater opportunity to pass on higher wage costs to the consumer than those with elastic product demand curves.

The relationship between general wage and price levels has an important bearing on the cost-revenue problem. Wages and salaries tend to increase less rapidly than prices during a strong inflationary trend. However, wage reopening and escalator clauses in collective bargaining agreements have probably taken some of the slack out of the lag. Unions also take anticipated price rises into consideration in making wage demands. On the other hand, wages generally lag behind downward swings in the general level of prices, so that the result is often a price-cost squeeze with serious consequences for companies with insufficient financial resources. A sound long run business venture cannot always remain solvent in the short run.

[16] *Ibid.,* p. 44. Significant variations in the percentages occur from year to year with changes in business conditions.

[17] Wotinsky, *op. cit.,* p. 68. Value added by manufacture is defined as the manufacturer's return for goods produced, minus payments for purchased materials, components, and energy.

[18] Imperfections in the sense that actual markets do not correspond to the abstract models of competitive markets portrayed in economic theory.

Plant and Equipment

Business firms have been spending over 80 billion dollars for fixed plant and equipment in recent years. Data for individual industries and companies are equally impressive. The steel industry has spent almost 30 billion dollars for capital expansion, modernization, and replacement since World War II. The expenditures of the American Telephone and Telegraph Company for plant and equipment totaled over 4 billion dollars in 1967. The General Motors Corporation has advanced well over a billion dollars a year for these purposes in the recent past. The plant and equipment expenditures of a sizable number of other companies can be counted in the hundreds of millions.

The acquisition of plant and equipment involves something more than providing the financial means. The construction of a major plant installation becomes a planning and procurement problem of great magnitude. For example, the Fairless Works of the United States Steel Corporation required approximately 800,000 cubic yards of concrete, 10,000,000 cubic yards of fill, 470,000 tons of various kinds of steel, 25 miles of concrete and tile sewers, 3 miles of belt conveyors, and some 80 miles of standard gauge track.[19] This construction project involved the services of 200 principal contractors, 2000 subcontractors, and the purchase of supplies and materials from 130,000 business firms.

A company sinks money into plant and equipment because it expects a positive rate of return over cost. The total return over the life span of such assets must be sufficient to cover the original money investment, implicit or explicit interest on that money, other operating costs, and enough profit to satisfy the businessman. The greater the original cost of an asset, the lower the rate of profit with given revenue expectations. However, revenue expectations are not constant and may rise as much as or more than costs. Business expenditure for plant and equipment continued at a high level during the postwar years in spite of a large rise in construction and other costs. The reason was that businessmen were generally optimistic about future revenue potential. Greater uncertainty in this respect would tend to make the cost of plant and equipment a much more strategic planning factor.

The cost of plant and equipment is determined by a variety of market factors and conditions. Contracts for the construction of plants and other

---

[19] T. J. Ess, "Fairless Works," *Iron and Steel Engineer,* Vol. 31, No. 6, June 1954, pp. F62–F92.

facilities are often awarded on a competitive bid basis. However, the size and nature of a construction project frequently limits the number of potential contractors. Only one or a few construction companies may possess the required financial means or have the specialized personnel and equipment for a particular project. It cannot be assumed that there is a going market price for the construction of plant facilities. Every plant is somewhat or significantly different from every other plant. The final price generally results from a great deal of bargaining between the company and the contractor or contractors about specifications and estimated cost data. Companies have an advantage when more than one qualified contractor is actively interested in the project. The contractor is often willing to cut his profit margin and take greater risks in his cost estimates during a recession period; a construction boom generally results in opposite propensities. However, the cost of the materials and labor required for construction tends to place minimax limits on this kind of flexibility. A construction company, like any other company, can find itself in a price-cost squeeze induced by price rises in markets over which it has little control. The whole process of cost determination can be traced back through a maze of markets to the original raw materials.

Some plant acquisitions result from the purchase of existing facilities that are either adequate for the intended purpose or adapted by construction. The cost of such facilities may range from nothing or almost nothing to an amount that is as high or higher than new construction. Communities often offer plant facilities as an inducement to companies seeking new locations. The sale of war surplus plants after World War II provided some real bargains. However, locational factors, the urgency of need, and construction material scarcities may raise the price of "used" plants to a high level. Plant facilities may also be acquired by a lease-back and other rental arrangements; such practices are particularly common in the merchandising field.

Many equipment items are purchased in the same manner that a consumer buys a hammer in a hardware store. However, a company can often gain important price concessions by quantity purchases. Specialized equipment and tooling are frequently purchased through the same procedures used in placing construction contracts. The sellers of such items can sometimes make a "monopoly profit" by virtue of patents and trade secrets. On the other hand, a company may gain advantages if it is the sole or a major purchaser from a particular supplier. The possibility of producing rather than purchasing such items as tooling may also be a bargaining element. Some specialized and complicated equipment, such as an electronic computing machine, is acquired through lease.

Raw Materials, Merchandise, and Supplies

A large percentage of company revenues is paid to other business firms. A manufacturing concern requires a continuous flow of raw material and parts from outside vendors. A retail establishment buys merchandise inventories for sale to consumers. Business firms also purchase supplies and services not directly used in the production process or sold to consumers. The amount spent for raw materials, merchandise, and supplies relative to other expenditures varies from industry to industry. Expenditures for these items may account for 25 per cent of the sales dollar for a railroad, 50 per cent for a manufacturing company, and as high as 80 per cent for a retailer. The number of firms supplying a company may range from a score into the thousands. The General Motors Corporation estimates that it has over 55,000 suppliers who furnish a large diversity of products, including steel, diapers, ground corncobs, rubber, baby bottle nipples, walrus hides, cattle tail hair, crushed walnut shells, and castor oil.

The economist has categorized market behavior by such analytical concepts as pure competition, monopolistic competition, oligopoly, monopoly, monopsony, oligopsony, and bilateral monopoly. These concepts afford some insight into the nature of the market forces that may be involved in buying goods and services. Thus, a manufacturer who buys steel is faced with a different price and supply situation than a meat packer who buys in the livestock market. The ability of a company to influence the price of the goods and services it buys may vary a great deal. A competitive market offers little opportunity to gain a price advantage relative to other buyers. On the other hand, significant price concessions may be granted a monopsonist (one buyer) or an oligopsonist (one of a few buyers). Monopoly power on the part of both buyer and seller may lead to a number of possible bargaining solutions. A variety of institutional and structural relationships makes for an almost infinite number of market situations.

Although price is an important factor, it is by no means the only consideration. Also important are such factors as quality, technical efficiency, the availability of parts, servicing, and advertising. For example, a furnace manufacturer may install a more expensive control device primarily because it is better advertised than another equally good device. The ability of a vendor to supply parts or raw material at a given rate is sometimes a vital factor. An automobile manufacturer, for example, might experience considerable difficulty if a supplier failed to deliver a sufficient number of spark plugs. Public and community relations may cause a company to buy from a local firm in spite of price or other disadvantages.

An important consideration in planning purchase programs is the possibility of price fluctuations. A rise in prices can result in large inventory profits; a price decline may lead to irreparable losses. Specific shifts in the overall price level and the prices of particular commodities cannot generally be forecasted with a high degree of accuracy. Companies sometimes attempt to avoid the speculation involved in purchasing inventories of raw materials, merchandise, and supplies by hedging in the futures markets. A flour miller buying wheat can hedge by selling an equivalent amount of wheat for future delivery. However, the large majority of purchases cannot be hedged either directly or indirectly. The uncertainty of general or particular price changes cannot be entirely eliminated in a dynamic economy.

Shortages in the supply of materials may disrupt company planning. Companies producing electrical equipment, power boilers, freight cars, heavy machinery and trucks, nuclear reactors, and bridges were faced with shortages of plate steel during the latter part of 1956.[20] Shipbuilders reported that they were able to acquire less than half their plate steel needs. The concern of some customers about the situation is indicated by their willingness to help finance the expansion program of one steel producer. Companies may also have difficulties finding a source of supply for unique and specialized items. Purchasing is not always a matter of sitting back and waiting for salesmen to arrive in the outer lobby. A company requiring a metal that will withstand extremely high temperatures, for example, may not readily find a supplier with the necessary know-how and facilities. The specifications of the purchaser can involve extensive research and development by the supplier.

Natural and Land Resources

The product of industry can ultimately be traced back to the contributions of nature. The economic development of nations has been greatly influenced by the amount of agricultural land, mineral deposits, and fuel and power resources found within their borders. The United States has been more fortunate than most nations in this respect. Yet, the attrition of two world wars and high levels of capital formation and consumption have reduced or depleted the supplies of some vital resources. Large amounts of iron ore, titanium, manganese, copper, bauxite, and other minerals have to be imported from abroad.

The adequacy of mineral and fuel resources may become a strategic planning factor for companies requiring such resources in the production

[20] *The New York Times,* December 30, 1956, pp. 1, 2.

process. Private companies have played a major role in the discovery and development of domestic and foreign sources of petroleum, iron, and other resources. Steel-producing companies, for example, have spent millions of dollars to develop large iron ore deposits in Canada, Venezuela, and Liberia. They have also devised techniques that make possible the utilization of lower-grade domestic deposits of coal and iron. The petroleum industry has extended its exploration and development activities to the oil-rich countries of the Middle East. Chemical companies import large quantities of barite, bauxite, chromium ore, and other minerals from abroad. The development and importation of foreign sources of raw materials may involve highly complex international political and economic factors. Trade restrictions imposed by foreign governments, a rising tide of nationalism in some areas, diplomatic moves and countermoves, and the specter of Communistic imperialism can play havoc with company plans and programs.

Companies also have to contend with scarcities imposed by the institution of private property and the market system. Thus, altough the domestic supply of coal is more than adequate to meet industrial needs, a mining venture may have to stop operations because it cannot acquire additional coal properties. A similar eventuality may face companies requiring mineral and fuel resources in the production process. An important reason for vertical integration [21] is to insure an adequate supply of raw materials. The United States Steel Corporation was undoubtedly motivated by this consideration in extending ownership control over large iron ore and coal deposits. But, at the same time, such control over basic raw materials may preclude entry by other firms. Companies who purchase mineral and fuel resources are faced with market forces similar to those that determine other prices. A possible difference is that the supply of some natural resources is highly inelastic. A period of rising demand can bring about exorbitant prices or absolute scarcities at a given price.

Except for firms engaged in agricultural pursuits, the acquisition of land is primarily a problem of location. The value of land is closely related to the factors that determine the location of company production and marketing facilities, such as nearness to raw material supplies, availability of labor, transportation facilities, market proximity, power resources, and community and other services. The price of land is partly dependent upon the extent to which companies seek the locational advantages offered by a given site. Another determinant is the availability of other sites with the same or similar inducements.

---

[21] Vertical integration means control of various steps in the production and marketing process.

Government and Business Planning

Business planning may be influenced directly or indirectly by government action. Antitrust policies, the regulation of competitive practices, government spending, and taxation are particularly important in this respect.

Federal Antitrust Laws

The hand of government may point an accusing finger at any business practice or activity that violates a vast body of antitrust laws and regulations. One example is the ruling of the Supreme Court in the government antitrust suit against E. I. du Pont de Nemours and Company and the General Motors Corporation. The Court contended that ownership of GMC stock (23 per cent) by Du Pont violated Section 7 of the Clayton Act, which prohibits stock acquisitions that tend to create monopoly in any line of commerce.[22] This case set a precedent by applying antitrust law to vertical as well as horizontal combinations. Many companies are concerned about the application of this interpretation to their particular situation. Business planning must contend with the possibility that something planned today may become unlawful in the future. The best corporation lawyers cannot accurately forecast the manner in which a court may interpret the many laws designed to restrain monopoly and enforce fair competitive practices. The public utilities find themselves in a somewhat different category with respect to government intervention. They are given certain monopolistic prerogatives, but their rates and operating practices are subject to regulation by governmental agencies.

Governmental Purchases

Federal, state, and local government expenditure is an important source of revenue for some business concerns. A decline in government spending can induce a general business recession if expenditure in the private sector is not increased by a sufficient amount.[23] Equally important is the impact of changes in the type of government expenditure upon the revenues of

---

[22] This stock had been purchased over forty years ago.

[23] If reduced government spending brings about lower taxes, consumer and business spending may rise. Lower public expenditure is sometimes necessary to ease inflationary pressure during a hyper-prosperity period.

particular companies. Such changes will affect some companies adversely and others favorably. A producer of military items may find himself on the losing end, but a highway contractor or an appliance manufacturer may win greater rewards. The uncertainties involved in gleaning revenues from government purchases are much the same as those experienced in the consumer markets. It is most difficult to forecast the actions that may be taken by politicians and administrators in Washington, D.C., Lincoln, Nebraska, or Belle Plaine, Iowa.

Business Taxes

Company profit margins can be significantly affected by income and other taxes. Indirect business taxes can reduce profit margins by increasing the cost of business operations.[24] Income or profit taxes transfer an appreciable portion of business earnings to government. However, the impact of taxes upon company planning is not limited to such direct revenue and cost consequences. Thus, although a corporate income tax may reduce the money available for investment, it may also tend to stimulate investment if accelerated amortization is permitted. A good example is the tax write-off program designed to increase capital expansion during the Korean War. Companies producing certain products were allowed to deduct the cost of new plant and equipment from income over a five-year period rather than the normal life of the asset. Much of the money that would otherwise have to be paid as income taxes could be used to purchase capital goods. Accelerated amortization of a capital asset increases expense and reduces profit. Since a large percentage of the greater profit without such amortization would have to be paid in taxes, the actual cost of plant and equipment may only be a fraction of the market cost. Corporate profits taxes can influence company planning and expenditures in other respects. The high excess-profit tax rates of the postwar years caused some companies to increase advertising budgets and permit more liberal expense accounts. With a tax rate of 85 per cent on the last increment of profit, the actual cost of an additional dollar spent for such purposes amounts to only fifteen cents.

Other Examples

There are many other ways in which government action may directly or indirectly influence business planning. Labor legislation has undoubtedly given impetus to the development of the "human relations" emphasis in management. Agricultural price support programs have an effect upon

[24] The ultimate consequence of a particular tax depends upon the extent to which it can be shifted and the manner in which it influences pertinent economic variables.

costs in such industries as meat packing and grain processing. The activities of the Federal Reserve System may cause changes in the supply and price of funds in the money markets. International trade agreements and import duties have a bearing on company price policies, foreign sales opportunities, and the amount of competition. Zoning ordinances and parking restrictions may become important locational factors.

Innovation as an Environmental Factor

The term "innovation" is used here to mean the introduction of new ideas and techniques that result in higher productivity, lower costs, or increased revenues. The executive must be constantly alert to innovations that relate to his field of endeavor. He must keep pace with innovations made by competitors if his firm is to prosper and survive. The process of innovation is characterized by a relatively continuous sequence of major and minor developments. Some innovations are revolutionary in their impact upon business operations and existing economic interrelationships. Others are like drops of rain, individually minute, but collectively of great magnitude.

Managerial and Operating Efficiency

A primary precept of a competitive system is that greater productive efficiency enhances the survival power of a company. The literature of management is replete with accounts of innovations that have increased productivity in a small or large measure. The development of line production, the self-service market, decentralized management, and automation express the innovation process in its most revolutionary form. The solution of some fundamental problem frequently gives rise to a number of related innovations in a short period of time. Such innovations as automation actually involve a cluster of major and minor innovations that form a systematic whole. A revolutionary sequence of innovations within a given area may be followed by a long evolutionary period involving relatively routine improvements in technique. However, not all innovation should be considered as a part of some major achievement. A great deal of progress is made by a series of small changes, such as an improved sequence of operations for producing a gasket or a better procedure for hiring employees. The importance of innovations outside the mechanical arts and sciences should not be neglected. The development of a better organizational technique or a more accurate employee testing program is sometimes more important than an improved production process.

The relationship between innovation and productivity may be difficult to measure. Some of the recently developed "human relations" techniques can be placed in this category. The oft-expressed idea that these techniques have improved morale does not necessarily lead to the further conclusion that productivity has been favorably affected. Many such conclusions are more the product of fairy tales than the hard realities of production economics. The hiring of preachers or psychologists as employee counselors, for example, has probably resulted in less inhibited workers, but there is little concrete evidence that output has been increased. However, improved human relations tend to have a more indirect relationship to productivity than other kinds of innovation. Thus, a company may experience fewer strikes in the long run than a competitor who uses the stick rather than the carrot to motivate his personnel. The social and other satisfactions that may evolve from better human relations can also be considered as a proper substitute for a higher output of goods and services. Productivity is not the only or, necessarily, the most important consideration in developing a program of human relations.

Innovation and Economic Efficiency

Innovation is concerned with economic as well as productive efficiency; the survival of a company is ultimately related to its success in the market. The most efficient operations will lead nowhere if people will not buy the product or service. Innovation may cause declines in the demand for existing products or services and give rise to entirely new industries. The development of the automobile dealt a death blow to the carriage and livery stable industry, but it gave birth to the giant automobile industry and a cluster of related industries. Air travel has become an important substitute for travel on railroads, bus lines, and ships. Some innovations have unfavorable consequences for industries that evolved from previous innovations. Thus, television has created serious difficulties for the motion picture industry. An innovation in one industry may bring about a need for innovation in another industry. The brassiere industry, for example, was handed the problem of providing sufficient support for the plunging necklines created by Paris and New York fashion circles.[25]

Companies should give constant consideration to the manner in which innovations may affect the demand for their products or services. A major innovation can significantly, and sometimes rapidly, reduce the revenue

[25] *Business Week,* April 4, 1964, p. 64.

potential of a company. Also important are the many relatively small innovations that mark the course of the competitive game. Annual model changes in the automobile industry provide a good example. During the past decade some rather sizable shifts in competitive position have resulted from innovations in body styling. Some automobile companies greatly expanded their styling activities and organized separate styling departments to keep ahead in the race.[26]

Advertising innovations have played an important role in many battles for competitive advantage. The major tobacco companies, for example, have been engaged in an "advertising gimmick" contest since the 1920's. Similarly, a new television idea may upset the competitive apple cart for companies in a diversity of industries. A novel installment buying idea, a new pricing system, a mechanical improvement, and the introduction of a new service represent other kinds of market-oriented innovations.

The problem of organizing production also involves economic considerations. Some innovations reduce costs without necessarily increasing physical productivity. One goal in combining such productive resources as land, labor, and capital is more efficient production. But there is also the possibility of reducing costs by substituting lower-priced resources for higher-priced ones. Thus, the substitution of capital for labor may result in short-run or long-run advantages. Companies that are more alert in this respect can charge ahead of their lagging neighbors.

Innovation and Uncertainty

Elaborate measures are frequently taken to prevent other companies from learning about important innovations. Nothing is more sacred in the lexicon of business than the term "trade secrets." Innovations are kept under cover until they cannot be successfully copied by competitors. Automobile styling and fashion design innovations often involve complicated security measures. The only recourse a company has under such conditions, aside from "mata hari" techniques, is to forge ahead with its own program of innovation.

Other Environmental Considerations

Such environmental factors as culture and weather may also significantly influence business planning. Although emphasis has been given to business

[26] A comprehensive account of automotive styling is found in: *Industrial Design*, Vol. 2, No. 5, October 1955, pp. 50–72.

enterprises, the environmental problems of nonbusiness organizations are similar.

Cultural and Social Factors

An understanding of cultural norms and social practices can be extremely important in effective planning. The nature of some of these problems was considered in Chapter 6. Attitudes toward racial segregation, the customs of different nationality groups, and religious beliefs and practices illustrate the kind of thing that may become pertinent in planning.

Weather Conditions

The state of the weather is particularly important in such industries as agriculture, construction, and air transportation. Restaurants, amusement parks, theatres, baseball clubs, and retail establishments also find that weather conditions affect their operations. Weather was a primary factor in setting the day of the Normandy invasion during World War II. However, forecasting difficulties limit the extent to which the planner can take weather conditions into consideration. Short-term forecasts may be rather unreliable and long-term predictions are highly conjectural.

Nonbusiness Organizations

Some of the environmental factors involved in planning the program of nonbusiness organizations, such as hospitals, churches, universities, and the military, are much the same as those of a business enterprise. The problem of acquiring personnel and material resources is similar in many respects. The revenues of nonbusiness organizations may be derived by making products or services available to "customers." A church offers religious satisfactions, a university retails an education, and hospitals cater to the sick and injured, in return for contributions, tuition, and fees. Many nonbusiness organizations plan their operations on the basis of "demand" forecasts. However, significant environmental differences can also be noted. The military is sometimes given a priority in the labor market by draft legislation. Churches generally cannot demand contributions from a sinner who receives religious enlightenment. Public-supported hospitals and universities have to contend with the politics of legislative bodies in obtaining revenues.

Environmental and Internal Planning Premises

Planning is premised on implicit and explicit forecasts or estimates of the future. The subject matter may range from a forecast of future sales to a forecast of paper towel requirements. Some forecasts are concerned with the various environmental factors considered in this chapter. Others are concerned with factors internal to the organization, such as employee morale, research potential, and the efficiency of existing production facilities. However, a strict dichotomy between environmental and internal factors cannot be maintained in practice. A cost estimate is based on factors internal to the organization, such as productive efficiency, and on external factors, such as raw material prices and wage rates. Furthermore, consideration must always be given to the extent to which the program being planned may influence the forecast. A forecast of demand should take into account the possible effect of sales promotion and advertising plans. A cost estimate is based on certain assumptions about the production program that is being planned.

The reliability of forecasts or estimates varies a great deal with the subject matter that is involved. Generally speaking, the behavior of things can be forecasted more accurately than human behavior. An engineer can often forecast with complete certainty. An economist usually has better hindsight than foresight. However, most forecasts are abstractions of a large number and diversity of material and human factors. They involve subtle interrelationships that often create havoc with any simple cause and effect approach. Some events are not considered in planning because forecasting them is almost impossible. International incidents, such as the invasion of Korea by the Communists and the Cuban missile crisis, frequently catch everyone by surprise.

In spite of the emphasis given to the importance of a scientific attitude and method, many of the factors that influence planning are highly subjective. The health of the president, the nagging of an executive's wife, or an incident at the club may directly or indirectly affect company planning. The executive who does the planning is a human being with the psychological properties of other human beings. He may not look into crystal balls or carry a rabbit foot, but he is not immune to other manifestations of magic and sorcery.

SELECTED REFERENCES

Theodore A. Andersen, "Regional Industry Forecasting," *California Management Review,* Vol. 8, No. 3, pp. 51–56 (Spring 1966).
Stephen H. Archer and Charles A. D'Ambrosio (editors), *The Theory of Business Finance.* New York: The Macmillan Company, 1967.
Joe S. Bain, *Industrial Organization.* New York: John Wiley and Sons, Inc., 1959.
E. Wight Bakke, Clark Kerr, and Charles W. Anrod, *Unions, Management and the Public.* New York: Harcourt, Brace & World, Inc., 1967.
Roy Blough, *International Business: Environment and Adaptation.* New York: McGraw-Hill Book Company, 1966.
Steuart Henderson Britt, *Consumer Behavior and the Behavioral Sciences.* New York: John Wiley & Sons, Inc., 1966.
The Business Man in Politics, Management Report No. 37. New York: American Management Association, 1959.
Joel B. Cohen, "Toward an Interpersonal Theory of Consumer Behavior," *California Management Review,* Vol. 10, No. 3, pp. 73–80 (Spring 1968).
Kalman J. Cohen and Richard M. Cyert, *Theory of the Firm: Resource Allocation in a Market Economy.* Englewood Cliffs, N.J.: Prentice-Hall, Inc., 1965.
Keith Davis and Robert L. Blomstrom, *Business and its Environment.* New York: McGraw-Hill Book Company, 1966.
Marten Estey, *The Unions: Structure, Development, and Management.* New York: Harcourt, Brace & World, Inc., 1967.
George Fisk, *Marketing Systems.* New York: Harper & Row, 1967.
Walter W. Heller, *New Dimensions of Political Economy.* Cambridge: Harvard University Press, 1966.
Walter Krause, *Economic Development.* San Francisco: Wadsworth Publishing Company, Inc., 1961.
Walter Krause, *International Economics.* Boston: Houghton Mifflin Company, 1965.
Ralph Linton, *The Tree of Culture.* New York: Alfred A. Knopf, Inc., 1957.
Otis Lipstreu and Kenneth A. Reed, *Transition to Automation.* Boulder, Colorado: University of Colorado Studies, Series in Business No. 1, 1964.
Huxley Madeheim, Edward Mark Mazze and Charles S. Stein, *International Business.* New York: Holt, Rinehart and Winston, 1963.
Campbell R. McConnell, *Economics: Principles, Problems and Policies,* 3rd ed. New York: McGraw-Hill Book Company, 1966.

Joseph W. McGuire, *Theories of Business Behavior*. Englewood Cliffs, N.J.: Prentice-Hall, Inc., 1964.

Chester A. Morgan, *Labor Economics*, rev. ed. Homewood, Ill.: The Dorsey Press, 1966.

Joseph W. Newman, *On Knowing the Consumer*. New York: John Wiley & Sons, Inc., 1966.

Roger M. Pegram and Earl L. Bailey, *The Marketing Executive Looks Ahead*, Experiences in Marketing, No. 13. New York: National Industrial Conference Board, Inc., 1967.

Wallace C. Peterson, *Income, Employment, and Economic Growth*, rev. ed. New York: W. W. Norton & Company, Inc., 1967.

Paul H. Rigby, *Conceptual Foundations of Business Research*. New York: John Wiley & Sons, Inc., 1965.

John K. Ryans, Jr. and James C. Baker, *World Marketing: A Multinational Approach*. New York: John Wiley & Sons, Inc., 1967.

Richard J. Schonberger, *Labor Market Survey: The Relationship Between Part-Day Employment and the Role of the Woman in the Home*. Rock Island, Ill.: U.S. Army Management Engineering Training Agency, 1968.

Irwin M. Stelzer, *Selected Antitrust Cases: Landmark Decisions*, 3rd. ed. Homewood, Ill.: Richard D. Irwin, Inc., 1966.

Scott D. Walton, *American Business and its Environment*. New York: The Macmillan Company, Inc., 1966.

chapter 15

THE DEVELOPMENT OF PLANNING STRATEGIES

Executives look into the future for forces that will promote or stand in the way of organizational success. When adaptation to environmental forces becomes necessary, they will either modify the organizational objective, or they may decide to push through a particular objective by modifying the forces that stand in the way. For example, the objectives of a business organization are partly determined by an analysis of consumer demand. If a decline in demand is anticipated, the organizational program may be adjusted accordingly. But another possibility is to attempt to increase demand through better product styling, technological innovation, and sales promotion. Organizational objectives may likewise be affected by such factors as inadequate plant facilities, excess capacity, poor employee morale, insufficient financial resources, a shortage of engineers or production workers, federal legislation, and the forces of nature. Not all factors can be readily overcome by organizational action. Agricultural firms can exercise little control over the weather; lobbying activities are not always successful in stopping adverse legislation; and sales promotion may have a limited effect upon sales during a major recession.

Planning for Profits

Strategic Revenue and Cost Factors: A Synthesis

Planning is given a conceptual unity by the fact that there are limited resources. The planning problem is to overcome the obstacles imposed by this condition. The problem is partly solved by successful planning at the consumer side of the business. Larger revenues enhance the ability of an organization to survive and provide a basis for growth. This aspect of planning is concerned with marketing strategies to improve the firm's revenue potential. The planning problem can also be solved with resource procurement strategies that reduce the cost of such resources as labor, raw materials, plant, and equipment. Still another approach to the problem of limited resources is to achieve higher productivity through improved methods and motivational techniques.

The manner in which planning strategies interact varies with different companies and at different times. Some companies experience periods of time when there is little possibility of increasing revenues through marketing strategies or reducing costs through more effective resource procurement. The only alternative under such circumstances is to reduce costs through improvements in operating efficiency. Changing economic conditions can alter the situation and bring about more alternatives in the areas of marketing and resource procurement.

A business firm cannot generally survive if costs are consistently greater than revenues. Management should take advantage of every possible opportunity to increase profits. Companies do not always take advantage of the alternatives available to them. The ease with which revenue can be earned during a prosperity period has resulted in a neglect of cost-reducing strategies. Far too many companies engage in highly marginal activities that do not benefit either the revenue or the cost side of the ledger. An important planning objective is to make a profit. Profits are both necessary and moral in a private enterprise society.

The planning problems of nonbusiness organizations are in many respects similar to those of business firms. Such organizations also have the problem of reducing costs through improved resource procurement and operating methods. The differences are on the "revenue" side. Legislative appropriations and charitable contributions are important sources of income for religious, political, educational, and military organizations. However, the techniques used to obtain such income do not differ in a marked degree from the marketing techniques of the business world.

The remainder of this chapter considers the three basic kinds of strategies that may be used to solve the problem of limited resources: (1) marketing strategies; (2) resource procurement strategies; and (3) efficiency strategies.

Marketing Strategies

Marketing strategy is concerned with the methods that may be used to improve a company's revenue position. It involves planned adaptation to market forces that cannot be controlled by the individual company and planning designed to overcome limitations imposed by the market.

The Company Product Line

To survive, companies must produce something that consumers are willing to buy. If the demand for a company's products or services seems destined to dwindle to little or nothing, executives should consider the possibility of shifting to other products or services. The specialized nature of plant and equipment may make such a move difficult, if not impossible, in the short run. A company may simply have to bear the consequences of a lack of foresight or an unexpected turn of events. However, there is frequently enough flexibility to make product line adjustments. Some demand shifts can be met with gradual changes over a long period of time.

Many companies have expanded their revenue potential through product diversification. Their products compete in a number of dissimilar markets. Such a situation requires a periodic appraisal of the relative profitability of particular products, and some may have to be dropped in the interest of economic efficiency. The decision of the International Harvester Company to quit the refrigeration business was at least partly motivated by this consideration. Another example is the Kaiser Company's decision to get out of the "mainline" domestic automobile industry. But products are also added to obtain a more favorable competitive position, to promote organizational growth, and to maintain a given scale of operations. The search may become particularly diligent when a company is faced with the problem of excess production and distribution capacity.

The cigarette industry found itself with a possibly serious product line problem with the publication in 1964 of the report of the Surgeon General's advisory committee on the relationship between smoking and health. The report noted that cigarette smoking definitely causes lung cancer and other health problems. The ultimate impact of this information on smoking habits is difficult to forecast. Some tobacco companies are not taking a chance. They began adding to their product lines even before the Surgeon General's report became a best seller. Shaving cream, razors, blades, candy, chewing gum, and fruit juice are some of the products with which tobacco companies have hedged the future.

The J. C Penney Company launched a drive a few years ago to become a full-fledged department store with a more comprehensive line of merchandise.[1] Its expanded product line will include major household appliances, automobile equipment and accessories, sporting goods, furniture, and hardware. Women will be able to put on a façade of glamour in Penney beauty salons and obtain a permanent record of the result in a photographic studio—both facilities under the same roof. In-home selling of such items as draperies and carpets will also be featured. A mail-order catalog with a complete line of merchandise is available for those who want to shop at home.

Companies do not always look to the outside for possible additions to their product line. Product research and development have provided important opportunities in this respect. The Du Pont Company, for example, has introduced literally hundreds of new products through an aggressive research and development program. In 1968, 45 of a total of 65 types of proprietary fiber products manufactured by Du Pont had been introduced during the preceding five year period. Union Carbide spends well over 80 million dollars a year for product improvement, new product development, and related purposes. During a recent period, scientific research at General Mills resulted in more than 30 new food products in addition to improvements in existing products. Research and development at the American Can Company created 8 new products during 1967.

The history of nylon, the first of many synthetic fibers created by Du Pont, testifies to the importance of product innovation. Nylon was introduced on a commerical basis in the late 1930's after ten years of research and development. During the first year, United States women bought 64 million pairs of nylon hosiery and screamed for more. Du Pont doubled production capacity the first year to meet the demands of hosiery manufacturers. The war years led to the use of nylon in military items, and the postwar years brought even higher levels of consumer demand. The technical and commercial achievement of nylon led the way to more synthetic fibers, such as orlon and dacron. These and other exploits in product development were highly instrumental in giving Du Pont the top rank in the chemical industry.

Price Policies

A company can sometimes enhance its revenue position by changing the price of its products or services. The revenue consequences of a price

[1] *Business Week,* February 2, 1963, p. 44.

change are dependent upon what economists call "elasticity of demand." The individual firm in a purely competitive industry cannot increase price above that of a competitor because its demand curve is perfectly elastic. A farmer who ships his hogs to the market in Omaha or Chicago cannot ask more than the prevailing market price if he wants to sell his product. However, the demand curves of the majority of companies are at least slightly inelastic, which makes possible some degree of price discretion. Under such circumstances a company can increase prices and not lose all of its sales to competitors. A monopolist is generally in a better position in this respect than companies that have to contend with producers in the same line of business. But even the monopolist cannot increase his price without sustaining reductions in sales. If the price of diamonds goes up too much, people will buy more rubies and emeralds.

The elasticity of demand concept means that company revenues may rise with price reductions and fall with price increases, or conversely. The reason is that *both* price and quantity sold must be taken into consideration in computing revenues. An elastic demand curve means that total revenues will rise with price reductions and fall with price increases. A reverse situation will prevail with inelastic demand curves. Thus, it cannot be assumed that an increase in price will always help a company solve a problem of insufficient revenues. A further consideration is the relationship between the quantity produced and operating costs. A company with high fixed costs and excess productive capacity can frequently gain a great deal of profit by a price reduction. The classic example is the Ford Motor Company's dynamic policy of price reductions during the Model T era. This policy was instrumental in building a mass market for the Model T, which in turn made possible a production line that turned out ten thousand automobiles per day. Ford recognized the importance of demand elasticity and the cost advantages that could be derived from large-scale production. A high price per unit policy would have stifled growth and reduced earnings. The Ford policy and experience have been duplicated in most of America's basic industries.

A company's price policy may be strongly influenced by possible reprisals from competitors. This consideration is particularly important when a few companies dominate a market. A price increase may result in a loss of sales if the rest of the companies do not follow. An attempt to gain an advantage by a price cut may result in even greater price reductions by rival companies. The gasoline price war provides a good example of this aspect of price strategy. Such wars generally begin with a price cut by one gasoline company in a particular market area. This move is immediately followed by similar actions by the other dealers. There is frequently a long sequence of price reductions until the original or a new price equilibrium is achieved; the price-cutter sometimes loses far more than he expected to gain originally.

Sometimes a price leader will emerge in an industry or a market area. As Richard B. Tennant has pointed out in his study of the cigarette industry, the leader "may be selected by chance, by agreement, by the power of the strongest firm to enforce its decisions on the rest, by the fact that one firm prefers a lower price than do the others, or by simple habit and custom." [2] Price leadership in various forms has existed in many industries, such as steel, cigarette, automobile, milk, and restaurant. However, it should not be assumed that uniform price changes in an industry necessarily involve collusion among the companies concerned—evidence of collusion might result in government antitrust action. Such pricing phenomena can be explained by the economic logic of profit maximization. A company may simply follow another in a price rise or price cut because it enhances revenue potential.

Companies sometimes refrain from a policy of "charging what the traffic will bear" for public relations reasons. The lurking stick of governmental antitrust policy also plays a role in this respect. There is a tendency, particularly on the part of the big corporation, to administer relative price stability in the short run. The big corporation need not and generally does not attempt to exploit a temporary market advantage. The large steel producers maintained prices at a lower than "competitive market level" during the period of short supply after World War II. The result was an extensive grey market in which steel sold far above the prices charged by the steel companies. Although motives are complex and illusive, there is every indication that possible adverse public opinion and the threat of government intervention were important factors. As Oxenfeldt has concluded: "They seem to balance the threat of increased regulation or nationalization against the prospect of profit, and pursue a course that does not give maximum profits at any given time." [3] But short-run price inflexibility does not mean that prices are equally inflexible in the long run. Price reductions have played an important role in the continued growth and development of big enterprise.

Many strategies and factors may be involved in a particular pricing situation. Prices may be set at a lower level than would be necessary for other reasons to keep potential competitors out of the industry. Companies sometimes attempt to increase revenues by selling the same product at

[2] Richard B. Tennant, *The American Cigarette Industry* (New Haven: Yale University Press, 1950), p. 282.

[3] Alfred R. Oxenfeldt, *Industrial Pricing and Market Practices* (Englewood Cliffs, N.J.: Prentice-Hall, Inc., 1951), pp. 510–511.

different prices to different categories of customers.[4] A price rise can be used to give dealers a larger margin with the idea that greater sales effort will cause a net increase in revenues. Uncertainty, inertia, and a fear of change are important elements in price determination. Why make a change if the present price results in a profit and causes no adverse action from government, competitors, and others? A price change might have all sorts of real and imagined consequences. Why tempt fate in the face of the unknown?

Advertising

Companies spend billions of dollars a year for advertising to promote sales and gain other advantages. The percentage of the sales dollar used for advertising and other sales promotion techniques ranges from a fraction of a per cent for some products to well over 10 per cent for others. The extent to which demand can be changed by advertising varies from product to product. Such products as cigarettes, drugs, soap, cereals, beer, liquor, and cosmetics rank high in this respect. At the other end of the scale are industrial machinery and equipment, metals, and crude oil.

How does a company determine the proper amount to spend for advertising? Should it spend $50,000, $100,000, or $1,000,000? The marginal approach of the economist provides a theoretical solution to the problem. An increase in advertising expenditures is appropriate as long as each additional dollar spent brings in more than an equivalent amount in revenues. The equilibrium point is reached when the two are equal. However, uncertainty and measurement difficulties preclude the application of precise marginal analysis in a practical situation. A major problem is that the effect of advertising upon revenues is difficult to determine. Advertising is only one of many factors that may cause a change in demand. An increase in sales cannot always be credited to advertising, and a decline in sales does not necessarily indicate an advertising failure. Furthermore, the long-term assets that may be created by advertising should be considered in computing the returns from a given volume of expenditures.

Another problem is to choose from among alternative advertising media and sales promotion techniques. Should a company buy newspaper advertising or should it put its money into a television show? Would higher expenditure for window displays or customer services offer a better alterna-

[4] A discussion of the economics of price discrimination is found in: Joan Robinson, *The Economics of Imperfect Competition* (London: Macmillan and Co., Ltd., 1946), pp. 179–208.

tive? The answer depends on the kind of customer the company wants to attract. Advertising in a trade publication might be better than newspaper advertising if the company sells to other companies; a television or radio program would have greater appeal to ultimate consumers. The scope of the market in which a company sells is another consideration. National television coverage would obviously not be appropriate for a company selling in a local market. The weekly newspaper is a more efficient medium for some purposes than a large metropolitan daily. A company should make adjustments in its advertising and sales promotion program until it obtains the highest possible returns from expenditures. Research, experimentation, and experience provide some basis for evaluating the alternatives, but the difficulties of measurement preclude a high degree of accuracy.

The standards used by companies to determine the size of the advertising budget are little more than "rule of the thumb" approximations.[5] One method is the use of a fixed or variable percentage of past or anticipated sales to determine the size of the advertising budget. Another is simply to spend all that can be afforded in the light of profit expectations and liquidity considerations. Advertising expenditures are sometimes handled as a capital investment that must compete with other capital expenditures on a rate-of-return basis. A technique that came into prominence during World War II involves estimating the cost of achieving a given objective by advertising. Thus, how much money must be spent for advertising to increase sales by 5 per cent? A widely used approach is to relate advertising expenditure to the amount spent by other companies in the industry. These methods generally give recognition to the idea that advertising expenditures should be judged by efficiency criteria, but they do not adequately measure the revenue consequences of particular advertising expenditures. The practical problem is that the factors that ought to be considered in planning an advertising program cannot be quantitatively measured. However, executives ought to be fully aware of the limitations of the methods that are being used. Furthermore, such methods should not become impediments to the application of better, though far from perfect, estimating techniques.

Advertising is frequently an important weapon in the competitive battle. Companies are sometimes forced to increase advertising expenditures to match the outlays of rivals. Such retaliation tends to nullify the competitive advantages sought in the first instance. Conceivably the process could continue until the combatants experience zero profits or even losses in their attempts to strike a final blow. One reason this does not occur is that there

[5] An appraisal of some of these methods is found in: Joel Dean, *Managerial Economics* (Englewood Cliffs, N.J.: Prentice-Hall, Inc., 1951), pp. 363–375. The methods presented in this section are taken from this source.

is undoubtedly some optimum point beyond which higher expenditures do not provide better results. Another is that each company recognizes the potential danger of this kind of cutthroat competition. Companies sometimes limit their advertising efforts for the same reason they do not engage in indiscriminate price cuts. But it should not be assumed that advertising never results in competitive advantages. A company may make large short-run (and possibly long-run) gains by an advertising innovation that cannot be readily duplicated. For example, a popular television show may be sufficient to swing the competitive battle. A contract with an Elvis Presley or an Elizabeth Taylor may be the wiggle that turns the tide in a competitive war.

There may be gains for all companies in an industry even when advertising efforts result in no competitive advantages. The big cigarette companies have been engaged in advertising skirmishes for many years with relatively slight shifts in competitive position. But the impact of this accumulated advertising appeal upon the overall demand for cigarettes has probably been significant. There is no way of knowing how many cigarettes would be consumed today without the advertising of past years. The difficulty that smokers experience in "quitting the weed" is one indication that advertising may have subtle psychological implications. Advertising and other sales promotion programs are sometimes designed to make major changes in social customs and habits. For example, a number of years ago ladies' hosiery producers tried to establish "leg consciousness" in an effort to pull up sagging stocking sales.[6] According to one consumer research report, women seemed to feel that the sexual significance of their legs was declining. The emphasis had moved away from the leg since the heyday of Marlene Dietrich and Betty Grable.

Products and Service Innovations

Product research and development, styling and design, and product engineering have become increasingly important functions. A primary purpose of these activities is to gain greater consumer acceptance by improvements in product performance and appearance. A consumer who owns yesteryear's model of a product is fully aware of industry's effort to create something better. The current model generally tempts him with some kind of innovation. It may offer him better mechanical performance, a more pleasing color combination, greater convenience, better operating efficiency, or improved design and styling. As has been noted in previous sections, product and service innovations are highly important instruments of competition. Companies are constantly seeking ways to keep the cus-

[6] *Wall Street Journal,* Vol. 37, No. 182, July 2, 1957, p. 1.

tomers they have, attract customers away from competitors, and bring in new customers.

American industry spends millions of dollars and employs thousands of specialists in many fields for product and other research. At the General Electric Company over 18,000 highly trained employees were engaged in research, development, and engineering in 1967; of this total some 1200 held doctoral degrees. The company maintains a centralized research and development center for the purpose of conducting advanced studies in major scientific fields. The Westinghouse Research Laboratories employs 1500 research scientists, engineers, and supporting personnel in a search for new knowledge and techniques. The Bell Telephone Laboratories has well over 10,000 persons assigned to tasks involved in basic and applied research. Equally impressive data are available about research in such companies as International Harvester, General Motors, RCA, Ford, IBM, and Sperry Rand. The small and medium-sized companies should not be neglected in this respect. The Maytag Company, a producer of automatic washers and household appliances, has always been active in product development and employs some 60 research people.[7] The laws of probability give an advantage to companies with large organized research facilities, but it should not be assumed that creative thought and imagination are the exclusive property of research specialists. Executives and operating personnel have made outstanding contributions in product innovation. Small companies should not be taken out of the race because they are small. They can frequently win it if executives give sufficient time and attention to the problem. However, the problem is sometimes ignored because of a lack of foresight or the pressure of operating problems.

Research cannot be divorced from the economics of doing business. It must result in some kind of increase in company revenues, at least in the long run. A good example of guiding principles that can be applied to this problem are the "house rules" developed by the Du Pont Company.[8] The first rule is to establish a broad commercial base for research activities because larger sales increase the amount that can be spent for research. A larger research budget tends to increase the statistical probabilities for successful research and the degree of specialization. Rule number two is to select research problems with great care and judgment. One Du Pont research division requires a unanimous vote of an eight-man committee before a project is authorized. The third rule is to recognize that a particular program may run five or six years if probabilities are to have any validity. The fourth rule is to know when to quit, which is the toughest decision of all. The research man may insist the answer is right around the corner. But management must frequently take uncertainty by the hand and call a stop.

[7] *Facts about The Maytag Company* (company publication, unnumbered pages).
[8] *The Story of Research* (E. I. Du Pont de Nemours & Company, 1951), p. 23.

How much time should executives in companies without specialized research activities devote to the problem? The only really safe answer to this question is that they should not ignore it. Some time should be set aside from normal operating activities for the development of ideas and plans for product improvement. Executives should study the pertinent trade and technical literature, attend some of the conventions and educational meetings of their line of business, and generally keep up with current trends. The importance of product innovation should be emphasized throughout the executive hierarchy. The ideas of operating personnel should be solicited through some kind of suggestion system.

Customer acceptance and capital obsolescence may place important practical limitations on the rate of innovation. Too much change in design or styling sometimes results in customer resistance. Many people seem to want the 1990 model in 1990 but not in 1969. Customer habits may change significantly over a period of time. The millions of people who bought black Model T Fords cussed about a great many things, but they did not seem to give a damn about styling. Today, an automobile producer has to make some changes every year if he wants to keep his customers, but, again, not too much change. The cost of capital obsolescence and replacement is a deterrent to innovation. Companies cannot afford a complete replacement of tooling and other equipment every time the model year rolls around. This factor tends to limit the extent to which companies use product innovation as a competitive instrument.

Resource Procurement Strategies

The influence of resource markets on business planning was considered in the previous chapter on environmental factors. To a great extent the problem is that of successful adaptation to external market conditions. An example would be planned adaptation to an anticipated rise or fall in the price of merchandise by changes in the level of inventories. But companies also use their economic and institutional power to influence resource markets. Thus, they may attempt to lower the price for a given item by forcing active competition between two or more sellers. This section suggests the kind of strategies that may be used to gain advantages in buying such productive resources as labor, raw materials, and supplies.

Labor Costs, Wage Rates, and Collective Bargaining

The price of labor is an important element in the successful solution of the cost-revenue problem. The problem is to achieve a sufficient spread between the amount that a company must pay in wages and the revenues it receives for its products. One aspect of this problem is the relationship between wage rates and prices. An upward spiral in wage rates without a corresponding increase in prices may have serious consequences for a company. A failure of wages to adjust downward during a period of falling prices presents a similar problem. This discussion is concerned with the manner in which such relationships affect a particular company rather than the broader economic implications that they may have.

The extent to which a company can control the economic and institutional forces that determine wages is definitely limited. The only alternative in some instances is to attempt to overcome the problem of higher wage rates by greater operating efficiency. However, companies should give constant attention to the means that may be employed to gain a more favorable margin between product prices and wages. Effective bargaining with union is a primary consideration in this respect for a majority of companies in the basic industries. Although market forces place limitations upon the discretion of both unions and management, there is generally a bargaining range within which either party may gain some advantage.

The appropriate management strategy in bargaining with a union cannot be defined by a definite set of rules applicable to every situation. Each bargaining situation involves a complex interrelationship of many factors, such as the personalities of executives and union leaders, the history of bargaining in the company, attitudes of the workers, and economic and institutional considerations. A strategy that works well in one case may produce opposite results in another. However, the following ideas may be helpful in developing a more positive and systematic approach to the problem. Contract negotiation generally begins with union proposals for changes in the existing agreement, although some companies make the first move by offering proposals to the union. Management will normally offer a number of counterproposals at a later date. The first thing that management should recognize is that the union usually demands more than it expects to gain. The management side of the table should be careful not to give the union reason to believe that it can exceed its original expectations. This problem should be kept in mind in framing counterproposals and in statements made during negotiation.

Management should plan its bargaining strategy in advance. It should attempt to anticipate the actual expectations of the union and think through the economic and noneconomic consequences of accepting them. Particular attention should be given to the long-run implications of a union demand. How will it affect the company's competitive position? What kind of difficulties may result with a change in general economic conditions? How may the acceptance of a particular demand influence future negotiations with the union? The implications of these and other questions should be carefully thought out by the management side. Where should management draw the line? When should it be willing to force a strike to temper union demands? The military maxim "it depends upon the situation" expresses the danger of giving a definite answer to these questions. On the one hand, management should not always satisfy the union's expectations. But it may also have to accept something it does not want to prevent even greater losses. The various parts of the problem should be viewed from the perspective of a total strategy. There is a time to fight and a time to refrain from fighting. A strike simply continues the bargaining in a somewhat different form. The implications of a strike should be given careful consideration. How much can be gained and how much may be lost? Strikes, like wars, should be planned ahead of time. Preparations should be made to increase the ability of the company to withstand the economic pressure that is involved. For example, companies sometimes build up the inventories of dealers to mitigate the impact of a strike.[9] Considerable thought should also be given to the strategy and tactics that may become appropriate during the course of a strike.

Management should remember that there are two sides in collective bargaining. As C. Wilson Randle has emphasized, management strategy should involve more than "an exercise in graceful retreat, a retreating without seeming to retreat. . . . Bargaining is and should remain a two-way street. Anyone who believes that only the union exercises initiative in collective bargaining is out of date in his approach to negotiation."[10] Companies should develop a positive program both in negotiating with the union and in the area of labor relations generally. The policies developed by L. R. Boulware at the General Electric Company provide one approach to the problem. "Boulwarism," as it has been called, makes a definite distinction between the union and company employees. It involves an aggressive promotion of the company's wage and labor relations program by advertising and other communication techniques. Emphasis is given to the fairness of the company program both during negotiations with the union and at other times. The idea is to strike a wedge between the union and employees and to enhance the prerogatives of management in the area of labor relations. Some management people believe that the Boulware plan goes too far toward the other side of the polarity and that it results in an undesirable amount of conflict. Although more subtle tech-

---

[9] However, such a move may also strengthen the union position because workers frequently receive overtime pay during the inventory build-up.

[10] C. Wilson Randle, "Bargaining on Big Labor's Big Demand: The Outlook for the Guaranteed Annual Wage," *Industry at the Bargaining Table,* Personnel Series, No. 156 (New York: American Management Association, 1954), pp. 18–19.

niques may often give better results, the fact remains that management can frequently gain by forcing the union to respond to its demands.[11]

Recruitment and Training

Companies spend a great deal of time and money selling themselves as employers. The personnel placement office of one large university reports that more than 500 companies were engaged in active recruiting over a period of a year. Many companies send a large volume of literature describing the company and the job and training opportunities that they can offer college graduates. The problem that the executive faces in this respect is expressed by Clarence B. Randall, former chairman of the board of Inland Steel.

In recruiting a senior he may be choosing the future president of his company. Having determined what sort of recruits he wishes, he then finds that he must go out and persuade them that his employment is desirable. No longer can he wait for young people to ring his doorbell. If he does, he will have only those candidates who have been rejected by those more skilled than he in the art of recruitment. It is a rude shock to him when he finds that young people turn down his offers, and this compels him to reappraise his whole plan and ask himself why intelligent candidates go elsewhere.[12]

Thus, the recruitment of personnel is an important aspect of the competitive game. This situation can be partly credited to the high level of economic activity during the postwar period, but there is every indication that the problem may have more fundamental roots. Such developments as automation have increased the importance of brainpower in the total picture. Industry will require relatively less brawn and more brains during the next few decades. Universities and colleges will probably not be able to meet the demand without a basic change in public attitude and appropriation. Many corporations have comprehensive training and educational facilities to help solve the problem. They have also been active in formulating cooperative research and study programs with educational institutions. All this gives emphatic testimony to the idea that material things and money are of little avail without human knowledge and skill. Companies must attract and develop bright young men to survive in a world of nuclear energy, intercontinental missiles, and electronic computers.

[11] An excellent evaluation of Boulwarism is found in: Herbert R. Northrup, "The Case for Boulwarism," *Harvard Business Review,* Vol. 41, No. 5, September–October 1963, pp. 86–97.
[12] Clarence B. Randall, *A Businessman Looks at the Liberal Arts* (White Plains, New York: The Fund for Adult Education, 1957), p. 8.

Material Procurement Problems

Companies can sometimes reduce costs by getting a better bargain in the markets for material resources. Such factors as price, quality, delivery schedules, the dependability of the vendor, and community relations should be taken into consideration. Companies frequently attempt to maintain more than one source of supply for some of the items they buy, a policy that mitigates the impact of such events as a fire or a strike in the vendor's establishment upon company operations. A company would find itself in difficult straits if the flow of some critical part or material were suddenly stopped. Buying from more than one supplier may also increase the company's bargaining power with respect to price and other matters. Good procurement strategy involves an interrelationship of many factors. The advantages reaped in one respect may result in disadvantages with regard to other matters. A company may expect to gain a price advantage by reducing its inventories, but this action reduces the extent to which the company is protected against a shortage of supplies during the operating period. Management must balance such advantages and disadvantages in arriving at an optimum procurement strategy.

Vertical integration or the extension of control over various stages in the distribution and production process is another possible strategy. For example, the Ford Motor Company during its early history favored a high degree of integration and extended ownership over timberland, lumber mills, steel-producing facilities, iron and coal mines, ocean freighters, and a railroad.[13] It produced its own glass, paper, tires, roller bearings, artificial leather, copper wire, cotton and woolen textiles, and other items. Ford policy in this respect began to change in the late 1920's as the result of difficulties in putting the Model A into production. Further changes occurred as the result of the reorganization initiated by the administration of Henry Ford II during the late 1940's. An argument for vertical integration is that it may give a company a more dependable supply of raw materials. Companies sometimes produce a portion of their total requirements of certain items to provide a cushion against interruptions in the flow of supplies from outside vendors. Such a policy can also be used to keep suppliers in line with respect to cost and quality. A threat to increase the extent of vertical integration may be a factor in bargaining with suppliers. A disadvantage of integration is that a company can easily become too unwieldy and complex. Also, it may be less profitable to produce a partic-

[13] An account of the Ford experience is found in F. E. Folts, *Introduction to Industrial Management,* 2nd ed. (New York: McGraw-Hill Book Company, Inc., 1938), pp. 181–189.

ular part used in production than to produce another consumer item. The arguments brought up under the heading of product line are pertinent here. Furthermore, an outside supplier can frequently manufacture an item at a lower cost because it can generally increase its volume by sales to other customers.

The possibility of substitution may offer important cost reduction opportunities. Many companies attempt to increase revenues by developing new consumer and industrial uses for their products. The aluminum industry is constantly adding to the more than 4000 uses of aluminum.[14] Aluminum is now being used in the production of wall and window panels, roofing, radar mast, ships and boats, railroad cars, automobiles, industrial equipment, farm machinery, paint, ladders, and a diversity of other things. The efforts of industries to expand markets can increase the substitution possibilities of companies using their products and materials in production. Companies may save considerable money by substituting aluminum for steel or copper, synthetic fibers for natural ones, and steel for lumber or aluminum. It should also be emphasized that companies may substitute machines for labor resources. Thus, a high price for labor could induce companies to increase the amount of automation in factory and office.

Inventory Policies

Inventories are a necessary feature of business operations, but they may represent unnecessary expense. How much inventory should a company maintain? The answer depends upon the nature of company operations and economic conditions. A company must maintain enough inventory to prevent disruptions in production and distribution. Interruptions in the flow of materials from suppliers can create havoc with the production program, and a failure to stock sufficient merchandise can cause customer dissatisfaction. There would seem to be some kind of an optimum level of inventories from a purely operating point of view. However, economic factors may cause a company to increase its inventories beyond this level or reduce them to an absolute minimum. An expected increase in prices may justify a higher than normal level of inventories. On the other hand, a company may reduce its inventories during a period of declining prices even though it may interfere with efficient operations. Further considerations in determining the appropriate level of inventories are the savings that may result from volume purchases, interest and storage costs, obsolescence and deterioration, and shortages in supply.

[14] *Expanding Markets for Aluminum* (New York: The Aluminum Association, 1955), p. 3.

The Problem of Location

Market proximity, nearness to raw materials, transportation facilities, adequacy of power resources, availability of labor, and community services are some of the factors that determine the proper location of distribution and production facilities. The relative advantages and disadvantages of these factors must be carefully evaluated in making a locational decision. It is generally difficult and costly to make a change after the installation has been constructed or purchased. A bad location can have a far-reaching effect upon a company's profit potential. The problem should be viewed from a dynamic rather than static perspective; the right location today is not necessarily the right location ten years from now. Technological innovation, population shifts, urbanization, and institutional and political changes can significantly influence the appropriateness of a particular location. Furthermore, management should not ignore the intangible assets that a company may possess in a particular location. A company may refrain from moving out of an area because it has developed an excellent reputation with the labor force, local suppliers, and the community. On the other hand, companies that have developed liabilities in this respect can sometimes gain by starting elsewhere with a clean slate.

Efficiency Strategies

The last two sections have emphasized the importance of product market and resource procurement strategies in solving the revenue-cost problem. Another alternative is to increase revenues or reduce costs by improvements in operating efficiency. The problem is that of technique, or how a given output of goods and services can be produced with a lower input of resources. A larger output from a given input is another way of saying the same thing. Productivity strategies are subject to the same economic logic as market and resource procurement strategies. The most efficient methods from a technological standpoint cannot always be justified from an economic perspective. When they involve expenditures for physical facilities, estimated costs must be compared with expected returns over the life of the asset. Another consideration is the cost already sunk into existing buildings and equipment; a company cannot generally afford to build a more modern plant if the existing plant is only a few years old. The possibility of eliminating activities that have doubtful revenue-producing properties can also reduce costs. Companies may overburden themselves with such activities when the horn of plenty is tipped their way and experience serious economic difficulties when a recession darkens the horizon.

The following sections are principally concerned with the technological aspect of productivity innovation. The work of Frederick W. Taylor at the Bethlehem Steel Company provides a good example of this aspect of the management problem. Taylor achieved a much higher output with a lower input of resources in both the shoveling and pig iron handling experiments. The introduction of automation, a complete overhaul of the material handling system, and setting up a new incentive plan exemplify some of the more drastic changes of this type. A great deal of progress may also result from a sequence of relatively small changes, such as a slight improvement in the procedure for making an employee transfer.

Factory and Office Building Design

A company with run-down and obsolete factories and office buildings operates under a serious competitive disadvantage. Such a situation may evolve from financial difficulties resulting from shifts in product demand or an economic depression. But it may also express a failure to appreciate the significance of efficient facilities or to properly plan their replacement. Expenditures for plant facilities (improvement or replacement) cannot be considered apart from alternative expenditure programs. Thus, under certain conditions, it might be more profitable to build up large cash balances or increase advertising expenditures. Companies do not have unlimited resources and, hence, cannot avoid the problem of discrimination among what sometimes seem to be equally profitable alternatives. Plant replacement and improvement should have a high priority in management's thinking. The long-term welfare of the organization should not be taxed in the interest of short-term gains. An adequate plant today may be highly inadequate in future competitive markets. The money available today may not be available at some future date. At any rate, it ought not to be frittered away on causes that have doubtful merit.

Improved plant and office facilities can reduce costs in a number of ways. There may be direct savings as the result of reduced maintenance costs, lower fire insurance rates, and more economical heating and cooling. Building design may lower costs by making possible a more efficient layout of equipment and furniture, and improvements in material handling. Also important are the contributions that improvements in design may make to better employee relations. The factories and offices of today are a far cry from the drab and sometimes dirty places that once dominated the industrial scene. Attractive colors and functional design, locker and shower rooms, cafeteria facilities, and landscaped grounds give the modern factory some of the attributes of a country club. Modern offices and furnishings also reflect the theme of pleasant surroundings and personal comfort. Office buildings often display more luxury than the mansions of our most opulent citizenry. The extent to which these improvements contribute to greater operating efficiency is difficult to determine. Some changes in the physical conditions of work are clearly related to the goal of higher productivity. Others can only be rationalized in terms of such illusive concepts as "better human relations," "better morale," and "public relations." The point is not that beauty and comfort should be eliminated from the business and industrial scene but rather that executives should give careful consideration to other possibly more productive alternatives. Thus, higher salaries and wages might give better results than carpeting in the offices or marble-lined factory rest rooms.

Equipment and Other Facilities

Trade publications are replete with advertising copy emphasizing the cost reduction potential of factory and office equipment and machines. For example, XYZ fasteners saved one company $95,000 during the first year. Time and labor cost cut 85 per cent by the use of ZIBERONES. Let the LIFTGIANT lower your material handling costs. Office efficiency can be increased 50 per cent by the use of EASYTYPE electric typewriters. Executives should not go on a shopping spree every time they read an advertisement, but they should make every effort to keep up with productivity innovations in their line of business. Although the problem of sunk costs places a barrier in the road to optimum technological efficiency, innovations may increase productivity enough to justify scrapping existing equipment. Some machines and equipment are additions to industry's arsenal of productive facilities rather than improved versions of existing equipment. Equipment innovation may involve comprehensive changes in a company's mode of operations over a relatively short period of time. Automation in factory and office provides a good example of innovation in its more revolutionary form.

But such major innovations as automation should not entirely eclipse relatively less dramatic, but important, contributions to productivity. A new electric typewriter for a secretary, an improved storage rack in the supply room, more efficient ventilating equipment in the foundry, a better material handling device, and an easier-to-handle tote box are examples of small changes that add up to a great deal.

Scientific Procedures and Methods

The development of improved operating procedures and methods is an important element in cost reduction. As used in this section, the word *procedure* has reference to the manner in which individual factory or office activities are linked together into a process or sequence within a department or among departments. *Method* is concerned with the way in which particular activities are performed.

The first step in devising better procedures and methods is an appraisal of the way in which work is now being done. Such a study can be facilitated by the use of systematic devices developed by industrial engineers and others. One such device is the process chart which can be used to record the sequence of actions that make up a procedure or process. A process chart shows graphically what happens to a person, part, material, or printed form as it proceeds from one selected point in the process to another. It can be used to indicate man and machine operations, transportation, inspection, delay, storage, or combinations of these categories. The time necessary to perform an operation, the distance something is moved, the department in which the work is done, and other information can also be recorded. A procedure or process is sometimes plotted on a scaled floor plan of the office or factory which may be helpful in making an improved layout of machines, work benches, desks, and files.

The analysis of a procedure begins with a series of questions. What is the purpose of an operation? Why does it need to be done? Can it be eliminated in whole or in part? Who does the work? Can someone else do it better? Is the work duplicated elsewhere in the department or in some other department? Can the operation be assigned to someone with less skill? Can the activity be delegated to a lower level in the management hierarchy? Will a change in the location at which something is done reduce the amount of transportation? Can the procedure be improved by changing the time sequence of operations? Should two or more operations be combined into one? These and other questions may lead to significant savings in space, time, and effort.

Procedure analysis is concerned with improvements that can be made in an overall factory or office process. The elimination of unnecessary operations and inspections, reductions in travel distance, improved factory and office layout, and reduced material or paper handling are some of the results that may be obtained from this kind of analysis. An intensive analysis of particular activities or operations in a procedure may also bring about cost-saving improvements. Although procedure analysis generally precedes operation analysis, a detailed study of operations frequently brings to light improvements in procedure. Thus, procedure and operation analysis should be viewed as mutually dependent rather than independent activities.

Operation analysis is concerned with the activities assigned to an individual factory or office worker. The point at which one operation begins and another ends in a procedure may vary from one plant or office to another and at different times. Operations may involve only human activity or a combination of human and machine activities. The analysis begins with a study of the present method for doing the work. An operation chart may be used to detail elemental right- and left-hand motions and the layout of fixtures, equipment, tools, and materials. Such a chart can be analyzed to determine a better set of motions to achieve a particular purpose. A more precise and complex technique for operation analysis is micromotion study, which involves the use of a motion picture camera. A frame-by-frame projection of the film permits a study of motion details that cannot be differentiated by simple observation. The speed of the camera or a special timing device indicates the time used to perform various types of motion.

Procedure and methods analysis frequently results in large increases in productivity at relatively little cost. A ten-dollar fixture may save as much as $2000 a year. It can cost as much or more to develop an inefficient procedure or method than an efficient one. Many improvements are made by people who are not specialists in methods and procedure analysis and without specialized devices and techniques. Factory and office supervisors and employees should not be neglected in the quest for work simplification. Many companies report that their employees come up with more good suggestions than do the specialists.[15] The problem is generally not a lack of ideas but of motivating people to contribute their ideas. A further problem is that workers sometimes refuse to give their full cooperation and resort to tactics that reduce the gains that can be made from work simplification.[16] Yet, improved procedures and methods undoubtedly result in some increased office and factory productivity even when serious cooperation difficulties are present.

Standardization and Simplification

A standard may be defined as a unit of measurement or a system of classification that is commonly accepted. Standardization is the application of standards in a group, organization, or society. It implies that scientific methods will be used to develop the best possible standards for particular purposes. It tends to promote simplification through the elimination of unnecessary "standards" and the utilization of uniform standards through-

[15] Herbert O. Brayer, "Experience of 300 Companies with Work Simplification," *American Business,* July 1955, p. 17.
[16] An analysis of this problem is found in: William F. Whyte, *Money and Motivation* (New York: Harper & Brothers Publishers, 1955).

out a company or industry. However, simplification may be pursued for its own sake together with or apart from a standardization program.

The form of a given standard depends upon the nature of the objects or activities to be standardized. Professor Jack Rogers has categorized standards in this way.

1. Physical models or prototypes to which reproductions may be compared to decide whether they are practical counterparts in terms of size, shape, color, finish, or other physical properties.

2. Written descriptions (including mathematical and symbolical description, drawings, and formulae) of the essential characteristics of an object to be obtained by manufacture or other means, or an action to be performed. (The use of written description ordinarily implies agreement on the meaning of terms and therefore necessity for definitions of nomenclature such as words used in a technical or restricted sense, symbols, and abbreviations. The inconstancy of oral standards is apparent. Verification of characteristics may be through performance of a particular set of operations, e.g., a test performed on an object.)

3. Devices for making specified comparisons. (Standards may be embodied in measurement or control apparatus designed in accordance with predetermined standards. A simple go, no-go gauge is an example: the gauge dimensions are derived from a more basic standard incorporating a decision on limits of variance allowed for the measured piece.)

4. Any combination of implements and instructions to be used in decision. (Industrial standards often are not pure in form, but rather are mixtures of the three foregoing means of conveying what is wanted and how it is to be done.) [17]

Standardization and simplification may significantly increase operating efficiency and reduce costs. Product line simplification by the development of standard models and designs and the use of standard interchangeable parts reduces the number of separate components and increases the size of production runs. Quantity production makes possible a higher degree of labor specialization and the utilization of relatively less skilled and costly labor. Much greater use can be made of specialized machines, equipment, and tools because the cost can be spread over more units of output. The turnover of raw materials and parts inventories is increased, volume purchases lead to lower unit costs, and savings may arise from lower supervisory, clerical, and selling costs.

Other benefits can be derived from the development of technical standards. Such standards promote uniformity in quality throughout a company. They tend to increase quality by imposing minimum requirements and to reduce costs by inhibiting the use of higher than necessary quality

[17] Jack Rogers, *Industrial Standardization,* Studies in Business Policy, No. 85 (New York: National Industrial Conference Board, 1957), p. 7. This source contains an account of standardization in a variety of business concerns.

standards. Closer tolerances may be good from a purely technical point of view, but they cannot always be justified from an economic perspective. The problem is to find an appropriate balance between the gains from higher quality and the increases in cost that may be involved. Uniform standards facilitate coordination by reducing conflicts among different functional interests on quality and other matters. For example, manufacturing and sales executives sometimes disagree with product designers and engineers on tolerances that should be maintained. Better coordination may result from the uniformity of information made available to different departments, such as engineering, manufacturing, purchasing, and sales. Each department is given a frame of reference for the performance of the responsibilities assigned to it.

There are dangers in carrying standardization and simplification to an extreme. The advantages of quantity production and lower costs may be negated by unfavorable consumer response. Consumers want quality products at low prices, but they also want some degree of diversification. Companies that offer too little diversification may find themselves losing the competitive game. However, standardization and simplification are not always the antithesis of diversification. A considerable variety of products can result from different combinations of standard interchangeable parts. As Professor Rogers has noted:

> The family relationship between a Chevrolet and a Cadillac or a Ford and Lincoln, which exists because some of their parts are the same, does not impair their individuality. Moreover, hundreds of combinations of standardized features such as body style, color, trim, and optional equipment can and do appear in each line. Providing uniformity where it is desirable is one thing; providing uniformity for its own sake is another.[18]

A dynamic environment imposes limitations upon standardization. Technological innovation can play havoc with attempts to standardize products, parts, materials, and processes. A company may find itself with an obsolete product if it refuses to change its standards. At the same time, changes in design and specification impede the development of an efficient system of production. The exact point at which one or the other consideration should take precedence is sometimes difficult to determine. Many industries have alleviated the problem by the "custom" of annual model changes.

Plant Capacity and Utilization

Average per unit cost of output can be greatly affected by the degree to which a company utilizes its fixed resources. This problem is partly a

[18] Rogers, op. cit., p. 5.

368 DECISION MAKING: PLANNING STRATEGIES

technological problem, that is, certain combinations of plant, equipment, labor, and other resources produce relatively more physical output per unit of input than others. Another consideration is that per unit fixed cost is lower with a higher output. A major difficulty is that companies cannot perfectly predict the future market for their products or services. As a result, they frequently overestimate or underestimate their fixed resource requirements. Short-term economic fluctuations also prevent perfect adjustment even though longer run market expectations are about right. Thus, short-run demand situations in steel have forced the industry to operate at 60 or 70 per cent of theoretical capacity during periods when longer range expectations dictated further expansion. Another problem is that some kinds of resources are not indivisible, that is, a company cannot vary the amount of fixed resources with different levels of output. For example, a railroad must build essentially the same trackage for one, ten, or fifty trains per day.

What can a company do to achieve a better relationship between demand and fixed resource capacity? The problem of excess capacity can be partly solved by more accurate market forecasting. Although long-range forecasts may be highly unreliable, some companies might gain by taking greater advantage of systematic forecasting techniques. Business executives sometimes become overoptimistic in planning plant expansion, particularly during a relatively long period of economic prosperity. However, their critics should remember that hindsight does not always reflect prior wisdom. Production to inventory and product diversification are sometimes helpful in solving excess capacity difficulties. However, the accumulation of inventories to prevent excessive variations in the volume of production may involve a great deal of cost and risk. This alternative is generally feasible only if demand can be estimated with a high degree of accuracy and then only for very short periods of time. Additions to the product line are possible only if fixed resources are not highly specialized. An automobile manufacturing company can readily shift to the production of army tank motors or aircraft parts during periods of reduced automobile demand. But the alternatives available to a steel-producing plant are practically nil. Companies with indivisible resources and large fixed costs have a particularly difficult problem. The solution is to increase the volume of output by strategies that increase demand. But, as is indicated by the experience of the railroads, there are many practical complexities. Thus, the railroads might be able to increase revenues if higher rates were approved by the Interstate Commerce Commission, but the result might shift more business to their competitors. Additional business might be gained by a modernization program, but such a program costs money which is what many railroads lack. The public welfare and other considerations force them to maintain services that cannot be justified from a purely economic standpoint. They are faced with stockholders who are anxious for dividend checks and railroad brotherhoods who want high wages and rules that keep costs high.

The Problem of Technological Unemployment

The long-run consequence of productivity innovation has been a higher scale of living for the population generally. But the fact that such innovations displace workers may create serious short-run employment problems. The adverse employment effect of productivity innovation is mitigated during a period of economic prosperity and expansion. But it cannot be assumed that prosperity is a perpetual phenomenon for a company, an industry, or the economy generally. The hue and cry of "technological unemployment" may again be heard from many quarters. One might argue that the real problem is a scarcity of employment opportunities caused by factors other than productivity innovation. Nonetheless, a worker who finds himself displaced by a machine or an improved method during a period of job scarcity has a problem whatever the ultimate cause. The extent to which a company can directly alleviate the situation is limited by the scarcity implications of the cost-revenue equation. A business organization cannot be managed with the philosophy of a philanthropic institution. However, companies can sometimes mitigate the problem by slowing down the rate of innovation. Innovation may be paced by the rate of normal labor turnover and, in some cases, by retirement rates. There may be a possibility of shifting some of the burden to other interest groups, such as stockholders and customers. Thus, workers can be given severance pay to help overcome some of the financial difficulties involved in displacement. The question of how the burdens and benefits involved in productivity innovation should be shared among the various interest groups does not have an easy answer. Management should generally view the problem from the perspective of the system as a whole. In other words, what kind of solution will best serve the welfare of the organization? The solution to the problem of technological unemployment rests partly with the general society. Executives should take an active part in the social debate; they should not hide their heads in the sand or refuse to face the reality of the problem. If executives refuse to raise their voices, union leaders, politicians, and crackpots will dominate the scene.

The Problem of Motivation

The motivation problem is an important element in achieving productivity. One aspect of this problem is the distribution of monetary rewards (wages, rent, interest, and profit) to resource contributors, such as workers, stockholders, and executives. But equally important is the creation and distribution of nonmonetary incentives, such as social satisfaction and status. These and related problems will be considered in Part VI of this book.

SELECTED REFERENCES

Walter Adams (editor), *The Structure of American Industry: Some Case Studies*, 3rd. ed. New York: The Macmillan Company, 1961.

Lee Adler, "Systems Approach to Marketing," *Harvard Business Review,* Vol. 45, No. 3, pp. 105–118 (May–June 1967).

Dean S. Ammer, *Materials Management,* rev. ed. Homewood, Ill.: Richard D. Irwin, Inc., 1968.

H. Igar Ansoff, *Corporate Strategy.* New York: McGraw-Hill Book Company, 1965.

Clifford M. Baumback, *Systematic Work Simplification,* Industrial Management Series, No. 2. Bureau of Business Research, College of Business Administration, University of Oklahoma, 1960.

Edwin F. Beal and Edward D. Wickersham, *The Practice of Collective Bargaining,* 3rd. ed. Homewood, Ill.: Richard D. Irwin, Inc., 1967.

Harold Bierman and Seymour Smidt, *The Capital Budgeting Decision,* 2nd. ed. New York: The Macmillan Company, 1966.

A. B. Blankenship and J. B. Doyle, *Marketing Research Management.* New York: American Management Association, Inc., 1965.

Francis J. Bridges and Kenneth W. Olm, *Business Policy,* Boston: Allyn and Bacon, Inc., 1966.

A. Lynn Bryant and Peter P. Schoderbek, "Line of Balance Revisited," *University of Washington Business Review,* Vol. 27, No. 2, pp. 28–37 (Winter 1968).

Robert B. Buchele, *Business Policy in Growing Firms.* San Francisco: Chandler Publishing Company, 1967.

J. Thomas Cannon, *Business Strategy and Policy.* New York: Harcourt, Brace & World, Inc., 1968.

Neil W. Chamberlain, *The Firm: Micro-Economic Planning and Action.* New York: McGraw-Hill Book Company, Inc., 1962.

John M. Champion and Francis J. Bridges, *Critical Incidents in Management.* Homewood, Ill.: Richard D. Irwin, Inc., 1963.

Robert H. Cole, *Consumer and Commercial Credit Management,* 3rd. ed. Homewood, Ill.: Richard D. Irwin, Inc., 1968.

James A. Constantin, *Principles of Logistics Management.* New York: Appleton-Century-Crofts, 1966.

Harold W. Davey, *Contemporary Collective Bargaining,* 2nd. ed. Englewood Cliffs, N.J.: Prentice-Hall, Inc., 1959.

Harold W. Davey, Howard S. Kaltenborn, and Stanley H. Ruttenberg (editors), *New Dimensions in Collective Bargaining.* New York: Harper & Brothers, 1959.

R. E. Gibson, "The Strategy of Corporate Research and Development," *California Management Review,* Vol. 9, No. 1, pp. 33–42 (Fall 1966).

Ronald R. Gist, *Management Perspectives in Retailing.* New York: John Wiley & Sons, Inc., 1967.

Ronald R. Gist, *Retailing: Concepts and Decisions.* New York: John Wiley & Sons, Inc., 1968.

Clyde T. Hardwick and Bernard F. Landuyt, *Administrative Strategy and Decision Making,* 2nd. ed., Chap. 9. Cincinnati, Ohio: South-Western Publishing Co., 1966.

Donald V. Harper, *Price Policy and Procedure.* New York: Harcourt, Brace & World, Inc., 1966.

Keith D. Harris, *Automated Production Line Balancing at the Basic Motion Level.* Rock Island, Ill.: U.S. Army Management Engineering Training Agency, 1968.

Roger H. Hawk, *The Recruitment Function.* New York: American Management Association, 1967.

John R. Hinrichs, *High Talent Personnel.* New York: American Management Association, 1966.

John G. Hutchinson, *Management Under Strike Conditions.* New York: Holt, Rinehart and Winston, Inc., 1966.

Thomas W. Jackson and Jack M. Spurlock, *Research and Development Management.* Homewood, Ill.: Dow Jones-Irwin, Inc., 1966.

Robert A. Lynn, *Price Policies and Marketing Management.* Homewood, Ill.: Richard D. Irwin, Inc., 1967.

Raymond R. Mayer, *Financial Analysis of Investment Alternatives.* Boston: Allyn and Bacon, Inc., 1966.

Ernest C. Miller, *Marketing Planning,* AMA Research Study, No. 81. New York: American Management Association, 1967.

Erwin E. Nemmers, *Managerial Economics.* New York: John Wiley & Sons, Inc., 1962.

William H. Newman, "Shaping the Master Strategy of Your Firm," *California Management Review,* Vol. 9, No. 3, pp. 77–88 (Spring 1967).

Herbert R. Northrup, *Boulwarism.* Ann Arbor, Mich.: Bureau of Industrial Relations, Graduate School of Business Administration, University of Michigan, 1964.

Cyril O'Donnell, *The Strategy of Corporate Research.* San Francisco: Chandler Publishing Company, 1967.

Alexander A. Robichek (editor), *Financial Research and Management Decisions.* New York: John Wiley & Sons, Inc., 1967.

Meyer S. Ryder, Charles M. Rehmus and Sanford Cohen, *Management Preparation for Collective Bargaining.* Homewood, Ill.: Dow Jones-Irwin, Inc., 1966.

J. H. Westing, I. V. Fine, and others, *Industrial Purchasing,* 2nd. ed. New York: John Wiley & Sons, Inc., 1961.

Max S. Wortman, Jr. (editor), *Creative Personnel Management: Readings in Industrial Relations.* Boston: Allyn and Bacon, Inc., 1967.

Max S. Wortman, Jr. and C. Wilson Randle, *Collective Bargaining,* 2nd ed. Boston: Houghton Mifflin Company, 1966.

chapter 16

DYNAMIC PLANNING I

This chapter considers the planning process from a number of perspectives. The manner in which lead time and the transformation period relate to the planning problem is discussed in the section that immediately follows. In the next section, the analysis turns to profits and other criteria that can be used to determine the appropriateness of plans. The importance of operations research and other techniques for effective planning is then considered. The final section is concerned with the manner in which subjective processes and techniques are involved in solving the planning problem.

The Time Horizons of Planning

How far should an organization plan into the future? A day, a week, a month, a year, a decade? The answer depends upon the nature of the environmental and organizational forces that are involved. A planning period of less than a day may be appropriate in some situations; a decade might not be sufficient for others. Closely related to these matters is the question of how much planning should occur. To what extent should preparations be made for a future eventuality?

To Plan or Not to Plan: The Problem of Lead Time

An important reason for planning ahead is that planning takes time. A long lead time is generally necessary to plan such major programs and projects as an expansion of manufacturing facilities, the development of a weapons system, and personnel development. A change in the scope or kind of objectives requires many specific changes, each of which is related in some respect to every other. Although lead time can be reduced by work division and cooperation, it cannot be completely eliminated. Another consideration is that some changes have to be completed before others can be begun. For example, tooling requirements cannot be determined until the product has been designed. Some of the delay that may be caused by this problem can be overcome by what has been called the *harmonious overlap*.[1] The idea was used to reduce the time required to develop the atomic bomb during World War II. Dr. Alexander Sachs, who estimated that the project would normally take twenty-five years, suggested that "when you start one part of the project, assume you have finished it successfully, and start the next as if you had."[2] In spite of the obvious risks, this approach may provide the time necessary to take advantage of some great opportunity or to avert adversity.

Planning enhances the ability of the organization to adapt to future eventualities. To paraphrase Professor Newman, the executive should not always sit back and wait for lightning to strike.[3] Planning is frequently essential even though the eventuality for which plans are prepared is not likely to occur. Much military planning could be eliminated if the time and locale of the next war were certain, but it would be foolhardy to stop military planning simply because the planner must operate under conditions of uncertainty. The prospect of defeat by a ruthless enemy is appalling enough to override even the arguments of the most avid economy-minded politician. A failure to plan may also have serious consequences for a business organization. One result may be a loss of important opportunities. For example, the time gained by forward planning may be sufficient to reap a large harvest of sales made possible by a sudden increase in demand. Planning may also be important in combating adversity. A planned contraction of operations is less costly and disruptive than makeshift contraction. Such emergencies as fires and floods have also emphasized the importance of planning.

If the future could be accurately predicted, executives could plan ahead without fear that their effort had gone for nought. Uncertainty always places limitations upon the practicability of forward planning. Furthermore, since the distant future is generally more uncertain than the immediate future, long-range planning may be extremely hazardous. The executive must constantly balance the benefits that may be derived from planning

---

[1] Ernest Dale, *Planning and Developing the Company* (New York: American Management Association, 1952), p. 33.

[2] Nat S. Finney, "How F. D. R. Planned to Use the A-Bomb," *Look Magazine*, March 14, 1950, p. 25.

[3] William H. Newman, *Administrative Action*, 2nd ed. (Englewood Cliffs, N.J.: Prentice-Hall, Inc., 1963), p. 66.

with the possibility that the time and effort so spent may have been in vain. There is little purpose in planning for the sake of planning. But planning for an eventuality that can be anticipated with reasonable accuracy may be highly desirable. However, the executive cannot always restrict the planning period because his crystal ball is hazy. He is frequently forced into long-range planning whether he likes it or not. The reason is that some decisions commit the organization for a long period of time. For example, the construction of a specialized plant involves an explicit or implicit projection of sales far into the future. Uncertainty makes such projections highly conjectural, to say the least. Yet such decisions cannot be avoided if the organization is to prosper and survive.

Some degree of stability is necessary in all organized endeavor. Effective coordination cannot be achieved without a common objective and a sense of direction. For this reason executives frequently undertake long-range planning in spite of the hazards that may be imposed by uncertainty. As one executive has said: "Accurate planning beyond one year is difficult at best, and long-range plans are very apt to be changed before completion. Nevertheless, they serve a definite purpose in setting up an orderly approach to the problems of long-range growth of the company." [4] Subjective considerations may also influence the executive in this respect. Long-range planning presents a challenge to organizational participants. It gives them a purpose beyond the ordinary and sometimes tedious tasks of today.

The Transformation Period

A dynamic environment in which uncertainty is the rule rather than the exception places a premium upon adaptability. But the ultimate consequence of planning is a reduced capacity to react to change. The reason is that it takes time to transform productive resources into products or services. This time period, which is often referred to as the *transformation period,* may vary a great deal with different resources. For example, it may take a period of twenty or more years to fully transform an industrial plant into products. On the other hand, raw materials and supplies can readily be transformed in less than a year. However, it is not the transformation period per se that creates the difficulty. A more fundamental consideration is the specialized nature of resources. Thus, if an industrial plant could be used as an office building, a bank, or a gymnasium, the problem would be essentially eliminated. But this kind of substitution is possible only to a limited degree. Hence, the transformation period must be viewed as a projection of a relatively stable objective into the future. The situation is

[4] "Industry Plans for the Future," *The Conference Board Business Record,* Vol. 9, No. 8, August 1952, p. 324.

further complicated by the fact that resources are a part of an integrated production process. They cannot be viewed as isolated units that are subject only to the transformation period pertinent to them. A single or a few resources may be sufficient to impede change in objectives. The existence of a specialized factory may force a firm to continue a certain line of endeavor for a longer period than would be warranted by the transformation period of other resources.

The problem may also be stated in terms of various time lags between cost commitments and receipts. It may take one, five, or twenty-five years of receipts or sales to compensate for costs that result from the contracts or purchases made in a single day. For example, inventories in the merchandising field are often purchased several months before the beginning of the next selling season. Such commitments are made with implicit or explicit assumptions about the quantity and kind of merchandise that customers will buy and the price that they will be willing to pay. The degree of restriction imposed upon future planning by past commitments varies over time. The planning process reduces the liquidity of the firm through commitments of actual and expected monetary resources by purchase or contract. Liquidity is regained through the translation of the specialized resources (buildings, plants, equipment, supplies, inventories) thus acquired into products or services. The firm loses and regains planning flexibility throughout the planning cycle. In other words, the extent to which objectives can be changed varies over time. During early stages of the planning period such changes may be practically impossible. But, as the flow of revenues reduces the indebtedness that may have been incurred or builds up depreciation reserves and retained profits, the adaptability of the firm is increased.

The Importance of Forecasting

The problems of lead time and transformation emphasize the importance of forecasting. Henri Fayol has said that "if foresight is not the whole of management at least it is an essential part of it." [5] Planning for eventualities that do not occur is obviously inefficient. Yet a failure to plan for future adversity or opportunity may have even more serious consequences. Although uncertainty can never be completely overcome, intelligent and systematic forecasting can eliminate some of the difficulty. Forecasting will never be an exact science, but it frequently affords better results than the pure hunch or guess.

---

[5] Henri Fayol, *General and Industrial Management* (London: Sir Isaac Pitman & Sons, Ltd., 1949), p. 43.

Industry Practices

According to a survey conducted by the National Conference Board, three to five years seems to be a common measure for long-range planning, although some companies think in terms of decades.[6] Many companies plan all activities for the same length of time. A target date is set and all planning is conducted with that date in mind. The planning period may vary with different kinds of activities, such as capital expenditures, research, and sales promotion.

Capital expenditures are more subject to long-range planning than any other planning area. Such plans frequently form the basis for all other planning. As one executive remarked: "We attempt to set our sights ahead as far as possible as to capital expenditures, and then each move that we make in other fields is in the direction of that plan."[7]

Working capital requirements, dividend policy, tax payments, marketing programs, research projects, raw material procurement, production allocation, and personnel development are frequently planned far in advance. One company plans its contributions to philanthropic organizations on a long-run basis.

The basic operating program is generally planned for a year. The plans for the first month or quarter are more definite and detailed than plans for the succeeding months or quarters. Appropriate changes are made in the over-all plan whenever necessary and possible. An unexpected increase in demand may lead to an upward revision of production and marketing schedules; a sudden shortage of raw materials would have an opposite effect.

Some companies contend that they do not plan at all. However, such a state of affairs evolves from semantics rather than reality. All executives and organizations engage in some kind of planning. To say otherwise is to repudiate the very essence of the executive function. Planning may be conducted in a haphazard way, or it may involve highly systematized procedures. Some of it may represent little more than reflective thinking by executives. The appropriate amount of planning cannot be determined without a careful appraisal of particular situations. Uncertainty sometimes makes any kind of long-range planning a marginal pursuit. Some companies undoubtedly plan too little, but still others plan too much.

---

[6] The Conference Board Business Record, *op. cit.*, pp. 324–328.
[7] *Ibid.*, p. 324.

Planning Criteria

The achievement of a favorable balance between revenues and costs is the criterion used in planning the program of a business organization. A sizable profit, particularly over a long period of time, is usually accepted as prima facie evidence that planning is in good hands. However, there is by no means a perfect correlation between profits and planning efficiency. The relationship between good or bad planning and profits or losses is more indirect than is sometimes assumed. The fact that uncertainty is always present means that the best possible plan may result in losses and a bad plan in profits. A further difficulty in measuring planning efficiency is that planning cannot be easily differentiated from other executive activities, such as communication and leadership. A mediocre plan that is well executed frequently provides better results than a good plan badly executed.

Assets and Liabilities from the Past

The mistakes of the past may have set the stage for ultimate disaster. Under such circumstances the most efficient planning may not significantly alter the final outcome. A large deficit for a current period does not mean that the planning that occurred during that period was inefficient. Japanese military planning during the last stage of World War II cannot be called inefficient only because it failed to avert defeat. The unsuccessful season experienced by the new football coach may have resulted from the failure of past coaches to recruit players properly. Students should not hang his likeness upon a tree until he has had the chance to make some mistakes of his own. The fate of executives and administrators is frequently not unlike that of the football coach. Executives sometimes refuse important positions because they recognize that they cannot possibly salvage the damage wrought in the past. Conversely, the success of the past may make possible a considerable amount of "living off the fat of the land." The assets built in the past are often sufficient to counterbalance the liabilities imposed by the inefficient planning of today. Even a nincompoop in executive attire can seem to have the properties of a genius for a short period of time.

The Profit Criterion

The foregoing discussion emphasizes the importance of evaluating each plan or adjustment in the organizational program on its own merit. As the economist would say, how much will it increase profits or reduce losses? Thus, a particular plan is efficient if it results in profits irrespective of whether overall operations produce profits or losses. However, it should not be assumed that business organizations always attempt to maximize profits. The profit criterion should be viewed as a rather elastic efficiency framework. The planner as a general rule does not deliberately plan negative profits, but neither does he necessarily plan to maximize profits either in the short or long run.

Expansion and Contraction

An implicit or explicit inventory of present resources places an initial limitation upon the scope of organizational activities. However, planning is concerned with the future potential of the organization. Business organizations, like religious, political, military, and educational organizations, are frequently inclined to practice a policy of expansion. Some companies are more aggressive than others in taking advantage of opportunities to expand. The following statement by a top executive of the General Electric Company represents one point of view on this matter.

It is the conviction of General Electric's management that the markets of the future will go increasingly to companies that plan ahead to meet customer wants by making daring investments in manpower, research, new facilities, and development of products and markets. Such investments are a risk—a major risk. But failure to make the investments would be an even greater risk.[8]

There is a time to expand and a time not to expand. The appropriate alternative is sometimes difficult to determine in a dynamic economy. Too much caution may mean the loss of important opportunities. For example, the Montgomery Ward Company experienced smaller postwar sales because its chief executive, who anticipated a severe recession, refused to launch an expansion program. On the other hand, the Sears, Roebuck and Company forged ahead to a dominant position by pursuing an expansionist policy. But it should not be assumed that a failure to expand always denotes inefficient planning. Too much fixed resource capacity can create difficulties during a long period of economic decline. A serious postwar recession would have made the Montgomery Ward policy an example of enlightened planning. What seems to be the best possible plan can become the worst possible plan by an unanticipated turn of economic events. However, companies should not necessarily make major changes in their long-range plans whenever recession darkens the horizon. There is frequently a tendency to overcompensate for short-run variations from a basic trend. The long view is difficult to maintain when the immediate situation seems to in-

[8] *Annual Report,* The General Electric Company, 1956.

dicate an opposite policy, but it may set the stage for expanded future sales and profits.

What are the ingredients of a successful expansion program? An organization's capacity to expand is obviously enhanced by expanding markets for its products and services. A generally favorable market situation may also enable a company to increase its scale of operations by entry into new markets.[9] But expansion involves more than the right kind of market conditions. It also requires a growing pool of human, material, and financial resources. The availability of such resources is partly dependent upon the economic efficiency of past operations. A large volume of profit makes possible the accumulation of liquid capital which can be used to finance expansion. It also increases the capacity of the firm to acquire additional financial resources in the money markets. Expansion involves procurement of additional material resources, such as plant, equipment, tooling, merchandise, raw materials, and supplies. The recruitment and training of managerial, technical, and operating personnel are other important problem areas. Companies may acquire some needed resources by buying existing companies with appropriate facilities. An increased scale of operations may also necessitate extensive changes in the organizational structure and in managerial and operating procedures.

The Impact of Executive Personality

A capacity for expansion or profits is not always translated into accomplishment. Some executives fiddle around with the insignificant while burning issues hang in the fire. They either fail to comprehend opportunities, or lack the opportunities or the courage and inclination to take action. It takes courage to cut through a web of inertial forces that impede change. It takes courage to plan into a future that is shrouded by the shadows of uncertainty. However, organizations have also been plagued by too much enthusiasm and resoluteness and too little intelligent planning. It is folly to deliberately plan the impossible.

Planning Techniques: Operations Research

Frederick W. Taylor first gave emphasis to the idea that scientific techniques should be substituted for intuitive and "rule of thumb" approaches

[9] For an excellent discussion of the problem of entry: Howard H. Hines, "Effectiveness of 'Entry' by Already Established Firms," *The Quarterly Journal of Economics*, Vol. 72, No. 1, February 1957, pp. 132–150.

to planning. More recent developments have given birth to "operations research," which, according to one of its proponents, "now brings to commerce and industry more powerful techniques of quantitative analysis and is an extension of Taylor's basic philosophy to possibilities probably beyond Taylor's vision, far-reaching as it was." [10]

Historical Background

The development of operations research as an integrated body of knowledge began during World War II.[11] The first comprehensive operations research studies were made in Great Britain and dealt with such military problems as the right depth at which to detonate anti-submarine charges, the proper size of merchant ship convoys, and the relationship between losses and the number of planes in a formation. Operations research emigrated to the United States in the early 1940's and was extensively used to solve tactical and strategic military problems. Successful applications by the military during and after the war gave impetus to the use of operations research techniques to study business problems. However, it should not be assumed that business had never before experienced anything like operations research. Many of the techniques used to study problems in such areas as marketing and production in the 1920's and 1930's were similar to those used by operations research. What was added by the developments that occurred during the war? One claim is that operations research approaches problems from a broader perspective than the earlier studies in scientific management. Another is that it brings into play "the sophisticated mathematical ability required for the solution of complex problems involving many variables." [12] Emphasis is also given to the advantages of using a "team" composed of people from different disciplines, such as mathematics, physics, psychology, and economics.[13]

The Nature and Importance of Models

The basic approach of operations research is to construct a model of the decisional problem under consideration. A model represents some aspects

[10] J. W. Pocock, "Management Consulting and Operations Research," in Joseph F. McCloskey and Florence N. Trefethen, *Operations Research for Management* (Baltimore: The Johns Hopkins Press, 1954), p. 82.
[11] Florence N. Trefethen, "A History of Operations Research," in McCloskey and Trefethen, *op. cit.,* pp. 3–35.
[12] *Ibid.,* p. 30.
[13] C. West Churchman, Russell L. Ackoff, and E. Leonard Arnoff, *Introduction to Operations Research* (New York: John Wiley and Sons, Inc., 1957).

of an existing thing, event, structure, or process.[14] Models can be classified into three categories: iconic, analogue, and symbolic.[15] An iconic model is a scaled reproduction of the essential features of that which it represents. Toy automobiles, model airplanes, and globes are examples of this type of model. Analogue models portray various properties of something by a different set of properties. For example, solid and broken lines are often used on a map to indicate the kind of surfacing that can be found on the roads. Contour lines are used to show the nature of the terrain found in the area encompassed by the map. The lines and other symbols of an analogue model take the place of the scaled reproductions of an iconic model. Models can be used to determine the most efficient layout and the nature of material flow. They also facilitate the study of comprehensive and complex situations. As Karl W. Deutsch has pointed out:

> The only alternative to their use would be an attempt to "grasp directly" the structure or process to be understood; that is to say, to match it completely point for point. This is manifestly impossible. We use maps or anatomical atlases precisely because we cannot carry complete countries or complete human bodies in our heads.[16]

Symbolic or mathematical models can be used to predict consequences to the extent that the logic of mathematics corresponds in some degree to the dynamics of the "reality" it represents. Pure mathematics is a completely abstract system concerned with number, quantity, spatial relationships, and other types of logical conceptions. "The certainty of mathematics," to use the words of Alfred North Whitehead, "depends upon its complete abstract generality. But we can have no a priori certainty that we are right in believing that the observed entities in the concrete universe form a particular instance of what falls under our general reasoning." [17] The models of pure mathematics are not directly concerned with empirical problems, and the results do not necessarily reflect "reality." The models of applied mathematics are directly concerned with "reality" and are attempts to derive practical conclusions by the use of abstract mathematical reasoning. The basic process begins with abstractions from "reality" which are

[14] A comprehensive treatment of models and model building can be found in the following sources: Karl W. Deutsch, "On Communication Models in the Social Sciences," *The Public Opinion Quarterly,* Vol. 16, No. 3, Fall 1952, pp. 356–380; Churchman, Ackoff, and Arnoff, *op. cit.,* Chaps. 4 and 7; C. H. Coombs, H. Raiffa, and R. M. Thrall, "Some Views on Mathematical Models and Measurement Theory," in R. M. Thrall, C. H. Coombs, and R. L. Davis (editors), *Decision Processes* (New York: John Wiley and Sons, Inc., 1954), pp. 19–37.

[15] Churchman, Ackoff, and Arnoff, *op. cit.,* pp. 159–162.

[16] Deutsch, *op. cit.,* pp. 357–358.

[17] Alfred North Whitehead, *Science and the Modern World* (New York: The Macmillan Company, 1926), p. 33.

then subjected to mathematical analysis. The mathematically derived conclusions are then related to "reality," and an attempt is made to predict the behavior of the real thing or process.[18]

The Construction of Operations Research Models

The fundamental purpose of operations research models is to measure the relationship between alternative courses of action and objectives. An important step in model construction is to formulate the objectives sought by management. Objectives must generally be expressed in quantitative terms, such as to increase profits, reduce costs, increase output, decrease labor turnover, and reduce distance traveled. Qualitative objectives must be translated into quantitative terms whenever possible. For example, the objective "to increase sales without engendering government antitrust intervention" can be expressed in terms of a quantity or a range of quantities at which intervention might occur.

Another step in model construction is to determine the factors or variables that will influence the achievement of the objective or objectives. Such factors are generally divided into those that can and those that cannot be controlled by management. This aspect of model building is closely related to the problem of determining objectives. Operations research can be used to determine which of two or more alternative courses of action is better or best. But it cannot solve a problem that has no possible solution in terms of the "reality" with which organizations must contend and the problem-solving techniques that can be used. Asking questions that can be answered has always been a prime prerequisite for successful scientific endeavor.

The variables that relate to the achievement of the objective must be translated into quantitative form. For example, the objective "to increase profits" might involve some of the following variables: cost of labor, raw material prices, inventory levels, productivity, advertising costs, price elasticities, size of production runs, and administrative costs. Such subjective variables as employee morale and consumer motives are expressed quantitatively as labor turnover rates, hourly output, advertising elasticities, and shifts in demand schedules. The variables are carefully scrutinized to determine their absolute and relative importance to the desired objectives. The final step in model construction is to identify the variables by the type of symbols used in algebra and formulate equations or inequations that express the relationship among the variables and between the variables and

---

[18] A discussion of the role of mathematics in scientific endeavor is found in: Coombs, Raiffa, and Thrall, *op. cit.*, pp. 19–37.

the objective. The model can then be solved in some of the ways that will be indicated below.

The Planning Problem and Operations Research

Executives must constantly contend with limitations imposed by the resources available to them and the competing and complementary qualities of alternative plans of action. Thus, sales objectives cannot exceed the capacity of company production and marketing facilities. An expanded research program cannot be launched if competent personnel is not available. The planner must also take into account the alternative strategies that can be used to overcome such limitations. For example, the revenue potential and the relative costs of possible variations in product line should be carefully evaluated. The planning problem involves a large number of competing factors that must be balanced if an optimum solution is to be achieved. For example, the use of plant capacity for product x reduces the capacity that can be used to produce product y. Lower inventories reduce production costs, but they can also reduce sales to customers. Advertising may increase sales, but it also increases costs. Larger output may reduce production and purchasing costs, but it tends to reduce revenues if demand is inelastic. The diversity of limiting, complementary, and competing factors that exist in actual planning situations presents an extremely complicated problem-solving situation.

Many of the factors and relationships in the planning problem are quantitative in nature and can be represented by algebraic or numerical equations or inequations. Equations can be designed to show the relationship between output and variable costs, revenues and advertising expenditures, plant utilization and fixed costs, and so on. Inequations can be used to represent restrictions imposed by plant capacity, size of production runs, financial restraints, and the tolerances set forth in product specifications. Inequations differ from equations in that one side is greater or less than the other side. Thus, $x = 3y$ (an equation) becomes $x < 3y$ or $x > 3y$ (inequations). An inequation offers a range of possible solutions within given restrictions. Examples of planning restrictions which would be represented by inequations in operations research models are: output must be equal to or less than plant capacity; raw materials are required on or before April 7; and specifications cannot be greater or less than a certain value.

An operations research model may contain large numbers of equations and inequations representing factors and relationships in the planning problem. The basic problem is to find the combination of plans and actions that best achieves the objective set forth in the model. Ordinary arithmetic and geometry are adequate to solve highly simplified models, but the more complex models generally used in operations research require more elaborate mathematical techniques. The reason is that there are a seemingly infinite number of possible alternative solutions. A change in any one part of the model will change the values in many other parts of the model. This fact presents serious difficulties because a "trial and error" substitution of values is inadequate for most purposes. Fortunately, a systematic procedure for handling this problem has been developed by operations researchers.

Model-Solving Techniques

The solution of various aspects of the planning problem may become apparent during the model construction stage. This stage may develop understandings and insights that were not evident before. Defining the problem frequently provides a part of the answer. This idea holds for operations research as well as other types of scientific endeavor. Thus, important solutions may be derived even when the research process stops with the completed model. However, models are generally "solved" by the use of analytical or numerical techniques. Analytical techniques involve the use of the logic of mathematics to derive abstract conclusions about the nature and dynamics of a real situation. Many theories that were originally developed by "pure" mathematical thinking were later substantiated by empirical research and experimentation. Mathematics has been useful in developing and improving methods for handling a problem and in indicating the directions that further research should take. The mathematician cannot be a hazy thinker because the rigid logic of his subject will soon catch up with him. However, it should also be pointed out that mathematics may give some highly "logical" wrong answers about the nature of reality.

Much of the work of operations research involves the use of numerical values to find solutions that can be used for actual planning purposes. As was noted in the last section, the solution is difficult in a complex model because a seemingly infinite number of possible alternatives are available. However, systematic "trial and error" procedures, usually referred to as "iterative procedures," have been developed to facilitate a solution. Such procedures make possible a sequence of computations that lead to better and better solutions until the best possible solution is achieved. Each subsequent trial leads to fewer errors, and, with the final step, error is entirely or almost entirely eliminated. Electronic computers can frequently be used to perform the large amount of computational work that may be involved in this procedure.

Many of the techniques and theories that have been developed by pure and applied mathematicians are used in operations research. For example, an important facilitating instrument in solving many models is the matrix, a rectangular array of numbers or symbols, which can be used to denote many combinations of variables. Some models involve special applications of mathematical sampling and probability theories. The neophyte is soon lost in a mathematical maze without some of the knowledge inferred by such terms as "the calculus" and "matrix algebra." A sufficient conclusion for purposes of this analysis is that the techniques of operations research make possible the solution of highly complex models. Operations research can indicate the appropriate values for a large number of variables relative to the objective formulated for the model. But it should be emphasized that the model and its solutions are not the same as the actual planning problem that is represented. The nature of the difference determines the extent to which operations research is a useful instrument in a particular planning situation. Some conclusions about this matter are made in the next section.

Some Basic Types of Problems

Operations research has given particular emphasis to certain classes or types of problems. Such problems have been defined by prototype models which can be applied to actual situations with modifications.[19] Some of the basic types of problems are discussed below.

INVENTORY PROBLEMS. Such problems are concerned with balancing the costs involved in holding inventories against the costs that may result from insufficient inventories. Loss of customers, delays in production from material shortages, relative costs of different-sized production runs, and the advantages of quantity purchasing are some of the variables that make up this problem. Inventory models can be helpful in determining how much and when inventory should be purchased or produced to achieve a minimum cost situation.

ALLOCATION PROBLEMS. A company can frequently use productive resources in different ways and for a variety of purposes. Thus, there are alternative combinations of processes that can be used to produce a particular product, or different combinations of products can be produced with the resources at hand. Allocation models can be used to determine the least cost combination of processes and the most profitable product line. Such restrictions as limited machine capacities, limitations in storage space, raw material shortages, and a lack of skilled personnel are taken into account in solving this kind of problem. Similar models can be used to determine

[19] Churchman, Ackoff, and Arnoff, *op. cit.*, pp. 184–189. A major portion of this book deals with models that have been developed to handle various classes of planning problems.

the most economical transportation routes for the shipment of company products. This problem becomes particularly difficult when routes must be planned for shipments between a number of plants and warehouses and to customers in various locations. The problem of selecting from alternative ways to meet a given set or sets of product specifications can also be categorized as an allocation problem. For example, gasoline used in automobiles or aircraft can generally be blended in various ways without hindering performance. The nutritional requirements of commercial feeds can usually be met by alternative combinations of ingredients.

WAITING-TIME PROBLEMS. One aspect of such problems are queues or lines of trucks at loading docks, busses at terminals, patients at doctors' offices, or customers at store counters awaiting service. Another view is that loading dock personnel, employees at bus terminals, doctors, and sales personnel are sometimes idle awaiting the arrival of trucks, busses, patients, and customers. Waiting-time or queuing models can be helpful in reducing the costs involved in the two kinds of waiting time. One approach is to improve the schedules of the things or persons requiring services, and the other is to provide additional service facilities. For example, a department store might use advertising techniques to increase the flow of customers during slack periods of the day and add sales personnel during rush periods to reduce customer waiting time. Trucks can often be dispatched and routed in a way that reduces the time drivers must wait at loading docks and, at the same time, reduces idleness on the part of loading dock personnel. Models can also be helpful in determining the proper order in which various kinds of work should be done. For example, if jobs X, Y, and Z are waiting for a drill press operation, what kind of sequencing will reduce time or cost?

REPLACEMENT PROBLEMS. Equipment becomes less efficient over time as the result of operation or innovation. A ten-year-old lathe is generally less efficient than a new one and even more so if major improvements have been made in subsequent design. An unused Model T Ford is better than one that has been driven 100,000 miles, but a new 1969 Ford is better than a new Model T. How often and when should a company replace such equipment as lathes, drill presses, typewriters, and trucks? Replacement models attempt to balance the costs involved in purchasing new equipment with the costs of lower efficiency and maintenance. Another kind of problem is to determine the replacement pattern for things subject to complete failure, such as light bulbs and electronic tubes. For example, how frequently should light bulbs in a large sign be replaced to minimize the cost involved in intermittent bulb failures and replacements?

COMPETITIVE PROBLEMS. Executives are frequently faced with decisions that must take into account the decisions that might be made by competitors. For example, the appropriate price policy is frequently dependent upon actions that competitors may take. A decision to cut prices to gain a larger share of the market may not pay because similar cuts will be made by competing companies. A decision to increase price can put a company into a disadvantageous position if competitors do not follow. A similar situation may prevail with respect to such decisional problems as advertising, wage policy, model changes, and service innovations. Competitive or "game" models have been developed to show the appropriate strategy or set of strategies in the light of alternatives available to competitors. The solution is generally "minimax" because countermoves by competitors make any attempt to maximize gains an extremely hazardous business. Thus, a large price cut to eliminate competition may lead to even larger price cuts by competing companies and large losses in revenues for the original price-cutter. Some decisional situations involve the use of "mixed strategies" to keep competitors from learning a company's strategy. A football quarterback generally mixes up the plays to confuse the opposition. A military commander may use a similar stratagem to hide his real intentions from the enemy. Mathematical models can indicate the best possible mixture of strategies, given the alternatives available to all parties and the objectives of the players.

All of the above situations involve a balancing of two or more conflicting or competing factors. The problem is to develop a strategy that maximizes results as measured by such objective criteria as profits, costs, output, and time. The prototype models that have been developed can be helpful in a number of directions. Some of them, as was noted, can be adapted to actual planning problems with modifications. Inventory and allocation models have been more useful in this respect than have the other types. Models can also be used to train executives and operations research specialists. They help define the nature of the planning problem even when they cannot be directly used to solve it. For example, competitive or "game" models give the neophyte insights that may be helpful in solving strategy problems.

Operations Research: An Evaluation

Operations research, like other innovations in human history, has had its share of zealots proclaiming the dawn of a new management order. Executives should be wary of attempts to make operations research sound as though miracles were somehow possible through the magic of higher mathematics. Mathematical techniques can facilitate the solution of empirical problems only if there is some relationship between the dynamics of the phenomena being studied and mathematical logic. The formulation of restrictive assumptions about the nature of reality has the effect of leaving unanswered the "solutions" that are assumed. The assumptions that have to be made in constructing some models are sometimes the critical elements in a decisional problem. Emphasis should be given to the idea that many problems cannot be solved by mathematical techniques. Mathematics is not useful in solving many of the uncertainty problems that face the executive.

In spite of limitations in logic and practice, operations research can directly and indirectly solve many decisional problems. It has reaffirmed the importance of using scientific measurement to the greatest possible extent. The degree of error in decision can undoubtedly be reduced even though perfect solutions are not possible. Particularly pertinent in this respect are problems involving a large number of quantitative variables. Operations research may also contribute toward better decision making by the emphasis that it gives to defining the problem. A better understanding of the nature of the problem, even when it cannot or can only partly be solved mathematically, may provide useful insights for more subjective techniques. A contribution can also be made by operations research in the area of executive development. Something about the basic elements that are involved in decision making can be learned through inventory, allocation, competitive, and other models. However, it should not be assumed that mathematical training necessarily makes a better executive. It can impede the development of decision-making talent by giving the student a much too stereotyped picture of the decisional environment. Mathematics courses generally give birth to better mathematicians but not always to more competent executives.

The success that has already been achieved indicates that the history of operations research will be similar to that of the earlier "scientific management." Frederick W. Taylor and some of his lieutenants were also inclined toward overoptimistic opinions about their innovation. They were right in certain respects and wrong in others. Operations research, like the scientific management that went before, will undoubtedly be more successful in solving decisional problems that relate to things as opposed to people. It will provide better answers to production and inventory problems than to personnel and market research problems. It will increase the objectivity of decision making in some measure, but it will not eliminate the need for subjective techniques. Executives will continue to provide answers to questions that have no answer.

Subjective Processes and Techniques

Much planning involves subjective processes that occur in some unknown fashion in the human brain. Yet, they frequently result in the solution of highly complex problems. Man seems to develop subjective insights that transcend the knowledge he can derive through scientific techniques and objective sources. There are physicians, physicists, chemists, mathematicians, psychologists, economists, and executives who have skills they cannot explain in objective terms. The president of a large metal producing company had this to say on the subject: "I don't think businessmen know how they make decisions. I know I don't." [20] A top executive from the steel industry came to a similar conclusion: "You don't know how you do it; you just do it." Another executive commented: "If a vice president asks me how I was able to choose the right course, I have to say, 'I'm damned if I know!'" A possible reason is provided by the president of a large manufacturing company: "It is like asking a pro baseball player to define the swing that has always come natural to him."

The Physiology of Subjective Problem Solving

What is the nature of subjective or intuitive processes? The difficulty in finding the answer is that relatively little is known about the functioning of the human brain.[21] Some research findings indicate that the brain operates in the manner of an electronic computer. The basic component of the system is the *neuron* or nerve cell which generates or propagates nerve impulses. There are billions of neurons linked together into an integrated whole which create complex patterns of nerve impulses. John C. Eccles, professor of physiology at the Australian National University, has described the process "as a patterned activity formed by the curving and looping of wavefronts through a multitude of neurons, now sprouting, now coalescing with other wavefronts, now reverberating through the same path —all with a speed deriving from the millisecond relay time of the individual neuron, the whole wavefront advancing through perhaps one million

---

[20] The statements that follow are reproduced from John McDonald, "How Businessmen Make Decisions," *Fortune,* Vol. 52, No. 2, August 1955, p. 85.

[21] The present state of knowledge in this area is indicated by the following: John C. Eccles, "The Physiology of Imagination," *Scientific American,* Vol. 199, No. 3, September 1958, pp. 135–146; Francis Bello, "New Light on the Brain," *Fortune,* Vol. 51, No. 1, January 1955, pp. 104 ff.; John von Neumann, *The Computer and the Brain* (New Haven: Yale University Press, 1958).

neurons in a second."[22] A major mystery is the nature and functioning of memory or the manner in which the nervous system stores and recalls information. John von Neumann, the mathematician, has written that "the presence of a memory—or not improbably, of several memories—within the nervous system is a matter of surmise and postulation, but one that all our experience with artificial computing automata suggests and confirms."[23] He concluded that it is difficult to see how the human nervous system could do without a rather large-capacity memory. Some possible physical embodiments of human memory are: (1) variability of the stimuli or impulses required to activate a neuron, (2) variation over time in the distribution of nerve connections, (3) genetic components (chromosomes and their constituent genes) may play a role and may possibly have a memory system of their own, (4) chemical changes in various parts of the body.[24] Dr. Eccles has this to say about the memory question.

Memory must be dependent on some enduring change that has been produced in the cortex [outer layer of brain] by its previous activation. Theory and even some experimental evidence favor the hypothesis that the initial activation of the synapses [connections between neurons] in a network brings about a lasting improvement in the efficacy of these junctions. As yet no one know just how.[25]

Subjective processes, even though their functioning is not well understood, represent an additional element in solving decisional problems. Some might argue that the filtering of objective data through the human brain generally results in a net loss because personal bias and emotion give rise to distortions. But the functioning of the human brain may also add something to the quality of problem solving. A sudden illumination from the so-called subconscious mind has been known to solve problems that defied a purely objective approach. Such illuminations generally occur during considerable mental activity about some unsolved problem. Dr. Eccles has pointed out in this respect:

One can deliberately seek to experience some new imaginative insight by first pouring into one's mind hypotheses and the related experiments and then relaxing to give opportunity for the subconscious processes in the brain that may lead to the conscious illumination of a new insight. Such illuminations are often fragmentary and require conscious modification, or are so erroneous as to invite immediate rejection by critical reason. Nevertheless they all give evidence of the creativeness of the subconscious mind.[26]

[22] Eccles, *op. cit.*, p. 142.
[23] von Neumann, *op. cit.*, p. 60.
[24] von Neumann, *op. cit.*, pp. 64–65.
[25] Eccles, *op. cit.*, p. 141.
[26] *Ibid.*, p. 144.

The human brain has the capacity to make subtle distinctions and complex integrations. It seems able to recall vast amounts of information with proper stimulus. It is the fountainhead for the innovations that gives man's future a different form than that which prevailed in the past. The manner in which the brain performs its functions is still largely a matter of speculation. The memory "system" may well contain a great deal of information that is not readily subject to conscious control or recall. Indeed, some information may become memory without conscious awareness on the part of the subject. One wonders in this respect how often students later recall parts of "unheard" lectures as new ideas. The interplay between a comprehensive memory system and flows of impulses in complex and changing patterns involving millions of neurons would seem to provide adequate means for the solution of problems by subconscious processes. It might also be reasonable to assert that subconscious processes may give better results than objective techniques under certain circumstances.

Subjective Decisional Techniques

Objective decisional techniques involve attempts to solve problems by the use of methods and measurements that have an existence apart from the mind of the decision maker. The conclusions that result can be verified by other persons using the same methods and measurements. But objective techniques are never completely devoid of subjective elements. Subjectively derived imagination and ideas are an integral part of the objective problem-solving process.

The extent to which subjective elements enter the decisional process is partly determined by the nature of the problem under consideration. For example, the executive is frequently forced to form an essentially subjective conception of what the future might hold. Previous experience cannot provide data that can be measured by the techniques of probability theory. The only alternative is to fill the void with subjectively derived solutions. However, subjective techniques may be appropriate even when the decisional problem can be solved by an objective approach. Many decisions become routine or habit for the experienced executive with resulting economies in time and cost. Executive decision also involves creativeness and innovation which are at least partly a product of subjective processes. Although objective techniques are important in solving decisional problems, subjective techniques also play a significant role in executive decision making.

The development of subjective decision-making theories and techniques would seem to be an important goal for future research. Professor G. L. S.

Shackle of the University of Liverpool has taken a step in this direction.[27] The Shackle theory assumes that the executive can best solve the problem of uncertainty by evaluating the alternatives until he arrives at a solution that seems to offer a minimum of "potential surprise." [28] In other words, the executive "feels" that the decision will not result in unpleasant surprises. The degree of error in any decision can be gauged by the degree of potential surprise. Somewhat similar to Shackle's conception is the regret criterion developed by L. J. Savage.[29] The decision maker will experience regret to the extent that he does not achieve a maximum possible payoff. The degree of regret is measured by the difference between the maximum payoff and the payoffs that would actually result under various possible conditions.

The following are other assumptions and approaches that can be used to contend with the problem of uncertainty.[30] One of these is a maximum criterion, suggested by Abraham Wald, in which the decision maker chooses a course of action which maximizes the minimum return. Each possible action is appraised by assuming that the worst is going to happen and that the optimal decision is to pick the best worst state. A second possibility is to follow the Laplace criterion, referred to as the principle of insufficient reason, which assumes that all possible acts are equally likely. Under this criterion, the decision maker would choose the action with the highest payoff. A third approach to uncertainty is the pessimism-optimism index criterion developed by Leonid Hurwicz. This technique involves the use of a weighted combination of the decision-maker's conception of the worst and the best results of particular courses of action.

The above criteria for solving uncertainty problems are not adequate for the planning problems that actually face executives. However, they repre-

---

[27] G. L. S. Shackle, *Uncertainty in Economics* (Cambridge: The Cambridge University Press, 1955); C. F. Carter, G. P. Meredith, and G. L. S. Shackle (editors), *Uncertainty and Business Decisions* (Liverpool: Liverpool University Press, 1954).

[28] The advantage of the "potential surprise" concept is expressed by Professor Shackle: "An unlimited number of rival hypotheses concerning any one question or experiment can all simultaneously carry zero potential surprise, and when any one such proves true, the judgment is fully vindicated. Should a hypothesis prove true to which a degree of potential surprise greater than zero had been assigned, the degree of misjudgment is exactly measured and represented by this degree of potential surprise." Shackle, *Uncertainty in Economics, op. cit.,* p. 34.

[29] L. J. Savage, "The Theory of Statistical Decision," *Journal of the American Statistical Association,* Vol. 46, 1951, pp. 55–67; Joseph W. McGuire, *Theories of Business Behavior* (Englewood Cliffs, N.J.: Prentice-Hall, Inc., 1964), pp. 128–129.

[30] *Ibid.*, pp. 124–133; R. Duncan Luce and Howard Raiffa, *Games and Decisions* (New York: John Wiley & Sons, Inc., 1957), pp. 275–298; David W. Miller and Martin K. Starr, *Executive Decisions and Operations Research* (Englewood Cliffs, N.J.: Prentice-Hall, Inc., 1960), pp. 85–94.

sent an important step toward a better understanding of the problem of decision making under conditions of uncertainty. The elementary formulations of today can become the basis for much more elaborate criteria in the future. Such criteria make possible computer programs that can be helpful in solving the really difficult planning problems.

The Creative Process

Creative thinking generally involves a blending of objective and subjective factors. Although little is known about the way in which the human brain generates new ideas and solutions, a systematic approach to creativity appears to be helpful in certain respects. Professor John F. Mee has set forth some of the steps in such an approach to creative thinking: [31] (1) *Attitude and concentration.* A person should have a positive attitude toward the formulation of ideas even though they may seem impractical and unorthodox at first. An effort should be made to concentrate on "thinking" rather than on a television program, last night's party, or a new Ian Fleming novel. (2) *Selecting or defining a problem.* Determine the purpose for which you want or need ideas. Pick a problem and then search for the solution with an open mind. (3) *Exploration and preparation.* This step in the creative thinking process involves a comprehensive survey of all existing knowledge about the problem. One reason for this step is that there is no point in rediscovering something that is already known. Another is that the examination and evaluation of existing knowledge will provide a basis for the "subjective" process that comes at a later stage. The missing link that solves the problem will be much easier to obtain if there are partial answers. (4) *Hypothesis, brainstorming, or wild thinking.* All possible applications and relationships of present knowledge are explored during this step. Charles S. Whiting has noted three approaches to this stage: an analytical approach, a forced relationship approach, and free association. The analytical approach involves the use of a pattern for determining possible relationships of knowledge to a problem. For example, can it be put to other uses, can it be modified, can elements be combined differently, is substitution possible, etc. The forced relationship approach involves lists of objects or ideas that can have some relationship to the problem and then considering each object or idea to every other object or idea. The free association technique is to generate ideas without giving thought to their possible use in solving the problem. Brainstorming illustrates this technique. (5) *Incubation or gestation.* During this step, the mental apparatus should be given an opportunity to work on the problem without conscious

[31] John F. Mee, "The Creative Thinking Process," *Indiana Business Review*, Vol. 31, No. 2, February 1956, pp. 3–7.

thinking. A person should think about other subjects, indulge in "light" reading, listen to classical music, or simply sit in the park and feed the pigeons. Give the unconscious mind a chance to solve the problem. (6) *Illumination.* This step often occurs at an unexpected time. A person may be shaving, eating, driving an automobile, or riding the elevator when some kind of solution to the problem suddenly appears. Ideas often come in rapid order; a tape recorder or pencil and paper can be helpful at this stage. (7) *Verification and application.* The final step is to adapt the new ideas to the problem that needs to be solved. Some ideas will turn out to be quite useless; others will be directly or indirectly useful in obtaining a solution.

Another systematic approach to creative thought is "brainstorming," which was developed by Alex F. Osborn, an advertising executive.[32] This technique has been widely used in governmental and private organizations and has been incorporated in the course offerings of some universities. The purpose of brainstorming is to reduce inhibitions that interfere with creative thinking by (1) ruling out criticism and adverse judgment until later; (2) "free-wheeling" or letting ideas, even wild ones, flow without restraint; (3) pouring out a large quantity of ideas—the more the better; and (4) combining and improving the ideas of others. Osborn also gave a great deal of emphasis to the importance of group interaction as a means for generating ideas through brainstorming. However, in spite of its wide acceptance and seemingly successful results, some aspects of brainstorming procedure and practices may actually inhibit the creation of new ideas.[33]

Some of the techniques presently used by executives and others in solving problems may offer insights that can be helpful in improving subjective decisional techniques. For example, one executive says that he makes his most important decisions at night or on weekends. Another "gets away by himself" on a hunting trip to think through important decisional problems. Some executives say they go to bed with the problem and wake up in the morning with the answer. Others speed up the process by waking up in the middle of the night with the solution. There is also the problem of determining when the subjective process should end. Should the executive spend a day, a week, or a month in attempts to solve a problem that has no objective solution? The problem may be related to the "feeling" the executive has about the matter. A feeling of dissatisfaction might indicate that

---

[32] A. F. Osborn, *Applied Imagination,* rev. ed. (New York: Charles Scribner's Sons, 1957).

[33] Donald W. Taylor, Paul C. Berry, and Clifford H. Block, *Does Group Participation When Using Brainstorming Facilitate or Inhibit Creative Thinking?* (New Haven: Department of Industrial Administration and Department of Psychology, Yale University, 1957), pp. 28–35.

more "thought" is required. On the other hand, a feeling that the decision is "right" might indicate that nothing more can be done. However, the nature of the subjective sensations that provide such cues possibly vary from person to person.

The development of subjective decision-making theories and techniques requires more knowledge about man's mental processes than is presently available. Research in the fields of physiology and psychology may ultimately provide a basis for better answers. But in spite of limited knowledge the subjective aspects of decision making should not be ignored. Attempts should be made to develop useful techniques through experimentation and experience.

SELECTED REFERENCES

Administrative Science Quarterly, Vol. 3, No. 3 (December 1958). The entire issue is devoted to decision making.

Chester I. Barnard, *The Functions of the Executive,* Chaps. 15 and 16. Cambridge: Harvard University Press, 1951.

Edward H. Bowman and Robert B. Fetter, *Analysis for Production and Operations Management,* 3rd ed. Homewood, Ill.: Richard D. Irwin, Inc., 1967.

Ray E. Brown, *Judgment in Administration.* New York: McGraw-Hill Book Company, 1966.

Elwood S. Buffa, *Models for Production and Operations Management.* New York: John Wiley and Sons, Inc., 1963.

Elwood S. Buffa, *Modern Production Management,* 2nd ed. New York: John Wiley and Sons, Inc., 1965.

Elwood S. Buffa (editor), *Readings in Production and Operations Management.* New York: John Wiley and Sons, Inc., 1966.

C. F. Carter, G. P. Meredith, and G. L. S. Shackle (editors), *Uncertainty and Business Decisions.* Liverpool: Liverpool University Press, 1957.

C. West Churchman, *Prediction and Optimal Decision.* Englewood Cliffs, N.J.: Prentice-Hall, Inc., 1961.

C. West Churchman, Russell L. Ackoff, and E. Leonard Arnoff, *Introduction to Operations Research.* New York: John Wiley and Sons, Inc., 1957.

Jay W. Forrester, *Industrial Dynamics.* The M.I.T. Press, Massachusetts Institute of Technology, and John Wiley and Sons, Inc., New York. 1961.

Albert Gailord Hart, *Anticipations, Uncertainty, and Dynamic Planning.* New York: Augustus M. Kelley, Inc., 1951.

Earl O. Heady, *Economics of Agricultural Production and Resource Use,* Chap. 15. Englewood Cliffs, N.J.: Prentice-Hall, Inc., 1952.

Leonard W. Hein, *The Quantitative Approach to Managerial Decisions.* Englewood Cliffs, N.J.: Prentice-Hall, Inc., 1967.

J. R. Hicks, *Value and Capital,* Part IV. Oxford: The Clarendon Press, 1946.

Frank H. Knight, *Risk, Uncertainty and Profit,* Chap. 7. Boston: Houghton Mifflin Company, 1921.

N. Paul Loomba, *Linear Programming.* New York: McGraw-Hill Book Company, Inc., 1964.

R. Duncan Luce and Howard Raiffa, *Games and Decisions: Introduction and Critical Survey.* New York: John Wiley and Sons, Inc., 1957.

Raymond R. Mayer, *Production Management*, 2nd ed. New York: McGraw-Hill Book Company, 1968.

Joseph F. McClosky and Florence N. Trefethen, *Operations Research for Management*. Baltimore: The Johns Hopkins Press, 1954.

John McDonald, *Strategy in Poker, Business and War*. New York: W. W. Norton & Company, Inc., 1950.

Joseph W. McGuire, *Theories of Business Behavior*. Englewood Cliffs, N.J.: Prentice-Hall, Inc., 1964.

David W. Miller and Martin K. Starr, *Executive Decisions and Operations Research*. Englewood Cliffs, N.J.: Prentice-Hall, Inc., 1960.

Robert W. Morell, *Analysis of Stages in Decision-Making,* Research Bulletin, No. 106. Detroit: Institute of Business Services, University of Detroit (January, 1958).

Marvin E. Mundel, *A Conceptual Framework for the Management Sciences*. New York: McGraw-Hill Book Company, 1967.

S. Benjamin Prasad, *Modern Industrial Management*. San Francisco: Chandler Publishing Company, 1967.

Herbert A. Simon, *Administrative Behavior,* 2nd ed., Chaps. 1, 3, 4, 5. New York: The Macmillan Company, 1958.

R. M. Thrall, C. H. Coombs, and R. L. Davis (editors), *Decision Processes*. New York: John Wiley and Sons, Inc., 1954.

Howard L. Timms, *Introduction to Operations Management*. Homewood, Ill.: Richard D. Irwin, Inc., 1967.

J. D. Williams, *The Compleat Strategyst*. New York: McGraw-Hill Book Company, Inc., 1954.

chapter 17

DYNAMIC PLANNING II

This chapter is concerned with the problem of planning the program of a particular organization. The nature of the planning process, the instruments through which planning takes place, and the impact of planning upon policies are considered.

The Past is Prologue

The planning process begins with an existing organization having certain human, material, and financial resources. As in a game of chess that is half over, future moves are restricted and influenced by the action that has gone before. Once an organization is committed to a particular objective, a major change in objective is difficult and sometimes impossible. An automobile manufacturing plant cannot be readily adapted to produce steel ingots. The tools and equipment in such a plant cannot be used to make pajamas or chicken pot pies. An educational institution would experience difficulties in shifting to the manufacture of bar stools or fly swatters. A religious organization cannot make major changes in its doctrinal position from day to day without serious consequences. A student cannot easily change his academic program during the last semester of the senior year.

The Cost of Change

As was pointed out earlier, a major restriction to change is imposed by the length of time necessary to depreciate some specialized resources. Such costs cannot usually be absorbed in the short run under normal economic conditions. The specialization of executive, technical, and operating personnel also inhibits change because such personnel cannot be readily reassigned to radically different activities. Although personnel can be replaced from the outside, the real and hidden cost is generally high. Much of the money spent in the past for training and morale-building programs will have to be written off as a loss. Furthermore, the development of inexperienced personnel into competent employees is expensive and time consuming. The cost of past advertising and other sales promotion effort may also go down the drain with a major change in objectives.

The disruptive impact of change on formal and informal organizational relationships is another consideration. People generally do not relish the uncertainty that accompanies status changes. Morale and productivity are sometimes seriously affected by such disturbing forces. The possible adverse consequences of change cannot always be measured in objective terms. Some costs are purely subjective and can only be expressed by such terms as apprehension, worry, and anxiety. They are sometimes sufficient to counterbalance more objective considerations.

The Futurity of Planning

To the extent that the consequences of past planning are irrevocable, they reduce the capacity of the organization to adapt to environmental changes. The obstacles placed in the path of change may have both beneficial and destructive properties. Some degree of stability is necessary in the conduct of all human affairs. People seem to have a limited capacity to absorb changes in their physical and social milieu. But an inability to adapt to external changes may destroy the organization. Thus, a reduced product demand may bankrupt a company because it cannot shift to the production of another product.

However, the past is important only to the extent that it gives a better understanding of the limitations placed upon future action. Planning is concerned with the problems of the future; the question is not, what has been done, but, what shall be done? The planner should view each problem in terms of what is now pertinent. The errors of the past should not be perpetuated into the future. As an outstanding executive has written:

We ask not only what a thing is *now* worth but what it *did* cost, often a fact interesting for deplorable reasons but utterly irrelevant to the present decision that the merchant must make—to sell it for what it is now worth or not sell it at all, whether he shall make a past error of decision the basis for a new error of decision or deal with present circumstances.[1]

[1] Chester I. Barnard, *The Functions of the Executive* (Cambridge: Harvard University Press, 1951), p. 208.

Some corrective action will always be necessary in an environment of uncertainty. The mistakes of the past are rarely fatal if executives act promptly and decisively.

The Scope of Planning

The scope of planning may range from a slight modification in the procedure for making customer refunds to a major change in the production program. A foreman who orders a worker to do something in a certain way is engaged in planning. Such planning is not as comprehensive as the planning involved in building a new plant or conducting a nationwide advertising campaign. But it is planning none the less. Planning activities are not restricted to managerial personnel. Workers plan the methods that they will employ in doing a job within whatever range of discretion is permitted. However, this chapter is concerned only with the planning responsibilities of management.

Some plans are made without a great deal of forethought. Others require a long period of reflection and deliberation. Every alternative is given careful scrutiny and considered in the light of all available information. The participation in a particular planning problem may range from one executive to scores of executives. The time period involved may vary from a few minutes to several years. Not all plans become a part of the organizational process. Some planning decisions may lie in abeyance for years before they are activated by the communication process. The military, for example, is always engaged in strategic and tactical planning for use during the next war. Existing plans are constantly being modified as the result of changes in military technology and the nature of warfare. The rate of obsolescence of military plans is exceedingly high. Many of them will forever remain in the filing cases of the Pentagon.

The Nature of the Planning Problem

The term "planning" is generally used with the supposition that scientific methods are, or at least ought to be, utilized. Scientific management or rationalization has been a prime motif of management philosophy during the past fifty years. The lack of a scientific approach in solving planning problems has been lamented in many quarters. A failure to develop a program of systematic planning may stem from ignorance and inertia. The achievement of a high degree of rationality in making some decisions is impossible. The solution of some aspects of the planning problem will remain outside the province of science. Thus, although the use of scientific techniques to the fullest possible extent is appropriate, the decision maker should recognize the distinction between objectively and subjectively derived solutions. Many problems are solved in the name of science when in fact they cannot be solved scientifically.

Maximizing and Satisficing

Executives generally satisfice rather than maximize in solving planning problems. As Herbert Simon put the matter: "Administrative theory is peculiarly the theory of intended and bounded rationality—of the behavior of human beings who *satisfice* because they have not the wits to *maximize*." [2] A satisficing solution is one that appears adequate or good enough to the planner. Such an approach becomes necessary because much planning is not susceptible to objective solutions. The problem of uncertainty is ever present.

Planning for Profits

The profit criterion is a highly abstract concept with many implicit definitions of appropriate organizational action. It does not directly indicate what needs to be done to make a profit. Profits are a consequence of organizational activity and will normally result only if that activity is well planned. The planning problem in a dynamic environment has been considered at length in preceding chapters. Planning involves adaptation to product and resource markets, governmental policies, and cultural and social factors. Equally important are the strategies devised by the organization to control and modify its environment, such as product line changes, price policies, advertising and sales promotion, product and service innovations, resource procurement strategies, and improvements in operating and motivational techniques.

Defining Expectations

In spite of the limitations imposed by uncertainty, the planner should take a positive approach and attempt to construct the best possible plan from the information available to him. Some of his forecasts and estimates will be little more than hazy probability judgments. Others will portray a highly reliable account of future events. For example, the capacity of exist-

---

[2] Herbert A. Simon, *Administrative Behavior,* Second Edition (New York: The Macmillan Company, 1960), p. xxiv.

ing and planned production facilities can generally be estimated with a small margin of error. Although plans are based on expectations rather than facts, the planning problem should be given "objective" content by a definition of expectations. In other words, the planner must decide what the future will bring even though actual events may prove him wrong by a wide margin. Effective planning would not be possible without such analytically induced stability conditions. Although some degree of flexibility can be incorporated into the program, it is generally impossible to plan for the total range within which expectations might be in error.

Limited Resources and Company Strategies

The planner should give careful consideration to the limitations imposed by internal and external factors. Thus, sales objectives cannot exceed the capacity of company production and marketing facilities. An expanded research program cannot be launched if competent personnel is not available. Additional production facilities cannot be constructed or purchased with inadequate financial resources. Although the planning problem always involves limitations in resources, the planner should take into account the alternative strategies that can be used to overcome such limitations. Some of the strategies that may be employed to increase revenues and reduce costs were indicated in Chapter 15. The revenue potential of product line changes, price increases or reductions, advertising and other sales promotion techniques, and product and service innovations should be evaluated. Careful consideration should also be given to strategies that reduce the cost of procuring such resources as money, plant and equipment, personnel, raw materials, merchandise, and supplies. The development of higher productivity through improved factory and office building design, better machines and equipment, more efficient procedures and methods, standardization and simplification, and more complete utilization of facilities represents another aspect of planning strategy.

Strategic or Limiting Factors

Effective planning is directed toward what have been called limiting or strategic factors.[3] A strategic factor is the missing link in whatever system of integrated conditions or actions is necessary to achieve a given objective. Such a factor "is the one whose control, in the right form, at the right place and time, will set the complementary factors at work to bring about the

[3] John R. Commons, *Institutional Economics* (New York: The Macmillan Company, 1934), pp. 627–633; Barnard, *op. cit.*, pp. 202–205.

results intended."[4] In the following oft-quoted saying, an insignificant little nail significantly influenced the course of events.

> For want of a nail the shoe was lost,
> For want of a shoe the horse was lost,
> For want of a horse the rider was lost,
> For want of a rider the battle was lost,
> For want of a battle the kingdom was lost—
> And all for want of a horseshoe nail.[5]

Although few kingdoms have been lost for want of a nail, the importance of this idea is illustrated by the bombing of German transportation facilities, ball bearing plants, and oil refineries during World War II. The destruction of any one of these vital resources, the planners reasoned, would seriously impede the German war effort. The following report by Theodore H. White on the views expressed by Willi Schlieker, chief of German iron and steel production, allocation, and control, indicates that the consequences were closely related to expectations.

Willi, looking backward, has told American bombing experts over and over again that they never succeeded in putting more than a minor dent in Germany's heavy steel production. What hurt were such blows as the bombing of gasoline plants, for by the time Germany was producing 3,750 aircraft a month she lacked the fuel to train pilots, or even keep her already trained pilots in the air. What hurt even more was the bombing of the railways. The Ruhr, says Willi, ultimately collapsed not because of the bombing of plants, mills and mines but because the railway exits were so clogged with blowouts, breaks and burned-out locomotives that they could not carry away the 30,000 tons of finished goods the Ruhr produced every day. The Ruhr strangled finally, in January and February, 1945, on its own production; it did not cave in under blast.[6]

These experiences from World War II illustrate the importance of directing attention to strategic factors. Thus, the bombing of German corset factories or breweries would have contributed far less to Allied victory. The strategic factor (or factors) constantly changes during the planning process. At one period of time, the strategic factor may be a shortage of a mineral resource, at another an inadequate organizational structure, at still another employee morale, and so on. For example, the General Electric Company, which launched a major expansion program in 1945, gave initial emphasis to such matters as organizational structure and production facilities. But, as the planning and execution of the program progressed, other

---

[4] Commons, *op. cit.*, p. 628.
[5] Benjamin Franklin, *Poor Richard's Almanack* (1758).
[6] Theodore H. White, *Fire in the Ashes* (New York: William Sloane Associates, 1953), p. 178. Copyright 1953 by Theodore H. White.

factors became relatively more important. This point was emphasized by a statement attributed to GE's Ralph Cordiner: "Not customers, not products, not money, but managers may be the limit on General Electric's growth."[7] The strategic factor may change as the result of changes in the environment and within the organization. Customers would be a more strategic factor during a serious recession than during a peak prosperity period. Furthermore, the planning process itself generates a sequence of strategic factors. For example, a short supply of iron ore may be solved by importing ore from a foreign nation. The strategic factor may then become that of transporting the ore or changing the location of the steel mill.

Computerized Planning Systems

Significant improvements in planning can occur through the use of comprehensive computerized models of the economic system or an industry. Some of the larger and more progressive companies make extensive use of econometric models for sales and other forecasting. Progress has also been made through models that simulate particular environmental and organizational realities. Alternative planning strategies can be tested to determine the manner in which they may influence profits and other planning variables.

Once organizational objectives (the sales forecast) have been determined, computerized planning systems can be most helpful in translating organizational objectives into subsidiary objectives. Much of the production planning and control problem, inventory and purchasing programs, budgetary process, and cost analysis and control can be effectively programmed for computer operations.

The electronic computer and all of the techniques that relate to it (such as operations research) will play an increasingly important part in planning the means necessary to achieve organizational objectives. Executives will be less concerned with means and will find themselves more directly burdened with the problems of uncertainty and values. Electronic computers will make many of the objective decisions, leaving for executives the decisions that can only be made through subjective techniques.

An Optimum Combination of Strategies

The problem of the planner in determining the organization objective is to plan the best possible combination of strategies. Some strategies are

---

[7] Edward C. Bursk and Dan H. Fenn, Jr. (editors), *Planning the Future Strategy of Your Business* (New York: McGraw-Hill Book Company, Inc., 1956), p. 46.

complementary in the sense that organizational action in one area requires actions in other areas. A market strategy designed to increase sales by a large percentage is obviously futile if no provision is made for necessary expansion of plant and office facilities or a larger volume of raw material flow. Other strategies are competing in the sense that attempts to achieve a greater advantage in one respect leads to disadvantages in other respects. Strategies that successfully promote market dominance sometimes compete with strategies that reduce the risk of government antitrust action. Thus, a company may deliberately plan a market strategy that gives it lower sales and revenues than another strategy because it fears a zealous government lawyer who wants to justify his salary.

Some of the variables in the planning problem can be synthesized by mathematical techniques—simple arithmetic computation is frequently all that is required. Sales forecast information can be used to determine production schedules which in turn may be used to plan the purchasing program. Alternative strategies can be evaluated in terms of revenue forecasts and cost estimates. However, the planner should remember that much of the quantitative data used in planning evolves from highly subjective forecasts and estimates. Some values are translated into quantitative terms even though they are essentially subjective judgments. For example, how will a styling innovation or a television program influence future sales? The planner must assess the impact of not only his own plans in this respect but also the unknown plans of his competitors. The logic of mathematics does not offer any final solution to problems of this kind; it is frequently more economical to simply "juggle things around." The only thing that is gained by mathematical techniques in some instances is a more precise wrong answer. Thus, although a quantitative and computational approach is useful, a more fundamental problem is to make judgments about the expectations that are being quantified. The final outcome under the best possible circumstances will contain some degree of error. Fortunately, many of the planning errors made today can be corrected at some future date.

The Organized Planning Process

Planning in companies beyond a certain size is an organized process involving the cooperation of many executives and specialists. The process can be analytically divided into two phases. The first phase is concerned with the formulation of organization and departmental objectives. It generally involves much formal and informal interaction among executives at different levels of the management hierarchy. A good illustration of this phase of the planning process is provided by planning practices in the General Motors Corporation. Executives who head functional staff sections and the principal operating executives actively participate in the formulation of overall corporation objectives. This system gives top management firsthand information about conditions, problems, and attitudes in various parts of the organization. It also taps a diversity of specialized knowledge and experience which can be used to advantage in developing the overall program. At the same time, operating and staff executives have an opportunity to view the planning problem from a broader perspective and obtain information and insights that will help them better understand the part their departmental units will have to play. Although this aspect of the planning process is not always formalized, executives in most companies follow a similar pattern in determining objectives. Only a genius or an idiot would fail to make use of the specialized knowledge and experience of subordinates.

The second phase of the planning process occurs after the organization objective has been given final approval. Although the top executive (an individual or a group) may solicit advice and information from subordinates and specialists from various parts of the organization, the final decision as to the nature of objectives to be pursued is his responsibility. Planning during the second phase follows hierarchical lines more rigidly than during the first phase. It involves a further refinement of objectives into more particular objectives as the process moves from the top to the bottom of the hierarchy.

The Organization Structure and Planning Responsibilities

In Part II some of the alternative ways in which organizations differentiate planning and other decisional responsibilities have been indicated. The amount of discretion exercised by various hierarchical levels varies with the extent to which decision making is centralized or decentralized. Operating executives are given a great deal of latitude in planning their departmental programs in such decentralized companies as the General Motors Corporation and Sears, Roebuck and Company. The type of departmentation determines the manner in which objectives are divided and subdivided as planning proceeds from the top to the bottom of the hierarchy. The organization objective may be divided into functional objectives (production, sales, purchasing, and personnel), product objectives (objectives of the Oldsmobile Division), regional objectives (sales objectives of the Eastern Division), and other kinds of objectives. The process of redefining broader objectives into more specific objectives comes to an end with the assignment of duties to operating personnel, such as salesmen, purchasing agents, personnel recruiters, and factory workers.

Objectives, Plans, and Policies

Organizational Objectives and the Planning Process

Organizational objectives and the plans that are developed to achieve them are mutually dependent concepts. Objectives determine the nature of the activities that will be necessary, but at the same time the activities that are planned operationally define the objective.[8] A given objective at the beginning of the planning process may be given different operational definitions if two or more plans are possible. Whenever the planner selects one alternative plan rather than another, he is in effect making a decision about objectives. The determination of objectives is an implicit or explicit problem throughout the planning process.

The planning process translates broad objectives into more specific objectives while transforming objectives into means. The higher levels in the management hierarchy give primary attention to organizational objectives. The intermediate levels are essentially concerned with the means that will be necessary. A great deal of emphasis is given to the solution of specific production, marketing, personnel, and purchasing problems. The planning problems at intermediate levels are much more structured than the problems handled by top management. They are generally susceptible to solution by the techniques of the scientific approach.

The determination of objectives always involves some consideration of the plans that are available to achieve them. But plans should not be permitted to dominate the situation. The failure of top management to give adequate attention to objectives can have the effect of "delegating" the problem to lower levels. Objectives will then be operationally defined by those primarily concerned with techniques. The values of a democratic society are closely related to the objectives of the organizations within its domain. The question of objectives should not become a mere by-product of a technological process. Executives should give careful consideration to the problem of objectives. They should play a positive part in making the

---

[8] An operational definition gives to an otherwise subjective concept objective qualities by defining it as a set of operations. For example, time may be defined operationally by changes in the hands of a clock, the life-span of man, or the distance from A to B. A light and delicately flavored cake is defined operationally by the recipe. The recipe indicates the ingredients, the measurements, and the activities that will be necessary to produce the cake. An excellent discussion of the operational concept is found in: P. W. Bridgman, *The Logic of Modern Physics* (New York: The Macmillan Company, 1927), pp. 1–32.

choices that will determine the future of the organization and, through it, the future of society. They should not relegate this responsibility to those who cannot resolve the matter on other than technological grounds.

The Sales Forecast

Organizations frequently define their objectives in the form of a sales forecast. Such a forecast may be defined as a quantitative projection of objectives over some period of time. It is generally expressed in both product unit and dollar value to meet the needs of over-all sales, production, and financial planning. The data may be differentiated by time period (month, quarter, year), geographical area (state, district, foreign), type of customer (industrial, ultimate consumer), and mode of distribution (wholesale, retail). Separate sales forecasts are sometimes prepared for major operating units, such as product divisions, manufacturing plants, and sales territories.

Sales forecasting and planning should be viewed as mutually dependent functions. On the one hand, the sales forecast is an important basis for planning the company program, and, at the same time, the plans being developed have a bearing on sales potential. A sales forecast involves far more than an appraisal of conditions in the product markets. It also reflects the manner in which other environmental factors, such as resource markets and governmental policies, may influence sales objectives and reflects the limitations that evolve from the productive capabilities of the organization. The problem is to make a sales forecast that yields some optimum relative to opportunities and restrictions imposed by the environment and the organization. The solution involves a consideration of many interrelated alternatives. One executive has described the procedure used in his company to determine the sales forecast.

We look at the first estimates to see if the predicted results are what we want. If they're O.K., fine; we let them go through. But maybe the estimates show that we won't have the necessary funds available, or that the forecaster has figured to sell more of a certain item than we can get the material to produce. Too, the projected profit may be unsatisfactory. In such cases, we go to work to juggle things around, as best we can, to get a set of estimates that we want. Sometimes we can decide to put on a new promotion, which would raise the forecasts, but other times nothing we can do would seem to improve the situation, and we have to let them go through.[9]

[9] Interviewed and quoted by C. M. Crawford, *Sales Forecasting Methods of Selected Firms* (Urbana, Ill.: Bureau of Economic and Business Research, College of Commerce and Business Administration, University of Illinois, 1955), pp. 38–39.

Subsidiary Objectives: Internal Forecasts and Estimates

A distinction is generally made in the literature between external and internal forecasts. External forecasts are concerned with economic, political, social, and other environmental conditions that must be taken into consideration in planning the company program. Such external conditions as product demand, the supply of labor, and raw material prices may significantly influence planning. Internal forecasts are more directly concerned with conditions within an organization. Some internal forecasts, such as the sales forecast, involve a blending of many external and internal factors. Internal conditions, such as the capacity of plant and office facilities and the productivity of personnel, are as important in projecting sales as external economic and market conditions.

The sales forecast is both the most widely used and the most important internal forecast. It becomes the "official" objective of the organization after approval by duly constituted authority and becomes a basis for other internal forecasts and estimates from which subsidiary objectives may be derived. For example, production schedules can frequently be directly developed from the approved sales forecast.[10] Production schedules can in turn be used to make inventory and purchasing plans, to estimate personnel requirements, to plan additional production facilities, and to determine financial requirements. Internal forecasts and estimates are generally prepared by functional specialists in production planning, engineering, industrial relations, accounting and finance, market research, and purchasing. They become the "official" objective of the departmental unit after they are approved by the department head. The approved forecasts at higher hierarchical levels provide information and limitations for the forecasts and estimates made at lower levels. For example, the production department must plan its program in terms of explicit and implicit conditions set forth in the "official" company sales forecast.

Budgetary Planning Systems

Budgets express organizational and departmental objectives in financial and nonfinancial quantities. They anticipate operating results over some future period or periods of time and provide a basis for measuring performance as plans are translated into accomplishments. A diversity of budgeting practices is found in different companies. Some companies have a comprehensive budgeting system that incorporates every aspect of opera-

---

[10] Companies that do not produce standardized products generally build up production schedules as customers' orders are received.

tions and finance into budgets. Other companies limit budgeting to certain phases of their activities, such as sales and production. Still others do not prepare formal budgets but have developed informal procedures that vaguely approach a budget system. It is not possible to plan a company program without some consideration of quantitative factors. The production department does not plan its program without some idea about the plans of the sales department. Purchasing does not go on a buying spree without at least some knowledge of production schedules. The difference between informal and formal budgeting is the degree to which budgetary procedures are systematized and integrated into the planning process.

Although there are variations in terminology and budget practices, the basic budgeting process is illustrated by the schematic presentation in Figure 17-1. The nature of the budgeting process and its relationship to planning and control will be given comprehensive consideration in Chapter 20.

Although budgeting is not necessarily the *sine qua non* of good planning, a budgeting program may facilitate planning and other aspects of decision making in a number of ways. Budgeting gives emphasis to the importance of planning and frequently leads to a more systematic approach to planning problems. It tends to promote the use of scientific methods in solving forecasting and other measurement problems. It forces executives to establish clear-cut objectives and to coordinate their objectives with those of other departments. It increases participation in the planning process and expedites the flow of information within the management hierarchy. It sets forth objective standards that can be used to evaluate the efficiency of managerial and operating personnel. However, budgeting should be viewed as a facilitating technique rather than a substitute for good planning. It is generally a consequence rather than a prerequisite for effective managerial action. An effective budgetary program is not possible without a sound organizational structure with clearly defined responsibilities, a systematic approach to the solution of planning problems, adequate external forecasts of product and resource market conditions, internal cost records that can be used for estimating future costs, and a cooperative attitude on the part of managerial and other personnel.

Mechanical Drawings as Planning Devices

Organizational and departmental objectives are often indicated by mechanical drawings of products and their component parts. An assembly drawing shows the complete product with all its parts in proper relationship. Subassembly drawings are concerned with particular groups of parts that make up the product. Detail drawings show each part individually and

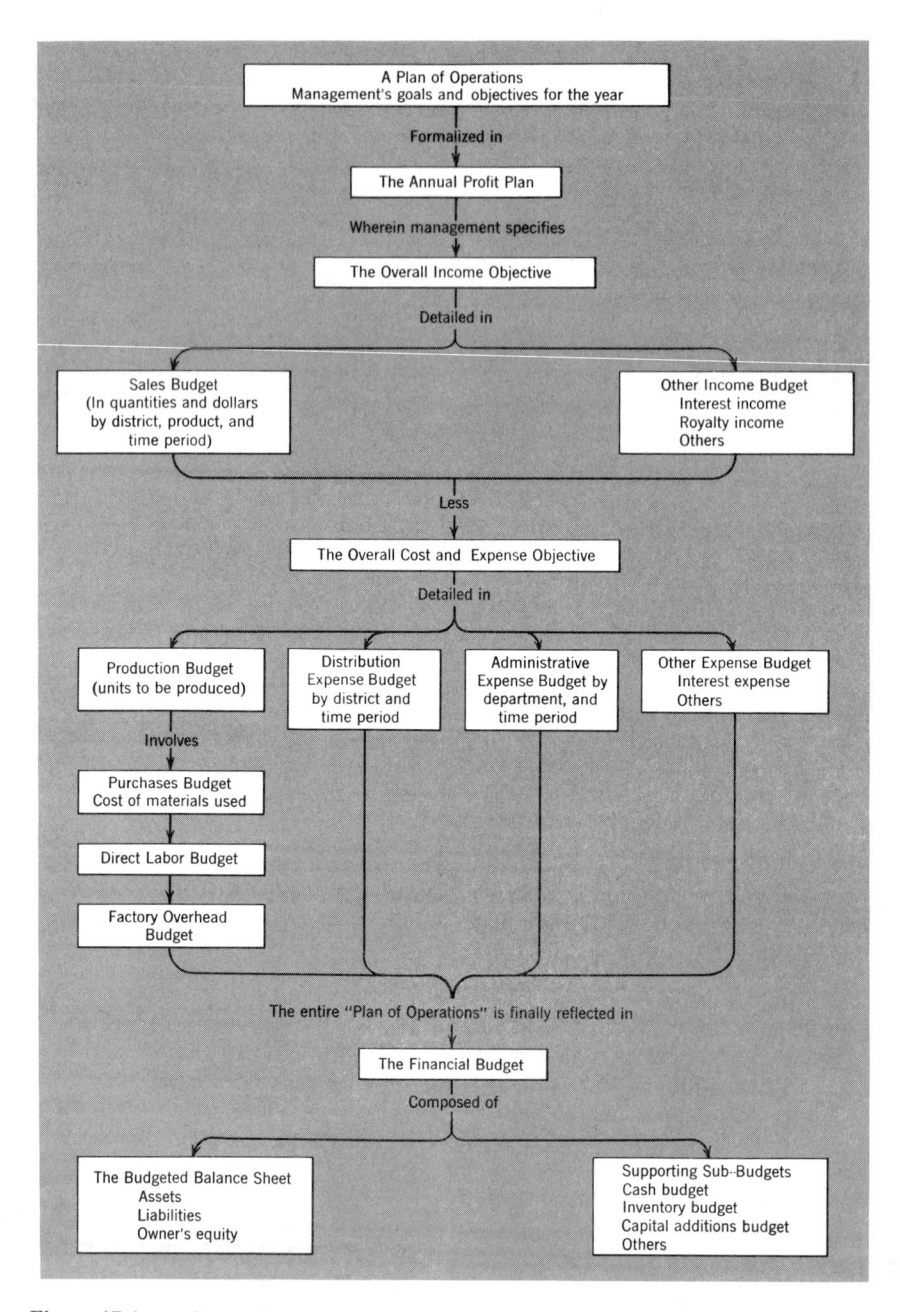

Figure 17-1. A chart of the development and composition of the annual profit plan. Glenn A. Welsch, *Budgeting: Profit Planning and Control,* 2nd ed. Copyright 1964 by Prentice-Hall, Inc., Englewood Cliffs, N. J. By permission.

indicate dimensions, material specifications, and other information. Much of the planning in manufacturing companies is based on the specifications provided by mechanical drawings. Departmental responsibilities are generally assigned on the basis of assembly, subassembly, and parts drawings. These drawings, together with data about the quantities to be produced, provide the basic information required for planning the production process. Nonmanufacturing departments may also formulate plans from mechanical drawings. The tooling department uses them to plan the tooling that will be required in manufacturing. The purchasing department can obtain information about the raw materials and parts that will have to be purchased from the "bill of materials" shown in the drawings. Mechanical and design specifications can also be used to plan aspects of the marketing program.

Analogue Models: The Gantt Chart and PERT

A highly useful planning technique is to build an analogue model of the activities that will be necessary to achieve an objective. This kind of model can be used to develop and improve plans before and during actual operations and can perform important control functions. The famous Gantt Chart plots activities and time along a horizontal scale. Planned activities can be compared with actual performance as the work progresses. Recently developed planning instruments utilize networks to show sequences of activities and the time that will probably be required to achieve planned objectives. A good example is the Program Evaluation and Review Technique (PERT) which was developed in 1958 to plan the Polaris Weapons System. PERT and related planning instruments have played an important part in United States military and space programs. Comprehensive consideration will be given to the Gantt Chart and PERT in Chapter 20.

Procedures and Methods

Managerial and operating personnel are sometimes assigned objectives with discretion as to the manner in which they will be achieved. On the other hand, objectives may carry with them explicit instructions about the procedures and methods to be followed. Procedures outline the manner in which managerial or operating activities are linked together into an integrated system of activities; methods are concerned with the way in which particular operations are to be performed. Executives at top levels of the management hierarchy are mainly concerned with objectives and only vaguely concerned with the problem of means. More and more attention is given to procedures and methods as planning proceeds from higher to lower levels. The ultimate consequence of the planning process is an elaborate network of procedures or interrelationships of operations. Some procedures involve only the operations that are necessary to achieve the objectives of particular departmental units. Others cut across departmental lines and relate the activities of one department to that of other departments. The whole system of procedures forms chains of human activity which are directly and indirectly concerned with the achievement of departmental and organizational objectives.

Standards or Norms

Plans set forth standards or norms to guide the behavior of managerial and nonmanagerial personnel. The profit norm is the basic planning criterion in business and industrial organizations. The planning process translates the profit norm into a variety of subsidiary standards. Some standards, such as profit and cost standards, are highly abstract with many implicit assumptions about appropriate behavior. Other standards, such as purchase specifications, quality standards, procedures and methods, and wage incentive standards, are more explicit behaviorial directives. An important problem is to develop standards that are effective from a communication point of view. They should provide sufficient information and accurately communicate the intentions of the planner. Information is transmitted in many different kinds of languages, such as written and spoken English, mathematics, accounting, and mechanical drawings. Some of these languages cannot be understood without extensive specialized knowledge. Furthermore, languages are not always absolutely consistent in what they communicate; that is, they do not always have fixed meanings. A comprehensive treatment of the importance of communication in planning and executing the company program is found in Part V.

Policies and the Planning Process

Policies represent the totality of standards or norms that govern the conduct of people in an organization. Some of them can be attributed directly to past planning activities. The norms set forth in a plan are organizational policies until they are implicitly or explicitly revoked. Other policies have a more nebulous origin and seem simply to exist. They evolve informally and become policies through implied acceptance by superiors, attaining "official" standing by the failure of executives to make a decision stipulating a different behavioral pattern. However, it cannot be assumed that executives are always aware of the policies they create by default. Indeed, insubordination may become company policy through a lack of information. Policies may be company wide in scope or have only limited applicability. Some policies are in effect over a long period of time and establish routine and habitual modes of behavior. Others are modified frequently in response to environmental and organizational forces. Policies may be set forth in such written instruments as corporation charters, organization manuals, annual reports, budgets, employee handbooks, and memoranda. They may also be expressed orally in training courses, committee meetings, and orders. Many policies are communicated informally or inferred from the behavior of others.

The policies that exist at lower levels evolve within a framework of broader policies determined at higher levels. However, the policies of one departmental unit may differ significantly from those of another. Differences in functional responsibilities provide one explanation. Although every worker in the production department may be required to wear safety glasses, such a policy would not be pertinent in the personnel or purchasing department. Policy variations also result from differences in interpretation and application. The personal qualities of executives cannot be eliminated from the problem, and overall company policies may be given different meanings by various departmental executives. As Professor E. Wight Bakke has written about a large telephone company: "A person moving from one organization, department, exchange, or work group to another will have to learn the emphases and definitions characterizing the general behavior traits rewarded and penalized in the groups to which he comes." [11]

Some policies continue to exist formally even though they have long been repudiated or modified by actual practice. The management of one company decided to give employees a ten-minute coffee break in the morning and afternoon. Employees gradually extended the time to fifteen minutes and management did nothing about it. What is company policy? The original order, which has not been formally revoked, sets forth a ten-minute limit. But, since there are no penalities for anyone who takes a fifteen-minute coffee break, a new policy would seem to have been established by implication. A similar situation was found during the Bank Wiring Observation Room Study at the Hawthorne plant during the 1930's. The output standard prepared by company engineers stipulated an output of 7312 units per day. The workers established a significantly lower informal output norm. The foreman thought that the workers' norm represented a satisfactory day's work. Higher management did not attempt to increase output even though there was evidence that the workers could have produced a larger amount. Thus, informally derived or modified behavioral norms may become company policy through implied managerial acceptance.

[11] E. Wight Bakke, *Bonds of Organization* (New York: Harper & Brothers Publishers, 1950), p. 112.

Considerable uncertainty may prevail about the nature of policy with respect to certain matters. Some superiors vacillate in the manner in which they apply norms. A norm may have different meanings at different times and with respect to different persons. A formally constituted norm may be ignored over a period of time and then suddenly become the basis for penalties. The enforcement of norms in an organization has a parallel in law enforcement in the general society. The law is not and cannot be enforced in any absolute sense. The number of drivers who exceed the speed limit is far in excess of the number of traffic tickets issued by police departments. A select few who are privileged to appear before the judge on a speeding charge serve to modify the behavior of drivers generally. However, the manner in which particular individuals and groups respond to the example of enforcement may vary somewhat or significantly. Thus, the policies of an organization or a departmental unit cannot be given an absolute definition. A great deal of subjective inference is generally involved in spite of the emphasis given to the scientific method.

The standards or norms that evolve from the planning process may result in some change of company policies. The degree of change depends upon the extent to which the norms set forth in the new program differ from those that now exist. Many policies remain in effect over a long period of time in spite of periodic planned changes. The specific changes that occur from one year to the next may not be noticed except by an alert observer. On the other hand, environmental or organizational forces can cause a major shift in some company policies. A new chief executive may radically depart from his predecessor's way of doing things; a court decision on "fair trade legislation" may prompt a major change in company price policies; a serious inflation or deflation may have an important impact upon inventory and purchase policies.

SELECTED REFERENCES

Marcus Alexis and Charles Z. Wilson, *Organizational Decision Making.* Englewood Cliffs, N.J.: Prentice-Hall, Inc., 1967.

Stafford Beer, *Decision and Control.* New York: John Wiley and Sons, Inc., 1966.

Ralph C. Davis, *The Fundamentals of Top Management,* Chaps. 3 and 4. New York: Harper & Brothers, 1951.

John E. Fleming, "Study of a Business Decision," *California Management Review,* Vol. 9, No. 2, pp. 51–56 (Winter 1966).

Frederick R. Kappel, *Vitality in a Business Enterprise.* New York: McGraw-Hill Book Company, Inc., 1960.

Preston P. LeBrenton and Dale A. Henning, *Planning Theory,* Parts 1 and 2. Englewood Cliffs, N.J.: Prentice-Hall, Inc., 1961.

R. Duncan Luce and Howard Raiffa, *Games and Decisions.* New York: John Wiley and Sons, Inc., 1957.

Ernest C. Miller, *Objectives and Standards of Performance in Marketing Management,* AMA Research Study, No. 85. New York: American Management Association, 1967.

Ernest C. Miller, *Objectives and Standards: An Approach to Planning and Control.* AMA Research Study, No. 74. New York: American Management Association, 1966.

Ernest C. Miller, *Objectives and Standards of Performance in Production Management,* AMA Research Study, No. 84. New York: American Management Association, 1967.

Philip Selznick, *Leadership in Administration.* Evanston, Ill.: Row, Peterson and Company, 1957.

E. Kirby Warren, *Long-Range Planning: The Executive Viewpoint.* Englewood Cliffs, N.J.: Prentice-Hall, Inc., 1966.

H. Edward Wrapp, "Organization for Long-Range Planning," *Harvard Business Review,* Vol. 35, No. 1, pp. 37–47 (January–February 1957).

PART V

COMMUNICATION AND CONTROL

chapter 18

INFORMATION AND COMMUNICATION

Effective planning cannot occur without information about alternative strategies and their consequences. The planner requires information about such environmental forces as product and resource markets, governmental policies, and technological innovation. Also important is information about such internal matters as plant capacity, inventories, labor productivity, and financial resources. The nature of the channels through which information flows was considered in Chapter 13. Other informational problems, such as forecasting and measurement, were considered in Part IV. Part V gives further attention to the nature of information and particular attention to information transfer or communication. Communication is an important aspect of the managerial process for several reasons. One is that the organized planning process requires extensive communication among executives and other personnel. Another is that effective communication is important in executing a planned program. Still another is that information about subordinate performance is necessary to determine whether planned goals are achieved.

Information, Communication, and Control

The subject of communication has been given a great deal of attention in recent years by mathematicians, physicists, electrical engineers, physiologists, and social scientists. The insights that were gained led to the development of a field of study commonly referred to by the terms "information theory" and "cybernetics." Norbert Wiener and Claude E. Shannon formally launched "the new science" in 1948 with separate publications on the theory of information and communication.[1] Wiener viewed information and communication as primary elements in man's efforts to control himself and his environment. He was concerned with the development of techniques that have general applicability in solving communication problems. His fundamental theory is helpful in understanding communication difficulties in the central nervous system, computing machines, organizations, and society. Shannon dealt with the problem of information and communication from the perspective of electronic communication systems. He was concerned with such problems as increasing the information potential of communication channels, more efficient encoding and decoding, and the elimination of channel noise. However, in spite of differences in perspective, the theories of Wiener and Shannon are closely related conceptually and approach the communication problem with similar analytical techniques.[2] Although a substantial part of the bridge between theory and practice must yet be built, information theory has provided a logical point of departure for the study of empirical problems in management and other areas of academic endeavor. Many of the ideas in this and the next chapter can be traced directly or indirectly to the contributions of Wiener and Shannon.

The Communication Problem

The communication problem is to transmit meaning from one person (or persons) to another person (or persons). Figure 18-1 indicates the nature of the problem and potential difficulties. If A seeks to communicate with B, he must first translate or code his perceptions into a message composed from a mutually understood language. The message is then

---

[1] Norbert Wiener, *Cybernetics: Control and Communication in the Animal and the Machine* (New York: John Wiley & Sons, Inc., 1948). Shannon's theory, originally published by the *Bell System Technical Journal* in 1948, has been reprinted in: Claude E. Shannon and Warren Weaver, *The Mathematical Theory of Communication* (Urbana: The University of Illinois Press, 1949).

[2] Both theories are founded on the idea that information is characterized by entropy similar to that found in the physical sciences. As used in information theory, entropy may be roughly defined as the tendency for a system to become more and more disorganized over a period of time. The concept of entropy is used to measure the efficiency with which given quantities of symbols, such as the English language or a cryptographic code, can be used to construct and transmit particular messages. The greater the entropy, the greater the information potential of a language system. This idea gives emphasis to the statistical character of information and the importance of probability in constructing message systems.

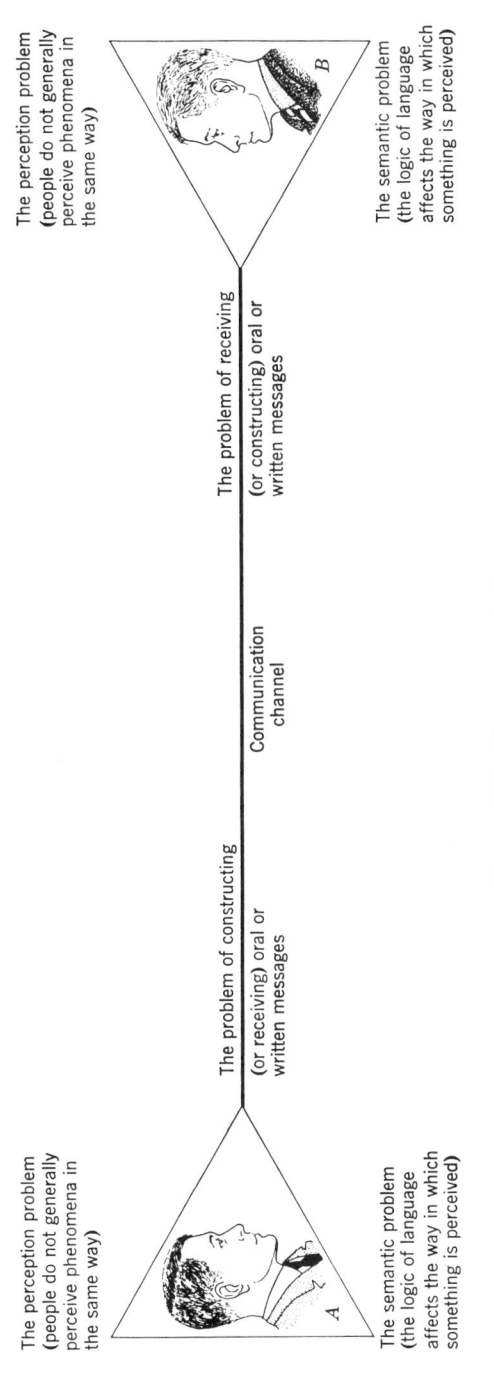

Figure 18-1. The communication process.

transmitted through a channel to B, who decodes the sounds or symbols into perceptions of his own.

Perceptions, language, and messages are related in a triangle because they are not as separable as they sometimes seem to be. Man perceives much of the universe in terms of learned symbols and substitutes a symbolic world for the real one; he has also created a symbolic world which does not exist in reality. Languages have evolved from this process of symbol formation and have influenced man's perception of the world around him. Ernst Cassirer has expressed the relationship between human evolution and symbolism in the following words.

> Man has, as it were, discovered a new method of adapting himself to his environment. Between the receptor system and the effector system, which are to be found in all animal species, we find in man a third link which we may describe as the *symbolic system*. This new acquisition transforms the whole of human life. As compared with the other animals man lives not merely in a broader reality; he lives, so to speak, in a new *dimension* of reality. . . . No longer in a merely physical universe, man lives in a symbolic universe. Language, myth, art, and religion are parts of this universe.[3]

The effectiveness of communication between A and B (Figure 18-1) is affected by a number of factors. One is that the two may not have the same perception about the "same" reality, even when they are able to perceive it directly. Another is that they may not have the same understanding of the language from which the message is formulated. Still another is that the message may not be well constructed or well received. Speaking and writing inadequacies and deficiencies in listening and reading are important barriers to communication. An additional factor is that channel "noise" can distort the message during the transmission phase.

Human communication often involves the use of electronic, mechanical, and other intermediate facilities. Telephones, teletype machines, the telegraph, closed circuit television, pneumatic tubes, typewriters, and the postal service may be used to solve spatial and other problems. Clerical and technical personnel who operate communication equipment and process information are also important links in the system. For example, an executive initiates a message by dictation to a secretary, who transcribes shorthand into typewritten symbols, thereby making up a memorandum which is delivered to another office by a company messenger, and so on. The processing, handling, and transporting of messages may involve a long sequence of machine and human operations.

---

[3] Ernst Cassirer, *An Essay on Man* (New Haven: Yale University Press, 1944), pp. 24–25.

The Perception Problem

Perception may be roughly defined as the awareness that a living thing has of its environment. Human perception cannnot be adequately explained in terms of purely sensory impressions. It involves integration, organization, selection, and interpretation of purely sensory phenomena. There are generally more elements in an environment than can be given attention at any one time. People tend to select the elements that are essential to their needs and to "recode" the diversity of elements into more abstract forms.[4] The learning process plays an important part in perception. People perceive particular learned patterns and not other possible patterns. Indeed, expectations derived from past perceptual experiences can cause people to insert "phenomena" that are not present in the thing being perceived. Perception is also influenced by motives. People sometimes fail to see things that conflict with preconceived ideas or things that might disturb them.

The primary purpose of this discussion is to show how *differences* in perception can affect communication. Two persons always form slightly or significantly different perceptions of the same situation. Perception may also be viewed as a group phenomenon. Persons in the same family, church, political party, fraternity, or school tend to have similar perceptions about many matters. But there are often large perceptual differences between persons in different groups. Some of the factors that lead to different perceptions between individuals and groups can be categorized as follows.

SENSORY FACTORS. People are not the same from a physiological point of view; there are significant variations in the ability to see, hear, taste, smell, and feel. A blind or a deaf person, to use an extreme example, has a different perception of reality than someone with sight or hearing.

AGE. Small children live in a different world than their parents because they have not had as much education or experience. There is also the physical fact that houses, tables and chairs, and adults themselves are much larger for children than adults. The world of the typical teenager may differ in a marked degree from that of his parents. Parents are frequently "old-fashioned," "behind the times," and they "just don't understand." The attitudes of grandparents generally differ in some degree from those of younger age groups.

SEX. The perceptions of men and women may differ for physiological

---

[4] Jerome S. Bruner, "Social Psychology and Perception," in Eleanor E. Maccoby, Theodore M. Newcomb, and Eugene L. Hartley, *Readings in Social Psychology,* 3rd ed. (New York: Holt, Rinehart and Winston, Inc., 1958), pp. 86-88.

and psychological reasons. Also important is that they learn to respond in terms of the roles prescribed for them by the culture.

EDUCATIONAL LEVELS. The attitude that people have on large number of subjects tends to vary with their level of educational achievement. College graduates often respond differently in public opinion polls on a wide range of subjects than people with only a high school diploma or a grammar school certificate.

ECONOMIC LEVEL. People from different economic levels frequently have diverse views on such matters as government intervention, taxation, social security, and education.

REGIONAL DIFFERENCES. The opinion that people have on many matters is influenced by differences between geographical areas. Persons in the Deep South often differ with Northerners in interracial relations. People from rural regions do not always agree with those who live in large metropolitan areas. Californians tend to have a greater interest in the Far East than the citizens of Illinois or New York.

RELIGIOUS AND OTHER LOYALTIES. Churches, political parties, labor unions, professional associations, and fraternal organizations generally make for uniformities in perception within the group and differences between groups. For example, Republicans normally prefer less government intervention than do Democrats. Labor union members often have a different image of business leaders than nonunion people. Catholics and Protestants differ on such matters as divorce and birth control.

ORGANIZATIONAL INTERESTS. Differences in organizational and departmental interests can cause people to view the same problem differently. Army, Navy, and Air Force officers often have three perceptions of the same military situation. Production executives do not always agree with sales executives on the reasons for reduced revenues. Subordinates sometimes have a significantly different conception of a situation than their superiors. Line and staff personnel frequently make conflicting conclusions about a problem.

PERSONALITY FACTORS. People generally have particular personal experiences which influence the manner in which they will respond to problems. The son of a tyrannical father, for example, may view "the boss" in a different light than other people.

Perceptions can be transmitted from one person to another through oral or written messages. The act of translating perceptions into a message and deriving perceptions from that message is an important aspect of the communication process. Effective communication cannot occur if the same message conveys different perceptions to different people. The perceptions that result from a message can be partly attributed to the factors considered above. But perceptions are also affected by the language from which the message is formulated. Languages can cause distortions in reality far beyond those that evolve from direct sensory contact. They may also construct a "reality" that has little content apart from the language itself.

Languages and Message Construction

Language may be defined as any systematic body of signs, symbols, or signals that can be used to transmit meaning from one person to another. English, French, German, Russian, Latin, Morse code, mathematics, statistics, accounting, mechanical drawings, standard weights and measures, and Indian signs are some of the languages that may be used for communication purposes. Some languages, such as English and French, are the product of a long period of cultural development. Their origin is a matter of speculation and their word content is to a great extent determined by "the accidents" of social usage and acceptance. Words are added and subtracted, and the dictionary meaning of words changes with the passage of time. The process of language creation and change is hardly noticeable at any point of time, but the long run may record significant modifications in content, form, and meaning. Languages may also be deliberately designed for some specific purpose. The artificial languages created to facilitate international communication and the cryptographic codes used by the military are examples of such languages. The history of mathematics has been characterized by innovations to deal with particular problems that could not be solved by existing techniques. For example, Sir Isaac Newton developed the differential calculus to facilitate the study of gravitation and motion. Many statistical and accounting techniques evolved from the problem of dealing with particular physical, biological, social, and organizational problems.

Communication generally involves the use of a social sign language which may convey as much or more meaning than the regular message content. Oral messages are generally accompanied by facial expressions, such as a frown or a smile, which represent additions to the message. The volume and pitch of speech and gestures may also play an important role. In written communication, additional information may be conveyed in various ways. A memorandum enclosed in a sealed envelope is often assumed to be more important than one that is not. A mechanically reproduced signature rather than a personally written signature has informational significance. Information may also be added by the fact that a message is sent by telegraph rather than third-class mail.

A message constructed from a language rather than the language itself performs the actual communication function. The best possible message must be selected from the totality of messages that could be used in a given situation. Most of the ordinary languages afford a considerable amount of choice in this respect. For example, the English language offers a large variety of words and word combinations that can be used to express essentially the same thing. There are often a number of equally good messages, but some messages are clearly better than others in particular communication situations. The achievement of clarity of meaning is partly a matter of proper word usage and grammatical construction. But this approach to communication and meaning is inadequate and incomplete. The relationship between language and the phenomenon it represents is an important aspect of the problem of meaning. The area of study that deals with this subject is generally referred to as "semantics" or "general semantics."

The Semantic Problem

Semantics may be approached from a number of different perspectives. Some people view semantics as a branch of logic which seeks to build an abstract theory on the relationship between symbols and what they mean.[5] Another approach conceives it as a branch of linguistic science, which is a systematic study of languages.[6] Still another approach is that of general semantics, which is concerned with the impact of language on many aspects of human life.[7] General semantics points to some of the difficulties that can arise from an improper use of language. The following discussion highlights some of the basic concepts that have been developed by this branch of semantics.

The Problem of Structure

A fundamental precept of semantics is that the structure of a language should be similar to the structure of the empirical world. Alfred Korzybski, a pioneer in the field of semantics, uses an analogy between language and

---

[5] For example: Rudolf Carnap, *Introduction to Semantics* (Cambridge: Harvard University Press, 1946).

[6] For example: Edward Sapir, *Language* (New York: Harcourt, Brace & Co., Inc., 1921); Benjamin Lee Whorf, *Language, Thought, and Reality*, J. B. Carroll, ed. (New York: John Wiley and Sons, Inc., 1956).

[7] Alfred Korzybski, *Science and Sanity: An Introduction to Non-Aristotelian Systems and General Semantics*, 4th ed. (Lakeville, Conn.: The Institute of General Semantics, 1958); C. K. Ogden and I. A. Richards, *The Meaning of Meaning*, rev. ed. (New York: Harcourt, Brace & Co., Inc., 1956); Irving J. Lee, *Language Habits in Human Affairs* (New York: Harper & Brothers Publishers, 1941); Wendell Johnson, *People in Quandaries* (New York: Harper & Brothers Publishers, 1946).

the map of a territory to present his idea. He begins with the proposition that a map is *not* the territory it represents, and that, in a similar sense, words are *not* the things they represent. If this proposition is true, and Korzybski asserts that it must be, then, in his words:

. . . the only possible link between the objective world and the linguistic world is found in *structure, and structure alone*. The only usefulness of a map or a language depends on the *similarity of structure* between the empirical world and the map-languages. If the structure is not similar, then the traveler or speaker is led astray, which, in serious human life-problems, must become always eminently harmful. If the structures *are similar,* then the empirical world becomes "rational" to a potentially rational being. . . .[8]

The validity of this statement is immediately evident to someone who has used a map to guide his travels in a strange territory. As long as the route and places indicated on the map correspond to the actual route and places, the traveler will have little difficulty in reaching his destination. But a structural difference between the map and the actual territory may cause a great deal of difficulty. Maps *A* and *B* in Figure 18-2 illustrate this idea. A New Yorker who uses map *B* to make a trip to Chicago will find himself in San Francisco. In a like manner, a failure of language structure to correspond to the structure of reality may cause serious difficulties. Korzybski has summarized the nature of the problem in these words.

Our only possible procedure in advancing our knowledge is to match our verbal structures, often called theories, with empirical structures, and see if our verbal predictions are fulfilled empirically or not, thus indicating that the two structures are either similar or dissimilar.[9]

The Imprint of the Past

Many languages have evolved over a long period of human development, and many of the theories formulated in the past about the nature of reality do not fit reality as man sees it today. But past theories have remained as an integral part of the language used in thinking and communicating. The structure of language has been molded in great part by the logic of Aristotle, the geometry of Euclid, and the laws of Newton. A failure to recognize this fact can lead to a serious distortion of reality. Einstein found that Aristotelian logic, Euclidian geometry, and Newtonian absolutes could not be used to describe some of his conceptions of reality. He was forced to develop a different kind of language to deal with a universe characterized by probability and relativity. The point is not that the languages that have

---

[8] Korzybski, *op. cit.,* p. 61. (Permission of Korzybski Estate.)
[9] *Ibid.,* p. 63. (Permission of Korzybski Estate.)

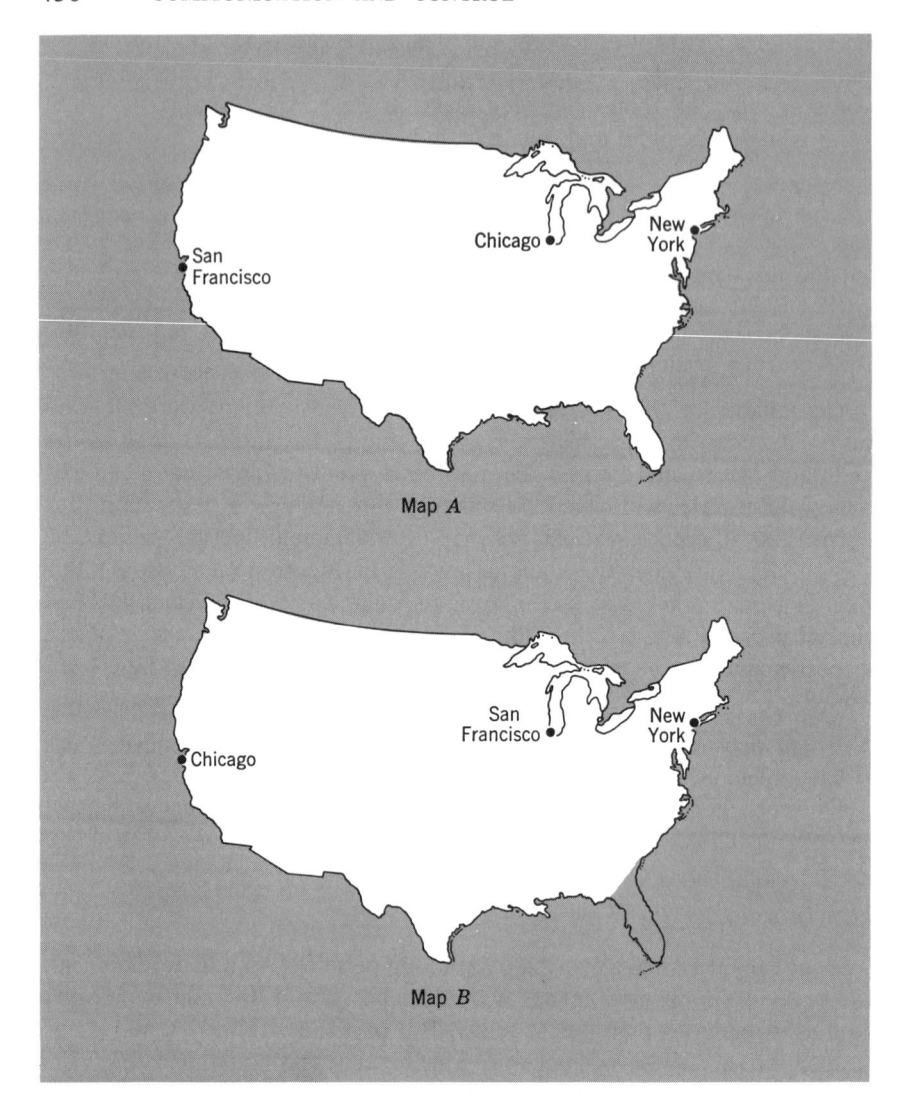

Figure 18-2. Two maps of a territory.

evolved from the past should be abandoned but that their limitations and the manner in which they may distort reality should be understood. Languages and words can also be deliberately used to create a reality that does not exist. People often respond to words without giving consideration to the manner in which they may or may not fit reality. The success of the propagandist can be attributed to such a lack of discrimination.

Aristotelian Logic

The following rules of logic developed by Aristotle have greatly influenced the structure of many languages. The first is the *law of identity,* or *A* is *A*; the second is the *law of the excluded middle,* or a thing is either *A* or not—*A;* and the third is the *law of noncontradiction* or something cannot be both *A* and not—*A*. These "laws" have significantly influenced modes of speaking and writing. One cannot assert that Aristotle's rules of logic are wrong as long as they are viewed as a pure system. They are as correct as the arithmetic rule that 1 plus 1 equal 2, or 3 minus 1 equal 2. But, *A* is *A* or 1 plus 1 equal 2 is not necessarily more correct than an arbitrary definition that *A* is *B* or 1 plus 1 equal 3. The rules of logic can cause difficulties when they are applied to empirical data. The fact that the structure of the English language is characterized by Aristotelian logic can create highly distorted perceptions of reality. The *law of identity,* for example, does not take into account the process of change that occurs through time. A man today is not the same man he was yesterday or five years ago. A flower garden changes in a marked degree as the growing season progresses. An iceberg slowly changes to water and water into icebergs. Man eats bird, bird eats worm, and worms eat both man and bird. Yet people often speak as though something were absolutely true or the same for all time. The *law of the excluded middle* leads into such two-valued conclusions as true or false, good or bad, rich or poor, conservative or liberal, pro-union or anti-union, and intelligent or stupid. This mode of speaking neglects the important in-between ground that often explains the actual state of affairs. The *law of noncontradiction* adds another link to the chain by forging such conclusions as someone cannot be both conservative and liberal, rich and poor, intelligent and stupid, etc. Actually a person may be conservative in some respects, liberal in others, and a blending of the two in still others.

The Problem of Abstraction

A map represents only a small part of the reality that a traveler will perceive in his travels. The location of trees, ruts in the roadway, a large rock by the side of the road, and many other features of the terrain will not be noted on a map. A complete map would be exactly like the territory and would have to contain a picture of the map itself. Languages and words likewise present a highly incomplete picture of the reality captured by man's sensory organs. A basic proposition of semantics is that a definite number of words must represent an infinite number of things. There are not enough words to adequately describe the totality of facts and situations that make up human experience. Thus, the use of language always involves some degree of partial representation or abstraction. Abstraction means that some of the details about a thing or an event are left out of the word picture.

A high order abstraction leaves out more details than a low order abstraction. The statement "morale is good in our factory" represents a higher order of abstraction than a well-written twenty-page report detailing worker behavior. Much of what we say and write involves the process of abstracting or making statements about statements about statements, etc. The difficulty is that different people may come to different conclusions as they move from lower to higher order abstractions. Thus, one person who reads a detailed report on the behavior of factory workers may conclude "morale is good" and another that "morale is bad." The details that people leave out in making higher order abstractions and the inferences that they make may differ from person to person. Some of the details that are left out may represent information that is vital to a proper understanding of a situation. Furthermore, some statements are highly subjective inferences that have little, if any, relationship to reality. As Wendell Johnson has written, people often create "verbal cocoons" that can lead to serious mental difficulties.[10] What do such words as "success" and "failure" really mean in terms of specific behavioral activities? A lack of adequate definition can result in the pursuit of goals that cannot be achieved in any sort of concrete way. Beating one's head against a verbal wall can have more serious consequences than contact with a real one. The process of abstracting can also cause serious communication difficulties. Thus, what does someone mean by such statements as "morale is good," "our workers hate the union," and "private enterprise is the only system"?

An Infinity of Meanings

The problem of meaning transcends the "meanings" indicated in the dictionary. Strictly speaking, a particular word or word combination has an infinite number of possible meanings. The perceptions that are formed in response to a word may change significantly over a period of time. The word "union" in 1969 does not portray the same thing it did in 1947 or in 1937. The words "Germany" and "Japan" generally create a different perception in 1969 than they did in 1944. The meaning of words also varies with the person using the word. Thus, the word "union" in 1969 may create different kinds of perceptions in different people. One person may think primarily in terms of racketeering union leaders who browbeat

[10] Johnson, *op. cit.*

workers; another may view unions as "guardian angels" who protect the interests of the working class. These variations in the inferences that people make seriously complicate the communication problem, so that two people engaged in a conversation sometimes fail to communicate even though the words they use have the same dictionary meanings. The response that is made to words may also vary with the social setting in which they are used. The words "hell" and "damn" generally have a different meaning when spoken by a preacher in the pulpit than when these same words are used by a putter who misses a putt.

Semantics and Executive Action

The executive should understand the manner in which language and its usage may influence human behavior. He should consciously use the insights gained from semantics to improve the effectiveness of communication. But, in spite of the semanticist's quest for greater sanity through language usage, there is still a wide gap between preachment and practice. Executives must contend with the "realities" of human behavior and cannot assume that every man lives by the rules of semantics. They would generally be ill-advised to forbid the "distortion of reality" through word manipulation. One reason is that such slogans as "Miss Shapely Torso buys Nogood cigarettes" and "Our toothpaste will make your teeth sparkle with sex appeal" sell more cigarettes and toothpaste than an elaborate array of scientific data. In spite of the emphasis given to a scientific approach to living, man lives and strives in a world of "unreality" created by words, partly because "reality" can be unbearable even for one who professes to be sane. The distortions created by words can have a constructive as well as a destructive consequence in human affairs. Propaganda can lead to the "Götterdämmerung" of a Hitler, but it can also lead to morality and profits.

Communication Centers: Their Nature and Functions

Communication channels, which were considered in Chapter 13, may be viewed from the vantage point of the persons and positions that form them. Each person and position is a communication center or the focus of an inflow and outflow of information. This section is concerned with the nature of such centers and the functions they perform in the communication process. Attention is also given to the importance of status instruments, the problem of planning adequate channel capacity, and the functions of specialized information processing systems.

Positions and Persons as Communication Centers

Informational and communication activities represent an aspect of the responsibilities that make up a position. Such activities are performed on an organized basis as are other activities necessary to achieve the organizational objective. Every position plays some part in an organized system of information processing and flow, with the nature of the position determining the quantities and kinds of information that have to be handled. Executive positions are particularly important elements in this system. Cooperative decision making requires a constant inflow of information and results in a corresponding information output. A large volume of information flow is necessary to integrate hierarchical decisional activities. A breakdown of communication at some executive position can affect a major portion of the organization.

An organized system of communication gives direction and continuity to the communication process. It impedes tendencies toward disorganization and gives order to what might otherwise become a purposeless "babble of tongues." It gives emphasis to the requirements of the organization apart from the persons who may hold a position. It mitigates the disruptive impact of changes in personnel. But it is people and not positions who form the vital links in the communication process. As Barnard has emphasized, the persons who occupy positions are the *means* through which communication takes place and "positions vacant are as defunct as dead nerve centers." [11] An executive position without an executive can be an important barrier to effective hierarchical communication. However, a position that is occupied by a number of persons, such as a committee or an executive with staff personnel, can function as a communication center during the absence of the primary occupant. A private secretary or other personnel can perform the routine informational functions of the position as though he were present.

Scalar and Functional Position

Position is an important determinant of the part that a person plays in the communication process. The functional and scalar relationship of a position to other positions is one consideration. A person whose activities cut across departmental lines tends to develop a broader range of contacts than someone who is exclusively concerned with the affairs of a single department. Personnel and maintenance work, for example, generally require

---

[11] Chester I. Barnard, *The Functions of the Executive* (Cambridge: Harvard University Press, 1951), pp. 217, 218.

frequent interaction with people in other departments. The position that a person occupies in the chain of command also influences communication patterns. Thus, vice-presidents communicate more frequently with the president than does a foreman or a worker on the production line. The physical mobility required in the performance of organizational duties is also important in this respect. A person whose work permits him to get out of his office and walk through other departmental areas has more communication opportunities than someone who sits in the office most of the day. As Keith Davis has noted from a study of one company, such persons can "walk through other departments without someone wondering whether they were 'not working,' to get away for coffee, and so on—all of which meant they heard more news from the other executives they talked with." [12]

In geographically dispersed organizations, travel between home office and branch offices and factories, or conversely, affords similar opportunities. At the same time, however, the location at which the work is done may isolate some persons from the main streams of communication flow. People in plants or offices a long distance from the home office generally have less information about organization affairs than those in installations located near headquarters. Working in a building away from the main area in which organizational activities are conducted also makes a difference.[13] The rotation of work on the basis of shifts also isolates some people from communication channels. Thus, foremen on the night shift have fewer opportunities to communicate with higher levels of management than those who work during the day.

Chain of Command Communication

An executive position differs from other positions in that it confers the right to transmit information as an order or a command. The expression "this is an order" gives an additional quality to the information that is transmitted. The differentiation of "chain of command" communication from other kinds of communication gives primacy to the objectives of the organization. It gives subordinates a basis for determining the manner in which they should respond to particular information. Subordinates are not required to obey orders from persons who do not occupy appropriate positions. For example, an informal group leader among factory workers may "give orders," but the fact that he does not hold an executive position reduces the effectiveness of his orders. The right to classify information as

[12] Keith Davis, "Management Communication and the Grapevine," *Harvard Business Review*, Vol. 31, No. 5, September–October 1953, p. 47.

[13] *Ibid.*, p. 48. E. Wight Bakke, *Bonds of Organization* (New York: Harper & Brothers Publishers, 1950), p. 95.

orders or commands increases the importance of the executive as a link in the communication system. Information can be so classified only if it passes through particular executive positions.

The Importance of Status Instruments

The instruments of status also facilitate communication within the organization and with outsiders. They are particularly important when the people who communicate are not personally acquainted. When a Mr. Smith receives a message from a nondescript Mr. Jones, many questions remain unanswered. Is the communication authentic? The authenticity of a letter of recommendation might be questioned if it did not contain a printed letterhead or the title of the person writing it. People who write their own fictitious letters of recommendation usually attempt to authenticate the letter by an assumed or real letterhead. Another problem concerns the reliability of the communication. For example, if Mr. Smith advises Mr. Jones that the design of the company's product ought to be changed, Mr. Jones might question Smith's qualifications to make such a recommendation. When Smith's title, "design engineer," is included in the communication, the recipient of the communication is told that Smith is probably qualified to make such a recommendation. The same idea applies to a communication from someone higher in scalar rank. The use of functional and scalar titles in organization also makes possible the wording of the communication in the language of the recipient. A communication to a research engineer is often expressed in a language that would completely baffle a foreman or a worker. The same communication must often differ considerably to make it intelligible to people at different scalar levels and with different functional duties. If only names were used, such necessary discrimination would be most difficult.

The status system facilitates communication in another way. In the words of Chester I. Barnard: "For very small organizations communication may effectively be addressed to persons, but for larger systems status becomes primary." [14] When the names of persons are used, a change in the person occupying a position would require a new message. If the communication reads Vice-president in charge of the Personnel Department rather than Mr. R. J. Smith of the Personnel Department, much confusion will be avoided when Mr. Smith is no longer the vice-president. The use of status designations in communication tends to create routine

[14] Chester I. Barnard, "Functions and Pathology of Status Systems in Formal Organizations," in William Foote Whyte (editor), *Industry and Society* (New York: McGraw-Hill Book Company, Inc., 1946), p. 66.

channels of communication that will not be disrupted with changes in personnel.

Importance of Personal Qualities

The personal qualities of the occupant may significantly alter the part that a position plays in the communication system. The fact that Smith rather than Jones holds a particular position always makes some degree of difference. A subordinate may be subjected to an avalanche of memoranda under Smith and hardly a trickle under Jones. The extent to which the telephone is used in communication may also vary from person to person. A similar statement can be made about the amount of oral communication that occurs. Socio-psychological factors are important determinants of the effectiveness of communication and the manner in which informational problems are handled. A gregarious person will generally create a more expansive pattern of personal contacts in performing his organizational duties. On the other hand, some people are communication isolates in that they receive and transmit information poorly, if at all.[15] Many specific factors may influence a particular situation. A newly hired executive, for example, does not immediately reach his full potential as a center of communication. A great deal of information will bypass him until others learn "what kind of a guy he is." Personal antagonism or friendship may greatly influence the manner in which people communicate with one another. The role a person may play apart from the position he occupies can be significant, for some people seem to attract information as honey does flies. They may become important communication centers even though their positions do not warrant such a status.

Planning Adequate Channel Capacity

The problem of adequate channel capacity is an important aspect of the organizing problem. Some of the relationships between organizational structure and communication were considered in the chapters in Part II. For example, too many levels in the management hierarchy can lead to informational delays and distortions. A high degree of centralization can unduly tax channel capacity and result in communication bottlenecks. Decentralization may eliminate some of these problems by reducing the volume of necessary information flow. Staff and committee organization can also be used to improve the dissemination of information within the management hierarchy. But, as has been emphasized before, executives

---

[15] Davis, *op. cit.*, p. 46.

should not ignore the importance of the channels of contact that are developed informally.

Informal communication channels frequently seem to have an infinite capacity for carrying information. Much of the information necessary for the proper performance of managerial and operating duties is derived informally. Although it may sound paradoxical, informal channels should be given explicit recognition in the organizing process. The organizer should take into consideration the manner in which his planning may affect existing informal channels. He should understand that the lack of a formal plan does not necessarily mean a lack of communication facilities. Thus, some companies have developed an effective "committee system" even though they have no formally established committees. Too many formal rules and procedures may impede rather than implement the development of effective communication channels. On the other hand, communication channels are sometimes established to overcome difficulties caused by informal communication. Rumors and gossip can spread a great deal of misinformation and create confusion within the ranks. Some organizations have planned more direct and faster formal channels to beat the grapevine and to counter false with correct information. For example, Westinghouse flashed the Bureau of Labor Statistics' latest cost-of-living data to more than 300 plants and offices in one hour.[16] Motorola, Inc., relayed information concerning a new executive appointment to all supervisors in Phoenix and Chicago, and within ninety minutes the news was disseminated throughout the entire organization. "We moved fast," said a company spokesman, "so the grapevine wouldn't have time to garble the facts." [17] Informal channels are essential elements in the communication system, but they may also cause communication difficulties. A great deal more knowledge about the nature and functions of informal communication is required for effective planning. The adverse consequences of the grapevine have been amply discussed, but too little attention has been given to the positive role that it can play.

Formal and informal communication channels are frequently used to disseminate purely personal information. Should management place some limitation on communication about personal matters during working hours? Such communication can obviously impede the efficient pursuit of organizational ends when carried to an extreme. Thus, some kind of action seems necessary if sales personnel or waitresses are constantly talking among themselves rather than waiting on customers. But management should also recognize that communication has motivational as well as information consequences. Banning idle chatter can create more problems

[16] *The Wall Street Journal,* Vol. 38, No. 124, April 8, 1958, p. 1.
[17] *Ibid.*

than it cures. Management should not assume that such activity necessarily reduces activity that promotes organizational ends. Emphasis should also be given to the idea that rumors and gossip, even when they disseminate gross misinformation, are not always detrimental to the organization. Some of them make the organizational life worth living and may do more good than damage.

Informational Functions and Communication Centers

The communication system has been described as a flow of information or messages through channels composed of people who act as communication centers. Each center is a focal point of message reception and transmission. But something generally happens to the message after it is received at a center and before it is transmitted to another center or its final destination. Thus, executives translate the information they receive about environmental and organizational conditions into decisions or messages about objectives and plans. The chapters in Part IV on the planning process were concerned with this aspect of the executive function. However, a great deal of information required for effective decision making is produced through the efforts of nonmanagerial personnel. Organizations produce the information needed for decision making and operations in much the same way they produce products or services. Information processing forms an integral part of the activities of many people. Some persons, such as accountants, draftsmen, stenographers, and inventory clerks, are almost entirely concerned with informational activities. Others perform such activities as an integral part of their primary activities. For example, factory workers are frequently required to report the amount of time they spend on various projects. Salesmen in the field generally make out detailed reports about various aspects of their activities, such as traveling expenses, inventory conditions, and their volume of sales.

Another important informational function is the storage of information for future reference. Some information about past activities, such as sales, net income, expenditure, and operating data, is recorded in written form and retained in files and other storage instruments for a period of time. However, a great deal of orally transmitted information is not converted into writing and cannot be physically stored. Such information is not lost to the organization as long as executives and others retain memories. The human brain thus becomes an important repository of information. This fact gives emphasis to the significance of particular people in the informational and communication system. Long tenure and experienced personnel can become highly strategic in this respect. The fact that some of them have confidential information, which might be of value to an outside company or person, is another consideration. Companies have attempted to hire the executives of competitors to gain such information, a possibility that increases the importance of personal loyalty to the organization as a qualification for promotion into and within the executive ranks.

The Problem of Information Distortion

Some of the things that happen to information do not serve the interests of the organization. Information is often deliberately or nondeliberately distorted by the persons who handle it. Some distortion evolves from a deliberate attempt of persons or groups to promote purely personal ends and to pursue organizational goals that differ from those prescribed by superiors. The semantic problem often interferes with the communication process through nondeliberate forms of information distortion. The mechanics of message processing, handling, and transmission can also give rise to distortions.

The Superior-Subordinate Relationship and Communication

The psychodynamics of the superior-subordinate relationship can lead to a number of communication difficulties.[18] Subordinates sometimes deliberately distort the information they send up the line to protect their interests and make their performance look good to superiors. A confession of mistakes may be good for the soul, but it does not generally lead to promotion and pay increases. Subordinates are inclined to take the sting out of failures by withholding and slanting information and to unduly emphasize any measure of success that may come their way. Another problem in upward communication is the tendency to cater to the likes and dislikes of the superior. Make the boss feel good even if it means stretching the truth a little or a great deal. Don't disturb his personal equilibrium with news he doesn't like to hear. The logic seems to be that a happy boss gives rewards and an unhappy boss exacts penalties.

Another communication difficulty is that superiors frequently communicate far more than they intend. Oral or written messages from superiors, particularly from high levels in the hierarchy, are generally given far more scrutiny than other messages. People tend to read between the lines and often infer something that is a far cry from what the superior really wanted

---

[18] Burleigh B. Gardner and David G. Moore, *Human Relations in Industry,* 3rd ed. (Homewood, Ill.: Richard D. Irwin, Inc., 1955), pp. 89–101; Perrin Stryker, "The Subtleties of Delegation," *Fortune,* Vol. 51, No. 3, March 1955, pp. 94 ff.

to say. The most casual remark or the failure to greet a subordinate can cause elation and satisfaction or anxieties and frustration. Superiors should make an effort to understand the feelings of the subordinate and attempt to reduce unnecessary anxieties.

Information that comes from higher hierarchical levels may also be deliberately distorted. An example of this sort of distortion is given by a World War II German officer, Major General F. W. von Mellenthin. As the American Forces advanced in Western Europe, Hitler ordered the fortress of Metz to submit to encirclement and fight to the last. However, a number of generals did not see eye to eye with the Führer on this subject. They minimized the effect of the order "by only allotting second-rate troops to the Metz garrison and by not giving them any tanks or assault guns."[19] Differences of opinion among executives as how best to promote the welfare of the organization is one reason for this kind of information distortion. The failure of higher executives to understand operating and social conditions at lower levels is another reason for making changes in messages. Deliberate distortion may also be used to facilitate the achievement of purely personal ends.

There is no easy solution to the problems considered in the above paragraphs. Some information distortion cannot be eliminated and must be considered as a price paid for an authoritarian system. However, the development of a feeling of personal trust and confidence between superior and subordinate is a step in the right direction. The two parties should attempt to understand the conditions and problems under which the other must operate. Communication should be viewed as a two-way process that involves both speaking and listening. The superior should be willing to listen to the problems of the subordinate and give him a chance to express his ideas and sentiments. Such an approach may promote a feeling of personal loyalty to the superior, which is another important factor. Communication involves a transmission of sentiment as well as information. A purely perfunctory approach on the part of either party cannot lead to effective communication.

The Problem of Semantic Distortion

Deliberate distortion involves a direct manipulation of the content of messages. A great deal of distortion is nondeliberate, however, in the sense that the parties intended to communicate but failed because of semantic difficulties. The semantic problem should be taken into consideration in deciding what to say or write and in listening to or reading messages.

[19] Major General F. W. von Mellenthin, *Panzer Battles* (Norman: University of Oklahoma Press, 1956), p. 329.

Executives should recognize that particular words or word combinations may have a different meaning for others. The importance of this idea is illustrated by a case history in which a foreman emphasized to his employees the necessity of working "as a team" to get the work out.[20] The president of the company later received a heated letter from one of the employees contending that she had been greatly abused by a foreman. Thorough investigation disclosed that the employee thought the foreman had called her a horse when he talked about teamwork. This particular case history will not be often repeated in an era of horseless carriages and team sports, but the problem it illustrates is by no means unique. Such words as "government," "taxes," "profits," and "unions" may invoke significantly different kinds of responses from different persons and groups. The word "government" may cause the executive to think about regulation, antitrust, and deficit spending; an employee may envision minimum wage legislation and social security. Such phrases as "we cannot survive without profits," "we must lower our costs," and "company investment raises wages" make good sense to executives. But they may be accorded little response from the workers in the factory and even cause some workers to think about the union "which will see to it that the damn company don't make too much or lay some of us off." To assert that workers ought not to be so unreasonable doesn't change the situation much. Some executive communication efforts result in reactions that are opposite from those intended and do more harm than good. A message that is food to one man may be fierce poison to another.

The executive should look beyond words in listening and reading. He should attempt to evaluate the information he receives from subordinates and others by asking himself questions. Are these the real facts? Does the communicator have direct access to the facts? To what extent is he relying upon information received from others? Does the message contain purely subjective judgments that may vary from person to person? In what respects may the message reflect individual or group vested interests? To what extent might the personality of the communicator have given the message a particular bias? These and similar questions can be helpful in determining the distortion that may be present in a message. Although deliberate distortion may also be involved, the present discussion is concerned with nondeliberate distortions evolving from semantic problems. In other words, the person doing the communicating is not consciously aware that his message is distorted. Thus, an individual who is normally optimistic honestly believes that his report about large future sales potential is valid. A pessi-

[20] This case was cited by Martin J. Maloney, "Semantics: The Foundation of All Business Communications," *Advanced Management,* Vol. 19, No. 7, July 1954, pp. 27–28.

mist might report and believe that exactly the opposite is the case. A foreman who has had personal difficulties with a union shop steward may tend to paint a rather black picture of company labor relations. Knowing this situation, his superior might well take the foreman's comment that "the lousy union is at it again" with a grain of salt, unless, of course, information from other foremen support the view. In a similar sense, a report from the vice-president of the sales division that the failure to achieve a sales goal was caused by production difficulties should be carefully scrutinized. The sales executive may be convinced that his report is unbiased, but nine times out of ten the production executive will present an equally unbiased report that such is not the case. It might be quite unfair to assert that the truth is not in them. Organizational and personal interests, psychological and social conditioning, particular personal experiences, and a diversity of other factors can give the truth a highly illusive quality. The executive is often forced to give a rather arbitrary solution to a problem and assert that the basis upon which action will be taken is thus and thus.

The flow of information through hierarchical levels involves the process of abstraction. More and more details are generally left out as information flows from the bottom to the top of the hierarchy. Many details are added during downward information flow. Such informational changes are subject to the judgments of executives in the chain of command. A foreman, in making a report to the production superintendent, tends to give emphasis to certain facts and not to others. The reports of the foremen are integrated by the superintendents, which involves additional normative judgments. The production manager synthesizes the reports of the superintendents, and thus the process continues to the top of the hierarchy. A similar sequence of judgments is involved as the information that flows from top to bottom levels is processed into more particular forms. A great deal of distortion can result as information passes upward or downward from level to level even when no deliberate distortion occurs. Every level tends to view a problem from a somewhat different horizon; something that seems highly important to the foreman may not be important from the broader perspective of the president. There are many different ways to synthesize and interpret information, and no two people will come out with exactly the same set of words in describing a situation. In extreme cases, top executives may be completely cut off from the realities of operations, and bottom executives may have no appreciation of the problems at higher levels. And yet the process of abstraction cannot be eliminated because to do so would be to negate the basic logic of cooperative executive action. The top executive, for example, cannot and should not concern himself with detailed information about operations.

Some distortion in the upward and downward flow of information can be eliminated by the use of information facilities that have some degree of independence from the chain of command. Thus, information obtained through an employee counseling program can be used to check information received through regular channels. A suggestion system may provide important additional information about the situation at lower levels. Staff assistants can be used to obtain information from various parts of the organization, but, of course, they should be careful not to give the impression that they are spying. Periodic personal visits with lower echelon executives and employees offer another approach. However, such techniques involve a shortcircuiting of the chain of command and can have adverse consequences if improperly done or carried to the extreme.

Attention should also be given to the need to amplify downward communication Much of the information that flows through the chain of command is concerned with specific functional responsibilities. Such information may give employees a sufficient basis for performing their duties, but it gives them little knowledge about the big picture. Although some might assert that the big picture doesn't concern them and "is none of their business," motivational and morale factors generally dictate a different point of view. Furthermore, the union may close the gap by presenting its own version of the truth. The following case history paraphrased from an account by a management consultant illustrates a management communication failure.

Joseph Zipotas (a pseudonym), an employee with twenty-five years service, was given a two hour interview by *Management Review* to find out how well he knew his company. He did *not* know the year the company was founded, the number of plants in the company, more than two of the over two hundred company products, the company president's name, the location of company headquarters, the source of a single raw material, except in general terms the operations that preceded or followed his own, and the meaning of free enterprise. But Joseph Zipotas did know the name of his union and the number of his local, the names of two columnists on the union paper, names of three out of five union officers, three direct benefits (only two could be credited to the union) the union had obtained for him, and a fairly good definition of collective bargaining.[21]

Joseph Zipotas would undoubtedly support the union rather than the company in a conflict of interests. A more comprehensive and enlightened company informational program might have shifted the balance in the other direction. Employees generally like to feel that they are playing a part in something more important and meaningful than the specialized tasks assigned to them. They are a vital part of the cooperative process and

[21] John A. Patton, "Management's Channels of Communications with Employees," *Modern Management*, Vol. 7, No. 8, November 1947, p. 20.

should be openly invited into the fold. However, it should not be assumed that mistakes of the past can be easily corrected. It takes a great deal of time and effort to change employee attitudes toward the company. There is little assurance of complete success, and even partial success may be difficult to obtain. An employee informational program should be viewed as a long-run project that offers many short-run disappointments and defeats.

Other Distortion Problems

The processing, handling, and transporting of messages can result in information distortion and other difficulties. For example, a secretary may not properly record a message formulated by an executive because of failures in speaking and hearing, i.e., the word "precedent" becomes "president." Errors may also occur during the process of transcribing shorthand symbols, listening to a dictaphone, and typing the message. The company messenger service may delay the delivery of the message or even lose it. Information distortion can sometimes be traced to inadequacies in electronic communication equipment. Examples are the "noise" or changes in signals or symbols caused by static (radio), line noise (telephone), distortions in shape and sound (television), and transmission errors.

Communication difficulties may be caused by personnel and facilities outside the organization. Telegraph and telephone companies, the postal service, printers, banks, and accounting services are sometimes vital links in the communication system. Airmail may be delayed by bad weather; a printer may make an error in printing the annual report; and a bank may improperly debit or credit an account.

SELECTED REFERENCES

E. Wight Bakke, *Bonds of Organization,* Chap. 4. New York: Harper & Brothers, 1950.
Janet H. Beavin, Don D. Jackson, and Paul Watzlawick, *Pragmatics of Human Communication.* New York: W. W. Norton & Company, Inc., 1967.
Colin Cherry, *On Human Communication.* New York: Science Editions, 1961.
Harold S. Geneen, "The Human Element in Communications," *California Management Review,* Vol. 9, No. 2, pp. 3–8 (Winter 1966).
Robert A. Hall, Jr., *Linguistics and Your Language.* Garden City, N.Y.: Anchor Books, Doubleday & Company, Inc., 1960.
William V. Haney, *Communication and Organizational Behavior,* rev. ed. Homewood, Ill.: Richard D. Irwin, Inc., 1967.
Clyde T. Hardwick and Bernard F. Landuyt, *Administrative Strategy and Decision Making,* 2nd ed., Chap. 14. Cincinnati: South-Western Publishing Co., 1966.
Mina M. Johnson and Norman F. Kallaus, *Records Management.* Cincinnati: South-Western Publishing Company, 1967.
Wendell Johnson, *People in Quandaries.* New York: Harper & Brothers, 1946.
Alfred Korzybski, *Science and Sanity: An Introduction to Non-Aristotelian Systems and General Semantics,* 4th ed. Lakeville, Conn.: The Institute of General Semantics, 1958.
Harold J. Leavitt, *Managerial Psychology,* 2nd ed., Chaps. 16 and 17. Chicago: The University of Chicago Press, 1964.
Irving J. Lee, *Language Habits in Human Affairs.* New York: Harper & Brothers, 1941.
C. K. Ogden and I. A. Richards, *The Meaning of Meaning,* rev. ed. New York: Harcourt, Brace & Co., Inc., 1956.
Claude E. Shannon and Warren Weaver, *The Mathematical Theory of Communication.* Urbana: The University of Illinois Press, 1949.
Herbert A. Simon, *Administrative Behavior,* 2nd ed., Chap. 8. New York: The Macmillan Company, 1958.
Lee Thayer, *Communication and Communication Systems.* Homewood, Ill.: Richard D. Irwin, Inc., 1968.
Norbert Wiener, *Cybernetics, Control and Communication in the Animal and the Machine.* New York: John Wiley and Sons, Inc., 1948.
Norbert Wiener, *The Human Use of Human Beings,* 2nd ed. rev. Garden City, N.Y.: Doubleday & Company, Inc., 1954 (Doubleday Anchor Books).

chapter 19

COMMUNICATION MEDIA: MESSAGE CONSTRUCTION AND RECEPTION

The first part of this chapter is concerned with alternative methods that may be used to transmit information. Particular attention is given to the problem of measuring the effectiveness of communication media. The problem of constructing oral and written messages and the importance of effective listening and reading are considered in later sections.

Communication Media and Methods

Oral versus Written Communication

Executives seem generally to make greater use of oral than written communication. Operational studies of executive work behavior indicate that a large part of the executive's working time is taken up by personal contacts with subordinates and others. The average executive probably devotes between 50 and 70 per cent of his time talking or listening to people. However, functional and personal factors cause a great deal of variation from the norm. Furthermore, executives have expressed a decided preference for oral communication as a means for gathering and disseminating information. A *Fortune* poll asked executives to select from among four methods the one they found most satisfying in gathering information about their business. Over 55 per cent preferred calling in subordinates for verbal reports; 37 per cent had a preference for inspection tours; about 18 per cent selected scheduled staff meetings; less than 25 per cent preferred written reports from subordinates.[1] In another study, the presidents of large corporations were asked to select the methods of communication they preferred for the transmission of "very important policy."[2] They were asked to select from five alternatives the two methods that were most likely to get the best results. The following preferences were selected by the fifty-one responding presidents.

Call a meeting of management personnel and explain orally	44
Hold personal interviews with key personnel	27
Announce policy in a management bulletin	16
Explain the policy in an interoffice memo	14
Explain the policy on the telephone or intercom	1

Twenty-one of the respondents selected oral methods in both of their choices, and none preferred written methods exclusively. However, thirty cast their vote for a combination of oral and written methods. Written messages are often used to supplement orally transmitted information. Although executives seem to prefer the oral method for most purposes, they also recognize that repetition and review in written form can be an important facilitating instrument.[3] In a similar sense, oral communication can be used to accompany or follow up written messages.

Written media are more effective for the transmission of certain kinds of information than oral methods. Few people can effectively transmit lengthy messages containing financial, production, or other data by oral means. Messages are often distorted as they flow through oral communication chains; written media provide protection against changes in the symbolic content of messages. However, the distortions of meaning that evolve from semantic problems are not necessarily avoided. Messages may be written for purposes other than the transmission of information. Written media are frequently used to provide tangible evidence that some event, agreement, or transaction has occurred. The statement, "I'll send you a memo (or a letter) to this effect," is a common one. Many future disagreements over what was said and by whom can be avoided by written evidence. A written statement may also be used to give *de jure* status to an

[1] *Fortune,* Vol. 34, No. 4, October 1946, p. 14.

[2] Paul E. Lull, Frank E. Funk, and Darrel T. Piersol, "What Communications Means to the Corporation President," *Advanced Management,* Vol. 20, No. 3, March 1955, pp. 17–18.

[3] *Ibid.,* p. 18; Helen Baker, John W. Ballantine, and John M. True, *Transmitting Information Through Management and Union Channels* (Princeton, N.J.: Industrial Relations Section, Department of Economics and Social Institutions, Princeton University, 1949), pp. 84–85.

arrangement arrived at through oral means. Thus, an orally transmitted decision giving a person certain prerogatives and responsibilities is generally followed or accompanied by a written proclamation. Written media are also used to protect the organization in relationships involving contractual obligations; orally transmitted orders from customers, for example, can cause legal difficulties if they are not confirmed in written form. Written records are frequently necessary to satisfy the requirements of tax and regulatory legislation.

Face-to-Face, Group, and Mass Communication Techniques

Oral communication on a face-to-face basis is generally considered to be more effective than other modes of communication. Face-to-face communication means that each person in a pair or group has an opportunity to respond directly to the other or others. An important advantage of this type of communication is that it encourages a two-way process of information exchange. Such a process offers a fertile ground for new ideas and a means for promoting cooperation. Disagreements and misunderstandings can frequently be resolved on the spot, which helps eliminate discord and dissension. Each party is given an opportunity to respond to and modify the views of the other. Superiors can learn something about the reaction of subordinates to a planned course of action and can use motivational and leadership techniques to break down barriers to effective cooperation. The information received from subordinates may bring about beneficial changes in a superior's orders or instructions. Face-to-face communication can help give the subordinate a sense of belonging and personal importance. The organization becomes something more than an abstract force that controls his destiny through impersonal messages from the executive suite.

Face-to-face communication may occur in a variety of unplanned and planned settings. Organizations generally rely heavily on informal contacts as a means of communication. As a top executive of a medium-sized company has said:

The fact is that we do nearly everything on an informal basis and because all of our executives are in such close touch with each other every day, no formal conference or communications plan seems necessary. We do constantly but informally endeavor to establish in the minds of our executive staff the management policies of the company.[4]

[4] William W. Mussmann, "Communication within the Management Group," *Conference Board Reports,* Studies in Personnel Policy, No. 80 (New York: National Industrial Conference Board, Inc., 1954), p. 3.

However, many executives believe that informal communication should be supplemented by planned individual and group contacts. One reason is that the informal approach may leave out people who are less gregarious than others or who may simply not be around at a particular time. A systematic program of planned meetings between two or more individuals increases the probability that vital information will be disseminated to those who need it. Another consideration is that planned contacts give the people involved an opportunity to make adequate preparations. Thus, a subordinate is given an opportunity to make a mental or written list of problems that require the superior's attention, and conversely. Preparation and planning may also make a committee meeting more effective than a haphazard informal meeting. The point is not that informal communication should be eliminated but rather that other techniques are generally required for adequate and effective communication. Furthermore, planned individual and group meetings can indirectly promote better communication by setting the stage for informal communication among the participating individuals.

Effective face-to-face communication cannot occur in groups beyond a certain size. Formal procedural rules and chairmanship become a more vital part of the process when the size of the group is increased to more than fifteen people. Although participation is still possible, it tends to be less dynamic and direct than in more informal situations. People are often less inclined to express their feelings and sentiments. Communication tends to become more of a one-way process of information transmission rather than a two-way process of information exchange. However, in spite of this tendency, a formal meeting that limits and directs participation can be an important communication medium. It represents a necessary compromise between the higher degree of participation possible in face-to-face communication and the completely one-way process of talks to large groups.

Speeches to mass audiences can be useful tools in the kit of communication techniques. They can be used to disseminate information rapidly and directly to large numbers of people. They make possible a degree of personal contact between organizational personnel and major executives, such as the company president. Periodic talks by executives can be important motivational devices and promote a greater unity of purpose. For example, a speech that announces some outstanding cooperative achievement or a major policy change can help make people feel that they are a part of and important in the total picture. But it should not be assumed that everyone is effective in addressing a large audience. Success in such an activity requires skills that few people possess in any great measure. The fact that the audience is captive and cannot respond presents another difficulty. Saying the wrong thing or even the right thing in a wrong way can create many misimpressions that are not easily corrected. Lower echelon executives may have to spend a great deal of time setting the matter straight. Furthermore, much of the effectiveness of even the best talks is lost by the fact that people do not have a high listening capacity.

The Design and Distribution of Written Information

A large volume of written information is composed of messages that are systematically distributed in terms of functional requirements. Such messages, designed for particular purposes and distributed only to those who require them to perform their organizational duties, are frequently written on standardized forms with blank spaces for the message and instructions on preparation and distribution. A disadvantage of forms and other standardized formats is that they place a limitation on the content of the message. However, the use of forms promotes uniformity in message content and quality and reduces the cost of information processing through the economies of "mass production." These advantages are generally sufficient to compensate for the restrictions imposed by forms. The problem is to design forms that provide adequate information for the majority of cases. Exceptional matters can be handled by supplementary informational channels and media, such as informal oral communication, committee meetings, or written memoranda.

Standardized messages should be distributed only to those who actually require the information in the performance of their duties. But the question as to whether a person really needs the information does not always have an easy answer. An experience in a large stock exchange house illustrates the problem that can arise in this respect.

The head of the accounting department questioned a thirty-seven copy report, asking each of the thirty-seven executives who received it whether it was necessary, complete and so on. All answers were emphatically affirmative. The next month he kept all copies in his file and not a question was asked. After several months he discontinued preparing the report. Many man and machine hours, not to mention the paper, have been saved. The surprising thing in this situation was that no question was asked even though all the executives had had the report called to their attention.[5]

In another company, a monthly report distributed to eight departments duplicated other reports that presented the same information in better form.[6] Yet, many years passed before anything was done to stop such

[5] Ben S. Graham, "Paperwork Simplification," *Modern Management,* Vol. 8, No. 2, February 1948, p. 22.
[6] *Ibid.*

unnecessary duplication. Many man-hours of work and dollars of profit were wasted preparing, distributing, filing, and storing a useless report. However, a great deal of money may be lost by a failure to provide a sufficient amount of information. Effective decision making and operations require adequate information about such matters as sales volume, production schedules, material requirements, design and specification changes, purchases and inventories, operating costs, and employee performance.

Some communication problems require a greater range of choice in message construction than is afforded by forms and other standardized formats. Letters, memoranda, reports, employee and management newsletters, and various types of publications can be used to handle exceptional matters. Written messages may also be specifically designed for and directed to particular persons or groups. For example, a letter or a memo may be used to commend an individual for an organizational or personal achievement. Bulletins and newsletters may be designed to serve the needs and interests of specific groups, such as engineers, chemists, foremen, or office supervisors. Other kinds of written media involve a shotgun approach which attempts to reach a wide audience. Company magazines and newspapers, mimeographed letters and memos, and notices on bulletin boards illustrate this kind of communication technique.

Alternative Message Transmission Techniques

Messages can be transmitted through many alternative transmission devices and systems. Thus, a particular message may be transmitted by telephone, bulletin boards, messengers, or airmail. One consideration in the selection of transmission techniques is the problem of time and distance. Telephones, telegraph, teletype, radio, and other electronic devices can be used to transmit messages over long distances. Such devices are extensively used to transmit vital information in organizations that are dispersed over a wide geographical area. Another consideration is the relative cost of alternative transmission techniques. The cost factor may determine whether long-distance telephone or first-class mail is used to transmit a message. A further consideration is that the effectiveness of the message may be reduced or increased by the mode of transmission. For example, oral communication on a face-to-face basis tends to be more effective than oral communication on the telephone. Only one of fifty-one company presidents surveyed about communication selected the telephone or inter-communication devices to explain important policy.[7] A large majority of the executives polled by *Fortune* reported that they used the tele-

[7] Lull, Funk, and Piersol, *op. cit.,* p. 18.

phone "an hour or less" on days they work in their offices.[8] However, although telephone communication may be less effective than a face-to-face approach, it may give better results than other communication media. The effectiveness of a message is also influenced by such alternatives as airmail versus third-class mail, general versus special delivery, and bulletin board posting versus an article in the company magazine.

Combinations of Media and Techniques

Although some modes of communication seem better than others, a combination of media is necessary to provide the communication potential required for effective operation and cooperation. No one communication medium can adequately serve the diverse functional and personal problems of organizational dynamics. Also important is that a repetition of ideas in different forms is useful in solving some communication problems. What kind of media combination is most effective? An attempt to construct a one best combination for universal or particular application is a hopeless project. There are undoubtedly many combinations that would give equally good results. Ideally, various media should be evaluated in terms of the additional costs and the revenues they produce. However, the problems of forecasting and measurement preclude a rigorous application of the economic calculus. A great deal of communication is concerned with the manipulation of highly subtle and complex socio-psychological forces. The consequences of particular communication efforts are often indirect and not immediately apparent. But the lack of perfect solutions should not deter management from giving consideration to the problem.

The effectiveness of communication media should be systematically and periodically appraised and reviewed. Particular media should be evaluated in terms of functional and motivational requirements. The possibility that specific decisional and operating failures resulted from a lack of information should be carefully scrutinized. Attention should be given to the manner in which media changes may affect particular motivational problems. Management should endeavor to eliminate any unnecessary duplication of communication efforts. Interviews and questionnaires can be helpful in determining the nature and solution of some of these problems. For example, the knowledge that only 6 per cent of organization personnel read a particular publication may well justify its elimination. The fact that a large number of people are not informed about certain company policies provides a basis for corrective action. The suggestions and opinions of

---

[8] *Fortune, op. cit.,* p. 14. Functional requirements and personality factors make for a great deal of variation from individual to individual.

managerial and operating personnel may also be helpful in planning media changes.

The personal qualities of executives should be considered in the selection of media. Executives should give recognition to their strengths and their limitations. Thus, the president should schedule weekly or monthly speeches before mass audiences of company personnel only if he is a reasonably competent speaker. It might be better for him to communicate his ideas through an informal newsletter or an article in the company magazine. Some executives may find that oral face-to-face communication is more effective for them than written memoranda. Others may find that their forte is written memoranda and formal meetings. Each executive should evaluate his communication successes and failures and plan a media program that best fits his qualities.

The Construction of Messages

The purpose of this section is to given some insights into the problem of constructing oral and written messages. No attempt is made to present a complete or detailed account of speaking and writing techniques. A person who wants more specialized knowledge about techniques can find literally hundreds of articles and books on such subjects as "how to write better business letters," "how to write better sales (credit, collection, or application) letters," "writing business memoranda," "better business and technical report writing," "more effective oral communication," and "preparing and delivering a talk." This discussion is concerned with basic ideas on the development of skills in message construction together with some of the factors that may influence their effectiveness.

Knowledge of Language

One aspect of communication involves the construction of oral and written messages from a language, such as English, French, accounting, and statistics. Although the message rather than the language performs the communication function, a knowledge of language is an important prerequisite for effective message construction. An understanding of words or symbols and the logic involved in combining them is a necessary first step. The potential messages that can be created by an individual are increased by his knowledge of language. A highly trained mathematician, statistician, or accountant has a far greater potential communication range than a neophyte in these specialized languages. The same thing can be said about such nonspecialized languages as English, French, and German. Language was an important barrier in the communication efforts of American soldiers in France and Germany during World War II. One could add that "never has so much been communicated with so few resources." However, language may also be a limiting factor among those who presumably speak and write the same language. Many people in the United States cannot effectively communicate because they lack knowledge of the English language, and, unfortunately, some executives and aspiring executives can be placed in this category.

The Importance of Vocabulary

Effective use of a language requires a knowledge of words and their various meanings and the contexts in which they can be used. The dictionary is helpful in achieving a better understanding of word meaning, but, as Bergen and Cornelia Evans have emphasized, the only way to really understand words is to experience their use in as many contexts as possible.[9] This idea indicates the importance of reading, writing, and conversing as instruments of effective vocabulary formation. How much and what kind of vocabulary should the executive possess? The executive should undoubtedly have a larger vocabulary than the average of the population, and higher executives generally require a more extensive vocabulary than lower level executives. The range of specialized areas of knowledge and the diversity of social situations with which the executive must contend make a large vocabulary a highly essential attribute. The executive's vocabulary should include a knowledge of technical terminology and the language of ordinary communication, but the relative emphasis that should be placed upon the two types of language is difficult to determine. Clarence B. Randall, former president of Inland Steel Company, has stressed the importance of the language training of a liberal education.

The communication of ideas is obviously a function of general education. One learns the effective use of the written word by studying the great literature of the past, and by infinite practice under skilled instruction. One learns to speak by hearing the spoken word of the masters, and by daily practice under guidance. Moreover, general education places emphasis on the speaking and writing of language as generally employed. This is not true in the technical institutions. There the inevitable emphasis is upon the particular terminology in that subdivision of science to which the scholar is devoting himself. Each specialist tends to express himself in the language of his own subject, and this goes so far sometimes that specialists in different branches of science all but lose the capacity of communicating with each other.[10]

[9] Bergen Evans and Cornelia Evans, *A Dictionary of Contemporary American Usage* (New York: Random House, 1957), p. v.

[10] Clarence B. Randall, "A Businessman Looks at the Liberal Arts," *The Randall Lectures* (White Plains, N.Y.: The Fund for Adult Education, 1957), p. 11.

It seems evident that people should learn the specialized language of their particular branch of knowledge. The difficulty is that often they cannot adequately read or write the English language. A student sometimes attains high academic achievement in the language of the accountant, mathematician, chemist, and engineer, but he requires a kind and sympathetic professor to pass "some highly useless and impractical" elementary English courses. If something must be sacrificed in the educational process, it would seem better for those who aspire to any sort of executive career to learn a little more English and a little less technical jargon. However, too little knowledge of the technical and professional languages can also be a problem. The two goals should not be considered as mutually exclusive; the problem is to achieve a better balance in some high school and university curricula. A major barrier for many students is a negative attitude toward any attempts to change the language habits that were learned from parents and home town cronies.

The Problem of Grammar

Grammar is concerned with the classification of words, changes in word form, sentence structure, and the functions of words. The grammarians of the past were often highly dogmatic in their views of how people should speak and write the language. They were concerned with what ought to be in terms of a rather rigid predetermined system. Much more attention is presently being given to the manner in which the language is actually used. Although formal grammatical logic is still important, the grammarian has been more willing to accept usage as a determinant of correctness. But the criterion of usage, if carried to an extreme, would sanction a large variety of modes of speaking and writing. The grammar of uneducated people could be called as correct as that of the educated. From the viewpoint of expressing meaning, "bad" grammar is frequently as effective as "good" grammar. However, grammar is only partly concerned with the problem of effective communication. The usage of formally educated people has been a major determinant of what is deemed to be proper in the formal sense. An important by-product is that language usage has important social implications. In the words of the Evanses:

There are some grammatical constructions, such as *that there dog* and *he ain't come yet,* that are perfectly intelligible but are not standard English. Such expressions are used by people who are not interested in "book learning." They are not used by educated people and hence are regarded as "incorrect" and serve as the mark of a class. There is nothing wrong about using them, but in a country such as ours where for a generation almost everybody has had at least a high school education or its equivalent few people are willing to use expressions that are not generally approved as "correct." [11]

The executive should use "correct" grammar because much of his work and life involves interaction with university graduates, but executives must also communicate with people whose mode of speaking and writing does not conform to this standard. Persons who speak differently in this respect sometimes have communication difficulties. The reaction of the one might be: "How can anyone who speaks in such an 'uncouth' manner have anything worthwhile to say?" The other might think: "He speaks fancy cause he's got 'book larnen' but he don't know nothing about practical things." They fail to communicate because each is evaluating in terms of inferred personal qualities rather than message content. An approach to this problem is to speak in the language of the person or persons being addressed. Politicians sometimes deliberately speak the language of "hill country people" or "street corner society" to get their messages across, but this technique can easily seem contrived when used by people who have never had close personal contact with the environment concerned. A person who has always spoken "proper" English should generally not attempt to speak the language of people who speak in a different manner. Also important is the social precept that a person should not depart too far from the role he is supposed to play. People expect an executive to talk like an executive for the same reason that most children frown when their parents mimic their speech.

Constructing the Oral or Written Message

The problem of message construction is to select a combination of words that most effectively transmits meaning. Message content is frequently controlled by planned message forms and formats. An application form or a purchase requisition indicates the kind of information that should be included in the message. Financial statements and reports are generally written in a standardized format. Many organizations make use of "canned" sales talks, ghost-written speeches, form letters and memoranda, and professionally written press releases. But the problem of message preparation cannot be entirely delegated to the professional, and the discretionary element cannot be completely eliminated by planned forms and format.

There is no easy road to effective speaking and writing. Books and articles on techniques can be helpful in overcoming some difficulties. They often present ideas that are useful to someone who must prepare sales

---

[11] Bergen Evans and Cornelia Evans, *op. cit.*, p. v.

letters, credit letters, public relations material, reports, and various kinds of oral presentations. Dictionaries and grammars are also important facilitating instruments in preparing messages. But a purely techniques-and-rules approach is not generally effective without a background of skills in speaking and writing. Such skills are partly developed through university courses in public speaking, debate, group communication, creative writing, and technical and business writing. Membership on student committees, holding an office in a fraternity, dormitory, or departmental club, participating in teas and other social events, and informal contacts with fellow students and faculty also afford excellent opportunities for developing communication skills.

A message should contain sufficient information to cover the subject matter and achieve the objectives of the speaker or writer. An important determinant of content is the capacity of the message recipient to impute meaning. A few words may be adequate for some people, but many words may not be enough for others. A supervisor may simply say to Jones: "The washrooms need cleaning." But Smith may have to be given detailed instructions on how to clean the washrooms, where to find the proper equipment, and also be told that cleaning activities should begin immediately. Another consideration in message construction is the importance of attracting and keeping the attention of the listener and reader. Humor, analogy, and illustrations are sometimes used to make conversation and speeches more interesting. The opening sentence in sales and other letters is often designed to catch the interest of the reader. Pictures, charts, color, indentations, and variations in type can be used to make written material more attractive.

Many books and articles on technique properly warn against the use of redundant and superfluous words or phrases. However, such words or phrases can sometimes be justified on the basis of social and business customs. For example, a failure to include a complimentary close ("Sincerely yours," "Yours truly," or "Cordially yours") in a letter might be viewed as bad form by a recipient. These words are not information in the ordinary sense, but they may imply a great deal.

The speaker or writer should give consideration to the problems of the other person in designing his message. For example, a subordinate should not involve the superior in a long rambling conversation if others are waiting to see him or when he is busy with an important matter. Written memoranda or reports should be written in a manner that reduces the workload of the reader. Many reports are far too long and written to impress rather than to inform. A brief summary at the beginning of the report, a table of contents, and the use of appendices for detailed data are usually appreciated by a busy executive who must digest a large number of reports. Messages can generally be improved if people do a little more planning and thinking before they speak or write. Too many people dash off a letter or a memorandum, compile reports, and utter sounds from the mouth in an unorganized and makeshift fashion.

Individual and Group Differences

Differences in background, interests, and motives should be considered in preparing messages to particular persons and groups. The employees in the factory should generally be approached differently than those in the office. Communicating with a group of foremen is not the same problem as communicating with vice-presidents or engineers. This idea also applies to communication with different individuals; a technique that works well with the production manager may not give good results with the sales manager or the credit manager. Such problems can be partly attributed to differences in functional responsibilities and professional or vocational interests. In addition, there are the unique personal qualities of individuals and the norms developed by social groups. Thus, one production manager will not react in exactly the same manner as another production manager or a third production manager, and so on. The foundry workers, foremen, or vice-presidents in one company do not generally have the same group norms as the foundry workers, foremen, or vice-presidents in another company. An ideal solution might be to design a different message for each individual or group in the organization. However, the extent to which this approach can be carried into practice is limited by considerations of time, effort, and cost. Another restricting factor is the lack of sufficient knowledge about psycho-sociological dynamics of particular individuals and groups. But in spite of these limitations executives give implicit, if not explicit, recognition to individual and group differences in their communication efforts. They usually develop a great deal of insight about the probable reactions of their subordinates and employ appropriate techniques.

Authoritative Communication: Giving Orders

An order differs from an ordinary message because it involves the authority relationship. It imposes an organizational responsibility upon its recipient and carries with it a threat of sanctions for nonconformity. But the fact that a subordinate is required to respond does not repudiate the ideas presented in previous paragraphs about message construction. An order is in one respect simply an oral or written message from a superior to a subordinate. Like any other message, an order should contain words that transmit the desired meaning and motivate the recipient.

Order-giving techniques may range from a direct order or command to an approach that indirectly implies that something should be done. Between this polarity are techniques inferred by the words "request," "suggest," "recommend," and "persuade." It is sometimes difficult to determine whether a message from a superior is an order or not. But the fact that it comes from a superior gives a message an imperative quality, however subtle, that invites a different kind of response than ordinary messages. The technique that should be used in giving orders varies with the kinds of personalities involved, the social situation, and the circumstances under which they are given. The use of such words and phrases as "please," "would you do this for me," and "I would appreciate" works wonders with many subordinates, but a tough foundry or construction worker might respond better to an order prefaced by a little lusty swearing. The norms developed in a particular social situation are important in this respect. Soldiers expect the first-sergeant to behave in a somewhat uncivil fashion and would probably not respond well to a highly courteous and tactful sergeant. A sergeant should behave like a sergeant, not like the manager of a haberdashery. Order-giving techniques may also vary with the environmental situation; an emergency, for example, often necessitates a more direct approach. The following general guides were prepared by one company to help superiors adapt their orders to particular situations.

A request doesn't offend the sensitive worker, while a direct order often antagonizes.

The direct order—if not used too frequently—stands out emphatically. It tends to shock a worker out of his lethargy, and may save a dismissal.

A request may partly melt the hard-boiled man, and is worth trying before a direct order.

The implied order usually gets best results from the dependable worker. But it is *not* for the inexperienced or unreliable.

The first time an error is made, *a request* to correct it adds the friendliness that keeps a man on your side. The *direct order* may be advisable on repetition of the error.

The *direct order* is appropriate for the chronic violator—and if most of your orders have been requests, the change to a direct order will carry emphasis.

The *call for volunteers* often is a challenge and produces good results where the job is disagreeable, calls for special effort or involves unpopular overtime. But *don't* use it to escape responsibility for making assignments in the best interests of production.

To develop ability and judgment in a promising employee, the *implied* or *suggestive order* is a good way of trying him out and putting him on his own. Close follow-up may be required, however.

The emergency usually requires a *direct order*.[12]

Courtesy, tact, and finesse are frequently more effective than a direct approach to order giving, but executives should not become "wishy-washy" in their dealings with subordinates. Subordinates generally expect the superior to give orders and behave like a leader. Subtle motivational techniques in order giving facilitate cooperation but only within certain limits. A failure to take a positive approach to order giving may result from inadequacies on the part of the superior. Some people do not like to tell other people what they ought to do, a deficiency that seems often to be rationalized in the name of human relations techniques. A so-called democratic approach is sometimes a sophisticated way to avoid responsibility.

Message Reception Problems

The construction of oral and written messages is only one part of the communication process. The best message is of little avail unless the person at the receiving end listens or reads and makes an effort to understand. We often speak without listeners and speak when we ought to be listening. And we frequently fail to find readers for the avalanche of words that make up the memoranda, letters, and reports of the organizational world. A partial solution is to speak less and say more and to write shorter, fewer, and better messages. But a great deal more attention should also be given to the development of listening and reading skills.

Toward More Effective Listening

Listening requires as much, if not more, mental effort and concentration than speaking. It is true that some speakers and subjects are not worth the effort, but listening can reap a large harvest of ideas and help promote cooperation. Effective listening involves more than hearing the words spoken by another person. The listener should look beyond the words for the meaning and sentiments the speaker is attempting to convey.

A major barrier to effective listening is the tendency of the listener to evaluate in terms of *his* rather than the speaker's frame of reference. The

[12] Reproduced in: M. Joseph Dooher and Vivienne Marquis (editors), *Effective Communication on the Job* (New York: American Management Association, 1956), p. 106.

listener's prejudices and beliefs, cued by the words or the person of the speaker, partially or completely inhibit any exchange of information between the two parties. Each party is essentially talking to and about himself rather than to the other person. As the psychologist Professor Carl R. Rogers has said:

Although the tendency to make evaluations is common in almost all interchange of language, it is very much heightened in those situations where feelings and emotions are deeply involved. So the stronger our feelings, the more likely it is that there will be no mutual element in the communication. There will be just two ideas, two feelings, two judgments, missing each other in psychological space.[13]

Such words as Herbert Hoover, Franklin D. Roosevelt, Republican, Democrat, income taxes, government, and Communist can create an emotional reaction that blots out anything else the speaker may have to say. People often react adversely to the speaker because he is identified with a particular organization or cause. Thus, some people cannot listen to anything Lyndon Johnson has to say, and others have similar difficulties with Richard Nixon. Walter Reuther might have a problem in getting his point across to an audience of N.A.M. members, and L. R. Boulware might not find too many listeners at a U.A.W. convention. This sort of barrier to effective listening can be partially overcome if people make an effort, in the words of Professor Rogers, "to see the expressed idea and attitude from the other person's point of view, to sense how it feels to him, to achieve his frame of reference in regard to the thing he is talking about."[14] The solution may sound simple, but it is not easy to bring about. Logical argument is generally not very successful in changing sentiments. Most people evaluate because they do not want to change their prejudices and beliefs. Little progress can be made unless a person has a genuine desire to become a better listener. Understanding the problem is also a major step toward a solution, and success in overcoming it is another element in the cure. But people should not expect too much in too short a time; a bad listener, like an alcoholic, overcomes his problem on a day-to-day basis. Third-party intervention may also help overcome emotional barriers to communication. This technique is often used in labor-management disputes, marital difficulties, and international conflicts.

[13] Carl R. Rogers and F. J. Roethlisberger, "Barriers and Gateways to Communication," *Harvard Business Review*, Vol. 30, No. 4, July–August 1952, p. 47.
[14] *Ibid.*, p. 47. Professor Rogers then considers some of the barriers to this kind of understanding and techniques for overcoming them.

Other Listening Problems and Techniques

Most people can think a great deal faster than a person can speak. A person can listen to a conversation, speech, or lecture, and, at the same time, periodically ponder about last night's poker game, a certain blonde bombshell, a forthcoming football game, the household budget, or picking green peas. Unfortunately, the mind often wanders too far and loses the speaker completely. A good listener does not let his mind drift away from what the speaker has to say. The following suggestions from an article on listening problems and techniques by Ralph Nichols and Leonard A. Stevens can be helpful in this respect.

Try to anticipate what a person is going to talk about. On the basis of what he's already said, ask yourself: "What's he trying to get at? What point is he going to make?"

Mentally summarize what the person has been saying. What point has he made already, if any?

Weigh the speaker's evidence by mentally questioning it. If he tells you facts, illustrative stories and statistics, ask yourself: "Are they accurate? Do they come from an unprejudiced source? Am I getting the full picture, or is he telling me only what will prove his point?"

Listen "between the lines." A person doesn't always put everything that's important into words. The changing tones and volume of his voice may have a meaning. So may his facial expressions, the gestures he makes with his hands, the movement of his body.[15]

People sometimes listen for words rather than ideas and may even attempt to memorize the specific sequence of words used by the speaker. A more effective approach is to grasp the main ideas the other person attempts to convey. The details should be synthesized into higher order ideas and meanings. If the listener needs to relate the ideas to others, he should translate them into more specific terms in his own mode of speaking. People may also reduce their listening capacity by taking detailed notes. University students, for example, sometimes attempt to write down every pearl the professor casts before them. They divert too much energy to the act of writing and become frustrated by an inability to record everything. A better approach is to listen carefully and then write down only the leading ideas. If necessary, such notes can be elaborated after the speaker

[15] Ralph Nichols and Leonard A. Stevens, "You Don't Know How to Listen," *Collier's,* July 25, 1953, p. 19. This article deals with a variety of listening problems and offers some useful techniques.

has relayed his message. The ability to remember the ideas presented in a talk or conversation is often enhanced by subsequent review and reconstruction.

People can generally present many "good" reasons for not listening. They behave much like the heavy smoker who feels he ought to quit for health reasons but who finally decides to keep the habit because "there is no real proof that cigarettes cause lung cancer or heart trouble" or "my uncle smoked fifteen cigars a day and lived to be ninety-two." A bad listener may rationalize his habit in some of the following ways: "I couldn't hear because the people behind me were making too much noise." "What can she tell me about raising children? She doesn't have any and she probably won't because no sane man would marry her." "How can an idiot like that give advice on foreign policy?" "He was way over my head the minute he opened his mouth." "What does he know about economics? He doesn't have a Ph.D." "I couldn't understand a word he said because he talked like a man with a mouth full of mush."

Such comments may reflect actual listening difficulties and express legitimate reasons for not listening, but they are often used to soothe the conscience of the lazy listener. People sometimes seem to expend more energy avoiding the problem than it would take to become a reasonably good listener. They may even go to great lengths to make the speaker believe they are listening or have listened. An eager and intense look and a periodic comment or a question is the usual technique. The inappropriateness of some of their queries does not bother them in the least because they have not listened to anything the speaker said. Such techniques do not generally fool the speaker and those who were listening. But more important than this is the loss of information that might have served vital vocational and personal goals. Furthermore, a genuine understanding of others is possible only by listening to what they say and feel.

The Importance of Listening in the Superior-Subordinate Relationship

Listening is as important as order-giving skills in obtaining appropriate behavioral responses from subordinates. Some executives unduly stress the importance of order giving in their relationship with subordinates. They assume that a breakdown in communication can be credited either to their failure to properly explain what and why something should be done or to inadequacies on the part of the subordinate.[16] A frequent consequence of

[16] Carl R. Rogers and F. J. Roethlisberger, "Barriers and Gateways to Communication," *op. cit.*, pp. 50–52. Professor Roethlisberger presented this portion of the discussion.

this approach is that the superior continues to explain to the point of exasperation, with the subordinate becoming less and less inclined to understand. Professor F. J. Roethlisberger believes that better results can be achieved if the superior gives less emphasis to explaining and more emphasis to listening. Such a technique will give the subordinate the feeling that he is understood and accepted as a person and that his sentiments are important. The subordinate frequently assumes a more cooperative attitude and may even willingly accept a condition or a command that imposes an extreme personal burden.

An Effective Open Door Policy

Executives sometimes have little information about the actual state of affairs at subordinate levels. The socio-psychological restraints of an authoritarian system cannot and should not be completely eliminated, but such restraints can seriously interfere with the planning and control process if they become too extreme. Subordinates, whether they be vice-presidents or foremen, should feel that they can express sentiments without the threat of direct or indirect sanctions. Disagreements by a subordinate with a particular departmental or company policy does not necessarily imply insubordination. Effective communication with subordinates requires a willingness to listen with an open mind to the ideas and sentiments they express. It involves more than a perfunctory statement that "my door is always open." Subordinates must feel that the man behind the door wants to hear what they have to say and that he will do something about their complaints and suggestions.[17] However, it should not be assumed that the superior should make every change suggested by a subordinate. Some complaints are highly unreasonable, and some suggestions unsound. But, even though the subordinate cannot be satisfied through direct action, he often responds favorably to the interest and recognition implied by a superior's willingness to listen. There is also evidence that "talking out a problem" to a good listener can help ease emotional tensions and frustrations. Another important consideration is that listening helps keep communication channels open. Superiors must listen if they want knowledge about subordinate attitudes and activities.

[17] A comprehensive discussion of the nature of the problem and some techniques that can be used to solve it are presented by William Foote Whyte in *Human Relations in the Restaurant Industry* (New York: McGraw-Hill Book Company, Inc., 1948), pp. 217–234.

Faster and Better Reading

Executives frequently complain that they do not have sufficient time to read the memoranda, letters, and reports that flow into their offices. They also lament their inability to keep up with the professional, business, and trade literature. The development of reading skills is one approach to the solution of this problem. The average reader reads at the rate of about 250 words per minute, very good readers from 500 to 600 words, and a few exceptional persons read at the rate of 1000 or more words.[18] But effective reading involves more than the speed at which something can be read. It also requires an ability to comprehend the meaning transmitted via the words. Improvements in reading speed must not result in reduced comprehension if anything useful is to be gained. However, there is evidence that higher reading speeds do not generally reduce the degree of comprehension and may somewhat increase it.[19]

How do people become more proficient readers? Some people are skillful readers because they read a great deal. They practice the preachments of the experts in reading techniques without conscious effort. Better reading habits can also be developed by reading-improvement courses, an approach used with good results by universities and business organizations. For example, a reading course given to executives and other personnel in a number of motion picture studios increased reading speed from an average of 250 to 300 words per minute to somewhat over 800 words per minute with a rather significant increase in comprehension.[20] Equally impressive results have been achieved in many other cases.

What are some of the basic elements that make for more effective reading? Reading is partly a matter of moving the eye over written material. Many reading-improvement courses give emphasis to techniques that increase the span of print taken in by the eye. Use is sometimes made of various types of optical instruments and reading-training films. This approach can help correct habitual eye movements that make for reading inefficiencies, but the idea that reading is essentially a mental process should not be neglected. As Professor Nila B. Smith has emphasized, "the eye movements are simply symptoms of the mental process which a person uses while reading." [21]

---

[18] Nila Banton Smith, *Read Faster—and Get More From Your Reading* (Englewood Cliffs, N.J.: Prentice-Hall, Inc., 1958), p. 3. This book contains many useful ideas and techniques that can be used to improve reading speed and comprehension.
[19] *Ibid.*, pp. 364–366.
[20] *Ibid.*, p. 363.
[21] *Ibid.*, p. 21.

Effective reading, like effective listening, requires a great deal of mental effort and concentration. A fast reader reads by lines, paragraphs, and even pages rather than one or a few words at a time. However, the basic problem is to grasp and retain the thoughts expressed by the words. A good way to start a reading venture is to make a quick survey of chapter headings, table of contents, the introductory chapter, graphs and illustrations, and the preface. Such a survey gives the reader some insight into the nature of the content and a basis for deciding whether a more detailed reading is worth the effort. It also provides a mental framework into which more detailed content can later be placed. Another good reading technique is to learn to read by paragraphs. The paragraph generally contains one leading idea around which supporting details are organized. The problem is to find this idea rapidly and then go to subsidiary ideas if necessary. Reading the main idea in each paragraph is sufficient for some purposes. If the details are important, reading proficiency can be increased by mentally organizing subsidiary ideas and facts around the central idea of the paragraph. Watching for directional words is helpful in guiding the reader. For example, words like "furthermore" and "likewise" suggest further elaboration of what has gone before; such words as "but" and "however" give warning that something is to be qualified. The really fast reader knows how to glean the essential ideas by skimming. These readers generally have a comprehensive knowledge of language and subject matter and have great facility in making a synthesis. Completely ignoring the trimmings, they seek out only the really essential or specific ideas and facts.

Even the best reader does not and cannot read everything at the same rate of speed. Some written material contains more meat or less chaff than others; a scientific article, for example, may require a slow sentence by sentence approach. Variations in reading speed also result from differences in reading objectives. Some things are read for details, others for the essential ideas, and still others to find a specific fact. A person who reads novels at a fast clip might slow down considerably with a book or an article in economic theory. But an economist can often read publications in theoretical economics as fast as other people read novels. The degree to which a person is motivated to read something is also a determinant of reading speed. A football or baseball enthusiast may read the sports section in rapid order but slow down considerably for other parts of the newspaper. Some university students read twenty pages of the latest issue of *Playboy* in a much shorter span of time than a five-page assignment in a management book. The kind of psychological barriers that impede effective listening also influence reading capacities. Many people respond negatively to an author's ideas because they evaluate in terms of their values rather than his. Some labor leaders would experience mental torture in reading a publication prepared by the National Association of Manufacturers. Similar trepidations might engulf an executive who ventures into the literature of the AFL-CIO.

Information Retrieval for More Efficient Reading

The presses of the nation produce a huge volume of published material providing potentially useful information for managerial and other professional purposes. A major problem is to locate the publications that would be most helpful for a particular organization within the constraints imposed by budgetary considerations. Many companies employ professional librarians, who work with managerial, professional, and technical personnel in solving this problem.

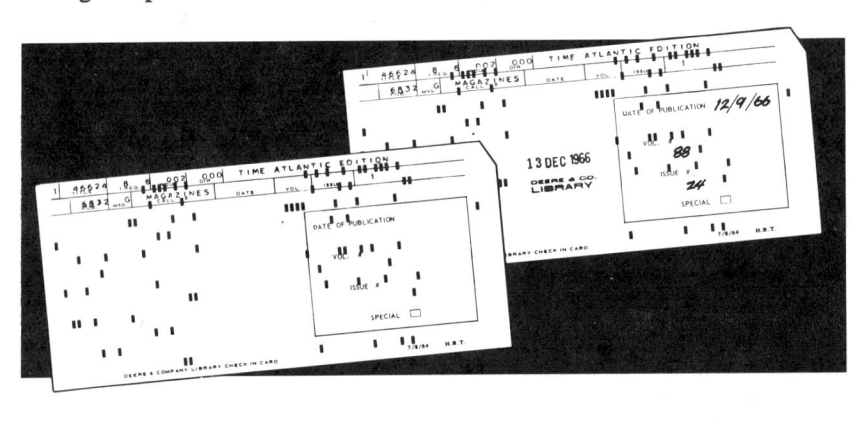

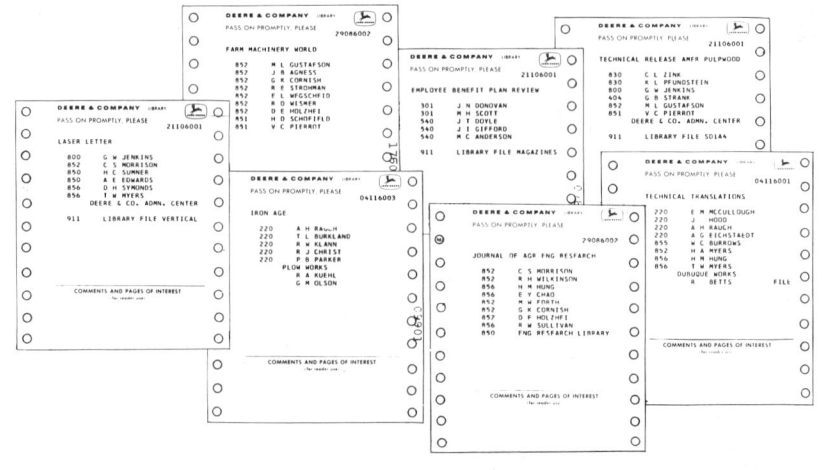

Figure 19-1. Check-in cards and routing slips. Courtesy of Deere and Company.

Some companies utilize electronic computers and related equipment to facilitate the distribution of routine information and to provide information for particular problems and projects. For example, Deere and Company uses a computerized system in the check-in and routing of some 3000 serial titles to about 11,000 persons. Punched cards for check-in and routing slips are produced by the computer on a bi-weekly schedule. Publication frequency (weekly, monthly, quarterly, etc.) is coded binarily; the code signals the computer to produce check-in cards and routing slips prior to the scheduled release of the publications. (See Figure 19-1.) This system can simultaneously provide information categorized by publication title, publisher, library holdings, subject-matter, library routing, and personnel receiving publications.[22] (See Figure 19-2.)

[22] Courtesy of Mrs. Charlotte L. Anderson, Librarian, Deere and Company. The coding system was developed at the Washington University School of Medicine, St. Louis, Missouri.

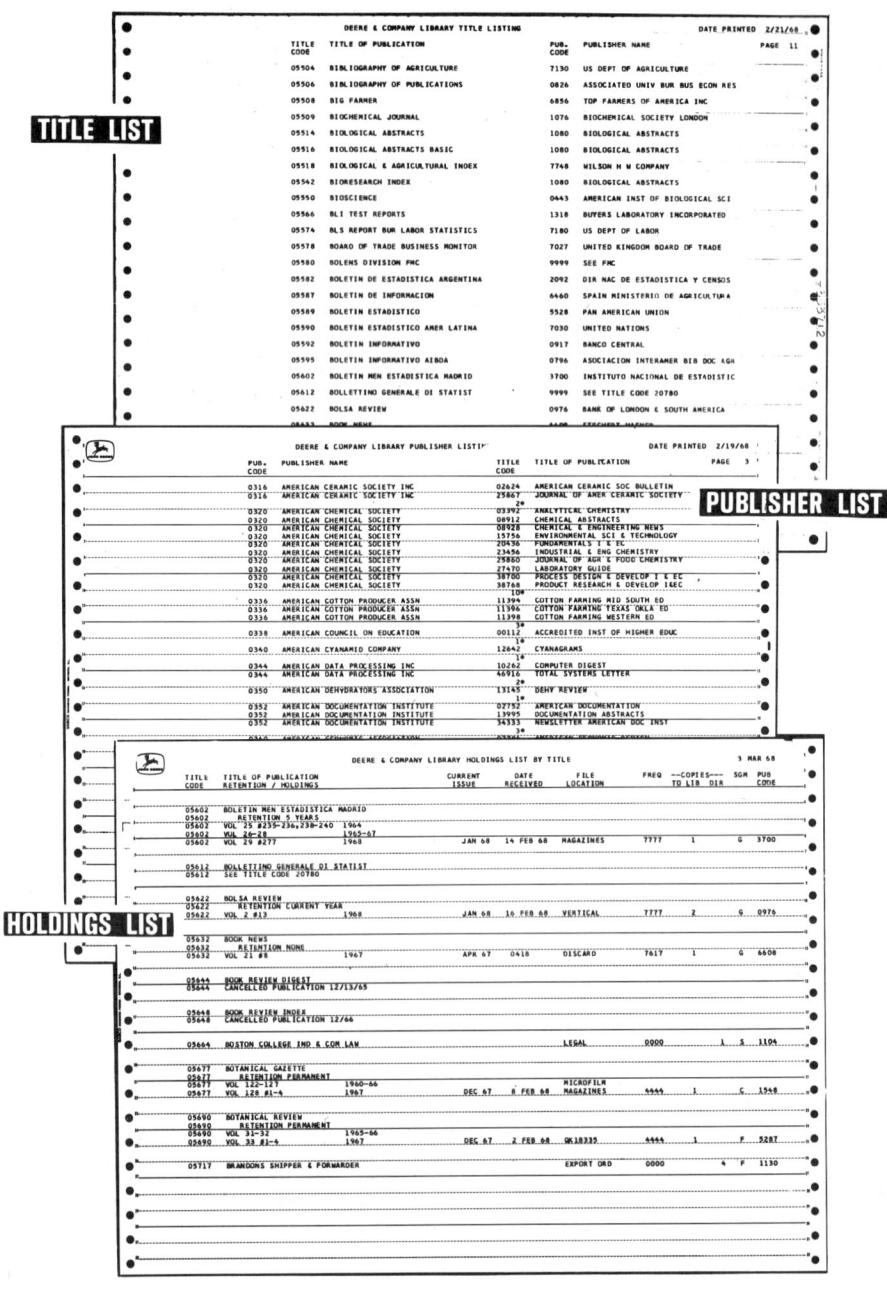

Figure 19-2. Computerized control lists. Courtesy of Deere and Company.

SUBJECT LIST

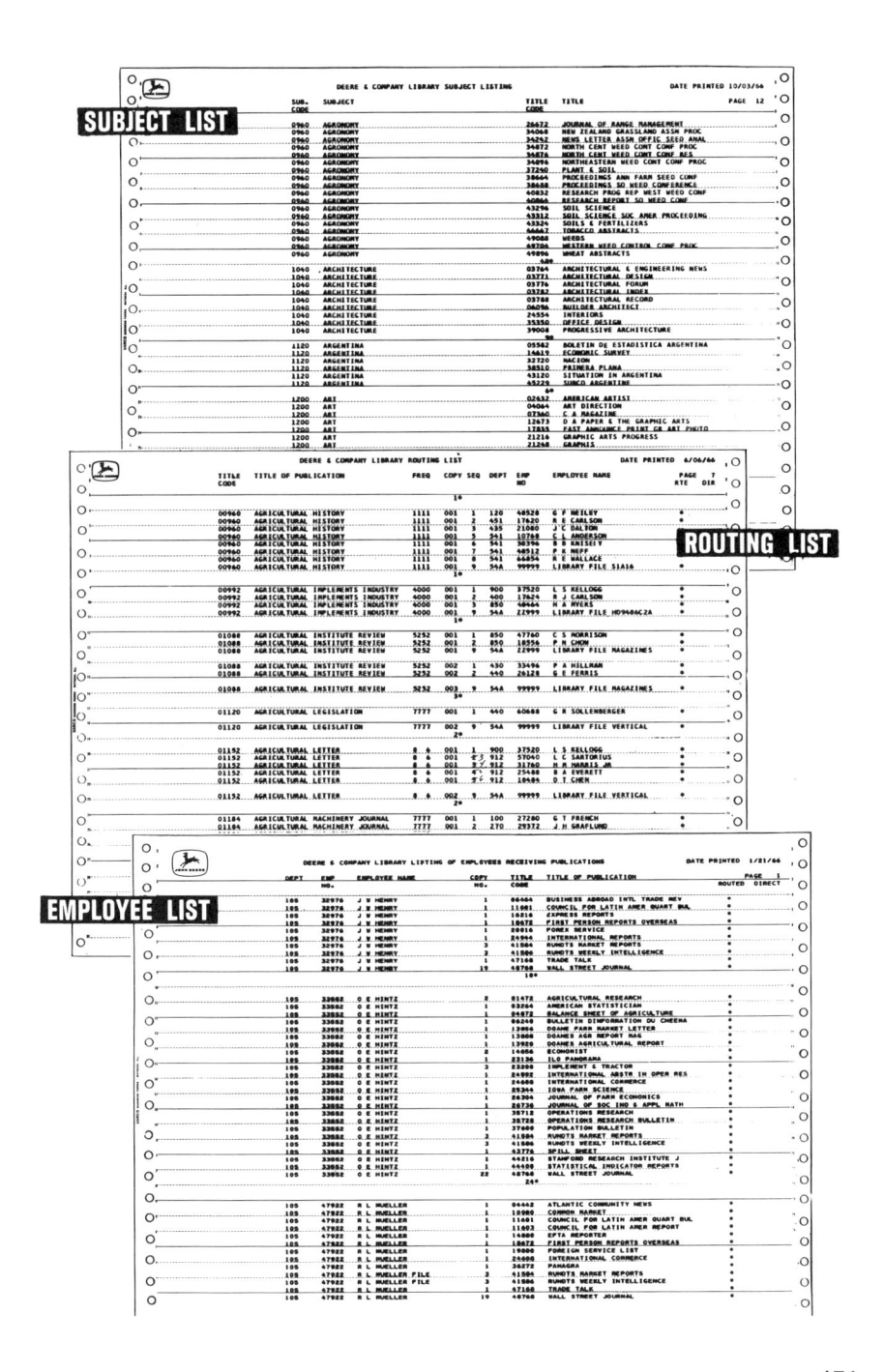

```
                    DEERE & COMPANY LIBRARY SUBJECT LISTING              DATE PRINTED 10/03/66
      SUB.   SUBJECT                          TITLE    TITLE                                    PAGE 12
      CODE                                    CODE
      0960   AGRONOMY                         26672    JOURNAL OF RANGE MANAGEMENT
      0960   AGRONOMY                         34068    NEW ZEALAND GRASSLAND ASSM PROC
      0960   AGRONOMY                         34252    NEWS LETTER ASSM OFFIC SEED ANAL
      0960   AGRONOMY                         34872    NORTH CENT WEED CONT CONF PROC
      0960   AGRONOMY                         34876    NORTH CENT WEED CONT CONF RES
      0960   AGRONOMY                         34096    NORTHEASTERN WEED CONT CONF PROC
      0960   AGRONOMY                         37260    PLANT & SOIL
      0960   AGRONOMY                         38664    PROCEEDINGS ANN FARM SEED CONF
      0960   AGRONOMY                         38668    PROCEEDINGS SO WEED CONFERENCE
      0960   AGRONOMY                         40832    RESEARCH PROG REP WEST WEED CONF
      0960   AGRONOMY                         40866    RESEARCH REPORT SO WEED CONF
      0960   AGRONOMY                         43296    SOIL SCIENCE
      0960   AGRONOMY                         43312    SOIL SCIENCE SOC AMER PROCEEDING
      0960   AGRONOMY                         43324    SOILS & FERTILIZERS
      0960   AGRONOMY                         46662    TOBACCO ABSTRACTS
      0960   AGRONOMY                         49088    WEEDS
      0960   AGRONOMY                         48704    WESTERN WEED CONTROL CONF PROC
      0960   AGRONOMY                         49896    WHEAT ABSTRACTS
                                               4##
      1040   ARCHITECTURE                     03764    ARCHITECTURAL & ENGINEERING NEWS
      1040   ARCHITECTURE                     03771    ARCHITECTURAL DESIGN
      1040   ARCHITECTURE                     03776    ARCHITECTURAL FORUM
      1040   ARCHITECTURE                     03782    ARCHITECTURAL INDEX
      1040   ARCHITECTURE                     03788    ARCHITECTURAL RECORD
      1040   ARCHITECTURE                     04096    BUILDER ARCHITECT
      1040   ARCHITECTURE                     24554    INTERIORS
      1040   ARCHITECTURE                     35350    OFFICE DESIGN
      1040   ARCHITECTURE                     39008    PROGRESSIVE ARCHITECTURE
      1120   ARGENTINA                        05562    BOLETIN DE ESTADISTICA ARGENTINA
      1120   ARGENTINA                        14619    ECONOMIC SURVEY
      1120   ARGENTINA                        32720    NACION
      1120   ARGENTINA                        38510    PRIMERA PLANA
      1120   ARGENTINA                        43120    SITUATION IN ARGENTINA
      1120   ARGENTINA                        45229    SURCO ARGENTINE
                                               6#
      1200   ART                              02632    AMERICAN ARTIST
      1200   ART                              04064    ART DIRECTION
      1200   ART                              07360    C A MAGAZINE
      1200   ART                              12673    D A PAPER & THE GRAPHIC ARTS
      1200   ART                              17835    FAST ANNOUNCE PRINT CB ART PHOTO
      1200   ART                              21216    GRAPHIC ARTS PROGRESS
      1200   ART                              21248    GRAPHIS
```

ROUTING LIST

```
                    DEERE & COMPANY LIBRARY ROUTING LIST                 DATE PRINTED 6/06/66
      TITLE                                                                                     PAGE 7
      CODE   TITLE OF PUBLICATION      FREQ    COPY SEQ  DEPT  EMP     EMPLOYEE NAME
                                                               NO                              RTE DIR
                                                    1#
      00960  AGRICULTURAL HISTORY      1111    001   1    120   46528  G F MEILEY
      00960  AGRICULTURAL HISTORY      1111    001   2    451   17620  R E CARLSON
      00960  AGRICULTURAL HISTORY      1111    001   3    435   21080  C L DALTON
      00960  AGRICULTURAL HISTORY      1111    001   5    541   10760  C L ANDERSON
      00960  AGRICULTURAL HISTORY      1111    001   6    541   30396  B B KNISELY
      00960  AGRICULTURAL HISTORY      1111    001   7    541   48512  P R NEFF
      00960  AGRICULTURAL HISTORY      1111    001   8    541   46854  R E WALLACE
      00960  AGRICULTURAL HISTORY      1111    001   9    54A   99999  LIBRARY FILE 51A16
                                                    1#
      00992  AGRICULTURAL IMPLEMENTS INDUSTRY 4000 001 1   900   37520  L S KELLOGG
      00992  AGRICULTURAL IMPLEMENTS INDUSTRY 4000 001 2   400   17624  R J CARLSON
      00992  AGRICULTURAL IMPLEMENTS INDUSTRY 4000 001 3   850   48464  H A MYERS
      00992  AGRICULTURAL IMPLEMENTS INDUSTRY 4000 001 9   54A   22999  LIBRARY FILE HD9484G2A
      01088  AGRICULTURAL INSTITUTE REVIEW    5252 001 1   850   47760  C S MORRISON
      01088  AGRICULTURAL INSTITUTE REVIEW    5252 001 2   850   18556  P N CHON
      01088  AGRICULTURAL INSTITUTE REVIEW    5252 001 9   54A   22999  LIBRARY FILE MAGAZINES
      01088  AGRICULTURAL INSTITUTE REVIEW    5252 002 1   430   33496  P A HILLMAN
      01088  AGRICULTURAL INSTITUTE REVIEW    5252 002 2   440   26128  G E FERRIS
      01088  AGRICULTURAL INSTITUTE REVIEW    5252 003 9   54A   99999  LIBRARY FILE MAGAZINES
                                                    3#
      01120  AGRICULTURAL LEGISLATION  7777    001   1    440   60688  G R SOLLENBERGER
      01120  AGRICULTURAL LEGISLATION  7777    002   9    54A   99999  LIBRARY FILE VERTICAL
                                                    2#
      01152  AGRICULTURAL LETTER       8 6     001   1    900   37520  L S KELLOGG
      01152  AGRICULTURAL LETTER       8 6     001   2    850   57040  L C SARTORIUS
      01152  AGRICULTURAL LETTER       8 6     001   3?    912  31760  H M HARRIS JR
      01152  AGRICULTURAL LETTER       8 6     001   4?    912  25440  B A EVERETT
      01152  AGRICULTURAL LETTER       8 6     001   5?    912  10484  D T CHEN
      01152  AGRICULTURAL LETTER       8 6     002   9    54A   99999  LIBRARY FILE VERTICAL
                                                    2#
      01184  AGRICULTURAL MACHINERY JOURNAL  7777 001 1    100   27280  G T FRENCH
      01184  AGRICULTURAL MACHINERY JOURNAL  7777 001 2    270   29372  J H GRAFLUND
```

EMPLOYEE LIST

```
              DEERE & COMPANY LIBRARY LISTING OF EMPLOYEES RECEIVING PUBLICATIONS    DATE PRINTED 1/21/66
     DEPT   EMP    EMPLOYEE NAME        COPY   TITLE   TITLE OF PUBLICATION                     PAGE  1
            NO.                          NO.   CODE                                        ROUTED DIRECT
      105   32976  J W HENRY             1     06464   BUSINESS ABROAD INTL TRADE REV
      105   32976  J W HENRY             1     11001   COUNCIL FOR LATIN AMER QUART BUL
      105   32976  J W HENRY             1     16816   EXPRESS REPORTS
      105   32976  J W HENRY             1     18672   FIRST PERSON REPORTS OVERSEAS
      105   32976  J W HENRY             1     20016   FOREX SERVICE
      105   32976  J W HENRY             1     24944   INTERNATIONAL REPORTS
      105   32976  J W HENRY             1     41584   RUNDTS MARKET REPORTS
      105   32976  J W HENRY             3     41500   RUNDTS WEEKLY INTELLIGENCE
      105   32976  J W HENRY             1     47168   TRADE TALK
      105   32976  J W HENRY            19     48768   WALL STREET JOURNAL
                                               1#
      105   33082  O E HINTZ             8     01472   AGRICULTURAL RESEARCH
      105   33082  O E HINTZ             1     03264   AMERICAN STATISTICIAN
      105   33082  O E HINTZ             1     04872   BALANCE SHEET OF AGRICULTURE
      105   33082  O E HINTZ             1     06240   BULLETIN D INFORMATION DU CNEEMA
      105   33082  O E HINTZ             1     13066   DOANES FARM MARKET LETTER
      105   33082  O E HINTZ             1     13080   DOANES AGR REPORT MAG
      105   33082  O E HINTZ             1     13929   DOANES AGRICULTURAL REPORT
      105   33082  O E HINTZ             1     14088   ECONOMIST
      105   33082  O E HINTZ             1     23136   ILO PANORAMA
      105   33082  O E HINTZ             3     23200   IMPLEMENT & TRACTOR
      105   33082  O E HINTZ             1     24992   INTERNATIONAL ABSTR IN OPER RES
      105   33082  O E HINTZ             1     24808   INTERNATIONAL COMMERCE
      105   33082  O E HINTZ             1     25344   IOWA FARM SCIENCE
      105   33082  O E HINTZ             1     26304   JOURNAL OF FARM ECONOMICS
      105   33082  O E HINTZ             1     26736   JOURNAL OF SOC IND & APPL MATH
      105   33082  O E HINTZ             1     35712   OPERATIONS RESEARCH
      105   33082  O E HINTZ             1     35728   OPERATIONS RESEARCH BULLETIN
      105   33082  O E HINTZ             1     37600   POPULATION BULLETIN
      105   33082  O E HINTZ             1     41584   RUNDTS MARKET REPORTS
      105   33082  O E HINTZ             3     41500   RUNDTS WEEKLY INTELLIGENCE
      105   33082  O E HINTZ             1     43776   SPILL SHEET
      105   33082  O E HINTZ             1     44216   STANFORD RESEARCH INSTITUTE J
      105   33082  O E HINTZ             1     44400   STATISTICAL INDICATOR REPORTS
      105   33082  O E HINTZ            22     48768   WALL STREET JOURNAL
                                               24#
      105   47922  R L MUELLER           1     04442   ATLANTIC COMMUNITY NEWS
      105   47922  R L MUELLER           1     10800   COMMON MARKET
      105   47922  R L MUELLER           1     11001   COUNCIL FOR LATIN AMER QUART BUL
      105   47922  R L MUELLER           1     11003   COUNCIL FOR LATIN AMER REPORT
      105   47922  R L MUELLER           1     14400   EFTA REPORTER
      105   47922  R L MUELLER           1     18672   FIRST PERSON REPORTS OVERSEAS
      105   47922  R L MUELLER           1     19004   FOREIGN SERVICE LIST
      105   47922  R L MUELLER           1     24808   INTERNATIONAL COMMERCE
      105   47922  R L MUELLER           1     36272   PANAGRA
      105   47922  R L MUELLER FILE      3     41584   RUNDTS MARKET REPORTS
      105   47922  R L MUELLER FILE      3     41500   RUNDTS WEEKLY INTELLIGENCE
      105   47922  R L MUELLER           1     47168   TRADE TALK
      105   47922  R L MUELLER          19     48768   WALL STREET JOURNAL
```

471

SELECTED REFERENCES

Harold B. Allen (editor), *Readings in Applied English Linguistics*. New York: Appleton-Century-Crofts, Inc., 1958.
Theodore M. Bernstein, *Watch Your Language*. Great Neck, N.Y.: Channel Press, 1958.
Leland Brown, *Effective Business Report Writing*, 2nd ed. Englewood Cliffs, N.J.: Prentice-Hall, Inc., 1963.
George de Mare, *Communicating for Leadership*. New York: The Ronald Press, 1968.
Frank J. Devlin, *Business Communication*. Homewood, Ill.: Richard D. Irwin, Inc., 1968.
John S. Fieden, "For Better Business Writing," *Harvard Business Review*, Vol. 43, No. 1, pp. 164–172 (January–February 1965).
Rudolf Flesch, *How to Write, Speak, and Think More Effectively*. New York: The New American Library of World Literature, Inc., 1963.
Improving Management Communication, General Management Series, No. 145. New York: American Management Association, 1950.
Raymond V. Lesikar, *Business Communication*. Homewood, Ill.: Richard D. Irwin, Inc., 1968.
John G. McLean, "Better Reports for Better Control," *Harvard Business Review*, Vol. 35, No. 3, pp. 95–104 (May–June 1957).
J. H. Menning and C. W. Wilkinson, *Communicating Through Letters and Reports*, 4th ed. Homewood, Ill.: Richard D. Irwin, Inc., 1967.
Ralph G. Nichols and Leonard A. Stevens, *Are You Listening?* New York: McGraw-Hill Book Company, Inc., 1957.
William M. Sattler, "Talking Ourselves into Communications Crises," *Michigan Business Review*, Vol. 9, No. 4, pp. 25–31 (July 1957).
William M. Schutte and Erwin R. Steinberg, *Communication in Business and Industry*, 2nd ed. New York: Holt, Rinehart and Winston, Inc., 1964.
Norman G. Shidle, *The Art of Successful Communication*. New York: McGraw-Hill Book Company, 1965.
Nila Barton Smith, *Read Faster—and Get More From Your Reading*. Englewood Cliffs, N.J.: Prentice-Hall, Inc., 1958.
William Strunk, Jr. and E. B. White, *The Elements of Style*. New York: The Macmillan Company, 1959.

chapter 20

SPECIALIZED INFORMATIONAL SYSTEMS

The functions of budgeting and accounting in the managerial process are considered in the first part of this chapter. This subject matter is approached from a managerial rather than an accounting perspective. The discussion is then directed to a selected number of informational systems involving the functional areas of management. Particular attention is given to the famous Gantt Chart and to a more recently developed planning instrument called PERT.

Budgetary Planning and Control Systems

As was pointed out in Chapter 17, budgets are frequently used to communicate plans to various parts of the organization. Some organizations have developed a comprehensive budgetary system encompassing every phase of planning and operations. The various budgets are quantitatively and logically related and form an integrated system. Other organizations have partial budgeting systems concerned with particular aspects of the planning problem. For example, budgeting activities may be confined to the preparation of a sales and a production budget.

Kinds of Budgets

The planning or operating budget is concerned with forecasted relationships between revenues and costs. The budgeting process generally begins with the preparation of the sales forecast, which becomes the *sales budget* after official approval. Companies with income sources other than sales (such as interest from investments and royalties) may prepare a budget estimating such income. The sales budget provides the data necessary to prepare the *production budget* and other subsidiary budgets. The production budget sets forth the quantities of finished products that must be produced to satisfy the sales forecast and provide the inventories desired at the end of the budget period.[1] The information contained in the production budget can be used to prepare materials budgets, purchase budgets, and the labor budget.

The *materials budget* lists the kinds and quantities of raw materials, parts, and supplies required to produce the finished products specified in the production budget. The *purchase budget* specifies the quantities of materials that must be purchased to meet production and inventory requirements together with estimates of purchase costs. Possible changes in material prices, necessary inventory levels to meet production schedules, and the market supply situation should be considered in constructing this budget. For example, an anticipated rise in the market price of raw materials or a possible shortage in supply may warrant a higher volume of purchases during the early part of the budget period. The *labor budget* specifies the amount of direct labor necessary to meet production schedules. Required hours of direct labor can be multiplied by estimated wage rates to obtain total and per unit labor cost. This information can be used by financial executives to estimate the funds needed to meet payrolls during the budget period. The personnel department can use labor budget information to plan recruitment, layoffs, and training. The factory overhead budget encompasses manufacturing expenses or burdens that cannot be directly allocated to particular products. Included in this budget are indirect labor costs, indirect materials costs, and such miscellaneous expense items as rent, heat, power, light, insurance, and depreciation. A considerable portion of total manufacturing expenses can be attributed to the activities of service departments, such as the time study department, the maintenance and repair department, the production planning department, and the inspection department. These departments generally prepare *service department budgets,* which set forth the estimated cost of providing their services at the projected volume of production.

The *distribution expense budget* takes into account the estimated costs of selling and delivering company products, such as advertising, sales promotion, direct selling expenses, packing and delivery, and record keeping.

---

[1] The quantities specified by the production budget will be higher or lower than sales budget estimates by the difference between inventories at the beginning and inventory levels desired at the end of the budget period.

Estimated distribution expenses are generally subdivided in terms of departmental responsibility, such as sales territory, branch and home offices, and other modes of departmentation. The *administrative expense budget* is essentially concerned with the expenses that result from the performance of general management functions. Included in this budget are top executive salaries and traveling expenses, corporate directors' fees, professional service fees, and office expenses.

The budgets described above contain the basic information necessary to construct an estimated profit and loss statement, a projected balance sheet, a cash budget, and other financial budgets. The estimated profit and loss statement, which is usually broken down into months and quarters, indicates the profit potential of the overall company plan. The estimated balance sheet shows the financial consequences of the operating plans and investment at the end of the budget period. Such estimates can be used to evaluate the effectiveness of plans from both an operating and a financial point of view. Appropriate planning adjustments can be made if the projections indicate unsatisfactory consequences or if actual results begin to show unanticipated variations from budget estimates.

Two highly significant subfinancial budgets are the *cash budget* and the *capital additions budget*. A lack of sufficient liquidity is an important reason for business failures. The primary purpose of the cash budget is to prevent a possibly disastrous depletion of funds needed for operations. The cash budget is an estimate of cash receipts and cash disbursements during the budget period. Its preparation involves estimating the amount of cash that will be collected from accounts receivables for a specified period (usually a month) and the backlog of cash available from previous periods. The labor budget, the materials budget, and the various expense budgets provide information about cash requirements at various times within the budget period. Difficulties that arise from variations in the relative flow of cash receipts and disbursements can generally be overcome by building up liquid reserves and the use of short-term bank credit. Capital additions budgets detail planned expenditures for additional plant, machinery, and equipment, improvements in existing facilities, and replacement due to depreciation and obsolescence. Many companies prepare a long-term capital additions budget encompassing a period of years. Such a budget is highly tentative because it involves a long-range forecast of product and money market conditions, assumptions about the consequences of company operations during the intervening period, and a distant projection of planning strategy. But in spite of the difficulties, a long-term capital additions budget gives emphasis to the importance of systematic forward planning and helps to focus the attention of management upon the problem. Short-term capital additions budgets can be used either separately or in conjunction with long-term budgets to specify planned expenditures during the current period.

Length of the Budget Period

The length of the budget period is influenced by such factors as the time necessary for a complete merchandise turnover, the duration of the production cycle, the timing of financial and purchase operations, and the pattern of seasonal variations. The extent to which the future can be accurately forecasted is a consideration, together with the willingness of management to engage in systematic forward planning. The length of the accounting period and the scheduling of tax liabilities may also play a role in setting the budget period. Such factors as the timing of legislative appropriations and charitable contributions are often important in nonbusiness organizations.

Some organizations budget ahead for a period of a year with quarterly and monthly breakdowns at the time the budget is prepared. Others divide the budget into quarters with a monthly breakdown only for the quarter that immediately follows. Quarterly revisions are made in the budgets if the original forecasts and estimates are not in accord with the actual course of events. Forecasting and planning difficulties cause some companies to make monthly revisions in budget values. A progressive or continuous budgeting system is sometimes used under such conditions. An annual, semiannual, or quarterly budget is maintained by adding another month after each monthly revision of budget estimates. Some budgets may involve longer or shorter time periods than the basic forecast and operating budgets. Plant expansion, research and development, and financial planning budgets may be set up for three-, ten-, or even twenty-year periods. Such budgets may be integrated with annual budgets or have an essentially independent status. Some special purpose and project budgets are adjuncts to the over-all budget structure and have a life-span of only a few weeks or months.

Fixed and Flexible Budgets

Too much budget inflexibility over too long a period of time can be extremely hazardous. The organizational and departmental goals set forth in budgets are based on forecasts and estimates that are not always accurate. An unanticipated decline in sales or cost increases often dictate corrective changes in existing plans and budgets. However, budgets should not necessarily be adjusted the moment a miscalculation becomes evident. Too many modifications can create more difficulties than they correct. Some degree of stability is necessary for effective planning and operations. Organizations generally attempt to mitigate the disruptive impact of too many changes by making periodic budget adjustments on a monthly or quarterly rather than a daily basis. Administered budget flexibility is essential under conditions of uncertainty and change. A failure to make appropriate planning changes can seriously impair survival power in a dynamic environment. Budgets should always be subordinate to the requirements of effective planning. They should not be permitted to stifle initiative and infuse stagnation.

Another approach to the problem of change is to use budgets with a built-in flexibility. Some budget values can be made to change with changes in the volume of business. A flexible or variable budget is premised on the idea that some cost or expense items vary with different levels of sales, production, or activity. Such costs as depreciation, insurance, and plant maintenance generally change less with changes in output than direct labor and direct material costs. The basic problem in constructing a variable budget is to determine the degree to which cost or expense items vary with output. Accounting records, statistical measures, and engineering estimates can be used to classify costs into various categories and calculate their amounts. However, it should not be assumed that every item can be rigidly classified as either fixed or variable. Many costs fall somewhere in between the two extremes, and they may also have different degrees of variability in different companies. Direct labor costs, for example, will tend to be less variable (or more fixed) in a company that maintains a large nucleus of permanent employees during seasonal slack periods. A step-budget method or a formula method can be used in a flexible budget system. The step-budget method results in a different budget for various levels of output. The formula method makes possible the computation of budget values for any level of output by adding fixed and variable costs. Thus, to use a simplified example, if fixed costs total $10,000 per month or quarter and variable costs $10 per unit, the budget amounts would be $20,000 for 1000 units, $30,000 for 2000 units, $40,000 for 3000 units, etc.

The Budgeting Process

The budgeting process generally begins with a meeting of the budget committee composed of top executives. The budget committee evaluates the manner in which various external and internal factors may affect the achievement of organizational goals. The final result is an estimate of the sales and production volume for the forthcoming period. Such estimates are sometimes given tentative approval by the chief executive, a top planning committee, or the board of directors. The executives who give such approval are frequently members of the budget committee and participate in the deliberations of the committee. The information provided by the budget committee will be the basis for the formulation of subsidiary budget estimates. The heads of line, staff, and service departments usually participate in the preparation of departmental budgets. A budget director, the controller, or the chief accountant is often given the responsibility for administering and implementing the budget program. Such a person serves in a staff capacity and performs advisory, scheduling, liaison, informational, and supervisory duties. The budgeting process is generally accompanied by a great deal of formal and informal consultation among executives. Differences of opinion and conflicts of interest are always present and must be resolved by compromise or compulsion. Effective budgeting involves more than the manipulation of accounting and other kinds of quantitative data. The budgeting process is fundamentally the planning process, and the budgets that are finally approved are messages about objectives and plans.

Budgets as Information

Budgets are messages that express organizational and departmental plans and anticipated consequences of future operations in quantitative terms. Their efficiency as communication devices is dependent upon the extent to which they transmit the same meaning to different people. Some aspects of a budgetary system are highly effective in this respect. For example, the quantitative information about material requirements found in material and purchase budgets transmits meaning in exact terms. But the quantitative preciseness of budgets does not eliminate semantic difficulties and other kinds of distortion. Budget information is often subject to different interpretations and may convey a variety of meanings. The president may view a reduction in a departmental budget as an inducement to higher productivity; the department head may see it as an unjustified attempt to curtail his department's activities; employees may feel that it threatens such dire consequences as wage reductions and unemployment.

Budgets, like messages in other languages, can be manipulated apart from the reality they are supposed to represent. As was emphasized earlier, a failure to change budgets with changes in actual conditions can lead to serious difficulties. The logic of finance and accounting is sometimes applied too rigorously and without an understanding of the complex economic, engineering, and socio-psychological problems involved in the planning problem. Revenues are not increased or costs reduced merely by juggling figures in an account book. Budgets are written in a highly abstract language and contain many implicit assumptions about appropriate managerial and operating behavior. They provide inadequate information about the manner in which objectives are to be achieved. They are generally supplemented by other kinds of messages to give subordinates a better understanding of their responsibilities. However, the lack of explicit information about appropriate managerial action makes budgets excellent devices for achieving decentralization. Thus, budgets can be used to indicate the superior's conception of the revenue and cost consequences of a particular line of activity. The subordinate can be left to his own resources in solving planning problems with little direct supervision from the superior. Control is achieved by an evaluation of the relationship between actual revenues and costs and budgeted estimates.

Forecasting errors, measurement problems, and semantic difficulties can cause nondeliberate distortions in budget information. Budgets may also be deliberately distorted by the people who participate in their preparation. Some departmental executives ask for more than they actually need to compensate for reductions that might be imposed by higher executives, which can lead to a guessing game as to how much budgets must be padded to make up for corrective cuts from above. Subordinates with higher budget estimates are sometimes able to win advantages over those who play the game straight. Empire builders are frequently highly skilled in the art of budget manipulation. Such interpersonal strategy not only seriously impedes the development of effective planning strategies but also reduces the effectiveness of budgets as efficiency measures and leads to unwarranted rewards or penalties. Thus, a subordinate who can push through higher expense estimates than other subordinates will have an advantage when estimates are compared with actual results. However, since too much discrepancy between estimates and results can lead to a reduced budget during the succeeding period, there is a tendency to shoot for a "reasonable" or "safe" margin. This dilemma is faced by many executives who work under a budget system. A favorable margin between budgeted and actual revenues and costs indicates managerial efficiency and generally results in rewards for the manager. But there is also the danger that future budgets will become more restrictive and reduce the likelihood of a reward situation. Executives and public administrators sometimes deliberately increase expenses in an effort to find a favorable solution to this dilemma.

Superiors should keep a wary eye on attempts to distort budget information, but they should not assume that the practice can be completely eliminated or that it always evolves from evil motives. The hierarchical planning process involves some degree of conflict about objectives and plans. Subordinates should actively promote the interests of their departments; a failure to do so can lead to an imbalance in the part played by particular functional, product, or territorial areas in the total planning process. For example, if the advertising executive takes a wishy-washy attitude with respect to budget requests, the result might be a reduction in company revenues for lack of advertising expenditures. Superiors should take the personalities of subordinates into consideration in approving budgets. They should bring the "empire builder" into line, but they should not neglect necessary upward adjustments. A low budget request does not always serve the organization better than a high one; a penny saved may be a dollar lost.

Budgets and Efficiency

Budgets can increase managerial and operating efficiency, but they can also reduce efficiency by disrupting cooperation. The budgeting process can become the focal point of conflict within the managerial hierarchy and between managerial and operating levels. An empirical study of the effects of manufacturing budgets upon front-line supervisors, sponsored by the Controllership Foundation, indicates some of the difficulties that can arise.[2] Supervisors and workers tended to view budgets as unreasonable pressure devices imposed by higher management levels. Many of them also resented what to them was an implication that they were lazy and needed to be pushed to do a good job. Interviews with top line and staff executives gave evidence of beliefs that constant pressure is required to counteract tendencies to restrict output. The reaction to what was assumed to be too much budget pressure was a variety of retaliatory and defensive moves. Workers banded together informally to provide a common front against management, more grievances were sent to higher levels, and the grapevine spread false rumors about management's motives. Supervisors attempted to shift the burden by blaming other supervisors and staff personnel for their failures to meet budget goals. The overall consequence of budget pressure in the plants studied was a negative attitude toward higher management and the company. Professor Chris Argyris, who participated in the study, concluded that "because of the effect of budgets on people, they tend to generate forces which in the long run decrease efficiency."[3]

How much is too much budget pressure, and what kind of measure can be used to find the answer? An approach is to measure the physiological and psychological fatigue that results from various amounts of managerial and other work, but the development of workload standards from studies of the incidence of fatigue does not necessarily lead to a higher degree of cooperation. A basic problem is that different people have different attitudes toward the norms set by budgets. It stems partly from the fact that

[2] Chris Argyris, "Human Problems with Budgets," *Harvard Business Review,* Vol. 31, No. 1, January–February 1953, pp. 97–110.
[3] *Ibid.,* p. 97.

the personal goals of various groups of organizational participants differ. The industrial worker is frequently inclined to view higher productivity as detrimental to his interests. Executives and budgeting people tend to view higher productivity in terms of the promotion and salary increase that might result. The supervisor's interests are similar to those of the higher executive, but he may also want somewhat lower productivity standards in order to eliminate the problems that result from worker resistance. Such conflicts of interests cannot be entirely eliminated and are present even when budgets are not used. The problem is to prevent interest conflicts that seriously disrupt the cooperative process.

The attitudes that people have toward budgets frequently evolve from highly nonlogical premises. Factual and logical arguments in support of particular budget values do not usually impress people with strong beliefs to the contrary; attitudes and sentiments are not easily changed once they become firmly established. The motivational consequences of budgets should always be considered. Executives should think twice before launching a budget program if subordinates have a completely negative attitude toward budgets. They should recognize that what they consider to be "reasonable" budgets may seem highly "unreasonable" to subordinates. Organizational and departmental goals are achieved through cooperative effort rather than through a mechanistic manipulation of budget data. The problem of achieving higher productivity is more complex than making arithmetic adjustments in budgets, and too much budget pressure can reduce rather than increase productivity through its effect upon cooperation. However, complaints about budget pressure may express symptoms rather than causes and denote dissatisfactions about other matters.

Executives should listen to subordinates and make an effort to understand their sentiments about budgets. Subordinates should be given an opportunity to express themselves, and their suggestions should be given explicit recognition. Participation in the formulation of budget values can be helpful in gaining acceptance and preventing conflict. But, as Professor Argyris has emphasized, "if top-management executives are going to use participation, then they should use it in the real sense of the word." [4] A perfunctory approach to participation can do more harm than good. However, superiors should not ignore the importance of leadership in the budgeting process. Subordinate participation without leadership is mobocracy rather than democracy and can have less to offer than a dictatorial approach. It should also be realized that some degree of resistance to budgetary and other kinds of change is normal and does not reflect a lack of cooperation.

[4] Argyris, *op. cit.*, p. 108.

Budgets as Control Instruments

The performance of managerial and operating personnel can be measured by a comparison of budget estimates with accounting and other data. However, a great deal of discretion should be used in interpreting the significance of such comparisons.

Accounting as an Instrument of Managerial Control

Accounting is a specialized language system that is used to measure the consequences of organizational activities and to communicate such information to executives and others. The logic of accounting has evolved over a long period of evolutionary and analytical development. Although records of business transactions can be traced to ancient Babylon, the modern method of double-entry bookkeeping was probably invented during the fourteenth century. The double-entry system is premised on the idea of an equation of business transactions and that every transaction represents a duality of elements. Something that has tangible or intangible value is received, but, at the same time, an equivalent value is given up. The value of each transaction is expressed in monetary units and results in increases and decreases in assets, liabilities, and net worth (owners' equity).

The Accounting Process

The information that flows into the accounting system is initially recorded into journals or books of original entry. Postings are made from journals in accounts which are combined in some systematic order into ledgers. Accounts are frequently arranged in the order that they will appear in such financial statements as the balance sheet and the income statement. They may also be classified alphabetically, by departmental units, according to geographical area, by budget classifications, and in other ways. Systematic numerical or alphabetical codes are often used to identify accounts in large and complex accounting systems. The problems of systematization and coding become particularly pertinent in companies that utilize electronic data-processing equipment. The changes that occur in assets, liabilities, and net worth as the result of business operations are recorded in the accounts as *debits* and *credits*. Debit has reference to the left side of an account and indicates increases in assets, decreases in liabilities, decreases in net worth, decreases in income, and increases in expense. Credit refers to the right side of an account and indicates decreases in assets, increases in liabilities, etc. The fact that every entry involves both debits and credits in equal amounts means that the two sides of an account or a system of accounts must always be in balance. A lack of balance can result only from errors.

Financial Statements and Reports

The basic problem of the planner is to achieve a favorable balance between revenues and costs. An accounting system accumulates information about the revenue and cost consequences of planning and operations. This information is presented to management and other interested parties in the form of financial statements and reports. The *balance sheet,* the *income statement,* and the *statement of retained earnings* (or surplus),[5] together with supporting schedules that may be appropriate, are generally sufficient to appraise the overall financial and operating condition of an organization. The balance sheet indicates the nature and amounts of assets, liabilities, and net worth at a given date as illustrated in Figure 20-1. The income statement reports income, expenses, and profits (or losses) for a given period of time. It also details some of the elements that make up total income and expenses as illustrated in Figure 20-2. The statement of retained earnings provides the connecting link between the other two statements, explaining the increases (from net income) and decreases (from net losses or dividends or both) in undistributed income during the period. Accounting information may also be detailed and classified to highlight specific aspects of business operations. For example, reports about such matters as manufacturing costs, purchases and inventory changes, sales returns and allowances, salary and wage schedules, cash requirements, and bad debts may be helpful in solving particular planning and control problems. The importance of financial reporting to stockholders, creditors, employees, and governmental agencies should also be emphasized. Such reports are necessary to satisfy the personal and institutional interests of those who contribute resources to the organization and to meet the requirements of the law.

---

[5] There has been an increasing tendency to discontinue the use of the word "surplus" because it has been subject to misinterpretation by nonaccountants. C. A. Moyer and R. K. Mautz, *Intermediate Accounting* (New York: John Wiley and Sons, Inc., 1962), p. 310.

PHILLIPS PETROLEUM COMPANY

Consolidated Balance Sheet at December 31, 1967

ASSETS
Current Assets

Cash	$ 141,466,000
Short-term investments, at cost	5,606,000
Notes and accounts receivable	
(less reserves: 1967—$3,976,000)	351,530,000
Inventories	
Crude oil, petroleum products, and merchandise	288,199,000
Materials and supplies, at average cost or condition value	30,781,000
Total Current Assets	757,582,000
Investments and Long-term Receivables, at cost	
(less reserves: 1967—$3,333,000)	290,313,000
Properties, Plants, and Equipment	
at cost, less reserves	1,709,674,000
Prepaid and Deferred Charges	29,664,000
	$2,787,233,000

LIABILITIES AND STOCKHOLDERS' EQUITY
Current Liabilities

Notes payable	$ 45,589,000
Accounts payable	220,229,000
Long-term debt—due within one year	49,890,000

Analytical Methods Used by Accountants

Accounting and financial experts use various methods in evaluating accounting information.[6] One approach is to study the absolute amounts of particular items in the various statements to determine what significance they may have. Another is to compare the same statements for two or more dates or periods or for different organizations, departments, geographical areas, etc. Such comparisons sometimes indicate important developments and problems to which management should be alerted. For example, a marked increase in certain expense items over a period of time may warrant managerial action. Percentages may be used to show the relationship between various elements of accounting information. Particular expense items or net profit may be expressed as a percentage of sales or some other

---

[6] A discussion of analytical methods and the interpretation of accounting information is found in Moyer and Mautz, *op. cit.*, pp. 482–498.

Accrued taxes	86,336,000
Other accruals	27,657,000
Total Current Liabilities	429,701,000
Long-term Debt	690,034,000
Deferred Credits	
Federal income taxes	67,317,000
Other	61,188,000
Total Deferred Credits	128,505,000
Reserve for Contingencies	27,568,000
Minority Interest in Subsidiaries Consolidated	15,859,000
Stockholders' Equity	
Common stock, $5 par value	
Shares authorized—50,000,000	
Shares issued (1967—35,914,051)	179,570,000
Capital in excess of par value of common stock	329,247,000
Earnings employed in the business	1,044,095,000
	1,552,912,000
Less treasury stock, at cost	
(1967—1,055,465 shares)	57,346,000
Total Stockholders' Equity	$1,495,566,000
	$2,787,233,000

Figure 20-1. Balance Sheet. Courtesy of Phillips Petroleum Company, Bartlesville, Oklahoma. Some of the details in the original are not reproduced in the above balance sheet. Inventories are priced substantially at cost (LIFO), which is lower than market in the aggregate. Other explanatory notes, which are an integral part of this company's financial statements, are found in the original report.

---

base. A comparison of percentages over a period of time or with industry and other information is sometimes used in determining problem areas. The fact that advertising expenses increased from 3 per cent to 6 per cent of sales or that net profit declined from 9 per cent to 5 per cent of net worth may have significance. A similar technique is to translate relationships into a ratio of one figure to another, that is, the ratio of current assets to current liabilities is 2 to 1. Accountants have given a great deal of attention to "ratio analysis" or a study of the relationship between various elements of accounting information. Some ratios or percentages have particular significance in evaluating financial and operating results.[7] For example, the ratio of current assets to current liabilities or the total of cash

[7] A list of ratios that are commonly used in the analysis of accounting information can be found in books on accounting principles. Some typical ratios are: current assets to current liabilities, merchandise to current assets, total liabilities to net worth, net profit to net sales, net sales to net worth, and net profit to total assets.

PHILLIPS PETROLEUM COMPANY

Consolidated Statement of Income and
Earnings Employed in the Business, 1967

Income	
Gross Operating income	$1,981,572,000
Other income	30,655,000
	2,012,227,000
Cost and Expenses	
Cost of sales and services	1,276,145,000
Selling, general, and administrative expense	245,896,000
Depreciation, depletion, and retirements	170,136,000
Interest and expense on indebtedness	42,954,000
Taxes other than income taxes	49,330,000
Provision for income taxes	63,751,000
	1,848,212,000
Income Before Extraordinary Item	164,015,000
Net Income	164,015,000
Earnings Employed in the Business at Beginning of Year	961,161,000
	1,125,176,000
Dividends Paid (1967—$2.35 a share)	81,081,000
Earnings Employed in the Business at End of Year	$1,044,095,000

Figure 20-2. Income statement. Courtesy of Phillips Petroleum Company, Bartlesville, Oklahoma. In addition, taxes were collected on the sale of petroleum products and paid to taxing agencies.

and receivables to current liabilities (the acid test) provides information about the organization's capacity to meet its current obligations as they mature. A ratio of net profit to net worth and net profit to sales, particularly when compared over a period of time and with other pertinent information, can afford important insights about organizational performance and return on investment. However, accountants and executives should be wary of placing too much emphasis upon the mechanics of ratio analysis to solve their problems. As Moyer and Mautz have written:

There is far more to both accounting and business than can be compressed into a few ratio results or into a single index as some would do. Ratio analysis is a useful tool to make accounting reports of business operations and conditions more readily understandable, but, unless the analyst knows (a) precisely what the ratio is intended to point out, (b) what a satisfactory ratio is for that company under the conditions that exist, and (c) any possible errors in the underlying data that might affect the ratio results, he is very likely to arrive at erroneous conclusions. And, unless all the financial data presented have been studied with a view toward comprehending the full significance of the data and their interrelationships, he may find himself tending to rely too much on a single fact or relationship which may be more than counterbalanced by other factors that he has overlooked.[8]

The Meaning of Accounting Information

Financial statements and reports are important instruments of managerial planning and control, but the information they provide cannot be understood without knowledge about the nature of accounting data, the manner in which the data are classified and combined, and accounting terminology. Executives must have an understanding of the language system if they are to understand the messages that are derived from it. They should also recognize that accounting reports, like messages in any other language, portray an abstract or incomplete picture of the reality of business operations. The significance of accounting information can only be determined by relating it to the environmental and organizational factors that affect organizational dynamics. For example, the information that net profits (as a percentage of sales or net worth) have declined over a period of time has little meaning without an understanding of the causal factors. Declining profits may indicate planning failures, or they may point to the need for control actions. But they may also evolve from environmental changes that cannot be attributed to a lack of effective planning and control. Lower profits may actually reflect greater rather than less managerial and operating efficiency.

The Accuracy of Accounting Information

The accounting profession has given a great deal of attention to the development of theories and techniques to improve the accuracy of accounting information. Much progress has been made in this respect, but a number of difficult problems preclude any sort of perfect solution.[9] A

[8] Moyer and Mautz, *op. cit.*, pp. 484–485.

[9] A comprehensive discussion of some of these problems can be found in: Howard C. Greer, "What Are Accepted Principles of Accounting?" *The Accounting Review,* Vol. 13, No. 1, March 1938, pp. 25–31. A similar critique was made in an address by Marquis G. Eaton, delivered before the Illinois Society of Certified Public Accountants, June 7, 1957, printed in: *Financial Reporting in a Changing Society* (New York: American Institute of Certified Public Accountants). The relationship between accounting concepts and data and managerial problems is given careful scrutiny by Joel Dean in *Managerial Economics* (Englewood Cliffs, N.J.: Prentice-Hall, Inc., 1951).

major problem is that the monetary unit (dollars) in which accounting information is expressed is not a constant measure of value. An analysis of accounting statements over a period of time can lead to erroneous conclusions unless price changes are taken into consideration. Estimating depreciation expenses and inventory values are difficult problems under conditions of inflationary or deflationary price movements. Net profits may be overstated or understated by large amounts unless appropriate adjustments are made in financial statements or by interpretation. Price fluctuations also create difficulties in appraising planning and operating efficiency. Profits or losses may evolve from unanticipated price changes rather than from effective managerial action or the lack of it.

Government regulations and tax legislation may directly or indirectly affect the manner in which business profits are determined. For example, the Interstate Commerce Commission and the Internal Revenue Code implicitly or explicitly stipulate accounting procedures and standards deemed appropriate for their particular purposes. The "profits" that evolve from such accounting practices may differ significantly from the "profits" that result from nonregulated accounting practices. Some companies give formal recognition to this distinction by following generally accepted accounting practices for financial and business operations and maintaining separate sets of information for tax and other purposes. Thus, a company may follow normal schedules for depreciation in its regular accounting system but compute depreciation on the basis of a "fast write-off provision" to take advantage of tax legislation. Other companies follow the accounting practices prescribed by government regulations and make appropriate adjustments for private use. However, the important consideration is not the way in which such problems are handled in the accounts, but a recognition on the part of executives and others that "profits" are not always what they seem to be.

Accountants generally follow what are termed "the accepted principles of accounting" in formulating information about financial and operating conditions. But, to use the title of an article on the subject, "What Are Accepted Principles of Accounting?" [10] There is general agreement that accounting should be based on a going-concern assumption,[11] that profits or losses should not be recognized until actually realized, that all transactions should be accounted for, that expenses should be allocated in the period in which they apply, and other such matters. However, the accounting profession would be the last to assert that the same transaction will be handled in exactly the same way by different accountants. There are sound

[10] Greer, *op. cit.*

[11] Without this assumption costs could not be charged against the revenues of future periods.

	Company A	Company B
Sales	$10,000,000	$10,000,000
Costs and expenses		
Cost of goods	$6,000,000	$6,000,000
Selling costs	1,500,000	1,500,000
LIFO inventory reserve	400,000	
Depreciation	400,000	300,000
Research costs	100,000	20,000
Pension costs	200,000	50,000
Officers' compensation		
Base salaries	200,000	200,000
Bonuses	200,000	
Total costs and expenses	$9,000,000	$8,070,000
Profit before income taxes	$1,000,000	$1,930,000
Income taxes	520,000	1,004,000
Capital gain (after taxes)	$ 480,000	$ 926,000
		150,000
New profit reported	$ 480,000	$1,076,000
Per share (600,000 shares)	$.80	$1.79

Figure 20-3. The Profit-and-Loss Statements for Companies A and B. Reproduced with permission from *Fortune*, Vol. 62, No. 6, December 1960, p. 145.

arguments to support more than one technique for dealing with particular problems. The extent to which accounting results may differ even when "accepted principles of accounting" are used is illustrated by two profit-and-loss statements used as a basis for a debate on accounting principles before members of the American Institute of Certified Public Accountants.[12]

The profit-and-loss statements were for two imaginary companies, A and B, with the same volume and kind of business. In spite of the similarity, B reported significantly higher earnings than A, as shown in Figure 20-3. The following are the differences in accounting technique used by the two companies: B used a first-in-first-out (FIFO) method in pricing inventory, and as a result had no need for the $400,000 inventory reserve set up by company A. B used straight-line depreciation, thereby avoiding a $100,000 charge against income; A practiced accelerated depreciation. B amortized research costs over a five-year period; A did not defer these costs. A funded all current pension costs by putting into a reserve an amount equal

[12] T. A. Wise, "The Auditors Have Arrived (Part II)," *Fortune*, Vol. 62, No. 6, December 1960, p. 145.

to the cost of the employee's current service and amortization of his past service. *B* funded only an amount equal to the discounted value of an employee's present interest in the pension program, with this amount not to exceed the company's current legal liability. *A* paid its officers a cash bonus; *B* gave them stock options, which are not charged to income (stock options can eventually reduce the amount of per-share income). *A* credited capital gains to earned surplus; *B* credited this amount to income.

The accounting profession has given constant consideration to improvements in measurement and reporting techniques. Like others in the business world, the accountant must contend with the uncertainties of a dynamic economy. Much accounting information is directly or indirectly based on forecasts and estimates that may be repudiated by actual events. Some accountants and economists have recommended a modification of accounting methods to handle such problems as price changes. One suggestion is the use of index numbers to reflect changes in price levels, and another is to completely revalue assets if major price changes occur.[13] However, the problem of determining appropriate index numbers and the vagaries of price movements present many practical difficulties. The accuracy of accounting data is also limited by the failure to fully compensate for such intangible elements as goodwill and trademarks. Accountants generally use objective measures, for example, cost and purchase price, to value these assets. However, actual values may be appreciably more or less than the amounts stated in the accounts. The validity and applicability of accounting information is also affected by computational limitations that make necessary a considerable amount of "averaging" and abstracting of data. Also important is that there may be a lengthy time lag between accounting reports and the events they represent. Recently developed mathematical techniques combined with electronic data-processing equipment are sometimes helpful in overcoming this difficulty.

Accounting provides highly useful information for planning and control purposes. But financial statements and reports can also communicate misinformation if their nature and the forces they represent are not properly understood. Executives should understand what accounting can do and what it cannot do. They should recognize that interpretation involves more than a mechanistic appraisal of accounting data.

Financial Reports and Reporting Systems

Accounting is a meaningless language unless the messages derived from it provide information that facilitates the solution of organizational problems. The informational requirements of executives, stockholders, credi-

[13] Moyer and Mautz, *op. cit.,* pp. 520–521.

tors, regulatory agencies, tax authorities, and employees differ in both nature and scope. Accountants should take cognizance of such diverse needs and interests in designing financial statements and reports. They should make allowances for differences between industries and companies in planning the reporting system.

Executives and accountants should recognize that the information potential of accounting is restricted by a number of considerations. A highly organized language system, accounting can communicate meaning more precisely than English, but its information potential is more limited. The accountant is restricted in what he can communicate to executives and others by the logical constraints of his language. He should understand the capacity of his language and recognize that some kinds of information cannot be derived from accounting. A further limitation is that message recipients sometimes lack a sufficient knowledge of the language. Nothing is gained from messages that will not be understood by those who receive them. Accounting messages may have to be simplified and supplemented by the use of another language.[14]

Financial reporting should be viewed as a dynamic rather than a static problem. The individual reports and the system of reporting that gave good results in the past may not adequately reflect the informational needs of today. Prosperity and recession, changes in product and resource markets, product line changes, expansion programs, technological innovation, and legislation may significantly affect the kind of information required for effective managerial action. The steps taken by one company to adapt its reporting system to changing conditions are described by the comptroller of a railroad.

1. While inventories of reports had been taken periodically, there was no mechanism for maintaining them on a current basis. Our minimum starting requirement was to be able to know *at all times* what information was available. Our first problem, therefore, was to provide a current inventory of reports and a mechanism for maintaining it—in other words, *a perpetual inventory* of reports.

2. Obviously, the proper time to start designing a new fire engine is not when your house is on fire. Our second problem, therefore, was to conform the existing reporting system to *current* management needs.

---

[14] Other factors may also restrict the discretion that can be exercised in constructing accounting messages. A high degree of uniformity is imposed by the need for comparative analyses of financial and accounting data within an industry or the economy. The development of professionalism among accountants and the requirements of education have also been important in this respect. The appropriate content of accounting messages is sometimes stipulated by the message recipient. For example, governmental tax and regulatory agencies generally set forth specific informational requirements. Banks, investment firms, credit rating concerns, insurance companies, and executives frequently request particular kinds of accounting information and indicate the manner of presentation.

3. We determined that there was a need for familiarizing our accounting organization with management problems at all levels. Only by doing this could we expect it adequately to fulfill its responsibility (a) for identifying data which were pertinent to those problems, and (b) for interpreting these data in language which would be understood by our management people. The development of these analytical and interpretive functions was related to our third problem: to convert our accounting and financial *statements* into useful and "used" management *reports*.

4. We recognized that the existing report structure, even when conformed to current needs and made more useful through analytical and interpretive services, would not necessarily fulfill future needs. Therefore, means had to be devised to keep us continuously conversant with the control techniques, programs, and objectives of our various sales and operating departments. This was a prerequisite to being able to design more effective new reports and reporting systems responsive to their foreseeable future needs.

5. Lastly, the report production process had to be simplified and expedited to the end that all management reports could fulfill the prime management requirement of being *completely timely*.[15]

The ideas presented in the above quotation have general applicability and pinpoint some of the basic requirements of effective reporting. Electronic data-processing and operations research may facilitate the solution of the time problem.

Cost Accounting

Cost accounting, which is generally categorized as a specialized branch of accounting, is concerned with the accumulation and analysis of cost information. The basic problem of cost accounting is to allocate costs on some kind of unit basis, such as products, services, subassemblies, parts, projects, and departments. Cost accountants generally use the following cost classifications in accumulating and allocating cost information.

Direct Material. Included in this category are the costs of materials that go directly into the product or are readily traceable to the product.

Direct Labor. Includes labor costs that can be charged to the production of a particular product.

Factory Overhead. This category takes into account all cost items that cannot be directly charged to a product, such as indirect labor (supervisory and clerical costs), indirect materials (fuels, abrasives, lubricants), depreciation, insurance, and power.

Administrative Overhead. Included are salaries of executives, staff per-

---

[15] Roger F. Brown, "Financial Data Reporting During Organization and Methods Transitions," *Reporting Financial Data to Top Management, Special Report, No. 25* (New York: American Management Association, Inc., 1957), pp. 112–113.

sonnel, secretarial and clerical personnel, and other nonfactory administrative expenses.

Sales Overhead. Expenses related to the marketing of the product, such as advertising and sales promotion, transportation and storage costs, and salaries paid to sales personnel.

Direct material and labor costs are by definition directly related to the production of a particular product. Such costs can generally be computed and charged from material requisition forms and employee time tickets. However, the cost accountant cannot always assume that such raw data are accurate. Behavioral studies indicate that factory supervisory and operating personnel sometimes deliberately distort information to protect and pursue individual and group interests. A number of methods and formulas are used to distribute factory, administrative, and other overhead expenses. The problem is to find a common factor that varies with the amount of overhead that can be properly assigned to particular products. Variations in direct labor costs, direct labor hours, direct material costs, and machine hour costs are often used to distribute factory overhead or burden. For example, if the total factory overhead is the same as total direct labor costs, one dollar would be added to every dollar of direct labor costs to cover factory overhead expenses. The basic logic of such techniques is to allocate overhead costs to products on an equitable or fair share basis. The intended result is an average unit cost that incorporates some or all elements of actual or historical costs.

Historical cost information can be helpful in determining the profitability of operations. However, distortions in the raw data, the problems of distributing overhead, and classification and computational difficulties can make such information highly inaccurate. The information provided by cost accounting, like other kinds of accounting information, cannot be understood without a knowledge of the nature of the data, the logic used in compilation, and the operations to which the data relate. Executives should also recognize that historical costs, developed by the techniques described in the previous paragraph, are not useful for some purposes.[16] One problem is that the kind of cost information required for planning is not directly provided by historical cost data. A simple projection of past costs into the future, like a projection of past sales data, is generally inadequate. Changes in the resource markets, technological innovations, motivational factors, and changes in plant utilization are factors that may significantly influence future costs. The uncertainties of a dynamic economy can cause estimating errors of great magnitude. Another difficulty is

---

[16] For a comprehensive discussion of costing concepts and problems: Dean, *op. cit.,* pp. 249–347.

that planning involves a consideration of alternative strategies and combinations of strategies. Estimating the cost consequences of the various alternatives presents difficult measurement and forecasting problems. The executive should not expect a high degree of accuracy in the cost information that can be derived about such matters. A rough approximation is about the best that can be achieved even with the most sophisticated mathematical and statistical techniques.

A number of techniques have been developed by accountants, economists, and statisticians to adapt actual and estimated costs to particular managerial problems. Some companies develop *standard costs* to measure efficiency, to serve as a guide for pricing and estimating bids, and for analytical purposes. Standard costs represent management's conception of what cost ought to be under certain assumptions. They are derived from analyses of past cost behavior, time study data, material specifications, and estimates of output level, prices, wages, and overhead expenses. A comparison of actual and standard costs (variance analysis) can be helpful in determining problem areas that require corrective action. Cost data are frequently classified by the degree to which they vary with changes in output for budgeting and planning purposes. Such classifications (fixed, semifixed, and variable costs) are used to construct flexible budgets (discussed earlier in this chapter) and break-even charts. A break-even chart shows the relationship between total sales income and costs at outputs ranging from zero to full plant capacity. Figure 20-4 presents a simplified version of the break-even charts used in business and other organizations. The sales line indicates the expected total income or revenue at different output levels and the total cost line shows expected total expenses over the same output range. The intersection point of the sales and cost lines is the break-even point or the point at which profits are zero. Total profits or losses for different output levels are also indicated on the chart. The need to absorb fixed costs is the primary reason for the losses that are shown for output levels to the left of the break-even point. Some of the break-even charts used by business concerns are constructed to show the manner in which particular factors may influence the total income and expense picture.[17] For example, a series of total cost lines can be used to indicate the manner in which changes in wages, material costs, and more efficient operations affect the profit situation. Break-even charts emphasize that planning involves incremental changes in the total program and that each change should be evaluated in terms of its contribution to profits. They can be used to estimate the income and cost consequences of particular planning alternatives, such as product line additions, changes in plant capacity, price changes, sales promotion programs, and changes in particular cost factors.

[17] The data on break-even charts can also be expressed in algebraic form.

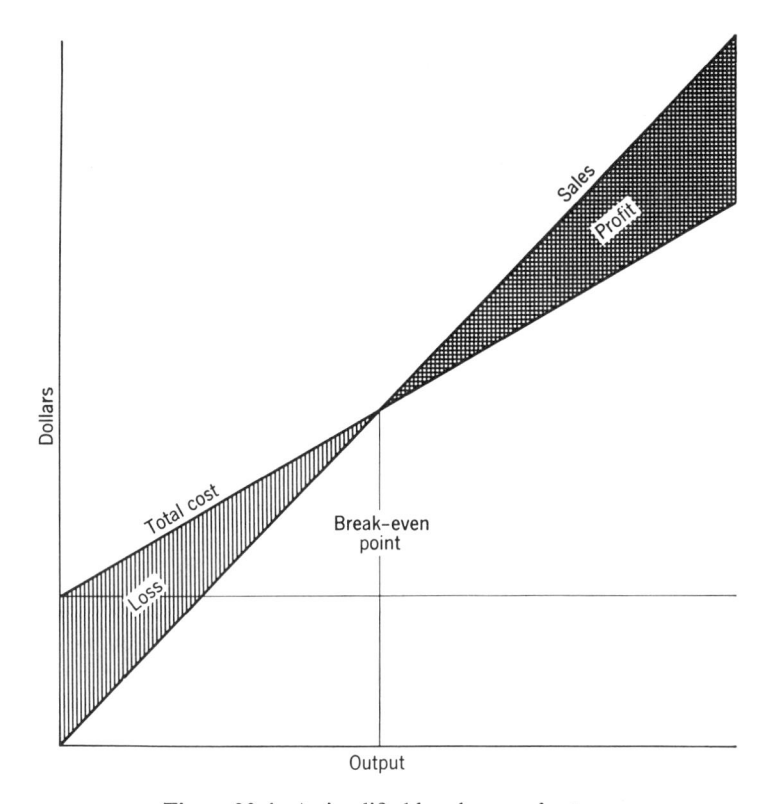

Figure 20-4. A simplified break-even chart.

However, executives should recognize that difficult estimating and measurement problems place limitations on the validity of the data that make up break-even charts.

Many other cost concepts, classifications, and computational techniques are used to formulate cost information that relates to particular managerial problems. For example, information about the extent to which costs are out-of-pocket (require current cash expenditures) as opposed to book costs (such as depreciation) may be helpful in financial planning. The advantages that may be derived from shutting down a sales office or a factory can be partly determined from a classification of costs into "escapable" and "unavoidable" costs. Information about the degree to which costs are controllable by a particular executive and the extent to which they could be cut is helpful in measuring managerial performance. Much of this information can be developed by a careful analysis of the nature of the data and the use of relatively simple computational techniques. Sophisticated statistical and mathematical techniques have been used to formulate some kinds of cost information. Such techniques have given important insights about cost behavior, but their use as a practical tool is limited by the time required to obtain results and the expense that is involved. However, a classification of cost data to fit the requirements of statistical techniques and the use of electronic data-processing equipment can help overcome these limitations.

The Auditing Function

Auditing may be defined as the examination and verification of financial and accounting records and reports. Narrowly construed, it seeks to determine whether bookkeepers, accountants, and others have accurately and honestly performed their duties and followed good accounting practices. A broader view is that the auditing function also involves a check on managerial performance in the light of appropriate and established policies, plans, standards, and procedures. Thus, the peering eye of the auditor may be focused upon matters that range from the moving hand of a clerk who dips into the till to a decision by a vice-president to buy copper from Alpha Company rather than Beta Company. Some organizations employ auditing personnel to conduct internal audits of financial, accounting, and related activities. Others rely exclusively upon external auditing by independent certified public accounting firms, and still others use both internal and external auditing facilities. In addition to factors relating to internal managerial control, external audits are particularly important when management is required to present financial statements and reports to private and public interest groups. For example, the management of a corporation is legally obligated to the stockholder; may be compelled under certain conditions to provide financial information to creditors, customers, suppliers, and unions; and is forced to contend with a vast array of governmental informational requirements. A professional stamp of approval by independent auditors has become an important factor in authenticating the financial statements and reports required for such purposes.

Budgeting and Accounting

Budgeting is concerned with the *expected* consequences of planning and operations, and accounting with the *actual* consequences measured in monetary and other quantitative terms. Quantitative variations between expected and actual results can be used to gauge planning and operating efficiency. An analysis of such variations is frequently useful in determining the kind of problem that may be involved. But a quantitative approach is inadequate without an understanding of the nature of accounting and budgeting systems and the manner in which they relate to environmental and organizational conditions. Why did the organization or a departmental unit fail to meet or more than meet the expectations set forth in the budget? The answer may involve a diversity of considerations that cannot generally be reduced to a simple cause-and-effect analysis. Forecasting and estimating errors, deliberate and nondeliberate distortions in the information, communication and motivational difficulties, technological factors, inflexibilities evolving from past planning failures, and inadequacies in current planning represent major categories into which causal factors can be placed. Appropriate corrective action is impossible if the behavior of budget and accounting information cannot be related to dynamic forces that they are supposed to represent.

Selected Functional Systems

Production Planning and Control

Production planning and control are concerned with these functions: (1) the *routing* of parts and subassemblies through an appropriate sequence of machine and human operations, (2) *scheduling* or designating the time sequences for the performance of various amounts and kinds of work, and (3) *dispatching* or assigning work in a manner that results in the best possible utilization of machines, equipment and tools, materials, and manpower in line with the requirements set forth by routing and scheduling. These functions may be handled on an informal and nonspecialized basis in small and simple production systems. In large and complex systems, they are generally performed by specialized personnel in production planning and control departments.

Informational Requirements and Interrelationships. Production planning translates a variety of information into the information required for manufacturing operations. Sales forecast and inventory information is used to formulate the overall (master) production schedule. Mechanical drawings of the product and its various components are used to determine the proper sequence of operations (production routing) and the types and amounts of necessary materials. Machine and manpower requirements can be derived from production routing information and time study data. Such information can be used to formulate other data needed for systematic planning. Machine load information can be developed to determine the adequacy or inadequacy of existing capacity. A lack of machine capacity can cause changes in the master production schedule, result in the purchase of additional facilities, bring about overtime or multishift operations, and other planning adjustments. Information about personnel and material requirements is ultimately translated into personnel requisitions (or layoffs) and purchase orders.

The Gantt Chart. A number of specialized informational and analytical devices have been developed to facilitate production planning and control. A highly useful device is the Gantt Chart, which was developed by Henry L. Gantt in 1917. The Gantt Chart has been called "the most notable contribution to the art of management made in this generation." [18] The innovation of the Gantt Chart was that it presented facts in their relation to time. Each division of space along the horizontal axis simultaneously represents: (1) equal divisions of time, (2) varying amounts of work scheduled, and (3) varying amounts of work completed. The vertical axis shows the human and machine capacities to which production and other activities can be assigned. The manner in which these variables are portrayed on a Gantt Chart is illustrated in Figure 20-5. The use of the Gantt Chart requires a plan of operations that can be expressed in quantitative terms. The plan is recorded along the horizontal axis of the chart in relation to increments of time (days, weeks, months). Actual progress is posted on the same axis, and the reasons for variations between plan and performance can be indicated by symbols denoting such factors as machine breakdown, lack of materials, power failure, absence of operator, and lack of tools. Gantt Charts can be designed to plan and control production activities by operations, machines, groups of machines, departments, or factories. They can also be used to schedule purchasing activities, personnel recruitment, transportation facilities, and many other activities.

PERT: A New Planning Technique. The last few years have brought into being a number of planning instruments which offer important advantages over the Gantt Chart for some purposes.[19] The new techniques have been particularly useful in programming large and complex atomic, mili-

[18] Wallace Clark, *The Gantt Chart* (New York: The Ronald Press, 1922), p. 3. This book was translated into French, Italian, Polish, Czechoslovakian, German, Spanish, Russian, and Japanese. In Russia alone 100,000 copies were printed and, according to some reports, the first "Five-Year Plan" was completely plotted on Gantt Charts.

[19] The following references provide a comprehensive analysis of PERT and related planning techniques: Federal Electric Corporation, *A Programmed Introduction to Program Evaluation, and Review Technique* (New York: John Wiley & Sons, Inc., 1963); Robert W. Miller, *Schedule, Cost, and Profit Control with PERT* (New York: McGraw-Hill Book Company, Inc., 1963); Richard A. Johnson, Fremont E. Kast, and James E. Rosenzweig, *The Theory and Management of Systems* (New York: McGraw-Hill Book Company, Inc., 1963).

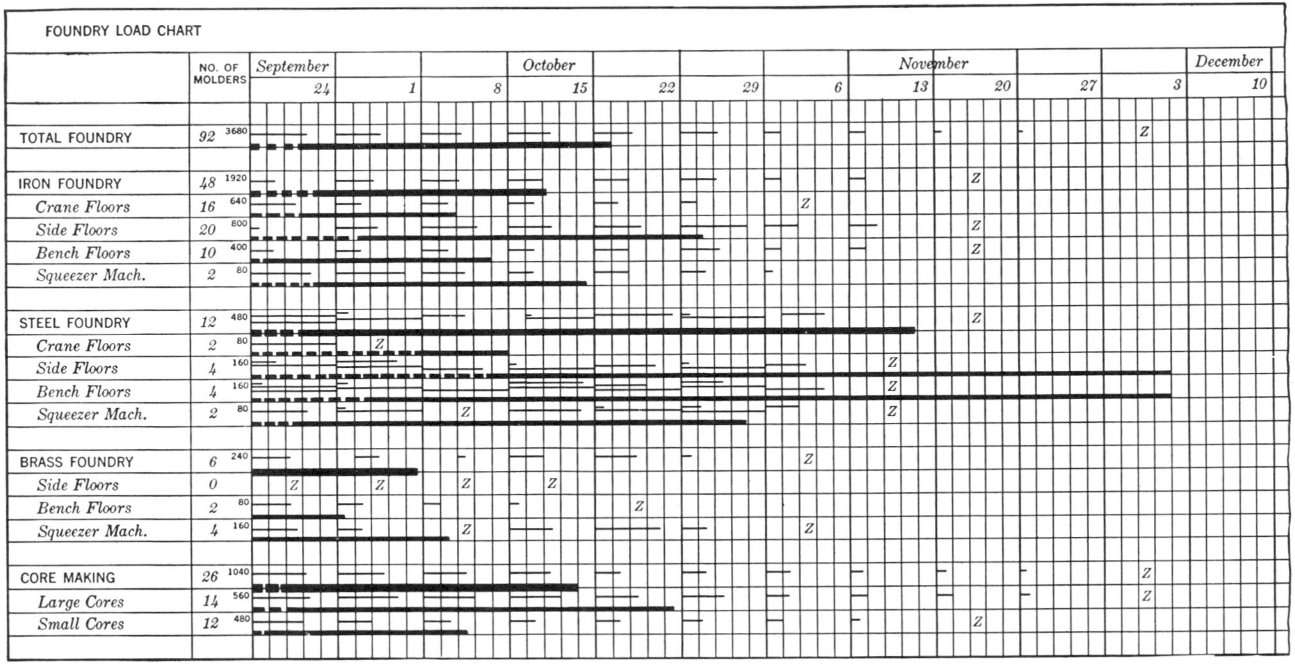

Figure 20-5. Gantt Chart for a Foundry. Reproduced with permission from Charles A. Koepke, *Plant Production Control*, 2nd ed. New York: John Wiley and Sons, Inc., 1949.

tary, and space projects. They have also proven useful in planning advertising campaigns, introducing new products, publishing books, constructing homes, and preparing theatrical productions. Probably the most noted of the many recent planning innovations is Program Evaluation Review Technique (PERT), which was developed in 1958 by the U.S. Navy's Special Projects Office. Two parallel planning techniques are the Critical Path Method (CPM), developed by the Du Pont Company, and Program Evaluation Procedure (PEP), which came from the U.S. Air Force.

PERT provides a means for improving managerial performance, but it does not take the place of effective management. Managers must make important judgments about objectives and methods before PERT can come into the picture. They may also have to translate highly subjective factors into an objective form. PERT requires concrete statements about intermediate and final goals and the activities that will be necessary to achieve them.

The first step in building a PERT network is to prepare a list of the activities that will be necessary to complete a project. An activity may encompass the work performed by a single operator, a departmental unit, or an entire organization. Activities must have definite starting and stopping points if they are to be plotted into a PERT network. Such points are called milestones or events, which represent a clearly identifiable achievement. A PERT event is the beginning or the end of an activity; it does not consume time or resources. Events are represented in the network by circles, squares, or other appropriate geometric devices.

A PERT network shows the interrelationship of the events and activities that are required to achieve an objective. Figure 20-6 represents a highly simplified PERT network. The events, represented by circles, are numbered for purposes of identification. The lines between the events denote activities, which are labeled by letters. Activities are the time-consuming

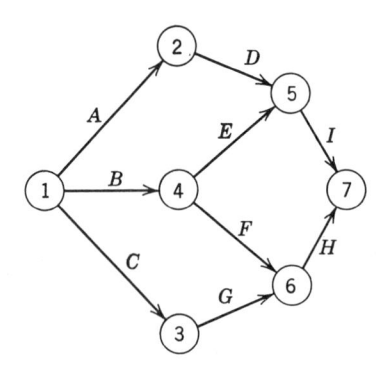

Figure 20-6. A simplified PERT Network.

aspects of the PERT network; they involve the expenditure of resources. The arrows in the network shown in Figure 20-6 indicate the order of events or the sequence in which the work must be done. Events must take place in a proper sequence—a house cannot be finished before the foundation is laid, an airplane cannot be flown before its engines are installed, and a television play cannot be presented until it has been written. In Figure 20-6, event 5 cannot take place until events 2 and 4 have been completed, event 7 cannot take place until events 5 and 6 are completed, etc.

After the PERT network has been built, the next step is to make estimates of the time (days, weeks, months, etc.) it will take to complete each activity. (See Figure 20-7.) The persons most familiar with the activity are generally asked to make three time estimates: (1) an optimistic estimate, a, or the time required for an activity if everything goes very well; (2) a pessimistic estimate, b, or the time required under adverse conditions, excluding acts of God; (3) a most likely estimate, m, or the most realistic time an activity might take. These three time estimates form the basis for a statistically weighted average time or expected elapsed time, t_e.

The expected elapsed times t_e for the activities can be used to calculate the earliest possible time T_E the events in the network can be expected to occur. (See Figure 20-7.) The t_e data can also be used to compute the T_L or the latest allowable date an event can occur without causing a delay in the project. The difference between the latest allowable time T_L and the earliest expected time T_E is the amount of slack in the project. Slack may be positive (ahead of schedule), zero (on schedule), and negative (behind schedule). The measurement of slack can be used to determine the critical path or the longest path in a network. The critical path, as the term implies, represents the sequence of events and activities that are most apt to upset the scheduled date of completion. All other paths in the network have more slack (time) or resources to achieve the objective.

The greater the uncertainty about an activity, the greater will tend to be the time interval between the optimistic and the pessimistic estimates. The uncertainty involved in particular estimates can be measured and used to formulate the probability P_R of meeting a scheduled date. A probability or P_R of 0.5 indicates that the project should be completed on time. A larger value for P_R means that too many resources are being used to achieve the objective. A smaller value is a sign that there may be difficulties in getting the work done on time.

The number of events in a PERT network may range from twenty to many thousands. Some 70,000 were required for the first PERT project, the Polaris submarine. A large project may involve layers of PERT networks from highly detailed networks to networks that include only major milestones. The arithmetic computations required for small networks with

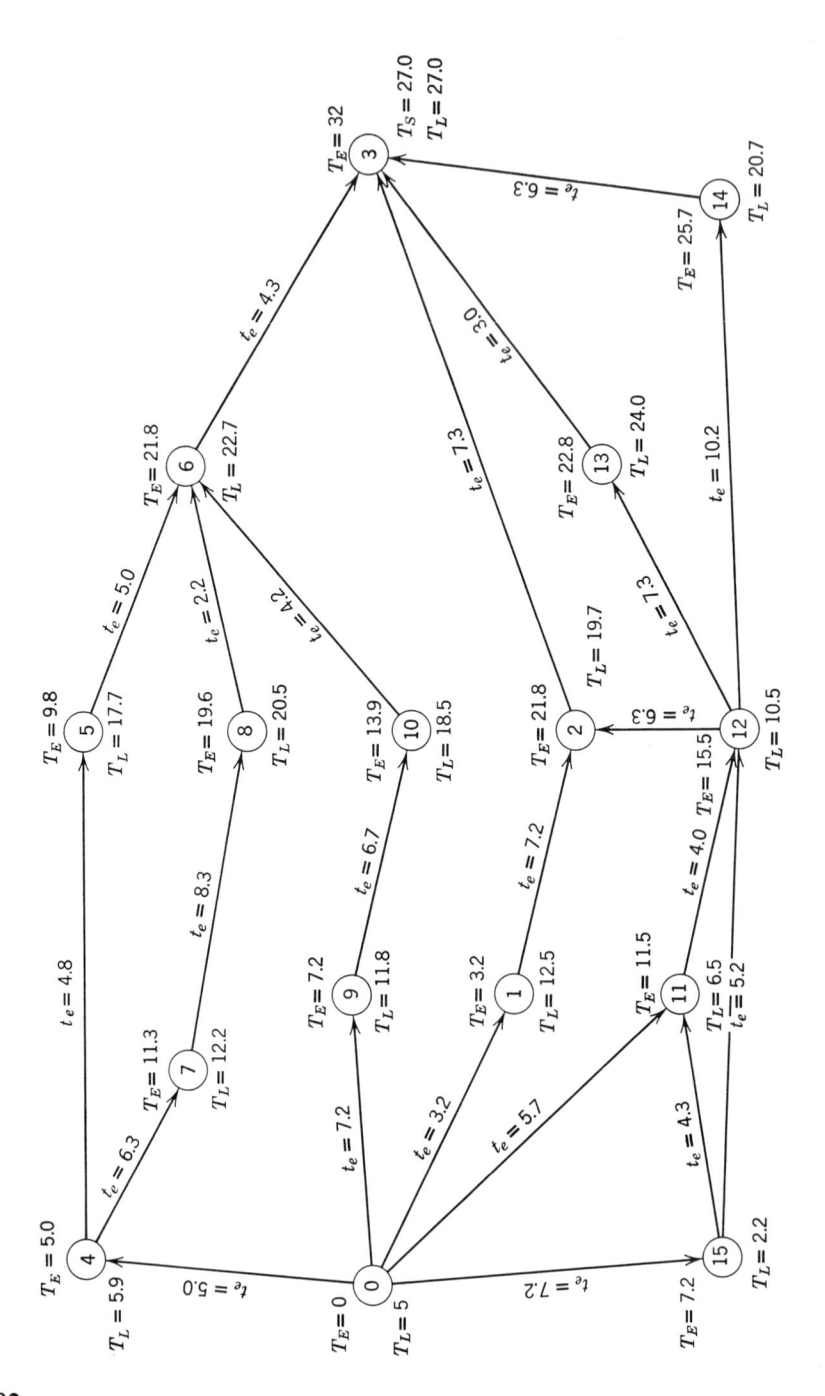

SPECIALIZED INFORMATIONAL SYSTEMS 503

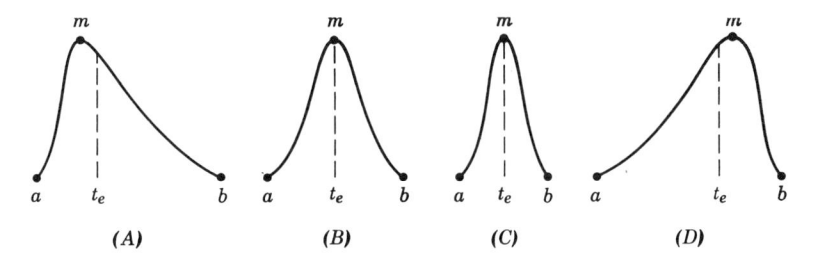

Figure 20-7. PERT Network (p. 502), Time Estimates, and Computational Procedures. Reproduced with permission from Federal Electric Corporation, *A Programmed Introduction to Program Evaluation, and Review Technique*. New York: John Wiley and Sons, Inc., 1963. Elements of the network are as follows:

A person familiar with an activity makes three estimates of the time necessary to perform the activity: *a,* an optimistic time estimate; *b,* a pessimistic time estimate; *m,* the most likely time an activity will take.

The t_e for the distributions shown in $(A) - (D)$ can be obtained by the equation

$$t_e = \frac{a + 4m + b}{6}$$

The variance or uncertainty in each distribution can be obtained by the equation

$$\sigma^2 = \left(\frac{b-a}{6}\right)^2$$

T_E represents the earliest possible time an event can be reached, which is computed by summing the t_e's of the longest (in time) activity path leading to the event.

T_L represents the latest allowable completion time and is computed by subtracting the t_e from the T_L of the last event in the network and working backward toward the first event. The smallest T_L is selected for an event if more than one T_L is possible.

$T_L - T_E =$ slack. Slack can be positive, negative, or zero. The lowest slack value determines the *critical path* of the network.

one or two hundred events can normally be done manually with ordinary equipment. Large networks should generally be programmed for a computer which can determine the various values in sufficient time for possible changes in plans.

PERT, like operations research and other planning techniques, forces all levels of management to think logically about a project and to give consideration to pertinent variables. It is highly useful in handling the uncertainties involved in nonrepetitive projects and has proven to be almost indispensable in planning the massive military and space programs of recent years. PERT directs constant attention to strategic factors through the information it provides about "slack time" and "the critical path." It can significantly reduce costs by indicating those aspects of a project that require attention. Resources can be shifted from activities that have slack time to activities on the critical path. As one executive noted:

In years past, when a program was in trouble, it was assumed that the *entire* program was in trouble, and most often everyone on the project was put on overtime. PERT now clearly shows that close to 90% of this crash effort was wasted, since it was applied to activities which were on slack paths where there was already time to spare.[20]

Management can often use slack time information to make necessary modifications in the plan. The time schedules in a PERT network assume a given level of resource input and technological capacity. A lack of sufficient time to meet a particular date can often be overcome by additional resources. The additional costs involved may be appropriate if the completion of the project is highly important. However, in some cases a change in objectives may be more desirable than higher costs. Variables other than time have been incorporated into PERT networks. For example, cost data may be obtained for many of the activities in a project. A major difficulty is that present accounting systems do not always serve the needs of PERT. Inadequate data often force highly tenuous assumptions about time-cost relationships.

PERT should obviously not be viewed as a panacea for all planning difficulties. It provides a systematic approach to planning; it does not eliminate uncertainty and related managerial problems. Executives must still make many decisions that involve highly illusive subjective factors. Such decisions make possible much of the apparent objectivity of the PERT technique.

Paperwork and Production. Many of the informational instruments used in production planning and control simulate the production process in abstract terms. One might say that production occurs on paper before it takes place on the factory floor. A Gantt-type chart portrays the expected consequences of production over some period of time. Route sheets indicate the sequence of operations necessary to produce a part, subassembly, or product. Operation sheets give detailed instructions about operation methods, tooling requirements, specifications, and related matters. These and many other devices are integrated into an informational system that activates the mechanical and human forces through which production objectives are achieved. The physical results are translated into control information that is used to evaluate managerial and operating performance.

Production Control Problems. Variations between the norms set forth in production planning information and the actual results as measured by control information can be helpful in determining problem areas. A failure

---

[20] Quoted in *News Front,* June 1963, p. 32.

to meet planned production schedules can be attributed to a diversity of possible factors, such as unanticipated shortages of raw materials, difficulties in hiring qualified personnel, a higher than average incidence of machine and equipment breakdown, or a slowdown by factory workers. A problem in one part of the production system can cause a chain reaction of difficulties throughout the whole system. For example, a shortage of a strategic part or subassembly can disrupt production activities generally and play havoc with planned schedules. Production failures can also be attributed to informational and communication difficulties. The information used in the planning process presents a highly abstract picture of the realities of the production process. Mechanical drawings, operation sequence information, standard time data, purchasing specifications, personnel requisitions, raw material and work-in-process inventories, and machine load data do not always provide completely adequate or accurate information for planning and operating purposes. The preciseness with which these devices seem to measure future requirements and results is partly a property of the measuring stick rather than what the stick measures. The data used in production planning contain assumptions and estimates that may be repudiated by actual events. Furthermore, some degree of deliberate and nondeliberate distortion of information results from processing and transmission activities. For example, an inventory of work-in-process may include defective subassemblies and parts because an inventory clerk failed to note this fact or because a supervisor wanted to cover up a mistake.

Quality Planning and Control

An important planning problem is to determine quality standards for products and services. A primary consideration in solving this problem is the relationship between revenues and costs. Additional quality must produce sufficient revenues to compensate for the costs that are incurred. Thus, the solution is not to achieve the highest possible quality but to meet the quality criteria implied by market forces. Furthermore, such factors as company, product, and management reputation may be more important than short- or long-run profit considerations. Governmental legislation, such as the Pure Food and Drug Act, and standards developed by industry associations also play a part in the quality picture.

Operational Definitions. Quality may be defined in subjective terms, as: "we give the best service," "we strive for quality, not quantity," and "built by craftsmen who know quality." However, such definitions of standards are subject to a variety of interpretations by managerial and operating personnel. Quality information should convey exact meanings and, if possible, should be expressed in language systems that define in operational terms. For example, the size of the product should be specified by the metric or other measurement system, its form should be shown by scaled drawings, color should be indicated by formula or samples, etc. Precise quality definitions or specifications are particularly important in manufacturing operations involving the assembly of interchangeable parts and subassemblies.

Specifications and Tolerances. The quality problem is a fundamental factor in the production planning process. Thus, product specifications indicated by mechanical drawings and other information are translated into processing, equipment, tooling, purchasing, and personnel specifications. The totality of production plans contains a diversity of implicit or explicit quality specifications or norms. However, physical and human factors preclude perfect uniformity in the things that flow from the production line. In other words, every item in a given quantity of items manufactured on the same production line will be somewhat different. For this reason, quality specifications must set forth an acceptable range of variation from norm. Specifications should indicate tolerances in precise terms.

Inspection. Quality control involves a comparison of planning specifications with actual results by inspection and other techniques. Inspection may amount to little more than a visual scrutiny of manufactured items by production or inspection personnel. However, it generally requires the use of predetermined tests and measuring instruments. The inspection process may be concerned only with finished products or it may include a number of inspections throughout the production process. Many companies check all purchased materials, inspect parts and subassemblies at various stages of production, and subject finished products to a final inspection. Inspection may involve a check of every item, or it may be restricted to a limited percentage of items. Statistical techniques are sometimes used to predict and control the range of variability that will result from a given process. Corrective action is taken whenever a sampling of items shows too much deviation from a predetermined distribution.

Control Considerations. One purpose of quality control is to keep substandard products out of the market. Another is to gauge the performance of managerial and operating personnel. Quality control can also be used to indicate planning deficiencies and techniques that can be used to overcome them. An evaluation of actual results may pinpoint technical and human problems that were not anticipated during the planning phase. Such problems sometimes result in a revision of quality specifications to meet the realities of the production situation. The quality control function is frequently given departmental status outside the production department. Quality and quantity objectives are not always in accord; the pressures of production schedules sometimes give rise to laxity in the enforcement of quality standards. However, the responsibility for quality planning and control cannot be completely centralized in a separate department. The ultimate responsibility rests with the people who plan and perform the physical acts of production.

Nonmanufacturing Areas. Quality planning and control have become specialized areas of endeavor in industrial management and engineering. The degree of specialization is indicated by university courses and professional literature that focus upon particular aspects of the quality control area, such as statistical quality control and specification writing. The theories and techniques of quality control specialists have found their greatest application in the manufacturing and purchasing fields. An important reason is that the technology of things is much more susceptible to precise measurement than the psychology of people, but this fact should not lead to the idea that quality is less important in other areas of endeavor. The problem of quality is an implicit or explicit property of almost every executive decision. A restaurant or a department store manager who instructs personnel on "proper" techniques for waiting on customers is dealing with a quality problem. However, there is no one set of techniques that will give the best results or fit every situation. Furthermore, such standards cannot be as precisely measured and communicated as the specifications that should be used in a lathe operation. Performance information may also be subject to a diversity of meanings. For example, customer complaints about a particular waitress or sales employee may indicate below-standard performance, but it could also reflect peculiar personality traits of a few customers who happened to sit at a particular table or shop in the lingerie department. Every other customer may have been more than satisfied by the service accorded them.

Procurement Planning and Control

Procurement or purchasing is concerned with the acquisition of merchandise, materials, supplies, and equipment required for managerial and operating activities. Narrowly construed, purchasing is the act of buying items at a price. More broadly defined, purchasing is an important aspect of managerial planning and involves activities other than buying. Some of the activities that may be included are:

The research and development required for the proper selection of materials and sources from which those materials may be bought; the follow-up to insure proper delivery; the inspection of incoming shipments to insure both quantity and quality compliance with the order; the development of proper procedures, methods, and forms to enable the purchasing department to carry out established policies; the coordination of the activities of the purchasing department with such other internal divisions of the concern as traffic, receiving, storekeeping, and accounting so as to facilitate smooth operations; and the development of a technique of effective communication with top management of the company so that a true picture of the performance of the purchasing function is presented.[21]

Informational Instruments. The importance of resource markets and procurement strategies in planning the organizational program was considered in Chapter 15. The present discussion deals with the nature of the purchasing process and some of the informational instruments that are commonly used. The process begins with a receipt of information from a user department or the stores department that various kinds and quantities of items are required at a particular time or over a period of time. An important informational device is the purchase requisition, which indicates the nature of requirements and authenticates the request by an appropriate signature. Requisitions may be routed to the stores department to determine whether existing stocks can fill the demand and then to purchasing if stocks are inadequate or lacking. Purchase requirements may also evolve from the production planning process and be derived from bills of materials, production scheduling information, and inventory data. In retail establishments, the managers of merchandising and selling departments frequently determine purchase requirements and perform the buying function, sometimes with guidance from specialists in such areas as market research and fashions. Budgetary systems can impose limitations on the amounts and types of items that can be purchased. The lack of budgeted funds may prevent the purchase of needed materials and equipment even though more than enough money is available for other things.

The Quality Problem. The problem of quality standards, discussed in the previous section, is a highly important element in purchasing. Quality requirements may be designated through brands or trade names, physical or chemical specifications, market grade, use or purpose, samples, and the names of vendors. They may be determined by operating departments (such as manufacturing or merchandising departments), the quality control department, the purchasing department, or through the joint efforts of two or more departments.

The Selection of Suppliers. The selection of companies from which purchases will be made is another important aspect of the purchasing process. The number of potential suppliers may range from one for some things to hundreds for others. The final selection depends on such factors as price,

[21] J. H. Westing, I. V. Fine, and others, *Industrial Purchasing: Buying for Industry and Budgetary Institutions,* 2nd ed. (New York: John Wiley and Sons, Inc., 1961), p. 2.

quality, capacity to meet delivery schedules, transportation costs, and the supplier's reputation. Actual purchases are made on a purchase order form which stipulates quantities, delivery dates, price, discounts, shipping instructions, and other information. Copies are retained by the purchasing department and distributed to other departments requiring them, such as accounting and receiving. The ordering transaction is formally completed after acceptance is received from the supplier. Many companies follow up orders with written reminders and personal consultations to assure prompt delivery. Shipments made by vendors are generally inspected to determine whether quantitative and qualitative standards have been met. Invoices, bills of lading, and other pertinent forms are compared with inspection information and the original purchase order.

Other Informational Requirements. An efficient purchasing system develops and maintains a large amount of information about such matters as sources of supply, prices and discounts, market and economic trends, past performance of suppliers, product specifications, and shipping costs. Informational techniques are also devised to facilitate a follow-up of quotation requests and purchase orders. The letters, forms, and other information relating to completed transactions are generally filed for a period of time.

Inventory Planning and Control

The time required to produce goods and services makes necessary an inventory or stock of merchandise, raw materials, work-in-process, manufactured products, tools and equipment, and supplies. However, inventories increase operating expenses and should not exceed whatever level is necessary to adequately perform organizational functions. Inventory strategy evolves from a consideration of such factors as the length of purchase, production, and merchandising cycles, the nature of technological processes, expected market and price trends, storage capacity, and anticipated shortages in market supplies. Inventory planning and control should be viewed as a dynamic problem involving a continuous inflow and outflow of stock as a result of operating activities. Changes in the relative rates at which items are purchased, produced, shipped, or sold will affect the level of physical inventories. Thus, higher sales will reduce inventories unless the amounts purchased are increased correspondingly. Such imbalances cannot always be immediately corrected, which means that inventory levels may fluctuate considerably in the short run. This problem also gives emphasis to the relationship between inventory planning and marketing, production, and purchasing programs. Planning inadequacies in other areas can impede attempts to develop efficient inventory plans.

Systematic Handling and Storage. Inventory planning and control require a systematic approach toward the handling and storage of merchandise and materials. The location and layout of storage space and the arrangement of stock on shelves, counters, and other storage devices should be carefully planned for efficient operations. Everything should have a place and be in place to facilitate the production and sales process and the identification and enumeration involved in a physical inventory. The things that make up inventories must be brought under physical control if the informational devices that measure inventories are to have any meaning.

IDENTIFICATION SYSTEMS. The translation of the facts of physical inventory into information requires a language system for identification purposes. Items are sometimes identified by the names that are ordinarily used such as hammers, hosiery, shoes, rivets, bolts, and tires. However, specialized identification systems are frequently used when inventories are large and complex. The following are some basic systems.

1. *Alphabetical:* the use of a letter or a group of letters according to some predetermined scheme.

2. *Mnemonic:* the use of letters in some such combination that they suggest the classification name of the particular item. Numbers may be combined with letters in the mnemonic system, particularly to suggest size or some generally accepted standard.

3. *Numerical:* the use of numbers to identify the particular item.

4. *Sign:* the use of symbols or signs to indicate items or operations. These have been extensively used in motion-study techniques.

5. *Combination:* the use of any of the foregoing systems in combination with any other one or all others to identify a particular item, service, or operation.[22]

Perpetual Inventory. Most organizations use some kind of perpetual inventory to provide information about changes in inventories. Such a system involves a corresponding informational adjustment when merchandise or materials flow into or out of storage. Balance-of-stores forms are commonly used to record the basic information required for this kind of inventory control. A separate form is maintained for each inventory item with information about such matters as the quantities ordered by purchase requisition, the quantities received by storage, the quantities issued by department or production requisition, and the quantities not issued but apportioned to production orders. The balance on hand and the number of items that have not been apportioned are generally computed after each transaction. A minimum inventory level or the ordering point together with the quantity that should be ordered is frequently indicated. The ordering point takes into account the time required to purchase the item and the

[22] William R. Spriegel and Richard H. Lansburgh, *Industrial Management*, 5th ed. (New York: John Wiley and Sons, Inc., 1955), p. 32.5.

amount that will be required during that period. In other words, the level of inventory must be sufficient to supply the needs of production, merchandising, and other departments during the purchasing cycle. The appropriate ordering quantity or the economic lot size is determined by balancing purchasing costs with the costs of maintaining inventory. For example, the costs involved in holding larger inventories are often justified by the lower costs of quantity purchases. Information about the value of the items in stock is also maintained on perpetual inventory forms for costing and other purposes. The data about inventory items can be combined and classified to meet the varied informational requirements of purchasing, production, budgeting, accounting, and marketing.

Physical Inventory. A perpetual inventory system would theoretically seem to eliminate the need for a physical count of inventory. However, the problem of information distortion cannot be completely avoided. A periodic physical inventory is necessary to correct the errors that arise in the informational system. Also important is that tax legislation requires verification of inventory information by actual count.

Personnel Planning and Control

The personnel or industrial relations department accumulates and maintains a diversity of information for planning and control purposes. Some of this information is concerned with the qualities of applicants for managerial and operating positions. Application forms, interview rating sheets, test results, recommendations, and medical reports can be placed in this category. Other information is concerned with the induction of personnel, providing them with facts about their position, the company, wages or salaries, promotion policy, rules relating to conduct, and other matters. Still other information deals with the performance of past and present personnel and includes reports and records on merit and performance ratings, transfers and promotions, wage and salary increases, disciplinary action, accidents and sickness, and termination of employment.

Job Information. Personnel recruitment and training require information about the nature of the positions that are to be filled. Position or job specifications are generally prepared by the personnel department with the help of information from industrial engineering and operating departments. Another problem is to evaluate positions or jobs for promotion and wage or salary administration purposes. Job evaluation is a systematic technique for measuring the relative importance of positions in terms of content. The job, not the person, is the focal point of the evaluation. The first step in the job evaluation process is to determine and define the nature of duties required for each position. The next is to select factors that are common to the positions being evaluated, such as the skill required (education, experience, etc.), effort requirements (physical and mental), the responsibility that is involved (equipment, material, safety of others), and job conditions (working conditions and hazards). Quantitative values are then assigned to various degrees or graduations of skill, effort, responsibility, and working conditions. For example, one year of education may be worth more than two years of experience, heavy physical labor may be valued higher than work requiring little physical effort, work under hazardous conditions may rate higher than work in comparative safety, etc. Each position is rated in terms of common factors and the extent to which factor values apply to it. The end product is a system of comparative values or rankings that can be used as a basis for planning wage and salary schedules and promotion policy. However, market conditions and collective bargaining play an important part in the final solution given to the problem.

Personnel Data and Reports. The administration of safety programs, suggestion systems, grievance systems, and personnel service activities have many informational requirements. Personnel departments also compile data and prepare reports on such matters as labor supply and wage trends, productivity, labor turnover, and absenteeism. Other informational needs evolve from collective bargaining, public relations, and government legislation.

Subjective Factors. Much of the above information contains implicit assumptions about the nature and predictability of individual and social behavior. For example, application forms and testing materials are based on the assumption that there is a measurable relationship between various specific stated or tested qualities and future performance. Some of the assumptions that are made in this respect evolve from highly tenuous logic. The meaning of such performance measures as merit ratings and disciplinary actions is frequently open to question. The apparent objectivity of some of this information may conceal subjective factors that were involved in the evaluation process. A similar statement can be made about job evaluation information. The values that persons with different backgrounds assign to such factors as working conditions and job hazards may vary a great deal. Since information concerned with the dynamics of human behavior is generally less reliable than information about things, psychologists and sociologists have not made as much progress in developing predictive theories as physicists. Executives should recognize the limitations of information that deals with individual, social, and institutional (such as unions) behavior. But they are also faced with planning and control problems that demand some kind of an answer. Many of the informational techniques developed by the behavioral scientists provide better results than a purely subjective approach. Thus, while it would be foolish to contend that psychological testing and other selection devices give perfect results, they undoubtedly are more reliable than phrenology.

Other Planning and Control Information

The importance of sales and other forecast information was discussed in the chapters in Part IV. Planning and control techniques used to develop improved procedures and methods were treated in Chapter 15. The manner in which organization charts, job descriptions, and job specifications facilitate organizational planning was given attention in Chapter 12.

SELECTED REFERENCES

Russell D. Archibald and Richard L. Villaria, *Network-Based Management Systems.* New York: John Wiley & Sons, Inc., 1967.

Chris Argyris, "Human Problems with Budgets," *Harvard Business Review,* Vol. 31, No. 1, pp. 97–110 (January–February 1953).

Nicholas Baloff and John W. Kennelly, "Accounting Implications of Product and Process Start-ups," *Journal of Accounting Research,* Vol. 5, No. 2, pp. 131–143 (Autumn 1967).

Clifford M. Baumback, *Patterns of Production Planning and Control,* Industrial Management Series No. 1. Bureau of Business Research, College of Business Administration, University of Oklahoma, 1957.

John E. Biegel, *Production Control: A Quantitative Approach.* Englewood Cliffs, N.J.: Prentice-Hall, Inc., 1963.

Elwood S. Buffa, *Modern Production Management,* 2nd ed., New York: John Wiley & Sons, Inc., 1965.

John Dearden, *Cost and Budget Analysis.* Englewood Cliffs, N.J.: Prentice-Hall, Inc., 1962.

Lester A. Digman, "PERT/LOB: Life-Cycle Technique," *The Journal of Industrial Engineering,* Vol. 18, No. 2, pp. 154–158 (February 1967). Also see: Peter P. Schoderbek and Lester A. Digman, "Third Generation, PERT/LOB," *Harvard Business Review,* Vol. 45, No. 5, pp. 100–110 (September–October 1967). The pioneering ideas that led to PERT/LOB were developed by John R. Moundalexis, Ray Thelwell, and James O. Jensen in an unpublished presentation by USAMETA to Interagency PERT and Line of Balance Coordinating Groups, August 2, 1963.

Gordon Donaldson, "Financial Goals: Management vs. Stockholders," *Harvard Business Review,* Vol. 41, No. 3, pp. 116–129 (May–June 1963).

Federal Electric Corporation, *A Programmed Introduction to Program Evaluation, and Review Technique.* New York: John Wiley and Sons, Inc., 1963.

David F. Hawkins, "Controversial Accounting Changes," *Harvard Business Review,* Vol. 46, No. 2, pp. 20–41 (March–April 1968).

J. Brooks Heckert and James D. Willson, *Business Budgeting and Control.* New York: The Ronald Press, 1967.

A. W. Holmes, G. P. Maynard, J. D. Edwards, and R. A. Meier, *Intermediate Accounting,* 3rd ed., Chaps. 24, 25, and 26. Homewood, Ill.: Richard D. Irwin, Inc., 1958.

William Travers Jerome III, *Executive Control—The Catalyst.* New York: John Wiley and Sons, Inc., 1961.

Mina M. Johnson and Norman F. Kallaus, *Records Management.* Cincinnati: South-Western Publishing Co., 1967.

Reginald L. Jones and H. George Trentin, *Budgeting: Key to Planning and Control.* New York: American Management Association, 1966.

E. H. MacNiece, *Production Forecasting, Planning, and Control,* 3rd ed. New York: John Wiley and Sons, Inc., 1961.

R. K. Mautz and others, *A Statement of Basic Accounting Postulates and Principles.* Urbana, Ill.: Center for International Education and Research in Accounting, 1964.

Donald E. Miller, *The Meaningful Interpretation of Financial Statements.* New York: American Management Association, 1966.

Robert W. Miller, *Schedule, Cost, and Profit Control with PERT.* New York: McGraw-Hill Book Company, Inc., 1963.

L. N. Morris, *Critical Path: Construction and Analysis.* Oxford: Pergamon Press, 1967.

C. A. Moyer and R. K. Mautz, *Intermediate Accounting.* New York: John Wiley and Sons, Inc., 1962.

Daniel D. Roman, "The PERT System: An Appraisal of Program Evaluation Review Technique," *Journal of the Academy of Management,* Vol. 5, No. 1, pp. 57–65 (April 1962).

William S. Shallman, *The Impact of Network Analysis Techniques upon Design Engineering Organizations.* Rock Island, Ill.: U. S. Army Management Engineering Training Agency, 1967.

"Uniformity in Financial Accounting," *Law and Contemporary Problems,* Vol. 30, No. 4 (Autumn 1965). A symposium sponsored by the School of Law, Duke University, Durham, N.C.

Glenn A. Welsch, *Budgeting: Profit Planning and Control,* 2nd ed. Englewood Cliffs, N.J.: Prentice-Hall, Inc., 1964.

T. A. Wise, "The Auditors Have Arrived," *Fortune,* Vol. 62, No. 6, pp. 144–148; 239–244 (December 1960).

Max S. Wortman, Jr., "Personnel Ratios and Personnel Departments," *Personnel Administration,* Vol. 26, No. 6, pp. 46–51 (November–December 1963).

chapter 21

COMPUTERIZED INFORMATIONAL SYSTEMS

The present and potential contribution of electronic computers to the informational process is now considered. The first part of the discussion deals with the nature of electronic computers and the manner in which they function. The discussion then turns to problems involved in the installation of computer systems. The section that follows describes the basic processes of computerized systems development and the kinds of systems that have been developed. Attention is then given to the problem of organizing for computers after which some conclusions are made about present achievements and future prospects.

Computer Functioning

What can electronic digital computers do? Fundamantally, they can read, remember, do arithmetic, make simple logical choices, and write. But they do not perform these tasks in a manner that can be called human. Computers do not read with eyes or write with fingers. An electronic data-processing system is composed of integrated or separate components that can be categorized as follows: (1) information input or "reading" devices, (2) memory or information storage instruments, (3) arithmetical and logical facilities, (4) information output or "writing" devices, and (5) operator control panels or consoles. The following briefly surveys the nature of some of the hardware that make up the above categories.

Input Devices

A number of devices can be used to feed instructions and data into a computer. One is a keyboard attached to the computer, which can be used either as the primary input mechanism or only to make modifications or corrections. Another is punch cards that can be converted through intermediate devices into paper or magnetic tape. Paper tape containing serially arranged perforated characters is another important input device. The fastest input medium is magnetic tape, which can hold several hundred characters per inch of length. Each of the above input devices has advantages and disadvantages from a business point of view. Thus, magnetic tape can be read by the machine at a rate that may approach several hundred thousand characters per minute, but it is subject to breakage and deterioration. Punch cards are read at a much slower pace but provide a better permanent record of business information.

Information Storage Devices

Information may be stored on instruments external to the computer, such as punch cards, paper tape, and magnetic tape. It may also be stored within the machine on such devices as magnetic drums, magnetic cores, cathode-ray tubes, and vacuum tubes or transistors. Internal devices store bits or units of information in particular locations or addresses in much the same manner as mail is stored in numbered postal boxes. Computers can put information into storage addresses, delete existing storage information, and transfer information to other addresses or into an output device. Storage facilities are used to store instructions to the machine, data received from external input devices, intermediate computing results, and the final answers derived from the computing process. A large enough internal storage system could theoretically maintain all information relating to past and present business operations. Files and other external storage instruments would no longer be a part of the office scene. Although such a state of affairs may prevail at some future time, technical imperfections and business requirements provide good arguments for a more tangible permanent storage instrument. A technical failure in the computer might destroy a large amount of vital and irreplaceable company records. Furthermore, legal, regulatory, and tax requirements place limitations upon the use that can be made of electronic storage. Extensive use is still being made of punch cards because they represent a compromise between technical and business requirements. Punch cards are reasonably efficient in feeding information into intermediate and internal input and storage devices. They also provide a type of permanent storage that is well adapted to present business practices and purposes.

Arithmetic and Logical Devices

Computers perform arithmetic operations by a flow of electrical current through electronic on-off switching devices. As current enters the system, numbers are accumulated in a series of electronic storage devices. The process is sequenced by off-on gates or switches that open when an appropriate state of computation has been achieved. Gating results in a transfer of totals in one accumulator to higher order accumulators. Computers can only add and subtract but, by repeated additions and subtractions, can also multiply and divide. Their computational capacity is no greater than an ordinary mechanical-type desk calculator with one important difference. Electronic on-off switching devices operate in terms of a thousandth (millisecond) or millionth (microsecond) of a second. Computers can make hundreds or thousands of arithmetic computations in less than a second.

Most computers use a binary (base 2) number system rather than a decimal (base 10) system in making arithmetic computations. A binary system, using the numbers 0 and 1, is well adapted to the on-off (off equals 0; on equals 1) switching devices that make up a computer. Computers generally convert a decimal number input into binary numbers and back again into an output of decimal numbers. Thus, the user can work in terms of a decimal system even though the machine uses a binary system internally.

Computers have the capacity to make logical choices automatically with proper instructions. That is, they can select the appropriate operation from the logical relationship that exists between two or more conditions. For example, if two sums are equal or their difference is zero, the computer will automatically select a particular sequence of operations. A different sequence will be selected if one number is larger than another or if a quantity is plus or minus. In other words, the computer automatically sequences operations in terms of such logical forms as: if "a" is true, then "b" is true; if "a" is true, then "b" is false. This built-in logical capacity is necessary because the exact values that may be fed into the computer and derived from various stages of computation are not known. The computer automatically selects alternative instructions on the basis of logical relationships in the information.

Output Devices

Electric typewriters can be used to print the output of the computer, but their lack of speed makes them inadequate for many purposes. Greater efficiency is sometimes obtained by recording the results on paper or magnetic tape and then feeding tapes into a number of electric typewriters and other printing devices. A great deal of attention has been given to the development of faster printing facilities. Printing speeds as high as 30,000 lines per minute have been made possible through a variety of mechanical and electronic innovations.

Control Devices

Computers have both internal and external control devices. Internal control is essentially concerned with the sequencing, timing, and coordination of computer operations. External control involves direct communication between the computer and a human operator. The operator can start and stop the computer, perform particular operations, determine values in storage or memory locations, put data into or take data out of internal storage facilities, regulate input and output devices, and control other aspects of computer functioning. The computer can also be designed or instructed to transmit information to the operator. For example, computers can indicate internal breakdowns or computational errors by printing the information, by flashing lights, by stopping, and in other ways. They can even point out the nature of the difficulty and identify the internal component that requires attention. Facilities may also be provided for checking out the adequacy or correctness of the instructions given to the computer. Some computers have the capacity to automatically bypass defective components and make periodic checks on the accuracy of computation.

The Problems of Computer Installation

Electronic computers have become virtually a necessity in medium-sized and large organizations. Many smaller organizations are taking advantage of computers through some kind of shared-time arrangement. But, in spite of the wide acceptance and application, some organizations are still involved in the difficulties of installing an electronic computer and others have yet to take the initial step. A brief review of some of the problems that plagued the pioneers of electronic data processing may be useful.

Pioneering Problems

An initial difficulty was that computers were portrayed as electronic wonders that would soon, if not immediately, eliminate office workers, accountants, and even the executive himself. The situation was not helped by rapid technological changes in the equipment and by the lack of experience in the use of computer systems. Manufacturers were faced with the problem of selling models that were being designed into obsolescence on their own drawing boards. Another difficulty was a lack of consensus on the part that might be played by computers in business. Some people viewed computers with the misty eyes of a missionary saving his first heathen, and others assumed the role of confirmed skeptics. Amateurs often dominated the scene because too few professionals had been developed. However, some degree of order seems to be evolving from the disorder that accompanies the first phase of development.

The Importance of Planning

The managerial problem is how to absorb a revolutionary innovation in an essentially evolutionary fashion. Executives should not order a computer simply because the advertising copy is appealing or because everyone is talking about computers. Some computer installations have been motivated by little more than "keeping up with the Joneses." Many companies have experienced difficulties because of a lack of adequate management planning rather than inadequacies in computer technology. It should be noted, however, that experimentation may be appropriate and necessary to overcome a lack of experience.

A Study of the Problem

The first step in making a decision about computers is to determine whether they can be effectively used. An individual or a committee should be given the responsibility for studying the situation. The computer market and the literature can be surveyed for information about technical and cost alternatives. Company operations should be analyzed to determine how and to what extent computers can be applied. Unless the answer is immediately negative, the planning may also involve a comprehensive operation and cost analysis. Computers have not repealed the need for a favorable relationship between revenues and costs. The purchase or rental of a computer involves costs that must be balanced by revenue considerations.

Training Personnel

The costs of programming, training personnel, and making a transition from existing methods should not be neglected by the planners. Computer consultants and manufacturers can provide useful guidance in solving many problems, but their advice should be carefully scrutinized in terms of company requirements. The difficulty is not so much that someone will deliberately distort the truth but that there is still a great deal to learn about computer applications. Manufacturers, universities, and professional associations have developed courses and programs concerned with various aspects of computer operations, but there still seems to be some lack of consensus on training requirements and techniques. The experience of other companies can be helpful in overcoming this handicap.

The Transitional Period

An organization should expect many unanticipated difficulties during the computer installation and the transitional period. The situation will be replete with systems development, programming, training, and operating problems that do not always have easy answers. Indeed, some executives will wonder why they ever considered the idea in the first place.

A major transitional problem is that of converting manual record-keeping systems into a form that can be handled by the computer system. There are usually many errors in manually-kept systems that cause rejection by the computer, which has a more exacting control system. Some of these errors may have been corrected at the time of usage, others may not have been important, but some of them undoubtedly caused serious informational distortions. The process of converting existing records to computerized information may take ten years or longer with many difficult problems for all concerned.

The developmental stage tends to create uncertainty and status problems among managerial and operating personnel. Personnel engaged in such activities as accounting and production control may become somewhat apprehensive about the manner in which the computer will affect their future. The fact that computers can and will change personnel requirements is obvious to even the lowliest clerical worker. Careful consideration should be given to the motivational consequences of a computer installation during the planning phase.

Emphasis should be given to the fact that computers and everything they imply are expensive. There may not be any cost reduction in informational processing for a long period of time. Indeed, management may become rather concerned about the seemingly endless sequence of costly additions in the form of hardware and software. Eventually there will be dividends in the form of lower processing costs as well as more timely and better information.

The Development of Computerized Informational Systems

The development of computerized information is viewed from a dual perspective in the pages that follow. The first relates to the basic processes that begin with computer systems design and end with computer operations. The second is concerned with the kinds of computerized informational systems that may be developed in an organization. Figure 21-1 portrays the nature of these interrelationships.

The Design of Informational Systems

The design of informational systems involves an analysis of informational needs of a department or an entire organization and a determination of the manner in which a computerized system can meet these needs. Figure 21-2 indicates the nature of a computerized production control system. The basic problem is to translate informational requirements into a form that can be effectively handled by an electronic computer. The conversion to a computerized system may impose limitations that were not present in an existing noncomputerized system. In some instances, a systems study will result in the conclusion that computerization cannot solve the informational problem. But a computerized system can provide information that would not otherwise be possible.

The systems designer is obviously concerned with the capacities of the computer in designing an informational system. But this requirement does not mean that the systems designer must be able to perform the detailed steps involved in computer programming. A broad knowledge of computer capacities is adequate for most purposes. It is generally more important for the systems designer to understand the nature of the specialized field for which the informational system is being developed. Systems personnel should have a good background in accounting, economics, finance, marketing, production, and personnel before they attempt to design a computerized informational system for such fields. The systems function is often further specialized on a functional basis. One company divides systems responsibilities into manufacturing and distribution systems; another has separate systems sections for manufacturing, marketing, and finance; and

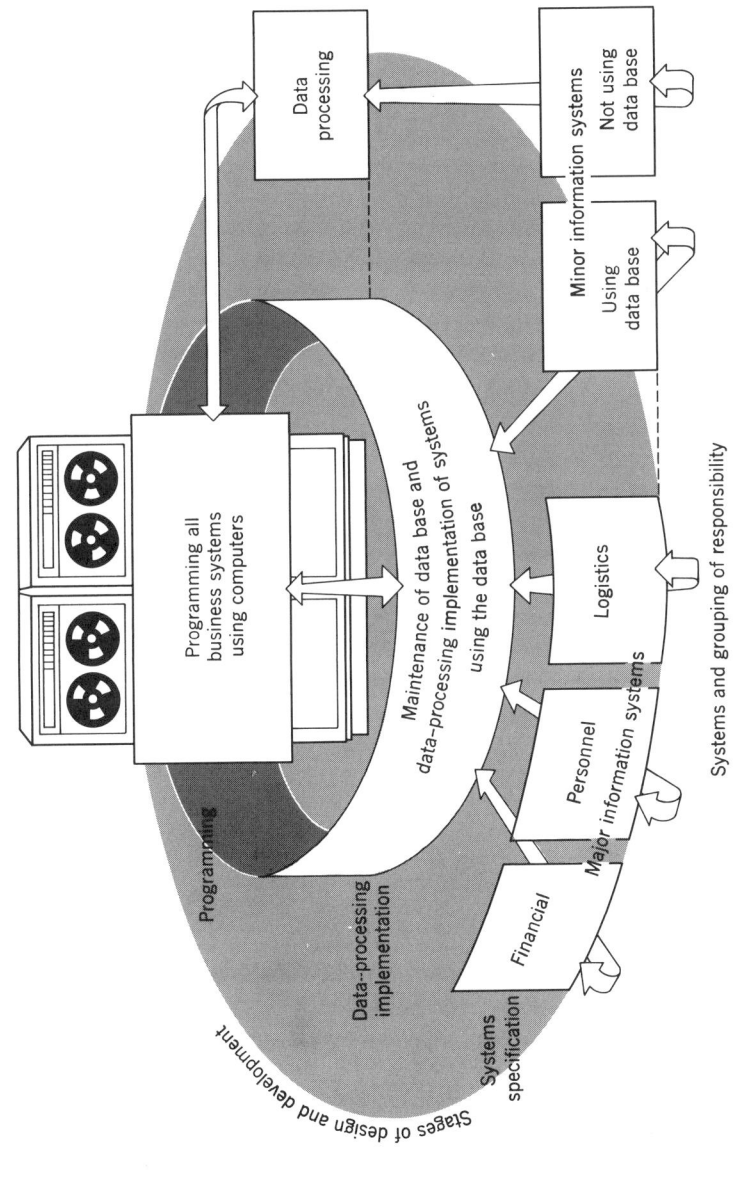

Figure 21-1. Generalized organization chart for systems and data processing. John Dearden, "How to Organize Information Systems," *Harvard Business Review*, Vol. 43, No. 2, March–April 1965, pp. 71. With permission.

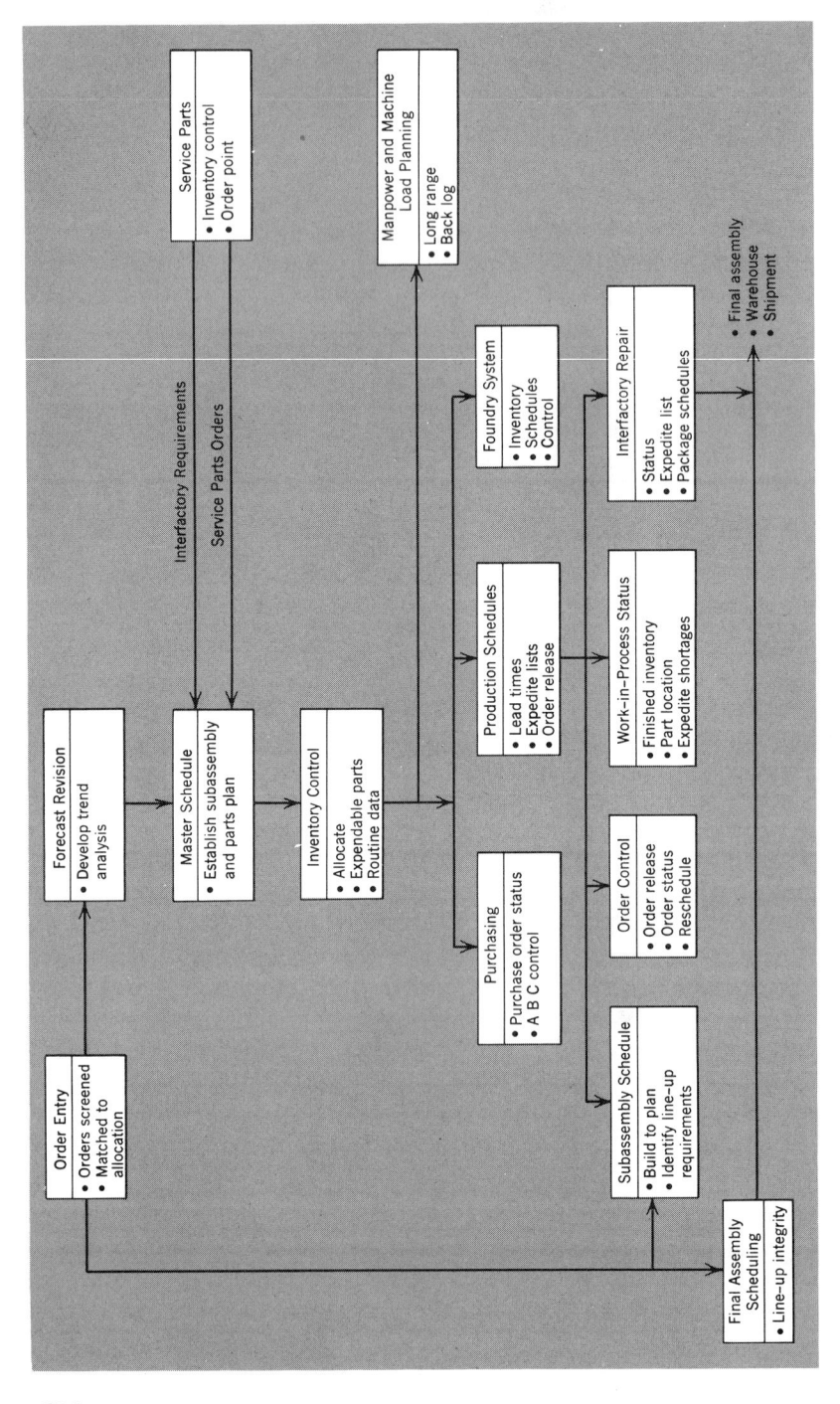

Figure 21-2. Basic elements of a total production control system. Courtesy: Deere and Company.

still another has categorized systems development under manufacturing and engineering, financial and relations, and marketing and distribution.

The interrelationship among informational subsystems within an organization, together with the tremendous capacities of the computer, means that systems design may transcend traditional informational boundaries. Some have even envisioned the development of totally integrated informational systems. Such a perspective means that the systems designer must have an understanding of the nature of the total management process. The philosophy of cybernetics becomes pertinent in an integrated informational approach. Impetus is given to the idea of systems theory as a separate and specialized field of endeavor. In other words, some systems designers will be primarily qualified in systems theory and practice rather than such specialties as accounting, production, or personnel. However, it should not be assumed that anything like total informational systems will soon be developed in any practical situation. The most that can be expected are partially integrated systems involving closely related subsystems. Nevertheless, such systems have opened a new dimension which will become increasingly important in the future.

Computer Programming

Most electronic computers are multipurpose and can be programmed to solve a wide range of particular problems. The programming difficulty is to translate informational requirements into a form that can be handled by the machine. Systems design indicates informational objectives and processes in generalized terms. Programming sets forth the necessary, detailed, step-by-step instructions to the computer. The language of the computer is a binary code (combinations of zeros and ones) that corresponds to the computer's off-on switching elements.

The problems of programming have been greatly simplified by the development of computer software. Computer hardware is the tangible equipment such as magnetic tape drives, central processors, and printers. Software is composed of the programs and programming aids provided by equipment manufacturers and developed by users. Software is an important ingredient for efficient hardware utilization.

A number of different techniques to assist the programmer can be noted. One is the assembly program that enables the programmer to use mnemonic designations in writing a program. In other words, one set of codes becomes another with the same or a similar meaning. The programmer must still think in terms of each machine operation, but he can write the specific instruction in something other than binary code. For example, he can write ADD or SUBTRACT instead of long sequences of zeros or ones. An assembly program will automatically translate mnemonic programming codes into machine or binary code. See Figure 21-3 for an assembly language listing.

Another important programming aid is the compiler program. An assembly program is a one-for-one translation device. For each machine instruction there is a corresponding mnemonic type code. Compiler programs are macro in the sense that they translate into many micromachine instructions. The programmer can set forth what needs to be done in much broader terms. He needs to be less concerned with the details of machine operation and can give more attention to the information procedure with which he is concerned.

Compiler programs through which the computer itself can be used to fill in the details have made possible programming languages that have greatly facilitated computer programming. A good example is COBOL (Common Business Oriented Languages), which can be used for a wide variety of organizational and managerial applications. See Figure 21-4. Another example is FORTRAN (Formula Translation), which is a scientific and engineering language. Other important languages could be noted, but the basic idea is the same. They all use macro symbols relating to the fields concerned, which can be translated into micromachine instructions through compiler programs. A word of caution is probably in order at this point. These languages have not made programming an amateur pursuit. Precise and complicated procedures must be followed in using them and the programmer must still have extensive knowledge about computer operations.

Still another important advance in the software area is the development of standardized application programs that can be used by many organizations. Computer manufacturers have developed programs of this kind for sales forecasting, capital investment, PERT, linear programming, production line balancing, inventory control, and many other systems. Such programs can often be used with a slight amount of modification to meet particular needs.

Computer Operations

A computer installation produces a large variety of information through hardware and software components. Hundreds of people may be employed in large data-processing departments. Some of the basic functions performed in such departments are the following. The preparation of input data for machine operations involves such activities as key punching cards with round or rectangular holes so that they can be "read" by machine input equipment. Punched cards may be duplicated, collated, and sorted in order to arrange or rearrange data for machine operations and other pur-

```
258     ENTER
259     MOVE        000CD4  D2 18 6 0B7 8 COC                MVC   0B7(25,6),00C(8)     DNM=6-398      DNM=3-215
260     PERFORM     000DDA  58 C0 D 1E0                      L     0,1E0(0,13)          VN=01
                    000DDE  5C CC D 1CC                      ST    C,1CC(0,13)          PSV=1
                    000DE2  58 C0 C 080                      L     C,080(0,12)          GN=016
                    000DE6  50 CC D 1EC                      ST    0,1E0(0,13)          VN=01
                    000DEA  58 10 C C38                      L     1,038(0,12)          PN=012
                    000DEE  07 F1                            BCR   15,1
                    000DFC                          GN=016   EQU   *
                    000DF0  58 00 D 1CC                      L     0,1CC(0,13)          PSV=1
                    000DF4  5C CC D 1EC                      ST    0,1E0(0,13)          VN=01
261     GO          000DF8  58 10 C 028                      L     1,028(0,12)          PN=08
                    000DFC  07 F1                            BCR   15,1
262     *SEQUENCE-CHECK
                    000DFE                          PN=06    EQU   *
263     IF          000DFE  58 10 C 0F4                      L     1,0F4(0,12)          GN=045
                    000E02  58 20 C C84                      L     2,084(0,12)          GN=017
                    000E06  95 40 7 066                      CLI   066(7),X"40"         DNM=3-23
                    000ECA  07 72                            BCR   7,2
                    000E0C  D5 C6 7 067 7 066                CLC   067(7,7),066(7)      DNM=3-23+1     DNM=3-23
                    000E12  07 72                            BCR   7,2
263     MOVE        000E14                          GN=045   EQU   *
                    000E14  D2 C7 7 066 C 190                MVC   066(8,7),190(12)     DNM=3-0        LIT+128
264     DISPLAY     000E1A  58 F0 C 004                      L     15,004(0,12)         V(IHDFDISP)
                    000E1E  05 1F                            BALR  1,15
                    000E20  0C02                             DC    X'0002'
                    000E22  10                               DC    X"10"
                    000E23  000C2C                           DC    X'00002C'
                    000E26  0C0C02CD                         DC    X"0C00020D"          LIT+253
                    000E2A  000C                             DC    X'0000'
                    000E2C  00                               DC    X"00"
                    000E2D  00000C                           DC    X'00000C'
                    000E30  0D0C01BC                         DC    X"0D0001BC"          BLI=1
                    000E34  0005                             DC    X'0005'
                    000E36  FFFF                             DC    X"FFFF"
266     IF          000E38                          GN=017   EQU   *
                    000E38  58 10 C 0F8                      L     1,0F8(0,12)          GN=046
                    000E3C  58 20 C 088                      L     2,088(0,12)          GN=018
                    000E40  95 40 7 06E                      CLI   06E(7),X'40'         DNM=3-59
                    000E44  07 72                            BCR   7,2
                    000E46  D5 C5 7 06F 7 06E                CLC   06F(6,7),06E(7)      DNM=3-59+1     DNM=3-59
                    000E4C  07 72                            BCR   7,2
266     MOVE        000E4E                          GN=046   EQU   *
                    000E4E  D2 06 7 06E C 194                MVC   06E(7,7),194(12)     DNM=3-35       LIT+132
267     DISPLAY     000E54  58 F0 C 004                      L     15,004(0,12)         V(IHDFDISP)
                    000E58  05 1F                            BALR  1,15
                    000E5A  0002                             DC    X"0002"
                    000E5C  1C                               DC    X'10'
                    000E5D  0C002D                           DC    X"00002D"
                    000E60  0C000239                         DC    X'0C000239'          LIT+297
                    000E64  000C                             DC    X"0000"
                    000E66  00                               DC    X'00'
                    000E67  0C0C0C                           DC    X"00000C"
                    000E6A  0D0C01BC                         DC    X'0D0001BC'          BLI=1
                    000E6E  0005                             DC    X"0005"
                    000E7C  FFFF                             DC    X'FFFF'
269     IF          000E72                          GN=018   EQU   *
```

Figure 21-3. Basic assembly language listing. Courtesy: Deere and Company.

```
00225  010100       READ SORTED-UNTIMED-WORK-FILE AT END GC TO END-OF-JOB.          P7129916
00226  010150 MONTH-CHECK-1.                                                        P7129916
00227  010160       IF PRODUCTION-MONTH IS > 6  THEN GC TC MONTH-CHECK-2.           P7129916
00228  010170       IF PRODUCTION-MONTH = 1 THEN MCVE 'NOV' TO CURRENT-MONTH,       P7129916
00229  010180           MOVE "DEC" TC NEXT-MONTH, GC TC CCNTINUE.                   P7129916
00230  010190       IF PRODUCTION-MONTH = 2 THEN MCVE 'DEC' TO CURRENT-MONTH,       P7129916
00231  010200           MOVE "JAN" TC NEXT-MONTH, GC TO CCNTINUE.                   P7129916
00232  010210       IF PRODUCTION-MONTH = 3 THEN MCVE 'JAN' TO CURRENT-MONTH,       P7129916
00233  010220           MOVE "FEB" TC NEXT-MONTH, GC TO CCNTINUE.                   P7129916
00234  010230       IF PRODUCTION-MONTH = 4 THEN MCVE 'FEB' TO CURRENT-MONTH,       P7129916
00235  010240           MOVE "MAR" TC NEXT-MONTH, GC TO CCNTINUE.                   P7129916
00236  010250       IF PRODUCTION-MONTH = 5 THEN MCVE 'MAR' TO CURRENT-MONTH,       P7129916
00237  011010           MOVE "APR" TC NEXT-MONTH, GC TC CCNTINUE.                   P7129916
00238  011020       IF PRODUCTION-MONTH = 6 THEN MCVE 'APR' TO CURRENT-MONTH,       P7129916
00239  011030           MOVE "MAY" TC NEXT-MONTH, GC TO CCNTINUE.                   P7129916
00240  011040 MONTH-CHECK-2.                                                        P7129916
00241  011050       IF PRODUCTION-MONTH = 7 THEN MCVE 'MAY' TO CURRENT-MONTH,       P7129916
00242  011060           MOVE "JUN" TC NEXT-MONTH, GC TO CONTINUE.                   P7129916
00243  011070       IF PRODUCTION-MONTH = 8 THEN MCVE 'JUN' TO CURRENT-MONTH,       P7129916
00244  011080           MOVE "JUL" TC NEXT-MONTH, GC TC CCNTINUE.                   P7129916
00245  011090       IF PRODUCTION-MONTH = 9 THEN MCVE 'JUL' TO CURRENT-MCNTH,       P7129916
00246  011100           MOVE "AUG" TO NEXT-MONTH, GC TC CCNTINUE.                   P7129916
00247  011110       IF PRODUCTION-MONTH = 10 THEN MCVE 'AUG' TC CURRENT-MONTH,      P7129916
00248  011120           MOVE "SEP" TC NEXT-MONTH, GC TO CCNTINUE.                   P7129916
00249  011130       IF PRODUCTION-MONTH = 11 THEN MCVE 'SEP' TO CURRENT-MONTH,      P7129916
00250  011140           MOVE "OCT" TC NEXT-MONTH, GC TO CCNTINUE.                   P7129916
00251  011150       MOVE 'OCT' TC CURRENT-MONTH.                                    P7129916
00252  011160       MOVE "NOV" TC NEXT-MONTH.                                       P7129916
00253  011170 CONTINUE.                                                             P7129916
00254  011172       MOVE CURRENT-MONTH TO CURRENT-MCNTH-1.                          K6310127
00255  011174       MOVE NEXT-MONTH TO NEXT-MONTH-1.                                K6310127
00256  011180       ENTER LINKAGE.                                                  P7129916
00257  011190       CALL 'CBDATE' USING CURRENT-DATE.                               P7129916
00258  011200       ENTER COBOL.                                                    P7129916
00259  011210       MOVE FACTORY-NAME TO H-FACTORY-NAME.                            P7129916
00260  011220       PERFORM NEW-PAGE.                                               P7129916
00261  011230       GO TO LIMIT-CHECK.                                              P7129916
00262  011232 SEQUENCE-CHECK.                                                       P7129916
00263  011241       IF STD            = SPACES THEN MOVE 1 TO STANDARD-HOURS.       P7129916
00264  011242           DISPLAY 'STANDARD-HOURS=SPACES-ASSUME 1, PART-NUMBER="      P7129916
00265  011243           PART-NUMBER UPCN CONSOLE.                                   P7129916
00266  011244       IF SCHEDULED        = SPACES THEN MOVE ZERO TO SCHEDULED-HOURSP7129916
00267  011245           DISPLAY "SCHEDULED-HOURS=SPACES-ASSUME 0, PART-NUMBER="     P7129916
00268  011246           PART-NUMBER UPON CONSOLE.                                   P7129916
00269  011250       IF DEPARTMENT-NUMBER > PREV-DEPARTMENT-NUMBER THEN DISPLAY      P7129916
00270  011251       'RECORDS OUT OF SEQUENCE' UPON CONSOLE, DISPLAY 'PREV:DEPT=' P7129916
00271  011252       PREV-DEPARTMENT-NUMBER ",SCHED HRS=" PREV-SCHEDULED-HOURS       P7129916
00272  011253       ',MONTH CODE=' PREV-MONTH-CODE ',CURRENT=' DEPARTMENT-NUMBER P7129916
00273  011254       UPON CONSOLE, GC TO OUT-OF-SEQUENCE.                            P7129916
00274  012020       IF DEPARTMENT-NUMBER < PREV-DEPARTMENT-NUMBER GC TC             P7129916
00275  012030           DEPT-CHANGE.                                                P7129916
00276  012040       IF SCHEDULED-HOURS > PREV-SCHEDULED-HOURS THEN DISPLAY          P7129916
00277  012041       'RECORDS OUT OF SEQUENCE' UPON CONSOLE, DISPLAY "PREV:DEPT=" P7129916
00278  012042       PREV-DEPARTMENT-NUMBER ',SCHED HRS=' PREV-SCHEDULED-HOURS       P7129916
00279  012043       ",MONTH CODE=" PREV-MONTH-CODE ",CURRENT=" SCHEDULED-HCURS      P7129916
00280  012044       UPON CONSOLE, GO TO OUT-OF-SEQUENCE.                            P7129916
00281  012060       IF SCHEDULED-HOURS  <     PREV-SCHEDULED-HOURS GO TO            P7129916
```

Figure 21-4. COBOL listing of machine loading programming. Courtesy: Deere and Company.

poses. They are also important information storage devices. Punched card information cannot be directly read by the computer; it must be first transferred to magnetic tape.

Computer programs and operating data are generally fed into the computer through magnetic tapes. The program is first put into the computer memory after which the data are inserted for operations. The computer console operator monitors the processing to check for programming errors, incomplete or incorrect data input, and other problems. The results of computer operation are recorded on magnetic tape, punched cards, or paper; high speed printers are used to provide much of the data output.

The problems that face other production facilities are also pertinent in data processing departments. Production planning and scheduling, quality control, maintenance problems (hardware and software), software storage, personnel supervision and training, and customer (user departments) relations are highly important managerial responsibilities.

Computer Applications

A list containing over 500 areas of computer application has been compiled and the list has by no means stopped growing.[1] Computers have been used to analyze costs, find criminals, design electric motors, schedule trains, land airplanes, wage war, fly a space ship, and play checkers. This analysis is primarily concerned with computer applications that relate directly to management; scientific and engineering applications are not considered.

Management Systems: Major Functional Categories

Three major kinds of informational systems can be found in most organizations.[2] One is the financial system that evolves from the flow of dollars through the organization. This system is highly conducive to computerization. Much of the data is historical in nature and generated within the organization. Important informational subsystems are accounts payable, accounts receivable, budgetary control, financial reports, general accounting, and payroll.

Another major informational system is the logistics system. This system is concerned with information about the flow of goods through the organization and encompasses the functions of procurement, production, and

[1] Edmund C. Berkeley, *The Computer Revolution* (Garden City, N.Y.: Doubleday and Company, Inc., 1962), Appendix 1.
[2] John Dearden, "How to Organize Information Systems," *Harvard Business Review*, Vol. 43, No. 2, March–April 1965, pp. 65–73.

1. *Payroll*

    Daily job incentive, weekly, hourly, monthly salary, and regional manager commission payrolls. Includes all employee efficiency and performance reports, payroll and deduction registers plus government tax reports and related labor accounting reports.

2. *Budget Accounting*

    Department analysis by account number reflecting actual against budget on a month and year-to-date base.

3. *Assets and Depreciation*

    Monthly control of all permanent assets including plant machinery, office equipment, dies, molds, buildings, and vehicles. Annual depreciation for buildings, vehicles, dies and molds.

4. *Invoicing and Accounts Receivable*

    Billing application for sale of all appliances and repair parts from Newton and field warehouses. Weekly analysis of accounts receivable by dealer supported by aging accounts.

5. *Marketing Unit Sales Analysis*

    Month and year-to-date analysis of sales for each appliance category (automatic washers, dryers, conventional washer, dishwasher, etc.) by dealer, county, regional salesman, branch office, etc. Monthly per cent comparison of Maytag sales versus total industry by county. Statistical records retained for 10 year period for marketing analysis.

6. *Financial Sales Analysis*

    Monthly distribution of dollar sales for repairs, appliances, Newton, and field sales into approximately 30 different analytical reports for financial department.

---

distribution. The functions involve the processing of large amounts of mostly internal information. Important informational subsystems are production planning and control, inventory control, purchasing, and PERT.

Still another major informational system involves the flow of information about personnel.[3] Such information is used for purposes of promotion, pay, work assignment, and transfer. The primary use of computer equipment is information storage and retrieval. Examples of subsystems are personnel records, manpower assessment, and skills inventory.

In addition to the three major systems, there are other important informational systems. Many companies maintain comprehensive marketing information on such matters as sales performance, customer credit, customer inventories, and advertising effectiveness. Some companies assemble and distribute information about the economic system, industry conditions, and research findings. See Figures 21-5 and 21-6 for listings of computerized informational systems developed by two companies.

[3] Richard T. Bueschel, *EDP and Personnel,* Management Bulletin 86 (New York: American Management Association, 1966).

7. *Purchasing, Receiving and Accounts Payable*
   The purchase, receipt, and payment of all materials required in the manufacture of our products. All purchase orders and accounts payable checks are processed daily with daily, weekly, and yearly vendor analysis accumulated.
8. *Warehouse Inventories*
   Weekly analysis and status of appliance inventories for each field warehouse. Daily analysis of shipments, production, and current inventory status by model for Newton Warehouse. Monthly analysis and replenishment of repairs for branch warehouses.
9. *Weekly Inventory Control and Daily Production Status*
   Based on current production forecast, reflects number of days coverage by part number for purchased and productive parts. Reports used by inventory controller to purchase necessary materials and production schedulers to schedule production.
10. *Quality Defects Reporting System*
    Daily analysis of rejects for the automatic and dryer assembly lines, paint, and porcelain departments. Allows for management concentration on high defect items and improved communications and control between inspection and production departments.

Figure 21-5. Computerized informational systems developed at the Maytag Company. Courtesy: The Maytag Company.

Forecasting and Planning Systems

Computerized informational systems have been particularly effective in providing information about what *has* happened. Accounting and financial reports, production and sales data, and labor turnover statistics are examples of this kind of information. Computers have also been helpful in preparing information about planned activities *after* management has made certain critical decisions. The processing of production planning and scheduling information provides a good illustration. Such plans and schedules incorporate some rather arbitrary assumptions about future sales. After management has determined organizational sales objectives, computerized systems can be most helpful in converting them into production plans and schedules, inventory and purchase programs, and financial budgets.

To what extent have computers been used to forecast the future and perform analytical operations to facilitate the planning process? This question is difficult to answer for the following reasons. One is that much of the literature on the subject is concerned with what should or what will happen rather than what has happened. Another is that surveys about company practices are generally subject to a great deal of misunderstanding and

Personnel Records	Engineering Project Control
Payrolls	Engineering Cost Analysis
Accounts Payable	Production Planning
Accounts Receivable	Manufacturing Orders
Financial Reports	Material Requirements
Operating Reports	Manpower Requirements
General Accounting	Machine Requirements
Reliability Analysis	Incentive Standards
Quality Control Analysis	Labor Analysis Reports
Sales Orders	Retail Note Acceptance
Sales Invoices	Retail Note Collection
Advice of Shipment	Retail Note Analysis
Order Analyses	Credit Company Insurance
Sales Analyses	
Inventory Control	Purchase Orders
Service Parts	Vendor Analysis
Complete Machines	
Work in Process	Sales Forecasts
Raw Material	Industry Reports

Figure 21-6. Major Computerized information systems developed at Deere and Company. Courtesy: Deere and Company.

semantic distortion. For example, how many purely engineering applications of computer technology are categorized as managerial applications? Nonetheless, there is some indication that increased use is now being made of computers for forecasting and planning purposes.[4] Computers have provided faster, more, and often better information for appraisal and analysis by human decision makers. The process of developing computerized informational systems has in many instances improved both the quality and quantity of information. The large computerized data banks that have been built during the past decade are a good base for mathematical and other analytical techniques. Many organizations are beginning to take fuller advantage of the available data and the capacities of their computer systems. The employment of specialists in operations research and related techniques

[4] Neal J. Dean, "The Computer Comes of Age," *Harvard Business Review,* Vol. 46, No. 1, January–February 1968, pp. 88–89; M. Valliant Higginson, *Managing With EDP,* AMA Research Study 71 (New York: American Management Association, 1965), pp. 47–84.

appears to increase as an organization gains computer experience. A sizable number of organizations are now using computerized information and computers to construct elaborate econometric models of the economy and of particular industries. Planning models that simulate important environmental and organizational factors have been developed to test alternative strategies. Similar models are being used to enhance executive development through a large variety of management games. Linear programming, queuing theory, and other mathematical models are extensively employed to solve planning problems. Analogue models, such as PERT, have been computerized for the planning and control of comprehensive projects.

A great deal of progress will undoubtedly be made during the next decade in applying computer technology to the problems of forecasting and planning. But it would be folly to expect too much. Human behavior presents many uncertainties which cannot be overcome by the computer. The assumptions that have to be made in constructing mathematical models are sometimes the critical elements in a forecasting or planning problem. The formulation of restrictive assumptions about the nature of reality has the effect of leaving unanswered the "solutions" that are assumed. In spite of the limitations, the new analytical and mathematical techniques will probably provide somewhat better solutions to decisional problems. The extent of error can undoubtedly be reduced even though exact solutions are not possible. Executives will continue to give answers to questions that have no answer.

Real Time Computer Systems

A great deal has been written in recent years about real time systems that can supply executives with completely up-to-date information about company operations. The term "real time" means that informational inputs into the computer occur at the time that operations occur. The only lag in such a system is the short span of time necessary to record information in computer memory. Some further delay might result from a possible queuing of information at the input point. The lags would generally not be longer than a few minutes. Such a system is "on line" in the sense that all information contained in the system is under the control of the computer. Information in the system is updated as operations occur and is immediately available in an appropriate form at a number of output stations.

One of the earliest and better known examples of a real time system is SABRE, the reservation system developed for the American Airlines.[5]

[5] A good description of this system is found in: R. W. Parker, "The SABRE System," *Datamation,* Vol. 11, No. 9, September 1965, pp. 49–52.

This system provides American Airlines reservation personnel with immediate information about available seats on future airline flights. A reservation can be made, confirmed, altered, or canceled at any point in the system, irrespective of where it was made, in a matter of a few seconds. A record is made of the passenger's name, itinerary, telephone number, and other pertinent information (such as special dietary needs), which is available to all American Airline agents.

In addition to maintaining a perpetual inventory of seating reservations and pertinent information about prospective passengers, SABRE automatically does the following things.

1. Notifies agents when special action is necessary, such as calling a passenger about a change in flight status.
2. Maintains and processes waiting lists of passengers wanting space on fully booked flights.
3. Sends teletype messages to other airlines for seating space, follows up if no reply is received, and responds to space requests from other airlines.
4. Provides the arrival and departure times for all flights for the day.[6]

Real time systems similar to SABRE have been developed for other airlines. The Pan American PANAMAC and the Delta Airlines SABRER are examples. Traffic control systems for railroads represent another application of the real time concept. The New York Central real time system, for example, maintains an up to the minute watch on 125,000 railway cars rolling over 10,000 miles of track.

Real time systems require expensive hardward and software. The SABRE system involved some ten years of experimentation and development at a cost of some $30 million. The cost of such a system is an important limiting factor at the present time. But even if costs are significantly reduced, there is still the question of whether real time information is required for every kind of informational need. Indeed, real time information may have little value for some management purposes. Professor John Dearden has suggested that the real time concept can generally be better applied to logistical rather than to financial or personnel informational systems.[7]

Some companies are beginning to use something approaching a real time system to provide relatively up-to-date inventory, production, and sales information. Strictly speaking, most such systems are not real time because they involve batching of input data and lengthy delays in output transmission. Sales personnel, for example, transmit sales data at the end of the day

[6] *Ibid.*, p. 49.
[7] John Dearden, "Myth of Real-Time Management Information," *Harvard Business Review*, Vol. 44, No. 3, May–June 1966, pp. 123–132.

to the computer system for processing. This information is made available to management in an appropriate form the next morning. Such a system has a lag of something like a day that could be reduced by a number of relatively simple techniques, but there would be little purpose in doing so. Management does not need to have the information on a "real time" basis. Much of the data required for planning and control does not need to be up to the minute. A lag of a day, a week, or even a month is not too long for many managerial purposes.

Some information is meaningful only if it is accumulated (batched) for some period of time. The revenues and costs for a particular day, for example, sometimes have little significance and can unduly distort the totals without some kind of an averaging process. Furthermore, the difficulty of forecasting under conditions of uncertainty gives any kind of corresponding standard an extremely tenuous quality. As Professor Dearden has written:

> Even assuming objectives could logically be calendarized by day or hour, we run into worse problems in calculating actual performance, and worse still in making the comparison of actual to standard meaningful. If the performance measures involve accounting data (and they most frequently do), the data will never be up-to-date until they are normalized (adjusted) at the end of the accounting period.[8]

Much planning and control, particularly at higher levels of management, involve relatively long time periods. It would be a waste of time for top and even divisional management to constantly compare plan and performance. The important consideration in many instances is whether something continues to persist over a relatively long period of time. The hour-by-hour changes are pertinent for some purposes, but have little meaning for others. A planning and control horizon of one hour, one day, or even one week is by no means always appropriate. Even if the technological and economic problems of installing a total real time system could be overcome, the system would still have to accumulate (internally batch) and analytically modify much of the data, thereby taking away at least some of the advantages of its real time properties.

Shared Time Computer Systems

Shared time computer systems evolve from technological and economic considerations. The tremendous speed at which the electronic computer performs computational and other functions means that a large volume of operations is necessary if there is to be no unused capacity. Large com-

[8] Dearden, *op. cit.*, pp. 126–127.

puter systems are generally more economical if they are fully utilized and have much more problem-solving and processing capacity than smaller systems. The difficulty is that many organizations are able to use only a small proportion of the potential of a large system. A solution is to share a large computer with other organizations. One approach is a joint venture in which several organizations participate. Another is to acquire a larger computer and lease a portion of its capacity to other organizations. Still another is to lease computer time from a company set up for that purpose in the manner of telephone, electric power, and other public utilities. Shared time systems have already shown that they can be successful, and there are good reasons for believing they will become more popular in the future.

Organizing for Computers

The section is concerned with the problem of organizing for computerized informational systems. The nature of the informational systems department and the manner in which it relates to other departments is briefly discussed. Particular attention is given to ways in which business and government have solved such organizational problems.

The Information Systems Department

Departments concerned with computerized informational systems are generally referred to by such names as the Electronic Data Processing Department, the Business Systems Department, and the Electronic Computer Department. They are generally organized on functional basis with the following primary units: (1) Systems Analysis and Design; (2) Computer Programming; and (3) Data Processing or Computer Operations. Other possible subsidiary units have responsibility for such functions as program maintenance and storage, planning, education and training, scheduling, and quality control.

A basic organizational structure for an information systems department and some variations of this basic structure are shown in Figure 21-7.[9] In some instances, systems development and programming are combined in the same departmental unit. One argument for such an arrangement is that informational systems should be designed so that they can be efficiently programmed. Another is that programmers cannot perform their functions

[9] *Administration of Electronic Data Processing,* Studies in Business Policy No. 98 (New York, N.Y.: National Industrial Conference Board, Inc., 1961), pp. 57–67.

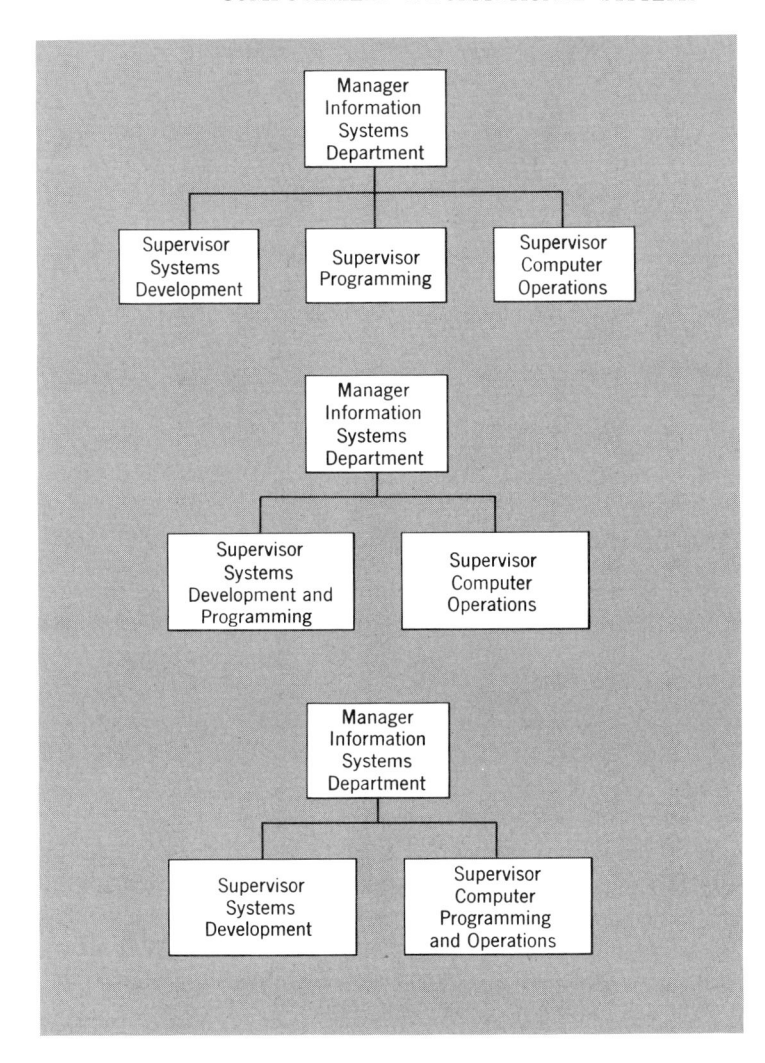

Figure 21-7. Alternative organizational structures for an information systems department.

properly unless they understand the purpose and logic of the system. Still another is that parts of the system can be programmed and checked to insure greater compatibility between the needs of the system and the programming problem.

Other organizations contend that systems design should be done in a separate departmental unit. The argument is that programmers might be too inclined to modify informational systems to simplify computer programming and operations. Some organizations have segmented the computer organization by placing the informational systems design function in a broader systems and procedures department. A possible difficulty is that systems design can become too far removed from the computer side of the schema. The result can be a lack of coordination and failures in cooperation.

Computer programming and operations are sometimes combined into one departmental unit. (See Figure 21-7.) The rationale is that efficiency in programming is an important prerequisite for efficient computer performance. Computer operations can then indicate the manner in which an informational system can be more efficiently programmed. Figures 21-8, 21-9, and 21-10 show the kind of specialization that takes place in systems and data processing departments.

Centralization and Decentralization

The extent to which managerial responsibilities relating to the electronic computer are centralized or decentralized is partly determined by the size of the organization. A small organization cannot generally afford the cost of duplicating electronic computers and specialized personnel. A single computer center creates conditions that make for some form of centralized control if computers are to be effectively utilized by more than one department. If the responsibility for computerization is placed under one department, such as accounting or production, there is often difficulty in gaining acceptance from other departmental executives at the same organizational level. Considerable support from higher management is frequently necessary to convince departmental executives that they should cooperate. During the initial phase of development, many organizations (both large and small) experienced strong resistance from operating and other executives. A lack of knowledge and the uncertainty of change were important in this respect.

The increasingly important part played by computerized information is indicated by the emergence of top level computer executives in many organizations.[10] According to a survey of several hundred companies by the American Management Association, the large majority of EDP managers report to the upper levels of management.[11] Almost three-fourths of

[10] Neal J. Dean, "The Computer Comes of Age," *Harvard Business Review,* Vol. 46, No. 1, January–February 1968, pp. 83–86; M. Valliant Higginson, *Managing With EDP,* AMA Research Study 71 (New York: American Management Association, 1965), pp. 34–35.

[11] *Ibid.,* p. 35.

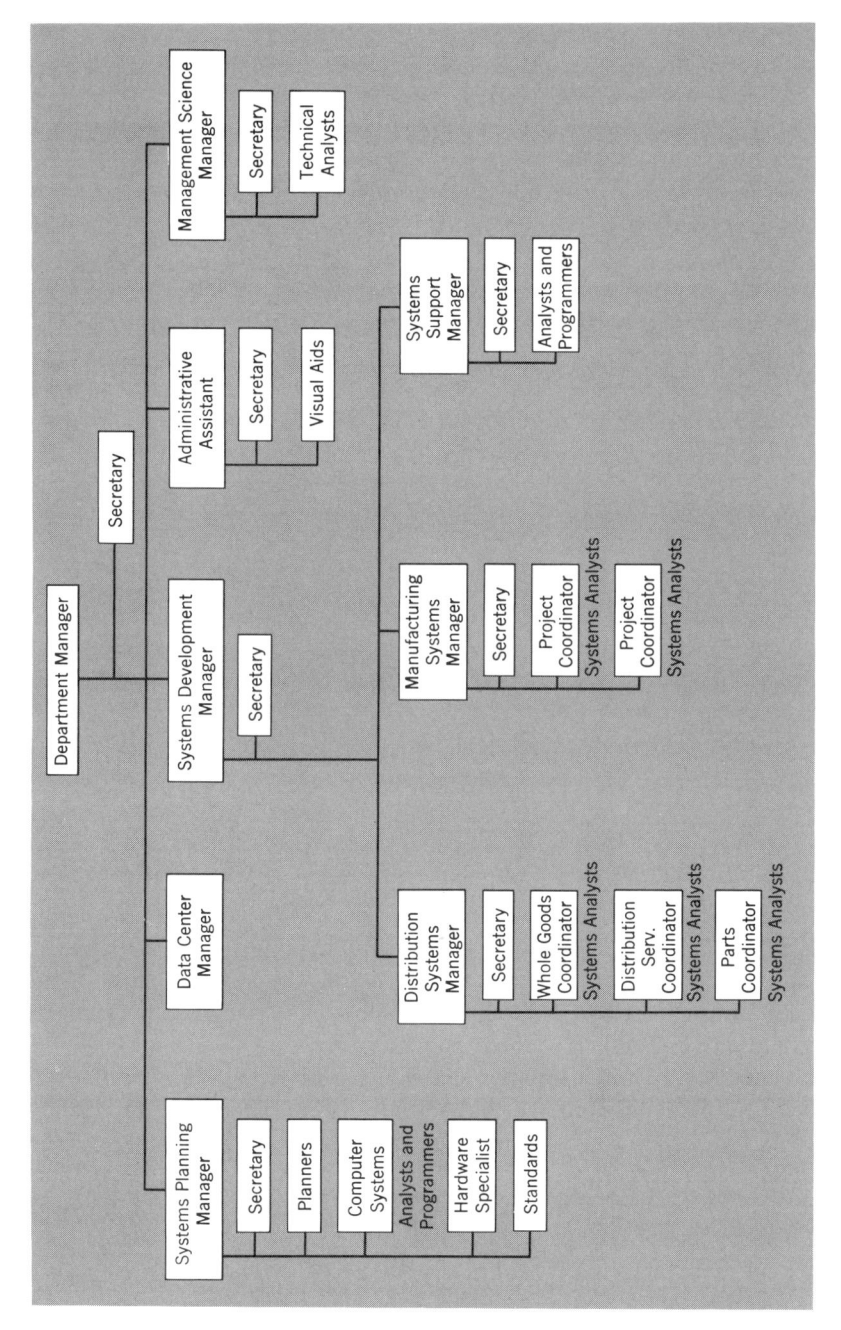

Figure 21-8. Business systems organization chart, Deere and Company. Courtesy: Deere and Company.

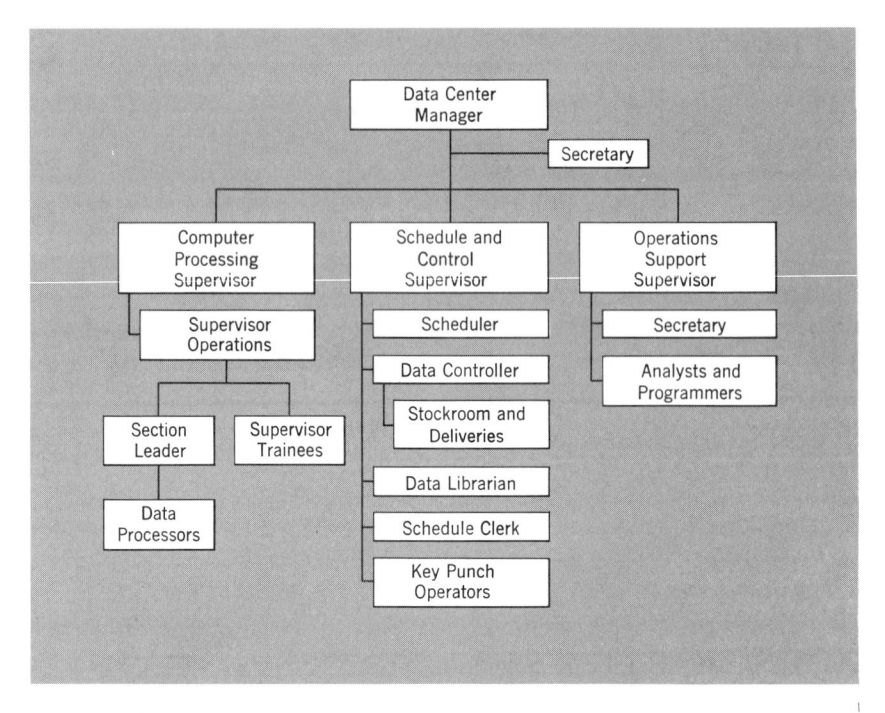

Figure 21-9. Data center organization chart, Deere and Company. Courtesy: Deere and Company.

them report to the president, executive vice-president, vice-presidents, controller, secretary, or treasurer. A similar result is reported in a study conducted by Booz, Allen and Hamilton, Inc., a management consulting concern. Of the 108 highly successful manufacturing companies studied, 97 had established a top level executive position with responsibility for the company computer effort.[12] About two thirds of these executives report directly to a vice-president or the president.

The majority of top computer executives still report to executives in some aspect of finance. In the AMA study noted above, 70 per cent reported to financial executives; the total was 60 per cent in the Booz, Allen and Hamilton research report. There is some indication that many electronic data processing departments have been moved out of the financial field. The pattern of change is illustrated by the experience of a large farm equipment manufacturing firm. For a period of about six years, electronic data processing existed as a section of the cost accounting department. An

[12] Dean, *op. cit.*, p. 84.

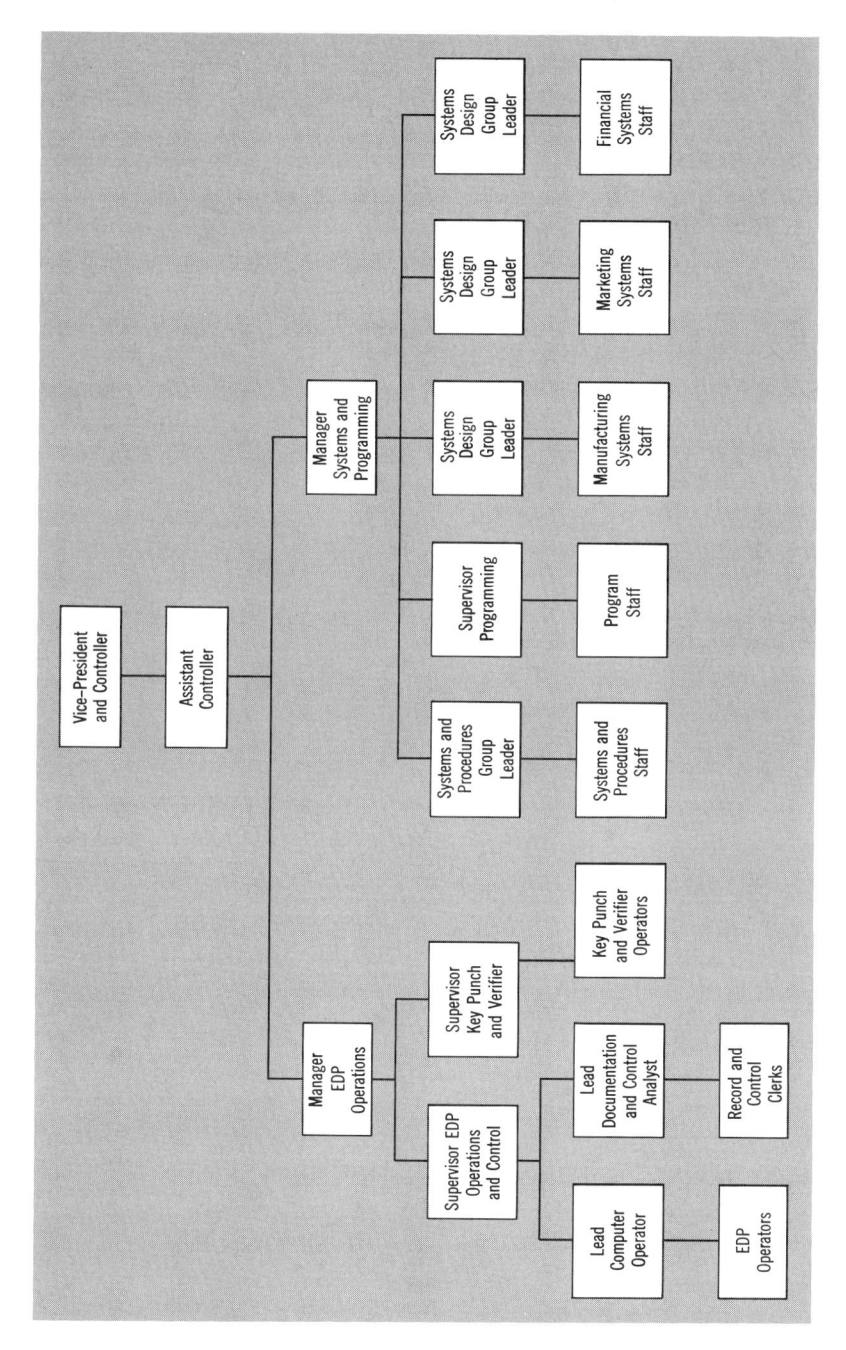

Figure 21-10. The Maytag Company—Systems and data processing organization. Courtesy: The Maytag Company.

important reason was that a large proportion of computer time was spent processing cost data. The application of computers to areas other than accounting gave rise to systems development and eventually a systems department. A company-wide systems department initially reported to the comptroller, but was almost immediately moved to a newly organized corporate planning and administration department. Similar changes have been made by many other organizations.

There has been a tendency to move computer executives into the center of the stage. The moves have not only been lateral, but also upward, which has tended to centralize data processing.[13] The very fact that EDP executives hold positions at the top management level indicates that the control of informational systems has been centralized even in organizations with decentralized informational systems. In other words, computerized informational systems tend to be relatively more centralized than the noncomputerized informational systems of the past.

The degree to which managerial responsibilities for computerized informational systems are centralized or decentralized seems to be closely related to whether other responsibilities are centralized or decentralized. Such a conclusion is given strong support by research conducted by Booz, Allen and Hamilton.[14] However, there are significant differences in the extent to which various kinds of informational responsibilities are centralized or decentralized. The amount of central direction in 97 well-managed companies is indicated in Figure 21-11. As might be expected, top level computer executives are generally charged with the enforcement of a basic framework of policies and standards for all computer activities within the organization. There are central management controls even when systems development and computer operations are highly decentralized.

The location of computer equipment has some relationship to the allocation of computer responsibilities. The existence of equipment at divisional or plant levels means that certain specialized personnel, such as computer operators, will also be located at that location. There is a tendency for such personnel to be under the direction and supervision of operating management. On the other hand, operating personnel will tend to report to someone in central management if the equipment is exclusively located at headquarters.

Some computer personnel is not as closely tied to equipment as others. Systems analysts and designers are probably the most flexible in this respect. They can perform their functions far removed from the computer equip-

[13] Higginson, *op. cit.*, p. 34.
[14] James W. Taylor and Neal J. Dean, "Managing to Manage the Computer," *Harvard Business Review*, Vol. 44, No. 5, September–October 1966, pp. 98–110; Dean, *op. cit.*, pp. 85–86.

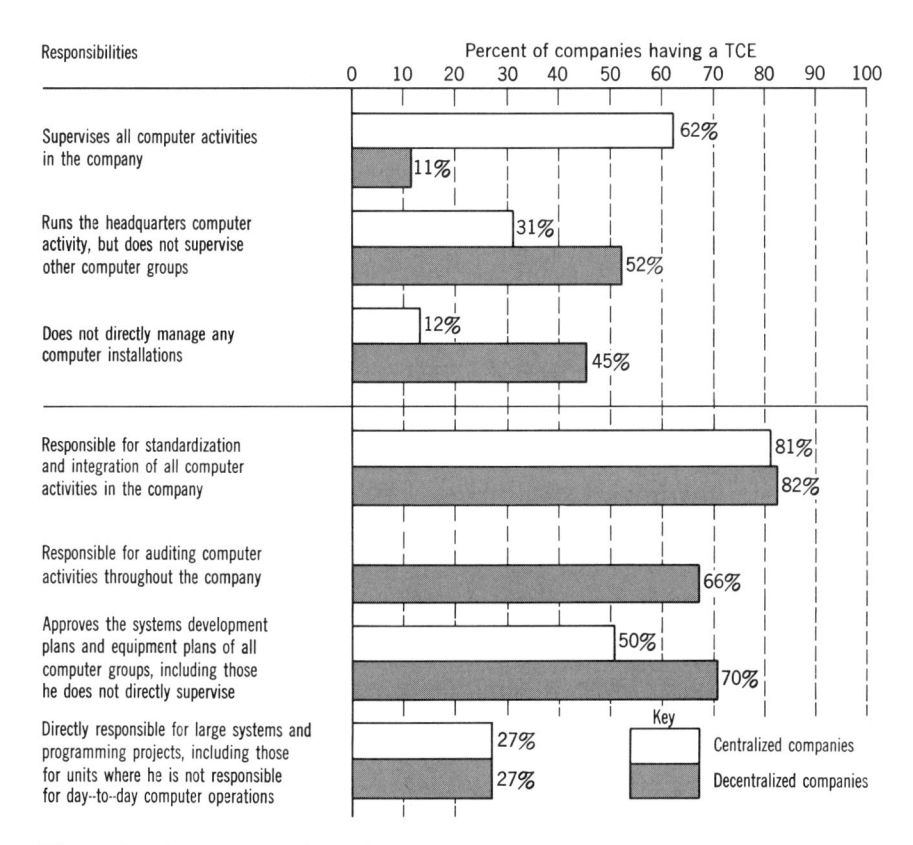

Responsibilities	Percent of companies having a TCE
Supervises all computer activities in the company	Centralized: 62%; Decentralized: 11%
Runs the headquarters computer activity, but does not supervise other computer groups	Centralized: 31%; Decentralized: 52%
Does not directly manage any computer installations	Centralized: 12%; Decentralized: 45%
Responsible for standardization and integration of all computer activities in the company	Centralized: 81%; Decentralized: 82%
Responsible for auditing computer activities throughout the company	Decentralized: 66%
Approves the systems development plans and equipment plans of all computer groups, including those he does not directly supervise	Centralized: 50%; Decentralized: 70%
Directly responsible for large systems and programming projects, including those for units where he is not responsible for day-to-day computer operations	Centralized: 27%; Decentralized: 27%

Figure 21-11. Responsibilites of top computer executives (TCE). Neal J. Dean, "The Computer Comes of Age," *Harvard Business Review,* Vol. 46, No. 1, January–February 1968, p. 85. With permission.

ment, and there is relatively less need to coordinate their activities with those of the programmers and operating personnel. Systems personnel may work at headquarters even though equipment is located at divisional or plant levels, and conversely.

As matters now stand the extent of centralization or decentralization of managerial responsibilities related to computerized informational systems does not radically depart from the prevailing patterns. Electronic computers and everything they imply have not been more conducive to either centralization or decentralization. To quote one report based on empirical research:

Our study has produced no evidence of a relationship between effectiveness of computer usage and centralization or decentralization. Both approaches seem to be able to concentrate the computer effort where it is needed. In companies where the normal management structure is highly centralized, a basically centralized computer system works best. Likewise, in decentralized companies, decentralized computer activities appear to work best. Managements have wisely sought to organize the computer function in much the same manner as they do other key operations of the business.[15]

Whether there are forces that make for more or less centralization of computer management in the future is not certain at this time. The need for greater uniformity of systems, the costs of unnecessary duplication in systems development, and potential advantages of company-wide informational integration may well lead to a higher degree of centralization. But, in spite of such considerations, there is little reason to believe that electronic computers, revolutionary though they are, will require a radically different organizational structure for effective utilization.

Computer Management: Line or Staff

Computer specialists usually have the status of staff and service personnel. The nature of their relationship to line executives is much the same as that of other staff specialists. Should computer specialists become something more than staff when they deal with operating executives? Should they have functional authority to give them more power to impose computerized informational systems upon operating executives? The answer to these questions would appear to be the same as that given in the past for other specialists, such as accounting and personnel. If operating executives are too reluctant to accept the help of specialists, top management may be forced to give strong support, possibly including full-fledged functional authority. However, the problem can generally be resolved within a line-staff framework. Staff status does not mean a lack of power.

A staff specialist who has the support of a top line executive can often obtain the cooperation of operating executives. Such support can readily be reduced or completely withdrawn if the activities of specialists become unduly disruptive. Formal functional authority is not essential except to reinforce higher line support. It serves only to give power the aura of authority.

During the initial phase of development, the computer specialist required considerable top management backing. Both operating executives and traditional staffs (such as accounting) were often opposed to computerized systems that departed far from the routines to which they were accustomed by education and experience. But as line and staff began to understand the new technology, they frequently became forceful advocates rather than

[15] Taylor and Dean, *op. cit.,* p. 104.

fearful opponents. Under such circumstances there are some good arguments for giving operating executives control of their own computerized informational systems.[16] If operating executives are to have responsibility for operating results, such an arrangement would appear to be highly appropriate. At the same time, some computerized systems should remain in the realm of top management. Systems that cross divisional lines or involve central control can be placed in such a category. A higher degree of centralization may result as informational systems become more integrated. The advantages of uniformity and costs of duplication are also important in this respect.

Future Prospects and Problems

This section attempts to build a bridge between present computer applications and future prospects. Computers have been tested on the firing line and have shown that they can solve important planning and informational problems. There is every indication that much more progress will be made in the future. But recognition should also be given to possible limitations and problems.

More Timely Information

Computerized informational systems have made possible more rapid communication of information about environmental and organizational conditions to management. The increased speed of information processing has given organizations a greater capacity to adapt to change. The planning period can in some instances be significantly shortened. However, more timely information is useful only if executives take advantage of it. The benefit of high speed processing can be negated by sluggishness in the planning and control process. A further consideration is that the costs of more timely information may more than offset their value. Also important is that instant information (such as real time) is by no means always necessary or even desirable.

The Problem of Informational Input

Electronic computers are essentially errorproof as far as the technical aspects of operations are concerned. They do exactly what they are di-

[16] Philip H. Thurston, "Who Should Control Information Systems?" *Harvard Business Review,* Vol. 40, No. 6, November–December 1962, pp. 135–139.

rected to do by their programs. But they cannot correct inputs of incomplete or inaccurate information. As one data processing executive put it, "The feeding of bad in-puts into faster and more capable equipments will only generate more bad information at a faster pace." [17] Production or sales personnel who deliberately or nondeliberately distort the data they provide are much the same problem they were before computerized informational systems were introduced.

Toward Integrated Informational Systems

There is little indication that organizations will soon have totally integrated informational systems. But a significant amount of integration has occurred within such functional areas as marketing and production.[18] In one survey of over 100 companies, a sizable number expect to have informational systems that tie together two or more functional areas. All of the companies in the survey expect their computer systems to be integrated to some significant degree in the future. Many companies reported that they are investigating the possibility and potential of a total informational system, but they do not intend to go that far in the immediate future.

Predictive Information and Models

A great deal of effort will undoubtedly be expended during the next decade to develop predictive and planning models. The high speeds at which computers perform their operations have probably improved the quality of accounting and statistical data. But the fact remains that such data are historical. Predictive and planning models are concerned with what will happen in the future. The human behavior reflected in data about the past can change significantly in a relatively short period of time. Computers have the capacity to provide a more accurate and complete history of human behavior, and they may well improve prediction of future behavior through their tremendous speed and computational capacity. But there is little likelihood that they will soon be able to improve upon the logical formulations that are presently employed by human behavioral scientists. The speed with which computers can solve logical and computational problems will not eliminate some of the more critical assumptions of predictive and planning models.

[17] Norman J. Ream, "Developing a Long-Range Plan for Corporate Methods and the Dependence on Electronic Data-Processing," presented at the Western Joint Computer Conference, San Francisco, California, March 3–5, 1959.

[18] Dean, *op. cit.*, pp. 89–90.

Socio-Psychological Problems

Some informational subsystems can be entirely controlled by computers, but man-machine interface cannot be avoided unless factories and offices are completely automated. The impact of machine-derived messages upon human receivers can have important psychological implications. Communicating with a machine can create problems that impede the communication process. In some cases communication may be blocked; in others, it may be improved.

Computers and all that they imply can have important motivational consequences. The pacing of mental operations by computers may create motivational problems among line and staff personnel. The amount of professionalization within the managerial structure will tend to increase as the personnel are upgraded. The larger percentages of college graduates and holders of advanced degrees in the personnel mix may significantly change the traditional authority and motivational situation.

The tremendous rate of technological change that characterizes the computer revolution has had a profound impact upon educational requirements. There is much more emphasis upon continuing education at all age and experience levels. Graduate education is for fathers and mothers as well as sons and daughters. A man can become as obsolete as a machine in a relatively short period of time.

The subject matter of education has also been affected by the computer and related technologies. Education in business schools, for example, has become less functionally oriented. Much more attention is now being given to mathematical and other analytical techniques. Such traditional fields as accounting and production control have been modified to cope with computerization. A greater fusion, in fact if not in name, will occur between business administration and engineering.

SELECTED REFERENCES

Lee Adler, "Systems Approach to Marketing," *Harvard Business Review,* Vol. 45, No. 3, pp. 105–118 (May–June 1967).

Allan H. Anderson and others, *An Electronic Cash and Credit System.* New York: American Management Association, 1966.

Robert R. Arnold, Harold C. Hill, and Aylmer V. Nichols, *Introduction to Data Processing.* New York: John Wiley and Sons, Inc., 1966.

Robert P. Bigelow, "Legal and Security Issues Posed by Computer Utilities," *Harvard Business Review,* Vol. 45, No. 5, pp. 150–161 (September–October 1967).

Rodney H. Brady, "Computers in Top-Level Decision Making," *Harvard Business Review,* Vol. 45, No. 4, pp. 67–76 (July–August 1967).

Donald W. Brewer, *The Impact of the Electronic Computer Upon the Production Control Function.* Rock Island, Ill.: U. S. Army Management Engineering Training Agency, 1968.

Warren B. Brown, "Systems, Boundaries, and Information Flow," *Academy of Management Journal,* Vol. 9, No. 4, pp. 318–327 (December 1966).

Richard T. Bueschel, *EDP and Personnel,* Management Bulletin, No. 86. New York: American Management Association, 1966.

Donald E. Cox and Robert E. Good, "How to Build a Marketing Information System," *Harvard Business Review,* Vol. 45, No. 3, pp. 145–154 (May–June 1967).

Neal J. Dean, "The Computer Comes of Age," *Harvard Business Review,* Vol. 46, No. 1, pp. 83–91 (January–February 1968).

John Dearden, *Computers in Business Management.* Homewood, Ill.: Dow Jones-Irwin, Inc., 1966.

Elias M. Ewad, *Business Data Processing,* 2nd ed. Englewood Cliffs, N.J.: Prentice-Hall, Inc., 1968.

Edgar C. Gentle, Jr., *Data Communications in Business.* New York: American Telephone and Telegraph Company, 1965.

Frank Greenwood and Erwin M. Danziger, *Computer Systems Analysts,* Management Bulletin, No. 90. New York: American Management Association, 1967.

Van Court Hare, Jr., *Systems Analysis: A Diagnostic Approach.* New York: Harcourt, Brace & World, Inc., 1967.

M. Valliant Higginson, *Managing with EDP,* AMA Research Study, No. 71. New York: American Management Association, 1965.

Richard A. Johnson, Fremont E. Kast, and James E. Rosenzweiz, *The Theory and Management of Systems,* 2nd ed. New York: McGraw-Hill Book Company, 1967.

A. E. Kollios and J. S. Stempel, *The Application of EDP to the Purchasing Function,* Management Bulletin, No. 83. New York: American Management Association, 1966.

George Kozmetsky and Paul Kircher, *Electronic Computers and Management Control.* New York: McGraw-Hill Book Company, Inc., 1956.

Hak Chong Lee, *The Impact of Electronic Data Processing Upon Patterns of Business Organization and Administration.* Albany, N.Y.: School of Business, State University of New York at Albany, 1965.

Lawrence L. Lipperman, *Advanced Business Systems,* AMA Research Study, No. 86. New York: American Management Association, 1968.

E. Jerome McCarthy, J. A. McCarthy, and Durward Humes, *Integrated Data Processing Systems.* New York: John Wiley and Sons, Inc., 1966.

Charles A. Myers (editor), *The Impact of Computers on Management.* Cambridge: The M.I.T. Press, 1967.

William E. Reif, *Computer Technology and Management Organization.* Iowa City, Iowa: Bureau of Economic and Business Research, 1968.

Eugene E. Rennekamp, *A Study of the Individual's Attitude Toward a Computerized Informational System,* Masters Thesis. Iowa City: The University of Iowa, 1967.

Fred J. Svec, *Organizational Placement of the Computer Systems Designer.* Rock Island, Ill.: U. S. Army Management Engineering Training Agency, 1968.

John N. Taussig, *EDP Applications for the Manufacturing Function,* AMA Research Study, No. 77. New York: American Management Association, 1966.

Stanley Young, *Management: A Systems Analysis.* Glenview, Ill.: Scott, Foresman and Company, 1966.

Stanley Young, "Organization as a Total System," *California Management Review,* Vol. 10, No. 3, pp. 21–32 (Spring 1968).

PART VI

LEADERSHIP AND MOTIVATION

chapter 22

THE PROBLEM OF MOTIVATION

Managerial decisions have been categorized as planning and motivational decisions. Planning decisions determine the organizational responsibilities of subordinate personnel. This aspect of the managerial process was considered in the chapters in Part IV. Planning becomes a part of the process through communication, which formed the subject matter of Part V. This chapter is the first of three chapters in Part VI concerned with the problem of obtaining appropriate behavioral responses from organizational participants.

Maintaining the Organization

The ultimate test of organizational success is its ability to create values sufficient to compensate for the burdens imposed upon resource contributors.[1] Each participant in organized endeavor engages in cooperative activity for personal economic and noneconomic satisfactions. If such satisfactions are not sufficient, he may no longer accept the responsibilities imposed upon him by the organization. An organization cannot long survive if it fails to satisfy the personal motives of those who contribute resources. The refusal of even a few participants to continue in a cooperative relationship is frequently a serious matter. The withdrawal of those who contribute an absolutely essential resource is often a fatal blow to the organization. A business organization that loses its customers cannot long survive. A church with too many vacant pews faces a similar problem. A university that fails to attract professors or students will soon become an

[1] Chester I. Barnard, *The Functions of the Executive* (Cambridge: Harvard University Press, 1951), pp. 56–59, 92–94, 253–255.

empty shell of stone and mortar. However, organizations do not always descend into the valley of the shadow of death with haste. Like old soldiers they frequently fade away very slowly. A university finding itself without qualified professors may attempt to fill this deficit by employing students who took the course last year under students who passed it the previous year. Furthermore, the ability of an organization to maintain itself may not be constant over a period of time. The scope and intensity of its activity frequently fluctuate a great deal. Adversity may be temporary and the prelude to an era of abundance.

The Technological Problem

The achievement of higher productivity through improved methods and techniques is closely related to the problem of survival. The greater the capacity of an organization to create values, the better it will be able to satisfy the personal motives of its members. The solution to this problem involves the application of a diversity of technologies, such as industrial engineering, accounting, traffic management, marketing, chemistry, and electronics. However, the highest level of technological efficiency may not be sufficient to prevent the decline or destruction of an organization. The values produced must correspond to the values demanded as a price of cooperation. Executives are fundamentally faced with two mutually related problems. One is the problem of technological efficiency or enhancing an organization's capacity to create values; the other is that of adapting to or modifying the values of present or potential organizational participants. Every kind of organization, whether political, military, educational, religious, or business, must contend with these problems.

The Economic Model: A Synthesis of Technological and Value Considerations

The problem of executives in business organizations is somewhat simplified by a market system that translates subjective values into prices. Product and resource prices are useful indices of the values that a firm must create and distribute to survive. The technological and value problems are successfully solved if a favorable balance between revenues and costs (including profits as an opportunity cost) is achieved. The values created by the organization are sufficient to satisfy the personal motives of all participants as long as revenues are equal to or greater than costs. However, it should not be assumed that the economic concepts of revenues and costs are completely adequate measures of organizational efficiency. As the welfare economist points out, such costs as smoke and fumes from industrial plants are not measured in the firm's cost accounts. Business organizations also create values that are directly consumed by organizational members. For example, the satisfactions derived from "craftsmanship" and social interaction are an important by-product of cooperative activity. Such values are not necessarily measured by productivity or cost data. The unmeasured values created by business organizations possibly exceed in some instances the values implied by costs and revenues.[2]

The Matter of Motivation

The ability to make effective motivational decisions requires knowledge about the motives which bring about purposeful behavior. The decision maker must have insights into the manner in which people will respond to particular conditions. Human behavior must be susceptible to the concept of causality if control is to become a possibility.

Human Motives: Physiological Drives

Motivation has its roots in motives within a person which induce him to behave in a particular manner. Human motives evolve partly from the physiological conditions that create sensations of hunger, thirst, pain, and sexuality. These motives will normally cause a person to respond by seeking food or water, eating or drinking, etc. Physiologically induced motives are modified by the customs and norms that prevail in a group or society. For example, babies are generally fed on a socially determined schedule that modifies the time and potency of "natural" hunger pangs. A similar kind of change is involved in the learning that eventually eliminates the need for diapers.

Human Motives: Conditioned Responses

Many human motives are acquired by a conditioning process that begins the day a baby is born. When people tend to react in a repetitious fashion, generally they are making a "conditioned response." In Pavlov's classic conditioning experiment, a dog was conditioned to respond to the sound of

---

[2] Economic theory takes such values into consideration through shifts in factor supply functions. For example, if the social satisfactions in an organizational situation are high, the employee would presumably be willing to work for a lower wage or salary. However, it is not reasonable to assume that actual markets adequately compensate for many of the utilities and disutilities that make up a work situation.

a bell as though it were a piece of meat. The ringing of the bell was followed by an offer of meat. The sight of the meat gave rise to the salivary mechanism in the dog. Eventually the dog would salivate at the sound of the bell and continue to do so for some time even though behavior was not reinforced by a reward of meat. The bell provided what psychologists call secondary reinforcement in spite of the fact that it does not directly satisfy the hunger motive. However, the secondary reinforcement tends to become weaker unless it is itself reinforced by the primary reward or reinforcement.

In other experimentation, chimpanzees have been conditioned to respond to poker chips with which they could later purchase food.[3] They would accumulate a large number of chips even when they could not be spent until a later date. They learned to distinguish between chips with different values and to select chips in harmony with thirst and hunger drives. Human beings seem to behave like chimpanzees in the way in which they respond to money. Money is an important reward for most people even though it does not directly satisfy their needs. It is a secondary reinforcement or reward which induces appropriate behavioral responses so long as it can be used at some future time to satisfy more basic human motives. Few people will accumulate or hoard money that has no value in the market for goods and services.

Cultural Norms and Human Motives

Man has an advantage over animals in his ability to create a culture which can be handed down from one generation to the next. A culture may be roughly defined as the totality of norms that govern behavior in a society. Cultures embody the achievements of the past and give humans greater capacity to cope with their environment. Man does not have to constantly begin anew; he has a store of knowledge from which he can draw.

Cultures are transmitted from one generation to the next through formal and informal modes of instruction and indoctrination. Basic human needs make for similarities among cultures, but there are significant differences in ways cultures solve particular problems. For example, polygamy and monogamy are different approaches to the satisfaction of sexual and survival needs. Beef, pork, horse meat, and dog steak are acceptable means for satisfying hunger pangs in some cultures, but they are taboo or disapproved

[3] John B. Wolfe, "Effectiveness of Token-Rewards for Chimpanzees," *Comparative Psychology Monographs,* Vol. 12, No. 5, May 1936, pp. 1–72; John T. Cowles, "Food-Tokens as Incentives for Learning by Chimpanzees," *Comparative Psychology Monographs,* Vol. 14, No. 5, 1937–1938, pp. 1–96.

in others. Hindus do not like beef, Moslems abhor pork, and Englishmen are not apt to relish a rare dog steak. Some societies abandon or kill their aged; others provide them free medical care and pay them pensions.

Cultural variations make for differences in human motives. Australian aboriginals would not respond to the rewards that motivate Americans, and conversely. There may also be significant differences in the motives of people from the same basic culture. Studies of underprivileged people in a large metropolitan area in the United States indicate they have widely divergent motives from those found among people with a middle-class background.[4] The motives of executives from lower-class backgrounds differed from executives born into high position.[5] Many other contrasts exist within broader cultural classifications and influence the way in which people respond to responsibilities and rewards.

Many cultural norms arise because man is a social being. Humans need affiliation—contact with their own kind. Gregariousness may be an intrinsic human motive or it may have been acquired over a long period of socializing. Some aspects of social behavior may have evolved from such basic physiological drives as sexuality and survival. Biological families and the various kinds of kinship groupings may have gradually brought about broader social systems. The economic and other benefits that could be derived from cooperative endeavor helped reinforce human social propensities. Social living gives rise to cultural norms and human motives which strengthen social bonds and help preserve the society. The need to defend the society against outsiders may give rise to aggressiveness. Dominative motives may be encouraged for those who are to perform the leadership functions that are required. A feeling of deference may be fostered so that certain individuals can more effectively fulfill the role of subordinates.

Many different kinds of human qualities make for effective social functioning and survival. Some are appropriate for some social goals and not for others. Achievement motives, for example, may promote a great deal of economic progress, but they may also engender high levels of social conflict. Societies have experienced difficulties because they did not have people with the appropriate motives for a particular purpose. S. L. A. Marshall, in an analysis of combat motivation during World War II and the Korean War, noted that many soldiers did not fire on the enemy. An important reason was the soldier's background, which Marshall described in the following words.

[4] Allison Davis, "The Motivation of the Underprivileged Worker," in William Foote Whyte, *Industry and Society* (New York: McGraw-Hill Book Company, 1946), pp. 84–106.
[5] W. Lloyd Warner and James C. Abegglen, *Big Business Leaders in America* (New York: Harper & Brothers Publishers, 1955), pp. 59–107, 144–176.

He is what his home, his religion, his schooling, and the moral code and ideals of his society have made him. The Army cannot unmake him. It must reckon with the fact that he comes from a civilization in which aggression, connected with the taking of life, is prohibited and unacceptable. The teaching and the ideals of that civilization are against killing, against taking advantage. The fear of aggression has been expressed to him so strongly and absorbed by him so deeply and pervadingly—practically with his mother's milk—that it is part of the normal man's emotional make-up. This is his great handicap when he enters combat. It stays his trigger finger even though he is hardly conscious that it is a restraint upon him. Because it is an emotional and not an intellectual handicap, it is not removable by intellectual reasoning, such as: "Kill or be killed." [6]

Some of the norms and motives that were developed during past periods and for particular purposes can become anachronistic with changing conditions. The motives that are necessary to obtain the proper behavioral responses differ in some degree as societies go from war to peace, from handicraft to mass production, from economic scarcity to abundance, and from ruralism to urbanism. Too much lag in modifying motives can cause an unduly large amount of conflict and disruption in a society. It can also give rise to an excessive amount of frustration, anxiety, conflict, and other psychological problems for individuals.

Human Motives: Similarities and Differences

There are similarities as well as differences in human motives. Cultural anthropologists have listed universal needs from which particular cultural norms appear to have evolved. Psychologists have also prepared listings of basic needs which reflect the motives that result in human activities. An analysis of human needs may begin with basic physiological drives—such as hunger, thirst, and sexuality—and attempt to relate these drives to the various motivational elaborations that exist in human societies. Many human motives seem to be an outgrowth of simple and complex forms of conditioning which substitute secondary rewards or reinforcements for the real thing. Some of these motives have evolved from the past and persist even though the reason for their existence may be lost to conscious awareness.

The impact of cultural norms on human motives is influenced by the extent to which the norms are enforced by social sanctions. Actual social behavior is not always in accord with cultural norms. The behavior of small groups and individuals may depart from cultural norms and social patterns of behavior. The enculturation and socialization processes do not bring about anything approaching complete conformity. Human motives

[6] S. L. A. Marshall, *Men Against Fire* (New York: William Morrow & Company, 1947), p. 78.

are apt to differ significantly in societies with freedom of religion, press, and speech. Differences in families, churches, schools, and other kinds of association make for a diversity of motives.

Human beings have a far greater capacity for reflective and creative thinking than their animal counterparts. Chimpanzees can be conditioned to respond to poker chips, but their ability to learn or create complex sets of symbolic relationships is limited. Man can choose to be a nonconformist, developing norms and patterns of behavior that depart from the dominant patterns of the society. Some uniformity in human motives makes for more successful social living and cooperative endeavor. But there is also a need for diversity in societies characterized by complex divisons of labor. Social and organizational specialization demands people with different motives to fit into diverse roles and tasks. Banks, churches, armies, universities, laundries, hospitals, and restaurants cannot all be manned by people cut from the same cloth. The organizational problem is to put a round peg into each round hole and a square one into each square one. The social problem is to have a sufficient supply of people who have appropriate motives for the jobs that need to be done.

The Problem of the Black Box

Man's mental apparatus is still very much a "black box" which translates stimuli into behavior in a manner that is not at all apparent. Certain psychological theories about the nature of the human mind should be categorized as science fiction rather than scientific fact. Some of the techniques that relate to such theories may even give satisfactory results, but for the wrong reasons. Such a state of affairs is not unusual in the behavioral sciences. Man has barely begun to understand himself and explain the reasons for his behavior. Many experienced executives probably have better intuitive insights about how to bring about appropriate behavioral responses than most behavioral scientists. However, this hypothesis does not mean that behavioral scientists should report to the nearest vocational rehabilitation office. Every effort should be made to build better theories even though there will be many false starts and exceedingly slow progress. Subjective skills must be translated into scientific knowledge if executive development is to be a successful pursuit. The resulting theories may not generally improve the skills of the experienced practitioner of human relations, but they can be helpful in bringing the neophyte to a higher level of proficiency earlier in his career.

Much of the knowledge about human motivation is partitioned into numerous partial theories. The difficulty with such partial theories is that they cannot provide more than a small part of the answer required in making motivational decisions. Solid scientific findings may appear to be wrong, and inadequate research results may seem to provide the answer. Another problem is that some theories are appropriate for decisions involving large numbers, but not helpful in solving a particular motivational problem. General behavior will tend to fall into a predictable pattern. This knowledge may not be helpful in deciding what to do about Thomas Murphy or Charles Smith.

Premises for Motivational Decisions

The problem of motivation should be viewed from the perspective of the cultural norms of the society in which the organization is situated. Although basic physiological and social needs make for uniformities in motives, there are many differences in the motives of people from different cultural backgrounds. The cultural heritage of Americans, for example, makes them more reluctant to accept authoritarianism than other groups. The emphasis on a democratic approach in the political sphere tends to be transferred to religious, economic, and other kinds of social endeavor. Emphasis should also be given to the manner in which cultural changes may affect motivation. The permissive educational philosophies of recent decades have undoubtedly influenced attitudes toward responsibility and authority. The shift from an economy of scarcity to an economy of abundance has significantly marked American attitudes toward consumption and saving, consumer credit, retirement, and leisure. Freudian and Darwinian ideology, the trade union movement, the Great Depression, the political philosophy of the New Deal, World War II, full employment, the specter of communism—these phenomena have modified American beliefs and hence American motives.

Some motivational assumptions are widely accepted as entirely valid even though they provide only a part of the answer. Douglas McGregor has categorized such assumptions under the label of Theory X, which he called the traditional view of direction and control.[7] One assumption is that the average human being has an inherent dislike for work and will avoid it if possible. Another is that the dislike for work means that most people must be threatened with sanctions to get them to put forth the effort necessary to achieve organizational objectives. Still another is that people generally prefer to be directed, attempt to avoid responsibilities, have relatively little ambition, and want security most of all. McGregor believes that recent research in the behavioral sciences has shown that the assumptions of what he calls Theory Y may be more valid than the precepts of Theory X.[8]

[7] Douglas McGregor, *The Human Side of Enterprise* (New York: McGraw-Hill Book Company, Inc., 1960), pp. 33–43.
[8] *Ibid.*, pp. 45–57.

The assumptions of Theory Y are described by McGregor in the following words.

1. The expenditure of physical and mental effort in work is as natural as play or rest. The average human being does not inherently dislike work. Depending upon controllable conditions, work may be a source of satisfaction (and will be voluntarily performed) or a source of punishment (and will be avoided if possible).
2. External control and the threat of punishment are not the only means for bringing about effort toward organizational objectives. Man will exercise self-direction and self-control in the service of objectives to which he is committed.
3. Commitment to objectives is a function of the rewards associated with their achievement. The most significant of such rewards, e.g., the satisfaction of ego and self-actualization needs, can be direct products of effort directed toward organizational objectives.
4. The average human being learns, under proper conditions, not only to accept but to seek responsibility. Avoidance of responsibility, lack of ambition, and emphasis on security are generally consequences of experience, not inherent human characteristics.
5. The capacity to exercise a relatively high degree of imagination, ingenuity, and creativity in the solution of organizational problems is widely, not narrowly, distributed in the population.
6. Under the conditions of modern industrial life, the intellectual potentialities of the average human being are only partially utilized.[9]

Theory X assumes that the personal goals of employees are incompatible with organizational objectives. It places major reliance on the use of authority as an instrument of command and control. Theory Y asserts that people have much to offer an organization if they can only be persuaded to accept its objectives. It attempts to take full advantage of the personal and professional potential of employees. The use of authority is assumed to impede the development of this potential, although authority may be necessary if people will not cooperate. The basic difference between the two theories is that Theory Y opens the door to motivational techniques that are precluded by socio-psychological restraints imposed by Theory X.

The behavioral assumptions of the economic theorist have been highly influential in the development of ideas about motivation. As was noted in Chapter 2, Frederick W. Taylor and many of his lieutenants assumed that the motivational problem was primarily a matter of satisfying economic motives. They also failed to recognize that informal groups could play a positive part in the motivational picture. Chester I. Barnard had the following to say on this subject: "Granting the utility of abstracting from social action that aspect which we call 'economic,' the relatively developed

[9] McGregor, *op. cit.*, pp. 47–48. Italics in original were deleted.

theories so effectively constructed by Adam Smith and his successors depressed the interest in the specific social processes within which economic factors are merely one phase, and greatly overemphasized economic interests."[10] The assumptions of economic theory are appropriate for many kinds of a priori analyses, but they are not appropriate for executives who must contend with a whole range of human motives.

People are not always consciously aware of the motives that give rise to behavioral responses. Attempts have been made to determine the nature of hidden human motives through various techniques. Nondirective interviews have obtained insights about people's inner motives, fantasy life, and "unconscious" motivation. Projective techniques, such as the Rorschach Ink Blot Test and the Thematic Apperception Test (TAT), have also been helpful in gaining knowledge on motivation. In the Rorschach test ten white cards showing unstructured ink blots are presented to the subject. From the manner in which he interprets the blots the subject's inner motives are inferred. In the TAT the subject is asked to tell a story about each picture, depicting probable action situations, shown to him. Somewhat underrestrained statements about what interview and projective techniques can do are found on the cover of a recent best seller.[11] The book announced that it would give the startling answers to such questions as: Why do men think of a mistress when they see a convertible in a show window? Why are women in supermarkets attracted by items wrapped in red? Why wouldn't men give up shaving even if they could? Why are automobiles getting longer and longer? It is interesting to note that about two-thirds of the cover of the book is colored red.

Depth psychology has offered some insights about human behavior. And even though it has not provided universally applicable answers, depth psychology has demonstrated that the cause and effect of human behavior has many, and frequently indeterminate, intermediate stages. The reasons for individual and social behavior are not always what they appear to be. Executives should not be surprised to find that many of their assumptions about how people will respond to particular situations were wrong.

Motivation: The Burdens and Benefits of Organized Endeavor

The analysis that follows takes advantage of the behavioral research of the recent past. It considers the basic problem of motivation in terms of the

---

[10] Chester I. Barnard, *op. cit.,* p. x.
[11] Vance Packard, *The Hidden Persuaders* (New York: Pocket Books, 1958).

burdens and benefits of organized endeavor. Executives should not impose unnecessary responsibilities, and they should attempt to reduce the burden of the responsibilities that are necessary. At the same time, they should make an effort to enhance the benefits or rewards that may be derived from the acceptance of responsibilities.

Adapting and Adjusting Responsibilities

One approach to the authority problem is to reduce the responsibilities of subordinates. For example, the territory of a salesman can be changed if he does not like the idea of being away from wife and children for long periods of time. Workers who are reluctant to work on the night shift can be given day work. Executives who do not like to live in a large metropolitan area can be assigned to the Iowa City plant. Some such adjustments are frequently possible, and they may favorably influence authority. The problem is partly a matter of taking advantage of individual differences in subordinates. The burdens imposed by the organization are reduced if such differences are taken into account in assigning responsibilities. Thus, the fact that Brown does not like to live in a metropolitan area and that Smith does should be taken into consideration. But some of the psychological hazards and handicaps that make up organizational responsibilities cannot be avoided. The superior may be forced to use the power of discharge against subordinates who do not perform the responsibilities that are necessary to maintain the organization. However, the defining of "necessary" may be subject to a diversity of opinion. For example, military training during World War II included the digging of what seemed to be an infinite number of foxholes in some rather solid soil. Some officers had the opinion that such responsibilities need not have been imposed because one enemy mortar shell will cause even an untrained civilian to dig deep and well. Other officers disagreed and contended that such responsibilities were necessary to condition recruits to accept the hardships and discipline of combat. The relationship between a superior's decision and the achievement of the organizational objective may be highly indirect. The appropriateness of decision must be judged in terms of many technological and socio-psychological factors which seem to work in combination. There is generally no simple cause and effect solution to the problem.

Responsibilities Relating to Purely Personal Conduct

Superiors may also impose responsibilities that relate to personal habits as well as work habits. For example, the subordinates of one executive are "compelled" to drink anywhere from five to seven very dry martinis before they are permitted to sup at his table. The subordinates of another dare not touch the stuff if they have inclinations to cash in on the company pension program. Changes in political and church affiliations have occurred because of real or imagined pressures from above. The social relations among the wives of executives may also be influenced by the hierarchy, with the social status of the wife frequently reflecting in some manner the position of the husband.[12] The wives of superiors have been known to affect appointments and promotions within an organization. The behavior of the subordinate's wife at social affairs is sometimes scrutinized by both the superior and his wife. Some careers have been cut short by the fact that the wife could not or did not properly play the part expected of her. Every subordinate must judge for himself the extent to which he will conform to the behavioral requirements of superiors. Although some degree of conformity is generally expected, subordinates should not assume that refusal to conform always results in disaster. The norms of superiors have been significantly modified by subordinates who directly or indirectly impose their conceptions of appropriate behavior. Conformity frequently goes far beyond the expectations of superiors.

Organizational versus Personal Affairs

The validity of norms that relate to personal behavior in nonorganizational situations has been questioned. Some executives contend that what a man does after working hours is his own business. However, there is no clear-cut line of demarcation between organizational and personal affairs. An obvious consideration is that personal conduct outside the organization may have implications in the area of public relations. A subordinate who is picked up for disorderly conduct in a public bar might properly be discharged, particularly if the matter is given wide publicity. Another consideration is that a person's private conduct may infer qualities that relate to behavioral requirements of the organization. For example, a failure to show some deference toward a superior at a social gathering may indicate a lack of respect for persons in authority. Still another consideration is that personal compatibility is related to teamwork within the management hierarchy and in the organization generally. Some degree of conformity to the mores of the group is a necessary feature of the total organizational life. A person to whom the personal habits of associates are repugnant will experience some difficulty in working with them. Such reasoning can also be applied to the wife who is not happy in social relations with company personnel and their wives. Her unhappiness with the situation might well

[12] William H. Whyte, Jr., "The Wives of Management," *Fortune*, Vol. 44, No. 4, October 1951, pp. 86 ff.

have some bearing on the husband's performance in the organization. A nagging wife can cause a man to dislike a job that he likes for other reasons.

The Benefits of Acceptance

Subordinates will accept the burdens imposed by superiors as long as the benefits or rewards are adequate. Authority may be favorably affected by actions that reduce burdens of organizational responsibilities. The discussion thus far has been concerned with this approach to the problem. Attention is now directed to the problem of increasing the rewards of acceptance. The rewards that may be used to maintain or enhance authority take many forms.[13] Some of the more obvious rewards are wages, salaries, bonuses, profit sharing, vacations and holidays with pay, health and retirement plans, and insurance programs. Somewhat less obvious are such rewards as reserved parking space, longer lunch periods, private offices, titles of rank and function, and other special prerogatives and privileges. These rewards can generally be categorized as formal or organizational instruments. They may also be viewed as penalties through the idea that they may be withheld.

The organizing and planning processes place limitations upon the discretion of the superior to allot responsibilities and rewards. One limitation results from the fact that monetary and other rewards available to achieve particular objectives are limited. The superior can influence the share allotted to his sphere of operations to the extent that he participates in planning. The amounts budgeted for wages and salaries in a department are generally affected in some degree by the superior's recommendations. Some superiors make better bargains in this respect than other superiors, which gives them an advantage in maintaining authority. The wages and salaries available in a particular department may be higher than necessary to induce subordinates to accept the responsibilities involved. Another limitation upon the discretion of superiors is imposed by the allocation of responsibilities and rewards in terms of positions. The organization of managerial positions into a hierarchy represents one aspect of this kind of limitation. The situation is subjected to further systematization by job evaluation, salary and wage classifications, employee rating systems for promotion and other changes in classification, and objective standards established by the planning process, such as sales quotas and time study rates. Although superiors play some part in the hierarchical process

[13] For a comprehensive listing of different types of reward and penalty in organizations: E. Wight Bakke, *Bonds of Organization* (New York: Harper & Brothers Publishers, 1950), pp. 124–125.

through which decisions about such matters are made, the discretion that may be exercised by particular superiors is limited by the actions of management as a group.

An organized approach to the allocation of responsibilities and rewards limits the discretion of the superior, but it does not eliminate him as a vital force in the superior-subordinate relationship. The superior may be forced to justify his actions in terms of the requirements of the system, but he wields a big stick through the power to recommend changes in classification and promotions in position. A subordinate's career can be affected far into the future by an adverse report or rating. Subordinate complaints about "unfair" actions by their superiors are not easy to effectuate. Bypassing one's immediate superior is generally frowned upon by higher executives, and such action may not be a good idea even when a formal appeal mechanism exists. Few soldiers register complaints about their noncommissioned and commissioned officers to the inspector-general. Some superiors have memories like the proverbial elephant; formal action against them can have dire consequences for the subordinate.

Social Satisfactions and Sanctions

Some of the burdens and benefits of organizational association are a product of social interaction among subordinates. The superior should understand the nature of the social system and the manner in which it may influence subordinate behavior. The foundation stone of the social system in organization is the small or primary group. Professor Charles H. Cooley, who first gave emphasis to the primary group as a sociological concept, presented his idea in these words.

By primary groups I mean those characterized by intimate face-to-face association and cooperation. They are primary in several senses, but chiefly in that they are fundamental in forming the social nature and ideals of the individual. The result of intimate association, psychologically, is a certain fusion of individualities in a common whole, so that one's very self, for many purposes at least, is the common life and purpose of the group.[14]

The first comprehensive study of a primary group in an industrial situation was the Hawthorne Study which was discussed in Chapter 2. A vast amount of subsequent research has elaborated on the importance of such groups in molding organizational behavior.

[14] Charles Horton Cooley, *Social Organization, A Study of the Larger Mind* (New York: Charles Scribner's Sons, 1909), p. 23. For a discussion of primary groups and their significance: *ibid.,* pp. 23–31.

The primary group evolves from interaction or doing something in close personal association with others over a period of time.[15] Interaction may be verbal or nonverbal. A baseball thrown from the pitcher to the first baseman, two persons shaking hands, a helper giving a board to a carpenter, and a waitress giving a menu to a customer are examples of nonverbal interaction. People engaged in a discussion or conversation are interacting verbally. The boundary lines of a primary group are determined by plotting the interaction that takes place among people. A plotting of interactions in a large organization, such as the General Motors Corporation or Yale University, would show many clusters of interaction. The people within such clusters interact more frequently with one another than they do with others in the organization. Each cluster of interactions indicates the boundaries of primary groups and cliques that may arise within such groups. An individual may and generally does belong to more than one primary group. He may belong to a group composed of people in his office or factory work area, a group with whom he eats lunch in the company cafeteria or executive dining room, a group commuting on the same train, and many others. The people in a primary group share common sentiments, feelings, and convictions about various things. They develop group norms of behavior which are ideas about how people in the group ought to behave. They rank the individuals in the group and tend to identify themselves with the group.

Individual, Group, and Organizational Goals. The group plays an important part in shaping the behavior of subordinates from vice-presidents to factory and office workers. The penalties that may be imposed by the group for failure to conform to its norms may significantly influence a subordinate's response to organizational responsibilities. A subordinate may refuse to obey an order because he fears the penalties of the group more than penalties that may be imposed by the superior. Thus, producing beyond the group output norm or informing on fellow subordinates may give rise to more severe penalties from the group than any that the superior might exact. Even the penalty of discharge is sometimes preferred because the group can make life in an organization a living hell. However, the impact of the group upon subordinate behavior is influenced by the psychological make-up of the individual. Some subordinates make a religion out of the group and adapt their behavior to group norms even though they may fail to reap other rewards. Others are at the opposite pole and behave in a highly "individualistic" pattern. For example, about 10 per cent of the employees in one industrial situation consistently violated group output

---

[15] George C. Homans made a noted contribution to primary group theory in *The Human Group* (New York: Harcourt, Brace and Company, 1950).

norms and were generally not responsive to group pressures.[16] The majority of subordinates fall somewhere between the two extremes. They are attracted by the social and other satisfactions that may be derived from conformity to group norms. At the same time, they do not ignore the rewards that can be conferred by the superior even though conflict with group norms may be involved. Individuals who are highly motivated by the prospect of advancement are generally more inclined to conform to the norms of those who occupy higher positions in the hierarchy. Their behavior may be significantly conditioned by such norms in spite of the fact that they do not frequently interact with higher executives. The ambitious subordinate may be caught in a web when the norms of higher groups conflict with the norms of fellow subordinates. His chances for advancement are enhanced by conformity to the norms of those above him, but they are also affected by his ability to get along with his peers.

Some superiors view the group as a disruptive force in their efforts to achieve organizational goals. Their ideal subordinate is the "rate buster" or individualist who does not respond to group pressures. The difficulty is that most people are not social isolates in a culture that gives so much emphasis to "togetherness" and social conformity. Whether people ought to behave in this manner is an interesting philosophical question. The superior may be able to reshape human behavior to some extent, but he should not attempt the impossible task of remaking mankind. Man seems generally to have propensities to socialize with his fellow man for reasons that need not be explored here.[17] Such propensities undoubtedly further the goals of organization more than they hinder them. An organization could not come into being without individuals willing to work in conjunction with other individuals. Organizations of complete "individualists" do not exist except in the minds of some economic and political theorists. Organization is a social process through which human beings cooperate to achieve a common purpose. It forces individuals into a context in which some degree of social behavior cannot be avoided. However, the socializing process through which organizational goals are pursued may be used to promote purposes other than those of the organization. It also provides an "organized" basis for opposing goals that seem detrimental to the interests of organizational members.

Groups as Positive Instruments of Leadership. The superior should not ignore the positive role that primary groups may play in promoting organizational goals. The following conclusion by the Army Studies in Social Psychology during World War II is pertinent in this respect.

[16] Melville Dalton, "The Industrial Rate Buster: A Characterization," *Applied Anthropology*, Vol. 7, No. 1, Winter 1948, pp. 5–18.

[17] Ralph Linton makes some interesting comments on this matter: *The Tree of Culture* (New York: Alfred A. Knopf, 1957), pp. 29–30.

The group in its informal character, with its close interpersonal ties, served two principal functions in combat motivation: it *set and enforced group standards* of behavior, and it *supported and sustained the individual* in stresses he would otherwise not have been able to withstand.[18]

Psychological research by the Army Air Forces among air combat units came to the conclusion that "the primary motivating force which more than anything else kept these men flying and fighting was that they were members of a group in which flying and fighting was the *only accepted way* of behaving."[19] A good commander was interested in the welfare of his men with respect to such things as food, living conditions, recreation, medical care, promotions, and awards. However, these factors "did not seem in themselves of primary importance in keeping the men flying and fighting."[20] The test of effective leadership, according to the researchers, was the ability to create and maintain group solidarity and group norms that promoted desired ends.

Similar conclusions were made by a research group from the Harvard School of Business Administration in a study of labor turnover and absenteeism in the California aircraft industry.[21] The aircraft industry had experienced a tremendous expansion in plant and personnel to meet the production demands of World War II. A major difficulty was the occurrence of over 175,000 terminations of employment between March and October of 1943. Statistical data indicated that some work centers had much less labor turnover and absenteeism than others. An intensive study was made of a work center composed of nineteen workers with an excellent attendance and production record. The workers in this center behaved as a group rather than a disunited collection of individuals as was found in other work centers. The researchers concluded that group solidarity had an important bearing on the problem being studied. The worker who attended regularly did so because he had a close identity with his group. He enjoyed the human association and took pride in group accomplishments. The group in turn imposed sanctions against individuals whose behavior threatened satisfactions that evolved from group living. The sanctions of the group seemed more effective in controlling absenteeism than direct action by management. A major factor in the development of this kind of team-

---

[18] Samuel A. Stouffer, et al., *The American Soldier,* Vol. II (Princeton, N.J.: Princeton University Press, 1950), pp. 130–131.

[19] John C. Flanagan (editor), *The Aviation Psychology Program in the Army Air Forces,* Report No. 1 (Washington, D.C.: U.S. Printing Office, 1948), p. 208.

[20] *Ibid.*

[21] Elton Mayo and George F. Lombard, *Teamwork and Labor Turnover in the Aircraft Industry of Southern California,* Business Research Studies, No. 32 (Boston: Division of Research, Graduate School of Business Administration, Harvard University, October, 1944).

work was that the immediate superior recognized the importance of group solidarity and gave attention to human as well as technical problems.

The importance of the group is also evident in these events that occurred in a Chicago restaurant. A waitress, named Jo, decided to quit because she disliked the hours. The waitress' sister, Ellen, who worked in the same restaurant, told the supervisor that she was leaving too. The supervisor tried to get the sister to stay, but was told: "Miss Jenkins, Jo and I have always worked together, and that's the way we want it to be." The matter seemed settled. The more Miss Jenkins talked to Ellen about staying the more resistance she got. The next day Ellen had changed her mind. Why? In her own words: "I'm staying. They talked me into it. Jo's quitting, but I'm going to stay awhile. Yes, it was the girls, Ann and the rest of them, they went to work on me. They told me I was foolish to quit. Well, I thought it over, and I thought after all I'll never have such a good bunch of kids to work with. I've been here eight months so I might as well stay another four and make it an even year." [22] The restaurant retained an experienced waitress. The satisfactions offered by the group were more important than the inducements offered by the superior.

Social satisfactions represent an important aspect of the totality of benefits that may evolve from organizational association. They may compete with other rewards in the sense that an increase in one results in a reduction in another. Thus, the amount that can be paid in wages and salaries is reduced if socializing (such as extended coffee breaks) reduces productivity. However, socializing may increase productivity without increasing the cost side of the ledger. The following situation illustrates this idea. The comptroller of a plant, who was in charge of the office workers, was concerned about social activity during working hours. He related the problem to Professor William F. Whyte in these words.

You know, I've just come back from a visit to the main office, and I want to tell you, the contrast is really unbelievable. They have an office force several times as large as ours, and it's all in one big room. But you could stand in that room any time of the day and hear a pin drop. Now, down here the place is in an uproar a good deal of the time. Of course, I realize that people sometimes have to talk to each other to get their work done, but I know lots of times when they are talking it can't be just about the work. I wonder, Dr. Whyte, do you think I should ask them to quiet things down? [Whyte asked how well the work was done.] Oh, I'm more than satisfied with that. Two years ago when I came here we had 62 people in the office; we now have 57, and still we are handling 40 per cent more orders than we were when I started. Why, last week they put out a volume of orders that I didn't think was possible. Whenever we have an

[22] William Foote Whyte, *Human Relations in the Restaurant Industry* (New York: McGraw-Hill Book Company, Inc., 1948), pp. 136–138.

emergency, I only have to ask them to put out a little extra effort, and everybody pitches in. Now, I'll bet you that, man to man, the main office doesn't begin to put out the volume of work we do right here. . . . But I don't know. It doesn't seem right. The place is in an uproar. . . .[23]

The comptroller did not take action to eliminate the uproar, but he continued to worry about the unbusinesslike atmosphere it created. His worry about the situation expresses the cultural precept that work is work and play is play and the two should not be mixed. Had he taken action to "correct" the situation, the result might well have been a reduction in output and a negative attitude toward him and management generally. The argument is not that organizations should be turned into social clubs but that the socializing involved in working with others may reduce the burdens and increase the benefits of organizational association. The superior cannot completely control the social situation, but he can take care not to destroy satisfactions that enhance the cooperative process.

Status as an Instrument of Motivation

The status system is an instrument of motivation; status is extremely important to most people. It is something the organization can offer to promote a greater degree of cooperation. The possibility of a loss of status is likewise available as an inducement to greater cooperation. This negative aspect of status, however, is generally a less effective motivational instrument.

Abilities and Aspirations. The status system should be closely related to the abilities and aspirations of people in an organization. When high status is conferred indiscriminately, the significance of status is reduced for people who have high status and those who seek higher status. An army with more generals than privates does not have an effective status system. An unduly large number of vice-presidents has a similar effect. Another problem arises when equal status is conferred on those who are not equal in ability. If two persons, who are not equally good accountants, are given the title of senior accountant, the result is frequently a great deal of friction and dissatisfaction. If should also be remembered that management is not the only judge of qualities. The informal social system may reverse a status decision by management by refusing to give it recognition from a behavioral standpoint. Since status is determined by an ability to get along well with others, the status of two people who are equally qualified from a technical point of view may actually be unequal. For this reason, social skills deserve consideration in making status decisions.

[23] Eugene Staley (editor), *Creating an Industrial Civilization* (New York: Harper & Brothers Publishers, 1952), p. 220.

Ideally the status system should reflect the differing aspirations of people in an organization. Such an equilibrium would maximize satisfaction in this respect and greatly facilitate cooperation. If the aspirations of a great many people cannot be satisfied by the existing status system, one possibility is to upgrade status by manipulating the instruments of status. Such a policy, however, presents a danger because status is relative. The result may be a net loss in the satisfactions offered by the system. Another approach is to strive for more realistic aspirations. Young college graduates, for example, often have unrealistic expectations about the role they will play in industry. Better use can probably be made of the employment interview and the orientation period to correct such difficulties. Sometimes people can be given the recognition they desire through other channels, such as a photographic contest, a hobby club, or athletic programs. Sufficient emphasis should always be given to the importance of a person's present role in the organization and the role he may play in the future. Future possibilities should, however, be realistically appraised, or the satisfactions created today may result in greater dissatisfaction later.

Conferring Recognition: de Jure or de Facto. Serious status problems are created by giving an individual recognition or promotion without conferring upon him the formal symbols and instruments of status. To make the man a division head without giving him the title of vice-president may create many personal and organizational problems. His scalar rank is equal to other division heads, but his status is not equal. Placing someone in a functional or scalar position without full status credentials should be done only on a temporary basis. Withholding formal status recognition may result in "jockeying for position." The individual feels insecure and attempts by political and opportunistic means to gain his rightful "place in the sun." Another serious problem may be caused by a long delay in filling a vacancy. To "keep them guessing" generally does not motivate the candidates in the direction of higher productivity. It often leads to all sorts of connivance, which does not serve the organizational ends. This kind of policy may cause a valuable executive to resign if he is not promoted. The longer he "campaigns" for the vacancy, the greater will be the possibility of resignation to "save face" before friends and followers. Some of the candidates for a vacancy may be unknown to management. Individuals may assume that they are qualified and being considered when such is not the case. Management should recognize such a possibility and make every effort to determine the possible candidates and reassure them that they have not been overlooked for the future.

The Deadwood Problem. The effectiveness of the status system can be seriously reduced by "bad" appointments. A short period of opportunism in making appointments or of failures in forecasting human propensities can plague the organization for many years. Universities sometimes have problems with professors who lose interest in teaching and research after they attain status. Corporate executives, governmental officials, and military officers are sometimes not unlike professors in this respect. Over a period of time an accumulation of such appointments can destroy the motivational significance of the status system and seriously disrupt teamwork. Who wants status if any idiot seems to achieve it? Why make an effort if no effort seems to be necessary? Executives should carefully scrutinize the appointment process at all times. It may be better to tax the present somewhat by a lack of personnel in order to safeguard the future welfare of the organization.

The problem of "deadwood" is complicated by the fact that a decision to confer higher status is not readily reversed. The difficulty increases when high status personnel, such as presidents, vice-presidents, generals, and admirals, are involved. When a person is removed from a position, the integrity of the appointing officials is at stake. For that reason, an executive is often "protected" even when it seems evident to others in the organization that an error in judgment was made in the appointment. Another important factor is the normal reaction to anything that tends to upset the status quo. The removal of an executive or a foreman even when justified may establish a "dangerous" precedent in the organization. The difficulty of reversing a status decision is further enhanced by "alliances." The removal of one executive may involve the removal of other executives. This problem may make necessary the retention of an incompetent executive to prevent a serious disruption in the executive ranks. To mitigate some of the above difficulties, the high status person is generally asked to resign and is not infrequently given a bonus.

The Problem of Status Anxiety. Many status problems are caused by management's failure to understand the significance that status has for people and to recognize a problem as a status problem. People do not always respond as a presumably rational person should. It is a serious mistake to assume that such behavior is not as it ought to be and, therefore, something to be ignored. The difficulties that can arise in this respect are well illustrated in a case reported by Roethlisberger.

The personnel of a certain department was moved from one building to another. In the new location, because of lack of space, it was found necessary to seat four people across the aisle from the remainder of the group. It happened that there were three women in the department who were to be transferred to other work. These three were given desks across the aisle so that their going would not necessitate a rearrangement of desks. The fourth person, a man, was also given a desk there, simply because there was no other place for him to sit. In choosing the fourth person, the supervisor was undoubtedly influenced by the fact that he was older than the rest of the group and was well acquainted with the three women. But, beyond that, nothing was implied by the fact that he was chosen. Now see how he interpreted this change. He felt that his supervisor regarded him as one of the women. The women were being transferred to other types of work; consequently he too would be transferred before long. Two of the women were being transferred to jobs in the shop. He, himself, might be transferred to the shop; and there was nothing he dreaded more. Having dwelt on speculations like this for a while, the employee recalled with alarm that his name had been omitted from the current issue of the house telephone directory. This omission had been quite accidental. The house telephone directory, however, constituted in this concern a sort of social register. Names of shop people below the rank of assistant foreman were not printed unless they were employed in some special capacity requiring contacts with other organizations. With the exception of typists and certain clerical groups, the names of all office people were listed. The fact that his name had been omitted now took on new significance. It tended to reinforce his growing conviction that he was about to be transferred to an unimportant shop position. He became so preoccupied with the problem that he could not work. He was completely demoralized.[24]

Some people might conclude that the man was "not very rational." That such a response is not an isolated case is indicated by the "status anxiety" expressed by a number of college professors when they were incorrectly listed in the university catalogue.

Who Else Calls Him Tony? People generally view their situation in relative rather than absolute terms. Thus, the status value of calling a superior by his first name is closely related to the number of people who assume this prerogative. John P. Marquand illustrated this idea well in the novel *Point of No Return*. The characters are Anthony Burton, president of the Stuyvesant Bank, Charles Gray, a young executive working for Burton, and Nancy, his wife.

"Look here, feller," Mr. Burton said, and he had blushed when he said "feller," "why not cut out this sir business? Why not just call me Tony?"

That was in 1941 but Charles still remembered his great joy and relief, with the relief uppermost, and that he could hardly wait to hear what Nancy would say.

"You know, Charles," Mr. Burton had continued, "Guthrie Mayhew and I have quite an idea. We're going to get hold of Tommy Mapes on the New Haven and see if he can't get us a special car on the eight-thirty. How about getting aboard? My idea is to call it the *Crackerbarrel*."

"Why, thanks," Charles had said. "I'd like to very much, Tony."

He had worked late that night and he could not remember what train he had taken home, but Nancy had been asleep when he got there.

[24] F. J. Roethlisberger, *Management and Morale* (Cambridge: Harvard University Press, 1947), pp. 34–35.

"Nance," he said, "wake up. I've got something to tell you. Burton's asked me to call him Tony." And Nancy had sat bolt upright in her twin bed.

"Start at the beginning," Nancy had said. "Exactly how did it happen, and don't leave out anything."

They must have talked for a long while, there in the middle of the night. Nancy had known what it meant because she had worked downtown herself.

"Now wait," she had said. "Let's not get too excited. Who else calls him Tony?" [25]

Nancy's last statement is also pertinent when applied to other things, such as a salary increase, a private secretary, a private office, an invitation to the boss's home, and a longer lunch period. A walnut-paneled office for one assistant vice-president will certainly cause comment if other assistant vice-presidents have ordinary offices. It is sometimes better to leave the walnut-paneled office vacant. Difficult status problems may be caused by wage and salary differences among those who consider themselves to be equal in qualification and contribution. One executive, for example, expressed delight with a salary increase. A few days later he found that a fellow executive had received a much larger increase. The result was dissatisfaction, which was not in the least compensated by the fact that he did get a significant raise. Management should be able and ready to defend its wage and salary policy; it should not and cannot depend on secrecy as a means for controlling this source of status difficulties. In some cases such a problem may result from an individual's unrealistic appraisal of his qualifications and accomplishments. Management may not be aware that a status problem exists. The solution to such difficulties lies in the maintenance of effective communication. Maintain a real "open door" policy. *Listen* to what your subordinates have to say. Let them tell you *their* problems. One of them may be a status problem.

The Telephone Directory as a "Social Register." The primary purpose of the company telephone directory is to facilitate the mechanics of internal telephone communication. However, the listing of names in the directory may have important status implications. The telephone directory sometimes becomes a sort of "social register" which confers higher status upon those who are listed. Since many people in the organization are not listed, the appearance of a person's name gives a degree of distinction. The status value of a listing is also influenced by the fact that high status people, such as the company president, are listed with lower status personnel.

Office Layout as a Status Factor. The arrangement of desks in an office is a matter of efficient workflow in the eyes of the industrial engineer. To people in the office, the position of a desk may have status implications.

[25] John P. Marquand, *Point of No Return* (Boston: Little, Brown and Company, 1949), p. 20.

The desks in the front row may have different status value than those in the rear of the office. Proximity to the supervisor's desk or office and the type of desk may also have status implications. For example, one walnut desk among metal desks can create a status problem.

The Status Value of Meat and Vegetables. In his study of the restaurant industry, Professor William F. Whyte found that different foods had different status values to the employees.[26] The preparation of fish ranked lower than the preparation of chicken or meat, and working with odds and ends had less status value than working with large slices. Highest in the vegetable field were luxury or decorative items such as parsley, chives, and celery; next came green beans and then spinach and carrots; after white potatoes came onions, which occupied the bottom of the scale. One worker made it quite clear to the researchers that she did not usually peel onions. The fish station in one restaurant presented an interesting status problem. The working supervisor, Gertrude, was a skilled and valuable employee in the kitchen. The importance of her work was enhanced by the wartime meat shortage. In spite of these facts, her position occupied the bottom of the status hierarchy because of the attitudes that the employees had toward fish.

A Blue Serge Suit and Dungarees. Clothing may be an important status symbol even when management makes no demands in this respect. Miller and Form found that the clothing worn by people in a small garage symbolized their status.[27] The owner generally worked in a business suit. The stock and order clerk removed his coat and worked in his shirt sleeves. The head mechanic also removed his coat, but he wore a nonfunctional white smock. The mechanics wore full-length blue jumpers; the apprentices and clean-up men wore overalls or discarded clothing of darker hues. The mode of dress was not formally planned or enforced by management, but it was scrupulously observed. Social sanctions were applied against anyone who attempted to rise above his status by wearing clothing "inappropriate" to his job. The same type of differentiation in the clothing worn by people of different statuses can be seen in every organization. Were this not the case, organizations would probably give greater attention to formalize status identities such as uniforms, insignia, and the like.

A Man's World. Professor William F. Whyte found that many status problems in restaurants arise when lower status individuals seek to originate action from those who have higher status. He found a great deal of friction between the bartender and the waitresses in one restaurant. The waitresses, in ordering the bartender to mix drinks for customers, were

---

[26] William Foote Whyte, *Human Relations, op. cit.,* pp. 35–41.

[27] Delbert C. Miller and William H. Form, *Industrial Sociology,* 2nd ed. (New York: Harper & Brothers Publishers, 1964), p. 483.

violating his conception of the role he should play in a man's world.[28] A possible solution to such a problem is indicated by the way a bartender in another restaurant handled the problem. This bartender lined up the orders and mixed enough of a particular kind of drink for all the orders. He would then call on the waitresses to get their orders. In this way the waitresses responded to him rather than the reverse. The bartender was dominating the scene as he thought a man should. Age, seniority, skill, sex, and pay were important factors in the status situation. Countermen disliked taking orders from waitresses. Highly paid and skilled cooks often resented taking orders from lower status men and from waitresses. Whyte found that some of the friction and tension between countermen and waitresses was eased by having the waitresses place orders on a spindle.[29]

These problems are not confined to the restaurant industry. One industrial plant found itself faced with a wildcat strike when a woman (who was well qualified) was given a job in an exclusively male department. A male tool-crib attendant in a manufacturing department composed primarily of women may result in a conflict situation. A young supervisor, who may be otherwise well qualified, in a department composed of older people may create serious status difficulties.

Titles and Rank Are Important. Management could give greater attention to the formal instruments of status than is sometimes the case. The expression, "We don't emphasize titles or rank in our organization," may reflect a healthy situation. But it may also ignore the positive role that titles denoting rank and function, formal ceremonies, insignia, and other status identifications can play in motivating managerial and nonmanagerial personnel. The formal status system should be given periodic scrutiny and viewed as a positive element of executive control.

Responsibilities as Rewards

Purposeful activity and the product it produces may become important sources of satisfaction. Some people enjoy accounting, selling, typing, operating a lathe, managing, and the many other responsibilities that make up organization. The world would truly be a vale of tears if work were actually the burden it is so often assumed to be. Much of what people say about work is the product of the learned and habitual responses that make up the culture. The idea that work is a burden is impressed upon people from early childhood. People seem generally reluctant to admit they enjoy work for the same reason most children say they dislike school. A distinction should be made between what people say about work and the satisfac-

[28] Whyte, *Human Relations, op. cit.*, pp. 78–79.
[29] *Ibid.*, p. 69.

tions that may actually be involved. Most sinners are against sin even when they are caught in the act.

A great deal has been written about the satisfactions that were presumably removed by the breakdown of crafts into routine and repetitive factory operations. The craftsman produced a complete product which gave evidence to the skills he possessed. The satisfactions that evolved from these creative efforts have not been measured by strictly scientific techniques, but it is generally assumed that work was more satisfying under such conditions than those that exist in modern factories. The technological and organizational innovations that reshaped the work of manufacture have also remolded the office. The modern office is much like a factory and the office worker has in many respects suffered the fate of the craftsman. A similar statement can be made about the manager who, unlike the "entrepreneur" of economic theory, performs only a portion of the total task of managing. Such consequences cannot be avoided as long as man seeks to reap the advantages of cooperative endeavor. Much of the work in modern organizations is undoubtedly as satisfying as the work performed by the craftsmen of old. However, some tasks do not seem to meet the requirements that give rise to a "pride of craftsmanship." The more routine and repetitive jobs are particularly vulnerable in this respect.

Some subordinates thrive on responsibilities and gain as much satisfaction from them as from monetary and other inducements. Even those who seem to dislike work and gripe a great deal may be motivated by an increase in responsibilities. Attention should also be given to techniques that make work more interesting and satisfying. Routine and repetitive tasks can sometimes be made less burdensome by enlarging the responsibilities involved in a position or job. Another approach is to limit the time an individual is assigned to such work, and still another is to change or increase responsibilities over a period of time. Superiors should not neglect the important part that words of appreciation and commendation can play in making work a more satisfying experience. Subordinates, whether vice-presidents or production workers, like to feel that they are needed and that they are doing a good job.

The satisfactions afforded by "pride of craftsmanship" have a parallel in another important source of satisfaction. Henry Dennison, the New England industrialist, wrote many years ago, "there may be a team craftsmanship which can make an even stronger appeal." [30] Such satisfactions stem from the idea that subordinates are members of a team producing an important product or performing a vital service. Superiors and organizations generally should emphasize the development of pride in team

[30] Henry Dennison, *Organization Engineering* (New York: McGraw-Hill Book Company, Inc., 1931), p. 86.

accomplishment. The satisfactions that may have been lost through a breakdown of the craft can often be replaced by the satisfactions of successful cooperative effort. Subordinates should be given an understanding of the manner in which they fit into the big picture. An effort should be made to provide a perspective that transcends the job and to give their efforts a meaning that has social significance.

The concept of team craftsmanship, which involves pride in the objectives of team or group effort, may encompass the entire organization. It may be carried a slight step further by the idea that people may assume a personal loyalty to a particular organization irrespective of the objectives pursued. Thus, a person who takes pride in producing automobiles may take particular pride in the fact that he is a member of the General Motors Corporation. Such statements as "I am a Yale man," "I boost the Cornhuskers," "I am a member of the Carpenters Union," "I am a Congregationalist," and "I am an American" suggest an identity with organizations that have characteristics distinguishing them from other organizations of a similar type.[31] Differentiating characteristics may be deliberately developed, or they may evolve as a by-product of techniques used to achieve other purposes. Organizations become unique "personalities" through such instruments as names (Ford Motor Company or Union Carbide), trade names (Wheaties or Lucky Strike), songs (I'm a Rambling Wreck from Georgia Tech), buildings (architectural form and size, such as tallest building in Chicago), advertising copy, traditions, quality products, a good labor policy, and many others. Every aspect of organizational operations may play a part in creating the image people have of an organization.

Motivation: A Dynamic Concept

The problem of motivation should be viewed in terms of a combination of complementary and competing factors. A motivational system must satisfy many different human motives if the organization is to survive. A lack of knowledge about motives precludes any kind of perfect solution to the problem. Fortunately, there are automatic adjustments which can help compensate for failures in motivational decisions.

Burdens and Benefits: An Integrated Approach

A strict dichotomy between the burdens of organizational responsibilities and the benefits of acceptance cannot be maintained in actual practice. Burdens are benefits for some subordinates, and benefits may become

[31] E. Wight Bakke, *op. cit.,* p. 152.

burdens. Thus, as was pointed out in the previous section, organizational responsibilities may take on the properties of reward through "pride of craftsmanship" and "team craftsmanship." The social pressures imposed by the group may turn an organizational reward into a penalty. Production beyond group output norms that results in higher wages or promotion may give rise to countervailing penalties by the group. The penalties that may be invoked from such external sources as unions, professional associations, religious organizations, and wives are also important in this respect. For example, a worker who refuses to participate in a slowdown "ordered" by the union may be rewarded by his superior but be penalized by union leaders and members. Rewards for the performance of responsibilities that interfere with a subordinate's obligations to his church may become a penalty. A higher salary or a promotion may not be worth the fires of hell to people with strong religious propensities. A promotion that involves a transfer to another city can become a penalty if the subordinate's wife dislikes the idea. Even a vice-presidency may not be sufficient compensation for tirades of discontent at home. General economic and particular market conditions can have considerable impact on organizational rewards. A salary increase may mean very little if other companies are offering 20 per cent more for the same kind of work. The threat of discharge is less potent when there are more jobs than job-seekers.

Subordinates generally view their situation in terms of the totality of burdens and benefits accorded them. They also tend to balance present burdens and benefits with those that may be offered in the future. A subordinate may accept burdens in the present for expected future benefits. He may also forsake a satisfactory relationship in the present for a lack of future opportunities. Subordinates are never completely satisfied or dissatisfied with a particular departmental or organizational association. They tend to react to a combination of burdens and benefits, each of which plays some part in the conception they form about their situation. Particular burdens and benefits add to or subtract from the totality of satisfactions, but there does not seem to be a simple cause and effect relationship between the elements and the whole.

Maslow's Hierarchy of Needs

Abraham Maslow has developed a theory of human motivation in which human needs are arranged in the form of a hierarchy.[32] At the bottom of Maslow's hierarchy are the basic physiological needs, which are the starting point for the most motivational theories. Security or safety needs, expressed by such phenomena as job tenure and insurance, are found at the

[32] A. H. Maslow, *Motivation and Personality* (New York: Harper & Row, 1954), pp. 80–106.

second level in Maslow's schema. The third level is taken up by what Maslow calls "the love and affection and belongingness needs," which may be generally categorized as social needs.[33] Next in line are the esteem needs, which involve both the need for self-esteem and the need to have the esteem of others (prestige and respect). At the apex of the Maslow hierarchy is the need for self-actualization or a need to fulfill what a person considers to be his mission in life. Self-actualization may take many forms: to be an ideal mother; to be an outstanding golfer; to be the top student; or to be the highest paid university professor or business executive.

According to this theory of motivation, lower level needs must be satisfied before higher needs become important. Maslow considers physiological needs to be the most potent of all needs. An individual "who is lacking food, safety, love, and esteem would most probably hunger for food more strongly than for anything else." [34] All other needs tend to be pushed into the background or to become nonexistent. However, after physiological needs are satisfied, they are no longer an important motivating instrument. In Maslow's theory, higher needs emerge as lower level needs are satisfied —safety needs follow physiological needs, social needs come after safety needs, and so on.

Human motives cannot be as neatly categorized as Maslow would have them. A need may become less important as a motivational factor after it is satisfied, but it probably retains some degree of potency by the fact that the rewards involved can be withdrawn. The higher needs undoubtedly play some part in motivation even when lower needs are not fulfilled. However, Maslow's theory of motivation has importance in spite of such modifications. All of the needs in Maslow's hierarchy should be taken into account in planning a motivational system. The relative potency of the needs at the various levels may vary a great deal from one situation to another. Differences among individuals, social groups, organizations, and societies are important in this respect. The principal consideration is that management should attempt to take advantage of the higher needs as well as the more obvious lower ones. Douglas McGregor's Theory Y involves such an approach to maximizing human motivation.

Monetary and Other Incentives

The problem of motivation may be viewed in purely monetary terms. The customer exchanges money for products and services; stockholders and creditors exchange money for an expected monetary return over a period of time; suppliers exchange material things for money; employees and executives exchange work for wages and salaries. Such exchanges are

[33] *Ibid.,* p. 89.
[34] *Ibid.,* p. 82.

generally made on the basis of monetary values determined by market and institutional forces. The importance of money as an instrument of motivation is sometimes undervalued. Money has a universal appeal because it embodies the means for satisfying almost every human motive. It can be exchanged for an evening at the theatre, Roquefort cheese, brown shoes, a dinner date, a week in Paris, a case of bock beer, an umbrella, a regimental tie, or a management book. The motivational problem is greatly simplified by a money system. Large-scale organized endeavor would be impossible without it.

Cooperative behavior is social and gives rise to social satisfactions which also have important motivational properties. The prospect of achieving higher status in an organization and in the society is another part of the picture. Also significant to many people are the satisfactions that come from the achievement of organizational and professional goals. Organizational behavior is motivated by some combination of these incentives. One individual generally requires a different combination than another. Some people are more highly motivated by money than by social satisfactions, status, or craftsmanship. Others accord a relatively lower rank to the values expressed by monetary rewards. There is little likelihood that a large number of people would respond well to only one of these incentives. An organization that seeks to motivate primarily through monetary incentives or social satisfaction would undoubtedly experience difficulties.

Modifying Motives: Personnel Replacements and Other Adjustments

Some adaptation to the incentives available in particular organizations is provided through recruitment and resignations. The recruitment process tends to bring in people who are inclined to respond favorably to particular combinations of incentives. Forced or voluntary resignations can also serve an important function in this respect. People willing to accept prevailing policies will stay; those unwilling to do so leave. There are obvious limits to this kind of adaptation. An organization may become so unpopular that it cannot attract sufficient personnel to maintain itself.

Organizations often change the motives of their personnel through education or indoctrination. They frequently spend large amounts of money to build a favorable image through advertising and other means. Stockholder and employee relations programs are highly important instruments for molding the motives of organizational participants. The inculcation of appropriate motives is also an integral part of many executive development programs.

SELECTED REFERENCES

Chris Argyris, *Personality and Organization.* New York: Harper & Brothers, 1957.
John R. Beishline, *Military Management for National Defense,* Chap. 16. Englewood Cliffs, N.J.: Prentice-Hall, Inc., 1950.
David W. Belcher, "Toward a Behavioral Science Theory of Wages," *Journal of the Academy of Management,* Vol. 5, No. 2, pp. 102–116 (August 1962).
Bernard Berelson and Gary A. Steiner, *Human Behavior: An Inventory of Scientific Findings,* Chap. 6. New York: Harcourt, Brace & World, Inc., 1964.
Roger M. Blough, "Business *Can* Satisfy the Young Intellectual," *Harvard Business Review,* Vol. 44, No. 1, pp. 49–57 (January–February 1966).
Richard F. Ericson, "Rationality and Executive Motivation," *Journal of the Academy of Management,* Vol. 5, No. 1, pp. 7–23 (April 1962).
David W. Ewing and Dan H. Fenn, Jr., *Incentives for Executives.* New York: McGraw-Hill Book Company, Inc., 1962.
Earl B. French, "Perspective: The Motivation of Scientists and Engineers," *Academy of Management Journal,* Vol. 9, No. 2, pp. 152–155 (June 1966).
Saul W. Gellerman, *Motivation and Productivity.* New York: American Management Association, 1963.
Robert T. Golembiewski, *Behavior and Organization: O & M and the Small Group.* Chicago: Rand McNally & Company, 1962.
Robert T. Golembiewski, *The Small Group.* Chicago: The University of Chicago Press, 1962.
I. L. Heckmann and S. G. Huneryager, *Human Relations in Management,* 2nd ed., Part IV. Cincinnati: South-Western Publishing Co., 1960.
Frederick Herzberg, "One More Time: How do you Motivate Employees?" *Harvard Business Review,* Vol. 46, No. 1, pp. 53–62 (January–February 1968).
C. Addison Hickman and Manford H. Kuhn, *Individuals, Groups, and Economic Behavior.* New York: The Dryden Press, Inc., 1956.
Robert E. Lane, *Faculty Unionism in a California State College,* Doctoral Dissertation. Iowa City: The University of Iowa, 1967.
Edward E. Lawler III, "Does Money Make People Work Harder?" *Yale Alumni Magazine,* Vol. 31, No. 7, pp. 40–43 (April 1968).
Harold J. Leavitt, *Managerial Psychology,* 2nd ed. Chicago: University of Chicago Press, 1964.
Rensis Likert, *The Human Organization: Its Management and Value.* New York: McGraw-Hill Book Company, 1967.

Fred Luthans, *The Faculty Promotion Process.* Iowa City: Bureau of Business and Economic Research, The University of Iowa, 1967.

A. H. Maslow, *Motivation and Personality.* New York: Harper & Row, 1954.

Douglas McGregor, *The Human Side of Enterprise.* New York: McGraw-Hill Book Company, Inc., 1960.

Malcolm P. McNair, "Thinking Ahead, What Price Human Relations?" *Harvard Business Review,* Vol. 35, No. 2, pp. 15 ff (March–April 1957).

Leon C. Megginson, *Human Resources: Cases and Concepts.* New York: Harcourt, Brace & World, Inc., 1968.

Theodore M. Mills, *The Sociology of Small Groups.* Englewood Cliffs, N.J.: Prentice-Hall, Inc., 1967.

M. Scott Myers, "Conditions for Manager Motivation," *Harvard Business Review,* Vol. 44, No. 1, pp. 58–71 (January–February 1966).

Michael S. Olmsted, *The Small Group.* New York: Random House, 1959.

Arch Patton, *Men, Money and Motivation.* New York: McGraw-Hill Book Company, 1961.

Waino W. Suojanen and G. C. Hoyt, "Differences in Motivation Among White-Collar Workers," *Personnel,* Vol. 34, No. 2, pp. 26–31 (September–October 1957).

Waino W. Suojanen, *The Dynamics of Management.* New York: Holt, Rinehart and Winston, Inc., 1966.

William Foote Whyte, *Human Relations in the Restaurant Industry,* Part IV. New York: McGraw-Hill Book Company, Inc., 1948.

chapter 23

DYNAMIC LEADERSHIP

Leadership may be defined in terms of the totality of functions performed by executives as individuals and as a group. Every chapter in this book is concerned with some aspect of leadership thus defined. Leadership is viewed from a more limited perspective in the discussion that follows. It is approached from the vantage point of the particular superior-subordinate relationships that make up the management structure. The responsibility of the superior is to direct behavior into channels that promote the achievement of organizational and departmental goals. However, the benefits that can be accorded subordinates for the burdens imposed by the superior are limited. To put the matter in economic terms, a given amount of revenue must be produced with a given amount of wage and salary cost. The wages and salaries paid to subordinates should equal their marginal revenue product under equilibrium conditions. However, such an equilibrium can be disrupted by variations in leadership capacity. Some superiors are able to produce more revenue with a given amount of wage and salary costs than others. In other words, the fact that A rather than B occupies a particular position may significantly influence the manner in which subordinates respond. The difference can be attributed to leadership or the capacity to make subordinates more willing to accept the burdens imposed by the organization. Executives can be said to have working capital in the form of the authority that evolves from their positions.[1] They may add to or subtract from this working capital through leadership or the actions they take with respect to factors that influence subordinate behavior.

[1] George C. Homans, *The Human Group* (New York: Harcourt, Brace & Company, Inc., 1950), p. 425.

Leadership: A Problem of Techniques

Much of the literature on leadership techniques has been concerned with relatively simple systems of superior-subordinate relationships. Leadership studies have stressed leadership in informal groups and the problems of first-line supervision. Such studies have provided a basis for the development of improved techniques. However, the leadership problems in complex hierarchies may differ in important respects from those found in simple systems.[2] The restraints imposed by a hierarchical system may force the leader to depart from what might otherwise be regarded as appropriate leadership techniques. Leadership in a formal hierarchical system is partly a matter of manipulating organizational instruments through which authority is maintained. Purely personal leadership qualities are important, but they are not always primary.

Maintaining the Authority of Position

An executive is a leader by virtue of the position he occupies in the hierarchy. Position is also a source of authority because, as Barnard has pointed out, people generally "impute authority to communications from superior positions. . . ."[3] The authority accorded an executive is not necessarily related to any personal leadership abilities he may possess. Some degree of authority may result even when the person occupying the position violates every known precept of personal leadership. Executives should recognize the importance of position in the authority relationship and promote "the authority of position" by appropriate actions.

Proper performance of the decisional responsibilities of the position is important in maintaining authority. The executive may consult his subordinates about possible alternatives, but he should make the final decision on matters that fall within his jurisdiction. Subordinates generally expect the leader to lead even when they have taken part in the proceedings. This idea has significance apart from its implications relative to personal leadership. The executive maintains the authority of position by creating the presumption that only he has the right to communicate decisions about certain matters. The ideas contained in a decision may have come from subordinate line and staff personnel, and it may sometimes appear that the

---

[2] George C. Homans gives recognition to the difference in developing "rules of leadership": *op. cit.,* p. 425.

[3] Chester I. Barnard, *The Functions of the Executive* (Cambridge: Harvard University Press, 1938), p. 173.

executive is a pilferer of ideas. However, a failure to impress upon others that his position gives him a monopoly on decisional information may have even more adverse consequences.

An executive in a hierarchical system should help maintain the authority of executives in other positions. Thus, a superior should not communicate decisions involving matters that have been delegated to subordinate executives. He may make suggestions, exert influence, and even make the decision, but it is important that he not give the impression that he rather than the subordinate made the decision. The decision should be communicated by the subordinate if it falls within his jurisdiction. All this is another way of saying that executives should respect the formal channels of command. They should not give themselves or others the license to openly subvert the integrity of the formal system of "authority."

Much communication in the management hierarchy is informal, and some such communication bypasses the formal channels of authority. Informal communication frequently compensates for the informational inadequacies of the formal chain of command. It provides an important means through which information pertinent to decision can be considered and communicated without a repudiation of the authority of position. Decisions are generally communicated formally by the appropriate executive even when the nature of the decision is already well known informally. Such action may seem like an anticlimax, but it helps maintain authority.

An open challenge to the authority of position cannot generally be tolerated even when the challenger is right by other standards. General Billy Mitchell was "right" about the future significance of air power in warfare, but he was "wrong" in publicly questioning the authority of his superiors. In other words, he did not abide by the accepted norms of behavior in the military hierarchy. An organization can be destroyed if incompetent executives are able to maintain their positions by imposing sanctions. Many might contend that generals other than General Mitchell should have been demoted and court-martialed, but an organization can be destroyed by a breakdown in the system of authority. Discharging subordinates for failure to obey decisions they know to be wrong and defending an incompetent superior may seem unfair; however, such actions are sometimes necessary if the system of authority is to be maintained.

Impersonalizing the Authority Relationship

The lives of subordinates may be greatly affected by the superior's power to impose sanctions. Superiors can obviously take advantage of the situation and invoke norms that are not related to the requirements of the organization. Tendencies in this direction cannot be avoided as long as organizations are composed of human beings, since some aspects of every superior-subordinate relationship involve responsibilities that relate to personal goals rather than organizational goals. But too much use of organizational power to serve the whims and fancies of a superior can disrupt teamwork and have adverse motivational consequences. Such power should be used to serve organizational interests and should not be destroyed by dissipation. Many subordinates reared in the traditions of the American culture are psychologically predisposed against the idea that the superior-subordinate relationship is a master-servant relationship. The behavioral norms that form a basis for imposing rewards or penalties should generally be susceptible to rationalization in terms of organizational responsibilities. The authority relationship becomes impersonal to the extent that the subordinate views his role and that of the superior from such a perspective. In other words, the acceptance of decisions by superiors becomes an obligation imposed by the organization rather than a personal obligation. Such a construction of the situation facilitates the maintenance of authority and explains why subordinates often obey the orders of a person they would disobey under other circumstances. Also important is that the burden of the superior is made less difficult by the idea that decision making is an organizational responsibility. The organization rather than the superior becomes the culprit when decisions repugnant to subordinates have to be made.

Motivating Subordinates Through Participation

Leadership in cooperative endeavor may be authoritarian, democratic, or *laissez faire*. An authoritarian leader makes all the decisions without subordinate participation. The *laissez-faire* leader, if he can be called a leader, gives the group complete freedom in determining activity. The democratic leader falls somewhere in the middle of the two extremes. He actively solicits suggestions from subordinates, frequently acts on their advice, and gives them a range of discretion in performing their activities. This terminology is used to categorize leadership techniques and does not necessarily relate to similar terminology in the political field. Thus, a leader in a "democracy" may use authoritarian techniques to promote the will of the people.

An experiment conducted by Lewin, Lippitt, and White at the University of Iowa attempted to find a relationship between types of leadership and group behavior.[4] Four groups of ten-year-old boys were recruited on a voluntary basis subject to various types of controls and organized into clubs engaged in such activities as mural painting, soap carving, and model

[4] Kurt Lewin, Ronald Lippitt, and Ralph K. White, "Patterns of Aggressive Behavior in Experimentally Created 'Social Climates,'" *The Journal of Social Psychology*, Vol. 10, No. 2, May 1939, pp. 271–299.

airplane construction. Every six weeks each group was given a new leader and variously subjected to authoritarian, democratic, and *laissez-faire* techniques. Table 23-1 defines the leadership techniques used in the experiment. Each of the four leaders used different techniques as they were

Table 23-1. Experimental Leadership Techniques

Authoritarian	Democratic	*Laissez Faire*
1. All determination of policy by the leader.	1. All policies a matter of group discussion and decision, encouraged and assisted by the leader.	1. Complete freedom for group or individual decision, without any leader participation.
2. Techniques and activity steps dictated by the authority, one at a time, so that future steps were always uncertain to a large degree.	2. Activity perspective gained during first discussion period. General steps to group goal sketched, and where technical advice was needed the leader suggested two or three alternative procedures from which choice could be made.	2. Various materials supplied by the leader, who made it clear that he would supply information when asked. He took no part in work discussions.
3. The leader usually dictated the particular work task and work companions of each member.	3. The members were free to work with whomever they chose, and the division of tasks was left up to the group.	3. Complete nonparticipation by leader.
4. The dominator was "personal" in his praise and criticism of the work of each member, but remained aloof from active group participation except when demonstrating. He was friendly or impersonal rather than openly hostile.	4. The leader was "objective" or "fact-minded" in his praise and criticism, and tried to be a regular group member in spirit without doing too much of the work.	4. Very infrequent comments on member activities unless questioned, and no attempt to participate or interfere with the course of events.

Source. Kurt Lewin, Ronald Lippitt, and Ralph K. White, "Patterns of Aggressive Behavior in Experimentally Created 'Social Climates,'" *The Journal of Social Psychology,* Vol. 10., No. 2, May 1939, p. 273.

shifted from group to group to control the impact of the leader's personality.

Autocratic leadership seemed generally to produce a great deal of tension and frustration. One of the autocratic situations gave rise to a large number of aggressive acts, such as carving on the posts of the clubroom, deliberately walking in a restricted area, leaving meetings early, and pretending not to hear the leader. The remaining four autocracies resulted in extremely nonaggressive behavior with an atmosphere described by such terms as dull, lifeless, submissive, and apathetic. There was little smiling, joking, movement, initiative, and general conversation. The boys still seemed to like their activities, but they were not genuinely contented with the situation. The repressive influence of the autocratic leader seemed sufficient to prevent a release of tension and frustration through aggressive acts. But when leadership was changed to the democratic or *laissez-faire* types, the groups tended to respond with sudden outbursts of aggression as though they had been under pressure. Aggression also increased when the autocratic leader left the room for short periods of time. *Laissez-faire* leadership gave rise to the largest number of aggressive acts, with democratic leadership falling between the one highly aggressive autocratic situation and the four nonaggressive autocracies. Interviews during the experiment and at the end indicated the following likes and dislikes. Nineteen of the twenty boys liked their democratic leaders better than their autocratic ones. The *laissez-faire* leaders were preferred over the autocratic leaders in seven out of ten responses. More favorable comments were made about democratic leadership than the other two types. The reactions were almost entirely dependent on the leadership techniques used rather than the person doing the leading. They were reversed when the same person used one of the other techniques.

A great deal of discretion should be used in generalizing from the above experiment. The sample was small, some variables were not controlled, boys are not adults, club activities are not the same as industrial activities, wages and other incentives were not used, and the time period of research was relatively short. However, it was an attempt at controlled experimentation, which is more than can be said for some leadership research. The results support the importance of leadership techniques and the idea that many people can become better leaders through training in techniques. They also indicate that democratic leadership techniques probably produce better results than autocratic techniques. The reasons, assuming the hypothesis is true, are not well understood at the present time. The participation involved in democratic techniques may motivate through "ego-evolvement" in a group purpose. Democratic techniques may also function indirectly through the social satisfactions made possible by greater freedom of action. The nature of the culture and social conditioning probably play an important part in the picture. Arbitrary leadership techniques seem generally to be frowned upon by people who have been reared in the traditions of "government by law" and "due process." Also important in this respect is the conditioning that occurs during the early years in the home and in school. It is interesting to note from the above experiment that the boy who liked autocratic leadership was the son of an army officer.

Actual leadership situations are rarely completely authoritarian or completely *laissez faire*. *Laissez-faire* groups seem to develop informal leadership and, in some instances, an informal hierarchy of leaders. Formally organized authoritarian systems, such as the hierarchies of business organizations, usually become somewhat democratic through formal and informal modifications. Subordinate participation may be promoted through such formal devices as committees, or it may evolve through informal interaction. However, a limitation is imposed by the concepts of work division and specialization. If carried to an extreme, subordinate participation repudiates the logic of hierarchical organization. What does the superior do if subordinates do most of the work? A lack of knowledge on the part of subordinates also places a limitation on participation. The superior cannot always act on the suggestions and ideas of subordinates. Motivational difficulties may result if subordinates, rightly or wrongly, begin to feel that their views are not taken into consideration. It might have been better not to invite participation in the first instance. Furthermore, it should not be assumed that subordinates always want to play an active role in the superior's realm; many people shun responsibilities and seem willing to let others assume the burden.

Keeping Subordinates Informed

Inappropriate behavior by subordinate personnel may result from a failure to provide them with sufficient information. Superiors sometimes fail to recognize the nature of the difficulty and attempt to "reestablish" authority by imposing penalties. Such actions can create serious motivational problems and cause subordinates to question the superior's capacities. Although the difference is not always apparent, superiors should distinguish between informational and authority problems. Measles are not cured by skin grafts or by taking out the appendix.

Subordinates should have knowledge of or access to knowledge about the norms defining appropriate behavior and the consequences of conformity or nonconformity. The functional requirements of the position and formal company policies should be explicitly set forth. Also important is information about the informal norms that pertain to the position. For example, the superior might discreetly point out that the president of the company likes well-dressed executives and that a certain residential section is "a nice place to live." Subordinates can acquire many insights from fellow subordinates who often provide information the superior cannot "admit" in his official capacity. The superior's wife and the wives of other executives can also serve an important informational role. The idea that communication is a two-way process should not be neglected. A lack of knowledge about norms can often be attributed to listening or reading failures on the part of the subordinate. It may also result from an inability to learn some of the more implicit and subtle rules of organizational living. Some people do not have sufficient social skills to respond to cues that may be obvious to others, and they may fail to advance in the organization or even be discharged for reasons they do not understand. Such consequences may seem unjust unless viewed in terms of organizational interests.

Consistent Interpretation and Enforcement

Superiors should generally be consistent in interpreting and enforcing norms. Subordinates cannot adapt their behavior to norms that are not susceptible to being learned. Unfair norms consistently enforced are sometimes more just than fair norms enforced in a capricious fashion. Erratic enforcement can create feelings of frustration, futility, insecurity, and distrust. A major problem is that some norms have highly subjective qualities. Professor E. Wight Bakke has concluded from empirical information on this matter, "the great bulk of behavior traits for which participants are rewarded and penalized is subject to personal judgment and not to objective standards."[5] Significant variations may occur in the manner in which norms are interpreted and enforced by different superiors. An appropriate mode of behavior for one superior may be inappropriate for another. Such variations may result from different conceptions of how best to achieve departmental or organizational objectives. They may also reflect differences in the personal backgrounds and goals of superiors.

Too many changes in superiors over a short period of time can have serious disruptive consequences. Each change requires some degree of adaptation on the part of subordinates with resignations, discharges, or transfers for those who cannot adapt. This problem can be partly solved by leadership training programs to promote more uniform standards. Uniformity is also imposed by the fact that lower levels of the hierarchy are subject to control from higher levels, and, to some extent, subordinate

[5] E. Wight Bakke, *Bonds of Organization* (New York: Harper and Brothers Publishers, 1950), p. 129. A discussion of this problem is also found in: *ibid.*, pp. 107–115.

executives are molded into the image of the superior. Promotion from within gives impetus to this phenomenon. It is generally more difficult to adapt to a superior who comes from the outside, since the norms in one organization often differ from those found in another. Variation in the interpretation and enforcement of norms cannot be avoided if personality differences exist. Such differences should not always be viewed in terms of good or bad leadership. Even a superior who violates many of the so-called rules of leadership may be successful if his approach is consistent enough to permit subordinate adaptation.

Understanding the Socio-Psychological Environment

An important prerequisite for effective leadership is knowledge of the socio-psychological environment. The psychological make-up of subordinates has an important bearing on the way in which they will respond to organizational responsibilities and rewards (or penalties). Some subordinates may be positively influenced by particular modes of leadership, and others may react in an opposite direction. The behavior of subordinates may also be significantly molded by the norms imposed by informal groups. The superior should become familiar with the nature of group norms and their pertinence to the problems with which he must contend. Some such norms may give support to the goals of the organization, and others may present difficulties. Superiors should listen to what subordinates have to say and make an effort to understand their conception of a situation. They cannot effectively control or change behavior without an understanding of the factors that may influence behavior. Also important is knowledge about the socio-psychological situation at higher positions in the management hierarchy.

Conflicting Organizational and Personal Goals

A hierarchical system is subject to conflicts about the appropriateness of organizational goals and conflicts between organizational and personal goals. Such conflicts can be resolved through decisions from superiors that can be enforced through the power to impose sanctions. But the power to impose sanctions should not be viewed in absolute terms. Subordinates may also impose "sanctions" through a refusal to cooperate. They may be fired, but they can also quit. Superiors are sometimes forced to adapt organizational goals to the personal goals of subordinates. Barnard's idea that executives should not make decisions that will not be obeyed involves this kind of problem.[6] It may be better to modify a decision than to be

[6] Barnard, op. cit., p. 194.

faced with an open challenge to authority. Such a challenge destroys authority and cannot generally be tolerated. A superior may be forced to fire a subordinate he would rather retain, a situation that can frequently be prevented by taking into consideration the possible reaction of subordinates to a decision. However, the fact that the superior must respond to decisions from higher levels may present difficulties in this respect. The superior is sometimes caught between the proverbial frying pan and the fire. Dire consequences may result if he openly disobeys his superiors, but obeying them may bring about serious difficulties with subordinates. Some might argue that obeying higher superiors is the best way out of the dilemma. They fail to recognize that subordinates can destroy a superior's career by a failure to give him support. This dilemma is generally resolved by adjustments that operate in both directions. As Professor Bakke has written, "the modification of the formal system by the inventiveness and adjustments of the very 'human' people in the organization, in response to personal and social as well as to operational needs, is extensive." [7] Such modifications are made at every level of the management hierarchy. Each superior-subordinate relationship involves a fusion of organizational and personal goals and an adaptation of one to the other. Much of this adaptation occurs with the tacit consent of higher levels, the result of which is a variation between the formally established norms and those that are actually enforced. Superiors may also deliberately distort decisional information from higher levels to compensate for problems at subordinate levels. This mode of adaptation was given comprehensive treatment in Chapter 18.

Some appropriate actions by superiors are highly indirect and may even seem contrary to the best interest of the organization. For example, a superior may recommend that an XYZ typewriter be purchased because a secretary has a preference for that particular brand. This typewriter may be less efficient and more expensive than another as measured by the standards generally used in purchasing, but the decision may better serve the organization than a more "logical" decision through direct and indirect motivational consequences. The superior can often gain more support from subordinates by showing a regard for the things that are important to them. As Professor Homans has noted about the superior, "it is only when he has shown by his actions that he accepts group norms that he can induce the group to adopt his own norms." [8] A superior may even respect group norms that conflict with those of the organization. However, he is sometimes forced to take action that reduces his effectiveness with subordinates as a group or as individuals. For example, he may have to impose penalties upon a subordinate who is an informal group leader or who is well liked by

[7] Bakke, *op. cit.*, p. 61.
[8] Homans, *op. cit.*, p. 426.

fellow subordinates in order to maintain the authority of position even though the offense may not be serious from other points of view.

Leadership: Strategic and Tactical Considerations

The specific action that should be taken in a particular situation cannot be determined without a knowledge of the many factors that are involved. Appropriate action in one situation may not be appropriate in another. The following discussion develops an understanding of some of the strategies and tactics that can be used to enhance authority.

The Use of Specific Sanctions to Enforce and Reinforce Authority

The effectiveness of specific sanctions is related to the degree to which subordinates are satisfied with the totality of benefits accorded by organizational association. The threat of discharge is less effective if many subordinates are on the verge of quitting. It may be more effective if employment in the organization or under a particular superior is highly valued. Specific sanctions are not often required when they are most effective because subordinates are generally less inclined to disobey orders. On the other hand, they may have to be used a great deal when they are least effective because subordinates are less apt to obey. There is a limit to the extent to which specific sanctions can be used to maintain authority. Specific sanctions, if properly used, can help reinforce authority, but they should not be viewed as the primary instrument of authority.

The relationship between authority and specific sanctions is somewhat paradoxical. The use of such sanctions indicates a breakdown of authority. Authority cannot be maintained if sanctions are constantly required. The organization ceases to exist if every subordinate must be discharged for failure to accord authority. Sanctions should not often be required to enforce a superior's orders. The use of severe sanctions, such as discharge or demotion, should be a rare rather than a regular occurrence. However, superiors should not take a completely negative attitude toward such sanctions. Some seem to have the idea that the need to impose sanctions can be avoided by "human relations" techniques. It is sometimes assumed that discharging a subordinate represents a failure on the part of the superior rather than the subordinate. Such a conclusion may be correct in some instances but certainly not in all.

A periodic use of specific sanctions to enforce decisions or reinforce authority may be good strategy on the part of the superior. Poker players who always bluff, traffic police who never make arrests, nations which are not disposed to fight, and professors who do not flunk students tend to become less effective in pursuing their purposes. The examples that are made of the few may have a pronounced socio-psychological impact upon the many. The following story about Frederick the Great, the Prussian military leader, illustrates this idea.[9] While making the rounds of his camp after "lights out," Frederick found a light coming from one of the tents. He entered and saw a Captain Zietern in the act of sealing a letter. The officer fell on his knees and begged to be forgiven. "Take a seat," said Frederick, "and add a few words to what you have already written." Captain Zietern obeyed and wrote as dictated, "To-morrow I die on the scaffold." The next day he was duly executed in the interests of discipline. The penalty may seem rather harsh for the offense involved, but not if it was necessary to maintain the security of the camp from enemy attack. The act of one man could have meant the death of thousands of soldiers. The execution of Captain Zietern also had a meaning beyond his act or fate. The authority of future orders with respect to "lights out" and other matters was undoubtedly reinforced.

A superior may sometimes deliberately seek an example with which to reinforce authority. Otherwise faithful subordinates frequently develop "bad habits," such as staying out too long for coffee, too much tardiness and absenteeism, or simply a lackadaisical attitude with respect to a number of matters. The situation can often be corrected with a little talk by the superior, but some situations may require more extreme measures. Appropriate action may consist of a general warning and a dismissal to make it stick. The superior might simply fire the first man who strays from the straight and narrow. However, this approach may result in the discharge of someone who is vitally needed. Such a consequence cannot and should not always be avoided, but a more selective approach may better serve the organization. One method is to pick a subject the organization can well do without and try to get him to hang himself. The person selected should not be too well liked by other subordinates. A word of warning: the superior must be able to justify his actions on some rational basis. He must not seem arbitrary or unjust to those who remain in the organization.

Two considerations are basic in the use of specific sanctions. One is the attitude of the subordinate or subordinates directly affected by discharge and other disciplinary actions. Another is the manner in which the use of sanctions may influence the behavior of other subordinates. The first consideration is relatively less important when the sanction of discharge is employed. However, the superior should attempt to make a dismissal as

[9] Sir Ian Hamilton, *The Soul and Body of the Army* (New York: George H. Doran Company, 1921), p. 100.

palatable as possible for public relations reasons. A discharged employee can help give the organization "a bad name" and create dissatisfactions among employees with whom he may interact socially. The superior should also recognize that some sanctions are equivalent to discharge. Such sanctions as a demotion or a reprimand may cause a subordinate to take a negative attitude toward the organization. The consequences that a sanction can have upon the future behavior of the subordinate concerned should always be considered. It is sometimes better to discharge or not take any action than to impose a lesser sanction.

Rapid Conditioning Through Sanctions

Superiors may deliberately impose many specific sanctions in an arbitrary fashion to rapidly condition subordinates to accept their decisions. Some aspects of military training illustrate this mode of developing authority. The recruit is conditioned to respond to decisions without question by a sequence of severe sanctions for nonconformity. Sanctions may even be imposed without "cause" with more severe sanctions for those who question the "unfairness" of the situation. The subordinate soon learns that the burdens of disobedience are far greater than the burdens of obedience. He also learns that the superior is "right" even when he is "wrong." The process is relaxed after a period of time partly because sanctions have fulfilled their purpose and partly to take advantage of the rewards implicit in a reduction in disciplinary action. A severe disciplinarian may seem less severe to subordinates than a lenient superior who becomes a little less lenient. However, superiors in business organizations may experience difficulties in using sanctions in this fashion. The majority of subordinates may quit the first time a superior begins to act like a first-sergeant. It is much more difficult to escape the long arms of the military police, and any attempts in this direction may have dire consequences, to say the least. Soldiers do not generally like confinement in a military prison, and they do not have unions to protect their interests. The chaplain is helpful, but he is apt to "give unto Caesar the things that are Caesar's." Yet, in spite of the differences in the ultimate power of the two organizations, superiors in business organizations should not ignore the possibility of using the above approach in a more restrained manner.

The Strategy of the Lenient Superior

Some superiors are more lenient in enforcing decisions and organizational policies than others.[10] A failure to enforce strict discipline may

[10] Peter M. Blau, *Bureaucracy in Modern Society* (New York: Random House, 1956), pp. 70–74.

result from psychological propensities that make the superior reluctant or unable to impose his will on others. The superior who has a psychological need "to be liked" may attempt to reap this reward by catering to subordinates. He may use his position and the power it involves to supplement inadequacies in personality and social abilities. Subordinates are sometimes inclined to take advantage of the situation and use the superior to gain unwarrantable personal ends. However, in spite of this limitation, the lenient superior may be a more effective leader than a severe disciplinarian. As Professor Blau points out, "leniency in supervision is a potent strategy, consciously or unconsciously employed, for establishing authority over subordinates, and this is why the liberal supervisor is particularly effective." [11]

The lenient superior goes along with many minor and some major infractions of official organizational policies. The fact that such policies can be enforced gives the superior a basis for imposing sanctions that would not otherwise exist. He can at any time turn to more rigorous enforcement, which subordinates are not apt to welcome. Such a relationship tends to produce a sense of obligation to the superior for the "favors" he has accorded. For example, if the superior looks the other way when Jones arrives at work an hour late, Jones is inclined to return the favor by doing something for the superior. Respecting the norms of the group tends to bring about a similar kind of relationship.[12] The fact that the superior does not listen to a "squealer" shows the group that he respects their norm against such behavior. The superior builds up a reserve of good will with individuals and the group which can be used to good advantage when he really needs support. Subordinates will tend to go out of their way to show their appreciation for the consideration shown them. They will also tend to protect the superior against adverse action by higher management. Thus, they may put in extra effort to get a job done to make their superior look good to his superiors. They attempt to maintain what to them is a satisfactory personal relationship.

A strategy of leniency is limited by the necessity for the superior to conform to substantive and procedural standards imposed and enforced by his superiors. The superior also has the responsibility of making decisions in the area delegated to him. It should not be assumed that the lenient superior forsakes his responsibilities to the organization. Leniency becomes lunacy if it is carried to an extreme or practiced without purpose. The strategy of leniency is to exchange one set of values for another. The superior must use the good will he creates to serve the ends of the organization. However, he should not view the problem as one of equal exchange or

[11] *Ibid.*, p. 71.
[12] Homans, *op. cit.*, pp. 426–428.

seem to be manipulating in a deliberate fashion. The fine art of leadership is to manipulate subordinates without their knowing it; in most instances an effective leader is not himself aware that he is engaged in this sort of game. Human beings tend unconsciously to justify or rationalize their actions through moral precepts with which they can live.

Somewhat related to the strategy of leniency is the idea of shifting the blame for unpopular responsibilities and rewards to the "system" or higher superiors. Subordinates may be less inclined to take a negative attitude toward the superior if they can vent their aggression upon someone or something else.[13] They may even develop a closer bond with the superior in their "fight" with a common "enemy." However, this approach, like that of leniency, is limited by restraints imposed by organizational responsibilities. The superior cannot entirely escape the fact that he represents the organization.

The Enigma of Leadership

Superiors should not expect to find any sort of perfect solution to the leadership and authority problems. They must contend with a complex interrelationship of socio-psychological factors that do not remain constant over time. As Barnard has pointed out, leadership may in practice mean an almost infinite number of possible combinations of variables.[14] It involves skills that cannot be neatly categorized into a logical pattern for purposes of education and training. Many leaders are highly effective or ineffective for reasons they and others do not fully understand. They seem to violate some of the intellectually derived precepts of leadership for the same reason that many aspects of physical phenomena do not fit the theories of the physicist.

There is a constant demand from executives, students, and others for definite answers. This demand has been instrumental in bringing forth studies that provided specific techniques of leadership. Some such studies probably caused Barnard to write that "leadership has been subject to an extraordinary amount of dogmatically stated nonsense." [15] The purpose of the preceding discussion was to promote an understanding of the leadership problem and provide an approach to leadership. To paraphrase Professor Homans, the leader does not need a definite set of rules but a method of analyzing the organizational situation in which he must act.[16] There are

[13] Blau, *op. cit.*, pp. 77–78.
[14] Chester I. Barnard, *Organization and Management* (Cambridge: Harvard University Press, 1952), p. 84.
[15] *Ibid.*, p. 80.
[16] Homans, *op. cit.*, p. 424.

many unanswered problems which have yet to be given scientific solution. But there may be some merit in knowing that knowledge is far from complete. The ignorant man who knows it all probably causes more damage than the intelligent man who knows so little.

Leadership Through Laws and Justice

An important principle of American and British government is the segregation of legislative, executive, and judicial powers. To what extent have these functions been segregated in business organizations? Mooney and Reiley had the following to say about the situation in the early 1930's.

Business executives are about the only present-day counterparts of the governor-judges of antiquity. Without intending any sinister implication, they may all be classed as modern Pontius Pilates, which means that they may initiate, judge, and then execute their own sentences.[17]

Mooney and Reiley believed that justice would be enhanced by separate "industrial courts" and predicted that they would eventually be established. However, they also warned that such courts should be organized "on some basis that will not interfere with the legitimate responsibilities of the executive." [18] Urwick, the British management philosopher, has recommended that a more definite distinction be made in business organizations between policy-making (legislation) and execution.[19] The legislative, executive, and judicial functions were also differentiated in Taylor's shop management plan.[20]

Separation of Powers Philosophy

The legislative, executive, and judicial functions can only be completely segregated by the appointment of three persons to each managerial position in the manner of Taylor's functional foremanship. One person would be assigned the task of legislating or making planning decisions; another, the functions of communicating orders, supervising the work of subordinate

[17] James D. Mooney and Alan C. Reiley, *Onward Industry!* (New York: Harper & Brothers Publishers, 1931), pp. 204–205.
[18] *Ibid.,* p. 206.
[19] L. Urwick, *The Load on Top Management—Can It Be Reduced?* (London: Urwick, Orr, & Partners Ltd., 1954), pp. 19–20.
[20] Frederick W. Taylor, *Shop Management* (New York: Harper & Brothers Publishers, 1919), p. 104.

personnel, and evaluating performance; still another, the function of judging cases involving a violation of the norms established through planning. Such segregation might result in improvements in performance through the advantages of specialization, but any gains made in this respect would undoubtedly be offset by difficulties resulting from a lack of unity of command. The political philosophy of segregation is more an expression of a fear of leadership than a means to enhance leadership. Some conflicts among the three branches of the United States government indicate that segregation does not always promote effective leadership. A lack of leadership can be hazardous during periods of national and international upheaval. However, too much concentration of political power may be even more hazardous.

Functional Segregation in Business Organizations

Although business and other organizations have generally solved the problem in an opposite direction, some degree of segregation has occurred in recent decades. The grievance procedure developed through collective bargaining gives recognition to the idea of judicial segregation. Some of the functions performed by personnel departments, such as the development of personnel rating systems, are also important in this respect. Explicit recognition is given in some organizations to the distinction between policy making and execution. For example, the Du Pont Executive Committee functions much like the Congress. The policies formulated by such committees are executed by executives at the operating level. However, it should not be assumed that policy making is restricted to the top level or that the judicial function has been completely taken over by personnel departments or grievance committees. Every executive from the top to the bottom of the hierarchy performs legislative, executive, and judicial functions in some combination. Lower levels are concerned less with legislation and more with execution than higher levels. Personnel executives spend a larger proportion of their time with judicial problems than some other executives.

The performance of legislative, executive, and judicial functions by the same person does not violate any fundamantal precepts of effective managerial organization. Executives should recognize the differences in the responsibilities involved and their importance in the managerial process. The ideas that follow should not be construed as a recommendation that business and other organizations adopt the philosophy of democratic government. Executives are not elected by subordinates, and they cannot and should not rule only to serve the interests of subordinates. The idea of "government by law" is important in business organizations but not necessarily for the reasons of the political philosopher.

Rule Through Law

How does decision making differ from legislating? They are the same, and yet there is a difference. Authoritative written and oral messages establish behavioral norms and have the essential properties of laws. The act of translating a decision into written form gives it an additional quality. It brings into being an impersonal instrument that may have important behavioral consequences. It represents the first step in the process of making a decision into a law. There is another quality that makes an authoritative written message a "law" rather than an ordinary norm. Laws seem generally to have an existence apart from the person or persons who initiated them. In other words, they cannot or are not attributed to the person of a particular superior.

An organizational system of law does not eliminate the need for direct oral and written messages from superiors to subordinates. Laws are ultimately implemented through the personal actions of the superior, but governing through laws may enhance subordinate acceptance of organizational decisions. Subordinates are given an additional basis for rationalizing the authority relationship. Obeying a superior becomes partly a matter of obeying a law rather than a person. Professor Whyte noted in his study of the restaurant industry that the relations between waitresses and kitchen personnel were influenced by the manner in which orders were transmitted.[21] Less conflict seemed to occur in several instances when waitresses used written orders. Higher status kitchen personnel were not required to respond directly and personally to lower status waitresses. The military idea that a soldier "salutes the uniform" rather than the person has a similar implication. Governing through law may enhance authority by virtue of the same logic.

The Judicial Process

A system of law may also give or at least seem to give a more objective quality to the control or judicial process. A higher degree of uniformity in the dispensation of "justice" tends to result. The superior is forced to view the situation from an organizational perspective. Purely personal factors may still enter the process, but they tend to be restrained in some degree. At the same time, subordinates seem generally inclined to view judgments based on law as more objective. What actually involves personal judgments

[21] William Foote Whyte, *Human Relations in the Restaurant Industry* (New York: McGraw-Hill Book Company, Inc., 1948), pp. 68–74.

by superiors is given an objective quality through instruments that seem to exist apart from superiors.

Business organizations should recognize the advantages that might be gained by a formal recognition of the legislative process. A formal distinction between legislating and decision making and between laws and other norms may have important motivational consequences. The impression that the superior governs through laws may significantly affect the subordinate's conception of the managerial process. Also important in this respect is the establishment of formal procedures for exercising the control or judicial function. Military and ecclesiastical courts are composed of executive officials, but, when they sit as courts, they become judges.[22] A distinction is also made between legislative and executive procedures and judicial procedures. Superiors need not wear the black robes of the judge, but they should seem to have a different quality when they make judgments. They should recognize that judging is not the same as legislating and executing the law. The judicial procedures of Anglo-American law have developed through a long evolutionary process. They do not always produce justice, and they sometimes give support to injustice. Nevertheless, they represent a high expression of man's efforts toward social justice and have been defended even to the death. Although the substantive content of justice may differ, the procedural concepts of justice developed by democratic society are applicable to judicial problems in business and other organizations. They represent a systematic and organized approach to the administration of justice and endow justice with an objective quality. They represent an important instrument of authority and cooperation to the extent that they give subordinates a more favorable conception of organizational justice.

[22] Mooney and Reiley, *op. cit.*, p. 204.

SELECTED REFERENCES

Chester I. Barnard, *Organization and Management,* Chap. 4. Cambridge: Harvard University Press, 1952.

J. D. Batten, *Tough-Minded Management.* New York: American Management Association, 1963.

John R. Beishline, *Military Management for National Defense,* Chap. 15. Englewood Cliffs, N.J.: Prentice-Hall, Inc., 1950.

Warren G. Bennis and Edgar H. Schein (editors) in collaboration with Caroline McGregor, *Leadership and Motivation: Essays of Douglas McGregor.* Cambridge: The M.I.T. Press, 1966.

Peter M. Blau, *Bureaucracy in Modern Society,* Chap. 4. New York: Random House, 1956.

C. T. Hardwick and B. F. Landuyt, *Administrative Strategy and Decision-Making,* 2nd ed., Chap. 2. Cincinnati: South-Western Publishing Co., 1966.

I. L. Heckmann and S. G. Huneryager, *Human Relations in Management,* 2nd ed., Part III. Cincinnati: South-Western Publishing Co., 1967.

Richard M. Hodgetts, "Leadership Techniques in the Project Organization," *Academy of Management Journal,* Vol. 11, No. 2, pp. 211–219 (June 1968).

George C. Homans, *The Human Group,* Chap. 16. New York: Harcourt, Brace and Company, Inc., 1950.

Alexander H. Leighton, *The Governing of Men.* Princeton, N.J.: Princeton University Press, 1946.

Norman R. F. Maier and John J. Hayes, *Creative Management.* New York: John Wiley and Sons, Inc., 1962.

Floyd C. Mann and James K. Dent, "The Supervisor: Member of Two Organizational Families," *Harvard Business Review,* Vol. 32, No. 6, pp. 103–112 (November–December 1954).

Alfred J. Marrow, David G. Bowers, and Stanley E. Seashore, *Management by Participation.* New York: Harper & Row, 1967.

Carroll L. Shartle, *Executive Performance and Leadership,* Chap. 5. Englewood Cliffs, N.J.: Prentice-Hall, Inc., 1956.

Robert Tannenbaum, Irving R. Weschler, and Fred Massarik, *Leadership and Organization: A Behavioral Science Approach,* Parts 1 and 2. New York: McGraw-Hill Book Company, Inc., 1961.

William Foote Whyte, *Human Relations in the Restaurant Industry,* Part IV. New York: McGraw-Hill Book Company, Inc., 1948.

Abraham Zaleznik, "The Human Dilemmas of Leadership," *Harvard Business Review,* Vol. 41, No. 4, pp. 49–55 (July–August 1963).

chapter 24

THE RESPONSIBILITY OF MANAGEMENT

To whom is management responsible? Is management primarily responsible to the stockholder, or should it assume a broader responsibility to other interest groups? Owen D. Young in an address given many years ago recognized the need for a concept of management responsibility.

If you will pardon me for being personal, it makes a great difference in my attitude toward my job as an executive officer of the General Electric Company whether I am a trustee of the institution or an attorney for the investor. If I am a trustee, who are the beneficiaries of the trust? To whom do I owe obligations? [1]

The first section of this chapter is concerned with legal, economic, and other conceptions of managerial responsibility. It is followed by a consideration of strategies for handling interest group problems. A final section indicates the importance of conflicting moral codes in developing a concept of managerial responsibility.

Conceptions of Managerial Responsibility

The Legal Theory of Responsibility

Under corporation law, management is required to manage in the best interests of the stockholder. This narrow conception of management respon-

[1] Quoted by E. M. Dodd, "For Whom Are Corporate Managers Trustees?" *Harvard Law Review*, Vol. 45, No. 7, May 1932, p. 1154.

605

sibility has not been unchallenged. Those opposing this view advance the idea that management should also assume responsibility to the public, the consumer, labor, and other groups.[2] A difficulty with this argument is that of legally enforcing the broader responsibility. The fear of those who oppose an abandonment of the theory of sole legal responsibility to the stockholders is that it will eliminate the only existing legal means for enforcing responsibility.[3] To expand the theory to include responsibility to other groups presents the danger of eliminating legal responsibility until a practical scheme of enforcement can be devised.

Is the assumption of a broader organizational and social responsibility compatible with the legal theory of management responsibility? One answer to this question is that the acceptance of a broader responsibility is merely an enlightened view of the interests of the stockholder. Another view is that the legal responsibility to the stockholder does not exclude the assumption of a responsibility to other groups and to the common enterprise. What is the purpose of the legal responsibility theory? It is designed to protect the stockholder's property from an irresponsible management that might seek to divert that property into its own pockets or the pockets of some other group. Its purpose is to prevent irresponsibility; it was not formulated to impede the development of a more constructive and comprehensive philosophy of management responsibility. Something more is involved in the development of such a philosophy than the abstract precepts of the law. The responsibility rests ultimately in business leadership itself. The law is essentially conservative; at the same time, it is not immune to the dynamic impact of social, economic, and political theories. The nature of the legal system dictates a search for a traditional precept of authority to meet the exigencies of change.

Economic Theory and Managerial Responsibility

In the theory developed by the classical economists, the problem of managerial responsibility is "solved" by product and resource markets which are assumed to be competitive. The individual firm plays a passive role in the determination of market values because it does not produce or purchase a large enough quantity to influence the market. The discretion of the entrepreneur or manager is limited by the requirements of the system.

[2] *Ibid.*, pp. 1145–1163.
[3] A. A. Berle, Jr., "For Whom Corporate Managers Are Trustees: A Note," *Harvard Law Review*, Vol. 45, No. 8, June 1932, pp. 1365–1372. Berle has written more recently that the argument has been settled, at least for the time being, in favor of the broader approach to responsibility. *The 20th Century Capitalist Revolution* (New York: Harcourt, Brace and Company, Inc., 1954), p. 169.

Competition forces productive efficiency and adaptation to the values of the market. The planning problem is solved by a series of adjustments or "decisions" which are essentially mathematical in nature. The symmetry and simplicity of classical economic theory should not delude students of management into thinking it had nothing to say about the problem of managerial responsibility. The theory was philosophically oriented toward the consumer even though other participants in the production process were not actually ignored. The primary purpose of the firm and of the economic system in which it plays a part was assumed to be the satisfaction of consumer wants. Every other aspect of the process was viewed as a means to this ultimate end.

During the last two decades, economists have all but destroyed the classical theory by constructing more realistic theories. Modern economic theories assume that an individual firm may be large enough to modify markets through its production and purchase programs. For example, a firm that produces 40 per cent of the supply in a market has some degree of monopoly control in that market. The new theories also recognize that firms may influence consumer wants through advertising and other means. Presumably they can induce consumers to buy products or services they do not "really" need or would not buy if they were not so influenced. The entrepreneur of the classical theory had no real decisional discretion, but in the new theories he has the power to modify market forces. In spite of such changes in the theory, the main stream of economic thought has not repudiated the idea that the primary purpose of economic activity is the satisfaction of consumer wants. The consumer is still the kingpin in the system even though the theory now assumes that this ideal is not automatically achieved. The managerial theory developed by Barnard, Simon, and others views the consumer in a somewhat different light. A distinction is made between the objectives of the organization and the personal aims of customers, suppliers, stockholders, creditors and others. The objectives of the organization are assumed to be the objectives of all of the participants in the cooperative process. However, as Professor Simon has noted, "the objectives of the customer are very closely, and rather directly, related to the *objectives* of the organization. . . ." [4] This conception is essentially in accord with the ideals of the theory developed by economists.

Laboristic Philosophy and Managerial Responsibility

The proponents of unionism and collective bargaining generally assume that the traditional market does not give the worker his proper share in the

[4] Herbert A. Simon, *Administrative Behavior,* 2nd ed. (New York: The Macmillan Company, 1958), p. 18.

distribution of income.[5] They contend that the employer has too much power under the usual state of economic affairs. A major consideration of the Congress in passing labor legislation favorable to union organization was that there existed an unfavorable balance of power between property and labor. Unionism and collective bargaining do not necessarily conflict with the conceptions of managerial responsibility developed in corporation law and economic theory. However, they present a potential area of conflict both in a philosophical and a practical sense. Powerful labor unions can make inroads into the income that might otherwise be paid to the stockholder. The unorganized stockholder seems to have become somewhat of an "underdog" in the total scheme of things.[6] The consumer may also have suffered some of the fate ascribed to the stockholder. Urwick has drawn the following picture of the situation.

> Over the last century, man has developed a complex of organisational forms for representing his interests as a producer, while his interests as a consumer have remained relatively unorganised save in so far as they could be protected by government or by the action of business managers. . . . The business manager . . . has found himself a trustee for the interests of man as a consumer under an increasing fire of criticism from the organisations designed to protect man's interests as a producer.[7]

A highly productive industrial system may well be able to afford some shift from the traditional emphasis on consumption. But, too much "consumption on the job" by a portion of the total population (unionized workers or others) may significantly affect the welfare of those who are not organized for power.

Management Responsibility: A Broader View

Many executives contend that management should assume responsibility to the organization and to all of the interest groups. This conception of management responsibility was well expressed by Frank Abrams, former chairman of the board of Standard Oil Company (New Jersey).

> We have a stewardship in a company like Jersey Standard and a personal pride. We would like to leave the company in a sounder and more assured position than when we took it over. We are not looking to the company just to support us; we want to make it healthy for future generations and for the employees

---

[5] This idea is usually stated in terms of the short run rather than the long run.

[6] J. A. Livingston has presented this thesis in *The American Stockholder* (Philadelphia: J. B. Lippincott Company, 1958).

[7] L. Urwick, *The Load on Top Management—Can It Be Reduced?* (London: Urwick, Orr, & Partners Ltd., 1954), pp. 7–8.

that will come along. We like to feel that it is a good place for people to work. We have equal responsibilities to other groups: stockholders, customers, and the public generally, including government. What is the proper balance for the claims of these different sections? What part of income should go to stockholders? What part to employees? What part to the customer in lower prices and improved quality? Keeping the proper balance in these things is one of the most important things that boards of directors have to consider. The corporation is a kind of team; it is a great moral drive of many persons.[8]

This statement and others like it indicate that many executives do not feel that their primary obligation is to serve the interests of the stockholder.[9] The customer has also been placed in a position of equality with employees, stockholders, the community, and other interests. Workers are not neglected, which represents some kind of challenge to the philosophical position of unions. Such conceptions of managerial responsibility represent a major shift in the philosophy of management. They reflect an historical evolution toward management by professionals who are psychologically oriented toward the organization as a cooperative system. The organization is viewed as something apart from the personal motives of its constituents. The problem of distributing the product of the cooperative process to the interest groups becomes less concerned with social ideology and more with organizational efficiency.

This conception of management responsibility means that management should oppose the efforts of any of the interest groups to obtain rewards that reduce the efficiency of the cooperative action. The interests of the consumer might be best served by lower prices, but a price reduction at the expense of stockholders or employees cannot be justified if the consequence is reduced efficiency. This logic also dictates a lower level of profits if higher wages would result in more successful cooperation. The same standard applies to management's part in collective bargaining. Union demands should be opposed or approved in terms of management's responsibility to the organization. To contend that the interests of the stockholder or the consumer will be violated by consenting to a union demand is a proper argument only to the extent that such interests are related to the welfare of the organization. Such a norm of responsibility means that an individual who owns considerable stock in the corporation in which he also holds an executive position may find himself in a dilemma. He may have to

[8] Quoted by Herrymon Maurer in "Boards of Directors," *Fortune*, Vol. 41, No. 5, May 1950, p. 107.

[9] Company creeds reflect a philosophy similar to that of Frank Abrams. Some examples are found in: Stewart Thompson, *Management Creeds and Philosophies, Research Study, No. 32* (New York: American Management Association, Inc., 1958), pp. 97–127.

subordinate his interest as a stockholder to his professional interests. But, if such a situation presents too much of a problem, the logical consequence of accepting sole responsibility to the stockholder group presents an even greater difficulty. If management limits its responsibility in this manner, it cannot contend that it has a greater right to manage than a labor leader. It is then, like the labor leader, simply a spokesman for an interest group. Management's status differs from that of an interest group representative only if it assumes a primary responsibility to the organization.

What happens to the welfare of society if the organization becomes the focal point of management responsibility? The classical economic theory assumed that organizational and social welfare were the same problems. The executive simply adapted to the values given by product and resource markets to serve the welfare of society through competition. The newer economic theories and the actual state of affairs endow the executive with a range of discretionary power that can presumably be used to serve the interests of the organization at the expense of society. What should management do when it is faced with a conflict between the interests of the society and the organization? Violations of the law are not involved in this question. Some people have contended that the business manager should place his duty to society above his duty to his company and above his private interest.[10] Such a conception of responsibility is difficult to translate into operational terms. There is no unified theory of social welfare to determine what kind of decision will best serve the society. The lack of such a theory gives considerable license for irresponsibility because there are no norms to indicate the nature of responsible behavior. Much of the difficulty is removed by making management primarily responsible to the organization. Such a conception pinpoints responsibility and provides a focal point for control.

The classical economic theory in which organizational and social welfare were not in conflict has been repudiated by many persons. Economists should be lauded for having developed more realistic theories to help explain economic phenomena. They should also be made to write a thousand production functions for having destroyed a theory that performed a vital ideological function.[11] The classical theory did not portray the actual state of affairs in the business world even when it was generally accepted as the gospel. But, as Professor Mason has written:

[10] For example: Robert W. Austin, "Code of Conduct for Executives," *Harvard Business Review,* Vol. 39, No. 5, September–October 1961, p. 60.

[11] Edward S. Mason, "The Apologetics of 'Managerialism,'" *Journal of Business,* Vol. 31, No. 1, January 1958, pp. 1–11. Also, Carl Kaysen, "The Social Significance of the Modern Corporation," *American Economic Review,* Vol. 47, No. 2, May 1957, pp. 311–319.

... for over a century, the philosophy was accepted by political, business, and moral leaders as gospel and effectively justified the ways of man to God. It cannot be too strongly emphasized that the growth of nineteenth-century capitalism depended largely on the general acceptance of a reasoned justification of the system on moral as well as political and economic grounds.[12]

It is doubtful that anyone will soon develop another such orderly picture of the economic process, for the same reason that the physicist will not soon recreate the symmetry of the Newtonian system. The realities of the universe and the economic world are shrouded with probabilistic characteristics that defy man's efforts to theorize a more orderly scheme.

It should not be assumed that the interests of the organization and those of the society are always in conflict. They tend to be compatible in the long run although the mechanism by which this is brought about is highly illusive. The society is not in danger of being destroyed by the organizations that live in its domain. The management of today seems generally less inclined than some of its forebears to profit at the expense of society. Organizations may modify markets and other aspects of their environment, but they would not long survive if they failed to adapt to important economic, political, and social forces. The nature of this process and its relationship to the objectives of organizations were detailed in Part IV of this book. Management cannot ignore the interests of consumers, stockholders, employees, creditors, suppliers, and society. Its discretionary powers are by no means absolute. It is forced to adapt to environmental forces as presently constructed, but it is also threatened by potential politically imposed restrictions if discretion is used without wisdom.

The Interest Groups: Management Strategies

Previous chapters have given a great deal of attention to the problem of interest groups. Interest group representation on boards of directors and other committees was considered in Chapters 9 and 10. The chapters concerned with environmental factors and dynamic planning (Chapters 14, 15, and 16) indicated the manner in which labor, creditors, customers, suppliers, and government influence organizational objectives. This section gives brief attention to some of the strategies that may be appropriate in dealing with the major interest groups. No significance is intended by the order in which they are considered.

[12] Mason, *op. cit.,* p. 6. Courtesy of University of Chicago Press. Copyright 1958 by the University of Chicago.

The Stockholders

The number of stockholders in a corporation may range from a few to well over a million. The interests of majority and large minority stockholders are generally well protected through either direct participation in the management or the real power to intervene if necessary. The millions of small stockholders who collectively own a large percentage of the total investment in corporate enterprises are in a much less favorable position in this respect. Such stockholders are generally content to collect dividends and let management do the managing. They take an active interest in what management is doing only if their dividends or assets begin to dwindle. In spite of the rights afforded by the law, the actual power of the small stockholder to protect himself from managerial actions detrimental to his interests is limited. Some managements may be inclined to take advantage of the situation, but such a policy tends in the long run to be contrary to the best interests of the organization. However, it should not be assumed that the best of intentions will keep every stockholder happy. The interests of different stockholders are not the same, and some stockholders may prefer a policy not preferred by others. Thus, stockholders who want income in the short run may not like a policy of plowing back a large part of earnings, but the interests of stockholders who think in terms of future equity and income prospects might be enhanced by such a policy.

Management should actively pursue a policy of promoting good relations with stockholders. Stockholders can play an important part in maintaining the corporation aside from the fact that they are willing to own its equity capital. They are frequently avid customers of the products or services produced by the organizations in which they hold stock. This idea is evidenced in the following comment by a shareholder at the Standard Oil Company (New Jersey) annual meeting: "I go ten miles with only one gallon of gas, to look for the Esso sign." [13] A shareholder may also influence his friends and acquaintances to buy and boost the company's product line. The part the stockholder may play in the area of public relations and in the political realm should not be neglected. Management sometimes laments the advantages that unions may derive from the political activities of their members without recognizing that they may also gain important support from thousands of stockholders. The idea is not that management should "organize" stockholders for political action but that a satisfied stockholder can be helpful in the precincts. Good stockholder

---

[13] Report on the 76th Annual Meeting of Stockholders, Standard Oil Company (New Jersey), May 28, 1958, p. 17.

relations may also facilitate the acquisition of additional financial resources that might be required at some future date. Present stockholders are themselves potential purchasers of new issues of securities and their past experience with a corporation is an important factor in bringing others into the fold.

Emphasis should also be given to the consequences that can result from a failure to uphold the interests of stockholders. The small stockholder is sometimes a strategic factor in a proxy battle organized to unseat management. Such battles may be launched by opportunists who are primarily motivated by personal power and financial gain. They may also result from dissatisfaction with the performance of management on the part of a powerful faction, such as a large minority stockholder. An inefficient management deserves to be defeated and unseated, but proxy battles do not always mean victory for the righteous. A lack of earnings or dividends cannot always be attributed to performance failures on the part of management. General and particular economic conditions sometimes make the best of managers look like the worst. Furthermore, stockholders may be induced to grant proxies on the basis of promises that never materialize. A history of good stockholder relations reduces the potency of such promises and represents an important barrier to opportunists who seek only personal aggrandizement. Management should also take into consideration the possibility of government intervention to protect stockholder interests. A large number of dissatisfied stockholders provides fertile ground for an ambitious politician.

The stockholder has the right to personally participate in the election of the board of directors. Imagine, a meeting of 300,000 or 1,000,000 shareholders! Fortunately, most stockholders are not inclined to sojourn to a distant city to meet other members of their species. And some corporations are highly pleased that they do not attend and make no effort to reduce the rate of absenteeism. The stockholder gets the dividend and the management the proxy, and little happens in between. However, recent years have witnessed a trend toward a more positive approach to stockholder relations.[14] Stockholders are invited to the annual meetings and are given a great deal of consideration if they do attend. The large majority who stay at home are remembered through letters from executives and publications informing them about company policy, products, profit, and potential. Every effort is made to make them feel they are important to and a member of the organization. But management should not assume that the techniques of Madison Avenue can really put a silver lining on what are really dark clouds. No amount of advertising copy can hide the fact that the postman failed to deliver a dividend check or that values have declined

[14] An account of some trends and techniques, Livingston, *op. cit.,* pp. 100–118.

on the Exchange. People generally respond well to the hard facts if they are honestly presented, and they may even forgive an honest error in judgment.

The Employees

The rise of powerful labor unions can be partly attributed to past failures by management to properly represent the interests of employees. Union organizers generally consider good employee relations as an important obstacle to their goals. However, no amount of speculation about what might have happened under other conditions will eliminate unions and collective bargaining as forces with which management must contend. It was emphasized in Chapter 15 that management should take a positive approach in negotiating with unions. But "a positive approach" does not mean cutting one's own throat to spite the union. Management should remember that union members are also company employees and that harsh measures may show up in employee and community relations for many years. There is no point in unnecessarily antagonizing company employees. Executives should negotiate forcefully and oppose demands they cannot accept, but they should not neglect employee relations even during a long strike. They should also recognize that union leaders may be helpful in advancing the company program. Management-union cooperation on many matters is possible under some circumstances and can bring important rewards.[15] Such cooperation has been practiced in such problem areas as accident prevention, labor turnover, job evaluation, methods improvement, and technological change.

Management should not neglect its responsibilities to unorganized factory and office workers. Unions will eventually fill the gap if management fails to act. Management must make employees feel that it is genuinely interested in their welfare and views. A perfunctory or a paternalistic approach to employee relations is not adequate. Furthermore, management should not assume that the loyalty of the employee can be bought by a give-away program. Employees want a "fair" wage and other benefits, but they also want to retain their self-respect.

Customers

Customers play a vital part in maintaining business and industrial organizations. Barnard includes customers in his scheme of organization and places them on a par with employees, stockholders, creditors, and sup-

---

[15] Ernest Dale, *Greater Productivity Through Labor-Management Cooperation,* Research Report, No. 14 (New York: American Management Association, 1949).

pliers.[16] Whyte has given emphasis to the manner in which customers may influence human relations within an organization.[17] Something more is involved in defining the term "customer" than the act of buying a company's products or services. A customer may be broadly defined as a person who has a favorable impression of a company and its products or services. A person may be categorized as a customer even though he has not committed the act of buying. Someone who owns a company product or has used its services may not properly be called a customer if he now has a negative attitude toward the company. Thus, a customer is as much a potential as an actual purchaser. He has a cooperative attitude toward the company and its products or services and represents an important company asset generally called "good will." The value of good will is frequently far greater than the evaluation given in the accounting records.

A variety of techniques is used to induce people to become a company's customers. Advertising and sales promotion programs, the use of trade names, price policies, product innovation, quality control, credit purchase plans, and customer servicing represent some of the more obvious techniques. The problem should be viewed in terms of a total approach that involves a combination of many techniques. People tend to develop an image of a company and its products or services that may be influenced by many direct and indirect ways. The techniques noted above are some of the more direct approaches to the problem, but management should also recognize the importance of actions not directly oriented toward customer relations. Thus, a speech on world affairs by the company president, the conduct of executives during a labor dispute, and participation or lack of participation in community affairs can significantly influence the situation.

The customer becomes an important variable in the human relationships that make up an organization. Whyte has noted, "when workers and customers meet, in the service industries, that relationship adds a new dimension to the pattern of human relations in industry." [18] Customers in banks, retail stores, restaurants, night clubs, barber shops, and many other types of enterprises come into direct face-to-face contact with employees. Planning and controlling the behavior of the customer frequently becomes an important area of management action. Customers are "trained" to accept specific behavior patterns in the manner of employees. For example, the customers of a bank are taught the accepted procedures for making out

---

[16] Chester I. Barnard, *Organization and Management* (Cambridge: Harvard University Press, 1952), pp. 111–133.

[17] William Foote Whyte, *Human Relations in the Restaurant Industry* (New York: McGraw-Hill Book Company, 1948), and *Industry and Society* (New York: McGraw-Hill Book Company, 1946), pp. 123–147.

[18] *Ibid.*, p. 123.

deposit slips, endorsing checks, and packaging small change. Restaurant patrons may be directed to a specific table by a hostess, are restricted by menus in what they can order, and may even be asked to leave if they insult the waitress. Customers in self-service laundries, grocery stores, automats, and drugstores become almost literally company employees. Many of the techniques that pertain to the supervision of employees apply with equal validity to customers.

The Management

The people who make up the management of an organization are themselves an important interest group. They will contribute managerial work only if their personal goals are satisfied. Their personal goals are in many respects similar to those of other participants in the cooperative process. Salary, status, and social satisfaction are important variables in molding executive behavior. However, the personal goals of executives seem generally to be more closely related to organizational or departmental goals than those of employees. In other words, the success achieved by the organization is a direct source of personal satisfaction. Higher levels of the hierarchy are probably more influenced by this consideration than lower levels. First-line supervisors are frequently inclined toward the attitudes of employees, particularly if they have been recruited from the ranks. University-educated managerial personnel tend to identify themselves with higher management and may play the part of an "organization man" even though they occupy a low position in the hierarchy.

The salaries and other compensation of lower levels of management are determined by higher levels subject to market and other forces. But who determines the compensation of the top levels of the hierarchy? To what extent can top executives simply set their own compensation without restraints from the outside? The degree of discretion that may be exercised in this respect varies. Top executive compensation is directly determined or influenced by large stockholders and financial interests in some corporations. Other direct and indirect restraints may be imposed by the government, the public, and the interest groups. The fact that information about top executive compensation is available for scrutiny by the public, labor unions, creditors, and other groups influences the situation. Thus, company public relations may suffer if executives put too much of a dent in company revenues. Labor leaders sometimes seek political and other advantages by loudly acclaiming the "unfairness" of executive compensation. They may also attempt to justify union demands upon the company by citing the privileges accorded the executive group.

Salaries and bonuses paid to top executives range from less than

$50,000 to more than $500,000 a year.[19] The amount of compensation differs considerably from industry to industry, and significant shifts may occur in the salaries paid to particular executives from year to year. However, the story is not complete without a consideration of the manner in which modes of compensation may affect the after-tax rewards of executive work. Deferred income plans represent an important approach to the problem of taxes. Such plans extend the time period during which an executive's salary is paid, thereby reducing the rate of tax paid on the last increment of income. It is obviously better for tax purposes to be paid $100,000 per year for five years than the total amount of $500,000 in any one year. Income may be deferred through retirement and pension plans, contracts to act as consultants after retirement, and in various other ways. Stock options may also be used to increase executive compensation and reduce the tax burden. Such options give executives the privilege of buying a given number of shares of company stock at stated values. Additional compensation results if the stipulated purchase price is below the price in the market. The taxes that may ultimately have to be paid on such compensation are affected by lower capital gains rates.

How much should executives be paid? When does the compensation paid an executive exceed a "reasonable" level? Such questions are almost impossible to answer objectively. The market for top executives does not provide much insight into the matter. Companies do make offers to executives in other companies, and executives may suggest the amount necessary to acquire them. But the result is more in the nature of an individual bargain than a prevailing market rate. The existing pattern of salaries in an industry or a company may play an important part in determining particular rates of compensation. However, what standards can be used to support the validity of existing salary levels? The problem is complicated by the idea that some executives have a monopoly on particular kinds of executive ability, much like outstanding people in other fields. There are many good composers and baseball players, but there is only one Bach and one Babe Ruth.

Some people contend that top executives make too much money because their salaries may be higher than that of the President of the United States or an outstanding physician or physicist. At the same time, executive compensation may seem low when compared with the salaries paid to some of the "talent" that appears on the television screen. The college professor laments the high salary of the football coach, the farmer frowns upon the wages of skilled labor, the retail clerk covets the income of the bricklayer, and women think they deserve as much as men. The views of one person

[19] The salaries and bonuses paid to top executives of corporations in various industries during 1967 are reported in *Business Week*, June 1, 1968, pp. 56–78.

on the appropriate rewards for various kinds of work may differ radically from those of another. The problem is solved through organized market systems that express the values of society relative to such matters and through a balancing of a diversity of social, economic, and political forces, which push and pull in various directions.

The lack of objective standards for determining the proper compensation for top executives does not preclude any standards whatsoever. Executives should give thought to the matter and attempt to develop standards that satisfy both introspection and inspection. Such standards should reflect their responsibility to the organization and to the other interest groups; they should take into consideration the sentiments of the society and the institutions through which they are expressed. However, executives should not respond to every pressure exerted against them. Labor leaders, professors, stockholders, clergymen, and politicians frequently disagree among themselves. They do not always understand the problems with which executives must contend. However, executives should not ignore a consensus among important leadership elements in the society. They should take cognizance of expressions of disapproval, but, what is more important, their actions should generally give rise to a vote of confidence rather than censure. Much that executives do in this respect must be categorized as an expression of moral rather than economic philosophy. Even if voluntary salary cuts in line with declines in dividends or wages may not be justified on purely economic grounds, they may be appropriate on moral grounds.

Creditors, Suppliers, and Other Interests

Some of the ideas expressed about stockholders, employees, and customers are also pertinent in the relationships involving creditors, suppliers, and other interests. Thus, a company might be ill-advised to take advantage of its suppliers in a buyer's market. The good will of suppliers and creditors is an important asset that should generally not be dissipated in the interests of short-run gains. Companies should have a similar attitude toward the communities in which their plants and offices are located. They should make an effort to gain the support of the community, and the executives should behave like good neighbors rather than bosses from the outside. Good will with respect to an interest group may reap many indirect rewards. Customers represent fertile ground for the sale of securities; stockholders frequently become buyers and boosters of company products and services; employees are potential customers and stockholders.

A Moral Responsibility to the Organization

The acceptance of a moral responsibility to the organization is an important, if not an essential, attribute of management. If management's primary professional and functional responsibility is assumed to be the accomplishment of the organizational purpose, a personal belief and faith in that purpose would seem to be an important facilitating faculty. Furthermore, the ability to create a sense of moral responsibility in others would be most difficult if done in a purely perfunctory manner. As Barnard points out: "Indeed, few can do it long except on the basis of personal conviction —not conviction that they are obligated as officials to do it, but conviction that what they do for the good of organization they *personally* believe to be right." [20] The ability to transmit faith in the mission of the organization is one of the highest attributes of leadership. Who will have faith if the leader does not?

Organizational Purposes and Personal Motives

Responsibility to the organization assumes a moral significance to the individual when it becomes an integral part of his personal ethical system.[21] The organizational purpose becomes an aspect of personal faith and belief. Hence, conduct that contradicts the accomplishment of the organizational purpose becomes immoral. Such moral responsibility to the organization is often described by such terms as "company man," "organization personality," and "bravery beyond the call of duty."

People engage in cooperative activity to satisfy a great many personal motives. The acceptance of a moral responsibility to an organization involves something more than the cooperation induced by the incentives of wages, profits, status, craftsmanship, and social satisfactions. A moral responsibility is present only to the extent that cooperation occurs because the achievement of the organizational purpose has become a personal purpose and motive. Some people do not seem to develop a personal loyalty to an organization, while for others loyalty may become an important reason for cooperation to the degree that the usual rewards become relatively unimportant. In extreme cases, people have given their lives, accepted persecution and torture, abandoned their families and

[20] Chester I. Barnard, *The Functions of the Executive, op. cit.,* p. 281.
[21] *Ibid.,* pp. 258–284. The discussion in this section is heavily indebted to Barnard's analysis of responsibility.

friends, and lived a life of poverty in order to enhance an organizational purpose. The history of military, religious, and political organizations affords many examples. But it should not be assumed that business and industrial organizations lack the attributes necessary to create a moral responsibility. Barnard illustrates the importance of organizational loyalty to a telephone operator.

I recall a telephone operator on duty at a lonely place from which she could see in the distance the house in which her mother lay bedridden. Her life was spent in taking care of her mother and in maintaining that home for her. To do so, she chose employment in that particular position, against other inclinations. Yet she stayed at her switchboard while she watched the house burn down. No code, public or organizational, that has any general validity under such circumstances governed her conduct, and she certainly violated some such codes, as well as some of her own. Nevertheless, she showed extraordinary "moral courage," we would say, in conforming to a code of her organization—the *moral* necessity of uninterrupted service. This was high responsibility as respects that code.[22]

Conflicting Moral Systems

No organization has single or complete sovereignty. An organization is constantly faced with competition for the loyalty of its members. The average person is simultaneously a member of a number of formal organizations, such as a church, a reserve military unit, an industrial concern, and fraternal organizations. He is also associated with informal relationships, such as friendship circles and family. The purposes expressed by these associations may become a part of his personal code of morality. In addition to the norms that evolve from group and organizational membership, people generally have purely personal norms that influence their conduct.

The conduct of the executive is guided by a variety of ethical norms, some of which are derived from his life outside the organization. The diversity of forces that influence management behavior is well described by Professor George A. Coe.

In one and the same act several of the following phases of mental dynamics always can be detected: Family affection, family pride, and anxiety concerning security and social standing; desire for recognition in the business world; the nursing of self-conceit; loyalty to a partner; pugnacity toward a rival; enjoyment of power; the exhilaration of a game; the thrill of originality; pride of workmanship; the glow of self-identification with an institution, enterprise or cause; the taking of a customer's interest as one's own; the feeling of responsibility for the welfare of employees; devotion to country. . . .[23]

[22] *Ibid.*, p. 269. The operator's mother was rescued.
[23] Quoted by *Fortune*, Vol. 37, No. 6, December 1948, p. 130. One of Professor Coe's professional interests is the psychology of religion.

The problem of resolving a serious conflict between two or more moral codes is sometimes a difficult one. During World War II, for example, many soldiers approached their chaplains with the question: "Is it right to kill the enemy?" The question implies difficulty in reconciling their responsibility to the army with the ethical norms of their religious belief.[24] Similar moral conflicts are implied in the following questions. Should an executive fire a friend of many years if this action enhances the welfare of the organization? If the demands made by the organization begin to interfere with a person's family life, should he seek another position? Should the employer assume a financial responsibility for employees who have to be temporarily discharged for reasons beyond the control of the employer? Should a manufacturer who believes in free international competition and trade oppose a restrictive tariff bill that would be helpful to his organization? Should a businessman refuse to sell at a high profit to a possible enemy nation? Should a subordinate refuse to obey an order if he believes that order conflicts with the purpose of the organization?

Decisions that involve a serious conflict between two or more moral codes or purposes are among the most difficult decisions that an individual or an executive must make. Some people do not seem to be able to make such decisions. The ability to resolve or compromise such conflicts for himself and others is an important quality of management leadership. As Barnard points out: "Neither men of weak responsibility nor those of limited capability can endure or carry the burden of many simultaneous obligations of different types."[25]

The Moral Responsibility of Management

Moral responsibility involves more than conformity. Management does and should play a positive role in man's quest for the better life. The people who do the managing are a product of the society in which they work and should understand the traditions and customs of that society, not only for purposes of conformity but also as a starting point for its further ethical development. Management should not be content merely to provide the means for social goals pronounced by consumers, politicians, labor leaders, religious leaders, or educators. Management becomes a creative force in society through the achievements of organized endeavor. It should give thought to the ethical implications of such achievements and become creative in the ethical sense to the same degree that it has demonstrated an ability to produce efficient techniques.

---

[24] For some interesting insights on this matter: S. L. A. Marshall, *Men Against Fire* (New York: William Morrow & Company, 1947), p. 78.

[25] Barnard, *op. cit.,* p. 272.

SELECTED REFERENCES

Robert W. Austin, "Code of Conduct for Executives," *Harvard Business Review,* Vol. 39, No. 5, pp. 53–61 (September–October 1961).

Chester I. Barnard, *The Functions of the Executive,* Chap. 17. Cambridge: Harvard University Press, 1951.

Chester I. Barnard, *Organization and Management,* Chap. 5. Cambridge: Harvard University Press, 1952.

A. A. Berle, Jr., *The 20th Century Capitalist Revolution.* New York: Harcourt, Brace and Company, Inc., 1954.

Howard R. Bowen, *Social Responsibilities of the Businessman.* New York: Harper & Brothers, 1953.

Thomas C. Cochran, "Business and the Democratic Tradition," *Harvard Business Review,* Vol. 34, No. 2, pp. 39–48 (March–April 1956).

Ralph J. Cordiner, *New Frontiers for Professional Managers.* New York: McGraw-Hill Book Company, Inc., 1956.

Peter F. Drucker, *Concept of the Corporation.* New York: The John Day Company, 1946.

Richard F. Ericson, "Looking Around, Should Management Be Idealistic?" *Harvard Business Review,* Vol. 36, No. 5, pp. 143 ff (September–October 1958).

J. D. Glover, *The Attack on Big Business.* Boston: Division of Research Graduate School of Business Administration, Harvard University, 1954.

Robert T. Golembiewski, *Men, Management, and Morality.* New York: McGraw-Hill Book Company, 1965.

Robert A. Gordon, *Business Leadership in the Large Corporation,* Chaps. 7–11. Washington, D.C.: The Brookings Institution, 1945.

Crawford H. Greenewalt, *The Uncommon Man.* New York: McGraw-Hill Book Company, Inc., 1959.

Challis A. Hall, Jr., *Effects of Taxation on Executive Compensation and Retirement Plans.* Boston: Division of Research, Graduate School of Business Administration, Harvard University, 1951.

Carter F. Henderson and Albert C. Lasker, *20 Million Careless Capitalists.* Garden City, N.Y.: Doubleday & Company, Inc., 1967.

Edward E. Lawler III, "The Mythology of Management Compensation," *California Management Review,* Vol. 9, No. 1, pp. 11–22 (Fall 1966).

Wilbur G. Lewellen, "Executives Lose Out, Even With Options," *Harvard Business Review,* Vol. 46, No. 1, pp. 127–142 (January–February 1968).

J. A. Livingston, *The American Stockholder*. Philadelphia: J. B. Lippincott Company, 1958.

Edward S. Mason, "The Apologetics of 'Managerialism,'" *The Journal of Business of the University of Chicago*, Vol. 31, No. 1, pp. 1–11 (January 1958).

Joseph W. McGuire, "The Finalite of Business," *California Management Review*, Vol. 8, No. 4, pp. 89–94 (Summer 1966).

Thomas H. Sanders, *Effects of Taxation on Executives*. Boston: Division of Research, Graduate School of Business Administration, Harvard University, 1951.

O. Glenn Saxon, Jr., "Annual Headache: The Stockholders' Meeting," *Harvard Business Review*, Vol. 44, No. 1, pp. 132–137 (January–February 1966).

Stewart Thompson, *Management Creeds and Philosophies*, Research Study, No. 32. New York: American Management Association, 1958.

PART VII

EXECUTIVE DEVELOPMENT

chapter 25

EXECUTIVE QUALITIES AND EXECUTIVE EDUCATION

A lack of executive talent may significantly affect the future of an organization. Death, disability, turnover, and retirement create a constant demand for executives. The problem is often accentuated by the personnel demands of organization growth. Business organizations have given increasing attention in recent years to executive development. The problems that relate to executive development are both organizational and social. Company educational and training techniques, recruitment, measurement and testing, and promotion policies are relevant variables. Also pertinent are the programs developed by the educational system and the attitudes that people have toward the executive role in the society. Thus, university and business school curricula have an important bearing on the problem, and the prestige of the profession may influence the number and kinds of persons who enter its ranks.

Leadership Succession

A distinction can be made between positions in a management structure and the people who occupy them. A position may be defined as a planned body of organizational responsibilities, powers, and privileges. It is activated by a person who together with persons in other positions makes up the managerial team. Leadership succession or the process by which hierarchical positions are filled is a highly important social and organizational problem. A position that is unoccupied or occupied by the wrong person may disrupt a vital aspect of the managerial process. But also important is that the people who occupy hierarchical positions become executives by virtue of their position. They possess power derived from the organization and the society which can become an instrument of terror if vested in a person with the psychological propensities of a Hitler.

The Problems of Organizational and Social Stability

The mutiny on the *Potemkin* and the later Communist Revolution did not leave the ship or the society without leaders. The ship elected a committee of the crew who served as "officers," and the society submitted to the leaders of the Communist Party. One set of leaders was replaced by another. Authority was reestablished by the acceptance of subordinates and by firing squads willing to fire on comrades not willing to accept orders. But leadership succession by revolution seriously disrupts the organized systems through which a society achieves its purposes. The vast array of hierarchies that direct the political, military, economic, and social affairs of people cannot function efficiently without an orderly system of leadership succession. Too many struggles for power dissipate the energies of organizations and disrupt the cooperative process. The Communist world and some South American nations have yet to solve this problem. Thus, the death of Joseph Stalin gave rise to a struggle for political power among various factions of the Communist Party. This struggle was not confined to top political positions but also affected many of the lower echelon hierarchies through which the Soviet society pursues economic, social, and other purposes.

The democracies that adopted the philosophical premises of British parliamentary government possess orderly systems of leadership succession. Although some of the political factions may not like the outcome of an election, they accept the leadership mandate of the "majority." The leaders thus selected are not always the best qualified by some standards, but they have the acceptance of a large portion of the populace and, by this standard, are the best leaders. The fact that they cannot long stay in power without this support emphasizes rule by the authority of acceptance rather than the power of sanctions. The development of a professional civil service has given further stability to the system of leadership succession by removing large areas of political administration from the realm of political conflict.

The high degree of autonomy given to economic and other areas of social endeavor has played an important part in leadership succession in democratic society. There is generally no direct relationship between changes in political leadership and leadership succession in business, religious, educational, and military organizations. The separation of church and state in the United States is one expression of this condition. The doctrine of *laissez faire* promotes this idea in the economic sphere. The organized entities that perform important social functions would tend to be seriously disrupted by a politically oriented leadership succession system. A major difficulty in the Soviet system is that a change in top leaders may force changes in leadership in such diverse areas as literature, biology, religion, and economics. The tenure of a church leader or a factory manager is constantly threatened by a failure to satisfy the political ideology of the ruling faction.

Direct political intervention in the process of leadership succession in nongovernmental organizations is a rarity in a democratic society. However, government supports particular procedures for resolving the problem. The laws that pertain to this problem are partly designed to protect the society from the avarice of the few, but they also emphasize the philosophy of private leadership as opposed to public leadership.

Private Property and Leadership Succession

The law of private property has played an important part in determining who will occupy managerial positions in business organizations. The property owner may himself perform managerial functions, or he may delegate such functions to others. Under corporation law, the owners or stockholders elect the board of directors, which is legally the top governing body. However, nonpropertied professional managers and other groups sometimes exercise the powers of property through legal and other devices. The persons in whom such powers are ultimately vested appoint one or a few top executives if they do not themselves assume such roles. Further delegation of managerial responsibilities occurs if the workload exceeds the capacities of the executives selected. Such delegation generally carries with it the power to select subordinates and other powers conferred by property rights. Thus, superiors from the top to the bottom of the hierarchy have the delegated power to impose sanctions upon those subordinate to them. This fact provides a basis for the idea that "authority" is delegated from superior to subordinate.

Property owners have ultimate control of management succession in many companies. They may delegate their prerogatives to others, but they have the potential power to intervene. However, professional managers and others [1] may exercise the prerogatives of property without the condition of

[1] Bankers, for example, have frequently taken a direct hand in managing a corporation and, in some cases, have selected top executives. It should be noted that bankers provide nonequity capital which does not confer the legal rights of the capital provided by stockholders. The influence of bankers in managerial affairs is discussed by Robert A. Gordon, *Business Leadership in the Large Corporation* (Washington, D.C.: The Brookings Institution, 1945), pp. 189–225.

actual ownership. The locus of power is sometimes difficult to determine, and proxy disputes and other tests of power sometimes occur to determine the identity of those who have ultimate control. Such tests are exceptions rather than the rule in spite of the impressions that may be given by publicity.

The Problem of Managerial Efficiency

The ownership of property does not automatically confer managerial talent. Property owners have not always given an enterprise the best management, and some companies have been destroyed by the incompetent offspring of a competent father or grandfather. At the same time, property ownership does not preclude managerial talent; indeed, the incidence of talent relative to the rest of the population probably lies on the positive side. There is certainly no conclusive evidence that the property owner is less qualified to manage or select managers than government, labor unions, customers, and other groups. The interests of the property owner are generally best served by a competent management. A large percentage of the total management group is selected on the basis of functional proficiency. Managers retain their positions because they are qualified to perform the functions of management. The management of today is far more professional than propertied.

The Responsibility of Business Leadership

The law of private property has endowed particular persons with succession rights to important positions in business organizations. It provides power to impose sanctions upon those who do not conform to the dictates of a legally established leadership. The law that evolved from the British tradition is essentially conservative. It is the custodian of social order and safeguards the society from the disruptive impact of revolutionary change. The process of change is evolutionary and rationalized in terms of traditional precepts. This system of law has promoted stability in leadership succession in business organizations and has served to insulate such organizations from political and other kinds of social conflict. For example, business leaders are not replaced whenever the incumbent political party is defeated in an election.

The conservatism of the law should not delude business leaders into believing they can ignore the social consequences of their acts. Social responsibility is partly a matter of successfully managing the enterprises through which society pursues its purposes, but a failure to assume a broader responsibility may have serious consequences. A particular leadership group can survive in the long run only if it takes into consideration the sentiments of the society from which its rights and powers are ultimately derived. The public may be damned in the short run, but it is rarely damned for long. What society has given, it can also take away. Succession to leadership positions and the power to impose sanctions are not absolute rights. The power of sanctions can be affected by laws that increase the power of those subject to the established leadership. The labor legislation of the 1930's is a good case in point. Succession rights can be taken away from one group and given to another. Socialization should not be viewed as an empty threat even in a society that has traditionally supported the idea of private business leadership. However, business leaders should not be crucified for every problem with which the society may be faced. They should not be made the scapegoat for social reformers who seek utopias that cannot be.

The Qualities of Successful Executives

What Is Success in Executive Work?

Profits, costs, budgets, and output are frequently used to measure executive performance. But, as was pointed out in previous chapters, such criteria are not always as objective as they appear to be and should be used with discretion. The problem of uncertainty, the impact of factors that cannot be controlled by executives, and the difficulties of measurement should be taken into consideration.

The fact that decision making is a cooperative process involving a hierarchy of executives presents a further complicating factor. An executive is not necessarily "successful" because the hierarchy in which he plays a part produces effective results. The capacities of the group may compensate for inadequacies on the part of individual members. Most hierarchies include a few persons who should not have been hired or promoted. The problem of deadwood cannot be entirely eliminated even with the best of intentions. There is also the possibility that a competent executive may seem to be incompetent as a result of failures in other parts of the hierarchy.

The career patterns of an individual or a group of executives can give useful information about competency. A history of continuous promotion and increases in salary frequently reflects successful performance.[2] Execu-

---

[2] William E. Henry, "The Business Executive: The Psychodynamics of a Social Role," *The American Journal of Sociology,* Vol. 54, No. 4, January 1949, p. 287.

tives with this kind of a career pattern from companies that have experienced profits over a period of time can reasonably be termed "successful." Errors that may occur with respect to particular individuals can be offset by the use of a large sample. A study of executives thus selected provides some basis for tentative ideas about the relationship between qualities and success.

The Problem of Determining and Defining Qualities

The qualities of successful executives are difficult to determine and define. One problem is that a set of qualities may result in success under some organizational and environmental conditions and not under others. Another is that particular qualities are parts of a combination of qualities. The significance of a given quality may be affected by the nature of other qualities and the manner in which they are combined. Still another problem is that much of the terminology dealing with this subject is highly subjective. What is meant by such terms as honesty, courage, loyalty, and intelligence? The suggestion that "honesty" means that executives never lie brought laughter from one group of executives.[3]

Executive qualities may be classified as skills and motives. Skills involve the application of "knowledge" to problem-solving and purposeful situations. They may be acquired through direct experiences with material and human phenomena. They may also result from a transfer of information from one person to another, if the techniques they imply can be reduced into objective terms. The idea that skills may be learned apart from the actual situation in which they will be used is highly important. It means that executives can be trained through a study of systematic bodies of facts, principles, and techniques accumulated by scientific and other methods. Such knowledge has played an important part in preparing people for executive work and in improving the skills of practicing executives. However, the systems of knowledge used for such purposes may not adequately describe or analyze the reality that is involved in actual situations. Furthermore, a person may possess the capacity to acquire knowledge but not have the skills (another kind of knowledge) required for application. Much skill becomes a matter of habitual response which can only be partially developed in situations that represent or simulate reality. Actual experience seems to be essential in mastering some skills.

Motives may be defined as subjective qualities that prompt an individual to action. Different kinds of motives lead to variations in the manner in which different individuals respond to situations. Since little is known

[3] This incident is related by Chris Argyris, "Some Characteristics of Successful Executives," *Personnel Journal,* Vol. 32, No. 2, June 1953, p. 50.

about the physio-psychological mechanics that give rise to motives, they must in general be inferred from behavior. Many motives seem to evolve from nurture rather than nature, which means that motives can be developed through education and training.

Some Qualities of Successful Executives

The qualities mentioned below have often been considered important for success in executive work.[4] They should not be viewed as absolutes and some of them may not apply to particular situations. Some overlapping occurs as the result of classification and definitional difficulties.

Organizational and Social Skills. Successful executives tend to view managment problems in terms of organization. It is interesting to note in this respect that much of the pioneering work in organizational theory came from practicing executives. Henri Fayol, James D. Mooney, Alan C. Reiley, Henry Dennison, and Chester I. Barnard, all of whom were experienced executives, stressed the importance of organization in the managerial process. A relatively small number of successful executives have translated their "knowledge" into systematic treatises. But they seem to have highly reliable subjective, if not objective, insights into the nature of organizational dynamics and apparently understand the manner in which such phenomena as status, authority, and informal group norms may influence behavior.

Experienced executives generally have a high ability to organize the activities of others and a willingness to accept the organizational restraints imposed upon them. As William E. Henry has noted from a study of the psycho-dynamics of the executive role, the successful executive views "authority as a controlling but helpful relationship to superiors . . . he does not see the authorities in his environment as destructive or prohibiting forces." [5] Executives interviewed by Chris Argyris understood the need for "unfavorable decisions" and discretionary limits imposed by superiors and the system.[6] They recognized "the rules of the game" and were willing to abide by them and accept the consequences. They seemed to have a large amount of skill in manipulating the instrumentalities of organization to achieve organizational and personal goals. While they tended to adapt to

---

[4] Henry, *op. cit.,* pp. 286–291; Chester I. Barnard, *Organization and Management* (Cambridge: Harvard University Press, 1952), pp. 92–102; Chris Argyris, *op. cit.;* Theodore O. Yntema, *A Liberal Education* (Dearborn, Mich.: Ford Motor Company, 1957); and Clarence B. Randall, *The Randall Lectures* (White Plains, New York: The Fund for Adult Education, 1957).

[5] Henry, *op. cit.,* p. 288.

[6] Argyris, *op. cit.,* p. 54.

the restraints imposed by the system when necessary, they also had the ability to use the system to advantage. Thus, an experienced executive is aware of the techniques that may be employed to "short-circuit" the chain of command should it become essential. He knows how to get around a rule without leaving evidence for those who may be inclined to use it against him.

The ability to permit participation by subordinates and others without a feeling of being "threatened" was a quality of the executives studied by Argyris.[7] This quality does not necessarily mean that successful executives are always "democratic" or that they encourage participation in the usual sense of that word. It implies that they are willing to accept the risks of social involvement and have a personal feeling of security in their own capacity to control the situation.

Successful executives seem to view relationships with subordinates "in a detached and impersonal way, seeing them as 'doers of work' rather than as people."[8] Such an attitude is much like that of other professionals. An experienced surgeon wields the scalpel without strong emotional ties to the owner of the gall bladder being removed. The scientist probes into the mysteries of the universe even though his activities may repudiate his personal prejudices and faith. Some degree of emotional detachment is important in any profession. It tends to increase objectivity and mitigate the impact of adversity.

Experience in executive work undoubtedly reduces the emotional impact of social relationships. Executives tend to develop an immunity to some of the stresses and strains that accompany the organizational life. They become more skillful in the art of handling people and less concerned about difficulties that cannot be avoided. They recognize that they may sometimes be labeled as the handiwork of the devil and that popularity may not be their greatest reward. However, it should not be assumed that executives never experience conflicts and tensions in contending with socio-psychological problems. Human relationships always have some emotional content for normal people.

Successful executives seem generally to have a greater feeling of personal attachment toward superiors than subordinates.[9] They tend to identify themselves with superiors and see them as symbols of their own aspirations. Subordinates portray the things that have been left behind and represent the past rather than the future.

Decision-Making Skills. The ability to make decisions is often categorized as an important executive quality. This quality implies that the

[7] *Ibid.*, p. 51.
[8] Henry, *op. cit.*, p. 290.
[9] *Ibid.*

executive has knowledge that can be used to solve decisional problems. Knowledge, used in this sense, may be defined as the information that makes up human memory. The nature of such information presents a number of complicated psychological, physiological, and philosophical problems that will not be considered here.[10] Knowledge may consist of facts, ideas, concepts, principles, and techniques derived through experience or education. Some knowledge may be directly used in the sense that the solution to a decisional problem is the same as or similar to that given in the past. Other knowledge provides means that can be used to derive solutions to problems that are different in kind and scope.

Emphasis is usually given to the importance of scientific methods in solving decisional problems. However, decision making and this kind of problem solving are not necessarily the same. Decision cannot always be delayed for the solutions that might ultimately be derived through scientific methods. Some decisional problems are not "scientific" problems because the variables cannot be objectively measured or because they involve ethical judgments. The executive is often forced to select from among what seem to be equally good alternatives. The capacity to come to a decision when there is no objective basis for determining the appropriate action represents an important aspect of decision-making skills.

Successful executives are generally willing to make decisions under circumstances that would put others into a quandary. This quality does not mean that executives necessarily make decisions quickly or on a "snap judgment" basis. Some decisions may require a long period of deliberation and others little or no deliberation. The qualities required for a scientific approach to decisional problems and the more subjective qualities involved in other approaches are not always compatible. The decisiveness of the executive and that of the scientist are not necessarily built on the same foundation. Scientific endeavor may make for indecisiveness through the emphasis given to "a questioning attitude." The scientist is usually unwilling to accept a solution until every aspect of a problem has been carefully scrutinized; his decisiveness is founded on faith in the objectivity derived through the scientific method. The decisiveness of the executive may evolve from the fact that the scientific method has been used to solve a decisional problem, but it also involves a willingness to come to a decision without the support of scientific knowledge. Decision-making skills have a subjective basis under such circumstances and represent a feeling of "conviction," "certainty," and "self-reliance." Executives must frequently speak with a feeling of certainty under what are actually uncertain conditions. A

---

[10] Some kind of encoding, recoding, and decoding system is undoubtedly involved in learning, memory, and recall. Knowledge may be learned, memorized, and recalled through conscious and "unconscious" processes.

loss of this quality may have serious consequences for the executive. Other executives begin to view him with apprehension, and he "seems to pass out of the socially defined role." [11]

Some decisions involve moral considerations that cannot be termed right or wrong by strictly scientific standards. Much has been said about the need for a high sense of moral responsibility on the part of executives. However, a moralist is frequently not very decisive as to what constitutes moral actions. A person who becomes too involved with the complexities of social morality and responsibility is apt to lack the decisiveness required for executive work. He may also experience an excessive amount of emotional conflict in making decisions that involve competing moral norms. Effective executive action sometimes requires a willingness to pursue particular social goals even though they may violate other social goals. A failure to do so can ultimately reduce the welfare of the society by changes in the relative importance of particular goals in the total scheme of things. Executives in their professional capacities are important spokesmen for the interests of the organizations through which society seeks some of its purposes. They cannot be crusaders for the large diversity of interests in the society. The emotional burden would soon sap their energies and preclude effective action in their own sphere of moral responsibility.

Communication Skills. The fact that a large part of executive work involves oral and written communication emphasizes the importance of communication skills. Clarence B. Randall, former president of the Inland Steel Company, has said in this respect: "The businessman today must be able to write and speak the English language with clarity and felicity, or stand aside and let his chair be occupied by someone who can." [12] Theodore O. Yntema, a Ford vice-president, has observed that "many men and women are sadly handicapped because they cannot write or speak effectively." [13] Other executives have made similar statements about communication skills. Little is known, however, about the specific skills possessed by successful executives and their relationship to success. For example, how many successful executives use "correct grammar" in speaking and writing, and what relationship, if any, does this quality have to success in executive work?

The basic elements of the communication problem and process were given comprehensive consideration in Part V. There is good reason to believe that many executives "understand" the nature of such problems as deliberate and nondeliberate distortion even though they may not be able to express them in objective terms. Successful executives undoubtedly

[11] Henry, *op. cit.,* p. 289.
[12] Randall, *op. cit.,* p. 11.
[13] Yntema, *op. cit.,* p. 10.

develop effective communication skills on an intuitive basis. Thus, the word "semantics" may be foreign to them, but they make good use of the ideas it implies. However, some successful executives would probably be more successful with a better understanding of the objective content of the communication problem. Although the relationship beween specific skills and success cannot be readily measured, it seems reasonable to assume that executives of the future will have to take full advantage of scientific progress in the area of communication and control if they want to stay in the competitive race. The qualities that make for success today may not be adequate for success in the world of tomorrow.

Leadership Skills. These skills are difficult to isolate from the totality of skills that make for leadership in the broader sense. In other words, what does "leadership" involve in addition to the skills considered in previous paragraphs? Barnard uses the terms "endurance," "vitality," and "persuasiveness" in a discussion of executive qualities.[14] Leadership seems to involve qualities of this kind, but, as Barnard points out, they are most difficult to describe in objective terms.

Motives and Other Matters. The qualities discussed next, which may be broadly classified as motives, also seem to have some relationship to success in executive work.[15] Successful executives are generally realistic in defining organizational and personal goals. They are not afraid to set high goals, but they tend not to overshoot their capacities. They are inclined to be somewhat aggressive in their relationships with other people but not without some well-defined purpose. They seem to have the ability to let the other person know their likes and dislikes, but they tend to be tactful and not overly hostile. They also show a capacity to accept similar treatment without feeling that the other person is out "to do them in."

Such terms as "active," "striving," "ambitious," and "drive" portray much of the personal and work behavior of successful executives. A "fear of failure" and "a desire for success" expressed by such things as money, position, and other status symbols seem to be highly important motivating factors. Many executives feel that they must constantly move forward and seem to thrive on past accomplishments. However, they also tend to control their emotions and not become "overexcited" about their successes. Some executives seem to have an ability to work effectively under frustrating conditions and take defeat without a feeling of being "washed-up."

The relationship between personal qualities and executive success should not be viewed apart from organizational and environmental factors. Some successful executives might well have failed completely under an even

[14] Barnard, *op. cit.*, pp. 93–95.
[15] The discussion that follows is indebted to the following: Argyris, *op. cit.*, and Henry, *op. cit.*

slightly different set of conditions. Executives may rise to high position even though they lack many of the qualities that "normally" seem important. Furthermore, some of the qualities that make for success may, under certain circumstances, reinforce the forces that lead to failure. For example, a great deal of drive may be an appropriate quality for success in executive work, but it may also be an Achilles' heel for those whose efforts are blocked by conditions they cannot control. As William E. Henry has written, "psychosomatic symptoms, the enlargement of interpersonal dissatisfactions, and the development of rationalized compulsive and/or paranoid-like defenses may reflect the redirection of this potent energy demand." [16] The problem of degree is important in evaluating some qualities. Thus, some "frustration tolerance" may be highly desirable, but too much of it may have adverse consequences.

The Education of Executives

This section directs attention to the problem of educating people for future executive positions. Primary emphasis is given to education in colleges and universities because secondary and elementary educational levels play a relatively small part in purposeful executive development.

The Formative Years

Much of the early period of human life is spent in learning the culture of the society. This aspect of the learning process is devoted in great part to the development of the routines of behavior that make up an orderly approach to social living. The family, schools, churches, Boy Scouts, and play groups are some of the formal and informal instruments through which society imposes restraints upon its members. However, there are significant variations in the kind of individual that is produced. One reason is that heredity does not give every individual the same start in the race to maturity. Another is that there are many subcultures within the total cultural complex found in a society. For example, the culture of urban communities is somewhat different from that of rural communities. Southern culture differs in some respects from the culture found in Yankee "society"; a factory worker may not transmit the same "culture" to his children as a physician; parents with a strong religious background produce different attitudes in their children than parents with agnostic inclinations. Furthermore, the restraints imposed by the group upon the

[16] Henry, *op. cit.*, pp. 289–290.

individual are by no means absolute. The individual generally has a rather wide range of discretion within which he can make choices, and he may also deliberately engage in acts of nonconformity.

The formative years have an important relationship to a person's future capacity to perform the executive function. Research in psychology and psychiatry indicates that this period of development may greatly influence a person's psychological propensities. The education and experience of later years may not be sufficient to remold attitudes and motives into those appropriate for executive work. Also important is that some experiences during the formative years may be more beneficial for purposes of executive development than others. For example, urban life frequently provides useful social experiences that may not be acquired by someone reared on a farm. A large high school may afford beneficial organizational experiences that are not available in a small high school. The son of a business executive can acquire important insights about executive work in his home environment. The argument is not that it is impossible "to take the farm out of the boy" but that some people acquire advantages by virtue of background.

Business organizations influence the learning process of the formative years in a number of ways. Advertising and public relations programs play a part in the development of attitudes toward business and its organizations. Political action and philanthropic activities by business enterprises undoubtedly have some effect on the manner in which society educates its children and performs other functions. But, except for the explicit emphasis given to executive careers by some institutional advertising, such activities have a highly indirect relationship to executive development. Although they undoubtedly help develop more favorable attitudes toward business organizations and the executives who manage them, there is little likelihood that they make any significant contribution to the development of the kind of skills and motives required for success in executive work. The forces that shape the individual during the formative years push and pull in many directions and produce a variety of products. Some people do not have the appropriate qualities for executive work even though they enter a college or university with the purpose of becoming an executive. Problems of this sort may be avoided by better programs of vocational guidance in high schools and universities and by screening applicants for positions through testing, interview, and other recruitment techniques.

More attention might be given by business organizations to the problem of developing a better understanding of the executive function in the society. The nature of the opportunities afforded by a career in executive work might also be given greater emphasis. Many high school students seem to be better informed about careers in engineering, medicine, dentistry, and science than an executive career. A large number of young people who have capacity for executive work are lost to other fields of endeavor. The society needs capable physicians, dentists, chemists, and engineers, but the importance of executive talent should not be neglected.

The Educational Background of Present and Past Executives

Some useful insights about the educational background of practicing executives are provided by a number of studies and surveys. However, the results achieved from such studies are not always comparable because of differences in the kind and size of the sample used and in research techniques. A study of 8000 top business leaders from different industries and geographical regions by W. Lloyd Warner and James C. Abegglen dealt with the matter of education.[17] The results of this study (1952) were compared with those of an earlier study (1928) of top business leaders by F. W. Taussig and C. S. Joslyn.[18] Such a comparison shows that the executives of 1952 were much more highly educated than the sample studied in 1928. Thirty-two per cent of the 1928 executives were college graduates, and an additional 13 per cent had some college credit.[19] Fifty-seven per cent of the 1952 group possessed college degrees, and a total of 76 per cent had either graduated from or attended college. But it is interesting to note that almost 15 per cent of the 1952 executives did not graduate from high school, and 4 per cent did not reach beyond the grammar school level.[20] A study of presidents and board chairmen from the largest railroad, public utility, and industrial corporations conducted by Mabel Newcomer follows the Warner-Abegglen conclusions in showing a marked increase in educational levels from 1900 to 1950.[21] Two-thirds of 1700 top executives surveyed by *Fortune* were college graduates, and one-fourth of those without degrees reported undergraduate work.[22]

Available data on the educational background of executives below the top level can lead to a variety of generalizations because of differences in the sample studied in particular surveys. One study of 562 executives from

[17] W. Lloyd Warner and James C. Abegglen, *Occupational Mobility in American Business and Industry, 1928–1952* (Minneapolis: University of Minnesota Press, 1955), and *Big Business Leaders in America* (New York: Harper & Brothers Publishers, 1955).
[18] F. W. Taussig and C. S. Joslyn, *American Business Leaders* (New York: The Macmillan Company, 1932).
[19] Warner and Abegglen, *Occupational Mobility, op. cit.*, p. 108.
[20] *Ibid.*, p. 98.
[21] Mabel Newcomer, *The Big Business Executive* (New York: Columbia University Press, 1955), p. 68.
[22] *Fortune*, Vol. 60, No. 5, November 1959, p. 139.

a number of industry classifications showed that 61 per cent of the top management were college graduates compared to 63 per cent for middle management and 62 per cent for lower management.[23] The positions studied ranged from the top to two levels above first-line supervision. A small sample studied by Daniel Starch showed that mid-level executives were slightly better educated than those at the top, but that lower levels were relatively less well educated.[24] Although studies show differences in both directions, there is a great deal of evidence to support the conclusion that the educational achievements of middle and top management are about the same. Executives at lower levels are not as well educated because much supervisory personnel is recruited from the ranks.

Industry, region, and size may also make for differences in the educational background of executives. The Newcomer study points to rather large variations in the education of executives from different industries. Public utilities ranked higher than either the railroads or the industrial corporations included in the sample.[25] The *Fortune* survey of 1700 executives from companies categorized as industrial, life insurance, commercial banking, transportation, utilities, merchandising, and others also showed significant interindustry variations.[26] The "most educated" executives were found in chemicals, insurance, and utilities. The possibility that there may be regional variations in the educational background of executives is indicated by an Alabama study of 319 managerial and professional personnel in 22 companies, which showed a somewhat different educational pattern than that found in other studies.[27] The various studies cited above do not indicate much variation in the educational background of executives from organizations of different size. However, one survey points to the possibility that executives in very small firms may not be as well educated as those in larger companies.[28]

As to the type of higher education, a little over one-third of the 1952 executives of the Warner-Abegglen study had received the bachelor of arts and a slightly larger proportion possessed a bachelor of science degree.[29] There were a significant number of law degrees, a few baccalaureate

---

[23] Frank C. Pierson et al., *The Education of American Businessmen* (New York: McGraw-Hill Book Company, Inc., 1959), p. 102. This information was derived from unpublished material supplied by Richardson, Bellows, Henry and Company, Inc.

[24] Daniel Starch, *How to Develop Your Executive Ability* (New York: Harper & Brothers Publishers, 1943), pp. 22–23.

[25] Newcomer, *op. cit.,* pp. 71–72.

[26] *Fortune, op. cit.*

[27] Pierson, *op. cit.,* p. 103.

[28] *Ibid.,* p. 101.

[29] Warner and Abegglen, *Big Business Leaders, op. cit.,* p. 55.

degrees in business, and a number of advanced degrees. Many of the executives, both with and without college degrees, received training in various business and commercial subjects by correspondence and other means. Fifty-eight per cent of the 1952 executives had some formal business training compared with only 29 per cent for 1928.[30]

Eight-five per cent of the college graduates among the 1700 top executives surveyed by *Fortune* majored in law, business, economics, engineering, or science.[31] There appeared to be an increase during later years (from 1952 to 1959) in the number of executives who had studied subjects in liberal arts. The data also indicated a relative drop in the number of science and engineering majors among top executives. An earlier *Fortune* study of 900 executives showed the following percentages for the college graduates: arts (8.9 per cent), law (14.8 per cent), business economics (30.8 per cent), and science and engineering (45.5 per cent).[32] The percentages changed rather significantly for the top executives under fifty years of age. Business economics majors increased to 38.5 per cent, and science and engineering declined to 28.9 per cent. Graduate degrees in business administration began to assume some importance in the early 1950's.[33] Although there is a lack of adequate information, middle and lower management in large companies seems to "include a heavy representation of all three of the principal educational backgrounds—engineering-sciences, humanities-social sciences, and business administration —the exact combination depending on the nature of the firm's product or function, its type of leadership, it most serious management needs, and the like." [34] Engineering and science have held a high place during past years, but there is some indication that business administration will be relatively more important in the future.

All studies support the conclusion that executives are better educated than the population generally. But the proportion of executives with a higher education is lower than for other "distinguished persons" as defined by *Who's Who in America*. Almost 93 per cent of those listed in *Who's Who* in 1952–1953 had some higher education, compared with a little over 75 per cent for the 1950 executives studied by Newcomer and about 80 per cent for executives of a more recent vintage.[35] Executives seem to be catching up in the educational race, with college education becoming increasingly more important as an aspect of executive development.

[30] Warner and Abegglen, *Occupational Mobility, op. cit.,* p. 112.

[31] *Fortune, op. cit.,* p. 139.

[32] Editors of *Fortune, The Executive Life* (Garden City, N.Y.: Doubleday and Company, Inc., 1956), p. 34.

[33] Newcomer, *op. cit.,* p. 75.

[34] Pierson, *op. cit.,* p. 105.

[35] Newcomer, *op. cit.,* p. 70.

The Need for Higher Education

A sizable percentage of the executives in the studies cited above did not have a university or college degree, and some achieved high positions with only a grammar school education. Thus, the lack of higher education is not an absolute barrier to success in executive work, and there is good reason to believe that this situation will prevail for some time into the future. However, the number of executives without a college degree will undoubtedly decline to a rather low percentage. Executives are being pushed up the educational ladder by a rise in educational levels for the total population and have to interact with people from other professional areas, such as accounting and engineering, which have increased educational requirements during the past decades. Even if it could be assumed that executive work does not require higher education, status problems and communication difficulties might still be a sufficient argument for more education. Still another reason for an increase in college degrees is that technological and other innovations have created a need for better-educated executives. The world of nuclear power, operations research, electronic computers, and moon rockets requires a higher level of intellectual competence than the world of the Model T and lye soap. The need for larger and larger numbers of executives is also an important consideration. Education may be helpful in speeding up the process of executive development and in providing a more reliable base with which to begin. The so-called practical man tends to spend a great deal of time rediscovering things that have already been discovered. He may also lack knowledge that has some importance even though it might not be absolutely essential for success.

Education for What?

The problem of educating for executive work is complicated by the lack of a clear-cut differentiation between managerial and other kinds of business responsibilities. For example, not all businessmen are executives, because some of them do not make decisions to which others must respond as a matter of organizational responsibility. A proprietor of a small grocery or shoe store makes decisions that are similar to those made by executives, but he cannot be categorized as an executive if he does not have subordinates. Furthermore, not all executives perform exclusively managerial tasks, which means that some executives are part-time executives and part-time something else. Such considerations invite the question as to how much executive work makes a person an executive. Although any definite answer is difficult to support logically, this matter has an important bearing on the problem of professional status and the related problem of education. It means that some part of the future executive's education and experience may involve areas other than executive work. It also presents the possibility of competing vocational and professional interests, since a part-time executive may also be a part-time accountant, engineer, or chemist. The interests of different professions are not necessarily in conflict, but the idea that they can be should not be ignored.

Professional Education for Executives

What kind of education is appropriate for those who perform the executive function as some part of their total responsibilities? To what extent should or can education for executives be differentiated from the education required for other business and industrial pursuits, such as accounting, actuarial work, engineering, market research, and plant layout? Does executive development require something beyond a liberal arts or a general business education? These and related questions will now be given consideration.

Many top executives have lauded a broad liberal arts education as a preparation for executive work.[36] At the same time, the people who represent them on the firing line of the market place have demanded increasing numbers of specialists in engineering, chemistry, production, marketing, accounting, insurance, retailing, and finance. The liberal arts graduate seems to come out second-best in the talent search of the business world. In addition, the universities themselves have given impetus to a decline in the relative importance of the liberal arts by the development of what William H. Whyte, Jr., has termed "the practical curriculum."[37] The Pierson and the Gordon-Howell reports also lament the lack of a broad education, the emphasis on vocationalism, and the extremes of specialization in much of the training provided by schools and departments of business.[38]

Some of the arguments about the relative importance of various kinds of educational programs are founded in a failure to differentiate among kinds of business needs. Business and other organizations require large numbers of specialists in such areas as accounting, insurance, engineering, market

[36] Randall, *op. cit.;* Yntema, *op. cit.;* "Industry and the Liberal Arts," *Saturday Review,* November 21, 1953, pp. 32–46.

[37] William H. Whyte, Jr., *The Organization Man* (New York: Simon and Schuster, 1956), pp. 78–100.

[38] Pierson, *op. cit.;* Robert Aaron Gordon and James Edwin Howell, *Higher Education for Business* (New York: Columbia University Press, 1959). These studies point to the need for introspection by business and related fields of study.

research, motion and time study, secretarial science, computer programming, and advertising. The tasks implied by such specializations are an important aspect of the work of the business world. Education for business and industrial careers involves more than executive development. There must be Indians if the chiefs are to have the resources to achieve their goals. Many specialists spend their working lives primarily in their area of specialization with little or no executive responsibility. Their educational needs may differ in some or many respects from the needs of those who climb the managerial ladder.

Some Basic Curricula Problems

The purpose of this section is to highlight problem areas in curricula development. Those seeking a more comprehensive and detailed analysis should refer to the Pierson and Gordon-Howell reports discussed earlier. The curricula development of the last few decades reflects a shift in emphasis from education for the sake of education to education for the sake of employment.[39] Some university educators feel that education has suffered in the process, but others contend that education has been helped. The consensus seems to be that both sides have an argument and that the problem is to find a proper balance between vocational and educational needs. A part of the solution involves the idea that the two interests are in many respects complementary rather than competing.

A major problem is the extent to which curricula should be adapted to vocational needs and interests. Business schools have developed courses in business English, business history, business statistics, and business law; engineering schools, in engineering management, engineering law, and engineering economics; agricultural schools, in agricultural economics, agricultural engineering, and agricultural physics. A similar vocationalism of curricula and course content is found in some liberal arts colleges. Some adaptation to vocational needs was undoubtedly necessary to compensate for a failure of the basic disciplines to meet legitimate needs. But too much "raiding" of this kind can result in a lack of resources for education in its broader aspects. It may also lead to courses that lack substantial content and instructors who lack adequate academic capacity.

Related to this problem are various other problems that plague business, engineering, and liberal arts departments. One is the extent to which the curricula should permit specialization in particular areas. How many courses should a university offer in marketing, production, personnel, or finance? Should universities develop courses in hotel front-office procedure, closing real estate transactions, operating a small store, and freight claims

[39] Pierson, *op. cit.*, pp. 16–23.

procedure?[40] Too much specialization may lead to a narrow perspective and takes time that might be better spent in other areas. Thus, a student who takes fifteen courses in marketing may not have time for a much-needed course in English or accounting. Another aspect of this problem is that of curricula and course content. What can be taught in the fourth course in credit, motion and time study, retailing, or production planning? The result is frequently far too much stress upon purely descriptive material that does not provide any really new insights or ideas. Universities should not teach everything demanded by vocational and other interests; some things are better taught at lower educational levels or in trade and commercial schools. For example, a course in horseshoeing, automobile mechanics, or raising bees would seem to fall within the realm of the trade school rather than universities or colleges. Some knowledge and skills can be gained through experience rather than education. Courses that encompass such mundane matters as how to make a date, how to buy bus tickets, and how to boil potatoes should not be offered at any educational level. Why teach the obvious when so much fundamental knowledge remains unlearned?

The educational and training responsibilities of business organizations must be taken into account in curricula development. Employers should not expect educational institutions to adapt their programs to particular job specifications, but the question as to where to draw the line is sometimes difficult to answer. For example, some curricula critics decry typewriting courses in university and college programs, contending that typewriting should be taught in high schools or commercial schools if at all. However, there are good arguments for courses in management, accounting, and finance for those who seek positions as office managers and private secretaries. It may be necessary as a matter of expediency to offer courses in typewriting, with or without degree credit, at the university level. High schools may not provide sufficient training, and commercial schools may not be located adjacent to the university campus.

The Universality of Knowledge and Skills

Some knowledge and skills are universal in that they are transferable from one kind of endeavor to others. For example, the scientific method is important in many different professional pursuits. Furthermore, a variety of educational programs may produce the qualities required for a particular profession. The scientific method can be learned in courses in chemistry (science), philosophy or logic (liberal arts), market research (business),

[40] Gordon and Howell, *op. cit.,* p. 140.

or thermodynamics (engineering). The ability to read and write the English language can be acquired in courses offered by the English department, but this kind of skill may also be learned in many other university courses. Reading the law and preparing legal briefs or reading economics and writing term papers can develop high capacity in this respect. The transferability of knowledge and skills may help explain why many highly successful executives have a diversity of academic backgrounds. It also infers that there is no one best academic program for purposes of executive development. A similar statement can be made about other professional pursuits. Such professions as medicine and law have a wider range of choice in curricula development than is often assumed. Medical schools borrow heavily from the basic sciences in their professional programs. It should also be noted that many outstanding advances in the profession of medicine have been made by persons who were not physicians or surgeons. The contributions made by economists and political theorists to legal knowledge provide other cases in point.

The pursuit of particular professional interests has played an important part in curricula development. The motives implied by such interests have been instrumental in upgrading the educational requirements of the professions. But professional interests may also involve "empire building" propensities that do not best serve either the profession or education. It is a difficult problem to develop curricula that meet the requirements of a diversity of professional and vocational interests within the range of resources available to educational institutions. Such professional pursuits as accounting, economics, and statistics, for example, have educational requirements that do not always meet the needs of executive development. The usual courses in beginning and intermediate accounting may be appropriate for future accountants, but they may not represent the best alternative for those who seek an executive career. The traditional courses in economic theory may be highly useful for prospective economists, but a different kind of course might be better for purposes of executive development. Similar situations prevail in such areas as statistics, operations research, market research, and industrial relations. This kind of conflict in vocational needs and interests has led to courses in managerial accounting, managerial economics, and managerial statistics. While they are probably more useful for executive development than are the traditional courses, these specialized courses for executive education may present problems similar to those that can result from courses in business English and agricultural economics. Executive development programs should give constant consideration to such problems as overlapping and duplication, deterioration in course content, and limitations in educational resources.

Education for Executive Development

The discussion below provides a point of departure for curricula development for purposes of executive development. It does not presume to give complete or concrete solutions. It is primarily concerned with education for executive work and does not stress education for other kinds of vocational objectives.

Knowledge Requirements. Potential executives should develop an understanding of the nature of the social, economic, and political environment with which organizations must contend. Basic courses in such academic disciplines as economics, sociology, social and cultural anthropology, psychology, and political science would seem to be highly useful in this respect. The program should also include courses that provide knowledge about the nature of organization (the hierarchy and its various aspects), the so-called functional areas of management (such as production, marketing, finance, and personnel), and the socio-psychological aspects of organizational behavior. Such courses will necessarily involve some description, but they should not attempt to describe every variety of factual information that may be required in actual employment situations. It should generally be assumed that one factory is much like any other factory, that credit institutions and markets have many common properties, that personnel problems in various industries may be similar, and so on. Thus, five or even two courses in production or finance would not seem to be necessary for purposes of executive development. However, the initial employment of many students who may ultimately want to become executives may involve highly specialized work. A number of courses in production or finance may be essential to meet this objective even though it may not further executive development.

Analytical Requirements. The courses indicated above should be used to develop analytical capacity. The development of actual knowledge involves the problems of classification and relationships, but such knowledge has little meaning without insights into the implicit and explicit assumptions that made a fact a fact or not a fact. Analytical skills can be applied in a variety of factual situations. Executives might gain more by learning them in courses in economics or production, but, if necessary, they can also learn them in botany or chemistry, even though the factual content may not be appropriate. Some colleges develop a solid foundation for executive work without any of the courses contained in a business school program.

English and Specialized Languages. Executive work requires knowledge of a number of kinds of languages together with skill in message preparation and interpretation. A problem in this respect is the relative emphasis that should be given to English and such specialized languages as accounting, statistics, and mathematics. The executive should speak with the grammar and vocabulary of the "educated" if for no other reason than that of social status. However, the appropriate level of competency is open to question. He does not need to have the facility of an H. L. Mencken or a George Bernard Shaw, but he probably requires a greater ability than that possessed by the average university or college graduate. Some graduates are well trained in some specialized languages, but they can barely speak, read, or write the English language. It might be proper to increase English requirements even if it means reduced requirements in accounting, statistics, and mathematics. However, business executives and others have also lamented the lack of facility in the specialized languages.

Some knowledge of mathematics and statistics would seem to be important for an understanding of the technological aspects of operations, quantitative economic and market information, the planning problem, and such recent developments as operations research and computer science. To paraphrase one executive, such mathematical concepts as rate of change, acceleration, rate of relative change, and the conditions for a maximum or a minimum have widespread application to the problems of business activity.[41] A mathematics course (or courses) encompassing such areas as the algebra of sets, matrix algebra, difference equations, and the basic elements of the calculus might be useful to future executives. Such a course should be taught at a high analytical level, but it should not presume to prepare people for a career in mathematics. Its purpose should be to develop a basic understanding of mathematical information and techniques and to improve logical capacities. Executives do not require as much mathematical depth as those who seek to become specialists in operations research, economic and market research, and statistics. They should, however, have enough mathematics to communicate with such specialists and to understand the implications and limitations of quantitative research and techniques.

The effective use of accounting information probably requires the level of knowledge attained in the traditional intermediate accounting courses. However, some accounting departments give too much emphasis to the preparation of professional accountants and neglect accounting as a managerial tool. A useful purpose might be served by courses in managerial accounting if adequate resources are available for this purpose. In many instances a slight shift in emphasis in present accounting courses might be sufficient.

[41] Yntema, *op. cit.,* pp. 7–8.

Simulation Techniques

To what extent can decisional, communication, socio-psychological, and other executive skills be developed on university and company campuses? The answer is partly dependent upon the extent to which the "realities" with which executives contend can be simulated or reproduced. The practice of decisional and other skills in such simulated environments provides a basis for the development of executive skills.

Skill Development: A Broad Perspective. Some aspects of higher education involve the development of skills that relate to the application of knowledge for vocational and other purposes. Analytical and communication skills may be derived from scientific experimentation and research, examinations, term papers, speech assignments, and class discussion. Organizational and social skills are practiced through student interaction with administrators, professors, and other students in classrooms, dormitories, fraternities, and student clubs. However, some educational critics contend that universities and colleges have not given adequate attention to skill development. The lack of faculty and the size of classes have created serious problems in this respect. Many basic courses are taught in large lecture sections that do not permit class discussion. Multiple-choice examinations have in great part replaced essay examinations because of the problem of numbers. Professors who are at all interested in research and reading have little time to spend with students. Such conditions do not facilitate the development of analytical and communication skills. The weekly letter to mother provides about the only writing experiences that some students have after they pass some perfunctory courses in "communication skills." Related to the problem of skill development is the possibility that the lack of opportunities for personal participation may have adverse motivational consequences. Higher education needs to give attention to these problems if its product is to be truly educated.

The Development of Professional Skills. Many of the skills required in various professional pursuits are developed as a part of the general educational program. Thus, many of the analytical and communication skills required by professionals in medicine, dentistry, accounting, engineering, and management are acquired before the student matriculates in the professional program. However, many professional schools make use of simulation techniques designed to provide skills specifically related to future professional activities. Military academies attempt to develop leadership skills through tactical and strategic war games. Law schools make use of "mock courts" to give trial experiences to prospective lawyers. Engineering schools simulate a variety of physical processes for a similar purpose. Medical and dental schools give emphasis to clinical experience in their educational programs. Business and other departments of learning concerned with executive development have also developed a number of simulation techniques designed to provide decisional and other skills. These techniques may be broadly categorized as the case method, role playing, and computer and noncomputer business games.

The Case Method. Under this method of instruction, the student is presented with a written description of concrete business situations that require some kind of decision. Some cases are of the problem-solving type in the sense that they have definite solutions that can be determined by the use of the scientific method. Other cases involve factors that require the exercise of a high degree of subjective decisiveness. Such cases have a number of what may seem to be equally good solutions to different "competent" people. John D. Glover and Ralph M. Hower of the Harvard Graduate School of Business Administration have this to say about the cases they present on human relations in business.

There are no "answers" in this casebook. Moreover, we insist that we, as instructors and as compilers of this book, do not have *the* "answers." Both of us do have *opinions* about these cases. To these opinions our students are always welcome. But our students are ever called upon to recognize our "answer" for what it is: *an* answer, but not *the* answer.[42]

Cases may be based on actual business experiences, hypothetical situations, or some combination of the two. They may be concerned with the problems of top management, situations involving the functional areas (such as personnel, production, and marketing), or the problems of "supervisory" levels. They may also be oriented toward the problems of particular industries and geographical regions. They may be used as a basis for class discussion, oral and written reports, and examinations. The case method may be the primary mode of instruction, or it may be combined with other teaching techniques.[43] It may be used in some areas of work, such as business policy, and not in others, such as economics. Some schools use the case method at all educational levels, and others use it only at upper undergraduate and graduate levels.

The case method forces students to view problems from the perspective of the executive. It gives them practice in dealing with complex situations

---

[42] John D. Glover and Ralph M. Hower, *The Administrator, Cases on Human Relations in Business* (Homewood, Ill.: Richard D. Irwin, Inc., 1949), p. 3.

[43] The Harvard Graduate School of Business Administration relies almost entirely on the case method, in contrast to the Chicago Business School which uses cases as a part of a more diversified program. Pierson, *op. cit.,* pp. 244–248.

and applying analytical problem-solving techniques. It may be used to point to the inadequacy of the scientific method and the importance of decisiveness as a subjective quality. It involves student participation as individuals and in a group which provides a basis for the development of communication and social skills. Participation may also have positive motivational consequences.

Attitudes toward the case method among educators and others range from a "missionary" optimism to militant opposition. However, the consensus seems to be that cases serve a useful purpose in some part of professional executive education. As the Gordon-Howell report points out, "the argument about the virtues of the case system is coming to be in good part a matter of emphasis." [44] Many educators believe that the case method requires strong support in the form of background knowledge. A student with little systematic knowledge of the socio-psychological, economic, and political phenomena with which he must contend may spend a great deal of time making obviously "wrong" decisions. Strong direction from the instructor may help overcome this problem, but it also repudiates other objectives sought through the case method. A major argument for the case method is that it facilitates the learning process through personal involvement. The student is in great part put on his own to find solutions and formulate generalizations that may be useful in solving future problems. But there is obviously a limit to the advantages that may be derived from this approach to education. For example, why spend two weeks with cases that may lead to the discovery that demand has price or advertising elasticities? It might be better to provide the student with this concept before he begins to work with problems involving it. In other words, there is much knowledge that need not be rediscovered to be useful or, for that matter, interesting. The case approach, if carried to an extreme, could lead to bathtubs full of students with the idea that they might discover Archimedes' principle before they graduate.

Role-Playing Techniques. Role playing, as the name implies, means to act out a role much in the manner of actors in the theatre.[45] Participants are given background information about a real or hypothetical situation and are then asked to play particular roles without prepared script or prior rehearsal. A person may be asked to play himself, he may be told to act out a position (such as personnel director or union shop steward), or he may

---

[44] Gordon and Howell, *op. cit.*, p. 368.

[45] For a more complete discussion of this technique: Norman R. F. Maier, *Principles of Human Relations: Applications to Management* (New York: John Wiley and Sons, Inc., 1952), pp. 87–172; M. Joseph Dooher and Vivienne Marquis (editors), *The Development of Executive Talent* (New York: American Management Association, 1952), pp. 191–209.

be required to act out a part with a given attitude (such as antimanagement, antiunion, distrust, or fear).

Role playing facilitates executive development in a number of directions. It can be used to help the future executive understand the manner in which his prejudices and emotions may adversely affect decisional and other situations. It can help develop skills in talking and listening to others and sensing their reactions and feelings. However, role playing, like other simulation techniques, can be given too much emphasis. It takes considerable time and can make heavy inroads into limited educational resources.

Computer and Noncomputer Business Games. More recently developed business games combine elements of the case method and role playing with additional features. They are like the case method in that they require decisions and like role playing in that they generally involve teamwork. The basic difference is that participants are given the results of their decisions and are forced to live with the results in subsequent stages of the game.

Game participants are generally divided into groups or teams, each of which "manages" a company operating in a simulated economic and market environment. The various teams may organize a hierarchy with each member performing some aspect of total decisional responsibilities. They then make decisions about such matters as product prices and mix, marketing expenditures, investment and plant utilization, and output and inventory within a framework of "game rules" and on the basis of data provided at the beginning and during intermediate stages. The game is played over simulated time periods that correspond to the planning, budgetary, and accounting periods of actual business operations. The results are given to participants at the end of each "time period" in the form of balance sheets, operating statements, and related informational devices. This kind of information is used in planning strategies for subsequent "time periods."

Business games require an "umpire" to translate the decisions of the various teams into results. This function can be performed by electronic computers or by human umpires using formulas, tables, and other computational devices. The complexity of some games and the time element make computers mandatory for all practical purposes. However, useful decisional experience can be gained from games that do not require computer facilities. A major problem is to design games that adequately simulate the "realities" of the business environment. It involves the construction of a model with variables and relationships that correspond to those that exist in actual decisional situations. The results of game decisions depend upon the values that are incorporated into the model. For example, if the model assumes a highly inelastic product demand curve, a decision to increase product price (all other things being equal) will increase revenues. An assumption of elastic demand would bring about reduced revenues if price were increased.

Business games may be classified in different ways.[46] General management games are concerned with the decisional problems of the whole enterprise from the perspective of top management. They may be specialized to simulate conditions in particular industries, such as petroleum, detergent, and steel. They may be competitively interactive in the sense that decisions by one team (company) affect the results achieved by the other teams. They may also be of the noninteracting variety in which teams or individuals "compete" in terms of the best results rather than with one another. Functional games are concerned with decisional problems in such functional areas as production, marketing, and finance. Games may be designed to simulate a large variety of particular problems, such as inventory, credit, scheduling, and sales problems.

Games may also simulate the hierarchical process through which decisions are made. Some games assign decisional responsibilities to a team without any specific organizational requirement. The various teams may themselves decide whether or not to organize a formal hierarchy. Other games indicate the appropriate structure and assign responsibilities to each team member. The quantity of decisions required in some of the more complex games force participants to organize if they are to operate effectively. An organized approach to planning is an important ingredient for successful performance in playing some games.

The primary advantage of business games over the case method and role playing is the element of feedback. The electronic computer has had an important part in the development of this type of simulation through the speed with which it can solve complex decisional models. A feedback of results gives participants insights into the manner in which past decisions may influence the decisional problems of subsequent planning periods. It helps to develop an appreciation of the impact of environmental changes and the importance of actions by competing companies. The cooperation and conflict that may occur within a game "hierarchy" afford useful sociopsychological experiences. The objective results (such as profits or losses) of decision making are translated into subjective expressions of success and failure. For example, a "losing" team may feel the pangs of remorse in emotional terms, and an individual team player may be similarly affected by group "censure" for a wrong decision.

Business games will play an important part in future executive develop-

[46] Descriptions of various kinds of business games are presented in: *Proceedings of the National Symposium on Management Games, May,* 1959 (Lawrence, Kansas: Center for Research in Business, University of Kansas, 1959).

ment in both university and company programs. They should, however, be used with discretion and should not be viewed as a panacea that makes other techniques obsolete. They seem to simulate many aspects of the reality the student will encounter in business situations. But, as critics point out, reality may be very much unlike some of the models used in business games.[47] It is not assumed that games need to be realistic to serve a useful purpose. The fact that they may not be realistic either by deliberate design or by inadequacies in knowledge poses a danger that should not be underestimated. Students may begin to assume that reality is a game model and make decisions that might not be appropriate in an actual situation. Some students may also enter industry with the idea that they now have all of the answers rather than just a few of them. Those who administer games should not give players the impression that games simulate various aspects of reality without scientific knowledge to back it up. Too much game playing can be as dangerous as too much operations research. It can foster the illusion that decisional problems are less complex or different than is actually the case. A great deal of progress will undoubtedly be made in developing better games, but the fact remains that some aspects of reality will not be effectively simulated.[48]

Business games may eventually be used to experiment with alternative strategies for purposes of practical planning. Thus, various alternative strategies may be programmed into a computer with a view of finding the best solution. The information derived from such experimentation may provide executives with a more objectives basis for decisions to the extent that the programs portray important aspects of reality. Business games may also become a means of testing applicants for executive positions. However, more knowledge is required for such adaptations of the gaming device. The difficulty is that we may fall into the trap of making right decisions for the wrong reasons. Much of what is concluded in the name of science is not really scientific at all. Some of this sort of thing may not be harmful under conditions of uncertainty that preclude any kind of scientific answer, but some useful purpose may be served by not kidding ourselves.

Simulation Techniques: Conclusions. Executive development programs should directly or indirectly incorporate some of these simulation techniques. However, the proper balance that should be maintained between such techniques and other educational techniques will depend upon the amount of resources and objectives of the program. One argument for the use of the techniques surveyed above is that they may facilitate the learning

[47] For example, *ibid.*, pp. II-6 and IV-16–17.
[48] S. L. A. Marshall's comments on army battle maneuvers are pertinent in this respect: *Men Against Fire* (Washington, D.C.: Combat Forces Press; New York: William Morrow & Company, 1947), p. 71.

process through the motivation that seems to evolve from participation. Another is that they do represent available means for developing various types of executive skills. Partial solutions are better than perfect solutions that cannot be obtained.

The Matter of Motives

Should educational institutions attempt to develop motives that make for particular professional responsibilities? Medical, military, and law schools give considerable stress to the inculcation of motives. There is a good argument for a similar practice in curricula concerned with executive development. However, too much indoctrination in a given direction can lead to difficulties in other respects. Thus, some students may become "antilabor" or even "antisociety" in the belief that such attitudes are a necessary product of being a "moral" executive. The problem is one of developing a sense of professional responsibility that does not result in a mental and moral myopia that blinds students to other worthy interests. An executive should not be "prounion" in dealing with the collective bargaining problem, but he need not hate unions in assuming a moral responsibility to his organization.

The Educational Problem: A Synthesis

Executives are important leaders in the society and should be informed about matters that may not relate directly to their professional development. They also require knowledge related to the development of a more fruitful life. An appreciation of music may add to the pleasures of living, and a well-conceived personal philosophy may help overcome life's strains and stresses. A failure to give executives a broad liberal education would deprive them of resources that would seem to be vital in a democratic and civilized society.

What is the proper balance between general educational and vocational goals within the limits of resources and time? This problem has been the subject of debate during many past years and has not been and probably cannot be resolved in any final way. However, the idea that broad educational goals are not necessarily in conflict with vocational goals should be affirmed. A liberal education may provide an important foundation for later professional development, and it may also directly produce important professional qualities. Many aspects of this kind of education may better serve the needs of executive development than the highly vocational courses of some curricula. The ideas presented in the foregoing section on the universality of knowledge and skills are pertinent in this respect.

The development of a program for executive education is complicated by the problem of balancing different vocational goals. As was emphasized earlier in this chapter, the executive function is frequently performed in combination with other kinds of functions. This fact means that business, engineering, and other areas of education must generally develop curricula that meet a number of vocational objectives. Many students who leave the groves of academia require preparation in two or even more vocational areas if they are to fit the needs of the business world. Some of them will eventually become full-fledged executives, but during the five, ten, or twenty preceding years they will be performing executive functions as a part of other responsibilities. Curricula development should be concerned with executive development, but it should not neglect the importance of such professional pursuits as market research, statistics, economics, production, personnel, accounting, and industrial engineering. However, it should be noted that education for one profession may also serve the purposes of other professions.

There does seem to be a trend toward the development of curricula that are exclusively concerned with executive development. Some of the Master of Business Administration (M.B.A.) programs are primarily concerned with education for executive work. They have many of the properties of professional schools of medicine and law. The ultimate development of such programs gives impetus to the professionalization of executives.

SELECTED REFERENCES

John W. Acer, *Business Games: A Simulation Technique.* Iowa City, Iowa: Bureau of Labor and Management, College of Business Administration, University of Iowa, 1960.

Robert R. Blake and Jane S. Mouton, *The Managerial Grid.* Houston, Texas: Gulf Publishing Company, 1964.

Floyd A. Bond, Dick A. Leabo, and Alfred W. Swinyard, *Preparation for Business Leadership,* Michigan Business Reports, No. 43. Ann Arbor: Bureau of Business Research, Graduate School of Business Administration, 1964.

A. Lynn Bryant, *Masters Degrees in Business and Government.* Rock Island: U. S. Army Management Engineering Training Agency, 1967.

C. Roland Christensen, *Management Succession in Small and Growing Enterprises.* Boston: Division of Research, Graduate School of Business Administration, Harvard University, 1953.

Dimistris N. Chorafas, *Developing the International Executive,* AMA Research Study, No. 83. New York: American Management Association, 1967.

William R. Dill, Thomas L. Hilton, and Walter R. Reitman, *The New Managers.* Englewood Cliffs, N.J.: Prentice-Hall, Inc., 1962.

Peter F. Drucker, *The Effective Executive.* New York: Harper & Row, 1967.

Richard F. Ericson, "The Growing Demand for Synoptic Minds in Industry," *Journal of the Academy of Management,* Vol. 3, No. 1, pp. 25–40 (April 1960).

Paul J. Gordon, "Administrative Strategy for a Graduate School of Administration," *Academy of Management Journal,* Vol. 10, No. 4, pp. 351–364 (December 1967).

Robert A. Gordon and James E. Howell, *Higher Education for Business.* New York: Columbia University Press, 1959.

Eugene Emerson Jennings, *Executive Success: Stresses, Problems, and Adjustment.* New York: Appleton-Century-Crofts, 1967.

Richard L. Kozelka, *Professional Education for Business.* Minneapolis: American Association of Collegiate Schools of Business, 1954.

Joseph A. Litterer, "The Simulation of Organization Behavior," *Journal of the Academy of Management,* Vol. 5, No. 1, pp. 24–35 (April 1962).

William D. Litzinger, "Entrepreneurial Prototype in Bank Management," *Academy of Management Journal,* Vol. 6, No. 1, pp. 36–45 (March 1963).

Fred Luthans, "Management Knowledge: An Untapped Resource for Academic Administration," *Advanced Management Journal,* Vol. 33, No. 2, pp. 83–88 (April 1968).

John B. Miner, "Psychology and the School of Business Curriculum," *Academy of Management Journal,* Vol. 6, No. 4, pp. 284–289 (December 1963).

David Novick, "The Mathematical Content of the Business School Curriculum," *California Management Review,* Vol. 8, No. 3, pp. 3–11. Also see comments by H. O. Steckler and G. H. Fisher which immediately follow this article.

Thomas R. O'Donovan, "Differential Extent of Opportunity Among Executives and Lower Managers," *Journal of the Academy of Management,* Vol. 5, No. 2, pp. 139–149 (August 1962).

Frank C. Pierson and others, *The Education of American Businessmen.* New York: McGraw-Hill Book Company, Inc., 1959.

Clarence B. Randall, "A Businessman Looks at the Liberal Arts," *The Randall Lectures.* White Plains, New York: Fund for Adult Education, 1957.

William G. Scott, "Executive Development as an Instrument of Higher Control," *Academy of Management Journal,* Vol. 6, No. 3, pp. 191–203 (September 1963).

Harold S. Sloan and Harold F. Clark, *Classrooms in the Military.* New York: Institute for Instructional Improvement, Inc., Bureau of Publications, Teachers College, Columbia University, 1964.

Erwin K. Taylor, "The Unsolved Riddle of Executive Success," *Personnel,* Vol. 37, No. 2, pp. 8–17 (March–April 1960).

Stanley C. Vance, "Higher Education for the Executive Elite," *California Management Review,* Vol. 8, No. 4, pp. 21–30 (Summer 1966).

E. S. Wengert, Dale S. Harwood, Jr., Lucian Marquis, and Keith Goldhammer, *The Study of Administration.* Eugene, Oregon: School of Business Administration, University of Oregon, 1961.

Frederic R. Wickert and Dalton E. McFarland, *Measuring Executive Effectiveness.* New York: Appleton-Century-Crofts, 1967.

chapter 26

COMPANY EXECUTIVE DEVELOPMENT PROGRAMS

The need for executive development should be evident to anyone familiar with the affairs of organizational and human life. Yet competent executives have shown reluctance in recognizing the importance of this problem.[1] Human beings do not always relish the idea that the bells may someday toll for them.[2] Many executives do not like the thought that the organization may survive without their unique contributions. The difficulty of measuring the revenue and cost implications of executive development also explains failures to take action. Executive development can frequently be delayed for a long period, but it can rapidly become a strategic factor as time makes inroads into the work-span of key executive personnel. The future can become better than the present only if the leaders of today help create the leaders required for tomorrow.

Position Responsibilities and Personnel Qualities

Descriptions of the responsibilities of present or planned managerial positions are useful in the development of recruitment, promotion, and training programs.

[1] L. Urwick, *The Elements of Administration* (New York: Harper & Brothers Publishers, 1943), pp. 23–24; Myles L. Mace, *The Growth and Development of Executives* (Boston: Division of Research, Graduate School of Business Administration, Harvard University, 1950), p. 5.

[2] This attitude has caused life insurance companies to avoid such terms as "death insurance." It is also reflected in the fact that many people do not have wills or own cemetery plots.

Position Descriptions

There are no definite rules on the amount of information that should be included in position or job descriptions. The descriptions should generally indicate the basic kinds of activities that make up the position. The detail that is necessary is dependent upon the information requirements of the user. An interviewer in the personnel department may need more specific information about a production planning position than someone from the production department. Position responsibilities should be expressed in operational terms whenever possible. For example, communication requirements might be described as giving speeches to large audiences of customers, preparing standard sales presentations, writing sales letters, and conducting classes for salesmen.

The nature of the duties performed by present occupants provides a basis for position descriptions. However, the fact that positions may be modified by socio-psychological factors should be taken into account. A different description might be appropriate for another person. As one executive put the problem: "When we evaluate the position of Mr. Executive Brown we evaluate the position as it *is done* by Mr. Brown. Mr. Smith, doubtless would perform it differently. Thus, we would in all probability have a different position if Mr. Smith were the incumbent."[3] Positions should not be so rigidly defined that they keep down a good man or keep out qualified persons who do not fit the exact pattern. As was emphasized in Chapter 12, a balance should be maintained between functional requirements and personal differences.

Executive Qualities

The appropriate qualities for a position can be inferred from position responsibilities. For example, the position of production manager requires knowledge about production processes and the position of research engineer demands an engineering background. Qualities can be categorized in various ways. Some common classifications are education, knowledge, skills, personal traits, responsibility, and physical characteristics. They may be more specifically defined by such requirements as university degree, years of college, high school diploma, kinds of education (business administration, engineering, or sociology), type and length of experience (three years' production planning experience), skill factors (communication or leadership), and particular personal traits (loyalty or self-confidence).

[3] R. H. Hoge, "Evaluating Executives' Jobs," *Personnel Journal,* October 1955, p. 167.

The manner in which qualities are related to a position is illustrated by the following statement of qualifications for a subsidiary manager in one company, Table 26-1.

These specifications involve inferences about the nature of and the relationship between various factors. For example, the "college graduate" requirement assumes something about the qualities that result from four years of higher education. The experience requirement is based on the premise that future performance can be predicted with a degree of accuracy

Table 26-1. Qualifications

	Minimum Qualifications
Education	College graduate with major in business administration, or the equivalent in practical business experience.
Experience	Five years' successful experience including Merchandise Manager, Operating Manager, or Controller.
Knowledge	Must have an appreciation of good merchandise and good customer service. Must have a good working knowledge of all phases of subsidiary activities. Should be thoroughly conversant with company policies and must understand and accept company objectives and standards.
Ability and skill	Ability to plan and organize work, supervise and direct people, delegate responsibility and authority wisely, and secure performance. Must be able to interpret company policies intelligently, and use good judgment in making decisions. Must be able to apply himself to details while directing a large organization.
Personal characteristics	Forceful leadership qualities. Analytical, thorough, cooperative, and aggressive. Must have good expression orally and in writing. A pleasing personality which inspires confidence, loyalty, and enthusiasm. High personal standards.
Physical requirements	Good health and businesslike appearance.

Source. Myles L. Mace, *The Growth and Development of Executives* (Boston: Division of Research, Graduate School of Business Administration, Harvard University, 1950), pp. 42–43.

from past experience. The subjective content of some of the terminology is another source of difficulty. Such terms as "pleasing personality," "businesslike appearance," and "forceful leadership qualities" may be given significantly different meanings by different persons. A businesslike appearance might mean a Brooks Brothers suit to one person and not to another. But scientific endeavor has provided few good definitions of what constitutes appropriate behavior for various purposes. The diversity of conditions found in particular situations also complicates the matter.

Forecasting Future Needs

A forecast of executive requirements is an important prerequisite for executive development planning. The forecast should take into account dynamic economic and technological factors. A company may need to double or triple its executive force during a relatively short period of time. Innovations such as electronic data-processing make for changes in the number and kinds of personnel required. Also important are planned modifications in the structure of the management hierarchy.

The accumulation of data about dates of retirement and estimates of preretirement disabilities and deaths has caused many companies to view executive development in a different light. The shocking revelation that most of the major executives will be gone in a few years is sometimes the straw that breaks the back of complacency.

The capacities of people at subordinate levels should also be given consideration in appraising executive requirements. The situation is often better or worse at one level of the hierarchy than another; there may be a large potential supply at lower levels but a dearth of persons fitted for top positions. Differences may also appear with respect to functional and other types of management specialization. They can result from the fact that executives in some departments gave more attention to executive development than those in other departments. The market supply of executive personnel can also contribute to this situation.

Development Programs

Companies seem to obtain good results from executive development programs that differ in marked respects. A number of factors make for variations in such programs. The extent to which executive development activities can be specialized is limited by the size of the company. A rapid rate of growth sometimes forces a company to avail itself of every possible means of meeting executive needs, and shortages in market supply may necessitate drastic increases in recruiting and training activities. The economics of revenues and costs can influence the situation in various ways. Companies with high profits can support and justify programs that might be marginal for companies with low or no profits. Some companies have to take chances with inexperienced personnel because they cannot afford to compete for top-notch people.

Companies should learn from the experience of others, but they should recognize that some or many aspects of established executive development programs may not fit their needs. They should not follow the Joneses into deep water if they cannot swim. The important consideration is to recognize the problem and develop an approach to its solution. Partial failures that result from planning are better than absolute failures resulting from inaction.

The Recruitment of University and College Graduates

The college graduate is the basic raw material for internal executive development programs. A company's supply of executive talent can be significantly enhanced by recruitment planning. Although this section is primarily concerned with college recruitment, many of the techniques apply as well to the recruitment of experienced personnel.

The Quality of Education

Recruitment planning should take into consideration the kind and quality of education in different institutions of higher learning. The relative emphasis given to liberal arts, science, and applied areas may be an important factor for some purposes. Institutions may have excellent faculties and facilities in engineering but not in the humanities or history, and conversely. The quality of graduates in terms of academic achievement may vary; a "B" grade average in one institution may be equivalent to a "C" average in another. However, some graduates from a substandard college or university have as much or more academic competence than the best from a highly rated institution. Companies should give explicit recognition to such factors in planning university recruitment programs and make appropriate adjustments. For example, they may hire more engineering or business administration graduates from one institution than another.

Recruiting Techniques

A variety of techniques are used in recruiting for potential executive capacities. One technique is to recruit specialists in such areas as engineering, chemistry, marketing, and purchasing with the idea that a sufficient number of them probably have executive capacities. Another is to recruit some persons who have adequate preparation in specialized areas but who also have qualities that make for success in executive work. Still another is to give primary emphasis to executive capacities with little regard for preparation in a specialized area. Such techniques can be combined with a variety of educational and training programs. For example, graduates may be recruited for executive work and spend the first year or two in a program planned for this purpose. They may also be hired for particular positions in production, accounting, purchasing, market research product engineering, or design and be selected for an executive development program later in their career.

Immediate and Future Needs

Companies are often faced with the problem of compromising immediate needs with the requirements of the future. A specialized education may be appropriate for the positions that are presently available but it may not give a company the personnel capable of promotion to higher functional or scalar positions. Explicit attention should be given to this problem in planning the recruitment program. It may be necessary in some instances to tax the present in order to better serve the needs of the future.

Inferring Qualities

A major problem in recruiting for executive development is to determine present and potential capacities from inferences that have varying degrees of reliability. The criteria that should be used for this purpose are dependent upon the qualities required for executive work and also upon the availability of information about a prospective graduate's personal qualities and past performance. The following kinds of information are frequently used as a basis for evaluating potential executive capacity.

Academic Performance. There is a diversity of opinion on the relationship between academic achievement and progress in management. Some contend that above average grades are not necessary for future success in a managerial career. Others have an opposite point of view on this subject.

EXECUTIVE DEVELOPMENT

Table 26-2. Rank in College Graduating Class as Related to Salary Progress (In Percentages)

	Top Salary Third	Middle Salary Third	Bottom Salary Third	
Top tenth of class	51	32	17	100
Top third of class	45	34	21	100
Middle third of class	32	36	32	100
Bottom third of class	26	34	40	100

Source. American Telephone and Telegraph Company, New York, N.Y.

Recent research by the Bell Telephone System has provided important insights.[4] This research related rank in college graduating class with salary progress for some 10,000 men at various managerial levels. The main criterion in the study was annual salary earned by a man as compared to that earned by others with the same length of service in the company. Adjustments were made for differences in salary levels in different parts of the United States and between different departments. The salary distributions for each length of service were divided into thirds and compared with rankings in college graduating classes. The results are indicated in Table 26-2.

The data indicate a significant relationship between academic ranking and progress in the Bell System. Fifty-one per cent of the men who graduated in the top tenth of their class and 45 per cent of those in the top third were in the top salary third. On the other hand, 26 per cent of those in the lowest third of their graduating class had attained this salary level. Only 17 per cent of the top graduating tenth and 21 per cent of the top third were found in the lowest salary third, compared with 40 per cent for those who were in the lowest rank of their college classes. These results are similar to those obtained in an earlier Bell System study made in 1928.

The quality of the college from which the manager graduated made some difference in the results. The middle third graduate from above average colleges was in the top salary third 38 per cent of the time, as compared with 28 per cent for the same category from average colleges. Extracurricular achievement was found to be somewhat compensatory for lower rank in the graduating class. The extent to which the graduate earned his own

[4] Data obtained from the American Telephone and Telegraph Company, New York, N.Y.

college expenses had no appreciable effect on salary progress. The major field of study (arts, sciences, business, and engineering) did not appear to have any relationship to managerial rank.

The Bell System warns against applying the above results in a mechanical way. Although academic achievement appears to be highly important in management progress, this conclusion does not close the door to all who stand upon the lowest rung of the grade point ladder. At the same time, the study indicates that some ideas on the importance of grades are based on tenuous assumptions. An oft-heard statement is that "C" students have "better" personalities for the practical affairs of business than "A" or "B" students. The truth of the matter undoubtedly points to the other direction. A "C" student may be more intelligent than some "A" or "B" students, but why did he fail to give forth the necessary effort to earn higher grades? Companies should be wary of intelligent graduates who have a lackadaisical attitude toward the matter of grades. It might be better to hire a "C" student with less intelligence but with enough ambition to achieve an important objective.

Formal university curricula do not generally afford much opportunity for the development and practice of social and leadership skills. Some extracurricular activities contribute more in this respect than the educational program. Active participation as members or officers in student government, fraternal and other clubs, debating societies, and such organizations as the Society for the Advancement of Management would seem to indicate important qualities for executive work. However, the lack of such experiences does not necessarily mean a lack of social and other skills. Some students deliberately ignore extracurricular activities to gain time for academic pursuits or part-time jobs with which to pay their college expenses. Part-time jobs provide opportunities for the development of skills important in executive work. This consideration does not mean a student should work if he does not need the money; the time can frequently be better used in the library or laboratory. The matter of part-time employment and extracurricular activities should be viewed in terms of the total situation. The important question is whether the applicant used good discretion in balancing the alternatives. For example, a potential "A" student who became a "B" student in order to engage in extracurricular activities did not necesssarily make a bad choice. A similar statement cannot be made about a low "C" student who worked a part-time job to maintain a sports car and participated in numerous clubs to become a "Big Man on Campus." But, a low "C" student who was forced by circumstances to work forty hours a week might be a better prospect than some "B" or "A" students.

Psychological Testing. Useful inferences about potential executive capacities can be made from testing information.[5] The tests mentioned below are often used in executive recruitment and for related purposes.

INTELLIGENCE TESTS. These tests attempt to measure learning capacity and the ability to adapt to situations. There is some question about the nature of intelligence and the extent to which it can be isolated from other qualities that may be involved in the test results. The "innate" potential a person may possess is subject to modification by the learning that has already taken place. Acquired knowledge and skills play a part in the results obtained in intelligence tests; the factors measured tend to be similar to the factors involved in achievement testing.

APTITUDE TESTS. These test differ from intelligence (general aptitude) tests in that they are concerned with specific aptitudes, such as the ability to perceive spatial relationships, memory capacities, and manipulative skills. They attempt to measure potential rather than prior learning through a simulation of the basic elements involved in a pursuit. For example, a person who can readily solve an abstract puzzle with certain spatial properties is assumed to have the capacity to perform tasks that have similar properties. In other words, the test is an abstract model of selected aspects of the realities of the work situation.

ACHIEVEMENT OR PROFICIENCY TESTS. These tests are designed to measure the knowledge and skill acquired from systematic educational and training programs. The examinations given in university courses illustrate this kind of testing.

VOCATIONAL AND OTHER-INTEREST TESTS. These tests seek to determine the nature of a subject's interests by the choices he makes from among alternative activities. For example, a person might be asked which he prefers to do most (or least): play football or watch a football game, compose music or play a musical instrument, read a book or watch a television show, hunt elephants or visit a zoo, etc. The basic assumption is that particular patterns of interests have a relationship to the qualities and motives required for particular pursuits. Thus, if most executives or physicians prefer mountain climbing over book reading, a person with a similar interest has "something" that may make for success in these professions. However, the nature of the "something" is open to question. People in some occupations seem to have different interests than those in other occupations, but there is doubt about the validity of some of the inferences that are made from interest tests. The problem of "cheating" also presents a difficulty. A person may indicate he likes to go to the opera or read books because such interests seem related to the job he is seeking.

PERSONALITY TESTS. These tests attempt to infer personality traits from

[5] The results of a study of executive attitudes toward testing and company experiences with various tests are reported in: Mace, *op. cit.*, pp. 83–91.

various kinds of information. The subject may be asked to make a choice from a number of alternatives, tell stories about a series of pictures, give impressions about ink blots, or simply to talk about himself. The responses are generally analyzed in terms of a personality theory and results obtained in previous testing. The statements that were made about the validity of interest tests and the "cheating problem" also apply to personality tests.[6] However, useful information can be gained from personality tests administered and interpreted by qualified persons.

Test Validity and Reliability. Psychological tests should be viewed as supporting instruments and used with discretion. Executives should consult with qualified psychologists and be wary of those who promise too much. They should endeavor to determine test validity (do they test for the intended purpose?) and reliability (are the results consistent?) as soon as sufficient information is available. They should also recognize that a testing program may provide good results for one purpose but not for another. Psychological tests do not eliminate the need for executive judgment and should not be used to avoid responsibility. However, they can sometimes be profitably used to justify unpopular changes.

Achievement or proficiency tests to determine writing skills should probably be given more emphasis than is presently the case. Many executives lament the lack of such skills in college and university graduates. The ultimate responsibility for this situation rests with educational institutions and there is no intent to shift it to business leaders. Companies should help themselves, however, while this unfortunate state of affairs continues to exist. A solution is to ask each applicant to write a two or three hundred word essay on some subject without help from a dictionary or any other source. This may sound too simple and even "unscientific," but it seems reasonable to assume that one way to discover a lack of writing skills is to have people write.

Interviews and Other Techniques. Interviews can be used to eliminate applicants who obviously lack appropriate qualities and to gain some general impressions. An applicant who shuffles into the interview with a cigarette dangling from his mouth and speaks in an uncouth manner might not be given further consideration. However, such extremes are exceptional, which means that the alternatives are not always so evident. Interview impressions should not be used as the only basis for eliminating an applicant, and they should be carefully evaluated. Well-qualified applicants are sometimes rejected for superficial reasons. There seems to be a tendency to give preference to the man with the right "look" and a friendly

---

[6] People with a Machiavellian bent might wish to read William H. Whyte, Jr.'s instructions on how to cheat on personality tests, in *The Organization Man* (New York: Simon and Schuster, 1956), pp. 405–410.

and "sincere" attitude. Every interviewer should be required to study a photograph of Abraham Lincoln and listen to a few Churchillian stutters before he marks his little book.

Letters of recommendation are generally of little value because they are either extremely favorable or they say nothing. The use of rating scales does not help the matter much because standards are apt to have different meanings to different people. Average is below average to one person, and above average is average to another. A telephone or a personal conversation with someone who knows the applicant generally produces better results than letters or rating sheets. Some companies invite selected applicants for an extended visit for interviews and consultations with personnel and other executives. As was pointed out above, a great deal of subjectivity is involved in these techniques; the "perfect" woman on a date does not always make an "ideal" partner in marriage.

Recruitment in Perspective

A high degree of uncertainty is involved in the selection of personnel for executive and other responsibilities. Mistakes cannot be entirely avoided, but they can be reduced through planning. Some companies do not give adequate attention to the problem; others "put on a good show" but do not properly use such techniques as testing and interviewing. Still others recruit in terms of immediate needs and give too little consideration to the long run. They fail to recognize that the requirements at lower levels may not serve future needs at higher levels. They might give greater emphasis to hiring persons who have potential "executive qualities" even though, for the present, they may be primarily engaged in nonmanagerial work. Furthermore, there should be less reluctance to hire the person who does not fit the stereotype expressed by such terms as "togetherness" and "other directed."

Recruitment of Experienced Personnel

Some companies have a policy of promotion from within and do not normally recruit for positions at higher levels. An oft-cited danger of bringing in people from the outside is that it has adverse motivational consequences, but the other side of the coin also has importance. Some competition from outsiders may motivate insiders to become more productive; promotions should not become a definite eventuality for those who stay around long enough. Some companies may even justify the promotion of unqualified people to show others that their opportunities will not be given to outsiders. Such a policy can be supported under certain circumstances, but it also invites dissatisfaction from those who believe that promotions, including their own, should be given on the basis of merit. Subordinates who have to work under an unqualified superior are apt to become disgruntled with their situations.

New Ideas and Personalities

Too much promotion from within or inbreeding can lead to inertia in the ranks of management. A periodic injection of new ideas and personalities is sometimes helpful in combating this problem. However, the dangers of too much disruption must be kept in mind. A necessary amount of stability should be maintained without engendering stagnation, but there are no easy or exact solutions.

The Evaluation of Past Performance

The problems in recruiting experienced executive and other personnel are similar to those involved in hiring neophyte university graduates, with the added element of the evaluation of successes and failures in previous places of employment. Reliable information about past job performance is sometimes difficult to obtain. Letters of recommendation and information given by the candidate may provide few useful insights. Furthermore, good or bad performance in one company does not necessarily mean a repeat performance in another. A person may experience failure in one environment and outstanding succcess in another. The elements of circumstance and chance are sometimes as important as knowledge and skills. There is probably too much reluctance to hire someone who expresses dissatisfaction with his present situation or who has changed jobs a number of times. A man who seeks another position in the middle of his career is not always foolhardy. He may have the initiative and courage required in a company that wants to go places.

Key Executives

Company sometimes seek an outstanding executive from another company because they want someone who is tried and tested for a particular purpose. They may also want to gain advantages from the personal contacts and influence of such an executive and the motivational impact of an important personage upon present personnel. A dynamic and experienced executive from the outside can help bring a company out of the doldrums and lift it to new heights. But far too much is frequently expected in too short a time and in situations that cannot be salvaged. The impossible is impossible unless the meaning of the word is changed. Good management, like good football, starts with fundamentals; an executive or a coach can be helpful if miracles are not expected. The cost of top talent is usually high. Other alternatives for the resources involved should be given careful consideration.

Executive Development Through Promotion

Some executives may be hired from the outside for purposes indicated in the previous section, but companies must generally meet much of the need for executive talent through promotion from lower positions. Career patterns in an organization can be categorized in a number of ways. Some people advance in status by becoming more proficient in such functional specialties as accounting, market research, and engineering. Others move up in scalar rank by assuming more and more executive responsibilities. A sizable proportion of line, staff, and service personnel will spend their working lives at middle and lower levels of the hierarchy. Such personnel frequently lack the capacities for higher positions or the ambition to put forth the necessary amount of effort. Many of them are content with such a career, which is in some respects a fortunate situation. There is not enough room at the top of a pyramid for everyone at the bottom, and experienced personnel is required at lower levels.

Selection for Promotion

A major problem is to determine which persons should be promoted or prepared for promotion to higher executive positions. Some companies attempt to classify personnel for future responsibilities at the recruitment stage. Others recruit personnel for particular positions without giving explicit consideration to promotion potential. Still others have a planned program of training and experience through which persons may advance to higher executive positions. There are no hard and fast rules for deciding which person or persons should be selected for actual or potential promotion.

Promotion Criteria

The recruitment stage provides information that may have value in later stages of a person's career. Some of this information may relate more to the requirements of the future than of the first position. Thus, the fact that X has a broad liberal arts background or a solid foundation in science may be particularly pertinent for promotion to some kinds of responsibilities. Recruitment information should be modified and magnified by subsequent information about performance. Some initial inferences may not have been appropriate in terms of later performance, and others may be supported by performance data. Subordinate performance should be systematically and periodically evaluated by superiors and others. However, the evaluation process should be carefully planned, and an attempt should be made to establish "objective" standards. As Professor Mace has pointed out, "slipshod and casual filling out of appraisal forms is potentially more dangerous than no appraisal system because of the possibly irreparable damage to the careers of men and because of the faulty management decisions resulting from misleading basic information." [7] Performance evaluations should generally be used together with other types of information such as educational achievements and test results. The idea that people change over time should always be kept in mind. Some people develop more slowly than others, and factors like family responsibility may result in a marked change in motives. Also important is that "good" or "bad" performances should be evaluated in terms of the responsibilities that are involved. An outstanding plant design engineer may not work out well in a position requiring executive talent. Furthermore, the capacities and motives required for higher positions are not the same as those required for lower positions. Performance and other kinds of information provide a basis for judgment about such matters, but they do not automatically provide the answer.

Company Educational and Training Programs

The years that followed World War II have witnessed a tremendous growth in company executive training programs.[8] Before that time the primary emphasis was on foremanship training, and little attention was given to the higher levels of management. A number of factors gave impetus to executive development through training and education. The earlier foremanship programs and the leadership training experiences of the military services and industry during the war demonstrated that effective

[7] Mace, op. cit., p. 82.
[8] Donald S. Bridgman, "Company Management Development Programs," in Frank C. Pierson and others, *The Education of American Businessmen* (New York: McGraw-Hill Book Company, Inc., 1959), pp. 537–541.

leaders can be rapidly developed through training techniques. Rapid economic expansion and technological innovation created a large demand for competent executive personnel, while government, the military, and other areas of endeavor made inroads into an already short supply.

Kinds of Training Programs

Management training may be used to increase competency in a present position, to prepare people for promotion, and to provide opportunities for self-development.[9] Training programs may be concerned with the problems at the various levels of management, such as first-line supervision, the junior executive level, middle management, and top management.[10] They may also give emphasis to the functional areas of management specialization and to particular staff, service, and technical functions. The length of the training period may vary from a few weeks to several years and may be intermittent or continuous. Training may be conducted on a part-time basis during regular employment, or it may involve full-time participation for several weeks or months. It may be administered by central management, by departmental units, or by outside organizations like universities and associations.

Educational Facilities

Some companies maintain special educational facilities and employ specialists; others rely upon regular personnel and facilities; and still others make use of both approaches for different types of training. A few companies operate their own educational plants with faculties in many fields of knowledge. The General Motors Institute at Flint, Michigan, and the General Electric Management Research and Development Institute at Crotonville on the Hudson illustrate this development. Management associations have generally increased their educational activities and conduct many conferences, seminars, courses, and workshops. The American Management Association, for example, maintains the equivalent of a residential college, the AMA Academy at Saranac Lake, New York, in addition to other facilities. "The Academy," according to an announcement of the Association, "is the most modern and completely equipped management education and research center in the world." [11]

---

[9] For a description of various types of programs: *Ibid.*, pp. 547–561.

[10] The distinction between the first-line supervisor and the junior executive is that the latter is usually a university graduate who is being prepared for supervisory responsibilities. A first-line supervisor, such as a foreman or an office supervisor, comes from the ranks and does not generally advance beyond this level.

[11] *Workshop and Orientation Seminars Program,* March–June 1960 (New York: American Management Association, 1960), p. 5.

Content of Programs

The content of management training programs varies from company to company and with the different purposes they are supposed to serve. Some programs involve a planned sequence of different subject-matter areas; others present pertinent aspects of various fields in an integrated course; and still others offer individual courses in subjects like accounting, job evaluation, and computer programming. Much company-administered training gives primary emphasis to knowledge and skills that can be applied to particular positions. The philosophy and practices of the company tend to become a major motif in the training program, and attention is generally concentrated on conditions that pertain to the company rather than to companies in general. A course in organizing, for example, may give almost exclusive consideration to the company's organizational structure. A course in accounting may use the company's accounting system as a point of departure. University and association programs for practicing executives are generally not adapted to the conditions of a given company, but many of them are oriented toward the problems of a particular industry.

Emphasis on Techniques

Management training has tended to emphasize techniques rather than the fundamental knowledge from which techniques are ultimately derived. It has also been more concerned with internal company problems than the economic, political, social, and cultural environment. However, the growth of training programs for higher executives has brought about some change in perspective. Greater emphasis has been given in recent years to the dynamics of the total organizational system and to the manner in which it fits into the environment. A few programs focus upon the humanities, with readings in classical and modern literature.

Instructional Methods

The instructional techniques used in management training programs are similar to those employed by educational institutions in undergraduate and graduate programs. Lectures, the case method, role playing, business games, and seminars and conferences are widely employed, with relatively more emphasis being given to student participation. The effectiveness of various techniques is dependent upon the purpose of the program and the

Effectiveness of Company Training

Some formal training undoubtedly improves executive performance and reduces the time required for adaptation to present and potential positions. It can be carried to an extreme. There is little in the way of objective measures to indicate exactly what is gained by various kinds of programs. Some programs are little more than superficial presentations of superficial material. They may seem like great sport, but nothing much is gained either by the participants or the companies. "Keeping up with the Joneses," company affluence, and tax deductions are probably important underlying motivations for some training programs. Programs sometimes reflect inadequacies on the part of educational institutions, for example, companies may have to teach junior executives to write the English language because high schools and colleges have not provided proper preparation. Company programs include subject matter that can be better handled by universities and colleges, and conversely. If more knowledge in the liberal arts is necessary, such preparation should generally fall within the domain of educational institutions. On the other hand, training in techniques can often be better handled by companies. Companies should generally not educate in the broader sense, and universities should not become too concerned with training for particular positions. This is not to say that definite jurisdictional lines can or should be drawn, but rather that educators and executives should give serious attention to their mutual problems and prevent wastes in limited educational and training resources.

University-Sponsored Programs

In addition to regular degree programs in which executives can participate with or without company support, higher educational institutions conduct executive programs, conferences, institutes, and courses. A number of universities offer "on campus" integrated programs that take a broad executive-development approach.[12] The duration of these programs ranges from two weeks to several months, the cost from $500 to over $2000 (with and without living costs), the size of the group from less than a score to over a hundred, and the participants from junior to senior executives. Program content includes such subjects as the management

---

[12] George V. Moser and Allison V. MacCullough, "Executive Development Courses in Universities," *Conference Board Reports,* Studies in Personnel Policy, No. 142 (New York: National Industrial Conference Board, Inc., 1954).

process, functional areas, human and public relations, and personal development (conference leadership, public speaking, and reading); instructional methods vary from exclusive use of the case method (Harvard) to combinations of lecture, case, seminar, and other techniques. Regular faculty members and specialists from business and from other universities make up the teaching staffs.

Colleges and universities have also established literally hundreds of residential and nonresidential courses in such areas as supervisory training, time study, quality control, cost accounting, computer programming, and production planning. These courses are designed to give executives specific knowledge and skill, to introduce new developments, and to refresh executive memories. Many of them serve a useful function, but some have little or nothing to offer. In more than a few instances, resources that are needed for regular degree programs are frittered away in large and small chunks.

Training Through Directed Experience

Companies frequently develop executive talent through what might be called "directed experience" with or without supplementary "classroom" training. In some situations, job experience is an integral part of the development program. A management trainee may be shifted from one department to another to gain a diversity of experience and, at the same time, attend formal training sessions. This approach is used in many different ways in general management programs and in the functional areas of specialization.

On-the-job training by superiors is another form of directed experience. This technique is often referred to as "coaching" and has been called "the most effective way of providing for the growth and development of people in manufacturing organizations. . . ."[13] The purpose of coaching is to develop subordinate potential, and it involves more than a set of training techniques. Coaching represents the conscious creation of an environment within which subordinates can learn to become better executives. Subordinates must be given rope but not enough to hang the company, and they should have the opportunity to make mistakes and learn from them. Responsibilities can be increased or decreased as the situation warrants, but this process should not seem deliberate. Superiors should "instruct" and counsel, but they should not appear to be intruding or interfering. At the same time, subordinates should feel that they can take problems to the superior without a loss of self-respect and status. In many ways, the superior must be willing to sacrifice his own ego for the interests and future of the

[13] Mace, *op. cit.,* p. 108. A comprehensive discussion of coaching methods and results is found in *ibid.,* pp. 107–175.

subordinate. Some otherwise successful executives are not able to assume this kind of role. The qualities that make for effective coaching are not necessarily the same qualities that make for effective leadership. Leaders are often successful for reasons other than their ability to coach subordinates.

Coaching also takes place in such situations as committee meetings and informal relationships. The McCormick Company, for example, uses committees of junior executives to provide insights into the problems at higher levels; staff or "assistant to" positions may accomplish a similar purpose.

The Importance of Nondirected Experience

If the present emphasis on education and training is carried to an extreme, a man might find himself in retirement before he has a chance to perform. Educational and training programs, and this includes directed experience, simulate reality; they are not the same as reality. The "hard-knocks" type of experience is still an essential ingredient of executive development. There is a thin line between directed experience and actual experience, but the line is highly significant. The psychological properties of the two are not identical as long as there is any awareness on the part of the subordinate that experience is planned in some fashion. Conscious coaching may be the exception if the fact that it is conscious can be hidden from the subordinate. Experience in executive work involves a personal burden that cannot be shared by others. Subordinates who have not been frustrated by uncertainty or who have not felt the pangs of failure have probably yet to pass through the executive portals.

The Problem of Stagnation

The management hierarchy has the inherent capacity to reconstruct itself in response to internal and external forces. Many organizations display a capacity to make appropriate changes over a long period of time, but such a system of self-generation can lead to difficulty. An already inefficient structure can gradually develop into an even more inefficient structure, and the vested interests of executives can inhibit corrective adjustments. The result is destructive rather than constructive changes. Organizations sometimes have to be revitalized by the dynamic force of new leadership if they are to survive. Many examples of organizational decline and revival can be found in the history of business and other organizations. The reforms of the Prussian military system by Scharnhorst, the development of an efficient United States military staff by Elihu Root, the reorganization of the General Motors Corporation by Alfred Sloan, Jr., the formation of a coalition cabinet by Winston Churchill during World War II, and the organizational changes made at the Ford Motor Company by the new management team headed by Henry Ford II all illustrate the impact of creative leadership. But such upheavals may not be necessary if the organization develops executives who have ideas and ideals and the courage to implement them.

SELECTED REFERENCES

Henry H. Albers and Lowell Schoer, *Programmed Organization & Management Principles*. New York: John Wiley & Sons, Inc., 1966.

Melvin Anshen, "Executive Development: In-Company vs. University Programs," *Harvard Business Review,* Vol. 32, No. 5, pp. 83–91 (September–October 1954).

Bernard M. Bass and James A. Vaughan, *Training in Industry: The Management of Learning*. Belmont, California: Wadsworth Publishing Company, 1966.

Marvin Bower (editor), *The Development of Executive Leadership*. Cambridge: Harvard University Press, 1949.

John W. Buckley, "Programmed Instruction in Industrial Training," *California Management Review,* Vol. 10, No. 2, pp. 71–79 (Winter 1967).

Lee J. Cronbach, *Essentials of Psychological Testing*. New York: Harper & Row, 1960.

M. Joseph Dooher and Vivienne Marquis (editors), *The Development of Executive Talent*. New York: American Management Association, 1952.

John W. Enell and George H. Haas, *Setting Standards for Executive Performance*. New York: American Management Association, 1960.

Don W. Garrison, *Executive Development in Business, Government, and Universities: A Comparative Study*. Rock Island, Ill.: U. S. Army Management Engineering Training Agency, 1968.

Edgar F. Huse, "Putting in a Management Development Program That Works," *California Management Review,* Vol. 9, No. 2, pp. 73–80 (Winter 1966).

G. Lawton Johnson, "Executive Development for Today's Business," *Michigan Business Review,* Vol. 11, No. 4, pp. 8–12 (July 1959).

Myles L. Mace, *The Growth and Development of Executives*. Boston: Division of Research, Graduate School of Business Administration, Harvard University, 1950.

William McGehee and Paul W. Thayer, *Training in Business and Industry*. New York: John Wiley and Sons, Inc., 1961.

Arch Patton, "The Coming Scramble for Executive Talent," *Harvard Business Review,* Vol. 45, No. 3, pp. 155–171 (May–June 1967).

Robert C. Sampson, "Train Executives While They Work," *Harvard Business Review,* Vol. 31, No. 6, pp. 42–54 (November–December 1953).

Don R. Sheriff and Jude P. West, "An Integrated Approach to Management Development for the Small Businessman," *Iowa Business Digest,* Vol. 35, No. 3, pp. 11–16 (March 1964).

Daniel Starch, *How to Develop Your Executive Ability*. New York: Harper & Brothers, 1943.

Fred Tickner, *Training in Modern Society*. Albany, N.Y.: Graduate School of Public Affairs, State University of New York at Albany, 1966.

NAME INDEX

Abegglen, James C., 557, 640, 641
Abrams, Frank, 609
Acer, John W., 658
Ackoff, Russell L., 62, 381, 382, 386, 397
Adams, Walter, 371
Adler, Lee, 371, 548
Albaum, Gerald, 315
Albers, Henry H., 39, 230, 680
Alexis, Marcus, 96, 417
Alford, L. P., 37, 41, 55
Allen, Harold B., 472
Ammer, Dean S., 371
Andersen, Theodore A., 343
Anderson, Allan H., 548
Anderson, Charlotte L., 469
Anrod, Charles W., 343
Anshen, Melvin, 680
Ansoff, H. Igar, 371
Archer, Stephen H., 343
Archibald, Russell D., 514
Argyris, Chris, 298, 480, 481, 514, 583, 632, 633, 634, 637
Aristotle, 429, 431
Arnoff, E. Leonard, 62, 381, 382, 386, 397
Arnold, Robert R., 548
Austin, Robert W., 610, 622

Babbage, Charles, 21, 32
Bacon, Jeremy, 236, 238, 239, 240, 241, 252
Bailey, Earl L., 344
Bain, Joe S., 343
Baker, Helen, 186, 197, 211, 315, 448
Baker, James C., 344
Baker, John C., 232, 233, 234, 240, 244, 252
Bakke, E. Wight, 61, 303, 306, 315, 343, 415, 435, 446, 565, 579, 592, 594
Bales, Robert F., 226, 227, 228, 229
Ballantine, John W., 315, 448
Baloff, Nicholas, 514
Bannister, Roger, 107
Barnard, Chester I., 6, 7, 8, 9, 46, 60, 63, 144, 255, 264, 269, 300, 307, 310, 311, 315, 321, 397, 400, 434, 436, 553, 561, 562, 586, 594, 599, 604, 615, 619, 621, 622, 633, 637

Barth, Carl G., 36
Bass, Bernard M., 680
Bates, George E., 237, 238, 252
Batten, J. D., 604
Baumback, Clifford M., 371, 514
Bavelas, Alex, 63
Beal, Edwin F., 371
Beavin, Janet H., 446
Beer, Michael, 118
Beer, Stafford, (2) 74, 96, 417
Beishline, John R., 184, 583, 604
Belcher, David W., 583
Bell, Gerald D., 298
Bell, William D., 23
Bello, Francis, 390
Bendix, Reinhard, 269, 298
Benge, Eugene J., 153
Bennis, Warren G., 177, 184, 298, 604
Berelson, Bernard, 583
Bergmann, Gustav, 72
Berkeley, Edmund C., 529
Berle, Adolf A., Jr., 29, 606, 622
Bernstein, Theodore M., 472
Berry, Paul C., 395
Biegel, John E., 514
Bierman, Harold, 371
Bigelow, Robert P., 548
Blake, Robert R., 658
Blankenship, A. B., 371
Blau, Peter M., 61, 298, 597, 598, 599, 604
Block, Clifford H., 395
Blomstrom, Robert L., 343
Blough, Roger M., 583
Blough, Roy, 343
Bond, Floyd A., 658
Boulding, Kenneth E., 29
Boulware, L. R., 357, 462
Bowen, Howard R., 29, 69, 70, 622
Bower, Marvin, 680
Bowers, David G., 604
Bowman, Edward H., 397
Brady, Rodney H., 209, 211, 548
Brayer, Herbert O., 365
Brech, E. F. L., 13
Brewer, Donald W., 548
Bridges, Francis J., 371
Bridgman, Donald S., 673

683

NAME INDEX

Bridgman, P. W., 408
Britt, Steuart Henderson, 343
Bromage, Arthus W., 143
Brown, Alvin, 153
Brown, Donaldson, 45
Brown, Leland, 472
Brown, Ray E., 397
Brown, Roger F., 492
Brown, Warren B., 548
Bruner, Jerome S., 425
Bryant, A. Lynn, 371, 658
Buchele, Robert B., 371
Buckley, John W., 680
Bueschel, Richard T., 530, 548
Buffa, Elwood S., 397, 514
Bunke, Harvey C., 29
Burck, Gilbert, 29, 252
Burlingame, John F., 116, 209, 211
Bursk, Edward C., 187, 189, 211, 308, 405
Bush, Vannevar, 21

Campbell, William H., 46
Cannon, J. Thomas, 371
Carey, Ernestine Gilbreth, 55
Carlson, Sune, 96
Carnap, Rudolf, 428
Carroll, J. B., 428
Carter, C. F., 393, 397
Cartier, Francis A., 184
Cassirer, Ernest, 424
Chamberlain, Neil W., 17, 29, 371
Champion, John M., 371
Chandler, Alfred D., Jr., 207, 208, 211
Cherry, Colin, 446
Chiselli, Edwin E., 153
Chorafas, Dimistris N., 658
Christensen, C. Roland, 658
Chrysler, Walter, 311
Churchill, Winston, 679
Churchman, C. West, 62, 381, 382, 386, 397
Ciaccio, Jack N., 328, 329
Clark, Wallace, 498
von Clausewitz, Karl, 31
Clay, Lucius, 308, 312
Cochran, Thomas C., 622
Coe, George, 620
Cogan, Morris L., 69
Cohen, Joel B., 343
Cohen, Kalman J., 343
Cohen, Morris R., 66
Cohen, Sanford, 372
Cole, Robert H., 371
Collins, Orvis, 52, 278
Collyer, John, 235
Commager, Henry S., 143, 156
Commons, John R., 403, 404
Constantin, James A., 371
Cooke, Morris L., 37
Cooley, Charles Horton, 566
Coombs, C. H., 382, 383, 398
Copeland, Melvin T., 232, 240, 243, 252

Copley, Frank Barkley, 32, 36, 41, 55
Cordiner, Ralph J., 405, 622
Costello, Timothy W., 64
Coubrough, J. A., 42
Cowles, John T., 556
Cox, Donald E., 548
Crawford, C. M., 323, 409
Cronbach, Lee J., 680
Cross, Hershner, 29
Crozier, Michael, 298
Curtice, Harlow H., 206
Cyert, Richard M., 343

Dale, Ernest, 44, 45, 61, 105, 106, 117, 118, 126, 127, 153, 184, 186, 188, 189, 195, 209, 211, 222, 225, 229, 273, 285, 287, 290, 291, 294, 295, 298, 311, 374, 614
Dalton, Melville, 52, 61, 275, 276, 277, 281, 298, 568
D'Ambrosio, Charles A., 343
D'Antonio, William V., 29
Danziger, Erwin M., 548
Dauten, Paul M., Jr., 72
Davey, Harold W., 371, 372
David, Donald K., 187
Davis, Allison, 557
Davis, Keith, 63, 304, 305, 315, 343, 435, 437
Davis, Ralph C., 47, 125, 153, 229, 417
Davis, R. L., 382, 398
Dean, Joel, 324, 352, 487, 493
Dean, Neal J., 136, 532, 538, 540, 542, 543, 544, 546, 548
Dearden, John, 209, 211, 514, 523, 529, 534, 535, 548
Delbecq, Andre L., 73, 96
de Mare, George, 472
Dennison, Henry S., 46, 271, 272, 578, 633
Dent, James K., 604
Dershimer, Frederick W., 108
Deutsch, Karl W., 382
Devlin, Frank J., 472
Dickson, William J., 48-55, 306
Diebold, John T., 39
Digman, Lester A., 514
Dill, William R., 658
Dimock, Marshall E., 298
Dodd, E. M., 605, 606
Dollard, John, 257
Dolvin, Wellborn G., 153
Donaldson, Gordon, 514
Dooher, M. Joseph, 229, 461, 652, 680
Doyle, J. B., 371
Drew, Franklin E., 168, 170, 286, 289, 290
Drucker, Peter F., 15, 190, 199, 203, 204, 211, 622, 658
Drury, Horace B., 55
Durant, William C., 45, 199, 311

Eaton, Marquis, 487

NAME INDEX

Eccles, John C., 390, 391
Eells, Richard, 29
Ehrlich, Howard J., 29
Einstein, Albert, 67
Eisenhower, Dwight D., 308
Embree, Edwin R., 191
Enell, John W., 680
Ericson, Richard F., 583, 622, 658
Ess, T. J., 331
Estey, Marten, 343
Ethe, Solomon, 237, 238
Etzioni, Amitai, 298
Euclid, 429
Evans, Bergen, 455, 457
Evans, Cornelia, 455, 457
Ewad, Elias M., 548
Ewing, David W., 583

Fairlie, John A., 143
Farquhar, Henry H., 133, 135, 155
Fayol, Henri, 9, 41-43, 47, 55, 59, 60, 104, 105, 109, 125, 135, 376, 633
Fenn, Dan H., Jr., 405, 583
Fetter, Robert B., 397
Feynman, Richard P., 25
Fieden, John S., 472
Fine, I. V., 372, 508
Finley, Ruth E., 6
Finney, Nat S., 374
Fisch, Gerald G., 118
Fish, L. S., 131, 132, 153, 229, 236, 243, 252, 286, 287, 290
Fisk, George, 343
Flanagen, John C., 108, 569
Fleming, John E., 417
Flesch, Rudolf, 472
Follett, Mary Parker, 48
Folts, F. E., 359
Ford, Henry, II, 359, 679
Ford, Henry, Sr., 13, 189
Form, William H., 576
Forrester, Jay W., 397
Forster, R. L., 302
Foster, Stephen, 6
Fox, Karl A., 320
France, Robert R., 186, 197, 211
Franklin, Benjamin, 404
Frederick, William C., 58
Frederick the Great, 31, 157, 596
French, Earl B., 583
Friedman, Milton, 29
Funk, Frank E., 448, 452

Galbraith, John Kenneth, 29, 269
Gantt, Henry L., 37, 40, 41, 498
Gardiner, Glenn, 132
Gardner, Burleigh B., 440
Garrison, Don W., 680
Gellerman, Saul W., 583
Geneen, Harold S., 446
Gentle, Edgar C., Jr., 151, 153, 548
George, Claude S., Jr., 55
Gerth, H. H., 44

Gibbon, Edward, 10
Gibson, R. E., 372
Gilbreth, Frank, 37
Gilbreth, Frank B., Jr., 55
Gilbreth, Lillian, 37
Gist, Ronald R., 372
Glaser, Comstock, 96
Glover, John D., 622, 651
Glueck, William F., 298
Goldhammer, Keith, 659
Golembiewski, Robert T., 583, 622
Good, Robert E., 548
Gordon, Paul J., 72, 658
Gordon, Robert A., 18, 29, 69, 72, 218, 236, 238, 252, 622, 629, 644, 646, 652, 658
Gore, William I., 96
Gorman, John A., 326
Gouldner, Alvin W., 61, 283, 292, 298
Graham, Ben S., 451
Graicunas, V. A., 60, 109-111, 118
Greenberger, Martin, 29
Greenewalt, Crawford H., 96, 622
Greenlaw, Paul S., 96
Greenwood, Frank, 548
Greer, Howard C., 487, 488
Gulick, Luther, 5, 29, 59, 60, 72, 166
Gustavus Adolphus, King of Sweden, 157

Haas, George H., 680
Haire, Mason, 153, 298
Hall, Carrie A., 8
Hall, Challis A., Jr., 622
Hall, George L., 168, 170, 286, 289, 290
Hall, Robert A., Jr., 446
Hamilton, Sir Ian, 104, 311, 312, 596
Haney, William V., 446
Hannibal, 9
Harbison, Frederick, 153
Hardwick, Clyde T., 372, 446, 604
Hare, Van Court Jr., 97, 548
Harper, Donald V., 372
Harris, Keith D., 372
Hart, Albert Gailord, 397
Hartley, Eugene L., 64, 425
Harwood, Dale S., Jr., 659
Hatch, McGlachlin, 162
Hathaway, Henry K., 38
Hawk, Roger H., 372
Hawkins, David F., 514
Hayes, John J., 604
Heady, Earl O., 397
Heckert, J. Brooks, 514
Heckmann, I. L., 583, 604
Hein, Leonard W., 397
Heisenberg, Werner, 66, 67
Heller, Walter W., 343
Henderson, A. M., 44
Henderson, Carter F., 252, 622
Henning, Dale A., 417
Henry, Guy V., 156
Henry III, King of France, 12

NAME INDEX

Henry, William E., 631, 633, 634, 636, 637, 638
Herzberg, Frederick, 583
Hickman, Addison C., 583
Hicks, J. R., 397
Higginson, M. Valliant, 137, 532, 538, 542, 548
Hill, Harold C., 548
Hill, Walter A., 179, 180
Hines, Howard H., 380
Hinrichs, John R., 372
Hitler, Adolf, 433, 441, 628
Hittle, J. D., 157, 159, 163, 184
Hodgetts, Richard M., 604
Hoge, R. H., 661
Holden, P. E., 131, 132, 153, 229, 236, 243, 252, 286, 287, 290
Holmes, A. W., 514
Homans, George C., 48, 53, 64, 567, 585, 586, 594, 598, 599, 604
Hook, Charles R., Jr., 272, 273
Hoover, Herbert, 462
Hoslett, S. D., 48
Hough, Richard, 258
Howard, John A., 321
Howell, James E., 69, 72, 644, 646, 652, 658
Hower, Ralph M., 651
Hoyt, George Calvin, 584
Hughes, Everett C., 269
Humes, Durward, 549
Huneryager, S. G., 583, 604
Hurwicz, Leonid, 393
Huse, Edgar F., 680
Hutchinson, John G., 118, 372

Iino, Haruki, 55

Jackson, Don D., 446
Jackson, Thomas W., 372
Jacobs, Walter, 323
Jaques, Elliott, 118
Jay, Antony, 30
Jennings, Eugene Emerson, 658
Jensen, James O., 153, 514
Jerome, William Travers, III., 515
Johnson, G. Lawton, 680
Johnson, Lyndon, 462
Johnson, Mina M., 446, 515
Johnson, Richard A., 74, 96, 498, 549
Johnson, Wendell, 428, 432, 446
Jones, Reginald L., 515
Joslyn, C. S., 640
Juran, J. M., 252

Kallaus, Norman F., 446, 515
Kaplan, A. D. H., 3, 4
Kappel, Frederick, R., 417
Kast, Fremont E., 74, 96, 498, 549
Katona, George, 83
Kaysen, Carl, 610
Kennelly, John W., 514
Kerr, Clark, 5, 343

Kircher, Paul, 209, 549
Klasson, Charles R., 153
Kneier, Charles M., 143
Knight, Frank H., 82, 397
Koepke, Charles A., 499
Kollios, A. E., 549
Koontz, Harold, 57, 58, 59, 72, 103, 118, 215, 252
Korzybski, Alfred, 3, 428, 429, 446
Kozmetsky, George, 209, 549
Krause, Walter, 153, 343
Kretsinger, Rose G., 8
Kruisinga, H. J., 211
Krupp, Sherman, 68, 72
Kuhn, Manford H., 583

Landsberger, Henry A., 48
Landuyt, Bernard F., 372, 446, 604
Lane, Frederic Chapin, (2) 11, 12
Lane, Robert E., 583
Lansburgh, Richard H., 47, 510
Lasker, Albert C., 252, 622
Lasswell, Harold D., 63
Lawler, Edward E., III, 583, 622
Leabo, Dick A., 658
Leavitt, Harold J., 65, 115, 116, 118, 209, 211, 250, 251, 269, 315, 446, 583
Le Breton, Preston P., 417
Lee, Hak Chong, 549
Lee, Irving J., 428, 446
Leighton, Alexander H., 604
Leithead, Barry, 235
Lerner, Daniel, 63
Lesieur, Frederick G., 252
Lesikar, Raymond V., 472
Lessing, L. P., 252
Letts, Malcolm, 11
Lewellen, Wilbur G., 622
Lewin, Kurt, 588, 589
Lewis, Wilfred, 36
Likert, Rensis, 61, 113, 298, 583
Linton, Ralph, 343, 568
Lipperman, Lawrence L., 549
Lippitt, Ronald, 588, 589
Lipset, Seymour Martin, 269
Lipstreu, Otis, 343
Litterer, Joseph A., 298, 658
Litzinger, William D., 658
Livingston, J. A., 608, 613, 623
Logan, James P., 211
Lombard, George F., 569
Loomba, N. Paul, 397
Louden, J. Keith, 252
Luce, R. Duncan, 81, 393, 397, 417
Lull, Paul E., 448, 452
Lundberg, Craig C., 96
Lurie, Richard G., 145
Luthans, Fred, 584, 658
Lynn, Robert A., 372

MacCullough, Allison V., 676
Mac Niece, E. H., 515
McCarthy, E. Jerome, 549

NAME INDEX 687

McCarthy, J. A., 549
McCloskey, Joseph F., 381, 398
McConnell, Campbell R., 343
McCormick, Charles P., 216, 221, 229, 248, 249
McDonald, John, 390, 398
McFarland, Dalton E., 153, 659
McGehee, William, 680
McGregor, Douglas, 9, 65, 177, 184, 293, 560, 561, 584
McGuire, Joseph W., 30, 344, 393, 398, 622
McHugh, Loughlin F., 328, 329
McLean, John G., 472
McNair, Malcolm P., 584
Maccoby, Eleanor E., 64, 425
Mace, Myles L., 232, 241, 242, 252, 660, 662, 668, 673, 676, 680
Machiavelli, 31
Madeheim, Huxley, 72, 343
Maier, Norman R. F., 604, 652
Maloney, Martin J., 442
Mangum, Garth L., 29
Mann, Floyd C., 604
March, James G., 31, 299
Marquand, John P., 575
Marquis, Lucian, 659
Marquis, Vivienne, 229, 461, 652, 680
Marrow, Alfred J., 604
Marshall, Alfred, 8
Marshall, S. L. A., 557, 558, 621, 655
Maslow, Abraham, 580, 581
Mason, Edward S., 610, 611, 623
Massarik, Fred, 216, 229, 604
Mastran, John L., 173, 174
Mathis, F. John, 153
Maurer, Herryman, 229, 235, 244, 252, 609
Mautz, R. K., 483, 484, 486, 487, 490, 515
Mayer, Raymond R., 372, 398
Maynard, G. P., 514
Mayo, Elton, 9, 30, 39, 569
Mazze, Edward Mark, 72, 343
Means, Gardiner C., 29
Mechanic, David, 256, 282, 283
Mee, John F., 55, 72, 394
Megginson, Leon C., 584
Meinhart, Wayne A., 30
Mellenthin, F. W. von, 441
Mencken, H. L., 280, 649
Menning, J. H., 472
Meredith, G. P., 393, 397
Merrill, Harwood F., 46, 55
Metcalf, Henry C., 48, 55
Miles, Nelson A., 156
Miller, David W., 393, 398
Miller, Delbert C., 576
Miller, Donald E., 515
Miller, Ernest C., 372, 417
Miller, Neal E., 257
Miller, Robert W., 498, 515
Mills, C. Wright, 30, 44

Mills, Theodore M., 584
Miner, John B., 659
Mitchell, Billy, 587
Moffitt, R. C., 132
Mooney, James D., 10, 11, 30, 45, 46, 60, 102, 122, 184, 600, 603, 633
Moore, David G., 440
Morell, Robert W., 398
Morgan, Chester A., 344
Morgenstern, Oskar, 62
Morison, Samuel Eliot, 156
Morris, L. N., 515
Moser, George V., 676
Moundalexis, John R., 514
Mouton, Jane S., 658
Moyer, C. A., 483, 484, 486, 487, 490, 515
Mundel, Marvin E., 398
Murphy, John A., 196, 211
Mussmann, William W., 315, 449
Myers, Charles A., 153, 549
Myers, Clark E., 56
Myers, M. Scott, 584

Nagel, Ernest, 66
Naum, Lionel, 56
Nelson, Edward A., 118
Nemmers, Erwin E., 372
Neumann, John von, 23, 62, 390, 391
Newcomb, Theodore M., 64, 425
Newcomer, Mabel, 237, 252, 640, 641, 642
Newell, Allen, 24
Newman, Joseph W., 344
Newman, William H., 211, 372, 374
Newton, Sir Isaac, 427, 429
Nichols, Aylmer V., 548
Nichols, Ralph G., 463, 472
Nixon, Richard, 462
Nordsieck-Schröer, Hildegard, 72
Norman, Albert, 156
Northrop, F. S. C., 66, 72, 79
Northrup, Herbert R., 358, 372
Novick, David, 659

O'Donnell, Cyril, 103, 215, 372
O'Donovan, Thomas R., 659
Ogden, C. K., 63, 428, 446
Olm, Kenneth W., 153, 371
Olmsted, Michael S., 64, 584
Oxenfeldt, Alfred R., 350
Osborn, Alex F., 395

Packard, Vance, 562
Parker, R. W., 533
Parkinson, C. Northcote, 30
Parsons, Talcott, 44
Patt, Henry, 118
Patton, Arch, 584, 680
Patton, John A., 444
Pavlov, I. P., 555
Pegram, Roger M., 237, 238, 344

NAME INDEX

Perlman, Selig, 17, 30
Person, Harlow S., 60
Peterson, Wallace C., 344
Petit, Thomas A., 72
Pfiffner, John M., 299
Piersol, Darrel T., 448, 452
Pierson, Frank C., 69, 72, 641, 642, 644, 651, 659, 673, 674
Plato, 31
Pocock, J. W., 381
Polak, J. J., 328
Polanyi, Karl, 30
Porter, Donald J., 153
Porter, Lyman W., 153
Prasad, S. Benjamin, 398
Pratt, John Lee, 45
Presthus, Robert, 30, 299
Price, James L., 299

Raiffa, Howard, 81, 382, 383, 393, 397, 417
Randall, Clarence B., 358, 455, 633, 636, 644, 659
Randle, C. Wilson, 357, 372
Raphael, Jesse S., 30
Rathe, Alex W., 37, 55, 72
Read, William H., 177, 184
Ream, Norman J., 546
Reed, Kenneth A., 343
Rehmus, Charles M., 372
Reid, Thomas R., 217
Reif, William E., 116, 117, 118, 182, 210, 251, 549
Reiley, Alan C., 10, 11, 30, 46, 60, 102, 122, 600, 603, 633
Reiley, DeWitt Ten Broeck, 46
Rennekamp, Eugene E., 549
Reuther, Walter, 462
Richards, I. A., 63, 428, 446
Richards, Max D., 96
Richardson, F. L. W., Jr., 118, 135
Rigby, Paul H., 344
Robb, Russel, 46
Robbins, Lionel, 79
Robichek, Alexander A., 372
Robinson, Joan, 351
Robinson, Richard D., 154
Rockwell, W. C., 46
Roethlisberger, F. J., 30, 48-55, 135, 306, 462, 464, 465, 574
Roll, Erich, 12, 13
Rogers, Carl R., 462, 464
Rogers, Jack, 366, 367
Roman, Daniel D., 515
Roosevelt, Franklin D., 374, 462
Root, Elihu, 158, 679
Rosenzweig, James E., 74, 96, 498, 549
Roy, Donald, 52
Ryans, John K., Jr., 344
Ryder, Meyer S., 372

Sachs, Alexander, 374
Sampson, Robert C., 184, 680
Sanders, Thomas H., 623
Sapir, Edward, 428
Sarachek, Bernard, 72, 73
Sarnoff, David, 27
Sattler, William M., 472
Savage, L. J., 393
Saxe, Maurice de, 31
Saxon, O. Glenn, Jr., 623
Sayles, Leonard R., 30, 73, 96
Scanlon, Joseph, 249
Scharnhorst, G. J. D., 157, 678
Schein, Edgar H., 604
Schlieker, Willi, 404
Schoderbek, Peter P., 75, 371, 514
Schoer, Lowell, 680
Schonberger, Richard J., 344
Schultz, George P., 136
Schutte, William M., 472
Scott, William G., 73, 299, 659
Scott, W. Richard, 298
Seashore, Stanley E., 604
Seckler-Hudson, Catheryn, 46
Selznick, Philip, 61, 417
Shackle, G. L. S., 393, 397
Shallman, William S., 515
Shannon, Claude E., 64, 422, 446
Shartle, Carroll L., 604
Shaw, George Bernard, 649
Sheldon, Oliver, 47, 55, 67, 94
Sheriff, Don R., 680
Sherwood, Frank P., 299
Shidle, Norman G., 472
Shull, Fremont, Jr., 73
Shultz, George P., 64, 154, 177, 182, 184, 209
Simon, Herbert A., 24, 30, 31, 78, 79, 80, 83, 84, 96, 107, 125, 257, 269, 315, 398, 402, 446, 607
Sloan, Alfred P., Jr., 44, 45, 55, 199, 206, 208, 211, 308, 311, 679
Sloan, Harold S., 659
Smiddy, Harold F., 56
Smidt, Seymour, 371
Smith, Adam, 18, 309
Smith, H. L., 131, 132, 153, 229, 236, 243, 252, 286, 287, 290
Smith, Nila Banton, 466, 472
Spence, Kenneth W., 65
Spriegel, William R., 56, 510
Spurlock, Jack M., 372
Staley, Eugene, 9, 30, 571
Stalin, Joseph, 628
Starch, Daniel, 641, 681
Starr, Martin K., 393, 398
Stein, Charles S., 72, 343
Steiner, Gary A., 583
Stelzer, Irwin M., 344
Stempel, J. S., 549
Steuben, Frederick von, 158
Stevens, Leonard A., 463, 472
Stieglitz, Harold, 287
Storrs, Constance, 41, 42, 105
Stouffer, Samuel A., 569

NAME INDEX 689

Strong, E. B., 279
Strunk, William, Jr., 472
Stryker, Perrin, 211, 311, 440
Sun Tzu Wu, 31
Suojanen, Waino W., 58, 73, 106, 107, 118, 584
Svec, Fred J., 549
Swinyard, Alfred W., 658

Tafur, Pero, 11
Tannenbaum, Frank, 30
Tannenbaum, Robert, 79, 96, 216, 229, 604
Taussig, John N., 549
Taussig, F. W., 640
Taylor, Donald W., 395
Taylor, Erwin K., 659
Taylor, Frederick W., 9, 13, 32-39, 40-41, 43, 45, 47, 48, 50, 56, 58, 60, 62, 67, 68, 115, 134, 135, 362, 380, 389, 561, 600
Taylor, James W., 543, 544
Tennant, Richard B., 350
Thayer, Lee O., 446
Thayer, Paul W., 680
Thelwell, Ray, 514
Thompson, Stewart, 70, 609, 623
Thompson, Victor A., 299
Thrall, R. M., 382, 383, 398
Thurston, Philip H., 545
Tickner, Fred, 681
Tilles, Seymour, 97
Timms, Howard L., 398
Tinbergen, Jan, 328
Tosi, Henry, 118
Towl, Andrew R., 232, 240, 243, 252
Trefethen, Florence N., 381, 398
Trentin, H. George, 515
True, John M., 315, 448
Turing, A. M., 23, 24

Udall, Jon G., 118
Urwick, Lyndall F., 13, 48, 56, 58, 59, 60, 107, 118, 133, 134, 135, 140, 158, 164, 167, 184, 195, 211, 272, 273, 600, 608, 660
Usher, Abbot Payson, 8

Vance, Stanley C., 659
Vaughan, James A., 680
Vaught, George, 235
Vergin, Roger C., 117
Villaria, Richard L., 514
Vogt, Leonard F., 136

Wadia, Maneck S., 154
Wagner, L. G., 211
Wald, Abraham, 393
Walker, Charles R., 118, 135

Walton, Clarence, 29
Walton, Scott D., 344
Warner, W. Lloyd, 557, 640, 641, 642
Warren, E. Kirby, 417
Watt, James, 13
Watzlawick, Paul, 446
Weaver, Warren, 64, 422, 446
Weber, Max, 43, 44, 61
Weinberg, Sidney, 234, 235
Welsch, Glenn A., 411, 515
Wengert, E. S., 659
Weschler, Irving R., 604
West, Jude P., 680
Westing, J. H., 372, 508
Whisler, Thomas L., 64, 115, 116, 118, 136, 154, 177, 182, 184, 209, 211, 250, 251
White, E. B., 472
White, Maunsel, 35
White, Ralph K., 588, 589
White, Theodore H., 404
Whitehead, Alfred North, 73, 382
Whiting, Charles S., 394
Whiting, Richard J., 73
Whorf, Benjamin Lee, 428
Whyte, William Foote, 61, 64, 249, 250, 252, 264, 269, 270, 271, 363, 436, 465, 557, 564, 570, 576, 577, 584, 602, 604, 615
Whyte, William H., 644, 669
Wickert, Frederic R., 659
Wickesberg, Albert K., 119
Wiener, Norbert, 20, 21, 27, 30, 64, 92, 97, 422, 446
Wilkins, Mira, 145
Wilkinson, C. W., 472
Williams, Charles R., 154
Williams, J. D., 398
Willson, James D., 514
Wilson, C. E., 235
Wilson, Charles Z., 96, 417
Winston, Clement, 323
Wise, T. A., 489, 515
Wolfe, John B., 556
Wood, Robert E., 235
Woodward, Joan, 73
Worthy, James C., 112, 113, 119, 135, 299
Wortman, Max S., Jr., 372, 515
Woytinsky, W. S., 329, 330
Wrapp, H. Edward, 417

Yntema, Theodore O., 633, 636, 644, 649
Young, Owen D., 605
Young, Stanley, 97, 549

Zaleznik, Abraham, 604
Zalkind, Sheldon S., 64

SUBJECT INDEX

Abbott Laboratories, 145
Abstracting process, semantics of, 431-432, 443
Academic degrees, 266, 280
Accelerated amortization, 337
Accounting, 482-497
  analytical methods of, 484-487
  and financial reporting, 490-492
  meaning problem, 487
  measurement problem in, 487-490
  principles of, 488-490
Advertising, 198, 340, 351-353
Alpha-numerical departmentation, 152
American Airlines, 534
American Association of University Professors, 263
American Can Company, 246, 348
American Institute of Certified Public Accountants, 489
American Management Association, 105, 126, 127, 137, 186, 222, 538, 540, 674
American Medical Association, 70, 263
American Society of Mechanical Engineering, 35, 36
American Telephone and Telegraph Company, 331, 666
Analogue computers, 21-22
Analogue models, 382, 413, 533
Antitrust laws, 19, 336
Aptitude tests, 52, 668
Aristotelian logic, 431
Arsenal of Venice, 11-12, 15
Artificial languages, 427
Assembly language, 527
Assembly program, 525
Association of National Advertisers, 46
Auditing function, 496-497
Authoritarian leadership techniques, 588-591
Authoritative communication, 459-461
Authority, and communication, 114
  defined, 255-256
  through leadership, 585
  the Milo plant, 275-278
  of position, 255-256, 267, 586-587
  and power, 255, 267-268, 274
  private property as a source of, 260

Authority, and professional associations, 262-263
  and sanctions, 258-260
  social conditioning for, 256-258
  social foundations of, 256-263
  and status system, 263
  and uncertainty, 267
  and unionism, 261-262
Auxiliary functions, 178

Balanced board of directors, concept of, 238-240
Balance sheet, 483, 484-485
Bank of America, 246
Bank Wiring Observation Room, 50-54, 306, 415
Behavioral sciences, 57-58, 64-65
Bethlehem Steel Company, 4, 33-36, 37, 39, 40, 62, 362
Black box, 68, 559-560
Board of directors, 230-244
  "balanced board" concept for, 238-240
  committees of, 244, 245, 246
  composition of, 237-240
  director's compensation, 240-241
  frequency of meetings, 241
  informal activities of, 234-235
  interest group representation on, 237-240
  legal status of, 230-231
  McCormick junior boards, 248
  managerial functions of, 231-233
  as philosophers of corporation, 244
  principal occupations of directors, 239
  size, question of, 235-237
  in small corporations, 241-242
Boeing Company, 4
Booz, Allen, and Hamilton, Inc., 540, 542
Boulton and Watt Company, 13
Boulwareism, 357
Brainstorming, 395
Break-even chart, 495
Brookings Institution, 143, 144
Budgetary systems, 410-411, 473-482
Budgeting process, 477-478
Budgets, and efficiency problems, 480-481

691

692 SUBJECT INDEX

Budgets, fixed and flexible, 476-477
  as information, 478-480
  kinds of, 473-476
  time periods for, 476
Bureaucracy, in Gypsum plant, 292
Bureaucratic theory, 43, 61
Business games, 653-656
  alternative planning models, 656
  feedback elements in, 654
  types of, 654
Business staff organization, 164-174
  General Motors Corporation, 171-173
  Radio Corporation of America, 173-174
  Standard Oil Company of California, 169-171
Business systems departments, 536
Business systems organization chart, Deere and Company, 532
Business taxes, 337
Business Week, 329

Capital expansion, 331
Carrier Corporation, 246
Case method, 651-652
Caterpillar Tractor Company, 246
Catholic Church, Roman, 10-11
  Curia Romana, 10
Centralization, 538-544
  conditions favoring, 190
  General Motors Corporation, 206
  importance of, 206
  policy formulation, 204
Centralization-decentralization, 45, 102, 115
  functional, 129-132, 195
  kinds of, 185
  nature of, 185, 187-188
  see also Decentralization
Chain of command, 301-302, 435-436
Chairmanship, 228, 243
Channel "noise," 424, 445
Channels, see Communication channels
Chesapeake and Ohio Railway Company, 246
Chicago Business School, 651
Child-training techniques, 257
Chrysler Corporation, 4
Classical economic theory, 18, 606, 610 611
Clayton Act, 19, 336
"Coaching," 677
COBOL, 526, 528
Collective bargaining, 17, 261-262, 355-358
Commentry-Fourchambault, 41
Committees, advantages of, 214-219
  boards of directors, 230-244
  chairman, role of, 228
  compromise and indecision by, 220
  and coordination, 215-216
  cost of, 219

Committees, defined, 212
  disadvantages of, 219-222
  Du Pont executive committee, 246-247
  effective operation of, 224-228
  and executive development, 218
  executive teamwork, 216
  versus individual action, 222-224
  informal meetings, 213
  and information technology, 250-251
  integrated group judgment from, 214-215
  interest group representation on, 217-218
  lifespan of, 213
  McCormick junior boards, 248-249
  membership of, 226
  and minority domination, 220-221
  nature of, 212-214
  operating level, 248
  procedures of, 214, 227-228
  responsibility problem, 221-222
  Scanlon plan, 249-250
  size of, 226-227
  Standard Oil Company of N.J., management committees, 247-248
  top-management, 245-248
Common Business Oriented Language, COBOL, 526
Communication, 89
  accounting systems as, 302, 482-497
  and authority, 114, 459-461
  barriers to, 461
  budgetary systems as, 473-482
  channel "noise," 424, 445
  and committees, 218
  control as, 63-64
  cybernetics, 64, 421-422
  and decentralization, 193
  defined, 422-424
  electronic devices, 424
  face-to-face, 449-451
  financial reporting, 490-492
  grammar problem in, 456, 636
  grapevine problems, 303, 438
  and information distortion, 440-445
  and information theory, 64, 421-422
  inventory planning and control, 509-511
  language defined, 427
  languages, types of, 427
  listening problems and techniques, 463-464
  as management function, 63-64, 591-592, 636-637
  mechanical facilities for, 424
  media and methods, 447-454
  message construction, 427, 454-461
  message distribution, 451-452
  message reception problems, 461-469
  nature of process, 422-424
  open door policy, 465
  oral versus written, 447-449
  order-giving techniques, 459-461

Communication, paperwork procedures in, 302-303, 306, 504
and perception, 424, 425-427
and personal qualities, 437
personnel planning and control, 302, 511-513
position, importance of, 434
positions and persons as centers of, 434, 439-440
process described, 422-423
procurement planning and control, 507-509
production planning and control, 302, 497-505
quality planning and control, 505-507
reading techniques and problems, 466-468
semantic problems, 65, 428-433, 437, 441
status instruments, importance of, 436-437
tall versus flat structures, 114-115
theory of, 421-422
titles, importance of, 436
vocabulary, importance of, 455-456
Communication centers, 433-440
Communication channels, 300-307
capacity problem, 437-439
of contact, 301
hierarchical, 301-302
informal, 303-306
Communism, and leadership succession, 628
Company training programs, 673-679
Compiler program, 526
Completed staff action, 162
Computer executives, line or staff, 544-545
Computer hardware, 517-518
location of, 542
Computerized informational systems, 516-549
Deere and Company, 532
design of, 522
development of, 522-536
integrated systems, 546
Maytag Company, 531
real time, 533-535
shared time, 535-536
Computerized planning systems, 405
Computer language, assembly language, 525, 527
COBOL, 528
compiler program, 526
FORTRAN, 526
Computer management, line or staff, 544-545
Computer programming, 538
Computer revolution, 20-28
and management science, 28
pace of, 27-28
Computers, *see* Electronic computers; Information technology

Computer technology, and management organization, 116
Conditioned responses, 555-556
Consumer sovereignty, 607
Continental Can Company, 312
Continental Oil Company, 246
Contract negotiation, unions, 356-358
Control, 90-93
centralized, 194, 205-206
cost of, 92-93
and decentralization, 188, 194
importance of, 43
inventory, 509-511
personnel, 511-513
procurement, 507-509
production, 504-505
quality, 505-507, 508
Controllership Foundation, 480
Cooperation, advantages of, 5-6
of formal organizations, 7
informal, 6-7
motivation for, 7
in organization planning, 296
survival problem, 553-554
technological problem, 554
and technology, 8
Coordination, advantages of, 140
interdepartmental, 133-134, 215
as management function, 42, 43
Corning Conference (1951), 9
Corporate taxes, 337
Corporations, and managerial control, 15-16
Correlation analysis, 322-323
Cost accounting, 492-496
CPM, 500
Craftsmanship, 578-579, 582
Creative process, 394-396
Creative thinking, 394
and brainstorming, 395
Creditors, 618
Critical Path Method (CPM), 500
Crown Zellerbach Corporation, 246
Curia Romana, 10
Customer departmentation, 141-142
Customers, 142, 614-616
Cybernetics, 64, 421

Data processing center, Deere and Company, 540
Maytag Company, 541
Data processing departments, 536-538
Deadwood problems, 297, 572
Decentralization, 538-544
centralized policy formulation, 204
and communication problem, 193
conditions for, 190-191
control problem in, 194
delegation problems in, 188-190
and executive development, 194
extent of, 186-187, 203, 206
of functional areas, 195-199

SUBJECT INDEX

Decentralization, General Motors Corporation, 190, 199-207
  geographical, 190
  operationally defined, 187
  see also Centralization
Decision making, 78-85, 313-314
  business organizations, 85-87
  defined, 78-79
  in a dynamic environment, 86-87
  and economic theory of firm, 85-86
  ethical elements in, 81
  functional, 167, 175
  hierarchical rules for, 309-311
  means and ends, 80
  and motivation, 88
  as organized process, 307-314, 406-407
  planning, 88
  planning and control, 93
  "potential surprise" concept, 393
  rationality of, 79-80
  risk and uncertainty, 81-82
  skills required for, 634-636
  subjective processes and techniques, 390-396, 635
  techniques, 83-85
  uncertainty criteria, 393-394
  types of, 83
  see also Planning
Decisiveness, importance of, 635
Decreasing returns to scale, 191, 192
Deere and Company, 124, 146-148, 469, 528, 532
  business systems department, 539
Delco Remy Division, GMC, 139, 171
Delegation, dynamics of, 311-313
  nature of, 188-190
  risk of, 189
  see also Decentralization
Delta Airlines, 534
Demand determinants, 320
Demand functions, 323
Democratic leadership techniques, 217, 588-591
Departmentation, alpha-numerical, 152
  customer, 141-142
  defined, 120
  equipment, 151
  functional, 122-137
  information systems, 536-538
  product, 137-142
  service, 141-142
  terminology of, 122
  territorial, 142-151
  time, 151-152
  types of, 120
Department of Defense, 4
Digital computers, 21-22; see also Electronic computers
Diminishing returns, law of, 192
Directors, see Board of directors
Du Pont de Nemours, E. I., and Company, 4, 108, 139, 168, 207, 208, 246, 336, 348, 354, 500, 601

Eastern railroads, rate hearings, 36
Eastman Kodak Company, 146-148
Economic forecasting, 321-322
Economic man concept, 39
Economic theory, classical, 18-19, 606, 610-611
Economic theory of the firm, 85-86, 554-555
Education, see Executive education
Efficiency, and budgeting, 480-482
  economic, 339-340
  managerial, 630
  operating, 361-370
  of planning, 378-380, 402
  and size problem, 191-193
Electronic computers, 76-77
  applications, 529
  arithmetic and logical devices, 518
  binary number system, 518
  and business schools, 547
  control devices, 519
  and creative thinking, 24
  development of, 21
  and forecasting, 546
  future prospects, 545
  as game umpires, 653
  hardware, 516-519
  and information retrieval, 468-469
  information storage devices, 517-518
  and information systems, 516-549
  input devices, 517
  installation problems, 519-522
  and management organization, 112-113, 207-210
  and motivation, 547
  nature of, 21-22
  operations, 526-529
  organizing for, 536-545
  output devices, 519
  pioneering problems, 520
  and planning, 405, 520
  planning models, 546, 655
  programming of, 525-526
  and reading efficiency, 468-469
  real time systems, 533-535
  shared time systems, 535-536
  speed and logic, 26-27
  and staff positions, 179-180
  standardized application programs, 526
  thinking machines, 22-26
  timely information, 545
  training personnel, 521
Employees, as interest group, 614
Endicott plant, IBM, 135
Entropy, 422
Equipment, cost of, 331-332
Equipment departmentation, 151
Ethical norms, 70
Executive compensation, 616-618
  deferred income plan, 617
  stock options, 617
Executive development, 69
  coaching technique, 677

SUBJECT INDEX 695

Executive development, in committees, 218
  company programs for, 663-664, 673-679
  curricula problems, 645-646
  and decentralization, 194
  education for, *see* Executive education
  forecasting future needs, 663
  formative years, 638-640
  motives problem, 637, 639, 656
  position descriptions, 661
  in product departmentation, 141-142
  professionalization, 69
  promotion criteria, 672-673
  promotion policies, 672-673
  qualities *see* Executive qualities
  recruitment problems, 358, 664-670
  simulation techniques for, 650
  university programs, 676-677
Executive education, 638-657
  company facilities for, 674
  company programs in, 673-679
  motives problem, 656
  nature of problem, 643-644
  past and present, 640-642
  and professional development, 71
  simulation techniques, 650
  universality of knowledge and skills, 646-647
Executive functions, 600
Executive performance, measurement of, 378-380, 631-633
Executive qualities, 631-638, 661-663
  communication skills, 636-637
  decision-making skills, 634-636
  leadership skills, 637
  motives, 637-638
  organizational skills, 633-634
  social skills, 633-634
Executive recruitment, 664-672
  interviewing, 669-670
  key executives, 671-672
  performance evaluation, 671
  psychological testing, 667-669
Exodus, Book of, 104
Expectations, defining, 402-403
External financing, 326-329

Face-to-face communication, 449-451
Factory system, 13-15
  defined, 14
Fair Labor Standards Act, 19
Fairless Works, U. S. Steel, 335
Fatigue, problem of, 107-109
Federal Reserve System, 218, 338
Federal Trade Commission, 19
Feedback, 91-92
Financial management, 197
Financial markets, 326-329
Flat management structures, 112-113
Ford Motor Company, 4, 101, 139, 145, 198, 207, 246, 349, 354, 359, 636, 679

Forecasting, 531
  economic, 321-322
  importance of, 376
  internal, 410
  sales, 321-322, 409
  techniques, 322-323
Foreign operations, 145-150
Formal organization, 7
Formula translation, FORTRAN, 526
FORTRAN, 526
The Fortune Directory, 4
Fortune magazine, boards of directors described by, 235, 247
  executives studied by, 447, 452, 640, 641, 642
France, military staff development in, 157
Functional centralization and decentralization, 129-133, 195-199
Functional decision-making, 167-168, 175
Functional departmentation, 122-137
  AMA study, 126
  centralization and decentralization, 129-132
  and information technology, 136-137
  interest conflicts, 133-134
  jurisdictional problem, 132-133
  parallel functionalization, 125
  personal conflicts, 134
  primary functions, 125-128
  secondary functions, 128
Functional foremanship, 134-135, 600

Game theory, 62, 387
Gantt Chart, 37, 413, 498
General Electric Company, 4, 101, 139, 168, 207, 295, 354, 357, 379, 404, 405, 605
General Electric Management Research and Development Institute, 674
General Mills, 348
General Motors Corporation, 4, 44, 45, 137, 138, 140, 141, 145, 168, 172, 178, 190, 199-207, 246, 294, 308, 311, 331, 333, 354, 407, 567, 679
General Motors Institute, 674
General semantics, 428-433
General staff organization, 160-162
General Telephone and Electronics, 4
Germany, military staff system in, 161
  in World War II, 404
Goodyear Tire and Rubber, 4
Gordon-Howell report, 69, 644, 645, 652
Government regulation, 18-20, 336-338
  to enforce competition, 18
  the labor laws, 19
Graicunas' theory, 109-112
Grapevine, 303, 438-439
Great Britain, management development in, 12-13
  operations research studies in, 381
Group dynamics, 566-571
Group norms, 53-54, 567-568, 594
Gulf Oil Corporation, 4

SUBJECT INDEX

Harmonious overlap, 374
Harvard University, 32, 33, 677
   Graduate School of Business Administration, 232, 569, 651
   Laboratory of Social Relations, 226, 227
Hawthorne study, 48-54, 250, 306, 566
   group norms, 53-54
   group output norms, 50-51
   illumination experiments, 48-49
   interview techniques, 49
   job trading and helping, 52-53
   psychological testing, 52
   regulated output patterns, 52
   small group research, 49-54
   social activities, 53
   Western Electric, 41, 48-54, 64, 65, 68, 415
Hoover Commission, executive report by, 105
Hourglass structure, 115-117

Iconic models, 382
"Ideal structure," 270
Illumination experiments, 48-49
Incentives, 581-582
Income statement, 483, 486
Industrial civilization, social problems of, 9
Industrial democracy, 261
Industrial jurisprudence, system of, 261
Industrial relations, 197-198
Industrial revolution, 12-13
   and capitalistic control, 14
   factory system, 14
   and management practices, 12-15
Informal communication channels, 303-306
   types of, 304-306
Informal cooperation, 6-7
Informal organization, 39-41, 213, 234-235, 270, 278-282, 292-293, 295-297, 303-306, 566-577
Information distortion, 440-445
Information retrieval, 468-469
Information systems, computerized, 516-549
   departments of, 536
   development of, 522-536
Information technology, 516-549
   and committee organization, 250
   and functional departmentation, 136-137
   and informal organization, 251
   and information retrieval, 468-469
   line or staff, 182-183
   and line-staff relationships, 179-183
   and management organization, 115, 136-137, 208-210
   operations research, 380-389
   and reading efficiency, 468-469
Information theory, 64, 421-428

Inland Steel Company, 358, 455, 636
Innovation, as environmental factor, 338-340
   product and service, 353-355
   technological, 8
Inspection, 506
Integrated informational systems, 546
Intelligence tests, 668
Interest conflicts, 133-134
Interest groups, 611-618
   on boards of directors, 218, 237-240
   committee representation, 217-218
   creditors, 618
   customers, 614-616
   employees, 614
   management, 616-618
   stockholders, 238, 612-614
   suppliers, 618
Interest rates, 328-329
Interest tests, 668
Internal financing, 326-329
Internal forecasts, 410
Internal Revenue Code, 488
International business, 145-150
International Business Machines Corporation, 4, 135, 145, 354
International Harvester Company, 139, 207, 347, 354
International management, 145-150
   cultural and social factors, 145-150
International Mining and Metallurgical Congress (1900), 41
International Shoe Company, 136
International Telephone and Telegraph, 4
Interstate Commerce Commission, 20, 36, 368, 488
Interview techniques, 49, 669-670
Inventory, physical and perpetual, 510-511
Inventory planning and control, 509-511
Inventory policies, 360
Invisible hand concept, 18
Iowa, University of, 588
Iterative procedures, 385

Job descriptions, 290
Job enlargement, 135
Job evaluation, 511
John Deere, 145
Judicial functions, 600-601
Judicial procedures, 602-603
Jurisdictional problems, 132-133, 222

Kaiser Company, 347
Kaiser Industries, 145
Korean War, government controls in, 20

Laboristic philosophy, 607-608
Labor legislation, 19-20, 337
Laissez faire, 18-19, 629

SUBJECT INDEX

Laissez faire leadership, 588-591
Land resources, 334-335
Language, computer, 527-528
  defined, 427
  imprint of past, 429-430
  and message construction, 427, 454-457
  types of, 427
Laplace criterion, 393
Leadership, consistent enforcement of norms, 592-593
  defined, 585, 637
  democratic, 217, 588-591
  enigma of, 599-600
  group dynamics, 566-571
  law and justice, 600-603
  lenient superiors, 597-599
  and motivation, 555-562
  reinforcing authority, 595-597
  as social responsibility, 630-631
  socio-psychological environment, 593
  strategies and tactics, 595-600
  techniques of, 586-595
  types of, 589
Leadership succession, 627-629
  political intervention, 629
  power struggles, 628
  private property, 629-630
Lead time, 373-375
Learned professions, 69
Legislative functions, 600-601
Lenient superiors, 597-599
Limited resources, 403
Limiting factors, 403-405
Line and staff, 544-545
Line and staff organization, General Motors Corporation, 171-173
  modified or hybrid form, 166
  Radio Corporation of America, 173-174
  Standard Oil Company of California, 168-173
Line and staff relationships, 163-164
  business organization, 164-174
  and information technology, 179-183
  military organization, 161
Line production, Arsenal of Venice, 11-12
Listening techniques and problems, 463-464, 576
Location, problem of, 361

McCormick and Company, 248, 678
McDonnell Douglas Corporation, 4
Machine systems, and human systems, 26
Management, a systems approach, 74-78
Management, antecedents to, 9-13
  Arsenal of Venice, 11-12
  Boulton and Watt Company, 12-13
  Catholic Church, 10-11
  early contributions to, 31
  as interest group, 616-618
  motivation, 64-65
  in the 1980's, 115-116

Management, professional status, 70
  Roman Empire, 10-11
  union challenge to, 17
Management functions, 59-60
  and cooperation in formal organizations, 7
  decision making, 78-85
  planning, 62-63
Management hierarchy, communication channels, 301-302
  flat structures, 112-113
  flat versus tall structures, 114-115
  informal chains, 304-306
  nature of, 101-103
  spans and levels, 103, 112-115
  stagnation problem, 678-679
  superior-subordinate relationships, 440-441, 464-465
Management process, 88-90, 94, 95
  concept of, 59-60
  universality of, 94-95
Management responsibility, 605-611
  conflicting moral codes, 620-621
  economic theory, 606-607
  laboristic philosophy, 607-608
  legal theory of, 605-606
  moral basis, 619-620
  organization perspective, 608-611
  social welfare, 610-611
Management science, and the computer revolution, 28
  and the systems concept, 74-78
Management systems, functional categories, 529-530
Managerial class, 15-16
Managerial organization, 41-48, 60-61, 89, 95
  authority and power relationships, 255-256
  early contributions to, 46-48
  fatigue problem, 107-109
  flat versus tall structures, 112-115
  functional theory, 270-271
  General Motors reorganization, 44-45
  General Motors Corporation, 407
  an hourglass structure, 115-117
  informal, 270-274
  and information technology, 136-137, 536-545
  levels versus spans, 103, 112-113
  long term changes, 207
  personality problem, 272-274
  Sears, Roebuck and Company, 112, 189, 407
  socio-psychological factors, 60-61
  span of management, 103-107
  street corner gang, 270
  strategy and structure, 207-208
  see also Bureaucracy; Management hierarchy; and Organizational structure
Managerial relationships, 109-111, 440-441, 464-465

SUBJECT INDEX

Managerial revolution, 15-16
Man-machine systems, 547
Market forecasting, 319-325
Market strategy, 347-354
Maslow's hierarchy of needs, 580-581
Master of Business Administration (M. B. A.), 657
Mathematical models, 62, 382
Maximizing, 402
Maximum criterion, 393
Maytag Company, 123, 354, 531
Meaning, infinity of, semantics, 432-433
Mechanical drawings, 411-413, 427
Merchandise, 333-334
Message, construction of, 427, 454-461
  distribution of, 451-452
  oral versus written, 447-449
  reception problems, 461-469
Metal-cutting experiments, 35
Method, defined, 364
Methods analysis, 364-365
Midvale Steel Company, 32-33, 37, 39, 50, 62, 134
Military staff organization, 155-164
  completed staff action, 162
  duties and procedures, 162-163
  field command staffs, 159-162
  functions of, 158-159
  general staff, 160-162
  historical development, 157-158
  legislation of 1903, 158
  modern United States, 160-164
  Normandy invasion, 155
  Prussian contributions, 157
  Scharnhorst reforms, 157
  Spanish-American War, 156
  special staff, 162
  U. S. Revolutionary War, 158
Military type organization, 134
Milo plant, authority and power relationships, 275-278
  formal structure, 275
  unofficial power structure, 276
Mnemonic system, 510
Mobil Oil Corporation, 4
Model building, 75-76
Models, 75-76
Monetary incentives, 581-582
Money markets, 326-329
Montgomery Ward Company, 379
Moral codes, and managerial responsibility, 620-621
Motivation, 64-65, 370
  burdens and benefits, of organized endeavor, 562-579
  integration of, 579-580
  conditioned responses, 555-556
  cultural norms, importance of, 556-558
  depth psychology, 562
  group dynamics, 567
  human motives, similarities and differences in, 558-559
  as management function, 64-65

Motivation, Maslow's hierarchy of needs, 580-581
  monetary and other incentives, 581-582
  nature of, 555-562
  physiological drives, 555
  responsibilities as rewards, 577-579
  social satisfactions, 566-567
  status as a factor, 571-577, 582
  theories X and Y, 560-561
Motivational decisions, 313-314, 560-562
Motorola, Inc., 438

National Broadcasting Company, 173
National Industrial Conference Board, 236, 237, 238, 245, 287, 377, 536
National Labor Relations Board, 20
Natural resources, 334-335
New Jersey Bell Telephone Company, 46
New York Central, 534
Normandy invasion, organization for, 155
Norms, 414
  cultural, 556-558
  group, 53-54, 567-568, 594
Norton gang, 270

On-off switching, 518
Open door policy, 465
Operational definitions, 408
Operations research, 62, 380-389
  future of, 388-389
  history of, 381
  iterative procedures, 385
  model building, 381-386
  prototype models, 386-388
  types of models, 386-388
Organizational objectives, 290, 345, 408-409, 593-595
Organizational responsibility, 563-564
Organizational society, 3-5
Organizational structure, functional theory, 270-272
  informal, 274
  personality problem, 272-274
Organizational systems, 74-95
Organization charts, 287-290, 291
Organization departments, 286-287
Organization identity, 579
Organization image, 579
Organization manuals, 290-291
Organization "personality," 619
Organization planning, 284-297
  administering plan, 286-291
  cooperation problems, 296-297
  development of plan, 284-285
  implementing plan, 285-286
  importance of, 284
  organization charts, 287-288
  organization departments, 286-287
Organization principles, 46-48
Organization size, 3-5
  business organizations, 3
  future prospects, 5

SUBJECT INDEX 699

Organization theory, 60-61
Organized decision-making, 307-314, 406-407
Organizing, 89
Output restriction, 39, 50-52, 415

PANAMAC, 534
Pan American World Airways, 534
Paperwork procedures, 302-303
Participation, by subordinates, 216-217, 588-591
Penney, J. C., Company, 207, 348
Pennsylvania Fruit Company, 246
PEP, 500
Perception, 424-427
  factors influencing, 425-427
Perpetual inventory, 510-511
Personal goals, and organizational objectives, 593-595
Personal power, 256
Personnel planning and control, 511-513
Personnel recruitment, 358
PERT, 413, 498-504, 526, 533
  critical path, 501
  network construction, 500-501
  time estimates, 501
Pessimism-optimism index criterion, 393
Phillips Petroleum Company, 246, 484-486
Physiological drives, 555
Piecework plan, 35
Pierson report, 69, 644, 645
Pig iron handling experiment, 33-34
Planning, 88, 90
  advertising strategies, 351-353
  budgetary systems, 410-411
  collective bargaining strategy, 355-358
  computerized systems, 405
  and control, 90-93
  and the cost of change, 399-400
  criteria for, 378-380
  defining expectations, 402-403
  environmental factors, 319-344
  equipment procurement, 363
  executive personality, 380
  expansion policies, 379-380
  factory and office buildings, 362-363
  forecasting, importance of, 376
  formulation of policies, 414-416
  the futurity of, 400-401
  harmonious overlap, 374
  impact of past, 399
  inventory policies, 360
  lead time problem, 373-375
  locational factors, 361
  and limited resources, 403
  market strategy, 347-355
  material procurement problems, 359-360
  maximising and satisficing, 402
  mechanical drawings, 411-413
  methodology, 62-63
  nature of problem, 345

Planning, nonbusiness organizations, 341
  operating efficiency, 361-370
  and operational definitions, 408
  operations research techniques, 380-389
  optimum combination of strategies, 405-406
  organized process, 406-407
  personnel recruitment, 358
  plant capacity and utilization, 367-369
  price policies, 348-351
  procedures and methods, 413-414
  product line policies, 347-348
  product and service innovations, 353-355
  resource procurement strategies, 355-361
  sales forecast, 409
  scientific procedures and methods, 363-365
  scope of, 401
  standardization and simplification, 365-367
  strategic factors, 403-405
  subjective techniques, 62-63
  transformation period, 375-376
  uncertainty criteria, 392-394
  see also Decision making
Planning decisions, 313-314
Planning models, 533, 546, 655
Planning periods, 377
Planning systems, 531
Plant capacity, 367-369
Plant expansion, 331-332
Plural executives, 223
Policies, defined, 414
Policy making, 88-89
"Potential surprise" concept, 393
Power, administrative skills, 280-281
  and authority, 255, 267-268, 274-283
  combination of factors, 282
  defined, 255
  determinants of, 278-282
  education and experience, 279-280
  ethnic factors, 278-282
  family background, 281
  the Milo plant, 276
  of subordinates, 256, 282-283
Prices policies, 348-351
Pride of craftsmanship, 578-579
Primary functions, 125-128
Primary group, defined, 566
Prince Potemkin, mutiny on, 258-259
Private property, 260
  leadership succession, 629
Probability, statistical, 82
  subjective, 82-83
  universe characterized by, 67
Procedure, defined, 364
Procedures analysis, 364
Procedures and methods, 413-414
Procedures, paperwork, 302-303
Procter and Gamble Company, 145

SUBJECT INDEX

Procurement, 359-360, 507-511
Product departmentation, 137-142
  control advantages, 140-141
  coordination advantages, 140
  executive development, 141
Production control, 524
Production management, 196
Production planning and control, 497-505
Product line policies, 347-348
Product markets, 319-325
Profession, defined, 69
  ethics of, 70
Professional development, 657
Professional education, 644-645
Professional management, 15-16
  knowledge for, 57-59
Profit norm, 378-379, 402
Profit taxes, 337
Program Evaluation Procedure (PEP), 500
Program Evaluation Review Technique (PERT), 413, 500
Programming, computer, 525-526, 536, 538
Property, and authority, 260-261
Proxy disputes, 630
Prussian staff organization, 157
Psychological fatigue, 107
Psychological testing, 52, 667-669
  achievement tests, 668
  aptitude tests, 668
  intelligence tests, 668
  interest tests, 668
  personality tests, 668-669

Quality planning and control, 505-507

Rabble hypothesis, 39
Radio Corporation of America, 4, 139, 168, 173-174, 301, 302, 354
"Rate busters," 567-568
Rate hearings, railroad, 36
Raw materials, 333-334
Reading techniques and problems, 466-468
Real time systems, 533-535
  SABRE, 534
Recruitment, personnel, 358, 664-670
Remington Rand Division, Sperry Rand, 46
Reorganization, 284-285, 293, 678
  costs and efficiency, 293
  earthquake approach, 285-286
  General Motors Corporation, 44-45, 294
  informal, 291-293
  results of, 294-295
  short- and long-run plans, 285-286
  the social system, 296
  Westinghouse Electric Company, 294
Resource markets, 326-335
Resource procurement strategies, 355-361

Retained earnings, statement of, 483
Revenues and costs, 346, 378, 483
Risk and uncertainty, 81-82
Robinson-Patman Act, 19
Role-playing, 652-653
Roman Catholic Church, 10-11
Roman Empire, 10
Rome, organization of, 10
Russia, and Communism, 628
  Gantt Chart used in, 498

SABRE, 533, 534
SABRER, 534
Salaries, executive, 616-618
Sales forecasting, 321-322, 409
Sales management, 196-197
Satisficing, 402
Scanlon plan, 249-251
Science, black box problem, 68
  of human behavior, 64-65
  and knowledge, 69
  and management, 67
  nature of, 66
  partial theories, 68
  philosophical roots, 66
Scientific American, 30
Scientific management, 33-41, 65-69
  the Bethlehem experiments, 33-34
  and human behavior, 39-41
  and management hierarchy, 38
  metal-cutting experiments, 35
  the Midvale period, 32-33
  pig iron handling experiment, 33-34
  pioneers of, 36-37
  and planning, 38
  shoveling experiments, 34-35
  and the systems concept, 74-78
  and Taylor, Frederick W., 32-37
Scientific method, 66
Sears, Roebuck and Company, 112, 145, 189, 207, 208, 379, 407
  Roebuck and Company experience, 112
Second industrial revolution, 20-28
Securities Exchange Commission, 20
Segregation, of legislative, executive, and judicial functions, 600-601
Semantics, 63, 428-433
  abstracting, 431-432, 443
  Aristotelian logic, 431
  distortion problems, 441-445
  and executive action, 433, 637
  general, 428-433
  infinity of meanings, 432-433
  imprint of the past, 429-430
  language structure, problem of, 428-429
  linguistic science, branch of, 428
  maps of a territory, 429
Service departmentation, 141-142
Service functions, 178
Shared-time computer systems, 535-536

SUBJECT INDEX 701

Shell Oil Company, 4
Sherman Anti-Trust Act, 19
"Short-circuiting," 301
Shoveling experiments, 34-35
Simonds Rolling Machine Company, 40
Simulation techniques, 650
Size, and economic efficiency, 191-193
Social responsibility, 244, 630-631
Social satisfaction, 582
  importance of, 566-571
Social Security Act, 20
Social skills, 9, 633-634
Software, 525
Span of management, 103-112
  the Exodus, 104
  Fayol's hypothetical hierarchy, 104-105
  Graicunas' theory, 109-111
  Hoover Commission recommendations, 105
  industrial spans, 105-107
  and military history, 104
Specialization, 5, 195
  and job enlargement, 135
  product, 139
  and size, 130, 191-193
  territorial, 144-145
Special staff, 162
Specifications, 506
Sperry Rand Corporation, 46, 207, 354
Splintered authority, 215
Staff assistants, 155, 165
Staff departments, 155
Staff functionalism, 164
Staff functions, 158
Staff organization, business, 164-174
  military, 155-164
  religious, 11
Standardization, 363-367
Standard Oil of California, 4, 168, 289, 290
Standard Oil Company (Ind), 4
Standard Oil Company (N.J.), 4, 207, 208, 247, 608, 612
Standards, defined, 363-367
  types of, 366
Statistical probability, 82
Status, 582
  and authority, 263
  and communication, 436
  defined, 263
  determinants of, 263-267
  education and experience, 279-280
  ethnic factors, 278-279
  formal ceremonies, 264-265
  informal determinants, 278-282, 573-577
  insignia, 265-266
  motivation instrument, 571-577
  privileges and special facilities, 266-267
  problems and policies, 571-577
  scalar and functional titles, 266, 577
Status anxiety, 573-574

Status system, 436
Stevens Institute, 33
Stockholders, 238, 612-614
Stock options, 617
Strategic factors, 404
Strategy and structure, 207-208
Subjective probability, 82-83
Subordinate participation, 216-217, 588-591
Subordinate power, 256, 282-283
Supervision, 112
Suppliers, 618
Supplies, 333-334
Supreme Court, Rulings by, 336
Sweden, military staff development in, 157
Swift and Company, 4
Sylvania Electric Products, 207
Symbolic models, 382
Systems, defined, 74-75
  and the electronic computer, 76-77
  and model building, 75-76
Systems management, 74-78

Tabor Manufacturing Company, 38
Taft-Hartley Act, 19
Tall management structures, 114
Taxation, and business planning, 337-338
Team craftsmanship, 578-579
Technological innovation, 8, 338-340
Technological unemployment, 369
Technology, and cooperation, 8
Territorial departmentation, 142-151
  and electronic computers, 150
  foreign operations, 145
  and jet travel, 150
  political organization, 142-144
Territorial specialization, 144-145
Testing, 52, 667-669
Texaco, Inc., 4
Theories X and Y, 560-561
Thinking machines, 22-24
Time departmentation, 151
Tolerances, 506
Trade unionism, 16-17
  philosophy of, 17
Traffic management, 198-199
Training programs, 673-674
Transformation period, 375-376
Trend-cycle analysis, 322
Trusteeship, 231, 605

Uncertainty, and innovation, 340
  problem of, 67
Unilever combine, 207
Union Carbide Corporation, 4, 348
Unionism, 261-262, 355-358, 614
  laboristic philosophy, 607-608
  and managerial control, 17, 261-262
Union-management cooperation, 249-251, 614
United States Air Force, 500

United States Army, military staff system in, 158
  operations research used in, 381
  psychological research by, 568-569
United States Navy Special Projects Office, 500
United States Steel Corporation, 4, 331, 335
Unity of command, 11, 134-135, 175, 301

Venice, Arsenal of, 11, 15
"Verbal cocoons," 432

Wagner Act, 19
Weather conditions, 341
Weber's theory of bureaucracy, 43
Western Electric Company, 4, 41, 48

Westinghouse Electric Corporation, 4, 246, 294-295, 354, 438
Who's Who in America, 642
Work division, 5
World War I, military staff organization in, 161
World War II, communication difficulties, 441, 454
  government controls in, 20
  operations research development in, 381
  psychological research during, 107-108, 568-569
  military staff organization in, 157-158, 161-162
  strategic factors in, 404
  time planning for atomic bomb, 374

Yale University, 567

PRINCIPLES OF MANAGEMENT: A MODERN APPROACH

THE WILEY SERIES IN
MANAGEMENT AND ADMINISTRATION

Elwood S. Buffa, Advisory Editor
University of California, Los Angeles

Peter P. Schoderbek
MANAGEMENT SYSTEMS

James L. McKenney and Richard S. Rosenbloom
CASES IN OPERATIONS MANAGEMENT

Henry H. Albers
PRINCIPLES OF MANAGEMENT: A MODERN APPROACH,
Third Edition